M000009553

"*A book worthy of any traders library, not only does this book deal with the trading environment in a clear format, it manages to do it in such a way that should enable even the novice trader to gain market understanding, experience and profitability.*"
—Martin Cole, www.learningtotrade.com

"*Clive Corcoran provides a hypothesis testing framework that will be a valuable tool for any serious trader. The book presents a blueprint for an analytical consideration of the markets that goes beyond pattern recognition and explores predictable and statistically verifiable precursors to the moves that traders look to capitalize on.*"
—Adrian F. Manz, MBA, Ph.D., Author of *Around The Horn: A Trader's Guide To Consistently Scoring In The Markets* and Cofounder of TraderInsight.com

"*With* Long/Short Market Dynamics, *Clive Corcoran has successfully managed to do what few other financial books have done . . . thoroughly explain advanced level technical analysis concepts in a manner that the average investor can understand. Just the right amount of trading psychology is also explained in order for investors to appreciate the inner workings of why certain chart patterns are effective. I highly recommend this book for anyone looking to get a more thorough understanding of technical analysis than just the tired basics covered in so many other books before his.*"
—Deron Wagner, Founder and Head Trader, Morpheus Trading Group

Long/Short Market Dynamics

For other titles in the Wiley Trading Series please see www.wiley.com/finance

LONG/SHORT MARKET DYNAMICS
Trading Strategies for Today's Markets

Clive M. Corcoran

BICENTENNIAL 1807 WILEY 2007 BICENTENNIAL

John Wiley & Sons, Ltd

Copyright © 2007 Clive M. Corcoran

Published by John Wiley & Sons Ltd, The Atrium, Southern Gate, Chichester,
West Sussex, PO19 8SQ, England
Telephone (+44) 1243 779777

Email (for orders and customer service enquiries): cs-books@wiley.co.uk
Visit our Home Page on www.wiley.com

Reprinted November 2007

All Rights Reserved. No part of this publication may be reproduced, stored in a retrieval system or transmitted in any form or by any means, electronic, mechanical, photocopying, recording, scanning or otherwise, except under the terms of the Copyright, Designs and Patents Act 1988 or under the terms of a licence issued by the Copyright Licensing Agency Ltd, 90 Tottenham Court Road, London W1T 4LP, UK, without the permission in writing of the Publisher. Requests to the Publisher should be addressed to the Permissions Department, John Wiley & Sons Ltd, The Atrium, Southern Gate, Chichester, West Sussex PO19 8SQ, England, or emailed to permreq@wiley.co.uk, or faxed to (+44) 1243 770620.

Designations used by companies to distinguish their products are often claimed as trademarks. All brand names and product names used in this book are trade names, service marks, trademarks or registered trademarks of their respective owners. The Publisher is not associated with any product or vendor mentioned in this book.

This publication is designed to provide accurate and authoritative information in regard to the subject matter covered. It is sold on the understanding that the Publisher is not engaged in rendering professional services. If professional advice or other expert assistance is required, the services of a competent professional should be sought.

Other Wiley Editorial Offices

John Wiley & Sons Inc., 111 River Street, Hoboken, NJ 07030, USA

Jossey-Bass, 989 Market Street, San Francisco, CA 94103-1741, USA

Wiley-VCH Verlag GmbH, Boschstr. 12, D-69469 Weinheim, Germany

John Wiley & Sons Australia Ltd, 42 McDougall Street, Milton, Queensland 4064, Australia

John Wiley & Sons (Asia) Pte Ltd, 2 Clementi Loop #02-01, Jin Xing Distripark, Singapore 129809

John Wiley & Sons Canada Ltd, 6045 Freemont Blvd, Mississauga, ONT, L5R 4J3, Canada

Wiley also publishes its books in a variety of electronic formats. Some content that appears
in print may not be available is electronic books.

Library of Congress Cataloguing-in-Publication Data

Corcoran, Clive M.
Long/short market dynamics : trading strategies for today's markets / Clive M. Corcoran.
p. cm.—(Wiley trading series)
Includes bibliographical references and index.
ISBN-13: 978-0-470-05728-5 (cloth : alk. paper)
1. Capital market—United States. 2. Investments—United States. 3. Stock exchanges—United States.
4. Risk management—United States. I. Title.
HG4910.C624 2007
332.64′273—dc22 2006036079

British Library Cataloguing in Publication Data

A catalogue record for this book is available from the British Library

ISBN 13 978-0-470-05728-5 (H/B)

Typeset in 10/12pt Times by TechBooks, New Delhi, India
Printed and bound in Great Britain by Antony Rowe Ltd, Chippenham, Wiltshire
This book is printed on acid-free paper responsibly manufactured from sustainable forestry
in which at least two trees are planted for each one used for paper production.

Contents

1
Coming to Terms with New Market Dynamics

The 1980s and 1990s saw a boom in public participation in the equity markets with spectacular growth in the number of mutual funds and unit trusts along with a global expansion of new enterprises and access to the exchanges that traded their securities. Since the NASDAQ collapse in 2000, the role of the retail investor has diminished, as has the prevalence of buy and hold strategies as advocated by investment gurus such as Peter Lynch. The innovations that have been taking place in the investment/trading strategies practiced by institutional asset managers, who now more than ever predominate, have led to a quiet revolution in the behavior of the capital markets.

The growing importance of derivatives, the heightened focus on proprietary trading by the major investment banks and the proliferation of alternative asset management strategies have all been reshaping the investment landscape. To cite just one example, the hedge fund sector alone is now estimated to be responsible for more than 50% of current stock market volume.

New transaction technologies have reduced the costs of trading, disintermediation has all but eliminated certain tiers of the market, and a low interest rate environment has forced a rethinking of many previously accepted canons of asset allocation theory.

The growing role of long/short strategies and derivatives means that many traditional market indicators simply don't work anymore. Increasingly stocks are being traded like commodities and many of the traditional decision support tools for analyzing stock market behavior have become obsolete. Paradoxically just as the markets have become more oriented towards purely technical trading, many of the legacy elements from technical analysis can actually be misleading and hinder the active trader who wants to profit in today's markets.

If you are an active trader or investor it is vital that you come to terms with the new modes of market behavior. You need new pattern templates and analytical techniques that will enable you to identify the chart formations that reveal these new dynamics at work.

This book is designed to show the individual trader or investor how to successfully analyze the morphology of modern markets and how to implement long/short strategies that enable the management of risk in a world and market that contain many new uncertainties.

We shall also be discussing some innovative techniques that are designed to capture some of the activity that occurs beneath the surface on a daily basis in the market place and which allow the trader to differentiate between the "noise" and the true dynamics of price development through price discovery. Along the way we will be examining some of the vital new forces and techniques that are influencing the way that markets behave. Some very bright and talented people are pushing innovations to the capital markets at a breakneck pace, and trying to monitor the research and new models that are being proposed and rapidly adopted is a challenging undertaking for finance professionals and traders alike. We shall also be examining a number of traditional techniques that, despite the major transformations that have taken place in the structure of the financial markets, have proved themselves to be remarkably resilient and effective at aiding the trader to discern the underlying value in market information.

In what follows we will look at stimulating research and analysis that is being done in the new discipline of econophysics, where models and quantitative techniques that have arisen in the study of the physical sciences are increasingly being applied to finance. The term "phynance" has been coined to reflect the fact that there is a growing constituency of PhDs from mathematics and pure science that are now working at major banks and hedge funds.[1] Affiliated with this is another source of new insights into the workings of the markets, their microstructure and *modus operandi*, and which can be called agent-based modeling. Inspired by ideas from artificial intelligence and algorithms that have been successfully applied in other models using computer simulations, there is a growing literature that provides insights into the complexity of behavior that *emerges* from modeling the markets as a dynamic and adaptive system with interacting agents whose "rules of engagement" are often stunningly simple.

Some might argue that very little of this research yields benefits that can be practically applied by the trader in real world situations, but we would suggest that there are invaluable insights and explanatory force behind ideas that have arisen in the science of complexity. We will serve notice now that we will not be applying chaos theory to the markets, and in reviewing the research for this book there seemed to be little of value to be taken from the finance community's love affair with this discipline in the 1980s and 1990s. However, we hope to show that the study of complex nonlinear systems in general, and more specifically the study of seismology, idealized sand piles, power laws, percolation lattices and other fascinating areas from the specialist literature, does have a payoff to the active trader. But we will return to these exciting and esoteric matters later.

To begin it would be good to think about the actual mechanics and practice of trading or what might also be described the "workflow of markets". Markets arise because people want to trade and the way they trade, the business process of placing trades and interacting with others in the conduct of their trading, should provide some important clues into the logic of price formation and the network dynamics that are markets. We also need to address the fact that there is a traditional notion of how markets work which is largely obsolete and handicaps an understanding of price formation and market dynamics. A more accurate notion of the contemporary trading workflow has to reflect the re-engineering that is constantly taking place in the trading process since the advent of ubiquitous computation technologies.

In 2006 as much as 30% of the trading activity that takes place each day in the U.S. equities market is performed entirely by software algorithms. While this automation of trading is ultimately supervised by the stakeholders in the markets, the actual trading process itself is conducted entirely by software algorithms and involves machine to machine communication. Equally as important for the price formation process is the fact that nominally trillions of dollars are committed to purely synthetic financial instruments that have a grounding in the real world economy of companies, customers, interest rates etc. but which are often only abstractly and remotely connected to a specific underlying variable that is widely understood by the nonspecialist. As an example the market for collateralized debt obligations (CDOs) is estimated to be worth more than two trillion dollars and allows those who know what they are doing, or at least demonstrate great confidence that they know what they are doing, to trade in the "risk" of corporate debt.[2]

From time to time when there is a derivatives scare there may be some attention to this gargantuan market in synthetic instruments in the financial pages of the mainstream newspapers, but most of the time these markets churn enormous amounts of capital obligations under the surface and in an unexciting manner. Indeed, we have to hope that the trading in these remains unexciting as the "malfunctioning" of these instruments has the capacity for very serious financial consequences. When the debt of GM and Ford was downgraded in 2005 there were some serious consequences for several hedge funds and banks that are exposed to the vagaries of these "securities". Much more seriously, the Russian debt default in 1998 left some of the world's most astute finance academics and previously successful traders paralyzed as they watched a meltdown in their highly leveraged portfolio of complex trades predicated on arbitraging cash and derivative instruments. Will there be more such incidents? Undoubtedly there will be. Could the next one bring the financial world to the brink of total collapse? We don't know, but we would suggest that for practical purposes we adopt the defensive posture of the unlikely asteroid scenario. If an asteroid that is headed toward Earth is discovered there would be widespread alarm and panic as it surely would be "the end of civilization as we know it" unless some technology is developed to deflect it. If another financial debacle and liquidity collapse presents itself we have to hope that central bankers will also be able to deflect the impact and fallout. However, for most of us there are more mundane concerns to keep us well occupied.

Let us examine the traditional notion of the financial markets that is still part of the folklore and can still be found in text books that are used in the teaching of finance and business studies. To older readers who recall trading in the 1980s and 1990s this will be familiar territory but to the newer generation of traders Figure 1.1 will seem truly archaic.

Our point in showing the graphic is to illustrate that traditionally markets involved human intermediaries. The placing of orders, their execution and the logging of trades was done with a human being aware of the whole process, even if there were automated steps along the way.

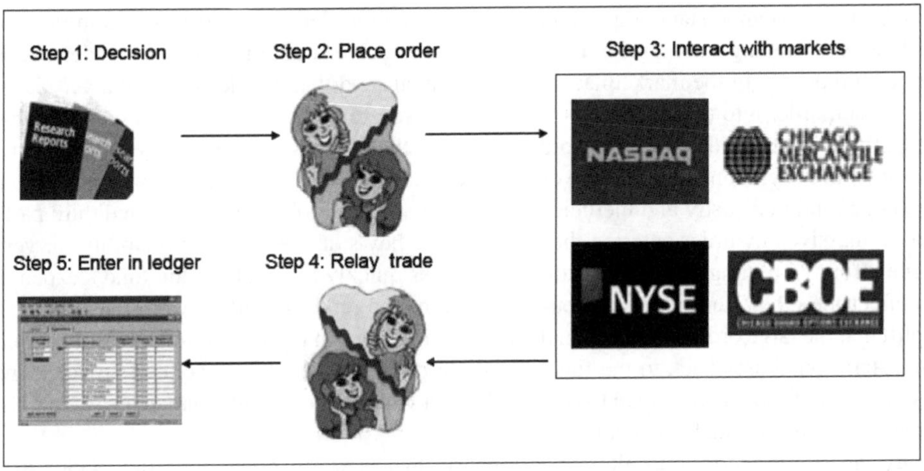

Figure 1.1 Traditional Trading workflow (*source*: TABB Group). Reproduced by permission of The Tabb Group LLC

Even today in the popular imagination when people think about markets they think of traders in the pits of the Chicago futures exchanges or the specialists stalls on the floor of the NYSE. These iconic images have a very powerful effect on our imagination and can subtly influence the way that we think about a business process or activity.

Why do news presenters stand outside the White House when discussing a news story about U.S. politics? Why does the monthly U.S. employment data need to be revealed on the steps of the U.S. Treasury building? Why does CNBC come "live from the floor of the New York Stock Exchange"? Why do stories about the entertainment industry often have the "HOLLYWOOD" sign that sits astride the Cahuenga Pass into the San Fernando valley? Most traders and financial decision makers do not literally work on Wall Street, more and more movies are made by people who do not live in Los Angeles or even depend on that city for their livelihood and why should we put greater credence in a news story if the presenter is standing outside the White House or U.S. Treasury? Iconic images serve a role as any good fiction writer, television producer or GUI programmer will attest but they sometimes have a way of confusing issues rather than clarifying them.

The reason we have gone through this exercise is that we sense that the icons and metaphors that creep into our thinking about markets have a way of distracting us from what is really going on. We deal with surface information and images, the "noise" of the markets rather than analyzing the underlying technical conditions of the market. If we are looking in the wrong places for the clues as to what the markets are telling us it is not too surprising that we will fail to get their message. Learning how to better understand what the markets are communicating can be one of the main payoffs from unraveling the elements in the new trading workflow.

To be specific, the contemporary financial markets have not only removed the human interaction at the level of order placement in the sense that orders can be executed directly into the market's order books by touching a screen or striking a keypad, but also that there is no need for a person to even touch a screen or "supervise" a fully automated process.

ALGORITHMIC TRADING

The best way to understand algorithmic trading is to consider the business problem that the technique of trading via algorithms was designed to solve. Large institutional traders leave large "footprints" in the marketplace. A large mutual fund that decides to place a very large buy or sell order into the market's order book runs several risks. The first kind of risk is that other traders will see the size of the order and know that there is an opportunity for exploiting the order flow by "front-running" the order which has the effect of moving the price away from the large fund in a costly and inefficient manner. If another brokerage or affiliated third party sees a massive buy order entering the books on the buy-side there is the possibility for very agile informed trading desks to position themselves quickly to benefit at the fund's expense. In effect the other participants are buying ahead of the fund, benefiting from the inevitable uplift that the large order will have on the price and taking a margin for ultimately selling their short-term purchases back to the fund at a slight premium. The fund may end up achieving the large purchase that it wished to achieve, but not without moving the market away from the price at which it wanted to execute the trade.

By digression there is an alternative scenario that is worth brief discussion which also illustrates the way in which order flow can be interpreted by market participants. This is the so-called "pump and dump" strategy in which a large fund or trading desk is keen to show to the market that it has a particular interest in a large order. After revealing its intention for all to see, let us assume that it is a large buy order, the market reacts to the move by following through with positive price action thinking that the buyer must have some superior knowledge about the attractiveness of the particular security that is being purchased. In fact the buyer is hoping to sell unwanted inventory into the strengthening market. This highlights a theme that we shall return to repeatedly which is that nothing influences price development more than price development. Another saying that seems apropos is the beautifully ironic remark that Wall Street is the only place that puts its prices up when it wants to have a sale.

Returning to the concerns that large institutions have had about exposing their orders to the market, a new type of automated process has been developed to disguise the true intent of these large fund managers. The process, known as algorithmic trading, not only facilitates the more efficient execution of large orders, but can even introduce subtle false signals into the procedure which are designed to confuse the markets about the underlying transaction objectives. For example, if a fund wants to buy a large quantity of a particular stock, the order is "sliced and diced" into a series of much smaller sub-orders and then executed over a period of time where the objective is to achieve actual price executions at the optimal cost. In other words, the algorithms are capable of scattering the original trade objective into a fragmentary process which should no longer be transparent to other market players. As part of the procedure the algorithms can also throw off contrarian trades that will from time to time reverse the original motivation by, for example, creating a selling phase within a large buy order:

> The most common type of algorithm, called Volume Weighted Average Price (VWAP), slices the parent order into a series of child orders over a certain time frame, attempting to conceal the true size of the parent order. These algorithms are dynamic and in response to current market conditions, cancel and replace live orders. Each time an order is canceled and replaced, the information becomes part of the market data environment. Therefore, the use of algorithms has not only increased the number of trades that occur, but it has increased the amount of intraday market data.[3]

One of the consequences of this innovation is that the microstructural behavior of markets is changing. There is far less transparency at the order book level and even when a series of orders do appear on the Level 2 or DMA screens there is a real question mark as to how firm these "orders" really are. Access to the order books was originally seen as a giant step forward in increasing market transparency and leveling the playing field for smaller traders, but as with most innovations there are usually ingenious techniques designed to defeat the purpose. Traders, both large and small, welcome transparency as a great principle but in practice they would rather be able to operate anonymously and stealthily in the marketplace (other than in the "pump and dump" mode we discussed).

There has been a lot of innovation regarding the complexity of the algorithms that buy-side traders are now using and the motivations have extended beyond the original desire to "hide" large trades. Another important driver of the trend is the changing landscape between the buy-side (i.e. the large pension funds, mutual funds etc.) and the sell-side (i.e. the large brokerage operations that are focused on taking a small (and smaller) margin or commission from executing the trades of the large players on the buy-side). Issues such as the competitive nature of commission arrangements, the separation of research and trading costs and activities and the confidentiality of trading motives are also pushing this agenda. According to the TABB

Group in late 2005, more than 60% of buy-side managers were experimenting with algorithmic trading techniques.

We need to clarify the significance of these new techniques and to differentiate them from the more "traditional" notions of computerized trading known as "program trading". Algorithmic trading has very different objectives to program trading which was a technique pioneered in the 1980s designed to exploit temporary arbitrage opportunities that arose in the trading of cash instruments such as the S&P 500 cash index and its major constituent stocks, and the futures contracts that trade in parallel with the cash market. When the derivative (the futures contract) and the cash index ("the underlying") become misaligned a risk-free arbitrage opportunity arises and program trading takes advantage of these temporary spread discrepancies:

> Algorithms are a step up from the more familiar program trading, which institutions for years have used to buy or sell bundles of 15 or more stocks worth a combined $1 million. Algorithms handle trades in individual stocks, and the exchanges don't ban their use when trading becomes extremely volatile, as they have done with program trades since the 1987 market meltdown. As the use of algorithms moves from hedge funds and Wall Street's trading desks to mutual- and pension-fund managers, it will account for more than 40% of total U.S. equities trading on all markets by 2008, up from about 25% today, according to Boston-based researcher Aite Group.[4]

To highlight this realignment of the workflow between the major market players, the brokerage and investment banking business, which, largely pioneered the algorithmic trading technology and uses these platforms for conducting its own proprietary trading activities, is morphing its role with respect to large buy-side players:

> Many bulge-bracket firms – the major brokerage houses that underwrite and distribute securities as well as produce research – are taking on a consulting role, helping buy-side customers choose algorithms. Brokers say they'll advise buy-side firms on which electronic strategies to apply for particular trading styles and develop customized algorithms, as well as pre- and post-trade analysis tools, for clients.
>
> In February, Goldman Sachs began providing a framework, known as the order-execution "Cube," to help buy-side customers classify their orders and segment their flow by methodology and venue. "The Cube maps orders into different execution strategies based on order size, liquidity, and trade urgency," says Andrew Silverman, head of U.S. algorithmic trading at Goldman Sachs, who explained the concept in April at a trading technology conference.[5]

Why should the individual trader be concerned about this issue? Surely it is only of relevance to the largest institutional players and has little bearing on the activities or concerns of the smaller fund manager and individual trader. But we would argue that because of these fundamental changes to the manner in which volume is recorded, and the fact that the use of algorithms has not only increased the number of trades that occur, but also the amount of intraday market data, there have been radical changes to the ground rules that are the basis for many technical indicators that are widely followed by practitioners of technical analysis. A substantial amount of the legacy indicators in technical analysis have assumptions about volume, money flow and other measures of accumulation and distribution. Can these be as valid today, given the nature of the obfuscatory intent of algorithmic trading, as they were when the traditional trading workflow paradigm was in place?

For intraday traders the situation may be more acute than for swing traders who take their cues more from end of day data than analysis of more high frequency data. If a large fund is executing a large order over several hours using a sophisticated algorithmic trading platform, which not only decomposes the order into smaller granularities but also uses some deliberate false signals designed to confuse, will this not invalidate a number of assumptions upon which volume analysis is based? What effect does the sudden removal from the order book of several "published" bids and asks have on intraday liquidity? Are the numerous avalanches and price cascades that can be witnessed during intraday trading connected to these algorithms?

We certainly are not trying to suggest that these techniques are "dangerous" any more than we believe that "program trading" was the much publicized culprit for the October 1987 market crash, but we think that to pretend that these technical innovations have not radically changed the ground rules for technical analysis is an untenable position. Does this invalidate methods that have been constructed to analyze money flow and accumulation/distribution, for example? We believe that there is much evidence that these indicators no longer work as effectively as they should and we will propose some modifications and new techniques that can play the role that these techniques were designed for. Before we move on to consider one more important aspect of how the traditional trading workflow has changed and how it impacts on the interpretation of the market's technical condition we should mention that the developers of algorithmic trading technologies may not have achieved exactly what they intended. There is some evidence that these algorithms may not have the "stealth" advantage that their promoters claimed for them:

> Some critics say that when less experienced hedge- or mutual-fund traders use the software they've bought from Wall Street, they inadvertently expose their trades. How? Canny traders, mainly those who trade on behalf of big banks and brokerages with the firms' capital, may be able to identify patterns of algorithms as they get executed. "Algorithms can be very predictable," says Steve Brain, head of algorithmic trading at Instinet, the New York City-based institutional broker.[6]

We want to return to the workflow diagram in Figure 1.1 and consider another revolutionary change that is taking place in the manner in which the trading process is changing and which has had, an impact on market behavior that should be of interest and value to all well-informed traders. There have been remarkable advances in the logging of trades and positions and more specifically with the real time monitoring of the interim profit and loss account, risk exposure, and compliance with the margin requirements of (say) a prime broker. TABB Group estimates that during peak cycles, top tier prime brokers could be hit with close to 150 trades per second and more than 10 times as many orders per second, imposing a tremendous burden on the applications that must update and disseminate this data across the execution platform:

> Each time a trade occurs, the prime broker's system must immediately update the accounts positions, usually stored in their database. Their system will examine the trade and determine whether to create a new position or close an existing position. Only when this is complete can the broker accurately calculate items such as unrealized and realized gains, and more importantly, the trading limit (the amount of capital the trading firm has at its disposal) on the account. When the fund places an order, the broker must make sure it falls within the account's current

> trading limit. Typically, trading limits include the value of the existing position, the leverage (the amount of money the firm can borrow against its current value), the amount currently being borrowed and the potential cost of the existing open orders. When a broker cannot calculate trading limits as fast as its clients are placing orders, one of two undesirable scenarios can occur: either the prime broker imposes conservative margin requirements, which limit trading, or the firm allows the trading to occur but takes on additional counterparty risk.[7]

As hedge funds diversify their strategies across multiple asset classes, across international markets in both cash instruments and derivatives, there are enormous challenges presented to the IT systems that have to monitor the net balances of all of the various positions. Many of these contemporaneously held positions need to be constantly marked to the market while some other holdings of a less liquid nature can only be updated periodically. Within the prime broker's IT infrastructure a margin engine has to be continuously updated with the overall exposure of a complex portfolio of long and short positions in a bewildering variety of asset classes. Delays in processing all of the current open positions could result in a situation where the prime broker and the client are more exposed to risk than they believed, where they are under their required margin and where the eventual realization of this could impact very negatively on the client's and the prime broker's account.

As the velocity of trading accelerates, as the activities of algorithmic trading become ever more complex, as the degree to which large hedge funds are participating in certain illiquid markets, the sheer burden of computing the net "real time" exposure is sometimes falling behind. When the IT systems that are in place to monitor this real time exposure "catch up" and if, to keep the example simple, the margin engine has underestimated the exposure and requires additional margin, this can sometimes lead to sudden abrupt moves in different markets as hedge funds "square" their various asset allocations. According to some reports that have been surfacing in the London markets during May and June 2006 there is a possibility that the "liquidity crisis" and financial contagion effect that began to affect global markets in late April 2006 and really picked up momentum in May could be attributable to precisely this kind of overloading of the systems designed to monitor in real time the exposure of certain major hedge funds:

> The market's slide, which accelerated towards the end of the trading day as hedge funds squared losing derivatives positions – what's become known as the "four o'clock shock" – followed heavy falls in Asian markets.[8]

The London markets cease trading each day at 4.30 pm and if the back office infrastructures are "struggling" to maintain the integrity with respect to all of a fund's varied and complex trade executions during a session, then it may be that in the last half hour each day the fund has to adjust its positions, perhaps dramatically, in order to remain in compliance with its obligations to the prime broker.

Other commentators have called this effect the "four o'clock cliff" and it is perhaps slightly ominous that during the period of May 2006 where the volatility of many different markets, equities, energy, metals and even currencies shot up dramatically there were several episodes that affected the London markets (and perhaps the New York and Chicago markets equally) that seemed to match this description.

We will examine financial contagion and "correlated liquidity crises" in what follows but our reason for spending the time we have on the impact of the various innovations in the "workflow" of the trading process is to highlight the fact that today's capital markets are fundamentally different than they were when a lot of trading methodologies and technical analyses were developed. There are some who may want to downplay these innovations and claim that the more things change the more they stay the same and that the fundamental characteristics of markets are just as they always were. Our view is different. We certainly do not wish to appear alarmist and hope that the reader is not sensing a knee jerk reaction to derivatives and computerized trading. That is most certainly not our intention, and in fact we have strong sympathies with greater accessibility to intermarket trading opportunities and the benefits of cross-sectional hedging strategies based on quantitative analysis of the wide variety of financial market instruments.

There are essentially two points that we would wish to make in concluding this brief review of the changed market landscape. The first point is that the dynamics and workflow of trading have changed so dramatically during the most recent 10 year period that there is reason to doubt that the legacy tools from technical analysis are still appropriate to analyzing and understanding modern markets. This does not mean that they are obsolete under all market circumstances but that they may have less to offer especially when markets are in critical or extreme conditions. The second point that we would make is that the innovations have been so rapid, the velocity of trading is increasing dramatically and the room for miscalculations is also increasing at a rate that could lead to some significant accidents. Throughout economic history there have been numerous crises and accidents so this is nothing new. Perhaps more than ever the operations of the capital markets and the financial economy are far removed from the understanding of most people. The traditional models and metaphors that have been used to educate and explain markets are based on outmoded concepts that now seem quaint and obsolete.

The trade in financial instruments, especially fixed income instruments and their derivatives, far surpasses the trade in physical goods and services. Market "fundamentals" such as price – earnings ratios and other ratios based on traditional economic and accounting principles certainly still have the capacity to shape and influence the markets but there is increasingly a sense that the financial economy is becoming a self-organizing entity which is detaching from the underlying "Main Street" economy. It is our view that, and we shall elaborate and develop some of these ideas more fully in what follows, the capital markets have become a highly complex game, played by very smart people (much smarter than those in the public sector that have to "police" their activities) that have access to almost limitless amounts of notional capital, vast resources of computing power and a social and political environment that does not really understand what these markets are doing but which cannot realistically allow them to fail.

The recent episodes of financial crisis – the Asian crisis of 1997, the Russian debt crisis and LTCM debacle, the collapse of the internet inspired "New Economy" stocks and the bursting of the NASDAQ bubble in 2000/1, the perilous situation of the financial markets from the summer of 2001 through to the Iraq invasion of March 2003, resulting in negative interest rates in the U.S. and Japan, and even more recent episodes such as the GM/Ford downgrades in May 2005 and the inflation scare and liquidity crisis of May/June 2006 – are all pointing to a changed financial system. When Alan Greenspan convened a meeting with the major U.S. investment banks in September 1998 to "rescue" the global financial system from the fallout of the LTCM collapse and when the world's central banks "inject liquidity" in overwhelming amounts at times of crisis to stave off the collapse of the markets it suggests that the main cultural and political priorities of our age are to protect the integrity of the capital markets, perhaps *at all costs.*

During the later years of his term as governor of the Federal Reserve, the notion of the *Greenspan put* became widely discussed and many would argue that it is a fact of modern economic life. This does not mean, of course, that the markets are a one way bet and that individual traders, both large and small, are immune to large doses of financial pain and failure. It does mean, however, that, because of the gargantuan nature of the contractual commitments that are implied in multi-party risk sharing and the interdependence of asset returns to the overall health of the financial system, we need to be more vigilant than ever. What may seem like a normal market episode at one point or from one perspective can very soon thereafterwards take on all of the characteristics of a full blown crisis.

It is the *immanence* of risk that has changed. As traders we have to live with the fact that highly unlikely events and big accidents are now more likely. Small accidents tend to cluster and previously observed low correlations between unlikely events can now turn on a dime, and suddenly all assets are moving together – downwards. Finally we will suggest crashes are probably best seen as corrections that didn't stop.[9] We may be in much the same position with regard to predicting market crashes and crises that we are with our ability to predict major seismic events. To the extent that we have learned something of the "signatures" of the underlying dynamics of these different kinds of critical events, we may be given some clues as to when a major event or "crash" is more likely than at other times. But for all practical purposes we are in the dark and at the mercy of unknown forces. But as anyone who lives in a seismically active region of the world knows, it is very prudent to always be prepared for the worse.

From our perspective the only sane way to approach contemporary markets as a trader is to recognize the *immanence of critical events* or "crashes" and always trade with a safety net. How this can be achieved in practice, how to devise strategies that always require your trading account to be somewhat immune from the overall direction of the market, lies at the foundation of the methodology that will be advocated. Not only can the use of a well-planned strategy of always having long and short positions in one's portfolio provide a large degree of protection from overall macro-market risk, but if properly implemented it can generate the other desirable requirement – positive alpha. How this strategy can be implemented with a methodology to enable one to select the most opportune trades and the correct portfolio construction techniques will be the central theme in what follows.

One of the great fallacies of investors is that they tend to believe that they can see far enough ahead to know when it is the right time to be seeking safety. Even if, as in the late 1990s, the markets were behaving irrationally and any company with the moniker "dot.com" was selling at absurd multiples, the average fund manager and trader thought that they could ride the wave of euphoric price development and know when it was time to get off the ride. There is also the complacent notion that we will somehow read warnings to get out of the way before an avalanche of selling occurs. There are no warnings, or if there are they are so well hidden that most market participants don't get out of the way in time.

The worst time to be looking to hedge one's exposure or liquidate one's positions is when the market is correcting wildly. This is why we emphasize that crashes are immanent. It is not that we are unduly pessimistic and have a tendency to expect the worst, rather it is a realization that we cannot expect any warnings. The best time to apply hedging techniques is during periods, which are the "normal" or typical times for the markets, when there is a lot of disagreement about the direction of prices, interest rates, outlooks and so on. In these circumstances, markets are fractious, they are multi-faceted with many traders operating in different time frames all seeking out a multitude of price targets and other agendas. In other words, these are times when the markets are liquid and when it is most prudent to putting a defensive or hedge strategy in place.

When markets lose this fractiousness and when all opinions about direction and outlook become aligned, they cease to have their "normal liquidity" and trading activity becomes extremely coherent. It is not always the case that in these circumstances that they are preparing to crash because sometimes the alignment of opinions can be of a highly positive nature and markets can be said to "boom". It is to these extreme trend days that we shall now turn.

2
Range Expansion and Liquidity

Nothing moves price more than price movement.

Why do traders, fund managers and scalpers suddenly form coherent views about price direction? We need to explain what this question is really asking before we can attempt to answer it. The emphasis in what follows will be an explanation of our view that the typical trading day shows little consensus or agreement about the near-term direction of prices. It is precisely this disagreement that facilitates trading. During a typical trading session there are willing buyers and sellers who will have different time horizons, liquidity preferences and strategic objectives and these different perspectives will find expression in a flow of transactions that is predicated on the fact that the different sides to a transaction disagree over the fitness of the prevailing price. A term that suggests itself in this regard is fractiousness as it conveys the notion that price discovery and the moment to moment movements of markets have an adversarial flavor. But if the typical trading session can be characterized as fractious, what are the circumstances that lead to a different kind of behavior on the part of a majority of market players? How does a more uniform or coherent view of price direction arise? What can we learn from these trading sessions in which there is a far more consensual view about the likely course of prices? It turns out that we can learn a lot.

Let us begin with stating what we believe to be the opposite case to the one we are asking about. Examining the intraday charts for the majority of trading sessions one will see that there are a series of price movements in different directions back and forth, the so-called zigs and zags, as one move is followed by a counter move and so on. These sessions are the most commonly found and allow the day trader to employ a host of tactics and strategies designed to "fade" price surges, buy pullbacks and various other momentum and price targeting techniques. But there are numerous sessions when the intraday price action is not like this, these are sessions in which, characteristically, a movement (in either direction) begins early in the session and is then sustained for the rest of the session with little or no retracement. These sessions are usually accompanied by above average volume and usually they mark the beginning (or continuation) of a period of range expansion.

RANGE EXPANSION

Ranked by Forbes magazine in 2005 as the 133rd richest American, Paul Tudor Jones,[1] who has consistently outperformed the benchmark returns for more than 25 years, provided some seminal clues as to his philosophy of trading and these will help us to document our claims about the importance of coherent trading sessions. Jones is fairly secretive and does not reveal too much about his trading strategy, but he did offer the following insights during an interview with Jack Schwager which is transcribed in the first collection of *Market Wizards*.[2] Asked about the nature of his trading system Jones remarked:

> The basic premise of the system is that *markets move sharply when they move.* If there is a sudden range expansion in a market that has been trading narrowly, human nature is to try to fade that price move. *When you get a range expansion, the market is sending you a very loud, clear signal that the market is getting ready to move in the direction of that expansion.* (Italics in the original)

Deciphering the "loud and clear signal" that the markets are sending when there is sudden range expansion will be the focus of this chapter. This discussion will allow us to introduce the phenomenon of trend days which provide some excellent profit opportunities for the correctly positioned trader. Moreover in unraveling the dynamics behind trend days we hope to reveal some vital characteristics of liquidity and price development.

When markets move sharply and coherently they display very distinctive features that are easily distinguished from the characteristics of more typical trading sessions. One of the most distinctive characteristics is a price pattern that we have decided to call the Coherent Closing Bias phenomenon. Although this will be analyzed in detail in what follows, the hallmark of a sharp and coherent move is that the closing price will tend to be at the extreme limits of the intraday range. On an upside move the price will tend to close at or near the high for the session and for a downside move the closing price will tend to be near the low for the session. Range expansion sessions that conform to this pattern have been called trend days by several market analysts and we shall follow this terminology. Later in the chapter we shall examine the converse behavior to a session showing range expansion, namely those sessions when the market is trading in a very narrow and constricted range. As will be revealed, there are some very useful interrelationships and dependencies between these contrasting modes of market behavior and there is a clearly discernible pattern where trend days are often found to follow immediately from narrow range sessions.

Trend days can be very valuable to the trader as long as they are recognized as such. Larry Williams, Toby Crabel and Linda Bradford Raschke among others[3] have written eloquently on these types of trading days and there are a lot of indicators that have been proposed to allow the trader to identify when such days are going to occur. Trend days differ from the majority of trading sessions in that the market becomes so one-sided for the duration of the session that the normal intraday swing patterns disappear. In other words, the usual back and forth price antics are largely absent and price proceeds in one direction throughout the session with few, if any, "corrective" periods or anti-trend behavior. Just how important such days are and how important it is to recognize them is brought out in this quote from Linda Bradford Raschke of the LBR Group:

> Traders must understand the characteristics of a *trend day*, even if interested only in intraday scalping. A trader anticipating a trend day should change strategies,

> from trading off support/resistance and looking at overbought/oversold indicators to using a breakout methodology and being flexible enough to buy strength or sell weakness. A trader caught off guard will often experience his largest losses on a trend day as he tries to sell strength or buy weakness prematurely. Because there are few intraday retracements, small losses can easily get out of hand. The worst catastrophes come from trying to average losing trades on trend days.[4]

From a day trading point of view the correct identification of such sessions can be highly profitable as price often moves a long way in either direction and if the trader is early to spot the trend day and patient enough to wait until the latter part of the session to exit, it is not uncommon to see a return of 5% or more from a single session. However, as the quotation brings out, the unwary trader who fails to understand the nature of trend days can also experience calamitous drawdowns by applying the normal day trading techniques in the middle of a strong trend day. Apart from the range expansion characteristics, on trend days the opening price and closing price are usually found at opposing ends of the intraday range. It is also not exceptional with trend days to find the closing price equal to the high or low of the day depending on which way the market was trending. And it is this phenomenon that we shall call the Coherent Closing Bias, for reasons that will become clearer as we move onwards.

To facilitate our understanding of the market dynamics underlying trend days it is worth spending some more time with the notion of coherent trading in which, at least for the duration of the session in question, there is a more or less uniform view of where the market wants to go. When we started out this chapter with the question "Why do traders suddenly form coherent views about price direction?" it may not have been apparent that we were really addressing the issue of liquidity. However, on trend days the market is really experiencing a loss of liquidity.

LIQUIDITY

Liquidity is one of the more important concepts in trading and finance and yet it is also one of the most difficult to define. Almost certainly it eludes any obvious way of being quantified. Sometimes it would appear that market commentators think of liquidity as some kind of macro-market variable that can be related back to the money supply or credit that is "in the system". We suggest that it is better not to view liquidity as having to do with money "sloshing around the system" but rather as having to do with the degree of disagreement among traders. The best way it can be observed, but often it is all too fleeting, is to review the depth of the market's order book. Expressed in overly simplistic terms, if the order book has depth and is layered in a multi-tiered manner then there is a "healthy" disagreement among traders about the most suitable price for the current time frame of reference. The market could be said to be operating with its normal degree of *fractiousness*. If the order book empties out very quickly and loses its fractal and temporal structure then the market has (temporarily at least) lost its liquidity. If there are very few, if any, bids and a preponderance of traders wanting to sell then either trading is going to grind to a halt or price is going to "jump" to a new level.

So we propose that liquidity is not a measurable variable of markets but is best thought of as a compressed way of describing the degree to which markets either facilitate transactions or inhibit them. For markets to work properly there need to be disagreements, different time horizons among the participants and different agendas and priorities. While some traders think that an asset is worth buying at a specified price there must be others who, for various reasons, think that it is worth selling at that same price. The two most common frameworks for financial markets are the open outcry model and the electronic order book and, in both cases, for sustained trading to take place there needs to be a fragmentation of opinions. Assuming that there are a dedicated group of traders that want to trade a particular asset, the more evenly divided opinions are regarding the suitability of the current price the more liquid the market will be. In very liquid markets buying and selling preferences will show a high degree of nonalignment. Trading stances will be dispersed and there will no obvious internal coherence to them. But when the fragmentation is replaced by a near-consensus view among traders the liquidity *evaporates* (notice again how the water-based metaphors seem to inform the way that liquidity is often discussed).

To summarize, liquidity disappears when long-, medium- and short-term investors all share the same market perspective eliminating a two-sided market. This is well expressed in the following quotation:

> Liquidity declines more than proportionally with the intensity of the demand for it. The more you need cash, the higher the price you have to pay to get it. And when average opinion comes to believe that average opinion will decide to turn assets into cash, then liquidity may be confidently expected to go to zero. By definition, no market can hedge this risk; no individual participant is rich enough not to need the hedge.[5]

EXTREME TREND DAYS

On trend days there is a range expansion and more importantly there is an unambiguous uniformity to the price action. In what follows we will be solely concerned with trend days in which there is a strong movement away from the opening price, in either direction. We are not screening for overnight changes between the open and the previous close but rather confining our attention to the cases where the extreme ranges are the result of purely intraday dynamics. Part of the reason for this focus is that we want to avoid the extreme trend days that are based purely on some overnight news or critical development that, accounts for the unusually coherent price behavior. This is not to say that an item of news/fundamental information will not arise during the day to instigate the strong directional movements we shall examine, but we want to make clear our qualification that we are not considering "overnight gap" events.[6]

Setting up the definitions for the pattern analysis we need to identify the following:

- The difference between the open and close is the metric used to determine the intraday P&L range. We call it the P&L range because this is how we want to consider the value – it represents the profitability of electing to take a particular directional bias at the beginning of the session and liquidating that position on the close. To that extent it does not include any intraday timing; it does not allow one to bale out of the position at any time after entry on the open until the market closes.
- The overall intraday range is defined simply as the difference between the high and the low for the session (which necessarily will be a positive amount, unlike the previous value which will be a signed value).
- The Intraday P&L Range as defined is then situated within the overall intraday range to provide the extension ratio for the day. Because the divisor can be a signed value the

extension ratio will also have a signed value and will lie within the interval of +100% to −100%.

- In the extreme positive case where the market opens on its low and closes on its high the extension ratio will be 100% and conversely if the market opens on its high and closes on its low this will show a value of −100%.
- Intermediate cases can be illustrated as follows. If the intraday P&L range is 75% of the overall intraday range, and the session closes higher than the open, then the value will be 75%. It is important to realize that this does not tell you that the close is in the upper quartile of the overall daily range but it does tell you that for those traders that bought the open and sold the close they would have enjoyed 75% of the possible gains to be had for the session.

To demonstrate the concept we have selected a sample case using the KLAC semiconductor stock which has traded since January 1993. The intraday P&L ranges have been filtered so that we only consider those that generated returns in excess of 5% or less than −5% and in each instance we have calculated the extension ratios discussed. If these paired values are plotted on an *XY* scatter graph we can see that there is a remarkable symmetry in the pattern observed (Figure 2.1).

Reviewing the chart the most striking feature is the absence of data points in the middle of the graph. This is not surprising in terms of the *x*-axis (the horizontal axis) as we have confined our attention to the more extreme changes but in the case of the *y*-axis (the vertical axis) we can see that there are extremely few data points in the +50% to −50% range. This is a highly significant finding as it shows that strong trend days are also strongly coherent and decisive. Whatever the precipitating factor, whether it is the release of key economic data or the market reaching a key technical target, once traders have "sensed" the impending new direction of price there is strong conviction and minimal retracement that accompanies such movements. In fact by exploring the more extreme moves we see that these are also accompanied by the highest extension

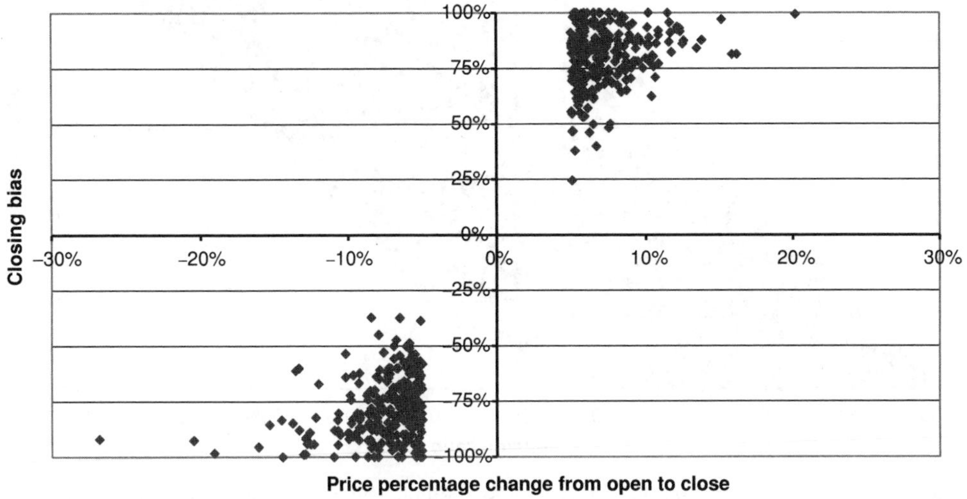

Figure 2.1 KLAC extreme movements – *XY* graph for intraday changes and the close position within the daily range 1993–2006

ratios indicating that there was almost universal consensus about the direction for the session. Universal consensus suggests a one-sided market without the normal fractiousness and that is why the moves are so unidirectional – the lack of disagreement causes a temporary collapse in liquidity. From a trading perspective such sessions produce quite different responses to those observed in a more typical session. Traders that are most attuned to the imminent nature of the decisive move will be doubling up on their positions and those that are on the wrong side of the market will be scrambling to reverse their positions. All of which will contribute further to the powerful dynamics behind trend days.

We decided to extend our investigation of the coherence of trend days by examining a further relationship. In addition to the extension ratio we have also calculated the position of the closing price for the day in relation to the available range for the day.

We will call this value the closing bias, and it is calculated very simply with the following formula: Close-low/(High-low). It will have a value between 0 and 100 which can be thought of in percentage terms. A value of 0% indicates that the closing price is equal to the low for the day and a value of 50% would indicate that the closing price was in the midpoint of the daily range and a value of 100% would indicate that the close and the high for the day were the same value.

We have ranked the daily returns for KLAC from absolute highest (i.e. we consider the magnitude of the move and not the sign) and then we have rendered two scatter diagrams. Figure 2.2 shows all absolute daily movements of less than 2% and Figure 2.3 covers the case for those absolute daily movements that are in excess of 4%. The charts are especially revealing for many reasons.

As is evident from Figure 2.2 the data points are highly scattered with no evidence that high or low levels of the extension ratio are associated with any particular bias with respect to where the close will be in relation to the daily range (i.e. the closing bias). Price and range

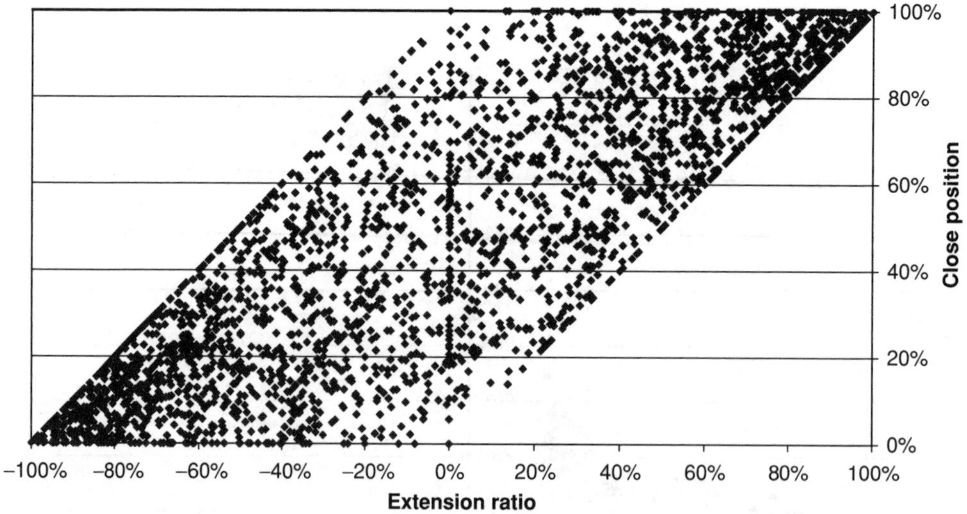

Figure 2.2 KLAC plot of extension ratio and close position – all intraday movements of less than 2% (absolute) since 1993

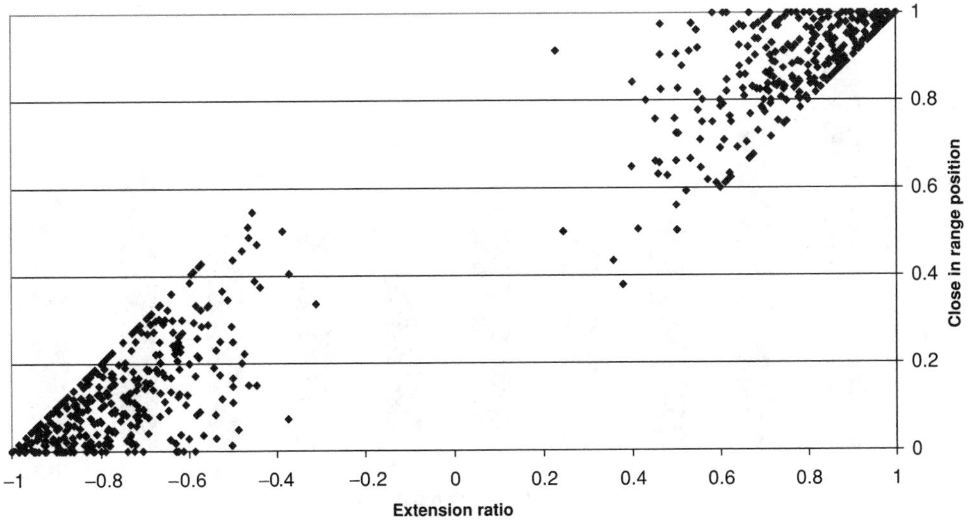

Figure 2.3 KLAC scatter plot for the extension ratio and close in range position – all intraday movements greater than 4% (absolute) since 1993

extension patterns are what might be called incoherently related and could in some sense be called noisy or random. Looking at this scatter plot one could easily conclude that for minor fluctuations there is a straightforward sense in which prices could be thought of as being randomly distributed. But, we are here talking about the smaller absolute daily changes of less than 2%. These are also the most typical of the series with almost 50% of the total observed daily data points falling into this category.

Switching our attention to Figure 2.3 this scatter diagram covers the other end of the spectrum as it shows only the absolute movements of more than 4%. The pattern is completely unlike the one we just examined and has much greater similarity with Figure 2.1.

What is very noticeable about Figure 2.3 is the absence of data points in the middle of the diagram. This time, however, this is even more remarkable than in the case for Figure 2.1. In the situation examined in Figure 2.1 the x-axis represented signed percentage changes for the intraday range and as we were only concerned about +4% or −4% changes the middle of the x-axis would necessarily have no values. In the case of Figure 2.3 the x-axis represents the normalized ratio of the (close-open)/(high-low) and theoretically values anywhere along the spectrum could be possible. But even more striking is the symmetrical nature of the association between large negative values on the x-axis with low values on the y-axis (the bottom left-hand cluster) and the association of high values for the extension ratio with high values on the y-axis (the top right-hand cluster).

Far from being random and noisy there is a remarkably coherent and structured relationship displayed in Figure 2.3. *When there is a strong move in either direction there is a correspondingly strong likelihood that the move will be accompanied by the closing price pushing towards the extreme of the daily range*. When the price is moving down the close will be tending towards the low of the day and when the price is moving up the close will be tending towards the high of the day. Almost never will an extreme price move see the closing price in the middle of the

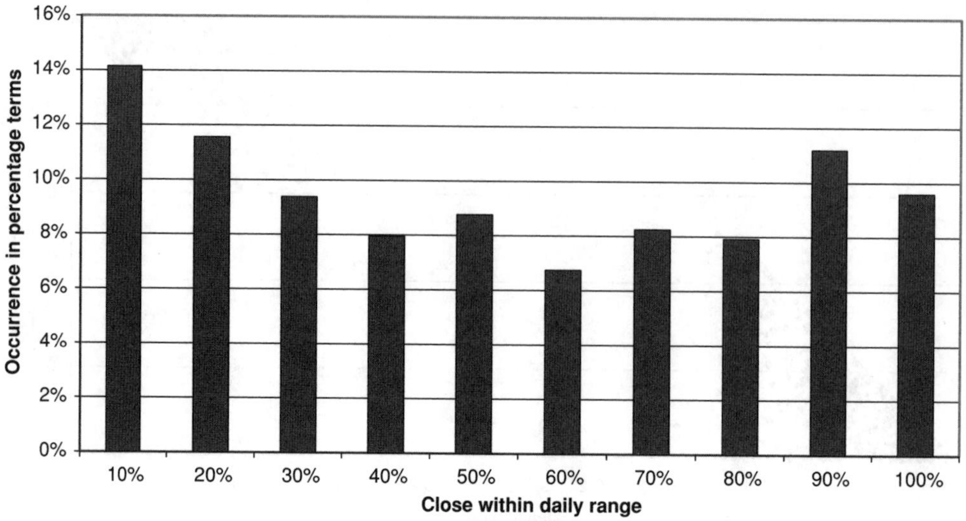

Figure 2.4 KLAC histogram showing position of close in the daily range – all data points since 1993

daily range and only rarely will it appear in the second and third quartile. When markets move decisively there is nothing tentative or neutral about their behavior. The market could be said to have put aside its "normal" fractiousness in favor of uniformity and coherence. The order book becomes one-sided and there is poor liquidity on the opposite side of the consensus view of price direction.

To further illustrate the manner in which coherent structure can be hidden or latent within an apparently random distribution we have created a frequency histogram showing the percentage occurrences of the closing bias for *all* of the data points that we have for KLAC – a total of more than 3300 such points.

The distribution for all of the trading sessions that we have analyzed, shown in Figure 2.4, shows that the closing bias is fairly evenly distributed across the 10 deciles where it might appear. If the probability of a particular decile appearance is approximately equal to its appearance in any other decile we can say that this variable is more or less randomly distributed. In other words, for all of the trading sessions one would expect the close within each decile of the range to appear about 10% of the time, which is almost the case in Figure 2.4 (but with a slight bias toward more frequent appearances in the lowest decile value). The situation changes dramatically when we just look at the extreme sessions or trend days that we have described.

In an examination of the frequency histogram for just those sessions when the intraday market move was 4% or higher (Figure 2.5) there is a very different distribution that emerges from the data. Remember this data is "included" (obviously) in the distribution for all of the data points in Figure 2.4, but one could be forgiven for not realizing that it was there! There were 347 occasions on which there was a 4% or higher intraday movement and that is approximately 10% of all of the data points that we have for KLAC. What we find is nothing like the even distribution across all the deciles but rather an obvious skew to the distribution with virtually no occurrences in the lower deciles and an obvious preponderance in the upper three deciles. In other words when the stock has moved up more than 4% in the great majority of cases,

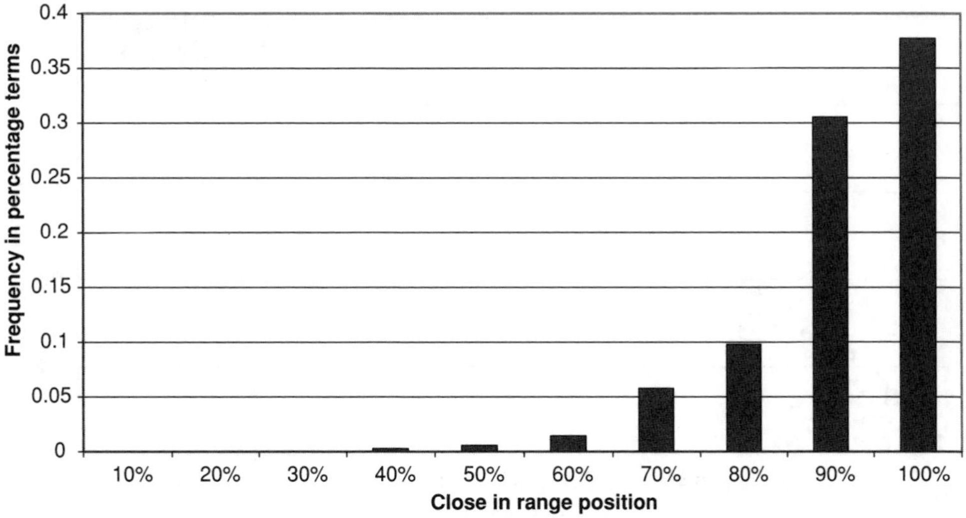

Figure 2.5 KLAC frequency histogram of extreme upside moves – all intraday moves greater than 4%

more than 75% of the time it will close at the upper end of its daily range (above the 80 percentile value).

With respect to the other side of the coin we now plot the frequency of occurrence (in percentage terms) of the close appearing in each of the deciles where the overall intraday market movement was greater than a 4% decline (i.e. $<-4\%$). There were 409 such occasions, more than 12% of the total data points and Figure 2.6 reveals the mirror image of Figure 2.5

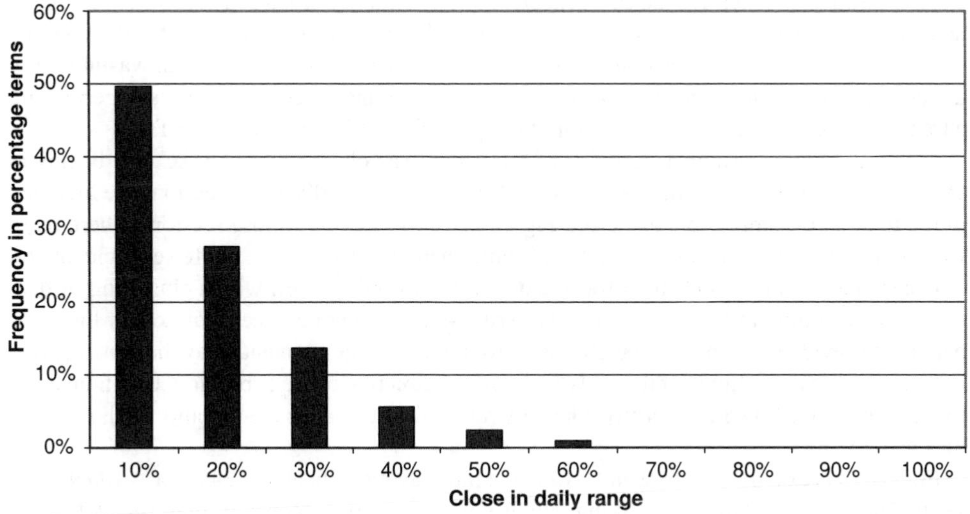

Figure 2.6 KLAC frequency histogram of extreme downward moves – all intraday moves of less than −4%

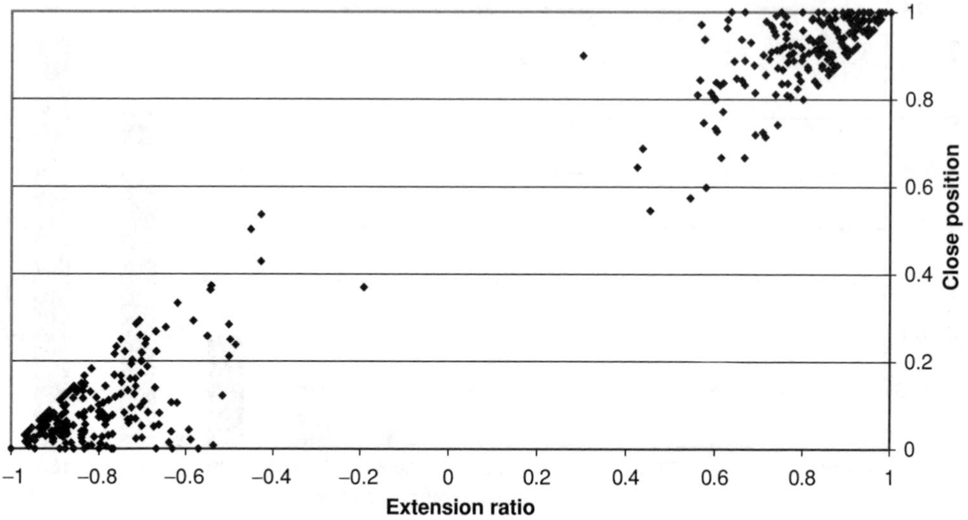

Figure 2.7 INTC plot of closing position and extension ratio – all intraday movements greater than 4% (absolute) since 1986

with the preponderance of values on the left-hand side indicating that on days when the market sells off after the open then it will tend to close near to the bottom of its overall intraday range. It is also interesting to observe that the slight asymmetry between the extreme up versus extreme down movements, with a bias toward more frequent extreme downward movements. In almost 80% of the cases where the market has dropped by more than 4% from its opening price it will close in the lowest two deciles with respect to its intraday range.

To reassure the reader that the coherent closing bias pattern is not just a peculiarity of KLAC and that its appearance is widespread two further charts have been included to illustrate the pattern. The chart template that most visibly portrays the pattern is the one that was in Figure 2.3 as it clearly displays the emptiness of the middle ground when a security is experiencing a trend day. Let us examine the same chart template for Intel Corporation (INTC).

Figure 2.7 covers a longer period for INTC than was observed for KLAC and begins in 1986 when INTC began trading on the NASDAQ. More than 5000 daily sessions are included in the total daily samples but as before Figure 2.7 only examines those sessions where there was an intraday movement (absolutely) of more than 4%. There were far fewer incidents on a percentage basis for INTC than for KLAC but the overall pattern with a clustering of data points in the bottom left-hand corner and top right-hand corner indicates that exactly the same pattern is in evidence. When a security has a pronounced range expansion day the closing price will congregate at the limits of the daily range in the direction of the expansion. One final chart for Amgen (AMGN) will hopefully allay any residual doubts as to the ubiquity of the closing bias pattern.

Figure 2.8 is exactly as before and covers the intraday movements of ±4% for AMGN since 1986. There were, relatively speaking, slightly more periods to consider than for INTC, but still fewer than for KLAC, but yet again the clustering of data points is clearly evident. Indeed one could make the case that for AMGN the center ground in the chart is even more void of data points than was observed for KLAC in Figure 2.3.

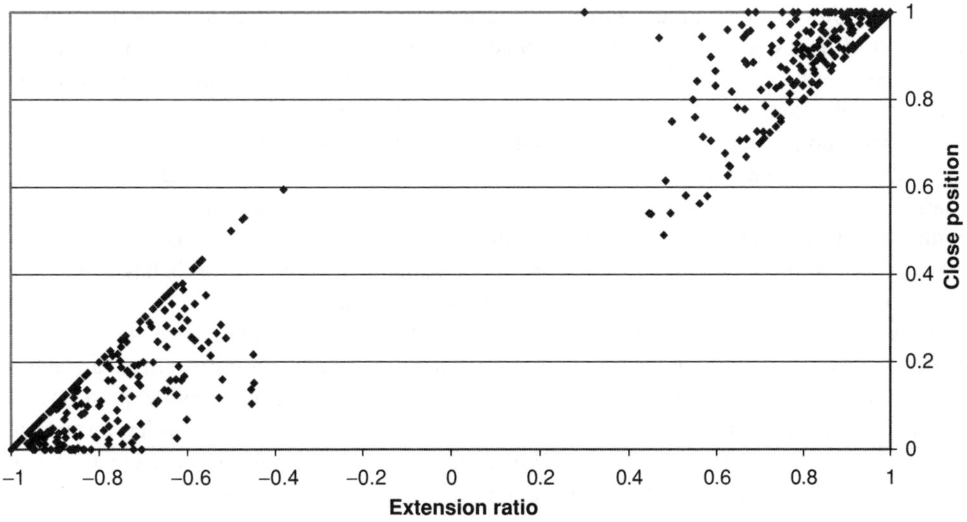

Figure 2.8 AMGN scatter plot of closing position and extension ratio – all intraday movements greater than 4% (absolute) since 1986

INTERPRETATION OF COHERENT CLOSING BIAS OF TREND DAYS

In considering the very striking difference between the distribution of the closing bias when all of the sessions are considered and only those that made it though the extreme filter, we can begin to formulate some hypotheses about the dynamics of price development. The coherent closing bias pattern lends itself to explanation by models that have been proposed from the worlds of econophysics and other disciplines focused on nonlinear systems.

In the natural sciences a "phase transition" occurs when a physical object that can take variable values passes through certain critical stages and its behavior or the behavior of its constituent parts and processes undergoes a transformation or change in its morphological characteristics. In effect quantitative changes to the variable, i.e. changes that can be measured, produce qualitative changes in which the variable's state changes so radically that it takes on entirely different qualities or attributes. The often cited example is the change in H_20 as it changes from ice to water to steam or vapor.

We have seen for KLAC, INTC and AMGN (and the behavior is typical of most time series data for equities) that there is a transformational change in each stock from its "normal" behavioral characteristics (i.e. how it performs in the majority of circumstances when the intraday movements are less than ±4%) to how it behaves in the more extreme sessions that we analysed. These extreme sessions can vary from approximately 25% of the total trading sessions in the case of KLAC to less than 10% in the case of INTC. But in all cases there is phase transition taking place. The price dynamics that are characteristic of smaller intraday fluctuations show a random quality that is strikingly absent when range expansion and larger movements are taking place.

When we consider all of the data series it would appear that the closing bias acts in a random (i.e. independent and identically distributed) fashion. The closing position with respect to the intraday range is, by and large, equally as likely to be in any one of the decile ranges. But as the magnitude of the intraday directional change grows, traders' opinions about the likely direction of prices begin to cohere, they become more and more aligned in their estimation of the near-term course of the market. There is a virtual unanimity of opinion that leads to a dramatic diminution of liquidity. Price takes the path of least resistance as even those who longer term do not subscribe to the prevailing view of the day, step aside to allow those in control of the agenda for that day to achieve their objective. During this trading session the market participants may have decided to suspend their usual fractious *modus operandi* (i.e. fading a trend after it reaches a certain point such as a moving average). This is not to overlook the fact that in the following session they may resume their more typical behavior or even decide to reverse the unidirectional nature of the previous session.

Why would normally argumentative and skeptical traders, who usually have very different views about the feasibility of the current price, decide to suspend their normal intraday tactics such as fading a price advance? This is a reformulation of the chapter's opening question and to come closer to an answer to it we need to discuss the reflexive notion of price formation. The classic treatment of the reflexivity in financial markets was proposed by the great English economist J.M. Keynes in his epic work, *The General Theory of Employment*:

> Professional investment may be likened to those newspaper competitions in which the competitors have to pick out the six prettiest faces from a hundred photographs, the prize being awarded to the competitor whose choice most nearly corresponds to the average preferences of the competitors as a whole; so that each competitor has to pick, not those faces which he himself finds prettiest, but those which he thinks likeliest to catch the fancy of the other competitors, all of whom are looking at the problem from the same point of view. It is not a case of choosing those which, to the best of one's judgment, are really the prettiest, nor even those which average opinion genuinely thinks the prettiest. We have reached the third degree where we devote our intelligences to anticipating what average opinion expects the average opinion to be.[7]

Once a certain price threshold is crossed (a tipping point) during intraday trading, the majority of market participants or average opinion begins to concur that for this particular day's trading average opinion has already chosen today's winner of the beauty contest. To use an expression taken from a totally different context but which can be adapted for the present purpose, it is as if for this trading session all have agreed that "There is nothing more powerful than an idea whose time has come." But the cynic would be right to add "Until the next day when everyone looks at the idea again and decides that it wasn't so clever after all." The usual market contrarians move to the sidelines and those positioned on the wrong side during a coherent session add fuel to the fire as they rush to correct their inappropriate positions. When average opinion realizes that average opinion is becoming increasingly uniform and coherent (e.g. a "bandwagon" is starting) it very soon becomes entirely coherent. Entirely coherent markets lose their liquidity, at least for the duration of the session in question. Liquidity could thus be said to go through "phase transitions" as opinions among market participants move along a spectrum of fractiousness $\rightarrow$ coherence.

PERCOLATION MODEL FOR UNDERSTANDING LIQUIDITY

The percolation metaphor can also be useful in this context as it helps to explain the quality of the order books when there are sudden changes in market liquidity. During the typical trading session where there is a wide diversity of opinions the order book will have a highly fractal quality (reflecting the fractious characteristics we have described) with many limit orders scattered through different price points. This fractal organization provides liquidity throughout the price spectrum and even though price can jump between different levels that have been identified by traders to be significant under normal conditions, there will be several layers at which market activity can be conducted without discontinuities arising. If, however, there is a sudden change in price or the sudden emergence of a much more coherent and united view of the price direction then many market participants will begin to change their order flow and cancel previous limit orders. A major realignment of orders takes place and they will all be tending towards the one side of the market which is becoming the prevailing direction. The scalpers who have been constantly caught out by trying to fade a move which does not want to be faded, the position trader who is on the wrong side of the market and is seeing the position P&L steadily moving against him and the momentum traders who see a locomotive that is gaining speed are all persuaded to climb aboard. Naturally inclined skeptics and contrarians either join the emerging consensus as well or step aside deciding that there is an irresistible force at work. Coherence and unequivocal opinion emerges and once certain price and volume thresholds are crossed then the degree of consistency in the estimation of near-term direction becomes not only something that the market notices but it becomes the phenomenon itself. At such points it can be noted that nothing influences price development more than the way that price is developing.

The extreme trending process becomes inherently self-aware and recursive in a process that is sometimes called positive feedback. In terms of the percolation model the normal fractious nature of the order book, by agents operating at different time frames with different price targets, starts to dissolve and large gaps open up in the granularity and position sizes of the order flow. Price changes not only percolate between time frames but there is an alignment across time frames as traders in all time horizons amend their orders. The percolation threshold expands beyond a critical level at which price movement becomes accelerated.[8]

RANGE CONTRACTION

Inside days

In 1988 Larry Williams published a book entitled *The Definitive Guide to Futures Trading*, which many (including this author) consider a landmark publication in the field of technical analysis. Williams' book outlines a pattern recognition methodology that he had been using successfully for many years in trading within the futures markets, and that was remarkably powerful and simple in its approach. After reading this book the present author became convinced about the importance of range contraction sessions in the market.

Earlier in this chapter, trend days were shown to have very distinctive features that make them attractive for the trader. Price moves quite decisively in one direction as range expansion is the underlying pattern that is being expressed. What is appealing about the insights that Larry Williams discusses in his work is his view that those sessions in which there is, in effect, a contraction in range may be just as significant as range expansion days. Also refreshing about the technique that Williams proposed is its simplicity and geometrical nature. Techniques which involve moving averages, standard deviations and so on, most certainly have a major role to play in quantitative and technical analysis of the markets but there is something refreshing and attractive about the idea that one can study markets by using the simple geometry of the OHLC data that is derived from each period of trading. Price geometry is perhaps best captured in the

Japanese candlestick techniques, which also have considerable value, but the simplest form of pattern recognition is based on cataloging the results of a sequence of OHLC formations and looking for those patterns which would yield the most profit potential.

Before examining the range contraction phenomenon the reader will hopefully indulge the present author in a brief autobiographical detour. Williams devotes Chapter 8 of his book to a study entitled "Patterns to Profits" and it would not be misleading to suggest that this core idea was a starting out point for me on my search over the last 20 years for a trading methodology that will not only generate consistent profits but would also provide intuitive understanding of the way in which markets behave. During this journey there have been many excursions into areas such as computational finance, genetic algorithms, self-organized criticality, Kelly money management techniques and much more,[9] but after each enjoyable detour I always return to what in some ways is the simplest and most important piece of the puzzle. *What can we observe about price patterns in the markets that will enable us to make more or less reliable forecasts about the near-term direction of prices?* Personally, I have forsaken the notion that longer-term market forecasting is a realistic possibility. Despite being persuaded (even enthusiastically) at different times that there is merit in such techniques as Elliott Wave analysis or a novel theoretical framework advocated by a cutting edge econophysicist, I have now set my expectations sufficiently modestly that I will be more than satisfied if I can make reliable forecasts that extend from a few days to a few weeks at most.

Let us return to Williams' chapter on "Patterns to Profits" and we shall quote from it quite liberally:

> Market folklore over the years has been that there are four basic patterns that are extremely reliable for trading . . . but I shall shatter some old traditions about what are supposed to be profitable patterns and will also reveal to you new patterns that are in fact profitable. (p. 179)

He begins by looking at one of the patterns that he believes and demonstrates has erroneously been considered as reliably profitable – a key reversal day:

> A reversal day is any day whose low was lower than the previous day, but whose close is higher than the previous day's close. This indicates a reversal since the market went down to new lows for the day, then came back, with buying pressure, closing higher than yesterday's close . . . Depending on which trader you talk with, this is either a phenomenally good, or an astoundingly good buy point . . . The records indicate otherwise. (pp. 180–181)

Based on back testing several futures markets Williams shows that the technique produces mixed and mediocre results at best. There is no need to rehash his findings or even to update his back testing by looking at more recent results of identifying the patterns. The point is simply to emphasize how the rather simple pattern recognition procedures that he describes and the extensive computerized back testing that he undertook produced results that were strikingly contrary to the market folklore. He separates the useful patterns that deliver profitable trades from those that are believed to be profitable but on close examination are effectively useless. He subjects various simple patterns to analysis including gap days, outside days and then inside days. And it is in the section on inside days that he reveals one of the secrets that made him a highly successful trader:

> Chartists and authors have not paid very much attention to inside days over the years. They have made note of them, but this is the first time, to my knowledge,

> that anyone has made a serious study of the impact of inside days. And wouldn't you just know it . . . inside days are one of the most reliable forecasting patterns to occur in the marketplace! (p. 218)

Williams proposes a variety of permutations that involve an inside day as a precedent condition and which is then followed by many other "geometrical formations". For example, he considers the following pattern – an inside day where the close is lower than the previous day and the low of the previous day is a 10 day low. This is the template for the pattern and in scanning across various markets (Williams scanned the futures markets) one can create a time projection/profit matrix showing how frequently the pattern leads to profits and how frequently it leads to losses. Regarding the pattern just mentioned and only to give the flavor of the Williams procedure it can be seen from back testing in 1988 (at the time that Williams was writing his book), in the case of the S&P 500, two days after the pattern occurs there were 71% times that one would be in profit and for U.S. Treasury bond futures the figure for three days hence would have been 87%.

Once again we do not need to spend too long on the actual historical data but rather to reflect on two issues. The first is a methodological one and it has to do with taking the simplest time series characteristics – the four elements of price OHLC only (no derived time series data such as EMAs or MACD data points) and using these as the basis for classification of pattern templates. The second point is that "hidden" within these patterns may be counterintuitive notions that defy the popular market folklore. Indeed by uncovering the reliability of certain permutations involving the inside day element to a two day pattern, Williams performed a significant leap forward in drawing attention to this particular aspect of market behavior. Moreover Williams' work has been seminal in underlining the fact that the occurrence of narrow range or inside range patterns are precursors to trend reversals or breakouts.

This has been taken up by many practitioners and one of the more notable is Toby Crabel who also came from a futures background. As we shall see later Crabel introduced some refinements to the idea that narrow range days have more forecasting power than had been previously acknowledged and proposed a methodology based upon the Opening Range Breakout.[10] Alan Farley acknowledges the influence of Toby Crabel's work in his own analysis of the importance of range contraction and expansion.[11] Farley has a pattern which he calls a coiled spring and it is based on Crabel's pattern of the NR7:

> This tiny signal represents the narrowest range bar of the last seven bars. The bar that immediately follows a NR7 often triggers a major price expansion. When price fails to eject immediately, the breakout may still appear one to three bars later. Sometimes the appearance of another NR7 on the next bar (NR7-2) rings a louder bell as odds increase for an immediate breakout event.[12]

In terms of trading with this pattern there is a compelling logic with regard to the risk/reward ratio in that the NR7 pattern is likely to appear before strong moves in either direction. If one is agnostic about the direction one can apply an ambivalent approach:

> Movement out of a NR7 should continue in the direction of the original violation. Place an entry stop just outside both range extremes at the same time and cancel one after the other order executes. This directional tendency permits a tight exit stop just beyond the opposite range extreme. Place this order at the level of the cancelled stop. This strategy takes advantage of price bar expansion regardless of market direction. Risk remains low because the NR7 range allows a very small loss when the trade fails.[13]

Before returning to the manner in which the impending breakout can best be applied it will be helpful to review several examples, from actual trading experience of how range contraction sessions are often associated with directional changes or breakouts. Some of the examples will show relatively short-term opportunities but there are others where the correct isolation of the key range contraction patterns were the precursors to large and sustained moves. While it may not be possible, contemporaneously, to differentiate the big opportunities from the smaller ones, if the trader is correctly positioned with the right money management techniques, then the small opportunities will give way to larger profit potential as one of the main features of the pattern is that the breakouts will be abrupt and decisive in nature.

The first chart (Figure 2.9) for Doral Financial (DRL) contains a mixture of signals based on range contraction events some of which are associated with minor inflection points and some of which are found at critical junctures when substantial profits can be earned in a very short time frame.

Figure 2.9 has many interesting chart patterns, some of which are examined elsewhere in this book but in this instance it is instructive just to focus on the narrow range sessions because many near-term turning points on the chart coincide with inside days and Doji formations. A Doji pattern is a very distinctive chart pattern that comes from the Japanese candlestick tradition. In essence the pattern reflects the situation within a trading session when the opening and closing price are virtually the same. The length of the upper and lower shadows (i.e. the distances to the high and low of the session) can take many different forms but the distinctive feature of the Doji is that the resulting candlestick looks like a cross. The formation is often found at market turning points and some have attributed its significance to the fact that traders are revealing their hesitation and indecision as they move price in both directions during the session but gravitate back to the starting point for the session.

The overall pattern for Figure 2.9 is of a complex topping formation with a third attempt in late March/early April 2006 to challenge the mid-February high (A) just above $12. Associated with A are two inside days which, when they occur soon after a new multi-period break to a new high or low, usually indicate hesitation and lack of conviction about whether to continue breaking to new ground. There was a lack of follow through at the $12 level and the stock retreated back to the $10 level by early March. Throughout March the stock rallies back towards its mid-February peak (A) but notably with waning momentum and declining money flow. The critical breakdown point is actually depicted at point B on the chart and yet again we find a revealing inside day just as the avalanche begins. Also worth noticing is the inside day at C which comes after several days of losses which brought DRL back to an area of potential chart support at $10. The inside day that was registered on this day again provides evidence that traders were hesitating at this point to see whether any buying support would appear to arrest the decline. As can be seen there was no attempt to rally and the stock continued down to a point on the right-hand side of the chart at $8.23 which is approximately 50% from the mid-February high. As an aside we could mention that there is an interesting interpretation of the bigger pattern to the chart for Doral. Some technicians might be tempted to identify a head and shoulders pattern in this chart and a plausible construction of this formation which is lurking within the data could be made. However, such large formations pose special problems for pattern detection algorithms and we have decided not to track this formation in our daily analysis of the markets.

The next chart (Figure 2.10) is for Office Depot (ODP) and shows a co-instantiation of three patterns that we have been reviewing. The candlestick found at B has all three properties; it is an inside day, it is a Doji formation and it is also an NR7 formation. What also makes the

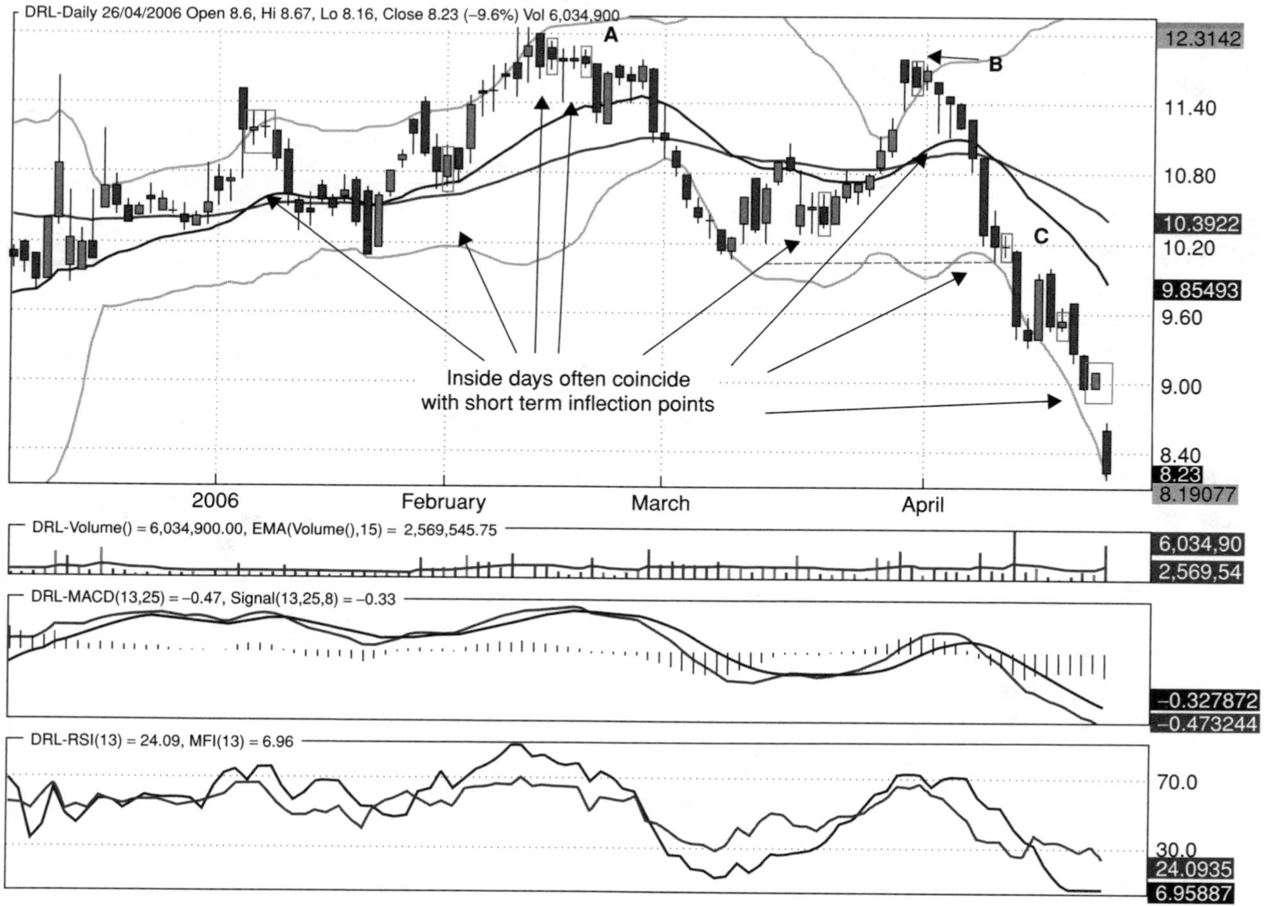

Figure 2.9 DRL showing inside days

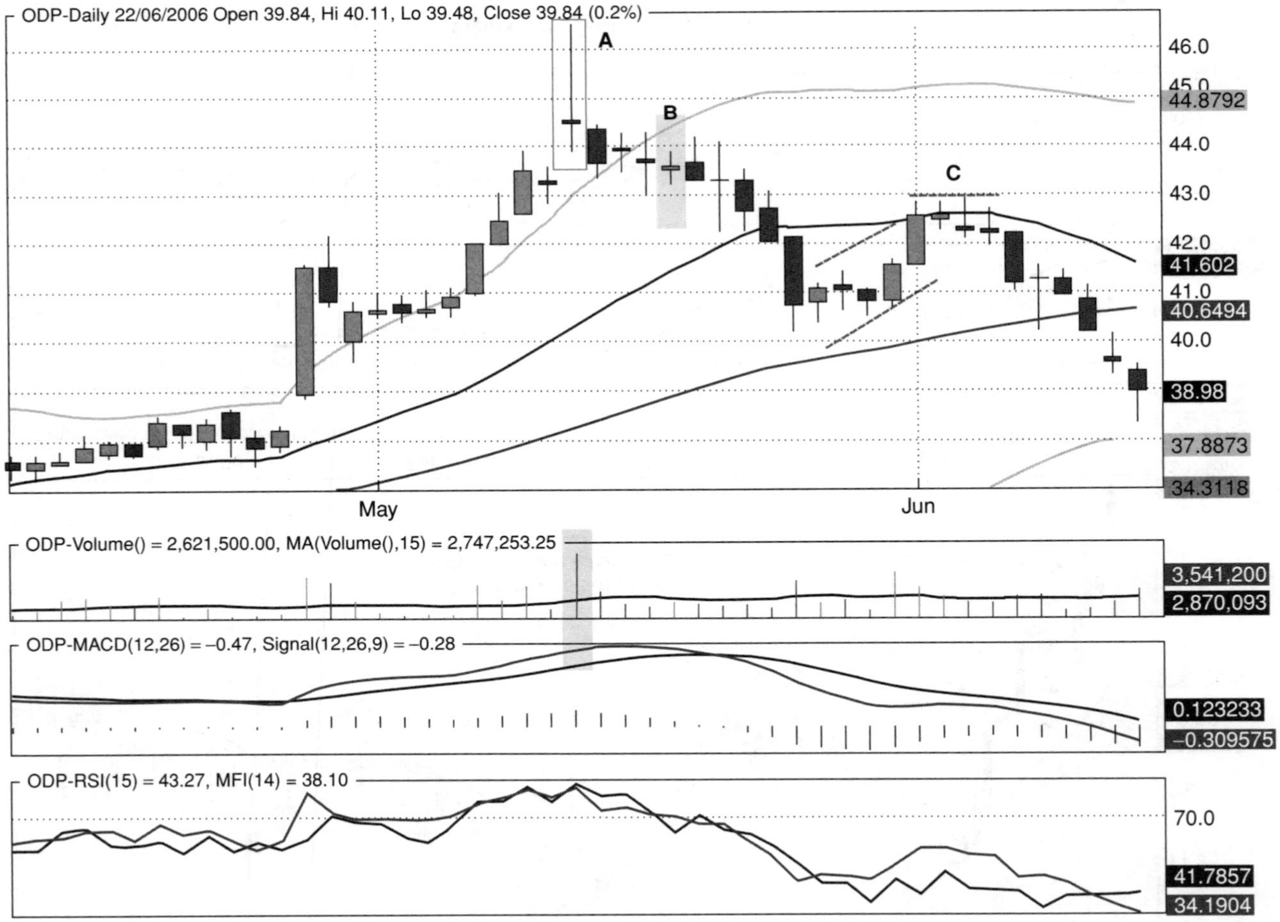

Figure 2.10 ODP inside days

pattern significant is that it occurs soon after the rather striking formation at A where ODP tried and failed to break above $46 with a powerful volume surge. The very long upper tail to the candlestick at A and the fact that the body of the candle is very narrow with a close that is nearer to the intraday low than the high suggests that there was a trend day in the making which reversed and failed. This is a warning signal that the overhead resistance is too formidable. What one wants to examine after such an occurrence is evidence as to how serious an effort will be made on an attempt to retest the breakout. When one confronts a very tentative pattern such as the one at B this suggests that the path of least resistance is a further retreat which is in fact what is observed. At the $41 level, which is an area with some previous resistance/support, the stock again tries to mount a new effort to revisit higher ground. A bearish looking pullback channel emerges and at point C we find the second very revealing inside day formation which occurs exactly at the 20 day EMA. The minor plateau that we have highlighted at $43 precisely illustrates the difficulty that ODP is encountering in its efforts to regain any positive momentum. This would have been an excellent entry point on the short side as there were three compelling reasons to be bearish on the stock.

The following factors would have contributed to a very reliable sell signal at point C:

- The earlier pattern at A and B shows clear overhead resistance at $46 and the rally back to C has the right characteristics for a bearish pullback channel.
- The momentum and money flow were deteriorating throughout May 2006 while the stock was trying to recover from the selling that emerges at B.
- The inside day at C followed by two more sessions in which price fails at $43 suggests that this is now the new overhead resistance barrier.

We would suggest that the perfect entry point would have been on the close of the day following the inside day at C as the stock failed to close above the level of the inside day. This would have provided an entry point just above $42 allowing for an approximate 10% profit within the next seven sessions.

In the next chart (Figure 2.11) for Disney (DIS) there are two examples of inside days that provide useful clues as to possible directional turning points. During April 2006 Disney had moved within a very narrow range between $27 and $28.20 with no exceptional volume sessions. At point A there was an attempt to break down below $27 which in hindsight can be seen as a fake-out in that it was clearly not in the direction that the stock was about to head. The three candlesticks at point A that coincide with the false breakdown are then followed by the highlighted inside day in which the lows below $27 are avoided. This suggests that for some traders, although the future course may be unclear and they are adopting a wait and see approach, there is at least some conviction behind the notion that there is support for the stock at $27 so there is no need to retest that level.

As we move forward the chart formation at point B is the most interesting and revealing. There is again, in similar fashion to what was observed on the ODP chart, a coincidence of three different patterns at point B – there is an inside day, there is a Doji candlestick pattern and, most strikingly, we find the NR7 pattern. The candle at B is tiny and we have learned to seek out these rather striking patterns as they are often important precursors to a major move. In this case we can see that the stock was about to enter a strong rally phase which begins three sessions later at C where the stock moved up on almost three times its average daily volume. The entire A $\rightarrow$ B pattern on the Disney chart is an example of a type of pattern that is often found in connection with turning points where we will find a false breakout in the opposite

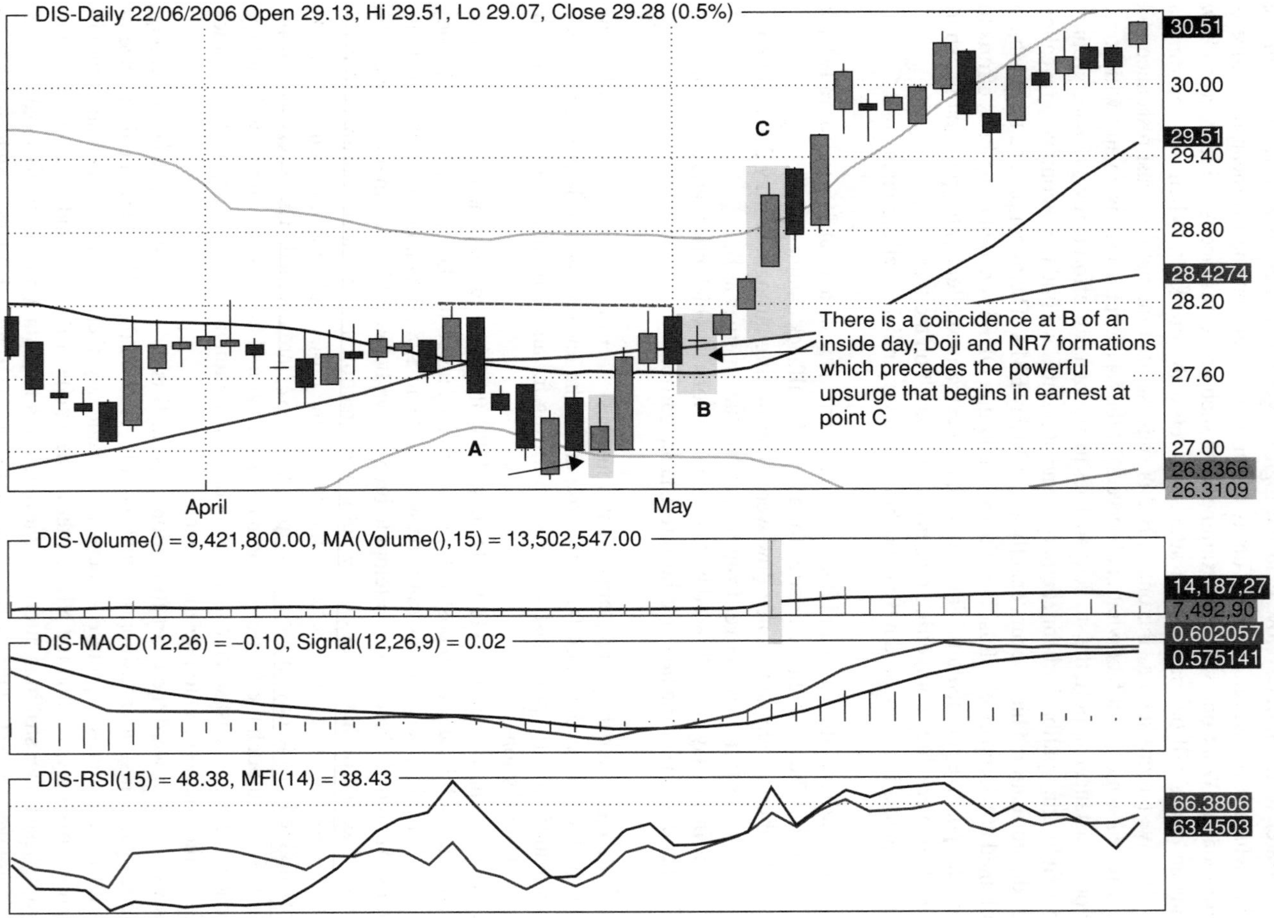

Figure 2.11 DIS inside days

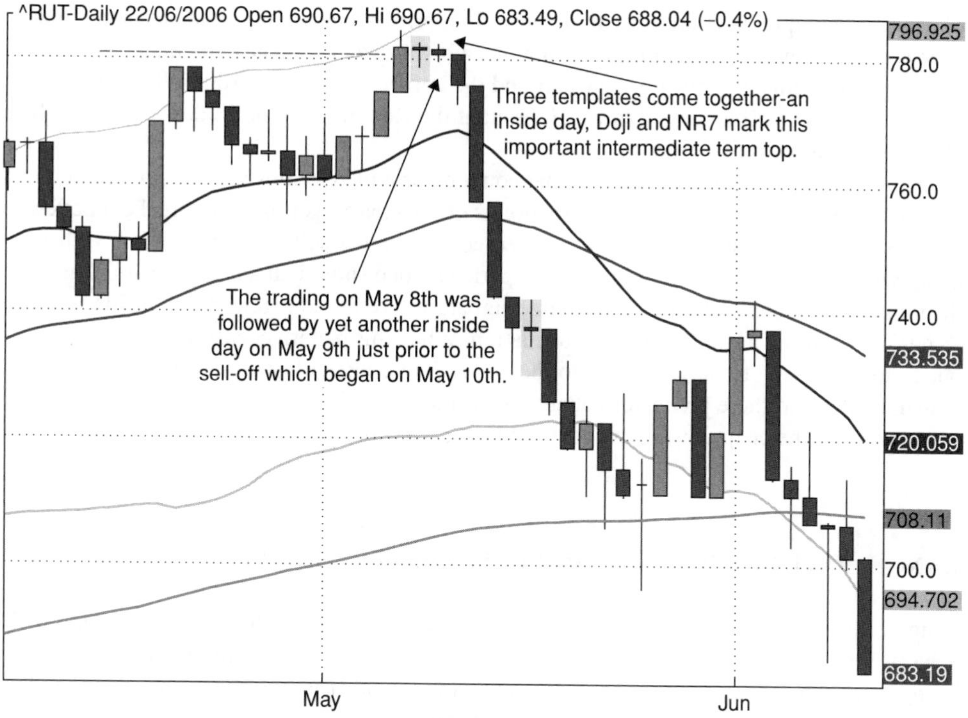
^RUT-Daily 22/06/2006 Open 690.67, Hi 690.67, Lo 683.49, Close 688.04 (–0.4%)
Three templates come together-an inside day, Doji and NR7 mark this important intermediate term top.
The trading on May 8th was followed by yet another inside day on May 9th just prior to the sell-off which began on May 10th.
796.925
780.0
760.0
740.0
733.535
720.059
708.11
700.0
694.702
683.19
May
Jun

Figure 2.12 Russell 2000 inside days

direction to the real one which is about to come, inside days at turning points and then a tiny candlestick which instantiates all three of the range contraction templates we have examined.

Continuing with the theme that tiny candlesticks can mark important turning points, the next chart (Figure 2.12) for the Russell 2000 index taken in May 2006 is also informative. During the early part of 2006 the small cap Russell 2000 index made a succession of new all time highs and in the session on May 5th 2006, which precedes the highlighted session, the index closed at 781.83 which was an all time high just exceeding the previous high from mid-April. So was there cause to celebrate a new further leg upwards? The chart formation that was registered on May 8th which we have highlighted is one that would have suggested caution rather than celebration. It is another example of all three patterns arising together – the NR7 formation, a tiny Doji candlestick and an inside day.

As it turned out the all time high on May 5th would have been a good time to be preparing to go short on the small cap index rather than believing that a new leg upwards was under way. Not for the first time (or the last) the markets would have confounded many players and misled a lot of index players that had been assuming a continuation of the bullish momentum to carry the index even further upwards. One possible way of interpreting the critical tiny candlestick that is highlighted is that it represents a reluctance to express any firm opinion on the future direction of price. Unlike the coherent trend days that we have examined in which liquidity conditions diminish because there is more or less a uniform view of the near-term price direction, in the case of these tiny candlesticks it would seem that there is no consensus view at all. Traders are demonstrating an unwillingness to take any kind of stand on near-term direction. The liquidity conditions at the prevailing price are not really tested as many traders appear to be sitting on the sidelines sensing that a big move may be just around the corner. As the chart shows this big move was just around the corner and on May 10th following another inside day the sell-off commences which brought the Russell 2000 index down by more than 100 points in just over one month.

There are numerous other examples that could be provided to illustrate the important point of this section which is that range contraction is often a harbinger of major breakout patterns. In the special circumstances that were observed for the Russell 2000, and also for Disney, along with many others from our trading experience, one should attach added significance to the range contraction pattern when all three signatures are found together – an inside session, an NR7 session and a Doji candlestick formation. When this pattern occurs the chart is sending out a clear message to pay attention to the impending course of price development. Having drawn attention to these precursor patterns we can now tie them together with the discussion from earlier in the chapter when we reviewed range expansion days.

RANGE CONTRACTION AS A PRECURSOR TO TREND DAY

Range contraction sessions are very often precursors to breakouts which often coincide with powerful trend days in which the trader who is forewarned can earn substantial profit within a single session. The attractiveness of the reward potential from trend days has commanded the attention of many well-known traders who have developed different trading strategies for anticipating breakouts and powerful range expansion sessions. In essence the technique is the same as the one that Farley alluded to earlier and that owes much to the suggestions of how to play the breakouts by Toby Crabel. Crabel's book is entitled *Day Trading With Short Term Price Patterns and Opening Range Breakout* and has become something of a cult classic. In essence the principle is that one determines certain price points, for the sessions that follow on from an NR7 session, that can act as automatic triggers which, if they are touched in the subsequent session, will leave a trader positioned to benefit from a strong trend day should it occur. The formula that has been proposed for determining an upward trigger by Crabel is the following. One finds the 10 day average of the minimum value between the following variables the high-open and the open-low and then one multiplies this resulting value by 1.1 (some other variations have been suggested).

An alternative method which allows one to be positioned on both sides is to set the triggers for the opening range breakout on both sides enabling one to benefit from both uptrend days and downtrend days. Once again Larry Williams has one of the simplest approaches which is to take the opening price on the session following an important range contraction event and then add (or subtract) a percentage of the previous day's true range. For a trigger to catch a bullish move the percentage could be 80% of the previous day's range and for a bearish move the figure could be to subtract 80% of the previous day's range.

A lot of articles have been written about the exact methods to follow to determine the opening range breakout with some believing that there is a magical formula that allows you to be sure of capturing the trend days when they should occur. But we would suggest that the more refined triggers suffer from a spurious degree of accuracy. It is interesting that Crabel's book has achieved almost mythical status with some traders and, since it is out of print, it can sometimes be found on eBay at prices measured in thousands of dollars.

We suggest that Larry Williams has it about right when he describes the mechanics of playing the breakout – "it is really just as simple as that, a pickup in range, substantially greater than yesterday's range implies a change in the current market direction . . . price almost always opens within the previous day's range . . . if there is an expansion or moving away from the opening, price will probably continue in that direction." This exactly echoes the point that John Paul Tudor Jones made in his interview with Jack Schwager. When markets speak with a united voice it makes a lot of sense to listen carefully to what they are saying.

There may not be the quantitative precision that one would need to program an algorithm to deliver the exact trigger points but essentially the simple rule of thumb is to put buy stops on either side of the opening price after an NR7 session that take into account a margin (based on the previous day's range) that prevents one from any obvious whipsaws. The next thing is to remember to be patient and to hold tight until the end of the session. As we have seen in connection with the Coherent Closing Bias phenomenon it is vitally important not to be impatient on a trend day as the chances are very strong that if you are correctly positioned for the directional surge you will want to exit on the close as it will probably be near the best levels of the day from the point of view of profitability.

3
Comparative Quantiles

Financial markets contain vital information about the way in which prices are likely to develop but the background "noise" is so distracting that the most revealing clues as to future likely direction remain largely hidden. Useful contributions to the vast literature of technical analysis have been motivated by the desire to develop the right techniques and methodology to enable the analyst and trader to separate the most pertinent information, the "nuggets", from the peripheral and information-less noise.

We shall contend that the primary reason why many quantitative techniques fail to unearth what is of most value to traders is that all data within a time series is treated as equivalently valuable or relevant. With tools such as moving averages and standard measures of dispersion, all of the applicable data is sucked into an algorithm or function, the data points are all treated equally and the output provides a vast array of statistical values, all precisely quantified, with the implicit promise that the essential information is now amenable to further analysis. However, our contention is that this process can capture too much data to be ultimately valuable to the trader. Because there is no differentiation as to the quality or appositeness of the data that is provided as input to statistical functions, we may find that the output statistics have only limited value in describing the data's key features.

To set the background for the cardinal issue that we will be making in this chapter we shall begin by examining an oft-quoted remark that points to the inherent limitations of the arithmetic mean – "My feet are in the furnace and my head is in the freezer so on average I'm feeling fine." What the remark is really pointing to is the fact that an average will "smooth" out extreme values to produce a rather bland ("middle of the road") numerical value that, taken on its own, gives no clues as to the extreme values that are included in its calculation. A human being would not be fine if his body extremities were exposed to such hostile conditions, and an arithmetic mean calculation that smoothes away the extreme, "outlier" events within a time series also fails to tell us what the series is really like. We can easily lose sight of the more interesting features of price data – the critical moments as the time series evolves – because these will tend to be subsumed in any averaging process. Instead of having a map with the critical contours and major peaks and valleys preserved an averaging technique produces an amorphous and monotonic pathway through the middle ground.

QUANTILES EXPLAINED

Our view is that markets are most revealing when they stray from the norm, which is why we focused in Chapter 2 on trend days and inside days. As we shall also discover with other market metrics such as volume, the quieter (low volume) sessions and the more active (high volume) sessions are usually more revealing than the sessions when there is more typical volume. With this in mind we propose that each market metric should be thought of as being best represented as a continuum or spectrum of values and that the value recorded for each session should be situated in that spectrum's range. Once such a continuum is assumed it becomes feasible to identify which segment of the spectrum each daily position occupies. There is a commonly used term within statistics that is applicable to the situation we have just described – a quantile. A quantile is a generic term that covers some better known specific instances which includes percentiles and deciles. The central idea behind quantiles in general is that data is ranked (i.e. sorted from lowest to highest) and then, depending on which quantile one is interested in, for example, the lower decile, the relevant quantile value can be identified from looking at the data values that lie within the appropriate interval. If we are focusing on the lower decile then we would be interested in the value that represents the demarcation point that separates out the lowest 10% of the values.

If this sounds too abstract let us be more concrete. What we are interested in can best be illustrated by thinking through one of the best known quantile values, which is the median value of a data series. To take a simple example if we have 101 people in a room and we rank them by their incomes, the exact midpoint of the ranking (i.e. the 51st person) will have the median income. Alas most things in statistics are not as simple as they seem and that is why we chose our sample size as 101 people rather than 100 because then the 51st person in the ranking has the median income. There are 50 people with incomes less than the median person and 50 people with incomes higher than the median person.[1]

The median value implicitly requires a ranking of the data unlike the mean value which simply sums the values and divides by the number of values. One of the main advantages of the median is that it is less sensitive to the inclusion of outliers. To revert to the example of the incomes of a small group, imagine what would happen if there is an addition to the group. Assuming that the members of the original group have incomes that are fairly typical of the general population the median value will, for the original grouping, also have a value that is very much in accordance with the median for the general population. But if a successful hedge fund manager is added to the group the arithmetic mean will jump dramatically and the mean value will no longer be similar to the typical income value of either the group or the population. However, the median value will not change as the ranking will ensure that the manager's income will be at the boundary of the ranking and therefore not be a factor in terms of the midpoint value. The median value can justifiably make claims to be the best indicator of the typical value in a series and it will usually correspond to an actual value (unless it has to be interpolated) as opposed to a theoretically derived value such as the mean.[2]

The vital point of this example is that the original data, whether it be a series of individual heights or incomes, closing prices, volume figures, MACD values, MFI values, log changes or even beta values, needs to be sorted and then subdivided according to the quantile that is specified. Users of software tools like Excel will be familiar with some of the functions that enable one to identify key quantile values such as the median, the quartile and the percentile values. With the appropriate Excel functions, for example =PERCENTILE(cell address, percent value), the parameters that are required by the function are the cell addresses or array

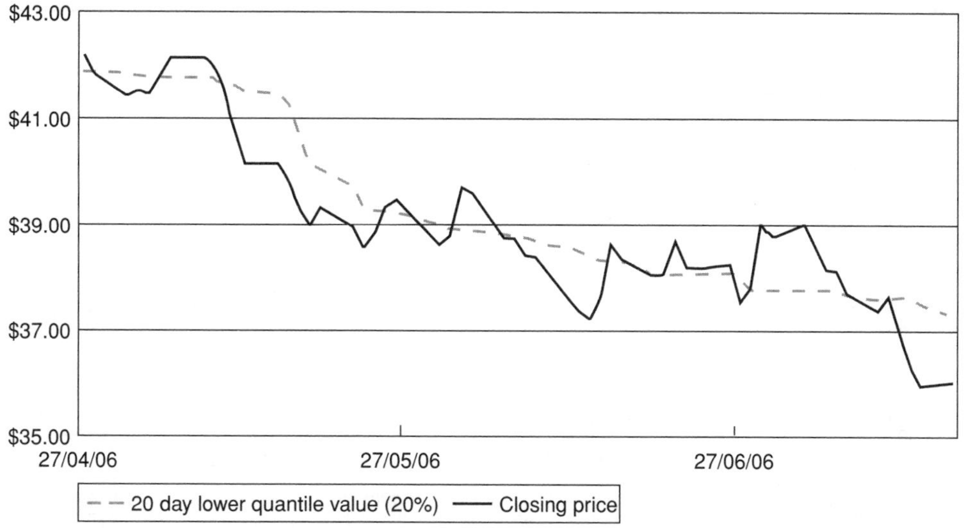

Figure 3.1 QQQQ April–July 2006 showing closing price and lower quantile values

that contains the values from which you wish to extract the quartile value and a specification of exactly which percentile value is required. This parameter can be specified in the interval between 0 and 1 so specifying 0.20, for example, would return the value that lies on the boundary for the lowest 20% of the values in the data series. It pinpoints the demarcation value for ranking the data so that the lowest 20% of values fall below the 20 percentile value.

In the case that follows we will set the lower quantile value at the 20 percentile value as we explore the price data for the NASDAQ 100 proxy, QQQQ. The period covers April through mid-July 2006 which corresponds with a period of overall market weakness and in particular a period when the NASDAQ 100 rather sharply underperformed the S&P 500.

Figure 3.1 has been kept as simple as possible to illustrate the lower quantile value. The dotted line corresponds to the 20 percentile value calculated from looking back at the closing price from the previous 20 sessions. For each session in the moving window the calculation is performed by ranking all of the data within the window and calculating the demarcation point that segregates the bottom 20% of values. All of these demarcation values are then plotted as a derivative time series in the same manner as the more familiar moving average. In the above example the quantile series is derived from the closing price series but it could just as easily be based on any number of variables. We might want to track the lower quantile for the daily lows or the daily volume or for other derived values such as the money flow values (as we shall discuss in Chapter 4). Once the value is computed we can easily detect those sessions when the variable of interest, in this case the closing price, is either above or below the designated quantile value. A cursory review of Figure 3.1 shows that, during most of the period in question, the closing price is below the lower quantile value. Price is seeking out even lower closes than the weaker closes indicated by the trailing 20 day window. Just as with a moving average the procedure can be tuned more exactly by selecting exactly the data window one desires and even weighting the quantile values in the same manner as an exponential moving average. In the discussion that follows in order to keep matters as lucid as possible we will proceed with pure vanilla quantiles and will normally use a 20 day window.

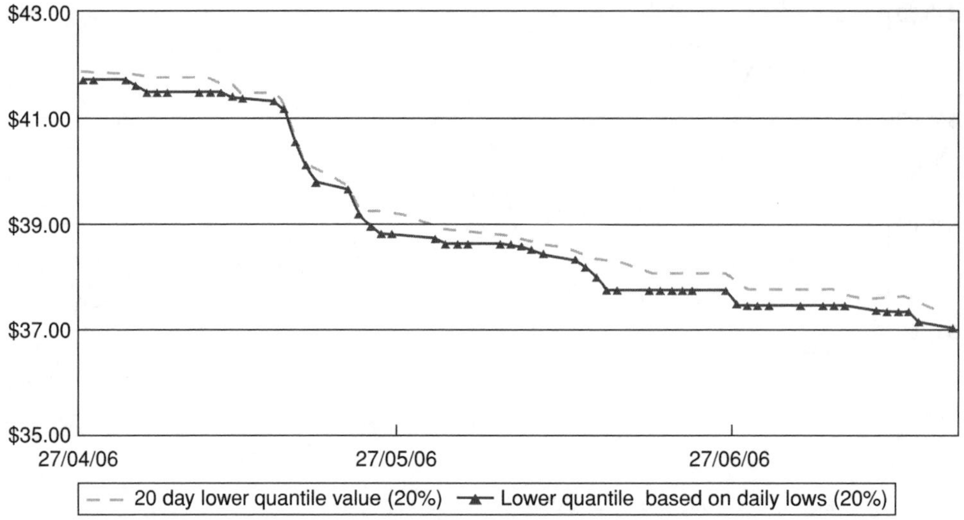

Figure 3.2 QQQQ April–July 2006 showing lower quantile values based on daily closes and lows

To further introduce the quantiles approach and provide more background to the more advanced techniques based on the comparative quantiles framework, the next chart in Figure 3.2 shows two series for the lower quantile value. The dotted line, as before, represents the 20 percentile for the daily closing prices, and the second line, with triangles, represents the 20 percentile for the daily lows during the same lookback period of 20 days. The envelope that is created between the lower quantile based on the closes and the lower quantile based on the lows has contained the closing price throughout the period. This suggests that the price lows achieved in the moving window are anticipating the upcoming direction of the closing price to a rather significant extent. In itself this can provide additional insights to the more customary charts involving moving averages and price envelopes created by volatility bands, for example. However, we are still introducing the concepts and will reserve our main discussion for those occasions when a primary data series value such as the daily closing price transgresses each of the separate quantile values that one is tracking. By tracking coincidental transgressions we can find important clues as to divergences and confirmations.

Figure 3.3 shows the envelope that is formed by the lower quantile for the daily closes (again based on the 20 percentile) and the upper quantile for the daily closes (based on the 80 percentile). The dashed line this time corresponds to the 20 day simple moving average and the closing price is also indicated as the line with the squares. As already intimated charts based on first order quantiles (i.e. the values inputted to the percentile function are the raw OHLC data) can have value in their own right, but the really fruitful use of quantiles is to be found in using derived time series data such as quantiles that track the closing bias that was discussed in Chapter 2 or quantiles that track the intraday range values.

At this point we need to step back and consider exactly how best to interpret Figure 3.3. The derived time series that corresponds to the upper quantile values is showing the trend from the previous 20 days of the highest closing prices (i.e. those that lie within the uppermost 20% when they are ranked). It effectively ignores the middle of the road values and captures what is occurring at the upper boundary. In terms of the ranking procedure there may be a constant

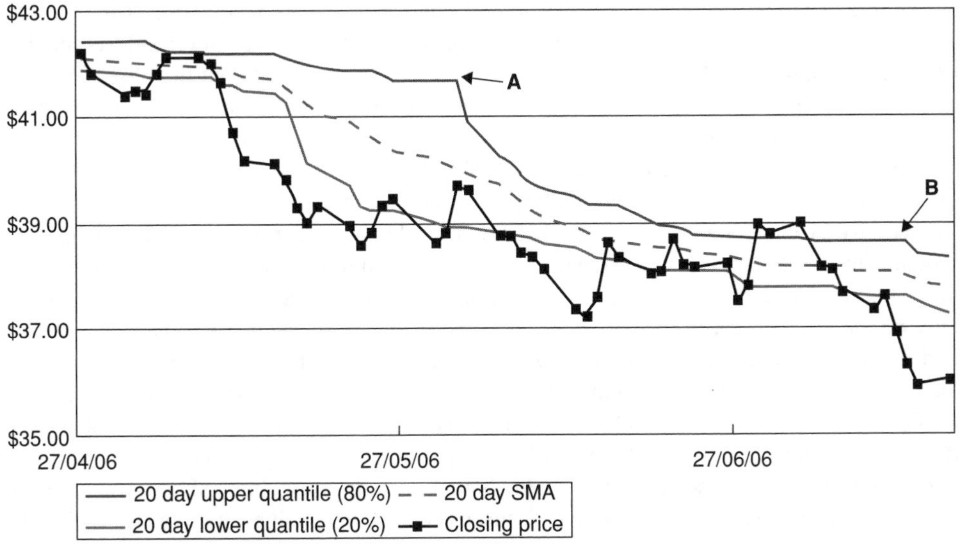

Figure 3.3 QQQQ April–July 2006 showing upper and lower quantile values

reshuffling of the actual instances of the closing price that are included in the upper quantile or there may be a kind of temporary "freezing" of the values. With respect to the upper quantile, if prices are deteriorating then there will be few additions, if any, of newer values to the upper interval as the time window moves forwards. The trend of the line revealing the upper quantiles may form a plateau which indicates that new higher prices are not being achieved and that the ranking is preserving a "stale" series of values. There will be sudden "cliffs" when the high values are dropping and the previously captured values slip out of the time window. This can actually be observed in Figure 3.3 especially at the point marked A, and, to a lesser extent, at the point marked B. The steepness of the cliff after a plateau gives a sense of how steep are the declines in the underlying price values under examination. By being selective about the data that is evaluated and only considering the boundary values one obtains a more responsive and pliable indicator of underlying market dynamics. As was noted previously one can avoid the tendency of averaging techniques to smooth away the rough edges that often contain the most valuable market data. Sometimes the smoothing effect of averages is exactly the behavior that is required from an indicator, but on other occasions it is very desirable to focus on the data from the untypical trading sessions.

DATA SELECTIVITY

Rarely, in reviewing the finance literature, do we encounter any suggestions that in analyzing historical time series data, it may be more useful to use a selective approach to data runs. Instead there seems to be an unspoken bias that the more all embracing a data run is the more efficacious it will be. If there is 20 years of high frequency data available on a particular asset, the view seems to be let's use it all in the belief that the more data that is used the more reliable the diagnosis will be. For certain purposes, the kind of hypothesis testing that uses all available data will be the most appropriate to use. But once one goes beyond trends and moving averages and tries to discern important information about turning points in price development, in other words, how markets behave during critical phases, we should put the obsession with comprehensiveness aside. Selectivity will allow us to zoom in on that part of the data spectrum that is likely to reveal the most useful information.

At this point we should anticipate a possible objection to the whole enterprise of data selectivity. An argument could legitimately be made that in analyzing the historical data for any security the data for all sessions should have equivalent status, and that we are on dangerous ground when we attempt to separate those sessions which have a "special" quantile status from those that are "ordinary" or typical. The argument could be that if we focus our attention only on the special occasions that show up in the quantiles of interest we may miss out on underlying price development trends that creep up on us during the ordinary sessions. But there is an important rejoinder to this argument which is that all of the data is considered in the comparative quantiles methods that we are advocating, it is implicit in the rankings. Even if a particular data point occupies the middle ground in the rankings its inclusion contributes to the delineation of the values that lie on the boundaries that are of interest. No data has been ignored but rather the spotlight has been focused on those data values that register within the quantiles which deserve the most attention.

Another paradoxical quality concerning data selectivity is worth commenting on as well. Much market analysis is confined to only the closing price and volume data in a historical time series. Returns can be easily calculated from only considering succeeding closes and since this provides the basic data for log change analysis the other dimensions of market prices – the open, high and low – tend to be ignored. Practitioners of technical analysis and actual traders themselves are keenly aware of the usefulness of the full range of OHLC data, and this richer data set has been used extensively in the construction of numerous technical indicators. True range, which we have found to be one of the more useful and relevant market metrics, can only be computed using OHLC data. Equally important is the notion of an intraday range or change and this can only be referenced by the change from the open to the close of the current session rather than the current close to the previous close. Without using the O, H and L it is impossible to get a perspective on intraday volatility as opposed to interday volatility and both of these metrics need to be determined for a proper analysis of volatility as we shall see in Chapter 6.

COMPARATIVE QUANTILES ANALYSIS (CQA)

Market behavior can best be thought of as falling into three phases – quiet, normal (or typical) and critical. Each phase has its own characteristics. Our analytical tools will focus on those quantiles that are designed to zoom in on the quiet and the critical (which will usually correspond for most variables to the lower and upper quantiles) and we shall pay less attention to the mid-range quantiles. As previously mentioned, this does not mean that we ignore the mid-range quantile values. If the typical values that occupy the mid-range quantiles were excluded from the data extraction process the ranking procedure that is implicit in the quantiles approach would fail to register the more interesting values that are pushed outwards to the boundaries by their insertion into the mid-range values.

Analysis based on comparative quantiles is concerned primarily with the time series data that falls within the boundary quantiles. What we are advocating is a systematically selective method of stratifying data points into those that are especially suited for a specific purpose. The specific purpose may involve volume analysis, range expansion, inside day analysis or whatever but the important issue is that by selecting the most relevant data for the specific purpose we are able to focus our attention on the critical or vital data rather than the overwhelming amount of background data which obscures what we are looking for.

The first intuition at this stage to help explain the CQA approach is to introduce the notion that quantile values can be extracted from two different but related sets of data points such as closing price and volume from a particular stock's history. When we use a moving time window approach where we look back at (say) the previous 20 data points for that specific series, we can then determine whether the current data point (or point that is being currently analysed by the algorithm) is above the quantile threshold, below it, or possibly equal to the specified quantile value. As soon as that marker has been established many different realms of analysis become possible such as a comparison between what may be happening in the upper quantile with respect to price but the lower quantile with respect to volume or the range for the session. It is for this reason that we call the methodology comparative quantiles analysis (CQA) and before explaining in more rigorous terms the precise procedures to follow we would like to provide a little more background to why we believe that the tools are so useful.

The example that follows is intended to illustrate the benefits of the technique and we hope to show that, even though the technique does require a fair amount of computation, it can be performed within an Excel framework. For those who are able to program in a language such as C++ or Java the algorithms are relatively simple to code and the great benefit is that the setup for different data series is much more straightforward than having to treat the data within the confines of a spreadsheet format.

CASE STUDY – NEWMONT MINING (NEM)

The first case study, as illustrated in Figure 3.4, will be for Newmont Mining (NEM) and the period selected is from January 2005 to the end of May 2006. During the period the stock experienced a major upward move from $35 in May 2005 to almost $60 at the beginning of 2006, but NEM also encountered a number of corrective episodes as can be seen on the chart. Figure 3.4 is a weekly chart of the stock's performance with the four episodes annotated as A, B, C and D which marked turning points that preceded corrective behavior.

The first correction that begins at A was the largest in percentage terms as the stock moved down 24% from almost $46 in March 2005 to $35 in May 2005. The correction that begins at point C in early February 2006 resulted in a 20% retracement and this was fairly closely mirrored by the separate correction that begins at point D. The brief and shallow retracement that begins at B led to only a 12% fall in October 2005.

The intuition that motivates the comparative quantiles approach is that turning points will be more readily identified and recognized by the focus on the upper and lower quantile values for specific variables. To test the effectiveness of the CQA methodology we need to see how well the signals that are generated conform to the turning points that are in evidence on the price charts.

With Figure 3.5 we will begin to witness the benefits that flow from the techniques of comparative quantile analysis. The chart will require some explanation as the material that is presented is unfamiliar. The time axis for Figure 3.5 is more or less the same period as that covered in Figure 3.4 with a slight delay on the left-hand side to allow for the trailing window

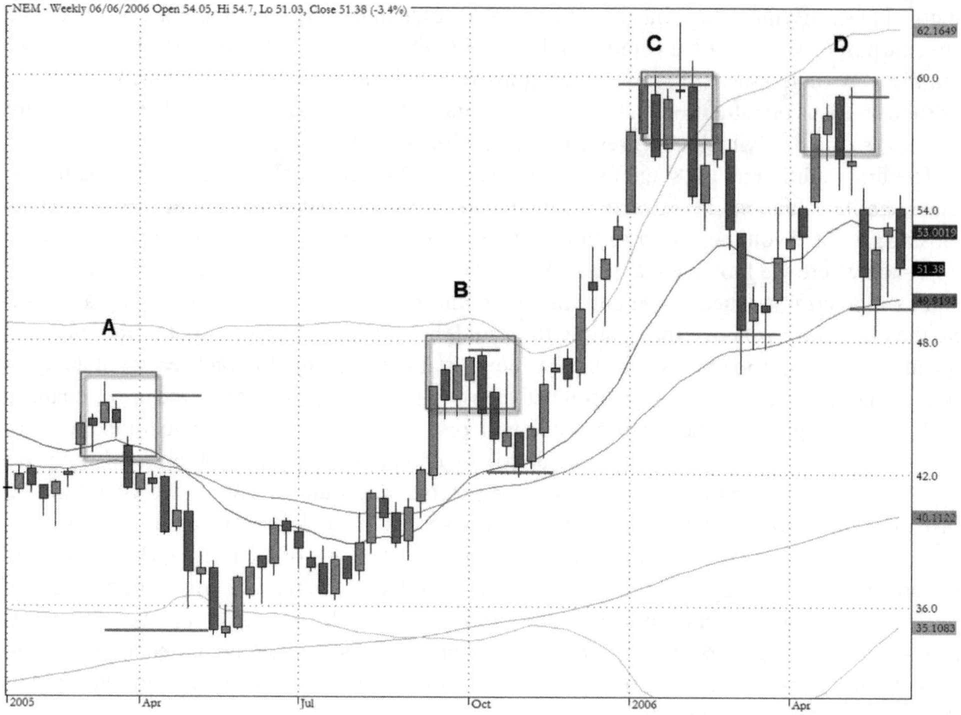

Figure 3.4 NEM correction turning points

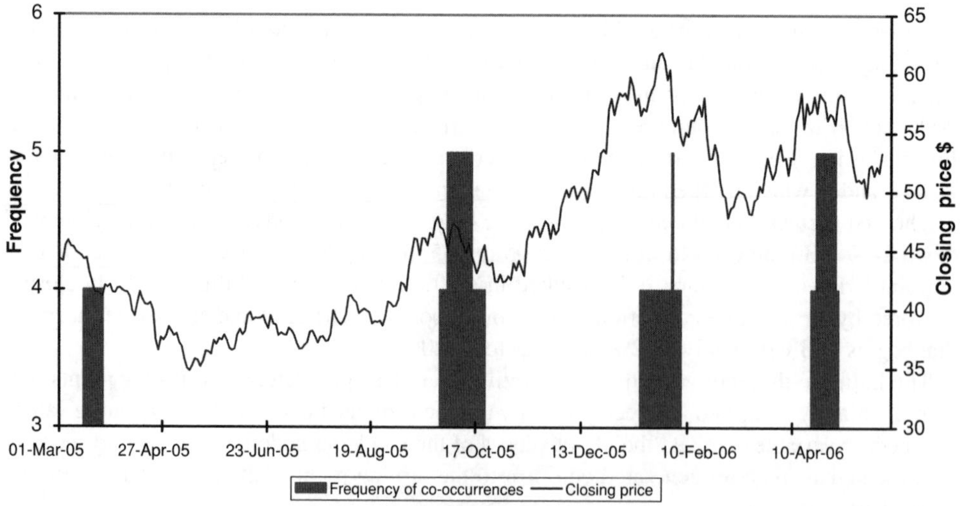

Figure 3.5 Newmont Mining (NEM) 20 day comparative analysis showing co-occurrence or alignment between upper quantile price and lower quantile closing bias

calculations. During the period just two variables have been tracked for NEM to show the dissonant activity that preceded each of the four corrections – A, B, C and D. The first of the two variables is simply the closing price and the second is the closing bias which was discussed in much detail in Chapter 2.

Before considering what is actually plotted in Figure 3.5 we need to examine the underlying calculations that are required for the CQA method. For each of the two variables – closing price and closing bias – a quantile value has been determined in accordance with a ranking analysis of the values that arose during the applicable time window being used – in this case the preceding 20 trading sessions. One calculation is for the upper quantile value for the closing price (UQ close) and this has been set at the 75 percentile value (i.e. this is equivalent to the upper quartile). The other calculation is for the lower quantile value of the closing bias (LQ closing bias) which has been set, in this example, at the 25 percentile value (this is equivalent to the lower quartile). For each session the next issue is to determine whether the closing price falls above the UQ close or not. If it does then a positive occurrence is registered otherwise the entry remains blank. Similarly for the closing bias in each session it needs to be determined whether the closing bias is in the lower quantile of values or not. If it is the positive occurrence is also registered separately otherwise the register is left blank. So there are two registers, one for UQ close occurrences and the other for LQ closing bias occurrences. Finally we can create an accumulation register which is given a positive value when, for the same session, there is a positive occurrence in both of the quantile registers. If we now use a moving 20 day window we can count the number of occasions that are to be found in the accumulation register. In essence we are monitoring the co-occurrence of events that arise in both of the opposing boundaries at the same time, and we accumulate these in a moving window.

The number of co-occurrences during a moving window is the crucial value that has been plotted in Figure 3.5. The threshold on the *y*- or vertical axis has been set to three so that only those occasions when the co-occurrence value is above or equal to three are shown. By setting the filter or threshold at three we eliminate a lot of the distracting noise in the data. What is so remarkable about Figure 3.5 is that only four periods register over the entire period and they strikingly coincide with the A, B, C and D periods from Figure 3.4.

We have screened out a lot of activity within the time series which is distracting and we have only registered the occasions on which the quantile threshold has been satisfied. As the frequency of the co-occurrence between the divergent indicators rises above the threshold so the diagram is suggesting that a there is a dissonant pattern underlying the price dynamics which needs to be resolved by a price correction episode. Going short on all of the occasions when the frequency of co-occurrences had attained a level of four on the *y*-axis would have captured each of the corrections that took place for NEM during the period. There were no false signals. The signals are a little bit early (better than being late) but there is additional fine tuning, as we shall see, that can be applied to make them even more exact. What is also important is that we are not being provided with too many signals and too many patterns to analyze further. *The closing bias could be seen as a leading indicator and when it diverges from "bullish" price behavior the subliminal message is that there are some market participants that are not acting bullishly but in fact selling into strength.*

Before moving to another case study there is another chart that can be useful to further explain the usefulness of the CQA approach. Figure 3.6 takes a different perspective on the frequency of co-occurrences that was featured in the previous chart (Figure 3.5).

Figure 3.6 is a slightly unorthodox regression between the occurrences of the close being in the upper quantile and the closing bias being in the lower quantile and could be construed as

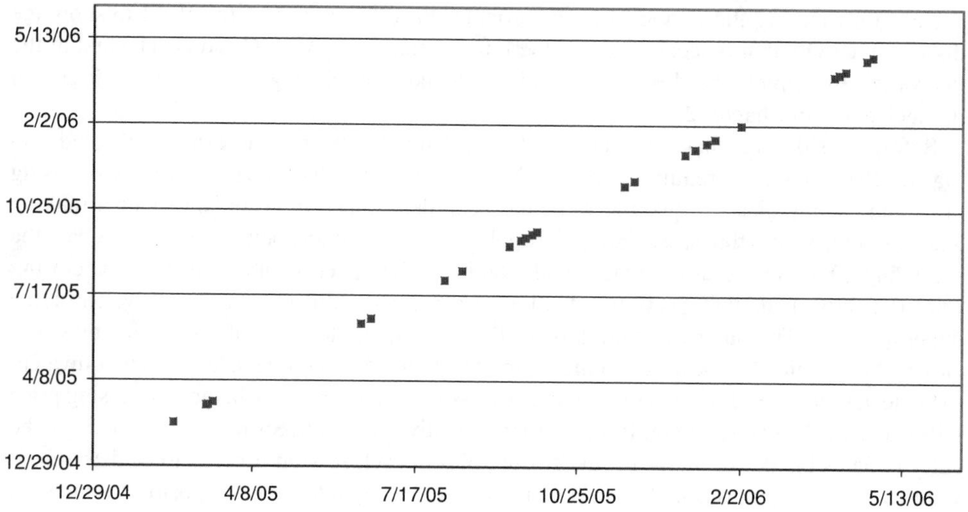

Figure 3.6 Newmont Mining (NEM) January 05–June 06 comparative quantiles regression showing upper quantile price and lower quantile closing bias

the regression of the closing bias on the actual price. But how was this regression created? The procedure is to mark each time that the variables registered within their respective quantiles with a date or time value for that occurrence. Any value could be used that marks a consecutive linear continuum for the time period under review, but in the case of an Excel spreadsheet the value that has been used is the underlying integer value that uniquely identifies each date based on a starting value of 1 for January 1st 1900. Where the two dates coincide a square appears on the *XY* scatter graph otherwise a value that is just below the minimum values for the *x*- and *y*-axes is recorded which means that the event does not appear on the diagram, but it still allows the "time line" to be revealed. The separate squares on the chart correspond to the frequency count which we observed in Figure 3.5 and as we can see they cluster at times along the time line. Just as in Figure 3.5, but this time with the different perspective provided by the pseudo-regression approach, Figure 3.6 enables us to identify those periods when we find a cluster of co-occurrences and this can act as a leading indicator of dissonance and a trade alerting protocol.

We have said that Figure 3.6 uses a pseudo-regression technique to illustrate the co-occurrences against integer data values so that they display on a time line but it needs to be stressed that this does not mean that it makes sense to perform an actual linear regression. There are too many periods when no co-occurrence is evident and the procedure will generate too many null values to be of value.[3] Interestingly, however, we can plot a correlation coefficient showing the co-occurrence during a 20 day window and the changes in the coefficient, if interpreted correctly, can also be used to anticipate potential turning points.

Figure 3.7 is slightly more difficult to interpret than the simple frequency of co-occurrences that is evident in Figure 3.6. However, significant turning points for NEM are subtly revealed in Figure 3.7 showing the value of using this alternative perspective on the data. Let us try to provide some additional intuition to what is revealed in Figure 3.7 as it will help to clarify the nature of the co-occurrence phenomenon. In the case of the two disparate quantiles we are

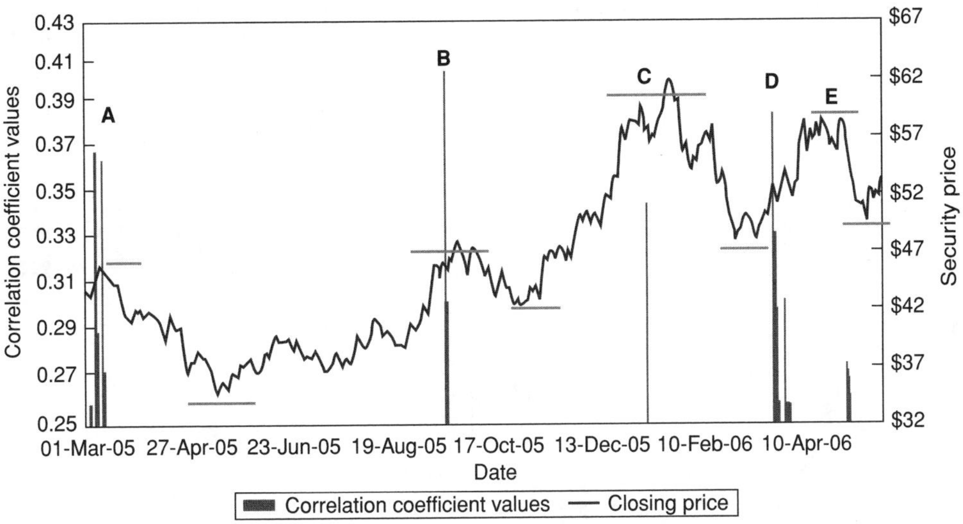

Figure 3.7 Newmont Mining (NEM) March 05–June 06 showing correlation between upper quantile closes and lower quantile closing bias

examining – bullish price action accompanied by weak closes – it should be expected that the frequency of the co-occurrences would be minimal. Even more strongly expressed, we would expect that co-instances would be absent or very rare, and that a correlation analysis would point to very weak correlation at best and most likely a negative correlation value should be observed. In fact this is the case in our analysis and that is why the threshold on the y-axis of Figure 3.7 has been set to 0.25. If the y-axis began at -1 which is the limiting case for negative correlation values, the lower half of the chart would be very busy indicating that most of the time the observed correlation is indeed negative. By setting the y-axis threshold at 0.25 all of this activity has been filtered out and we can concern ourselves only with those occasions when the coefficient value becomes significantly positive. Each of the jumps above the 0.25 level indicate that the far more typically weak or negative correlation is giving way to bouts of positive association or alignment between the two disparate quantiles.

By comparing the column peaks to the actual closing price of NEM, which is captured on the right-hand vertical axis, it becomes easy to evaluate the efficacy of the spikes as a system for generating trade alerts. Moving across the chart from left to right we can see that the alert at point A on Figure 3.7 would have led to substantial profits, and additional profits also could have been taken at points B and C. The alert that lies at D would have been a false signal and would have led to a loss. Point E would have been a good signal for the last price correction that is indicated on the right-hand side of the chart and which saw the price drop from \$58 to just below \$50. Taken together it would seem that the spikes in the coefficient value provide a good alerting system to price turning points that would have proven profitable on the short side. In other words the column peaks in Figure 3.7 provide an alternative method of discerning a critical dissonance condition that will often lead to a change in the price direction.

In summary we have so far shown that the CQA techniques applied to NEM have been highly reliable in anticipating major turning points that preceded price corrections. The incongruities between apparently bullish price action and increasingly negative divergences from the closing

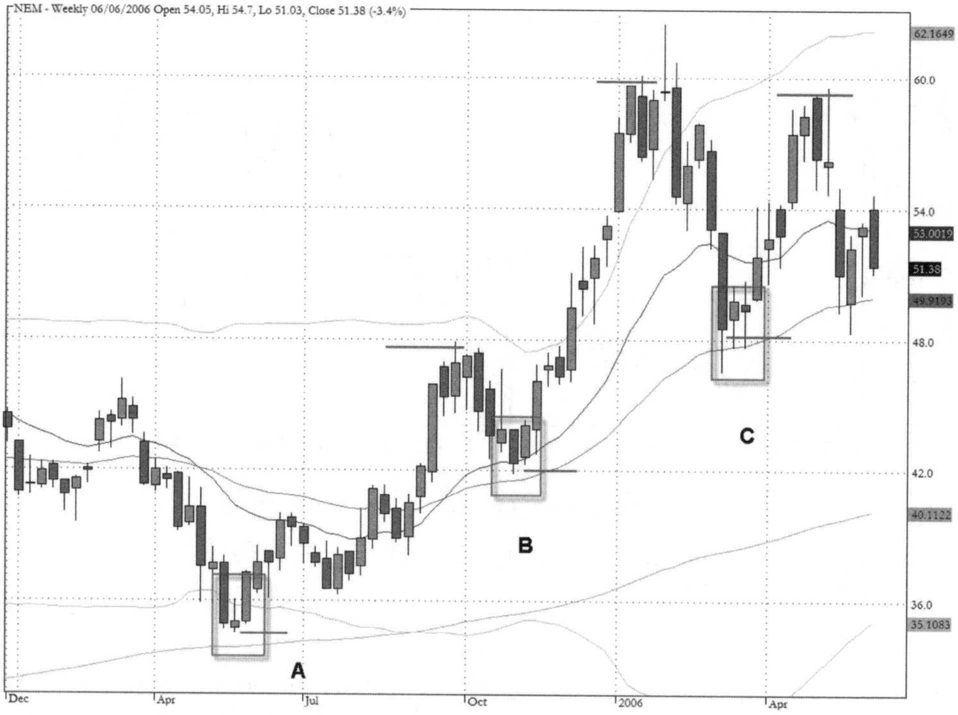

Figure 3.8 NEM turning points for bullish moves

bias values were clearly captured in Figure 3.5. Using the threshold of four co-occurrences within a 20 day lookback period it would have been plausible to have been correctly positioned for each of the four corrections that occurred during the period under review. Extending the analytical techniques to include the correlation analysis that we have just reviewed would have sharpened the focus somewhat and provided additional opportunities on the short side. Now we want to see whether the converse of what we have just examined is just as reliable. Can we use the lower quantile values for the closing price and upper quantile occurrences of the closing bias to anticipate turning points ahead of major bullish moves?

In Figure 3.8 there are three turning points identified that preceded bullish moves for NEM in the period from January 2005 to mid-2006. The most powerful bullish move is the one that begins at point B in November 2005 and culminates in the move up to the highest close in January 2006 just below $60. The rally that begins at C after the February/March 2006 correction moves from the $50 level back towards (but significantly just below) the late January high. The rally that begins at A is less acute and contains a minor retracement in July 2005.

For Figure 3.9 we have flipped the analysis that we undertook to unearth turning points that preceded corrections to show the situation where price is in the lower quantile and the closing bias is in the upper quantile. Exactly the same procedure has been followed where the co-occurrences within these disparate quantiles have been registered and Figure 3.9 shows the times when the co-occurrences have exceeded the threshold of three times within a 20 period lookback window.

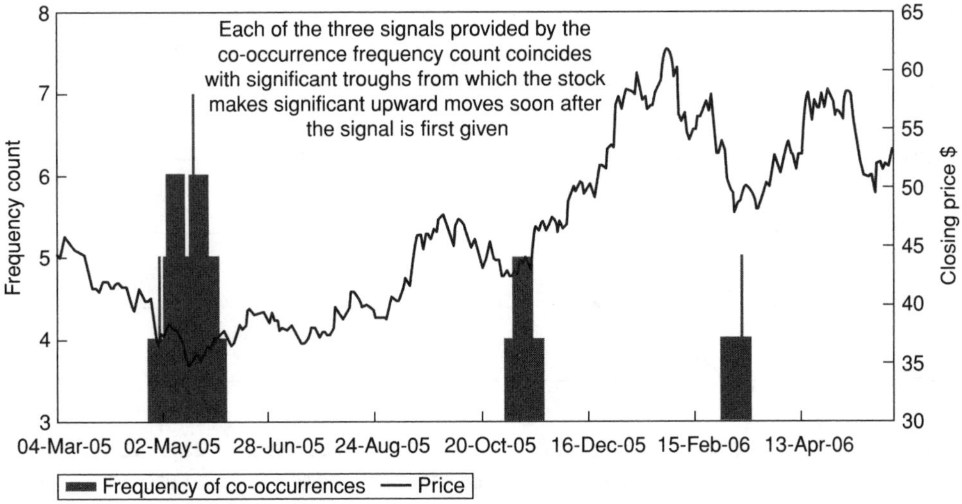

Figure 3.9 Newmont Mining (NEM) 20 day comparative quatiles analysis showing co-occurrence or alignment between lower quantile price and upper quantile closing bias

Demonstrated again in this example is one of the strengths of the CQA approach in that only few signals are generated. Only three separate clusters need to be considered and as can be seen from the NEM closing price, which has been plotted on the same time axis, the three clusters correspond convincingly with three noticeable price troughs that preceded periods of substantial price gains. Referring back to Figure 3.8 we can see that the three clusters of co-occurrence correspond to the A, B and C periods that were identified. The clusters in November 2005 and also in early March 2006 coincided with the two occasions during the entire period under review when the stock mounted sizable rallies and in both cases the signals gave adequate warning of the probability of an impending directional change. In both cases one would have been entering the long trade just ahead of the two major rallies. The left-hand cluster is notably more dispersed than the other two and the number of co-occurrences rises to six and seven on some occasions. Remember that this is the rally that was identified as beginning at point A in Figure 3.8 and the price formation was more complex than for the other two rallies at B and C. In fact the cluster that touches a co-occurrence value of four in late April 2005 would have proven to be premature as NEM continued downwards until mid-May and one could have sustained a loss by entering when the signal (i.e. on reaching the level of four) was first given. However, the very convincing nature in which we would have been alerted to the other two major rallies at B and C is sufficiently encouraging that we can assert with validity that the CQA techniques are adept at discovering turning points ahead of bullish moves as well as the corrections that we previously examined.

As was seen with Figure 3.6 the same co-occurrence data that is displayed in the preceding figure (3.9) can again be presented in the manner of a pseudo-regression line as previously explained. Figure 3.10 shows the *XY* scatter plot for the coincidences of the events within the two quantiles. All of the co-instances are plotted in this presentation and it can be seen that they remain relatively rare with the exception of the cluster in April/May of 2005 which as was just noted has some problematic implications. The clusters in November 2005 and March 2006 are

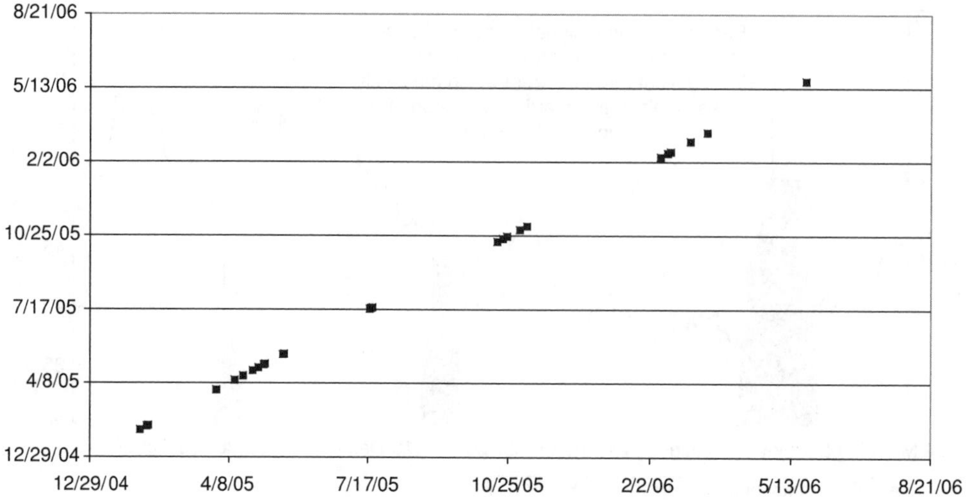

Figure 3.10 Newmont Mining (NEM) January 05–June 06 comparative quantiles regression showing lower quantile price and upper quantile closing bias

relatively isolated and as was seen they more accurately disclosed the incongruities between bearish price action and bullish action as revealed by the closing bias values. For the interested reader there is a refinement to the CQA techniques which relates the co-occurrence for individual securities to macro-market variables but this will have to wait for another occasion.

CASE STUDY – LEHMAN BROTHERS (LEH)

We want to switch our attention now to another case study to further gauge the reliability of the CQA technique for identifying potential short candidates for temporary (or longer-term) corrections. The stock selected is Lehman Brothers (LEH) and Figure 3.11 shows the weekly closes from the beginning of 2005 to early July 2006. Being able to identify tradable corrections and retracements in what is, for the most part, a very bullish chart should present some challenges to the CQA methodology. In particular we need to inspect how reliable the techniques prove to be in anticipating the major correction which begins at point D in Figure 3.11.

The most notable feature of Figure 3.11 is the unusually positive nature of the price development that begins in late June/early July 2005 and takes the stock from \$48 to \$75 in early April 2006. As we have annotated on the chart there is only one violation of the 20 week EMA during this whole period which is quite extraordinary. Three minor corrections at A, B and C and one major correction which begins at D have been identified. The turning point in late April 2006 which coincides with D produced a 20% correction by July 2006. Given this contextual background how reliable did the CQA techniques prove to be in identifying these turning points?

In Figure 3.12 we only have two signals provided by the comparative quantiles analysis. The first signal was provided by divergences that are indicated during the latter part of September 2005. The actual price top prior to the correction occurred on October 3rd and the threshold

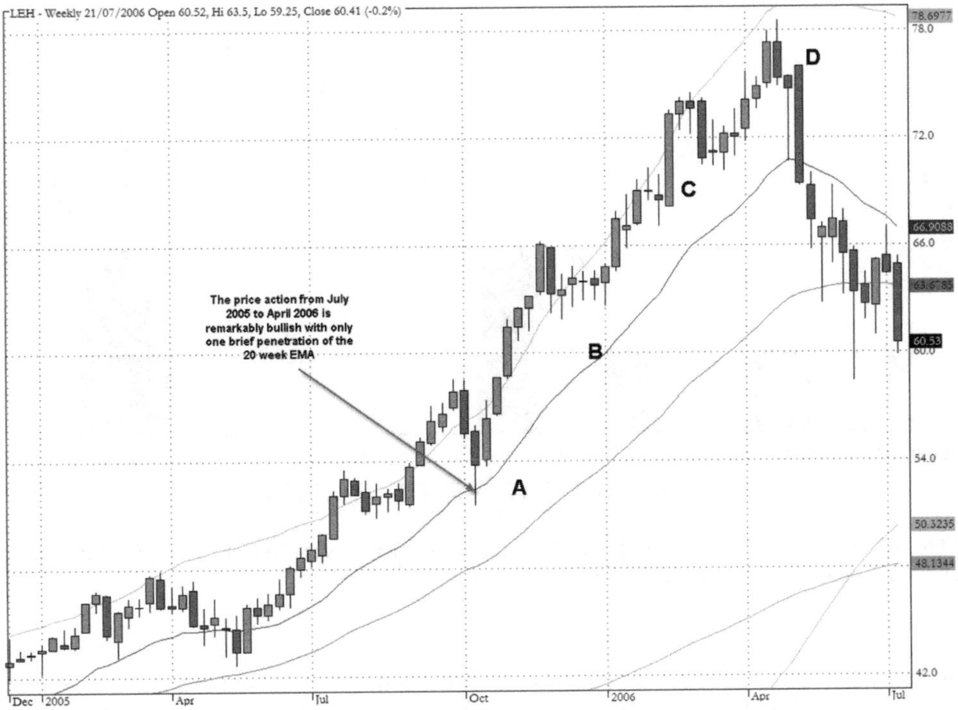

Figure 3.11 LEH weekly closes January 2005–July 2006

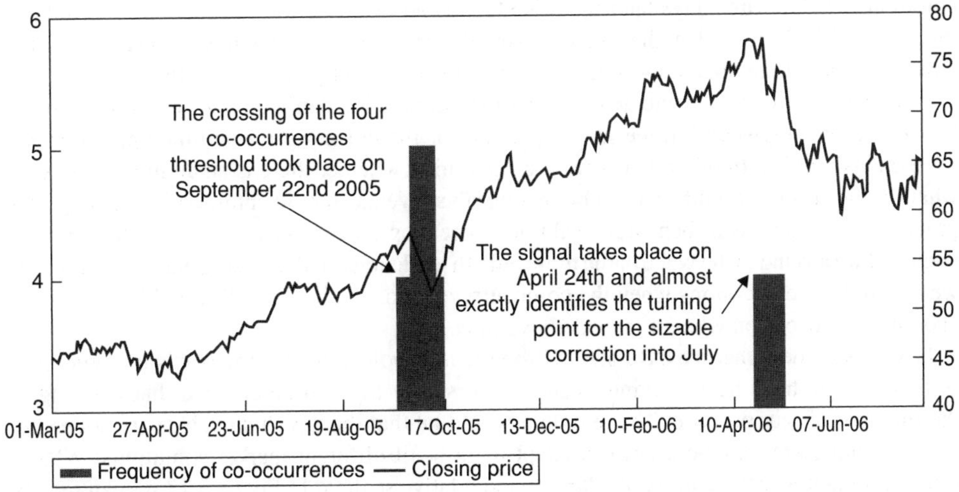

Figure 3.12 Lehman Brothers (LEH) 20 day comparative quantiles analysis showing co-occurrence or alignment between upper quantile price and lower quantile closing bias

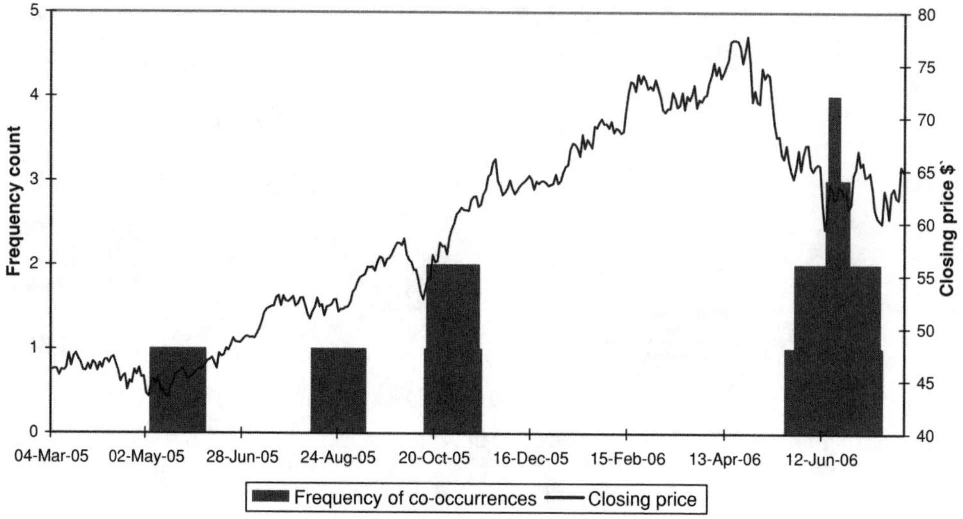

Figure 3.13 Lehman Brothers (LEH) 20 day comparative quantiles analysis showing co-occurrence or alignment between lower quantile price and upper quantile closing bias

of four was crossed initially on September 20th when the stock closed at \$56.74. The price went on to climb to \$58.57 on October 3rd so the first signal (the crossing of the four level) was several sessions early but the price peaked at less than \$2 higher. The only other signal was generated in April 2006 and timing for this is uncannily accurate. The first session when the frequency of co-occurrences crossed the threshold value of four was April 24th when LEH closed at \$76.75. Three days later the price top ahead of the serious correction occurred and this was at \$77.75 just \$1 higher than the signal alert price. Over the next two sessions LEH gave back more than \$6 and by June 13th 2006 it had fallen by more than 20%.

If we now move to the incidence of bullish signals we can examine the co-occurrence between events registered in the lower quantile for the closing price and the upper quantile for the closing bias. In other words we are examining whether there is an alignment between what on the surface would seem to be incongruous events. As our intuitions have suggested previously this divergent behavior could be suggesting that the bearish price action may be about to turn around in the wake of the more bullish tendencies of the closing bias. In Figure 3.13 we find only two occasions when the co-occurrence moved above the threshold value of two and only one occasion when it moved above three.

It will be evident that we have had to drop the threshold value for the *y*-axis in Figure 3.13 or there would have been nothing to show. But surely it could be claimed that is changing the rules to suit our purpose. The rejoinder would be that the threshold values are not etched in stone and there may be a need to adapt them to fit different market conditions. What is most important is that we think of adaptive and relative scaling. In Figure 3.13 we can see that there are extended periods when no co-occurrences at all was registered so the incidence of two occurrences becomes, relatively speaking, a significant event. If we confine our attention only to the two occasions when the threshold value of two was attained we can see that late October 2005 was a good time to be taking a long position in LEH and the mid-June 2006 period would have captured the bounce that followed from the severe correction. Again to be wholly consistent the June 2006 signal would have been premature and waiting until the co-occurrences had amounted to three times within the accumulation register would have been more accurate.

CASE STUDY – EBAY

The third case study for testing the validity of the CQA techniques involves the online auctioneer eBay (EBAY) and Figure 3.14 shows a chart of the weekly closes from the beginning of 2005 until July 2006. The stock begins the period under review with a very severe sell-off, there is a recovery rally from June 2005 to the end of 2005 (which contains some further corrective phases) and the weakness re-emerges in early 2006 and persists until the summer of 2006. During the period under review the price falls by more than 50% and the chart follows broadly an A B C wave decline in the Elliot Wave lexicon. The chart has very different characteristics to the one for Lehman Brothers that we examined and should provide a different set of hurdles over which the CQA methodology will have to prove itself.

Turning to the analytical charts the first to be examined tracks the co-occurrences of price in the upper quantile and closing bias in the lower quantile. Figure 3.15 illustrates that there are only three signals generated where the frequency of occurrences rises above the level of four. The closing price has been mapped on the same time axis and is measured on the right-hand vertical scale. The benefit of this charting technique is that it becomes very apparent whether the signals suggested by the comparative quantiles analysis do in fact coincide with key turning points. In reviewing Figure 3.15 it can be seen that there is a remarkably good fit between the occasions when the columns first attain the level of four co-occurrences and the suitability of taking a short position in EBAY. All three signals occurred just before significant declines. The right most signal would have alerted the trader to the substantial retreat which began in late November 2005 when EBAY was close to $46 and produced profit opportunities throughout December. The final hurrah in price development for the stock occurred in mid-January 2006 and the price would barely have exceeded the price level at the time of the alert. Whether the trader would have been patient and resisted the earlier opportunities to take profit is a separate money management issue. However, a scaling out of the trade by taking a portion of the profit in December and maintaining a longer-term interest in the trade would have enabled some exposure to at least part of the long decline that ensued from mid-January onwards.

If we now turn to the long side and evaluate the opportunities that were presented by the CQA methodology we can see in Figure 3.16 that three signals were generated again. The signals broadly coincide with three of the turning points that were annotated on Figure 3.14 and the notable exception is the late October 2005 rally which saw EBAY move from $38 to a level just above $46 in late November. If one is looking for exact timing then the two left most signals alerted in Figure 3.16 are somewhat early and in both cases although the anticipation of significant turning points was valid there would have been a risk of being stopped out before the move. It is for this reason that some of the CQA alerts are best not considered as appropriate for traders with short time horizons. The third cluster on the right which coincides with the later part of May 2005 would have allowed the trader to catch the only meaningful upward move in the entire first half of 2006.

Plotting the correlation between the different quantiles as opposed to counting the frequency of co-occurrence provides a different perspective and although there will be overlapping signals, the correlation approach sometimes will reveal additional information of value. In Figure 3.17

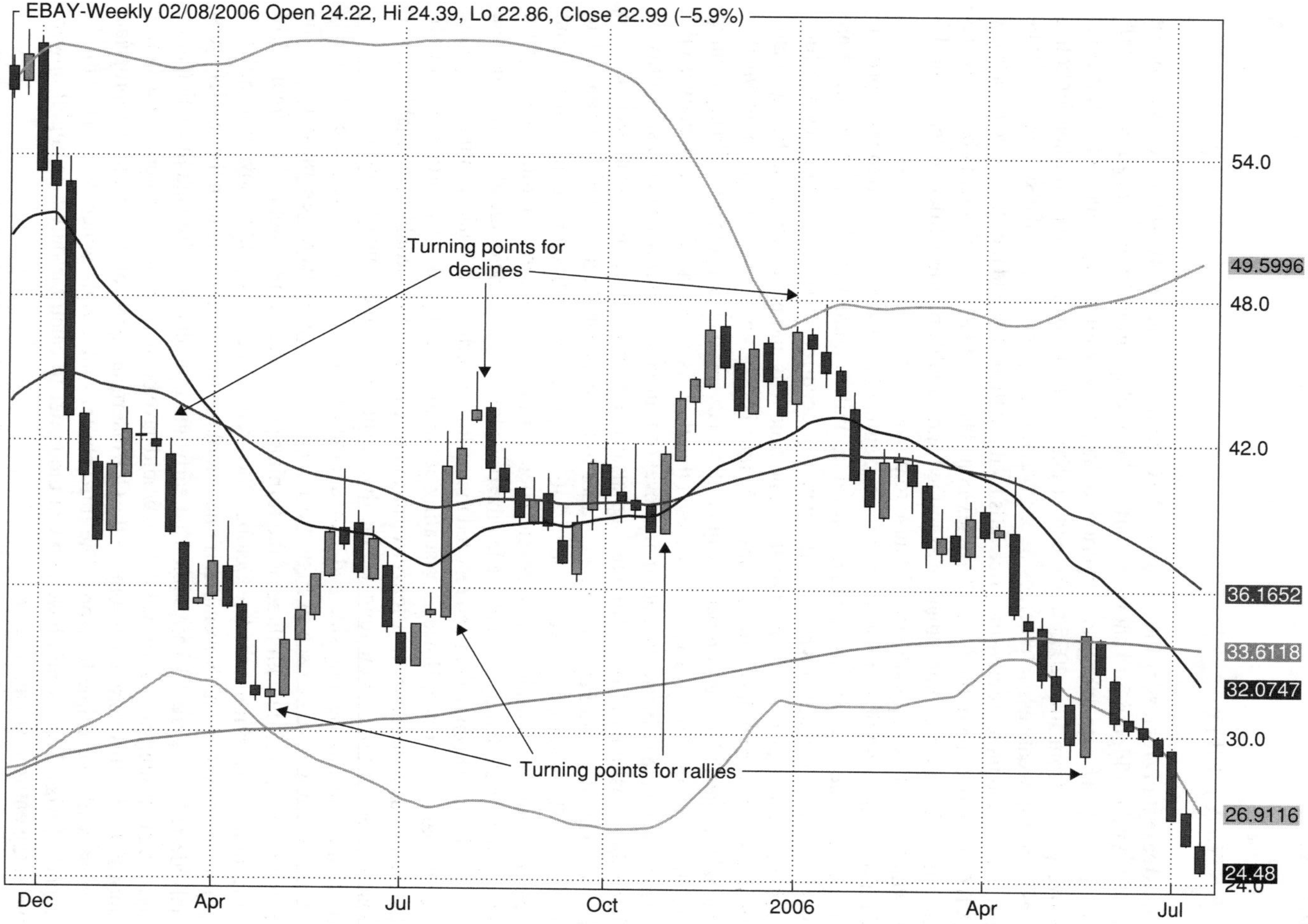

Figure 3.14 EBAY weekly chart January 2005–July 2006

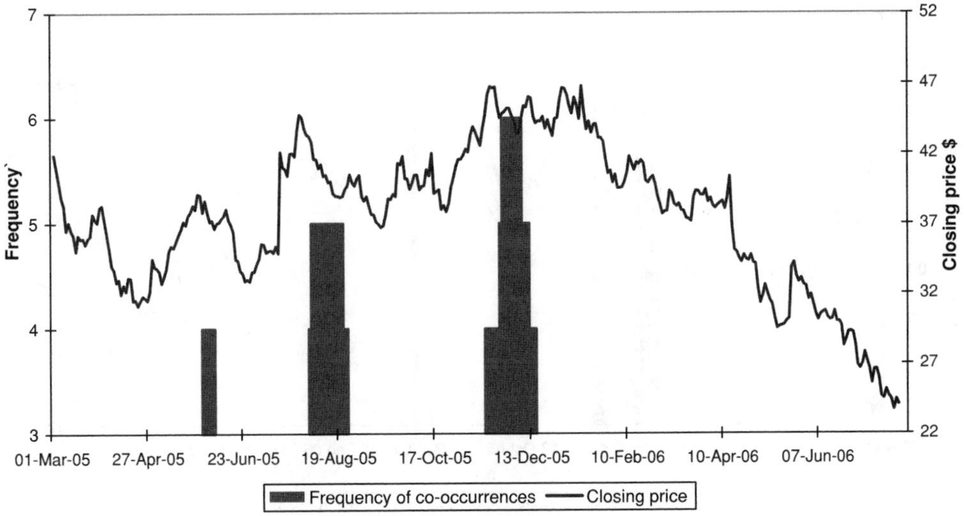

Figure 3.15 EBAY 20 day comparative quantiles analysis showing co-occurrence or alignment between upper quantile price and lower quantile closing bias

we can observe the spikes that bring the correlation coefficient value above zero from its more customary values below the threshold value of the left-hand vertical axis. In the case being displayed the presumption is that when the correlation spikes above zero there is a dissonance between the bullish price behavior and the fact that the security is closing weakly in terms of the closing bias. There are three occasions when the coefficient value rises above 0.3 and if only these had been followed with short trades all of the trades would have been profitable.

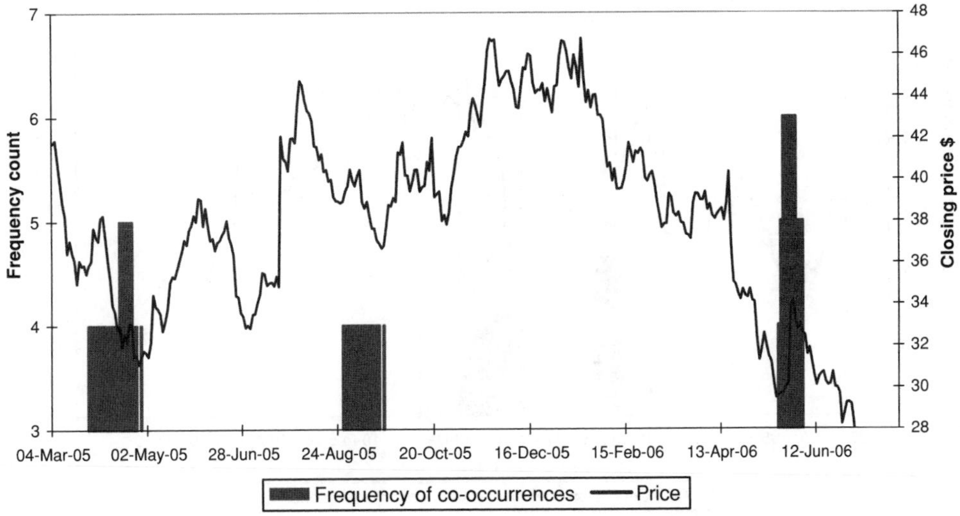

Figure 3.16 EBAY 20 day comparative quantiles analysis showing co-occurrence or alignment between lower quantile price and upper quantile closing bias

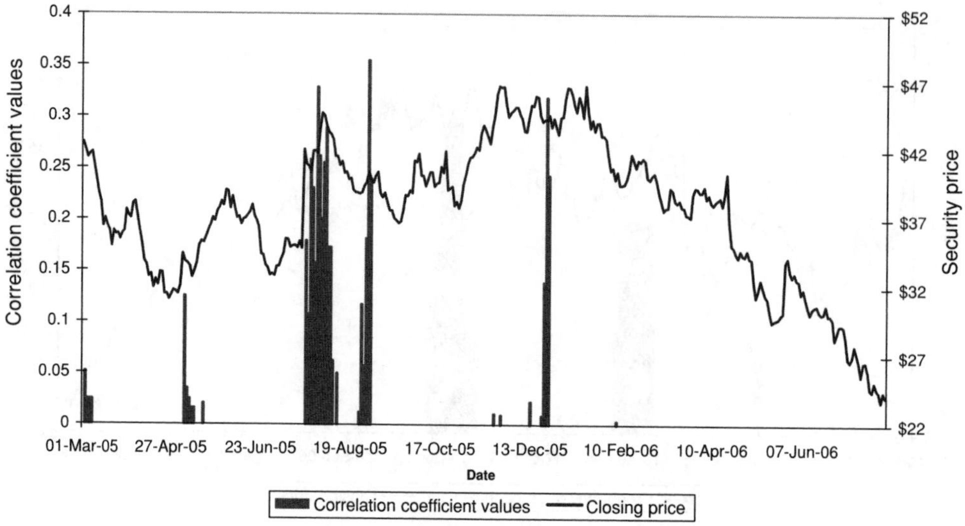

Figure 3.17 EBAY March 2005–June 2006 showing correlation between upper quantile closes and lower quantile closing bias

Figure 3.18 contains the flipside of what is seen in Figure 3.17 and indicates dissonance between poor price behavior (i.e. in the lower quantile) and strength being revealed in the closing bias. The clustering of signals throughout November 2005 would have been profitable on the long side and perhaps it is what is not revealed on the chart that is most relevant. There are no correlation spikes registered at all in 2006 and this would have kept the trader away from any temptations to trade on the long side during the protracted decline.

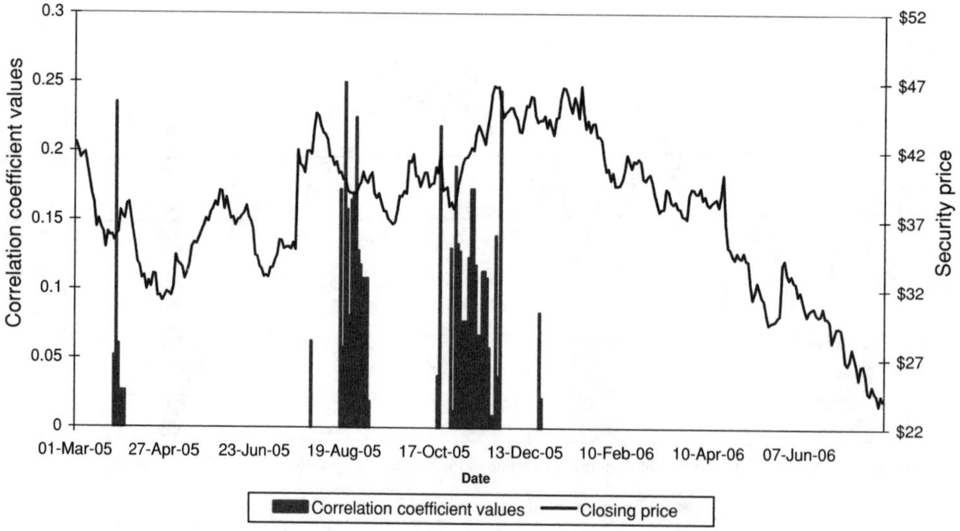

Figure 3.18 EBAY March 2005–June 2006 showing correlation between lower quantile closes and upper quantile closing bias

SUMMARY

We believe that when taken together the results of each of the case studies and all of the charts that we have considered provide convincing validation for the CQA methodology. There is much further work to be done with the basic framework but we believe that the evidence points to the proposition that *when unexpected alignments within incongruous quantiles appear there is a strong possibility that a directional change is imminent.* We receive relatively few signals from the CQA indicators but the ones that we do receive have been broadly coincidental with observed turning points in the price development. The CQA is not intended as a day to day timing tool but is reserved for those turning points when divergences have surpassed certain key values. There needs to be some flexibility in deciding on the key threshold values and the simple rule is that in each individual circumstance it needs to eliminate most of the data as inconsequential and only focus on exceptional values that have proven to be reliable in the past.

4
Volume as a Leading Indicator

If "volume precedes price",* as is often suggested, then it should be possible to apply analytical techniques to certain volume attributes that will have some predictive capabilities with regard to future price development. Rarely do the markets offer such promise in the form of a nonproprietary leading indicator. Using various techniques that come under the general heading of money flow analysis it becomes feasible to decide whether a particular security is being accumulated or distributed and this will be seen to be the most useful outcome from volume analysis. To paraphrase the opening citation slightly we will see that a security that is undergoing accumulation can be expected to gain in price and a security that is displaying the characteristics of distribution will probably offer opportunities on the short side. Equally, it can be very informative to see whether there are divergences between the security's price behavior and its volume behavior. This chapter hopes to throw light on how we can measure accumulation and distribution and how we can identify divergences between the rates of accumulation and/or distribution and the rate of change in price development.

Historically, some of the most relevant contributions to the literature on accumulation, distribution and money flow are due to the work of Joe Granville who pioneered the concept of On Balance Volume (OBV) in the 1960s and 1970s.[1] There have been many indicators that have been motivated by his analysis and today many technicians still rely on this indicator in their prognosis of the markets. There is an underlying intuition regarding the OBV indicator that has had a substantial influence on the thinking about volume, and also about the usefulness of indicators that point to a divergence between price action and other less visible market dynamics that are operating "beneath the surface". We shall explain the basic OBV technique and try to throw light on the intuition.

The formula for calculating OBV is remarkably simple:

- If the current close is greater than the previous close, then the current volume is added to the previous OBV as it is considered to be up volume.
- If the current close is less than the previous close, then the current volume is subtracted from the previous OBV as it is considered to be down volume.
- And if the current close is equal to the previous close then the current OBV is considered to be equal to the previous OBV.

Let us look at one of many examples where, despite (or should that be because of) its great simplicity there is often great value in the OBV analysis. Figure 4.1 shows the daily price development for Intel Corporation (INTC) during the second half of 2005.

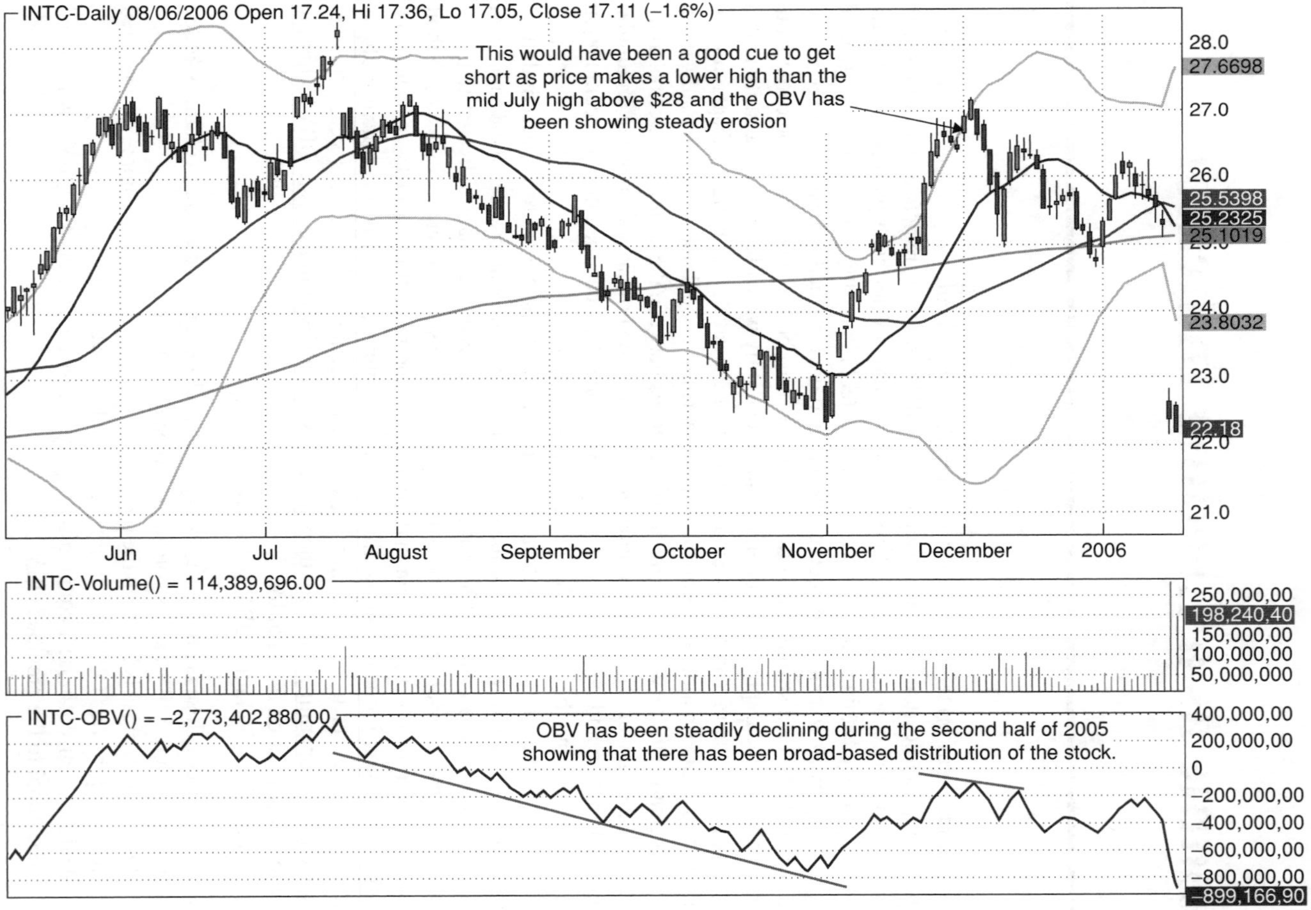

Figure 4.1 INTC OBV analysis

It can be easily seen from the chart that the stock is not performing well from a price point of view, but perhaps more telling is what is revealed in the OBV chart. Following the price peak in mid-July 2005 just above $28 the stock begins a steady descent into late October. It rallies in November 2005, very much in sympathy with the broader market, reaching a peak around the U.S. Thanksgiving holiday. As can be seen the stock stalled at $27 failing to regain the mid-July high value and thus setting up the potential for a lower high and rally failure. The OBV chart clearly reveals that during the second half of 2005 there is ongoing distribution indicated by the steady decline in the OBV values. Even during November when the price rallies the OBV fails more notably than price to recapture the OBV levels shown in the July period. This would be considered a good example of money flow and price acting divergently and could have provided the cue for a successful shorting of the stock in early December 2005 around $26. Following the gap down in early January 2006 to just above $22 this trade would have yielded a better than 15% return within a month.

One thing to notice about the OBV values is that they are raw positive or negative volume values representing the continued accumulation of actual volume based on the rules we have seen. The values are not expressed as an index which makes it more difficult for trading algorithms to interpret them easily. There is a variant of the OBV which does represent a similar value to the OBV in index terms but this has not been widely adopted.[2]

SMART MONEY

The On Balance Volume indicator also rests upon another widely held belief that many market technicians subscribe to, which is the view that there is both smart money and dumb money ("the crowd" or even more pejoratively this is sometimes expressed as "the herd") in the markets. Needless to say the task undertaken by OBV-inspired analysts has been to attempt to uncover or disclose what the smart money is doing and then align oneself with the smart money positioning before the crowd catches on. According to the OBV theory the evidence of what the smart money is up to can be found in learning how to read volume charts correctly and when the public or crowd finally become aware of what had been occurring to a security "beneath the surface" they will push prices even further in the emerging direction. Here in a nutshell is the essence of the idea that volume precedes price and also reference to the idea that it is the so-called smart money that paves the way through its accumulation of a security to eventual significant price increases. If the smart money is equated with major institutional players such as large mutual funds then the motivation for the trader might be simply to align oneself with a trend that shows that large institutions are accumulating a particular security. On the contrary, if a particular security has entered a distribution phase in which larger institutions do not appear to be participating actively with new commitments of capital while the price is rising, this is a useful signal that the security may be ready for a price correction.

We need to examine some different twists that have been applied to the notion of smart money to prepare ourselves for what we believe is the most useful tool in volume analysis – money flow based on our own comparative quantiles approach which we will come to later in the chapter.

There is a danger when using the term smart money that the definition becomes somewhat circular. There are two issues. First, can we identify the actual sources of the volume prior to the breakout (i.e. is it large pension funds or hedge funds for example)? If not we are really saying little more than this – there was some accumulative activity prior to the price increase and since it was correctly positioned to take advantage of the increase it must have been "smart" money. But it doesn't take much reflection to realize that this is only true in a circular fashion. The second problem relates to the control group issue in testing experimental hypotheses. How can we distinguish between the simple contrary cases, i.e. volume increasing with price rising and volume increasing with price falling? The smart money theory advocate might say that volume increasing with prices falling is actually an example of a security that is being distributed. But if this answer is acceptable then we seem to go round in a circle back to the idea that the classification of whether a security is under accumulation or distribution can only be made after the price development outcome is known. It would seem that one can neither be sure about the correct classification ahead of knowing the outcome nor have a theoretical framework that is falsifiable.[3] But let us see if the smart money concept can be made more rigorous.

To make the notion of smart money useful in our trading we need to find patterns that enable us to track its signature or footprints. This leads us in turn to questions about the possible institutional identity of the smart money in the market, and to some other difficult questions that need to be addressed before we can benefit from the important insights behind OBV and money flow:

- Who, or what, is the smart money? Is it the mutual funds (surely the surrogate for the public in many ways), is it the hedge funds, or is it the trading desks of Goldman Sachs and Lehman Brothers?
- Who is the dumb money? There seems to be a presumption that the dumb money or the crowd is in some vague sense "the retail" investor or trader who is trading via his or her own brokerage account. But the problem with this notion is that there are not enough such players in today's highly organized markets for them to be a serious factor in moving markets.
- How, if at all, can one differentiate between new institutional money that is being put into a security on an accumulation basis versus hot money that is looking for a swing trade that may last for hours or days at most?
- How, if at all, can one differentiate between new buying and short covering?
- Is there any method enabling one to distinguish between liquidation of existing long positions and new short selling?
- With algorithmic trading platforms so abundant how can one really attempt to unravel the nature of the buying and selling which is designed to confuse and conceal as to the principal's intentions?

In searching for answers to such questions we are setting ourselves an ambitious agenda but we hope to show that the comparative quantiles framework we have introduced in Chapter 3 provides us with an opportunity to tackle some of these issues.

QUIET VOLUME SESSIONS

Continuing with the smart money/dumb money dichotomy there are a couple of approaches to volume analysis that are worth considering cursorily in the light of the capabilities for a selective procedure to volume analysis that are offered by the comparative quantiles technique. Norman Fosback introduced the concept of the Negative Volume Index (NVI) in his book *Stock Market*

Logic.[4] The central assumption behind this index is that informed or smart investors tend to be dominant during quiet sessions (i.e. when volume is decreasing from the previous sessions) and the uninformed crowd will tend to predominate during the more active sessions when volume is increasing. Under this hypothesis at least, there is an implicit criterion for separating the activities of the smart and dumb money. According to the theory the smart money only gets counted when the volume is declining so the Negative Volume Index, following Fosback, is our way of tracing the footprints of the smart traders and market players. The methodology for the Negative Volume Index interestingly does not include volume directly in the actual calculation of the index but only as the criterion for deciding on what does get added to the index. Here is the simple rule. If the volume for the current session is below the volume for the previous session then the Negative Volume Index is augmented with the (current close – previous close)/Previous close and if the volume exceeds the previous volume a zero is added to the previous NVI value. The Positive Volume Index (PVI) works in a similar fashion except that the criterion for how to adjust the PVI is determined by whether the current volume is higher than the previous volume.

The real value for the NVI and PVI, as with many indicators including the OBV, is to be found not so much in the absolute values of the index or OBV values, but rather with trends and the rate of change in the values. If we compare the current value of the NVI to a moving average, say with a 50 day window, then if the value is above one it suggests that accumulation is taking place and vice versa. When the index increases above this value, the implication is that the smart money has been increasing its appetite for this security, adding plausibility to the idea that future price advances are expected by well-informed investors. When the NVI falls below one then the smart money is losing its appetite for the security and is probably engaged in distributive activity which could be a harbinger for lower prices ahead. It may well be that there are not too many followers today of the NVI as it has been eclipsed by more complex money flow techniques but it can still be used in an attempt to identify broad market trends by looking at overall market volume. Fosback claims that there is a 95% probability of a bull trend when the NVI is above its one year moving average, and drops to 50% when the NVI is below it.

One further and related approach to the issue of tracking the activity of smart money is to be found in the work of Lynn Elgert who initially expounded his views some years ago in an article that appeared in *Barron's* magazine.[5] The procedure culminates in a market metric called the Smart Money Index (SMI) and the basic idea behind its construction is that the dumb money is most active during the initial period of a market session whereas the smarter and more informed traders and investors are more active during the final hour of trading each day:

> The Smart Money Index is based on the idea that emotional, news-driven investors tend to trade during the first half-hour of trading, while the more rational, professional investors tend to trade during the final hour after evaluating the day's action in the markets. The Index is calculated by subtracting the change in the Dow-Jones Industrial Average during the first half-hour of trading from the change during the final hour, and then cumulating.[6]

Whether this observation is as true today as it was in the 1980s when the SMI was devised is open to some doubts. We would suggest that the nature of trading has changed so radically and there must be a real question mark over the notion of the participation of the "uninformed investors and traders". However, this has not diminished the enthusiastic way in which some commentators and promoters of proprietary trading techniques embrace such attempts to detect what the smart money is up to:

> More recently the Smart Money Index provided advance warning of the July 1998 market top, the October 1998 market bottom, the January 2000 DJIA/March 2000 NASDAQ tops, and the September 21, 2001 bottom. Thus, this Index has a stellar record of providing advance warning of important stock market turning points.[7]

Great things have been claimed for this index, which we are unable to comment upon and our only reason for mentioning this particular technique is to highlight more of a methodological perspective rather than to pass judgment on whether the supposed fact that smart money is more active in the latter part of the trading session is true or not.

Before we outline what we believe to be a new and improved methodology for money flow analysis we want to review the traditional notion and construction of the Money Flow Index and show how, in some instances, it can be used successfully in trading.

THE MONEY FLOW INDEX (MFI)

The Money Flow Index is a volume-weighted version of the Relative Strength Index. The indicator compares the total transaction values traded on days with upward price movement to the transaction values traded on days with downward price movement.

The steps involved in calculating the Money Flow Index are:

- Decide on the time window or lookback period of interest
- Calculate the Typical Price for each of the periods, i.e. (High + Low + Close)/3
- Determine the total transaction amount or Money Flow for each period, i.e. Typical Price * Volume
- Determine the Positive Money Flow amount, i.e. accumulate a Positive Money Flow amount for each of the periods, within the time window, when the Typical Price moves up from the previous value
- Determine the Negative Money Flow amount, i.e. accumulate a Negative Money Flow amount for each of the periods, within the time window, when the Typical Price moves down from the previous value
- Determine the Money Flow Ratio, i.e. Positive Money Flow/Negative Money Flow
- Determine the Money Flow Index, i.e. 100 − 100/(1 + Money Flow Ratio)

There are essentially four separate procedures:

- Decide upon the correct pricing value to be attributed to each session. Rather than simply using the closing price there is an attempt to capture the price spread during trading and to arrive at a typical price for the session. Once this has been calculated and multiplied by the observed volume one has the transaction value for the session which can then be accumulated.
- For each session one needs a criterion to decide whether it is a positive day or a negative day. The simplest criterion would be to use the Typical Price with a value in the current session above the previous typical close counting as a positive day and vice versa. It is also possible to use variants on the (H + L + C)/3 formula.

- After allocating the sessions to a positive or negative accumulation register one can then determine the positive/negative ratio.
- The Money Flow Ratio can be normalized and expressed in an index format.

The great advantage of the MFI is that it has been widely implemented in most of the well-known software packages used by traders for technical analysis. It can be used by position traders and swing traders that use end of day data primarily as well as for day traders that are monitoring intraday charts. In the author's own trading experience the MFI has been used extensively with considerable success and in certain specific circumstances there is undoubtedly a valuable edge that is provided by this indicator.

MFI is most valuable when a security is in a relatively quiet phase of volume and price development. This can best be illustrated with the following example, which proved to be highly profitable, and which arose for Martha Stewart Living (MSO) in late August 2005. The setup for the trade is displayed in Figure 4.2. Notice especially the price congestion during most of August 2005 in which price activity was confined to a very narrow range between $26 and $27. During this period of price stagnation there is clear evidence of accumulation taking place in the MFI chart segment below the price chart. Also noticeable is the manner in which the steepness of the MFI slope stands in contrast to the much gentler slope of the RSI slope. On August 25th the stock broke out on heavy volume and over the next four sessions moved from $26 to $34.

It is the dissonance or divergence that is revealing and which provides short-term trading cues. We are suggesting that the pattern below can provide us with the foundations for a reliable template or pattern recognition algorithm using the MFI. When price has been trading within a very narrow range for several periods but there is unmistakable evidence of positive money flow indicating accumulation, be prepared for a potentially major price breakout. This is essentially a short-term pattern in that one is not monitoring for any longer-term evidence of accumulation but rather looking for a trading pattern that should arise typically within a 10 to 20 day period. In the case of MSO the trader who had observed the unusually positive MFI prior to the breakout on the 25th could have achieved a 25% return within four trading sessions.

Another example of a very similar setup can be seen in the chart for AMGN (Figure 4.3) at the end of June 2005. There is again evidence of accumulation during the month of June as highlighted in the steepening slope of the MFI especially visible during the second half of June. Also very noticeable in the AMGN chart is the fact that the stock moved sideways within a very narrow range for the remainder of the month of June. Another noteworthy feature of the charts is that all three exponential moving averages, the 20, 50 and 200 day EMAs, had converged at or close to the $60 price level. When reviewing longer-term charts for AMGN it can be seen that this price level has proven to be fairly pivotal for the stock historically and certain institutions will have specific filters and screens set up to take a closer look at a stock that is trading at an area of important chart support. Also significant perhaps is that the period under review in the chart coincides with the end of the second calendar quarter, which is a period during which portfolio managers are overhauling their holdings and often engaging in some new acquisitions and portfolio cosmetics. The fact that there was little day to day volatility during this period suggests that the stock was probably not featuring as a priority for many day trading desks and it is precisely this relative calmness of this period of trading that is the hallmark of the pattern we have found to be so useful.

On July 5th, following a long holiday weekend the stock broke out from the period of price congestion with a 2.7% upward move to $62.51. This was then followed by a series of further

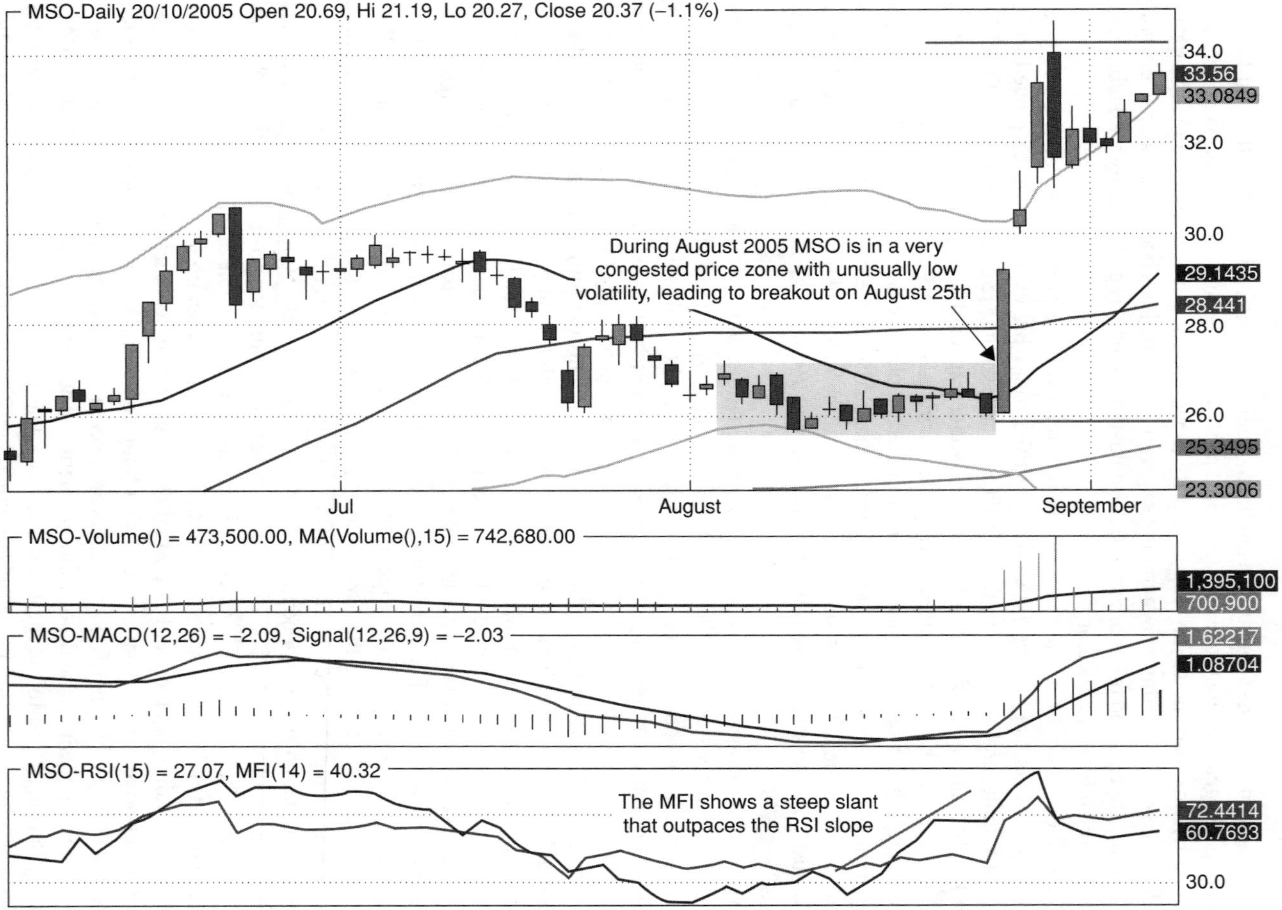

Figure 4.2 MSO August 2005

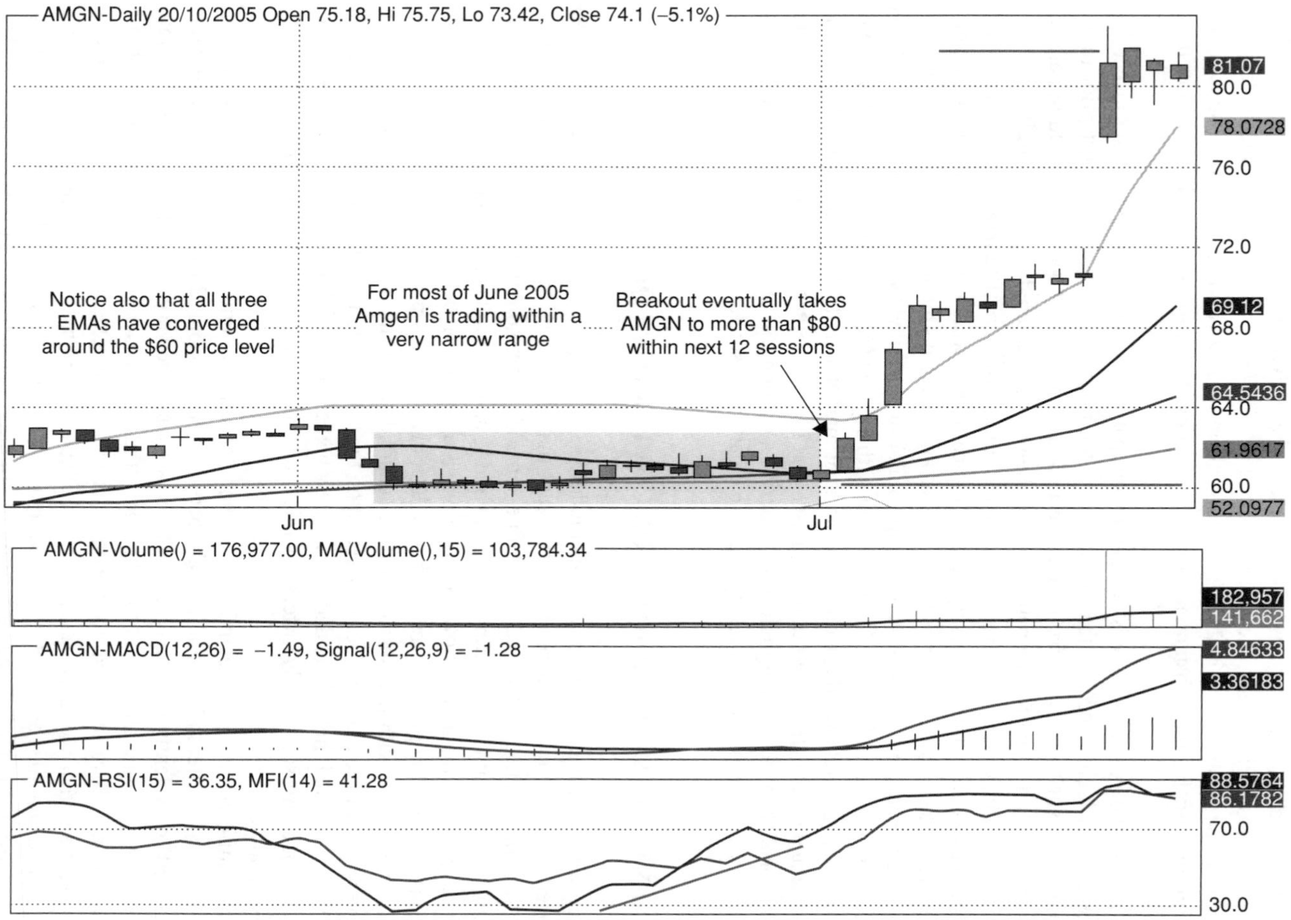

Figure 4.3 AMGN June 2005

upward moves including the major upwards gap on July 20th which enabled the stock to close above $80 representing a 33% advance from the price breakout at the beginning of July. There is a revealing dissimilarity between this chart and the one for MSO that we previously examined which in some ways would have made the AMGN opportunity more attractive. As can be seen from Figure 4.3, the price breakout for AMGN was less abrupt and traders that understood the dynamics that had led to the July 5th upward move still had plenty of opportunity to climb aboard for the substantial short-term profits that were to be realized within three weeks.

In each of the examples there is one key factor that becomes evident upon closer inspection of the charts which is the fact that in each case the price action is subdued just prior to the breakout and yet there is a very noticeable increase in the MFI values. An additional, not mandatory, requirement for the pattern is that the price has entered a zone where it is close to one or more of its key moving averages or an area of previous chart support. This suggests that the optimal circumstances for using the MFI indicator is in what we would call quiet markets. When the market is thrusting or experiencing strong trend days there are too many dynamics at work for a meaningful segregation of the up volume and the down volume. On those occasions where there are lots of fireworks in the market with big trending days we think that it is next to impossible to separate out these different forms of market activity. It is only when the markets or individual stocks are in their quieter phases that it becomes easier to attach the appropriate proportionality to the volume indicators to derive a meaningful ratio indicating whether there is accumulation or distribution taking place in a particular stock.

MONEY FLOW ANALYSIS BASED ON COMPARATIVE QUANTILES

Before we can properly introduce the methodology of comparative quantiles analysis (CQA) we need to take care of some preliminary issues that involve the basics of money flow from a high level perspective and we need to define some key terminology including the true range, closing position with the true range, signed volume and accumulation windows.

At the center of the money flow methodology is a distinction between positive and negative sessions where if the price closes up that is designated to be a positive session and all of the volume associated with that session is then accumulated in the positive or bullish camp and vice versa. The ratio that emerges is based upon the relative volume values of the positive and negative camps and this is intended to suggest whether there is a bullish or bearish bias to the security. Or expressed slightly differently this is intended to provide evidence of accumulation or distribution.

But in differentiating between the positive and negative volume sessions there has not been any attempt to differentiate qualitatively between the sessions. In other words all sessions are treated equivalently and the coherent trend sessions, the very quiet sessions and the more "typical" sessions are all lumped together and either added to the positive or negative volume accumulator. This raises precisely the same issue of data selectivity based on the character of the sessions that we discussed in the last chapter where we laid out the basic case for a comparative quantiles approach. We need to address again the same objection that we previously confronted regarding the selectivity of attention that is integral to this procedure. The argument could legitimately be made that from a volume perspective all sessions should have equivalent status and that we are on dangerous ground when we attempt to separate those sessions which have a "special" quantile status from those that are "ordinary" or typical. If we focus our attention only on these special occasions we may miss out on underlying volume trends that creep up on us during the ordinary sessions.

As we have indicated before the normal sessions are not ignored in a quantiles-based method; they occupy the middle ground in the ranking procedures. It could even be claimed that positioned as they are in a ranking procedure they help to push out the more consequential sessions towards the boundaries – both upper and lower. This also helps to clarify that we are not just, in the case of volume, concerned with the upper boundary sessions when volume is particularly heavy but also with the converse when volume may be unusually light.

Even more justification for the selectivity is that when examining money flow with quantiles it is the price quantiles that drive the methodology rather than the volume quantiles. What we mean by this is that we do not perform our basic filtering of sessions on the volume quantiles *per se*. Instead we single out the sessions that are of primary focus from the price or closing bias quantiles and then secondarily we would consider the quantile that the accompanying session volume falls into.

TRUE RANGE

A simple view of the session's range is to subtract the low from the high of the session and often that value is sufficiently useful. However, a more accurate reflection of whether a stock is experiencing more volatile conditions when the range is expanding is to use the quantity that was introduced into the technical analysis literature by J. Welles Wilder and featured in his book, *New Concepts in Technical Trading Systems*.[8]

The true range is useful for measuring more volatile periods in the markets and where stocks are experiencing "gaps" from the previous session's trading. Its original application was in the commodities markets where large price gaps and even limit moves are to be found and where the simple intraday range calculation is inadequate for quantifying the presence of range expansion. Although the limit move does not occur in the stock market, except under very rare circumstances, the principle is worth noting as it points to the insufficiency of the intraday range in extreme conditions. A limit move occurs when a commodity opens up or down its maximum allowed daily move and, assuming that it does not come back within the daily range limit amount, no trading is permitted in the current session.

While limit moves are not a problem with individual stocks, certainly opening gap moves are frequent enough to make the true range calculation a worthwhile improvement to the simpler intraday range measurement. The true range is expressed quite simply as the greater value of the following:

- The current high less the current low.
- The absolute value of the current high less the previous close.
- The absolute value of the current low less the previous close.

It is worth tracking this value in all trading sessions and then one can derive an average true range value for a specified lookback period or window. In our discussion regarding the flags and channel formations we typically suggest that the period for determining a range expansion session is to find a session where the current true range is at least 150% of the simple average of the true range values during the preceding 15 sessions.

CLOSING POSITION BIAS

The closing difference is the difference between the closing price for the current session and the closing price for the previous session. It will be a signed value depending on whether the stock gained or declined relative to its previous price.

The closing position bias is simply the signed closing difference divided by the true range and reflects where the current closing price is in relation to the range of trading as delimited by the most recent two sessions. If the value is $+1$ then the stock closed up from the previous session and at the high for the day, if the value is -1 then the stock closed down for the day and at the low for the day. If the value is zero it almost certainly means that the stock closed at the same price for the current session as the previous (although it is theoretically possible to get a zero value if the true range was zero, which is very unlikely). Intermediate values provide a useful barometer of the "strength" of the close. To take another instance a value of 0.5 would indicate that the closing price was above the previous close and is to be found at a level equivalent to the point three quarters of the true range whereas a value of -0.5 would suggest that the close was at a point below the previous close and at one quarter of the true range.

SIGNED TRANSACTION VOLUME

The sign value of the volume (i.e. whether it is positive or negative) depends on whether the closing bias is above or below certain thresholds. Our normal procedure is to set the threshold for attaching a negative sign to the volume at values for the closing bias, which are less than $-.0.5$ since the stock not only closed down but was also in its lower quartile (i.e. the 25 percentile value) with respect to its intraday range. The upper threshold for qualifying as a positive volume session can then be set where the closing bias is above 0.5 which shows not only that the stock closed up but was also in the upper quartile of its true range. There will then be an intermediate zone that approximately corresponds to the middle quartiles for closing bias that can either be considered to have a neutral volume sign or a zero value which effectively means that they do not register in any accumulation.

The next issue relates to what should be the actual value to accumulate within the positive and negative camps. As we have seen the value which is used in the Money Flow Index is determined by multiplying the session's volume by the typical price for the session. In our own calculations we have found that the following value has proven to be most useful in indicating turning points: Closing price $\times$ signed volume (which can be zero) * True range for the session (in dollar terms). By including the true range value the signed volume that is used in the CQA methodology takes on a weighting that is commensurate with the degree of intraday price movement.

ACCUMULATION WINDOW

This term is used frequently in the CQA methodology and specifically in regard to the money flow analysis it represents the period during which the signed transaction volume is to be accumulated. In the case of the co-occurrences between events in different quantiles it is similar to the above but enables us to count the number of occasions on which events registered in the designated quantile for one variable overlap with those for a second variable's quantile.

CASE STUDY – NEWMONT MINING (NEM)

To demonstrate the features of the quantile-based approach to volume analysis and highlight the manner in which it allows us to anticipate price turning points, both positive and negative, we will examine the gold mining stock Newmont Mining (NEM) which trades on the NYSE.

Figure 4.4 covers the weekly closes for Newmont Mining from January 2005 to June 2006 and shows the more obvious turning points in price development for the stock. From its low in May 2005 at around $35 NEM moved up to the $60 level in late January 2006, partly reflecting the bullish developments in the price of the precious metal that it extracts. There was a corrective period in October 2005 but the price action following that, at the end of 2005 and throughout January 2006, was very positive. The price topped out at the end of January when a more severe corrective episode began. Also clearly visible on the weekly chart is a bearish flag formation. Finding such well-defined formations on a weekly chart is somewhat unusual and the pattern takes on added weight because it is followed by NEM stalling at a lower high in late April 2006.

Figure 4.5 is the first of our quantiles-based diagrams and it maps the same period as the price chart covered in Figure 4.4. The four corrective episodes have been indicated in Figure 4.5 by A, B, C and D. What can be seen in Figure 4.5 is that where the gray and black columns are most closely aligned this corresponds with the more bullish price phases for NEM, and as the gray and black columns are diverging from each other, often associated with the gray columns descending below the zero lines, NEM is correcting. There is a very close match between all of these points which have been arrowed in Figure 4.5 with the observed weakness in NEM. The May 2005 weakness at point A is clear as is the temporary setback in November 2005 marked at point B. Most critically the more serious correction that appears at the end of January (point C) is anticipated by the gray columns moving below the zero line at the end of January 2006 prior to the price high which actually occurred at $61.83 on February 1st. If one had adopted the crossover below zero as a trading trigger point for a short trade one could have entered a short trade on January 27th when the price was $59.09 which would then have yielded a 10% profit within the next 10 trading sessions. The final corrective phase is marked at point D on Figure 4.5 and corresponds to the late April/early May slump and it also coincides with a substantial nonalignment of the gray and black columns.

Not only are the correction turning points signaled by nonalignment but the periods when the gray and black columns are showing their most alignment correspond to the periods of price strength. Adopting a policy of buying NEM if the two columns are aligned and more critically when the gray column has moved above the zero volume level after a period below it would also have been a profitable strategy. We should emphasize at this stage that our focus is on the big picture rather than specific signals and triggers that might have been generated in accordance with the analysis underlying Figure 4.5.

Let us pause and digest the calculations behind Figure 4.5. The black columns represent the volume that has been accumulated during a 20 day window only in the case where the closing price is in the upper quantile (set at the 75% level). The actual volume that is registered has a positive signed value where the volume occurred in conjunction with a strong close (i.e. above the 0.5 closing bias threshold) or a negative value when the volume occurred in

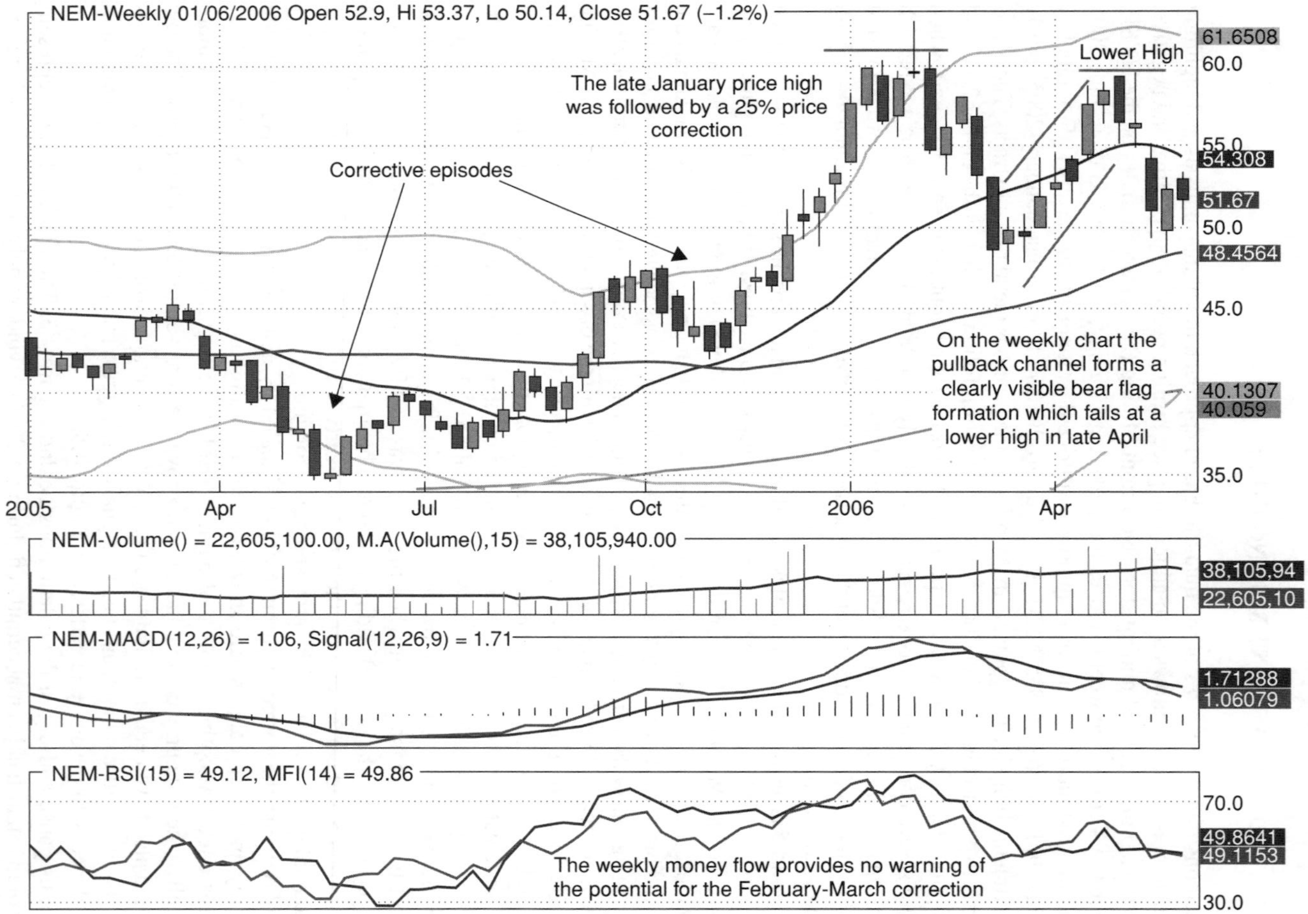

Figure 4.4 Weekly chart of NEM January 2005–June 2006

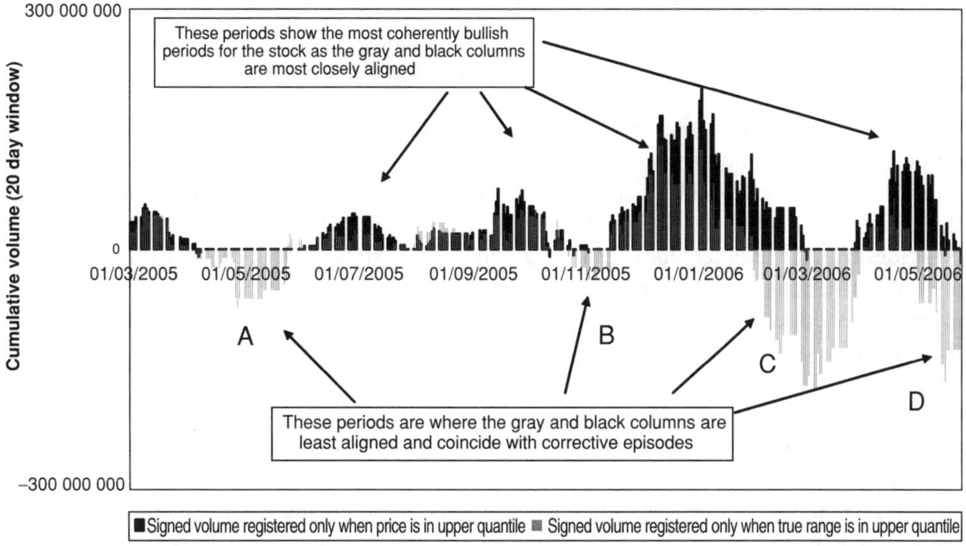

Figure 4.5 Newmont Mining (NEM) upper quantile-based signed volume analysis based on the period January 2005–May 2006

connection with a weak close (i.e. below −0.5 in terms of closing bias). Both positive and negative amounts will therefore appear in the accumulation and *the sign of the net volume figure will show on balance the degree to which upper quantile price activity is conforming to strong closes*. Looking at Figure 4.5 it is also apparent that there are several periods when there is an absence of any black columns as the prevailing price is failing to register in the upper quantile. The gray columns are constructed according to whether the true range values observed for each session are above the upper quantile value for true range (also set at the 75% level). Once again the values accumulated will tend to show whether range expansion is occurring in conjunction with strong closes or weak closes since this is the basis on which the sign value is attributed to the volume.

When the gray and the black columns in Figure 4.5 are aligned and above the zero volume level this conveys three separate but related items of useful information:

- The closing price is behaving relatively well (i.e. in the upper quartile of its recent performance).
- Closes are relatively strong (i.e. they are in the top quarter of the daily range).
- The expansion of range is, on balance, associated with strong closes.

A lot of valuable information is revealed by these conjunctions and provides an assurance that the bullish price action is being well supported by other below the surface dynamics that are constructive.

Alternatively when the gray and black columns are least aligned and the gray columns are moving below the zero volume line the underlying dynamics are revealing the following:

- The closes are relatively weak which is causing more negative volume to be accumulated than positive volume.
- The range expansion is, on balance, being associated with weak closes where the position of the close is near the bottom of the daily range.

- The activity of the closing price is deceptive if it is registering at all.
- If there are no black columns this shows that price has been performing poorly for at least the number of sessions in the accumulation window.

From the two different scenarios that have just been outlined it becomes possible to develop a framework for timing turning points and this can be more or less precisely tuned. There is a further scenario to consider which can also be followed by looking at the relative sizes of the columns in Figure 4.5. One of the best timing signals that emerges from the NEM chart coincides with the re-emergence of black columns after extended periods when they have been absent and the gray columns moving above the zero line when they have been below it for an extended period (at least 10 sessions). When both of these occur together the chart is showing that weakness is giving way to stronger closes and range expansion is also in the direction of the nascent price recovery.

Now that the overview has been established it will be helpful to drill down to a micro-analysis of a key turning point for NEM which is the late January 2006 sell-off which can be clearly seen on the price chart (Figure 4.4) and which is also marked as point C in Figure 4.5.

To highlight this excellent trading opportunity on the short side we have zoomed in on the relevant time period in Figure 4.6 to show how the gray columns were descending in a clear downward trend during January 2006 and slipped below the zero line during the last few days of January. This is in marked contrast to the behavior of the gray and black columns during December 2005 where there is positive alignment of the two columns.

As we have just commented the positive alignment demonstrates that when range was expanding it was associated with strong closes and this was closely tracking the accumulation of positive volume based on the bullish price action. As we move through January we find that the opposite begins to emerge which is that on days when the true range values are in the upper quantile there is, on balance, more negative volume being registered which reflects the

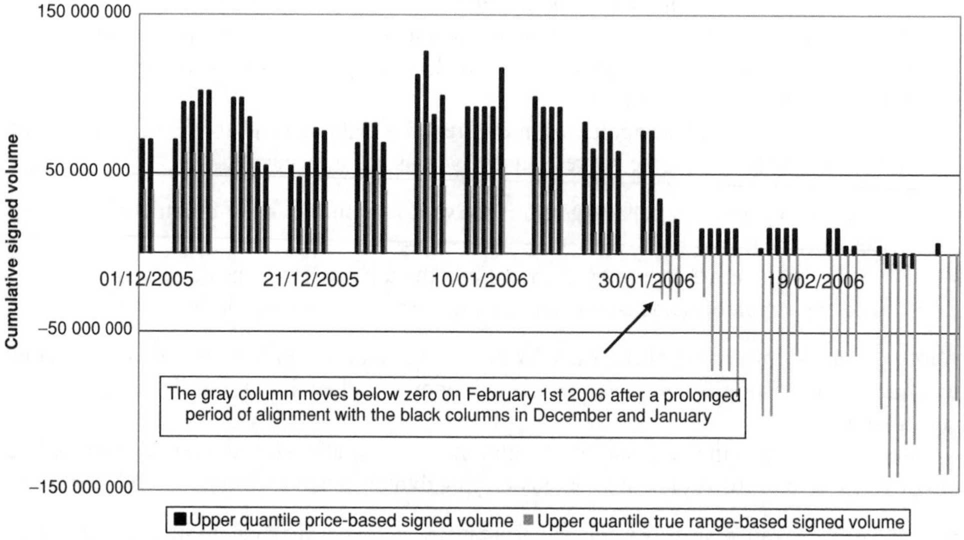

Figure 4.6 Newmont Mining (NEM) quantile-based volume analysis – focus on December 2005–early March 2006 showing divergencies

fact that the closing bias on these sessions was in the lower reaches of the session's true range. The signed volume associated with price performance in the upper quantile is still revealing that there is a bullish tone to the price development but the underlying volume and money flow dynamics are diverging. The gray column drops below the zero point on the vertical axis on February 1st 2006 which coincides perfectly with the price top before the February correction which brought NEM down to $48 for more than a 20% correction.

Figure 4.7 zooms in on the price action during the same period as that covered in the chart shown in Figure 4.6 and the late December/January price action coincides with the period showing strong alignment between the two columns. As the price chart shows the exact top for the bull move takes place on February 1st and this would have been alerted with uncanny accuracy by the action of the gray column in Figure 4.6.

The divergence and evidence of dissonance that is revealed precisely in Figure 4.6 highlights the key benefit of the CQA approach. Using a traditional MFI chart it may be possible to observe some evidence of divergence but we cannot easily quantify the degree to which the price action, considered alone, is not being supported or confirmed by the closing bias and range expansion/contraction. The CQA technique provides a clear and systematically useful method of determining whether the stock's price action, which manifests itself at the surface level, is in harmony with, and aligned with, the undercurrents that are either supporting the price momentum or are pointing to an eventual directional change.

CASE STUDY – GOOGLE (GOOG)

The second case study analyzes the price development for Google (GOOG) during a slightly longer period to the one that we examined for Newmont Mining, as it continues to the end of July 2006. The price chart will set the context for the CQA charts that follow.

Figure 4.8 illustrates the powerful upsurge that took Google from $180 in early April 2005 to a price peak of $475 which occurred in January 2006. There are four pullbacks on the chart, three of which have been designated as minor and the major one which has been highlighted on the chart. The largest decline began in early January 2006 and price declined by almost 30% within the next few weeks until price stabilized close to $340 in March. Using the same CQA approach that was used previously with NEM could these turning points leading to price corrections have been anticipated? Let us review the quantiles-based charts to see.

Figure 4.9 has been constructed on exactly the same premises as Figure 4.5. The periods when the alignment between the columns (gray and black) is most prominent coincide very closely with the periods of most bullish price behavior, and the periods that have been identified as showing the gray column moving below the zero level on the vertical axis and the least alignment match up closely with the periods of weakness on the price chart. Taking our cue from the price chart let us focus on the early January 2006 period to see whether an enlarged version of the CQA would have provided the clues as to the impending major correction.

Figure 4.10 focuses on the period from January 3rd to early April 2006. The gray and black columns track each other closely on the left-hand side of the chart and on January 19th the gray column moves below the zero line and does not move above it again until March 28th. This hiatus corresponds very closely to the severe price correction that was noted in connection with Figure 4.8. The actual price top for the entire move up in 2005 occurred two days prior to the move below the zero line and the recovery began on March 24th, which was three trading days after the gray column had moved above the zero line. The correspondence is remarkably close

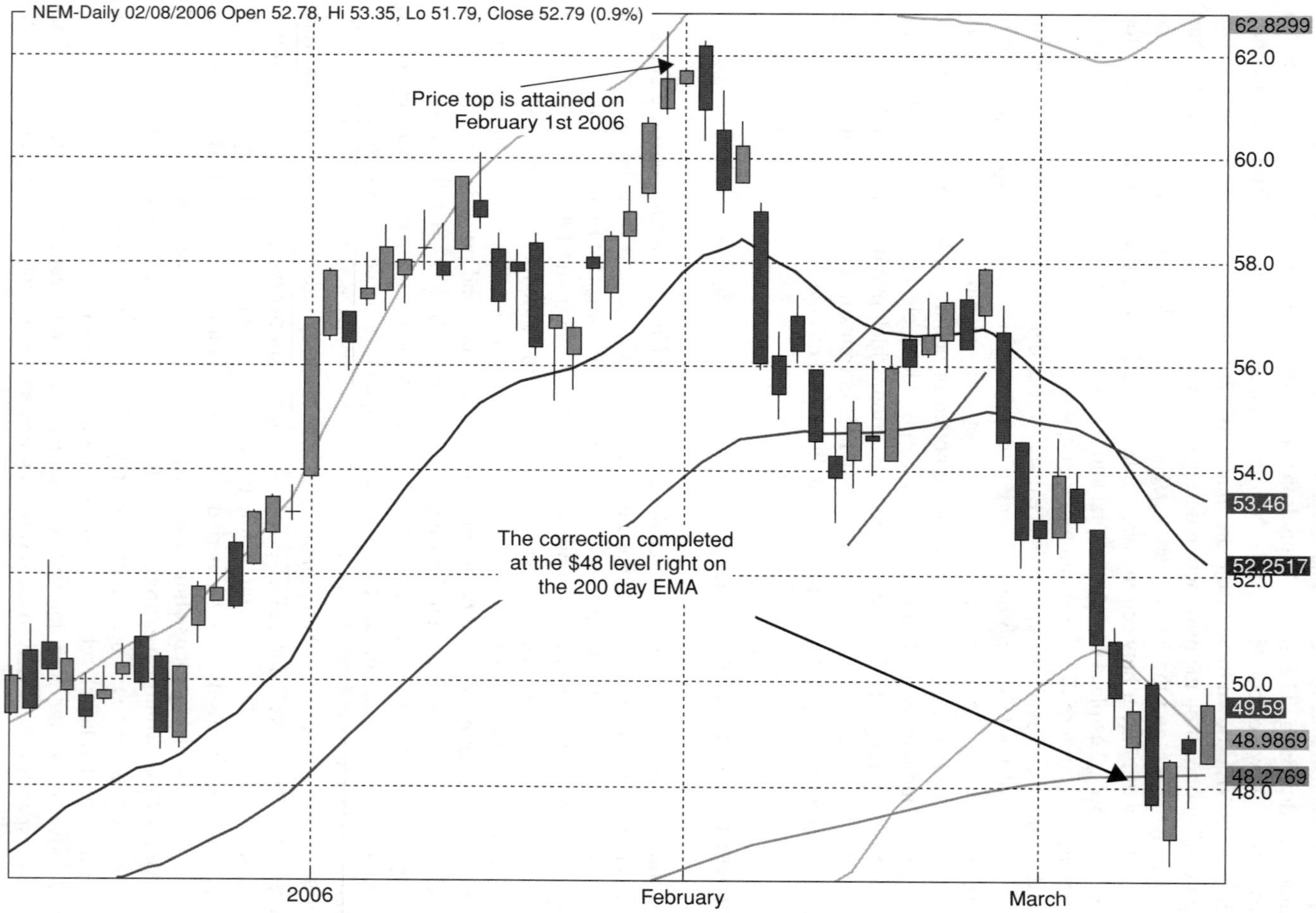

Figure 4.7 NEM February 2006 correction

Figure 4.8 GOOG weekly chart January 2005–July 2006

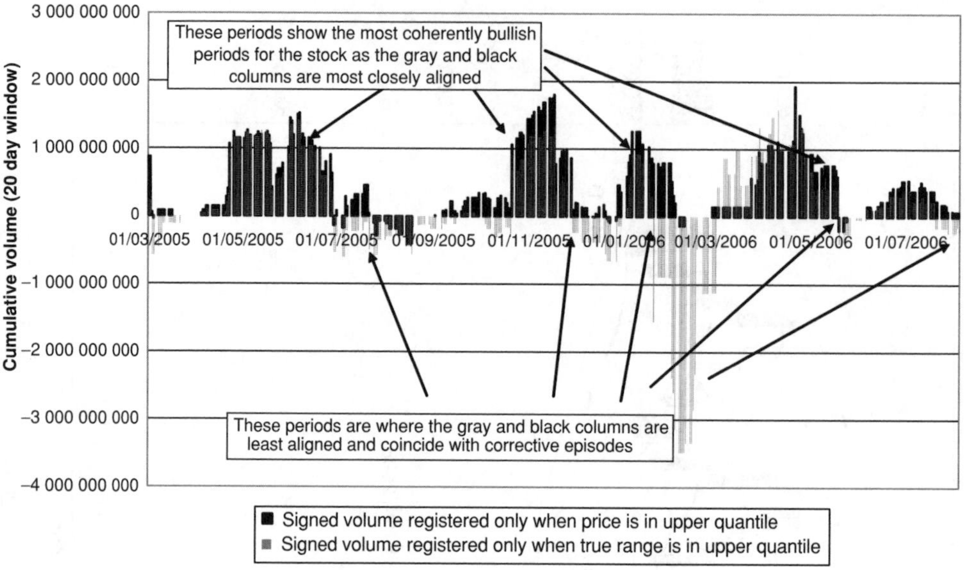

Figure 4.9 Google (GOOG) upper quantile-based signed volume analysis based on the period January 2005–July 2006

and using the penetration of the zero line as the signal would have allowed for virtually full participation on the short side and subsequent reversal to a long side. It is also noteworthy that during most of the period when the gray column was below the zero level on the y-axis there is no visibility for the black columns. However, these also make a reappearance coincidentally with the crossing of the zero volume level from below.

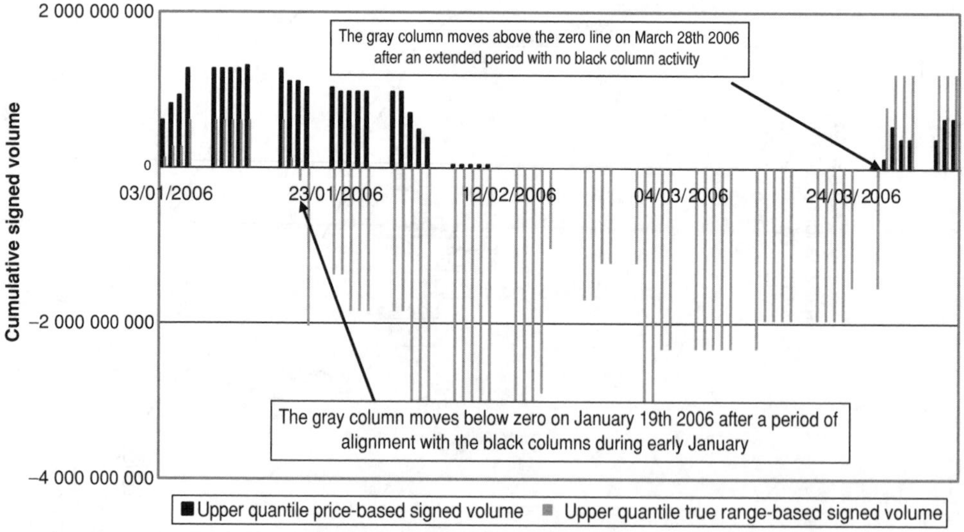

Figure 4.10 Google (GOOG) quantile-based volume analysis – focus on January 2005–March 2006 showing divergencies

CASE STUDY – OVERSEAS SHIPHOLDING GROUP (OSG)

Figure 4.11 is a weekly chart for Overseas Shipholding Group (OSG) from January 2005 to July 2006. The chart has more of a sideways character than the ones that we observed for NEM and GOOG although it also contains the powerful bullish move that begins in May 2006 and which appears set to challenge (at the time of writing) the previous highs that were registered in 2005. In this case study we have decided to focus on the three rallies that coincide with A, B and C that have been noted on the chart. The rally that begins at C is definitely the most powerful and B has more of an appearance of a temporary bounce. But we shall examine each of them with the CQA tools that we have previously used.

Figure 4.12 shows a similar CQA analysis as was used previously with all of the same parameters. The three periods that correspond to A, B and C on Figure 4.11 have been noted on the chart. In each case there is an almost exact correspondence between the turning points when rallies began and the point where the gray columns move above the zero line on the vertical axis. Noticeably there are fewer occasions for A and B where the crossing of the zero line is followed by a resumption of the black columns but this is far more evident on the right-hand side of the chart in connection with point C. In general there is less visibility for the black columns (i.e. indicating upper quantile price activity) than on the charts for Newmont Mining and Google which concurs with the overall sideways pattern.

The very powerful upward move that was observed as beginning at point C in Figure 4.11 is featured in the more detailed analysis that is provided from Figure 4.13. The first crossing

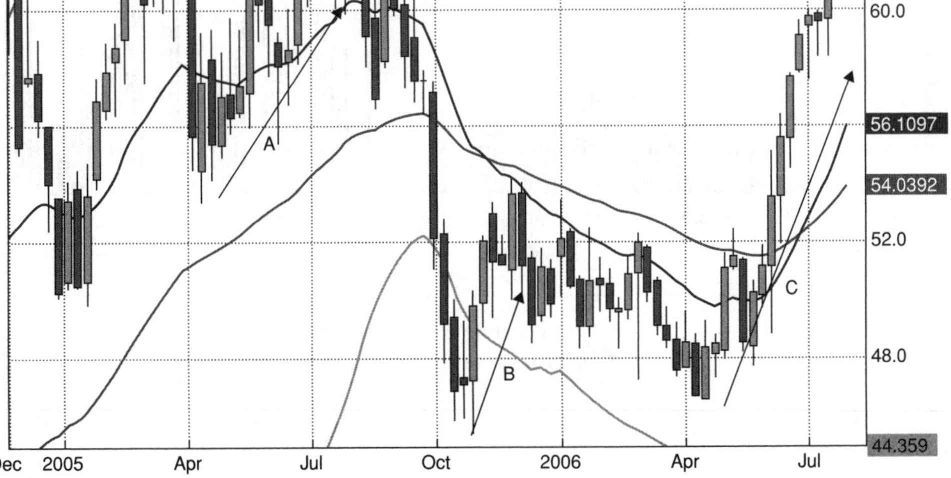

Figure 4.11 OSG weekly chart January 2005–July 2006

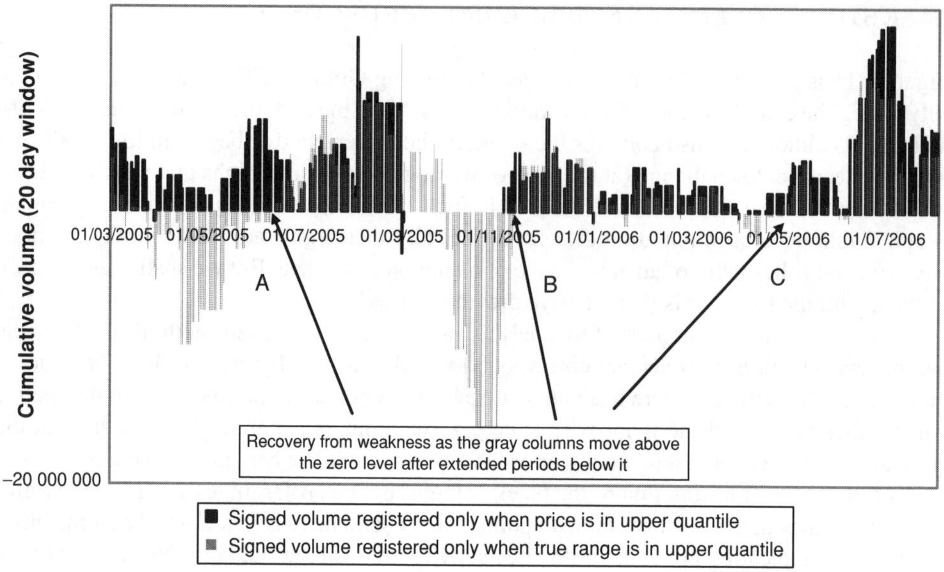

Figure 4.12 Overseas Shipholding Group (OSG) upper quantile-based signed volume analysis based on the period January 2005–July 2006

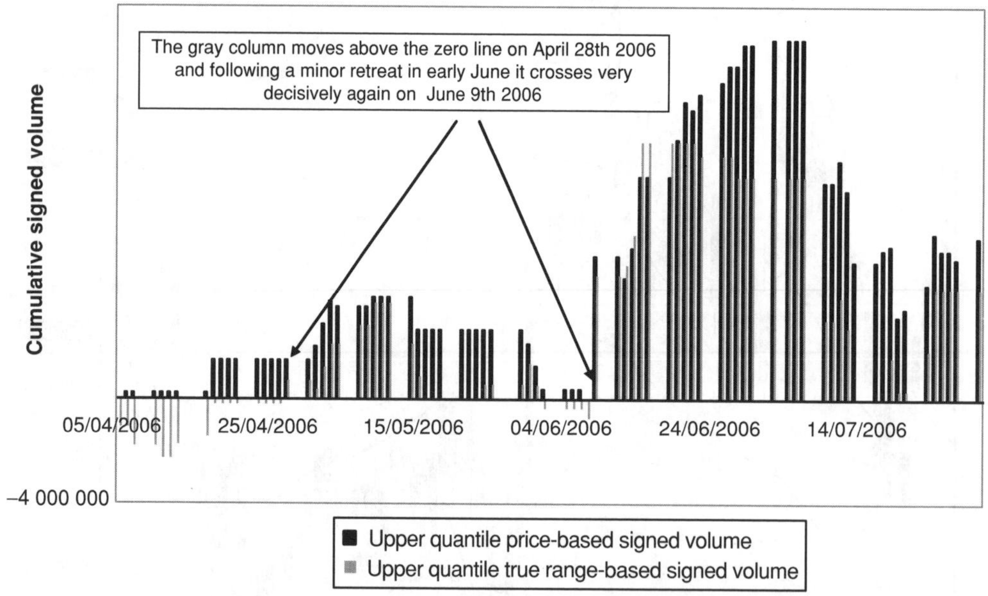

Figure 4.13 Overseas Shipholding Group (OSG) quantile-based volume analysis – focus on April–July 2006 showing divergencies

above the zero line takes place on April 28th 2006 which coincides very closely with the low price that precedes the major impulse upwards. However, there is a minor retracement which takes the gray columns temporarily below the zero line again only to be followed by the more decisive recrossing which occurs on June 9th. In checking the price chart in this time frame it can be seen that this coincides with the price action exactly and the full blown impulse wave commences after the price has broken above $52 which matches exactly with the second crossing of the zero line on June 9th. In terms of refining the trading signals that the CQA techniques offer, it is not unsurprising that these recrossings will occur and if the second crossing of the zero line is more forceful than the first (which it definitely is in this case) this will prove to be the more reliable. In chart formation terms, the situation that we have just observed coincides with the minor price retracements that are seen in cup and handle patterns.

CASE STUDY – LEHMAN BROTHERS (LEH)

Figure 4.14 shows a weekly chart for Lehman Brothers (LEH). Perhaps the most notable feature of this chart is the strong upward move that begins with the price breakout above the previous range bound trading in late June 2005. The move continues almost uninterrupted until late April 2006 and during the period LEH moves from $48 to $78. There is a minor retracement in August 2005, another in early October 2005 (coinciding with point A on the chart), a third in December 2005 (point B), a fourth and more acute in March 2006 (point C) and a fifth and far more severe one that begins towards the end of April 2006 (point D). During the major

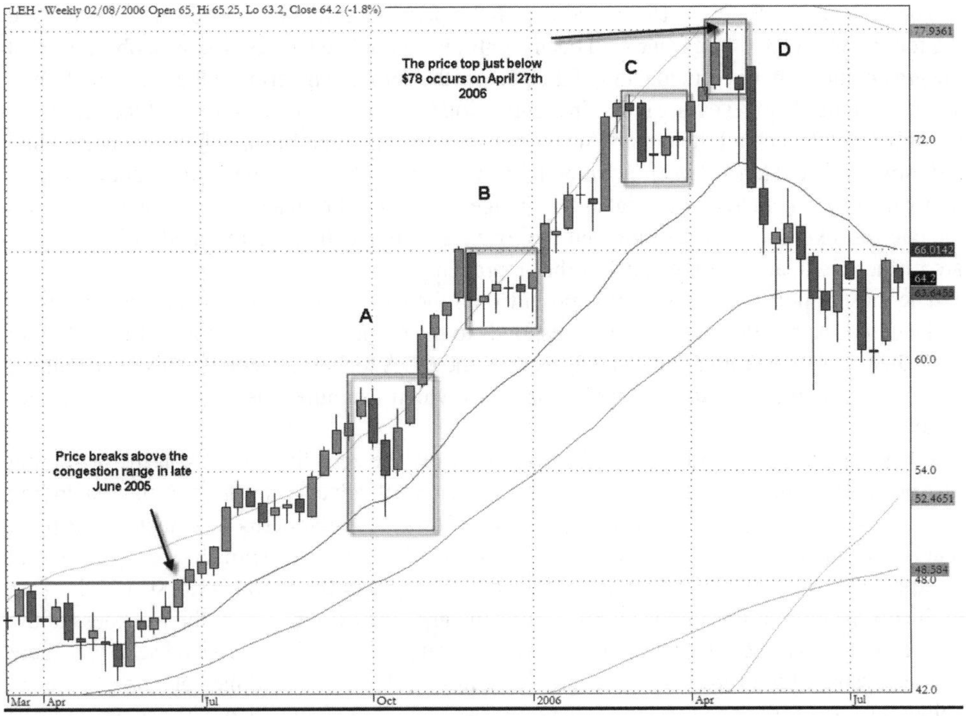

Figure 4.14 LEH weekly chart January 2005–June 2006

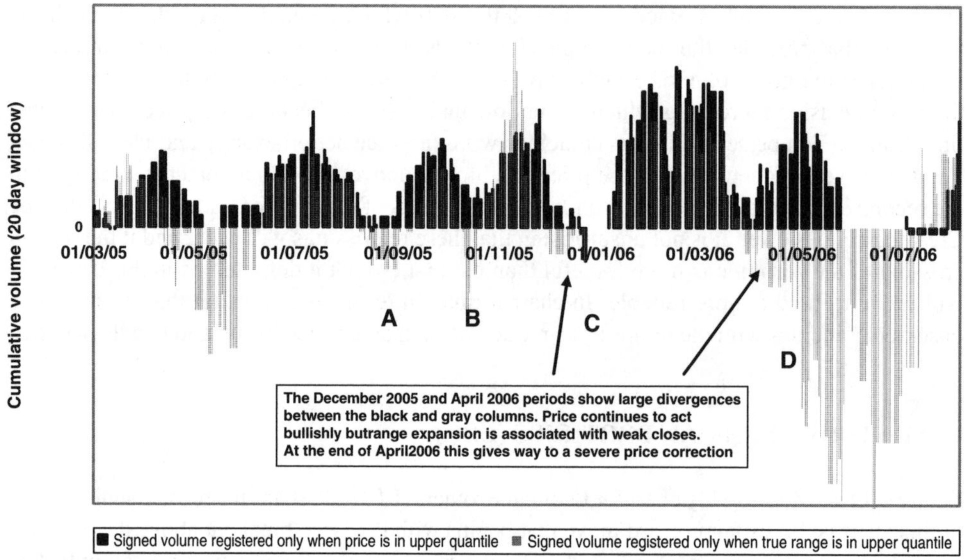

Figure 4.15 Lehman Brothers (LEH) upper quantile-based signed volume analysis based on the period January 2005–July 2006

upward move LEH manages to remain above its 20 week EMA throughout and only drops below it during the correction that begins in late April 2006.

The time axis of Figure 4.15 coincides with the price chart that has just been described and the four points A, B, C and D have all been identified again. In each case it can be observed that the gray columns have coincidentally fallen below the zero line in terms of the accumulation of signed volume. Also revealing is that in conjunction with these four episodes the black columns are still in evidence and the nonalignment between the gray and black columns is portending a dissonant mismatch between price activity which is still registering in the upper quantile interval and weaker closes associated with range expansion. From a trading perspective this is the cue for taking a short position and the four clear signals that are revealed in Figure 4.15 are further vindication of the value of this approach.

The most opportunistic short trade provided on the LEH chart is clearly the one that arises at the end of April 2006 and which corresponds to the point D on both Figure 4.14 and Figure 4.15. Just how well from a micro-analysis does the CQA technique identify this opportunity? To answer this we need to examine Figure 4.16 which examines the circumstances in finer detail.

It has been noted that the gray columns slip below the zero line initially at the beginning of April 2006 which would have given possibly too much advance warning of the impending decline. However, as was noted in the discussion of this particular period in Chapter 3 the price that is associated with the early April signal was just $2 below the eventual price top at the end of April. But what seems most noticeable about the April 2006 period is the strong showing of the black columns during the month despite the growing evidence from the weakness of the gray columns that the underlying dynamics were deteriorating. It can also be seen that there is a recrossing of the zero line by the gray columns on April 27th and then an abrupt reversal below it for the following session. This session – April 28th – coincided with the actual price top and over the next two sessions the price dropped by more than $6.

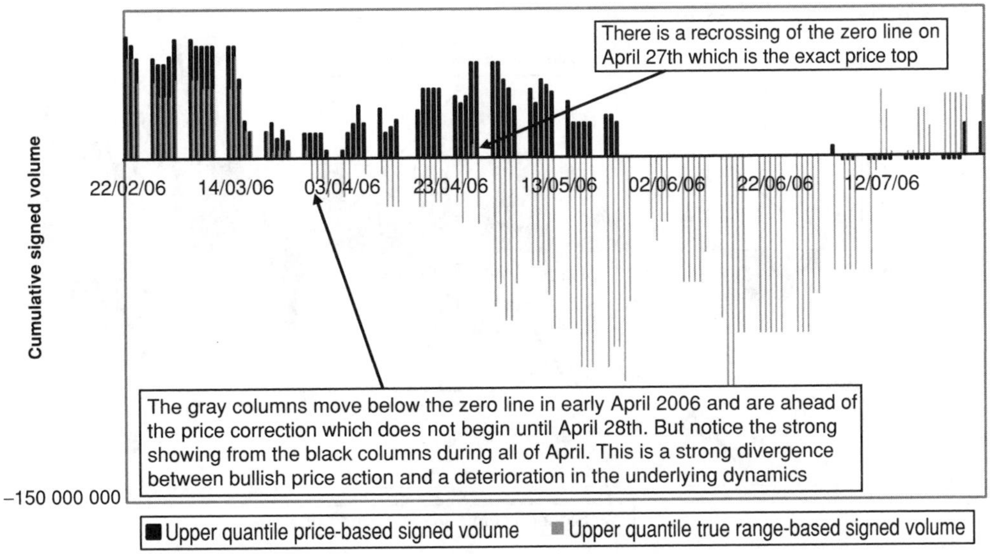

Figure 4.16 Lehman Brothers (LEH) quantile-based volume analysis – focus on April–July 2006 showing divergencies

In reviewing the price chart it can be seen that price had reached a plateau in the vicinity of \$72 during most of March 2006 and then in April there was a breakout to \$76 which created a lot of new entries to the upper price quantile. However, during the March/April period in the sessions when there was range expansion this was coinciding with more restrained volume and a tendency toward weaker closes. This is the classical dissonance pattern that can lead to the most profitable trading opportunities. The emergence of the gray columns below zero is a useful alert but the validity of the signal is reinforced when this coincides with a strong disconnect with the price activity. If the pattern persists, and even if there is a temporary recrossing before the discordant pattern reasserts itself, it points to a potential breakout failure. False breakouts will often bear this CQA signature and after the struggle between the traders attempting to push price higher despite deteriorating momentum dynamics is "lost" there can often be a substantial correction which is exactly what happened in this instance.

USING A SIGNED VOLUME MEASURE ON ITS OWN

The CQA methodology is extremely versatile and we have, with the several case studies that we have just reviewed, used one of the most useful techniques to illustrate its capacity for alerting traders to important turning points. We want to turn next to a simplified version of the preceding analysis that reduces the two column approach to a single metric which has also proven to be very effective. This section focuses on a separate signed volume amount which should also be monitored for when it moves back and forth below the zero level on the vertical axis.

The attribution of a signed value to the volume is exactly as before so volume that arises in connection with a strong close (i.e. where the close is positioned within the upper quadrant of the daily range) is considered positive, volume with a weak close is given a negative sign, and all

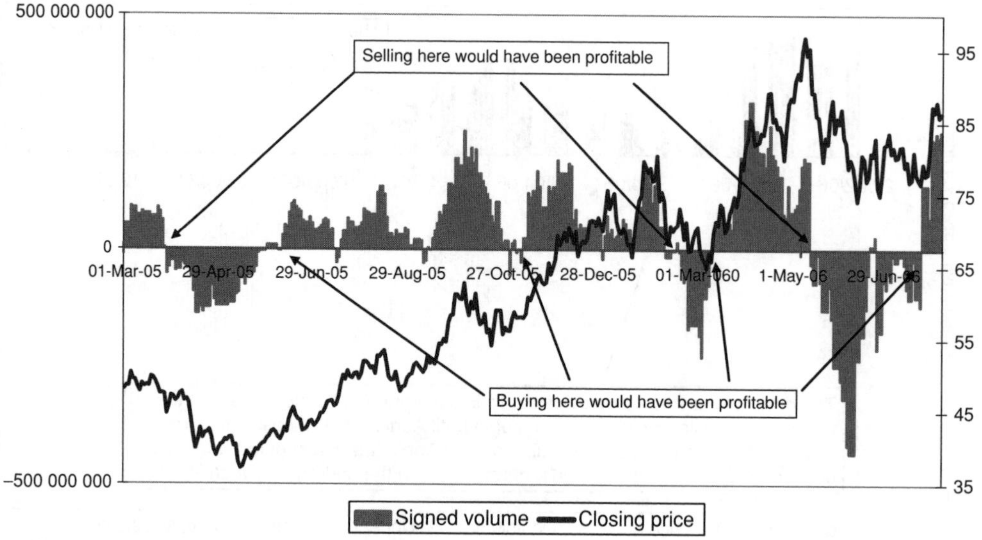

Figure 4.17 Phelps Dodge (PD) March 2005–July 2006 signed volume analysis

of the intermediate values are not accumulated. Two separate volume registers are maintained. One register accumulates within a moving window the signed volume when price is above the median value (for the last 20 periods). The other register accumulates signed volume when the true range is above the median value for true range (for the last 20 periods). Both registers can be showing at any moment a net cumulative volume that can be either negative or positive according to the preponderance of weak or strong closes.

The final volume value that is tracked is the sum of the moving totals at each interval.

To demonstrate the approach we shall move quickly through three charts that have been annotated with the appropriate signals and the benefit of the graphical presentations is that the price development of each security is included on the same time axis and the coincidences of the signals with the subsequent price action can easily be monitored.

Figure 4.17 shows the signed volume behavior for Phelps Dodge (PD) and the associated price action. There are three buy signals and three sell signals and in each case they are corroborated by the ensuing price action.

Figure 4.18 takes the same approach for Google (GOOG) and supplements the analysis that was already provided in the individual case studies. The major price turning points are also in harmony with the signals generated.

The third chart in this section (Figure 4.19) is for Martha Stewart Omnimedia (MSO) and each of the three sell signals and four buy signals are well corroborated by the subsequent price action.

AN ALTERNATIVE VERSION OF QUANTILE BASED MONEY FLOW

In this section, which can be construed as a stand alone item with respect to the chapter, we will present the reader with an alternative approach to volume analysis that is based on our

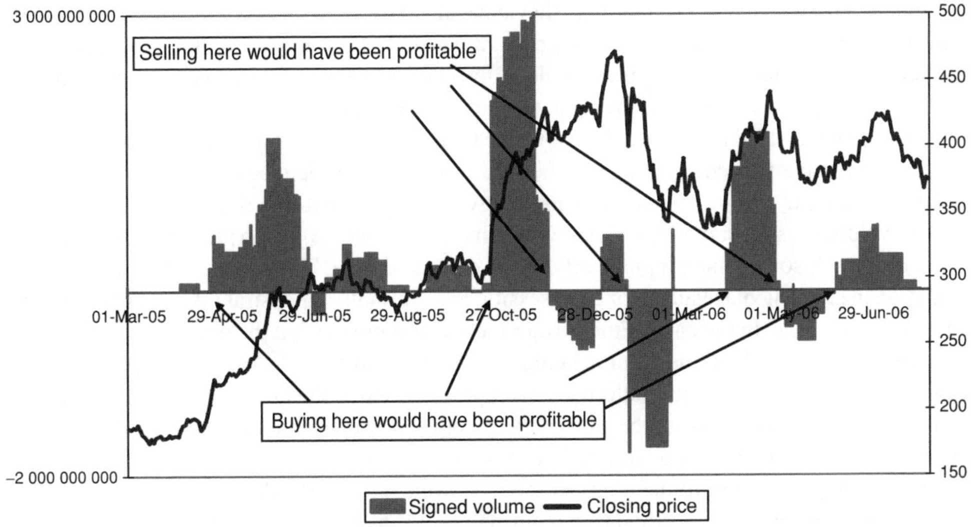

Figure 4.18 Google (GOOG) March 2005–July 2006 signed volume analysis

original application of the quantiles inspired methodology to money flow. We have offered it as a separate method because it is simpler than the versions previously outlined in this chapter, and because, from a historical point of view, it was the author's first attempt to refine the standard MFI methodology using quantiles. Th technique only requires us to classify and accumulate volume associated with the appearance in the appropriate quantile of price and the closing bias. We also do not attach a signed value to the volume and we are no longer required to register values based on which quantile is occupied by the intraday range. While the

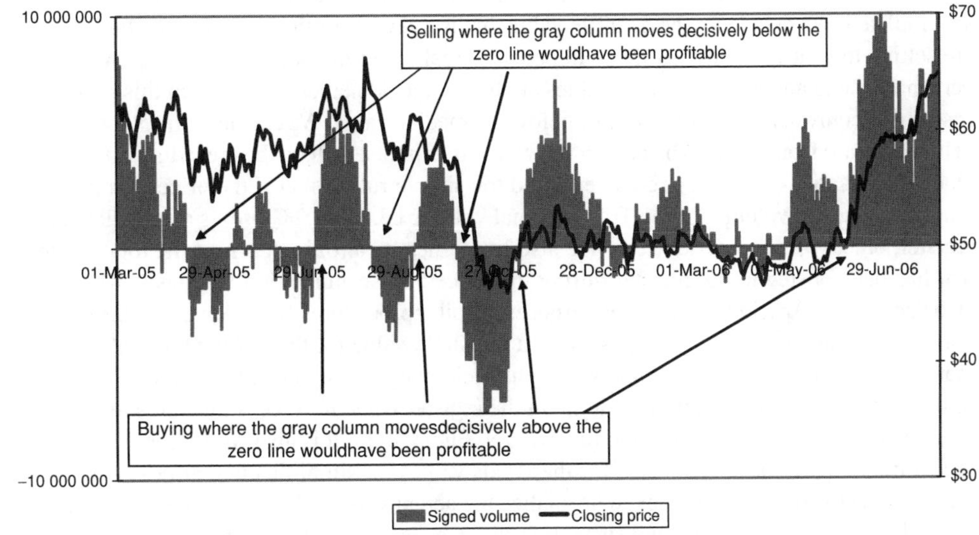

Figure 4.19 Martha Stewart Omnimedia (MSO) March 2005–July 2006 signed volume analysis

results require different interpretations, they have also proven to be very effective and we shall illustrate their usefulness in the case of the examples of AMGN and MSO that were mentioned earlier in the chapter. Once again we shall be looking at those circumstances where there is a discrepancy between what is occurring at the surface level and what is taking place beneath the surface and which leads to a kind of dissonance that often portends price breakouts. According to this alternative procedure it will be helpful to distinguish between two kinds of volume accumulation that can be registered using CQA techniques, but this time we simply assume that all volume has the same signed value. The first kind is based only on price performance and shall be called, somewhat simplistically, price driven volume. The second kind of volume is based on the closing bias values for each session and we shall call it, straightforwardly, closing bias driven volume. In the case of the former the presumption is that the primary motivation or explanatory factor behind the volume being registered is attributable to a surface phenomenon which is the way that the price pattern is developing – whether the closing price is making new multi-session highs or lows. In the case of the latter the key contributing factor for the tracking of volume is a phenomenon operating beneath the surface which is the strength of the closes – whether they are nearer to the highs of the day or the lows of the day.

The intuition behind the method is that during periods of quiet accumulation the volume that accompanies sessions with strong closes (i.e. when the closing bias is within its upper quantile value) will tend to show an edge and outpace those that are only based on the closing price being in the upper quantile. Our purpose is to reveal the activities of those traders who are quietly and somewhat stealthily ("smart money") building a long position in the stock. Additionally there are further clues provided by the framework for estimating the quality of the price breakout and whether it may be sustainable. For the present we shall only be considering the circumstances preceding upward price breakouts and moreover only those that occur within the context of the quiet volume sessions that we discussed earlier in the chapter. We shall again be reviewing the two previous examples of AMGN and MSO where we found that a period of price inertia and quiet volumes lead to explosive price breakouts to the upside, and later we shall examine a slightly different case where momentum factors were at work as well.

As a quick refresher on the CQA methodology here is how the price driven volume will be accumulated. We decide on the quantile value that is relevant for the exercise – in this case we are setting the bar quite low so we shall consider that upper quantile values are above the 50 percentile value and lower quantile values are below the 50 percentile value. In this particular case this is equivalent to being above or below the median value. We calculate the 50 percentile value (median) from our lookback window which in this case will be the preceding 20 periods. Once the quantile value has been determined the simple rule is that if the price is above that quantile value the volume (or the Transactional volume i.e. Price * Close) is accumulated in a register, otherwise we register, zero. We also keep track on a rolling basis of the total volume that has been posted to the register during the preceding accumulation window – which has also been set at 20 periods for present purposes. Similar procedures are followed for the closing bias except that we can, optionally, specify a threshold value for the closing bias value rather than the quantile value. For example we might decide on a threshold value for the closing bias of 0.5 and we will only count the volume in the register when it exceeds this threshold.

In the chart that we shall examine for AMGN, Figure 4.20. It is also worth mentioning that raw volume figures have been used for the *y*-axis values for simplification purposes although it is possible to construct an index to normalize the actual values. However, the key idea is that one is looking for discernible and sustaining divergences rather than at the absolute levels of volume that are involved. Also it has been decided to use an additive/subtractive relationship

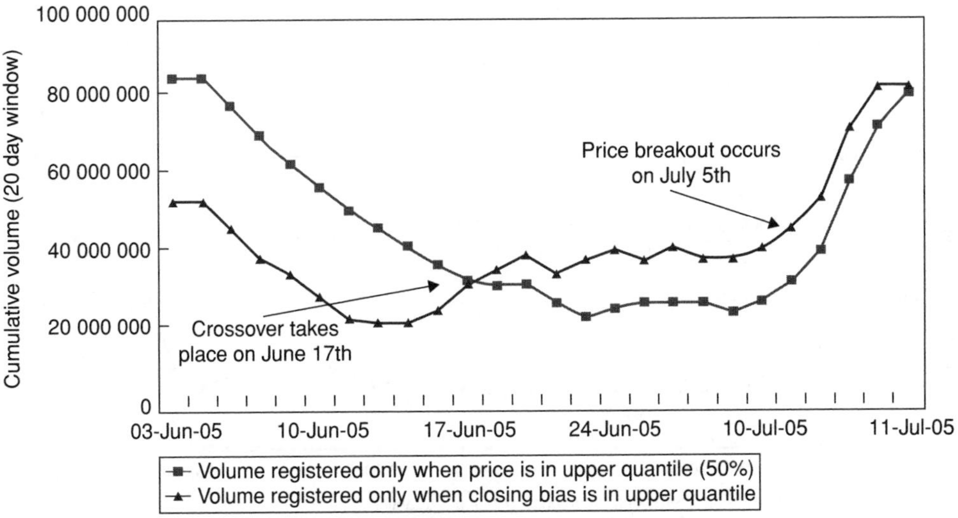

Figure 4.20 AMGEN June 2005 volume analysis

rather than dividing one set of volume by the other as the presence of low volume values in the denominator would produce erratic and mathematically monstrous values in the comparative analysis.

The vertical or *y*-axis represents the accumulation of transactional volume for a 20 day period prior to the actual data point that has been plotted for each of the two variables. The line with embedded squares – the price driven volume-shows the cumulative transaction volume for those days when price is in the upper quantile (i.e. in the current chart this has been set at the 50% level). The line with embedded triangles – the closing bias driven volume – shows the cumulative transaction volume for those days when the closing bias is in the upper quantile of that series of values. As can be seen the price driven volume has been descending steadily from early June indicating that day to day trading activity is not rewarding the stock with any positive volume accumulation characteristics. This can be typical of a quiet period for a stock as there is little inducement for momentum or swing traders to show much interest in a stock which is in a price congestion zone. As is evident the closing bias driven volume starts to turn up around the middle of June, it crosses the price driven volume line on June 18th and remains above it for the remainder of the month. In itself the crossover generates an alert for the methodology but it should not be acted upon until other factors are also present which are considered below. The price breakout point on July 5th has been noted on the chart and after this point it becomes all too apparent to the momentum or price driven traders that the price dynamics and range expansion favor further gains and the price driven volume line rapidly catches up with its counterpart – the closing bias driven volume line.

Let us next examine a similar chart for MSO, Figure 4.21, and we shall also examine how tuning the percentile value will generate slightly different results in this instance. Incidentally, in the case of the AMGN chart tuning the percentile value up to 70 has little effect on the pattern but the crossover occurs a little later than for the 50 percentile level we selected.

We observe a similar pattern to the one we have looked at for AMGN and this time it is noticeable that the price driven volume is actually "flat-lining" at zero during the mid-August

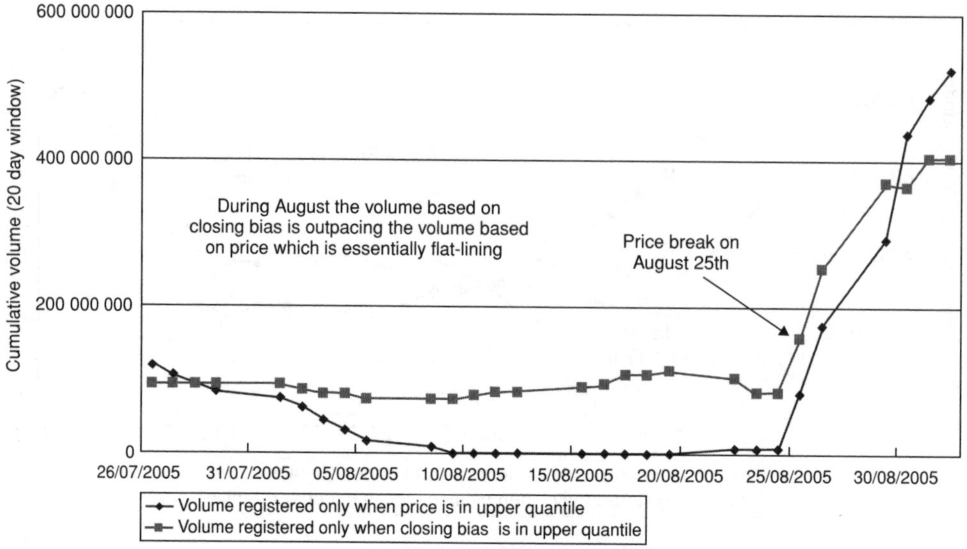

Figure 4.21 Martha Stewart Living Omnimedia Inc. (MSO) August 2005 volume analysis

period showing that the stock is failing to register in the upper price quantile; therefore no volume could be accumulated. But the line based on closing bias in Figure 4.21 (i.e. the one with embedded squares) is showing that the quiet money is steadily accumulating the stock during August and that the gap between the two lines widens as the month progresses. The price breaks out rather explosively on August 25th and at this point the momentum traders cause a rapid escalation in the gradient of the price driven line so that it has already surpassed the closing bias driven line by the end of August. This action can be construed as indicating that at this stage in the accumulation/distribution cycle the quiet, "early movers" (as expressed by the closing bias driven volume) are starting to distribute to the relative "latecomers".

How sensitive is the CQA approach to the quantile values selected for comparison? In Figure 4.21 the quantile for price was set at the 50 percentile value but what happens if this were to be increased to the 75 percentile value, while retaining the closing bias value set at 0.5? The results of setting the bar higher for inclusion in the price driven line can be seen in Figure 4.22. What is immediately apparent is that the "flat-lining" that was previously noted begins even sooner showing that for almost three weeks prior to the breakout on August 25th the stock failed to close within the upper quantile of its price performance during the preceding 20 day period. The zero volume characteristic for the price driven volume is an important element in the alerting procedure for the strategy and when it is observed in the context of the overall quiet conditions that we have witnessed for AMGN and MSO and there is accompanying evidence of stealth accumulation based on closing bias we have a bona fide case for a price breakout.

The flat-lining is not an absolute requirement of the pattern as we saw in the case of AMGN but rather it is the extended outperformance of the quiet money, as evidenced by the relative gradient of the closing bias driven line, that is the crucial ingredient. It is even plausible to conjecture that an extended period of zero values for the upper price quantile could indicate that short sellers are in control of the market from the day to day trading perspective but on those occasions when the closing bias is in the upper quantile or above the 0.5 threshold there is stealth accumulation occurring.

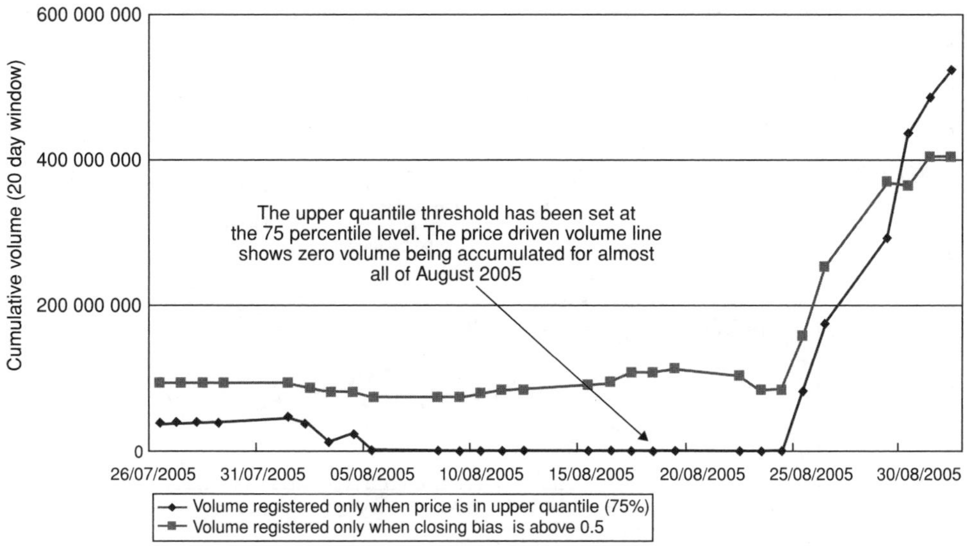

Figure 4.22 Martha Stewart Living Omnimedia Inc. (MSO) August 2005 volume analysis

Let us now review the inverse of what we have been examining during this period for MSO. We shall now examine the registration of transactional volume when price is in the lower quantile – in this case set at the 50 percentile level – and the closing bias is also below its 50 percentile value (again both values are determined using a 20 day lookback period). In Figure 4.23 the price driven volume accumulation is indicated by the line with embedded diamonds, and the volume accumulation based on closing bias is represented in the diagram by the line with embedded squares.

The time frame for Figure 4.23 has been extended to the end of September 2005 so that developments can be monitored in the comparative quantiles during the period when the late August price breakout is superseded by a serious bout of weakness for MSO. Starting on September 13th the stock begins a pronounced decline that continues into late October and which sees the price cut in half. Are there clues revealed in Figure 4.23 that this is imminent? Can the pattern of the relationship between the lines after the price break on August 25th be helpful in anticipating the steep correction that lies ahead? We believe that these questions can be answered affirmatively and that this provides further support for the case behind the CQA methodology.

During the latter part of July and early part of August the price driven volume line in Figure 4.23 shows that traders have been increasing their rate of selling despite the relatively weaker prices, which is usually considered to be a bearish development although it could be also be showing an increasing level of short-selling. Even as we move into the second half of August for those sessions when price is in the lower quantile there is still a substantial amount of transaction flow although it is fair to say that it is declining from its peak on August 10th. Meanwhile the closing bias driven line reveals much less activity. Cumulative transaction volume is declining steeply as the month progress and reaches its nadir just around the time of the price breakout on August 25th. What is also very striking in the diagram is that immediately following the price breakout the line based on closing bias starts to move up abruptly. We would propose that this could be interpreted as a follows. Prior to the breakout the quiet money traders whose footprints are revealed in the closing bias volume had been quietly accumulating MSO

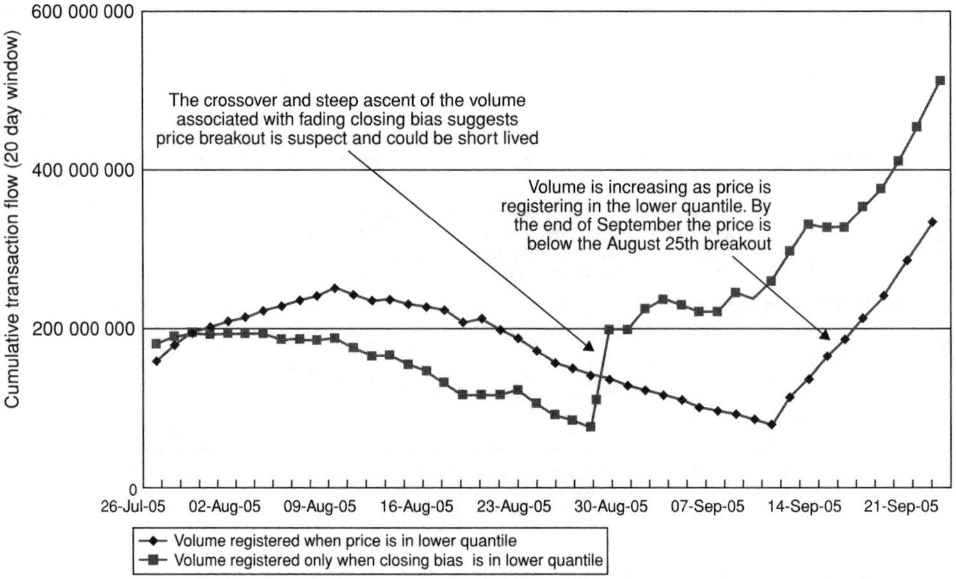

Figure 4.23 Martha Stewart Living Omnimedia Inc. (MSO) August–September 2005 showing volume registered in lower price quantile and lower closing bias quantile

in anticipation of positive news and an ensuing scramble to cover by short sellers. As soon as the price breakout occurs the same traders who had engineered the bear trap wanted to realize their profits quickly without having any longer-term intentions to "own" the stock. They are distributing quickly to the price and momentum driven traders.

In reviewing many such charts it is often the case that the volume accumulation based on closing bias changes direction suddenly after a breakout but it will then often stabilize after short-term profits have been taken. When this stabilization happens it is usually an indication that the breakout was based on a positive outlook for the stock rather than simply an opportunistic move designed to trap some overly enthusiastic short sellers. If the volume being registered in the accumulator based on closing bias in the lower quantile switches direction abruptly and continues to build as the closes continue to show relative weakness this is not, as in the case for MSO, indicative of a firm foundation for the price breakout. There is reason to question the longevity of the rally that accompanies the price breakout and should you have been attracted by the trade on the long side it would be prudent to take profits quickly, and even contemplate an eventual short position in the stock. This is a somewhat conjectural analysis of Figure 4.11 but the important point to note is that there is a very definite divergence between the activities of traders relying purely on price level and the "stealth" money that is flowing into a security which manifests itself in the volume register based on the closing bias characteristics.

Another example shares some of the characteristics that we have observed previously for AMGN and MSO but there are some interesting differences as well. The principal difference is that in the case of both MSO and AMGN the explosive price breakouts followed in the wake of periods of quiet accumulation which, as we have indicated earlier in this chapter, reflects the circumstances when, in our experience, the mainstream MFI indicator has proven to be most useful. Figure 4.24 is for Atherogenics Inc. (AGIX) and covers the months of November

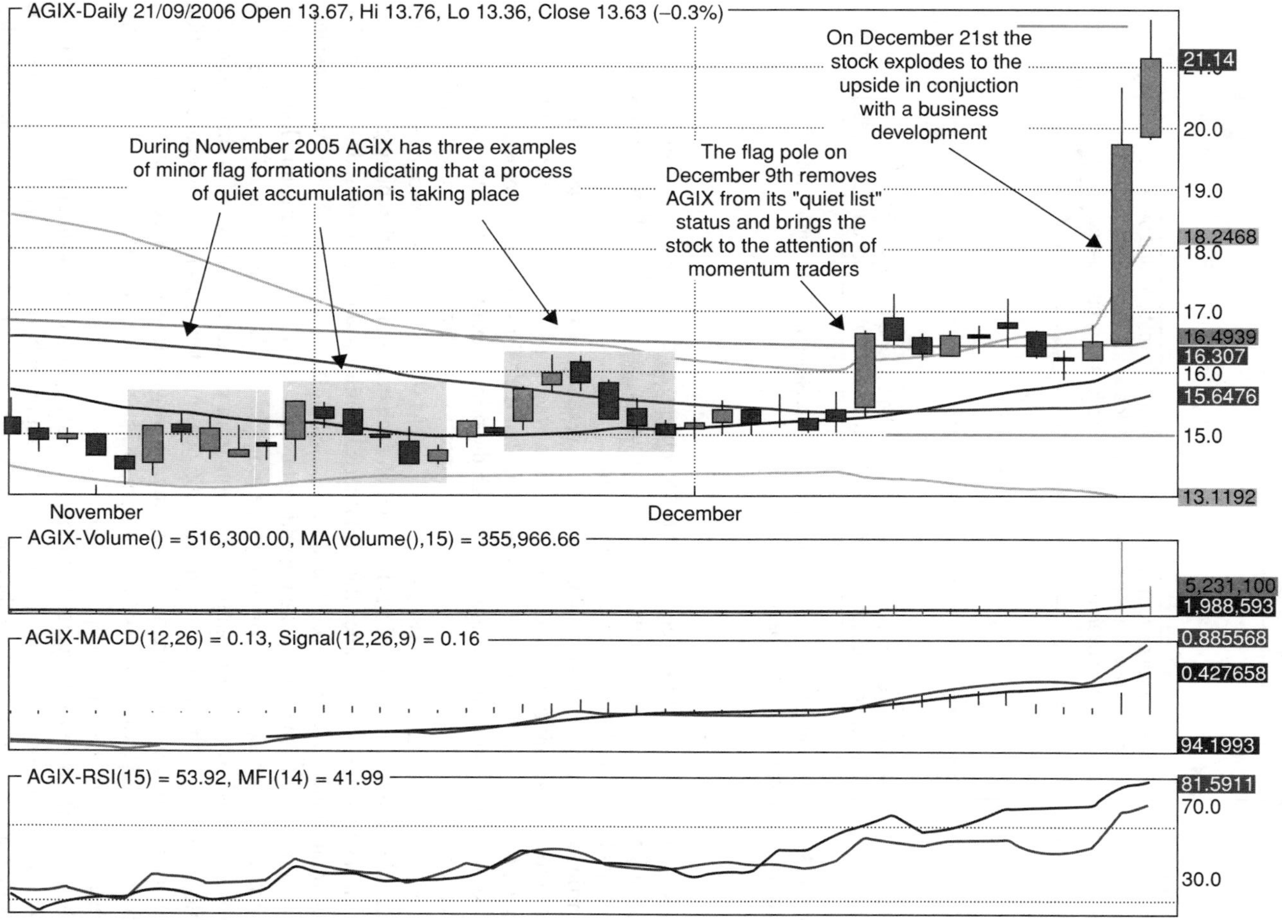

Figure 4.24 AGIX November–December 2005

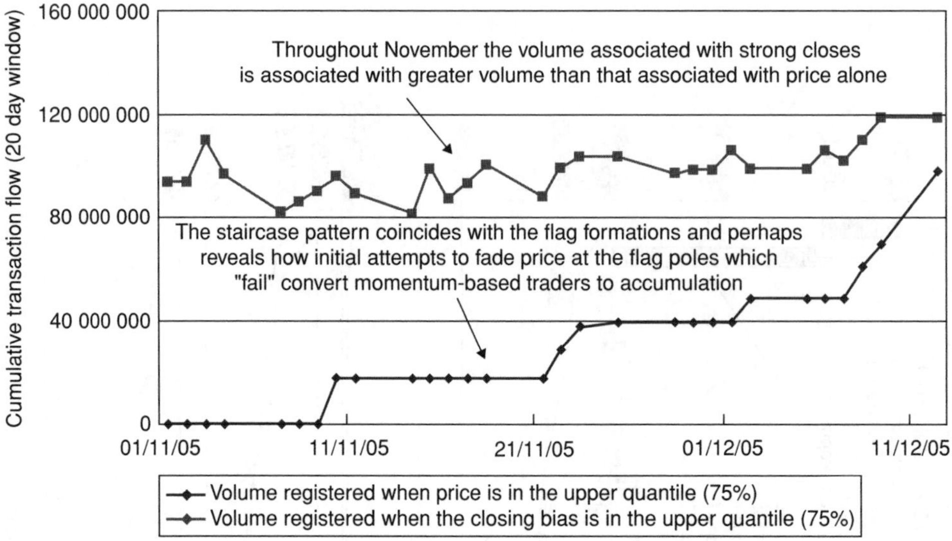

Figure 4.25 Atherogenics Inc. (AGIX) money flow analysis November–December 2005 based on upper price quantile and upper closing bias quantile

and December 2005. From December 8th to December 23rd the stock gained more than 40% and in a single session on December 21st there was a gain of 19.6% that coincided with a significant business development announcement.

Starting in early November the chart for AGIX reveals a series of bull flag formations that pointed to the possibility that some accumulation was beginning to take place in the stock. Unlike the charts for AMGN and MSO the gradient of the MFI slope during most of November 2005 shows a more gradual rise and even though the price is exhibiting relatively low volatility the presence of the flag formations points to proportionally greater range values for the stock during November than we witnessed for AMGN and MSO. As November progresses the series of flagpoles followed by pullbacks is followed on each occasion by further buying interest in a gradual staircase fashion. As noted the MFI is slowly building during the period as well, and in these circumstances it is plausible to make the case that there could have been some "insider" buying as those who knew about the impending business story were building up a long position in the stock. The breakout of the narrow range took place on December 9th and from this point forward the stock was clearly gaining attention from momentum traders. To that extent the profile for this stock as we enter December 2005 does not demonstrate the quiet accumulation characteristics that we have previously examined. However, using the comparative quantiles methodology it is possible by reviewing Figure 4.25 to witness clearly useful clues as to the volume characteristics prior to the breakout.

The line with embedded squares in Figure 4.25 is above the line with embedded diamonds throughout the period and especially so at the beginning of November when the case could be made that only the quiet money is showing any interest in the stock, as the line with embedded diamonds is registering zero volume at the beginning of November. As the flag formations begin to appear and the quite money continues to accumulate there are a series of step-ups on the line with embedded diamonds showing that there is growing interest in the stock from momentum traders. By the time of the first price breakout on December 9th the line with diamonds has pulled up closer to its counterpart and there is no considerable power behind the accumulation activities that clearly helped to spike the stock up on December 21st. We have tuned the upper quantile in this instance to the 70% level to make the situation slightly clearer but even at the 50% level a similar pattern is discernible.

Our discussion of money flow has ranged over many case studies and we have explored some different flavors to the CQA techniques. What unites the approaches is that all have been inspired by the analytical power of using statistical quantiles to unearth divergences. The CQA methodology needs to be extended and refined and we hope that this novel framework will inspire readers to produce further innovative indicators. There are a lot of further refinements that are required to sharpen the exact trading rules that can be profitably employed as a result of the CQA methods but these would require a book in their own right.

5
Alignments and Divergences

In Chapter 3 we introduced the idea that one of the motivational forces behind comparative quantiles analysis is the opportunity to examine whether co-movements or alignments are to be found in the array of variables that are available to describe and quantify a security's price development. These variables can include the actual raw data – OHLC and volume – but can also include derived variables such as closing bias, true range for the session, volatility, momentum as measured by MACD, money flow and even the security's beta value which has to be calculated in conjunction with a benchmark index. At each interval, in any time series, the selected variables for inclusion in a quantiles analysis can be calculated, stored in the appropriate registers and then accessed in pairs, triples etc. So to give a very straightforward example, if we want to test whether a price move is associated with range expansion we can perform a quantiles analysis in which we would register occasions when the price is in the upper quantile (using a moving 20 day window) and also register occasions when the true range is in the upper quantile. We can then calculate the number of co-occurrences for each of the separately registered events again using a suitable accumulation window. If we find that the co-occurrences exceed a certain threshold level which might be, say, four times within a 15 or 20 day lookback window then we can, depending on the co-occurrence hypothesis we are testing, be alerted to some highly reliable trading signals. The co-occurrence threshold parameter will be dependent on the context, and can also be tuned to conform to underlying market conditions.

In the case cited of comparing the registers for the upper price quantile and the upper quantile for true range, if we found a better than expected frequency of co-occurrence we could plausibly argue that we expected price to continue to outperform or have a tendency to remain in the upper quantile as it was accompanied by range expansion. The essential point is that we have a framework for testing a variety of hypotheses where we can confirm that an expected alignment is in evidence or absent. Looked at slightly differently we can also test hypotheses where an unexpected (or perhaps counterintuitive) alignment is in evidence. An example of unexpected alignments, which was already discussed in some detail in Chapter 3, was the discrepancy between the closing price appearing regularly in the upper quantile register and the closing bias appearing regularly in the lower quantile register. We saw that this can be a very reliable indicator of price deterioration and that the converse (i.e. where price is in the lower quantile and the closing bias is in the upper quantile) is equally as reliable in anticipating price advances.

In this chapter we want to focus on the cases where there are alignments between variables which are inconsistent or suggestive of an underlying discrepancy or disharmony. If one starts with the presumption that the foundational element in time series analysis is the price development pattern then we shall be zeroing in on some of the cases where the associated patterns which arise for other variables such as momentum or closing bias are acting discordantly with the price patterns. We shall refer to these anomalies or inconsistencies as being incongruous or dissonant. Another term that is often used in this context is divergence and we shall use it sometimes ourselves because it is so widely used in the technical analysis literature, but it does not quite match the flavor of the comparative quantiles approach. The terminology that most closely reflects the comparative quantiles technique is alignment or confirmation and non-alignments or nonconfirmation. One of the better known examples of non-alignments or divergences in technical analysis arises in regard to the widely used momentum indicator MACD. The indicator has been widely covered in the literature and we shall not embark on an elaborate explanation as to its construction.[1] In terms of its usage there are several techniques that are used ranging from the MACD signal line crossing its moving average line to the signal line crossing zero etc. In our own trading experience we have found that the most profitable application of MACD is provided by looking for divergences or non-alignments between price peaks and price valleys and the shape of the accompanying MACD line. The technique can be best illustrated by looking at Figure 5.1 which shows a daily chart for the last quarter of 2004 and early 2005 for American Express (AXP).

In early November 2004, AXP broke out from a trading range in the vicinity of $46 that had been in effect during the preceding month and then began to consolidate in a price plateau formation just below $49 in early December. During this period the MACD chart shows that there was a clearly discernible upward trend to momentum in early November and that this had also reached a plateau and began to decline as December progressed. The critical dissonance on the chart is illustrated by the break to a new price high just above $49 in the latter part of December but the action in the MACD chart shows that momentum is not supporting this move and can be said to be showing negative divergences with price. In the last few trading days of 2004, AXP makes a further, unsuccessful effort to penetrate the $49 level on typically subdued end of year trading volumes but as is clearly evident the MACD indicator is revealing a noticeable divergence to the price activity. When trading resumes in January 2005, the divergences give way to an abrupt price correction which brings AXP back down to the pre-breakout trading range levels from October 2004.

Divergences such as that for AXP are found fairly frequently on price charts and can have predictive validity, but often the divergence in the indicator needs to be placed in the context of potentially other important signals which may or may not lend weight to the divergence being resolved with the expected outcome. In the case of AXP we can see that the divergence in the indicator would have provided a very useful trading cue as the stock sold off throughout December right after the "false" price breakout. In fact the justification for using the term "false" breakout is provided not only by the eventual decline but also because of the MACD divergence.

Conversely there are occasions when the price has moved down to a new low and the MACD chart is revealing positive divergences showing that if one draws a slope from the previous valley on the MACD chart when price was previously making a low to the current valley on the MACD chart where price is breaking lower there would be an upward slant and this will often (but again the context and state of other indicators is important) be pointing to higher prices as gathering momentum is at odds with the new price low.

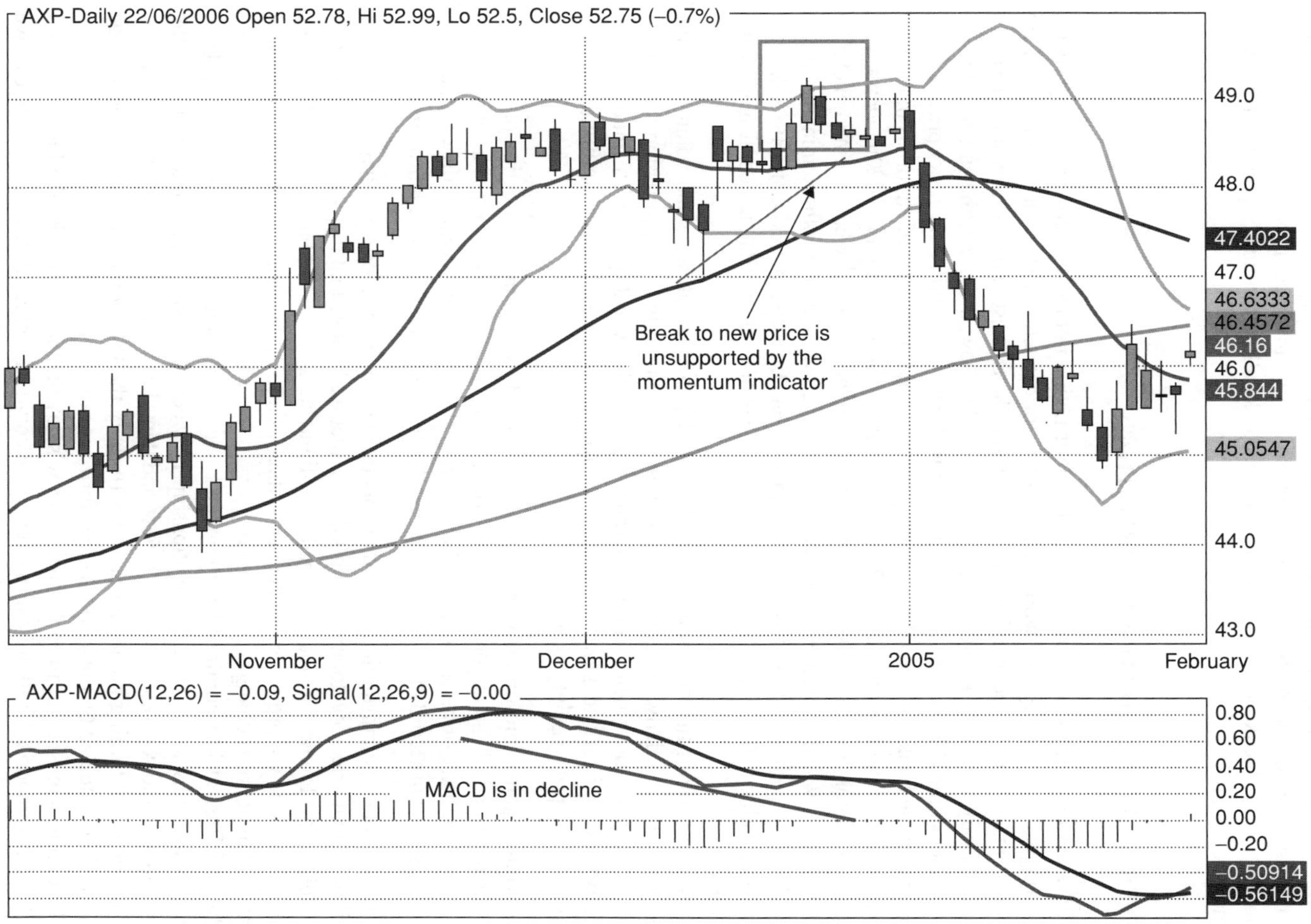

Figure 5.1 AXP showing negative MACD divergence

Figure 5.2 shows the converse situation to AXP and covers the period of August/September 2005 for Citibank (C). The breakdown in the closing price at the end of August is accompanied by a clearly discernible upward slant in the MACD indicator suggesting a positive divergence and nonconfirmation of the price deterioration so, in this instance, it is feasible to call this episode a "false" breakdown. As can be seen the stock rallied through September right after the nonconfirmation.

CONFIRMATION AND NONCONFIRMATION

We have used the terms confirmation and nonconfirmation in the same context as alignments and divergences and it might be worth just a brief historical detour to look at the origin of these two concepts within the technical analysis literature. The earliest known usage of the terms in technical analysis is to be found in the works of Charles Dow, the late 19th century publisher and founder of the Dow Jones Company and the *Wall Street Journal*. Dow never presented his ideas in a single book but instead recorded his observations in a series of editorials in the *Wall Street Journal* around the turn of the 20th century. After Dow's death in 1902 his views were collated in a book by S.A. Nelson, *The ABC of Stock Speculation*,[2] where the nomenclature of Dow Theory was first proposed. We are less concerned with an in-depth examination of the Dow Theory, which has been served well for many years by a disciple, Richard Russell,[3] than we are in looking at the legacy of some of the key ideas of confirmation, nonconfirmation and divergences.

Dow was perhaps the first to articulate the interdependence of price and volume and the importance of the relative magnitude of volume providing either a confirmation or nonconfirmation of price movement. Another seminal figure in the world of technical analysis, John Murphy, has summarized Dow's views on the role of volume in either confirming or not confirming the price activity as follows:

> Volume must confirm the trend ... Volume should expand in the direction of the major trend. If the major trend is up volume should expand or increase as prices move higher. Conversely volume should diminish as prices dip. Again if the volume fails to act in accordance with this simple rule then again there is non-confirmation.[4]

By placing volume confirmation as so fundamental in his market theory Dow has informed our intuitions about price development to this day. In fact we believe that the converse notion that when price development is not confirmed by volume behavior, as we have seen in the money flow analysis that we proposed in Chapter 4, there is a reliable basis for anticipating turning points and directional changes for a security.

Richard Russell has continued to propound one of the other central tenets of the Dow Theory which has to do with the relationship between the Dow Jones Industrials and the Transportation Index. In essence Dow's view, and it has been echoed over the years by Russell, is that significant turning points in one index (usually the Dow Jones Industrials) need to be confirmed or validated by the associated performance of the Transports.

The averages must confirm each other. In Dow's day this had to do with the Industrials and the Rails. No important bull or bear market signal could take place unless both averages gave the same signal. In other words, both averages had to exceed a previous secondary peak in order for a bull market to begin. The signals do not have to occur simultaneously but the closer

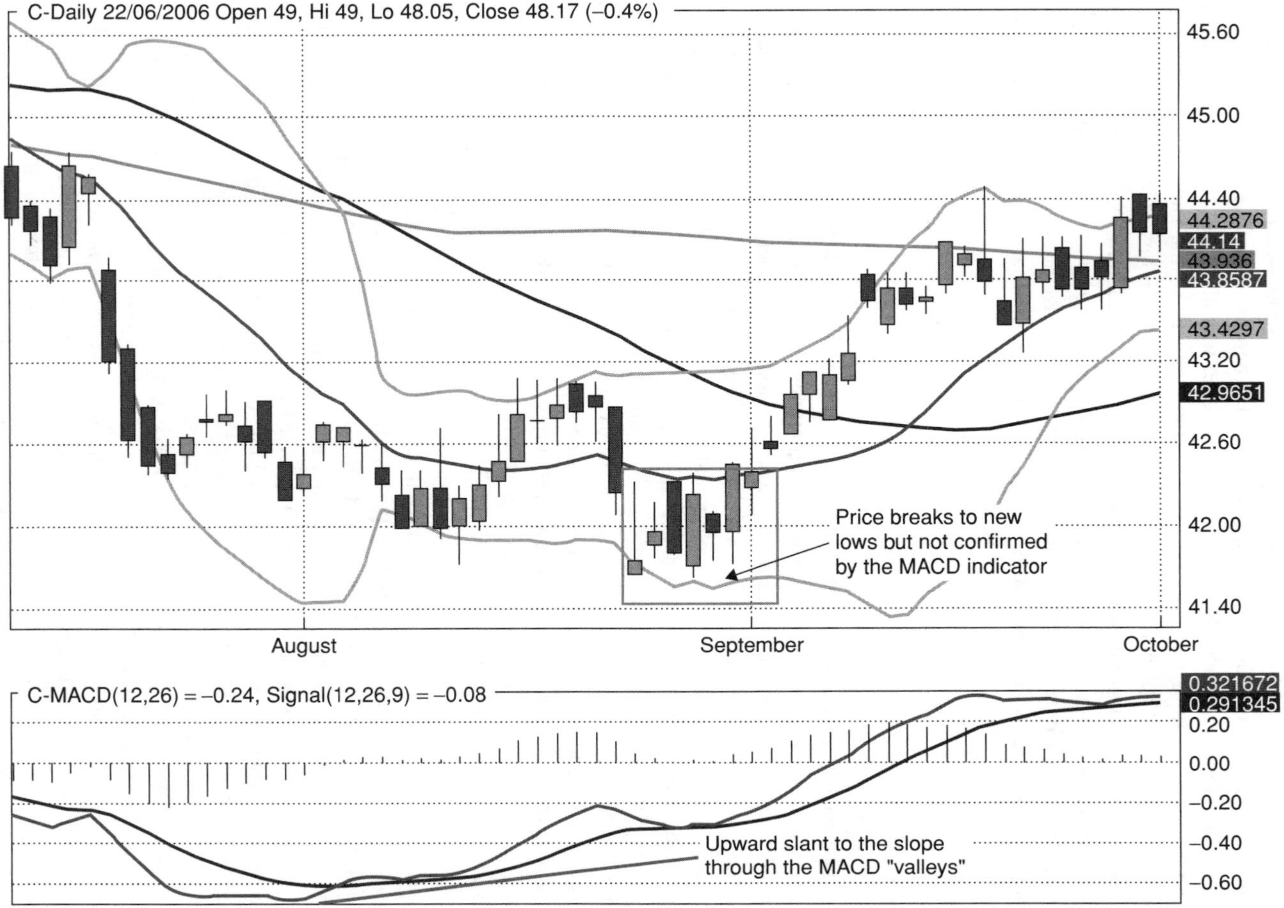

Figure 5.2 Citibank showing positive MACD divergence

together the better. If only average gives a signal then there is said to be nonconfirmation or divergence.[5]

Russell has been publishing his Dow Theory Letters for almost 50 years and has amassed a very good track record based on his interpretations of the market largely in accordance with the legacy tools from Dow. According to Mark Hulbert, who has been tracking the calls of market commentators since 1980, Russell's newsletter was in overall second place in late 2005.[6] One does not have to subscribe to all of the elements of the Dow Theory, such as the pivotal role of the Transportation Index, but see it rather as a historical curiosity. When Dow was writing the Rails (the previous name for the Transportation Index) had the same large significance as technology stocks have today and we suspect that an undue emphasis on the role of the Transportation Index is entirely attributable to this. But we do carry away from Dow's seminal contributions to thinking about markets the critical importance of confirmations and divergences.

DISSONANCE

Dissonance, as the term is most widely used, is a mental state in which the person experiencing dissonance is conflicted, is entertaining different thoughts or beliefs that are essentially contradictory. We have extended the meaning so that it is no longer a property of a human mind but can be the property of a collective mind which is a fairly good metaphor for a financial market. Dissonance with respect to the price development of either an individual security or the overall market is the manifestation of discordance among the most salient dynamics that underlie price activity. Whether it is a nonconfirmation by volume with respect to price or a divergence between the MACD and momentum characteristics and closing price, the divergences and disharmony will lead to a state that we can describe as dissonance.

Returning to our statement of the benefits for comparative quantile analysis we believe that an excellent handle on these dissonances is provided when examining the boundary quantiles for disparate or incongruous chart variables. This can be further illustrated by looking again at the examples we have already considered in connection with the MACD divergences for AXP and Citibank. Let us first consider the example of Citibank which as our analysis of the price and MACD chart was pointing to a positive momentum divergence in August 2005 as price was pushing down to new multi-period lows. If we set the lower price quantile register to count all values where price is below the 25% level based on a 20 day window we find that for Citibank we would observe that in late August 2005 the price would have frequently been within the lower quantile. If we also track the actual observed points traced by the MACD line during the same period we find that, based on using the same 20 day time window, there were several occasions when the MACD value was in the upper quantile. Here we are testing for the opposite of what should intuitively be expected, that is price and momentum should rise and fall together, but when we find that not only are the expected co-movements not aligned but in fact that divergent co-movements are confirmed, we can point to a nonconfirmation or dissonance which will require a resolution. The manner of resolution will be for price to "catch up" with momentum and the dissonant signal generated from the comparative quantiles technique would have provided an excellent profit opportunity. When we look at the contrary example for American Express (AXP) we find just the opposite situation in December 2004 where the upper quantile register is showing a preponderance of occurrences and the lower MACD quantile register is showing that many of the MACD readings are in this category.

These last two examples raise fundamental questions about the manner in which dissonance and nonconfirmation can actually be monitored. Traders that have a predilection for searching out evidence of dissonance can usually find several examples each day from looking at many daily charts. As we saw in the cases of American Express and Citibank the slopes of the MACD and the coincidental price action are fairly easy to observe once you know what you are looking for. But rather than having to look at hundreds of charts every day there are algorithmic procedures that enable a computer to identify candidates that conform to certain dissonance templates. These candidates can be brought to the attention of the trader for a final "sanity check" to be satisfied that there is a valid instance of the template. Armed with an array of such pattern recognition algorithms the trader would be able to decide on the best strategy for exploiting these dissonant patterns.

However, in our experience of developing trading systems and pattern recognition algorithms it is notoriously different to design a program that will identify certain kinds of dissonance such as the MACD divergences that we showed above. Determining the appropriate length for the time window is one of the issues as the divergences have quite variable extension characteristics. But even more problematic is finding an algorithmic procedure to discern subtle differences in the gradient of the slopes or the magnitude of the price variations as matched by the MACD variations. After experimenting with many techniques, which were somewhat reliable but always needed to be very carefully screened before instigating any action, the breakthrough for our ability to identify patterns such as the MACD divergences came with the realization that the slope divergence is closely tracked by the quantiles divergence. If the MACD values are registering in the converse boundary quantile to the price we have the foundation point for exploring further with other algorithmic procedures to see if we can identify a definite and significant divergence. Yet another benefit of this approach is that it can eliminate a lot of unnecessary pattern analysis since if one drives the quantile comparisons from the point of view of the registering of events within the boundary quantiles for price then one is confining the examination of the MACD values to only those which might be applicable for observing divergences. The MACD value taken on its own is not a useful statistic but when embedded within the quantiles comparison it can become a very valuable piece of information. Tracking to see whether the MACD is in a boundary quantile or mid-quantile can be the tip-off to further exploration, both algorithmic and visual, as to whether a dissonant pattern is present. As noted before the methodology is to separate the relevant conditions and information that the market is revealing from the background noise. Most of the time the actual MACD value is an inconsequential piece of information but when it is placed into the appropriate framework it takes on far more value.

TRADING SUCCESS COMES FROM DISCOVERING DISSONANT PATTERNS

We come now to one of the key ideas within this book which is that, in our belief, the best approach to trading markets is to identify dissonant patterns within the price charts and technical characteristics of individual securities and indices. Looking for dissonance becomes a forensic exercise that is greatly assisted by using the right methodology and like all good detectives we need to be looking for clues beneath the surface. We can develop various templates that are associated with dissonance and subsequent price breaks; the MACD example is such a template, and when we find a lot of supporting evidence that we have an instance of the template we go to the next challenge which is one of combining the individual trades in a systematic fashion to achieve the long/short goals that are outlined later in this book. In our experience there are usually as many special situations available on the long side as there are on the short side, and, when one puts aside the predisposition to trade only in what is perceived as the underlying direction of the market, we can exploit these long and short instances of dissonant behavior irrespective of what the trend within the overall market happens to be.

Because of our belief that dissonance is the most valuable information that the market reveals we have also learned to question and suspect a lot of patterns that on the surface appear to be saying one thing but on closer examination are saying something else which is often exactly the contrary. One obvious candidate is the "false" breakout pattern in which price breaks up or down above a well-recognized area of support or resistance. It may be that the breakout is legitimate and confirmed by the underlying dynamics of the move, but very often it is suspect and this can be discovered by finding dissonant patterns. It is sometimes observed that markets have a tendency to prove the majority of traders wrong and this is highlighted by the fact that too many market participants use surface information to make their key trading decisions. Another factor that is especially relevant is the tendency of market makers/specialists to "fade the crowd" and we shall see how this kind of market characteristic manifests itself in such patterns as pullbacks and flags in the next section. We shall identify the defining characteristics of pullback channels, usually but not always associated with flag formations and suggest that this is one of the most reliable market patterns. Traders need to become adept at spotting false breakouts, finding the differentiators that distinguish them from genuine breakouts, and to develop a variety of techniques to enable them to attempt to determine when securities (and indices) may be poised to change direction and perhaps even when underlying volatility conditions are likely to change.

DISSONANT PATTERNS IN THE MARKET INDICES

The same factors indicating dissonance that are manifested in the charts for individual securities are also found in the charts of the overall market and indices. A good example of the incidence of MACD nonconfirmation is provided by looking at the chart for the S&P 500 that coincides with the period at the end of 2004 where we previously examined the negative divergences for American Express.

Figure 5.3 is a daily chart for the S&P 500 index covering the period from November 2004 to January 2005 and, as we saw in the case of AXP, there is a strong upward movement in price during November, perhaps partly triggered by the resolution of the 2004 U.S. election in early November. There is a small plateau followed by steadily increasing prices again through December until the end of the year but as is also evident this was unsupported by momentum. The burst of momentum which propelled price higher in early November is dissipating throughout December. Price and momentum had effectively disconnected. Perhaps fund managers were keen to preserve the gains that they had made in November to improve their year end performances, perhaps it was just seasonal factors, but whatever the reason the price appreciation was clearly not in harmony with the underlying market dynamics. When 2005 begins the overall market suffered some rather severe declines which continued throughout January and this was not entirely unexpected given the degree and persistence of the MACD divergence that is revealed on the chart.

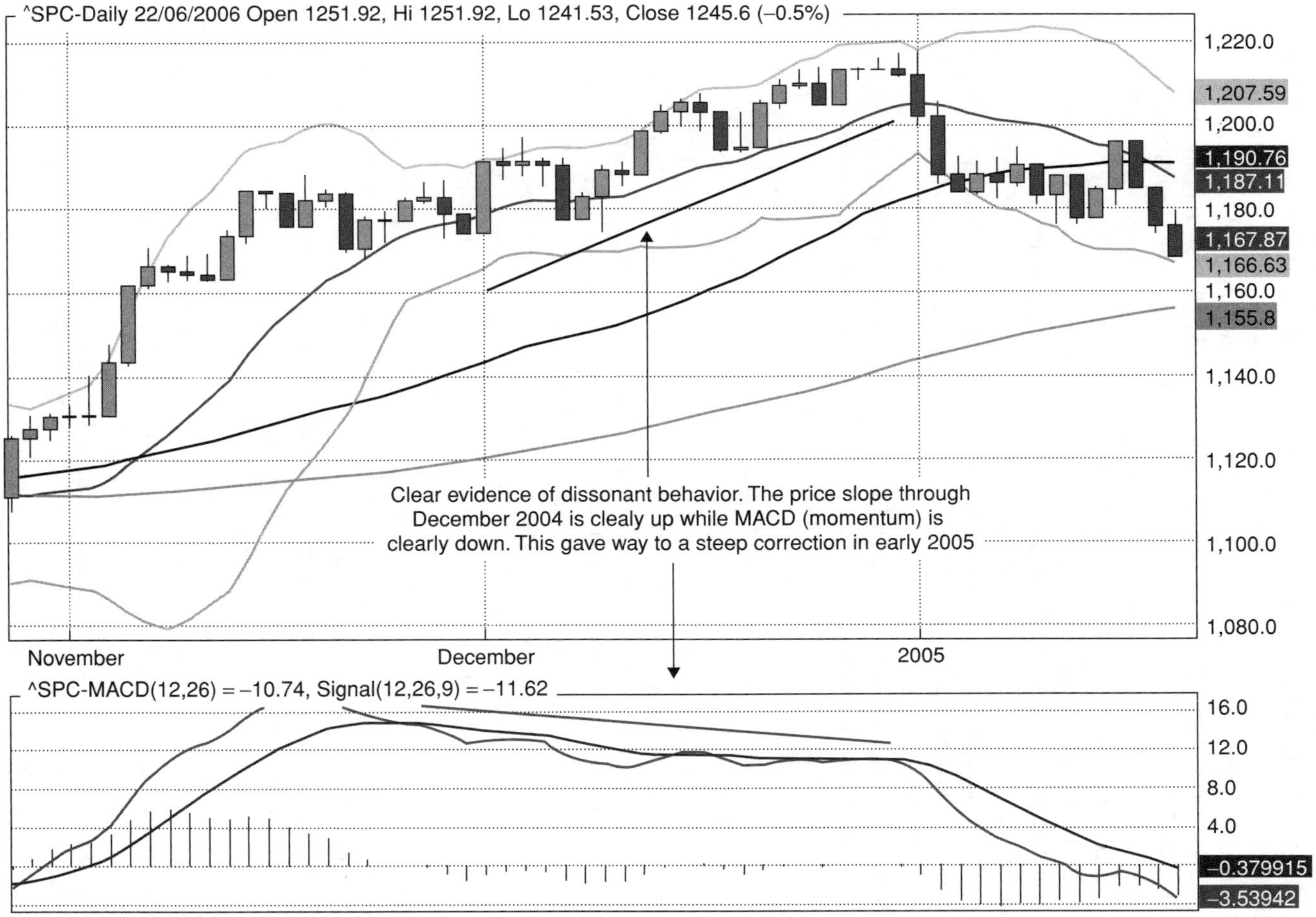
^SPC-Daily 22/06/2006 Open 1251.92, Hi 1251.92, Lo 1241.53, Close 1245.6 (–0.5%)
1,220.0
1,207.59
1,200.0
1,190.76
1,187.11
1,180.0
1,167.87
1,166.63
1,160.0
1,155.8
1,140.0
1,120.0
1,100.0
1,080.0
Clear evidence of dissonant behavior. The price slope through December 2004 is clealy up while MACD (momentum) is clearly down. This gave way to a steep correction in early 2005
November
December
2005
^SPC-MACD(12,26) = –10.74, Signal(12,26,9) = –11.62
16.0
12.0
8.0
4.0
–0.379915
–3.53942

Figure 5.3 S&P 500 at year end 2004

Interestingly a different scenario unfolded for the broad market indices in late 2005. As if anticipating a repeat performance of the year end exercise in portfolio cosmetics that had occurred in 2004, many asset managers and hedge funds played their hands earlier in 2005 and, as Figure 5.4 reveals, most of the strong gains occurred during November 2005. Prices reached their zenith just prior to the Thanksgiving holiday at the end of the month.

During December 2005 the S&P drifted within a narrow range and there is evidence in Figure 5.4 of MACD divergences that may have contributed to the faltering attempts to drive higher around the middle of the month. But the divergence is less acute than the one that was observed in Figure 5.3. The minor correction which eventually took place right at the end of 2005 prepared the way for a rather strong rally that appeared at the beginning of 2006. During December many asset managers were relying on portfolio insurance to preserve the gains that they had made from late October/November and were unwilling to commit a lot of new capital to purchasing equities at the end of the year. The very last trading day of 2005 saw a rather nasty sell-off that brought the key indices down to critical levels of support and was perhaps a well-orchestrated attempt by the bears to spook some unhedged portfolio managers into last minute liquidations.

The beginning of January 2006 saw a fairly explosive rally which could be explained by two factors. First, the short sellers that had been attempting to scare some money managers at the end of 2005 had to cover their positions. Second, money managers that had decided to lock in their gains from Q4 2005 by going short on index futures or purchasing put options were then eager to reverse their hedges at the start of trading in the New Year. The combination of these two separate but related activities (i.e. in both cases there were short trades that needed to be covered) led to a very quick and dramatic rally that saw the index move up 50 points within eight sessions. The essential point that we are making is that, when contrasting the performances of the broad market at the two year ends, there had been a persistent non-alignments between price and momentum at the end of 2004 which led to a very sharp sell-off in the first few sessions of 2005, whereas this was absent at the end of 2005. A minor negative divergence that had arisen in early December was "worked off" during the latter part of December 2005 and when trading resumed after the New Year holiday asset managers were not as exposed to the kind of liquidation and short-selling that characterized the trading at the start of 2005.

Even if one resists this possible overconstruction of motives it can be useful to adopt a forensic approach to the broad market indices, especially in the latter part of the year when trading conditions are thin and there is pressure on large institutions to show strong relative performance. By focusing on non-alignments between key variables such as closing price and MACD it may be that one will uncover the fact that the market is exhibiting a form of cognitive dissonance. In the same way that human beings have the capacity to embrace contradictory cognitions, major market actors such as pension funds, insurance companies and mutual funds may engage in a form of self-deception especially towards the end of the year. They may turn a "blind eye" to some kinds of divergences or make rationalizations that the incongruities are ephemeral and transient. Opportunistic traders will often find profit potential from the divergences that arise at the end of each trading year.

We want to continue now with a class of patterns that have characteristics that often occur in conjunction with evidence of market dissonance. They are often precursors to significant market turning points and often also reveal times when many market participants are caught off balance. The patterns share a common feature or template which can best be described as a pullback.

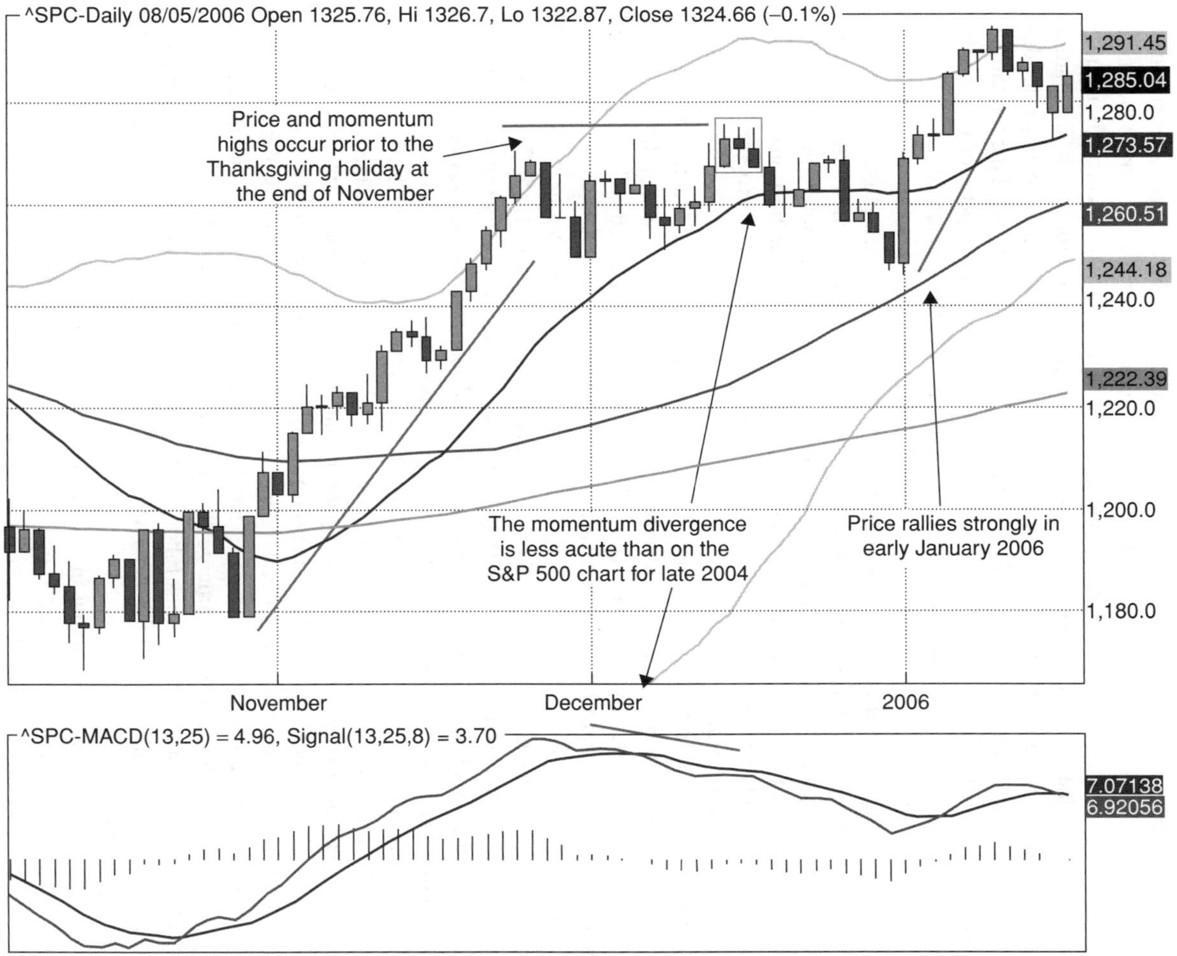
^SPC-Daily 08/05/2006 Open 1325.76, Hi 1326.7, Lo 1322.87, Close 1324.66 (–0.1%)
Price and momentum highs occur prior to the Thanksgiving holiday at the end of November
The momentum divergence is less acute than on the S&P 500 chart for late 2004
Price rallies strongly in early January 2006
1,291.45
1,285.04
1,280.0
1,273.57
1,260.51
1,244.18
1,240.0
1,222.39
1,220.0
1,200.0
1,180.0
November
December
2006
^SPC-MACD(13,25) = 4.96, Signal(13,25,8) = 3.70
7.07138
6.92056

Figure 5.4 S&P at year end 2005

PULLBACKS AND RETRACEMENT FORMATIONS

We can define a pullback as a retracement pattern following a previous strong move, perhaps a trend day move, which has the effect of pulling back from or fading the surge upwards or downwards that was seen on the strong movement or impulse day. The impulse day can sometimes be associated with a gap movement but will almost certainly be a range expansion day. This provides us with the first element in the ensuing pattern which follows on from the initial impulse move. It is the shape of the retracement pattern that enables us to correctly identify and differentiate the kinds of pullback formations that are most useful for identifying trading opportunities. It is paramount that there are very clear and unambiguous classification rules that make it possible to identify an instance of the formations that we are studying. If the formations are not susceptible to precise definitions then there is not a clear decision path for making the classification in the first place, and we cannot claim to have a useful and robust template.

Some traders will operate with a fairly relaxed requirement as far as spotting pullback patterns and find opportunities after general retracement targets have been satisfied. Often the key Fibonacci ratios of 0.382 and 0.618 are used by traders to anticipate when a pullback may have, at least temporarily, run its course. Sometimes, the precise chart points from which the ratios can be determined are unambiguous and susceptible to precise identification by a pattern recognition algorithm. If this is the case then it becomes relatively simple to programmatically determine the retracement thresholds.

A good example of a retracement within a bullish upward move that ran exactly 38% before resuming its upward momentum is provided by the example in Figure 5.5 which shows a daily chart for the homebuilder Toll Brothers (TOL). The stock began a sustained bull move in early October 2004 that ran until July 2005 but we shall focus on the first pullback pattern that arose in April 2005. We have identified the swing low for the move in early October at $20.82 and the swing high for the initial move up at $45.59 which took place in early March. The extent of the move was $9.46 and if we subtract 38% of that move from the swing high amount we find a retracement level of $36.12 and in reviewing the actual retracement that was observed we find that this is remarkably prescient as TOL retreated almost exactly to this level in mid-April 2005 before resuming the uptrend which eventually took TOL to $55 in July 2005.

One of the reasons why this example is so "convincing" from a Fibonacci perspective is that there is a clear and easily identifiable chart pattern that enables us to extract the key turning points from a swing perspective. When the turning points can be ascertained so clearly, and when the key retracement levels can be targeted on traders' screens, there is almost a self-fulfillment impetus at work as traders can "game" the support levels as it is anticipated that renewed buying interest is likely to emerge at well-known Fibonacci levels. Sometimes there are false recovery efforts at the obvious Fibonacci levels and it becomes necessary to seek out the less obvious "extensions" and this is a tactic that we shall review later in connection with Gartley patterns.

One final observation worth noting in regard to the TOL chart is the evidence of negative momentum divergence that is annotated on the MACD chart at the beginning of March 2005 which coincides with the onset of the corrective episode that brought the stock down to $36. The price peak in mid-February coincides with the MACD momentum peak and by early March as price is making another run to break above $45 the downward slope shows the kind of nonconfirmation that is often to be found at intermediate turning points. Simply by using the two techniques that we have discussed so far in this section it would have been possible to identify a very plausible opportunity to take up a short position at the end of February or early

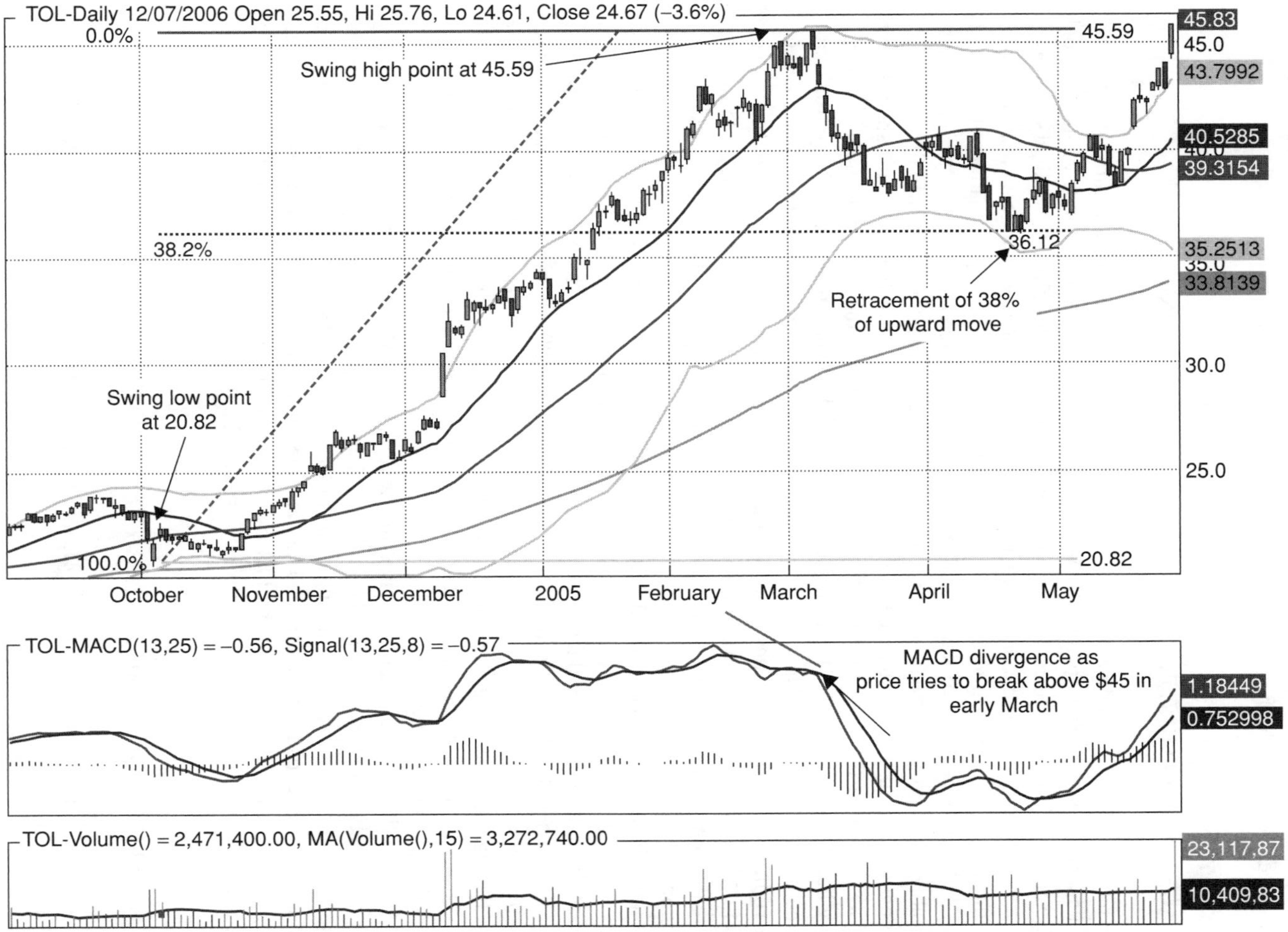

Figure 5.5 Toll Brothers showing Fibonacci retracement

March and by using the 38% retracement target one could have estimated a feasible profit target. Notwithstanding the rally effort in early April it would have been very plausible to have expected a first order correction of 38% given the magnitude of the upsurge from early October 2004 to early March 2005.

FLAGS – A RELIABLE PULLBACK CHANNEL PATTERN

We have discussed the pullback formation in general terms but let us now turn our attention to a specific variant of the pattern – the flag formation – which has, as one of its principal characteristics, a channel formation that contains and delimits the pullback. We shall summarize the key requirements for the pattern in a moment but let us start with a general overview. In coding pattern recognition algorithms for machine detection of flag formations it becomes very helpful to systematize the classification rules and to screen for all of the appropriate variables to be present. The first and fundamental screen to apply is to identify the flagpole of the pattern and to devise a template for recognizing instances of the pole. This should have vertical ascent or descent characteristics and the first stage in the formation should involve a price bar or candlestick which registers at least one and one half times the average true range of the trailing 20 periods. Once this initial rule has been satisfied the next test is to screen for the right volume characteristics. The volume on the range expansion day should be at least 1.5 times the simple moving average volume for the trailing 20 periods. The flagpole can take more than one session to be confirmed, although on some occasions it can present itself in one session.

Figure 5.6 is a daily chart for OSI Pharmaceuticals (OSIP) covering April–August 2005 and provides a good example of how the flagpole template is instantiated. The highlighted pattern in mid-June 2005 reveals a flagpole that took two days to form. The first thrust occurred on June 16th when the stock moved up 7.7% on 1.5 times the 20 day average volume. The next day the stock moved another 5% on almost three times the average volume. In this particular case the high achieved on the second day marked the top of the flagpole as the third day, which also shows as a green candle, was an inside day with the high being slightly less than the second day's intraday high.

Once the flagpole has been identified the next aspect of the overall template for the flag formation relates to the nature of the pullback channel. In the case of Figure 5.6 there is, as required for the pattern, a descending channel formation as OSIP pulls back from the price surge and range expansion that created the flagpole. In the case of a bearish flagpole, the pole itself is inverted and the pullback will have an ascending channel formation as price attempts to recover from the downward thrust which created the flagpole.

SUMMARY OF THE FLAG PATTERN TEMPLATE

Alan Farley in his seminal work, *The Master Swing Trader*, has the following definition for the flag formation

> Flag patterns appear as countertrend parallelograms between waves of strong trend movement ... Bull flags decline against the rally in uptrends, and bear flags rise against the sell-off in downtrends.[7]

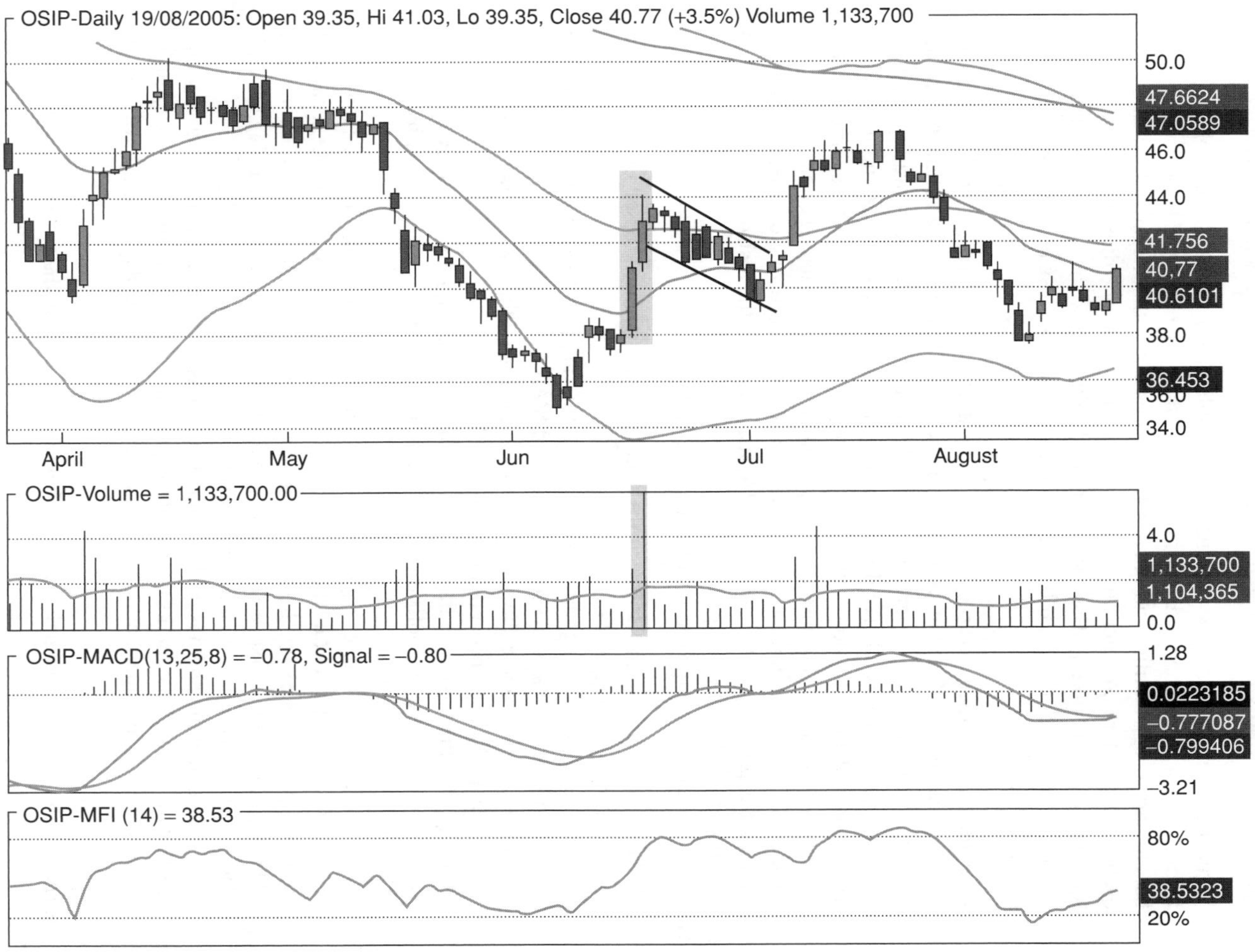

Figure 5.6 OSIP bull flag formation

Our only reservation with respect to this approach is that there is a danger of over defining the criterion for the pattern and looking for more symmetry and perfection in the shape of the formation than is warranted. However, in the remaining section devoted to the main features of flag formations Farley provides a clear account of some of the other defining characteristics:

> Vertical price movement precedes the most reliable flag patterns. Strong volume from the prior trend should drop off sharply as the range evolves. Expect price bars to narrow as volatility and interest flat-line, as with other negative feedback events. Near pattern completion, volume should increase in the direction of eventual breakout and spike just as the new trend begins. Flags should yield to new trends in no more than 15–20 bars. Bear flags tend to take less time to conclude than bull ones.[8]

We have refined our classification criteria so that the focus is not only on the price characteristics but also on the appropriate money flow and volume characteristics. The following are the separate component features – a flagpole, a pullback channel, a retracement threshold, a price target, volume characteristics, money flow characteristics and ideally a trigger point. There is also a need to be vigilant for the co-occurrence of other patterns that may either support the flag interpretation or invalidate it because of more potent conflicting signals. For example, a bull flag formation that develops in the region of previously observed strong overhead resistance, such as a previous price top or the 200 day EMA, may "fail" as the resistance pattern proves to be more dominant than the flag pattern.

The flagpole should have the following characteristics:

- Volume should be at least 150% of the average daily volume – based on a 20 period simple moving average (SMA).
- The initial day of the flagpole should have a true range that should be 1.5 times the average true range – also based on a 20 period SMA.
- The top of a bull flagpole should be a multi-period high – there are no hard rules about how many periods are needed for this to qualify.
- The day after the top of the flagpole should have a lower high than the previous high.
- The "top" of a bear flagpole should be a multi-period low – there are no hard rules about how many periods.
- The day after the bear flag "top" should have a higher low than the previous low.
- Gaps often mark the start of the flagpole and the base of the pole should be measured from the previous session close to the gap event. In all other cases the base for a bull flag is the low for the first session on which the pole forms and for a bear flag the high for the first session on which the pole forms.
- The retracement threshold is the base of the pole plus or minus a tiny marginal amount.
- Ideally the session that marks the top of the pole in a bull flag should have an up close.
- Ideally the session that marks the top of the pole in a bear flag should have a down close.

The rising or descending channel following flagpole should have the following characteristics:

- During the pullback phase volume should be relatively light and ideally below the 20 day SMA. If there are large volume days within the pullback channel this should cancel the pattern.

- There should be a series of descending highs in the pullback channel for a bull flag.
- There should be a series of ascending lows in the pullback channel for a bear flag.
- In a bullish flag formation if there is an intraday high that penetrates the top of the flagpole or a low that penetrates below the base of the pole the pattern is invalid.
- In a bearish flag formation if there is an intraday low that penetrates the top of the flagpole or a high that penetrates above the base of the pole the pattern is invalid.
- During a descending pullback channel (i.e. part of a bull flag formation) ideally one would like to see evidence of increasing money flow showing that despite the price retracement there is more money moving into the security than flowing outwards.
- During an ascending pullback channel (i.e. part of a bear flag formation) ideally one would like to see evidence of decreasing money flow showing that despite the price "recovery" there is more money moving out of the security than flowing into it.

The duration of the pullback channel:

- Should be at least three sessions following the completion of the flagpole.
- Should typically occur within 12 sessions – can last longer but the reliability decays with the passage of time. This can be qualified somewhat so that channels may be more extended in overall sideways markets.

The breakout trigger can be any of the following (or undefined):

- Touching a major pivot point such as the EMA values for the widely followed periods – 20, 50 and 200 periods.
- A Doji or Spinning Top candlestick.
- An inside day or NR7 session.
- An extremely low volume session.

The price target is traditionally set as follows:

- For a bull flag the target is the price at which the break from the channel arises plus the length of the flagpole.
- For a bear flag the target is the price at which the break from the channel arises minus the length of the flagpole.
- Often the price chart will point to other targets which are achievable within a few sessions of the channel breakout so one needs to retain flexibility

The abandonment procedure.

- If the price violates the retracement threshold (as defined) the position should be abandoned.
- If price remains within the pullback channel for more than 15 sessions the position should be abandoned unless the overall market has been in a sideways pattern for some time. In this case patience can sometimes be rewarded but there can be periods of slow attrition that culminate in a return to the retracement threshold and that tie up trading capital.
- If there is an increasing volume trend while price remains within the pullback channel the position should be abandoned.

Figure 5.7 is a daily chart for Taser International (TASR) showing the breakout from the descending reaction channel that formed after the stock moved up on January 26th which is the highlighted candle with an expanded range and more than 50% above the daily average volume.

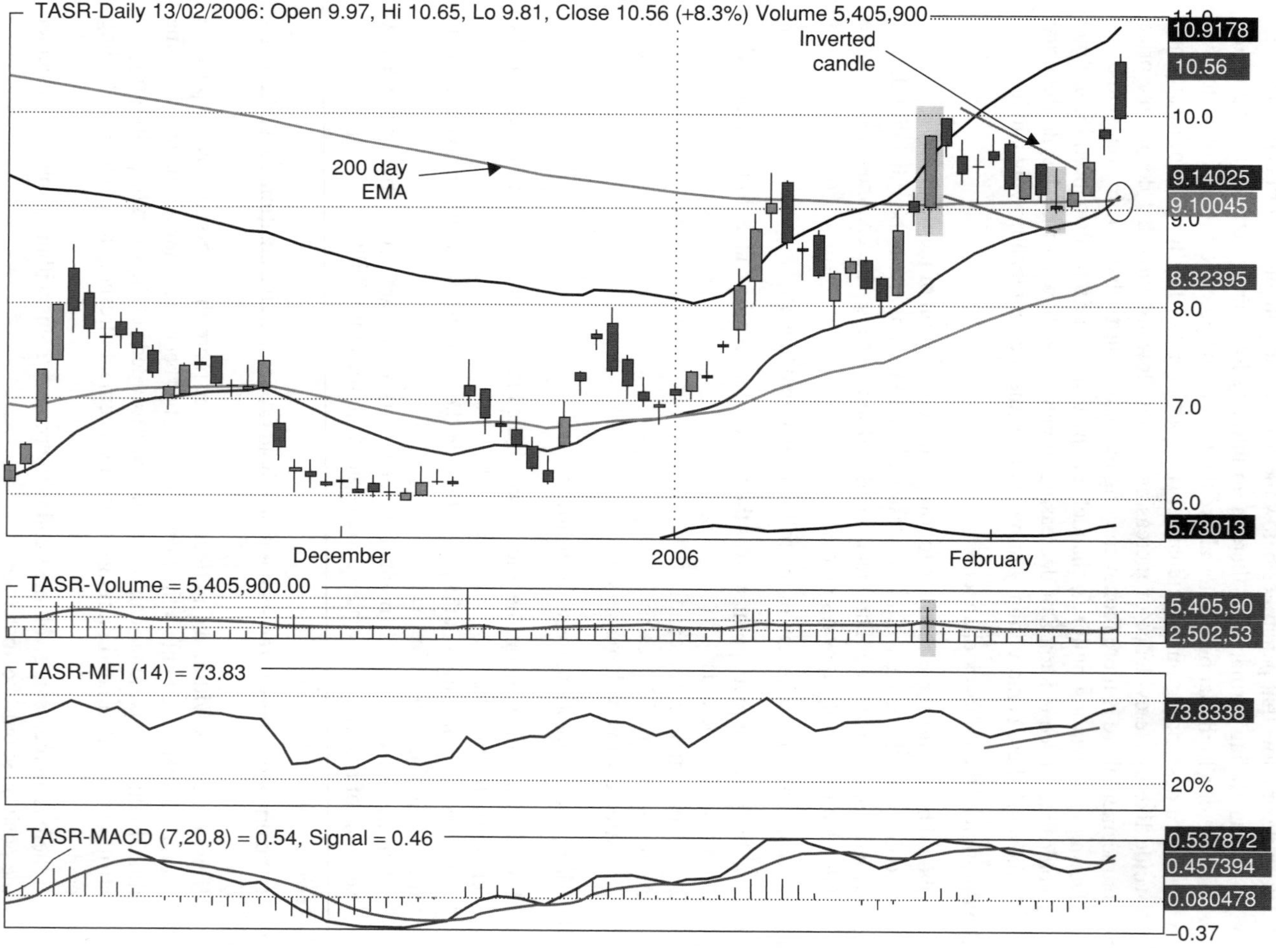

Figure 5.7 TASR bull flag formation

The actual top of the flagpole was formed in the next session when the stock retreated from a new breakout high and closed below its open registering the small red candle. The subsequent pullback was in a fairly well-defined descending channel and throughout the duration of the channel the volume was light and did not once exceed the 20 day SMA. The second of the highlighted candles is for an inverted hammer that closes right on the 200 day EMA. In the next session there is a pick up in volume but it takes until the next session before we begin to see the breakout from the channel and a renewal of the buying pressure that first arose on January 26th. As the circle indicates the 200 day EMA at this point has intersected with the 20 day EMA. Once the breakout has occurred there is a high volume day on February 13th which takes the stock up 8.3% and above the previous highs from January 26th/27th. Also noticeable in Figure 5.7 is the rising slope to the money flow on the MFI chart coinciding with the pullback channel. Although this is not a vital requirement for the pattern, when it is observed it does lend further weight to the interpretation.

Now that we have examined the technical characteristics let's think about the behavioral elements of the flag pattern. There are three psychological elements to the pattern. First, there is the initial range expansion and price breakout. *It is important to the methodology that we do not try to associate this technical event with any kind of news event.* It only needs to be observed and classified as a range expansion on significant volume event. If we look for reasons then we are likely to confuse ourselves and probably prejudice our view as to the remainder of the pattern.

The second element to the pattern is the fade or pullback element. In this phase there is a noticeable diminution of volume accompanied by a slow retreat in the opposite direction to the original price impulse. This can be explained as the result of one or more forces operating in combination. First of all the traders who instigated the move may be liquidating part of their initial positions (so-called "profit-taking"), and perhaps even reversing their positions so as to accelerate the pullback. Second, there are the breakout players who attached to the breakout perhaps as it was peaking and who are now being stopped out of their positions as the price reverses. The third element is the contribution of the market makers who act as intermediaries within the ongoing order flow and whose tactics will often involve fading the price direction so as to obfuscate and unnerve the breakout players.

An important question with regard to flag formations is what can be called the "time to wait" issue. Because the pattern recognition steps involved in identifying flags can often provide an early alert to an emerging pattern the challenge is trying to determine when the pattern is sufficiently "ripe" to enter a trade. The pullback channel may continue for an indefinite number of periods and there is considerable latitude as to when the breakout may occur. Of course the breakout may not occur or it may be in the contrary direction to that anticipated. In an overall trending market one should expect a resolution of the pattern within 5 to 12 sessions but there is a danger of proposing false precision in this regard. In a quiet or sideway market the channel can persist and there is often a need for patience to allow the initial impetus to resume. The key to managing positions that arise from this pattern is to be flexible in positioning stops and not placing them too rigidly or at obvious places where they will be challenged. It is in the nature of the pullback phase that there will be contrary and conflicting cross-currents that will trick the methodical stop loss traders and yank them out of the position at exactly the wrong time.

A clear price violation occurs if the price drops below the base of the flagpole. The base is set at the pre-breakout level. So, for example, if the closing price on the day before the range expansion/volume surge was $35.20 and the day of the breakout the price gapped up and closed at $37, the base of the flagpole should be considered as $35.20. If price, during the channel phase, spikes below this level the trade should be terminated. Looked at from the other perspective the trade also becomes suspect if, during the pullback phase, there is an intraday penetration above (or below) the channel that exceeds the top of the flagpole. A peek above or below the channel line may also be sufficient to contravene the pattern. The key to smart execution with this pattern is to look for certain likely trigger points to time the trade but not to become too concerned about timing the trade to the exact day. Using a multiple time frame analysis (i.e. end of day charts, 60 minute charts and 15 minute charts) will also assist in identifying potential inflection points that may arise during intraday trading. However, experience has shown that in many instances the eventual breakout will occur at the beginning of a trading day. In such cases the 60 minute or 15 minute patterns from the preceding day may provide clues as to the impending trigger point.

The advantage of the flag pattern is that one is not being a hero but rather taking advantage of the counterthrust pullback to hitch a ride on a smart trade. The initial impulse move is an alert to the trader that something is afoot and this is especially valuable if there is no obvious news item that accompanies the development of the flagpole. We like to think of it, metaphorically, as the first rupture in the market's fabric, perhaps, extending the metaphor from the earth sciences, the first rumblings or fissures from a volcano that has stirred to life. The pullback and quiet volume phase creates the appearance that the original impulse may have just been an aberration and that things have returned to normal. This is why the pullback channel phase needs to be monitored carefully to confirm whether the volume characteristics are in accordance with the pattern. For market movements, unlike seismic movements in the physical world where the processes unfold without intentionality, there is a more or less awareness of what is unfolding and there is a capacity for intentional intervention to enhance the feedback process.

The initial rupture may be the result of "subterranean forces" (perhaps the actions of "insiders" who are privy to certain information that the market is not) but as the consequences and ripple effects manifest themselves the technically oriented traders are able to intervene to enhance and/or dampen the consequences. Often the very same players can be found on both sides of the feedback process as they attempt to push the price discovery process toward a critical state that requires resolution. This is why one should wait for the pullback and never jump on the breakout itself. There is no need to rush but wait for the evidence to show the nature of the pullback channel first. It is better to occasionally miss out on a flag pullback that is in a hurry than to be misled by the original pattern and then come to realize that the pullback does not have the required characteristics. During the channel development one needs to be vigilant for evidence that the initial rupture was providing a clue as to underlying forces that want to move the price further in the direction of the impulse move. The challenge is that when the market makes its next move this will tend to be an abrupt move and probably will not provide an easy opportunity to climb aboard. Picking the right time to enter a flag trade is never easy but there is some comfort in that, if one is wrong about the pattern, there is usually a good opportunity to abandon the trade without great loss.

THE METAPHOR OF RUPTURE DYNAMICS

Beyond the mathematical contributions that have been made to the study of finance by researchers with a background in complexity theory, we can also find the development of a rich new metaphorical framework for thinking about market dynamics and price development. Use of metaphors and models in thinking about the way that markets behave is inevitable, and sometimes prone to error as we discuss elsewhere, and it is the quality of the metaphors and their suitability for the purpose that is likely to lead us to greater understanding of how prices evolve and how, as traders, we can harness this superior insight, to anticipate critical opportunities. The flag formation is itself a model as it enables us to think about price in a geometric and pictorial fashion. As we explore the nature of the flag pattern we not only learn more about the correct classification procedures but also about the intentions and psychology of the dynamics that give rise to flag formations. This is why we favor the term morphology as providing a framework for detailing the important stylistic features of price patterns and as an encouragement to think about the underlying dynamics behind the formations in a systematically analytical manner.

The contributions that have been made to the understanding of market crashes, and the possible dynamics that lead to such critical behavior, by geophysicists such as Didier Sornette[9] provide, we believe, some metaphors and mental models that are especially suitable for understanding extended price patterns where flags, often found in nested formations, are an integral feature. We would like to propose the term *rupture dynamics* as being metaphorically descriptive of the kind of behavior that can be found quite frequently in the markets and when the essential ingredients are correctly identified can lead to major profit opportunities on the short side.

An illustration of the potency of the metaphor of ruptures is provided by Figure 5.8 which shows the precursors to a critical collapse for the stock F5 Networks (FFIV) in April 2006. Let us examine the events and ruptures/fractures that led up to the eventual plunge on April 21st. We have separated the price and volume charts from other indicators initially to clarify the top line events first.

The first feature we would draw attention to in Figure 5.8 is the trend-line through the lows from the beginning of 2006. We can see that this line was violated by the long red candlestick on April 4th (B) also associated with three times the daily average volume. At this point we can see two days of recovery, the first is an inside day followed by another attempt to recover back to the 20 day EMA.

This was followed by two further long red candles bringing us to point D. It is at this point that the ascending channel formation begins as the flagpole "top" is in place. During the channel phase there follow six modest volume sessions leading to point E which is critical for several reasons:

- The candle straddles the 20 and 50 day EMA.
- The high for the candle would have enabled a recovery to the extension of the trend-line through the lows.
- Volume was twice the moving average.

The second chart for FFIV (Figure 5.9) covers the same period as before but this time includes the MACD chart as well as charts showing the MFI and RSI values during the critical period at the end of March 2006. It can be seen that there are negative momentum, MFI and RSI divergences during the rally to a new high in the middle of March (point A on Figure 5.9). Price closed above $72 followed by a retracement or pullback for several sessions bringing the price back below $70. The critical two sessions are those highlighted. In candlestick terms both are examples of the Spinning Top formation, with long lower and upper shadows which is a formation that is often found at turning points for a security. The first of the two also has a very narrow body pointing to a Doji formation in addition to the Spinning Top classification which reinforces the notion that FFIV is at an inflection point. Will it be successful in rechallenging the previous from point A or will it become victim to lower high failure pattern? The price action

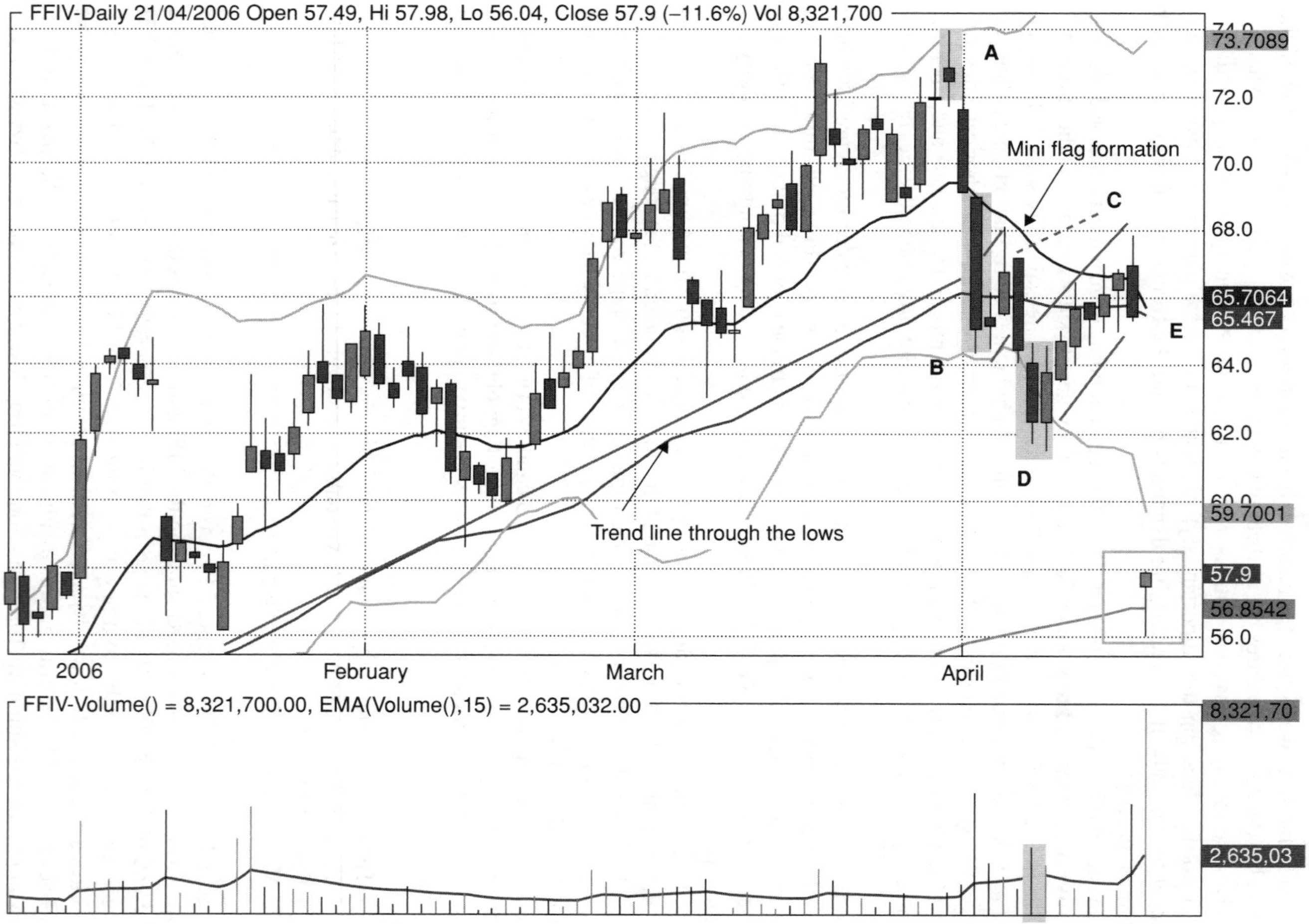

Figure 5.8 FFIV bear flag formation

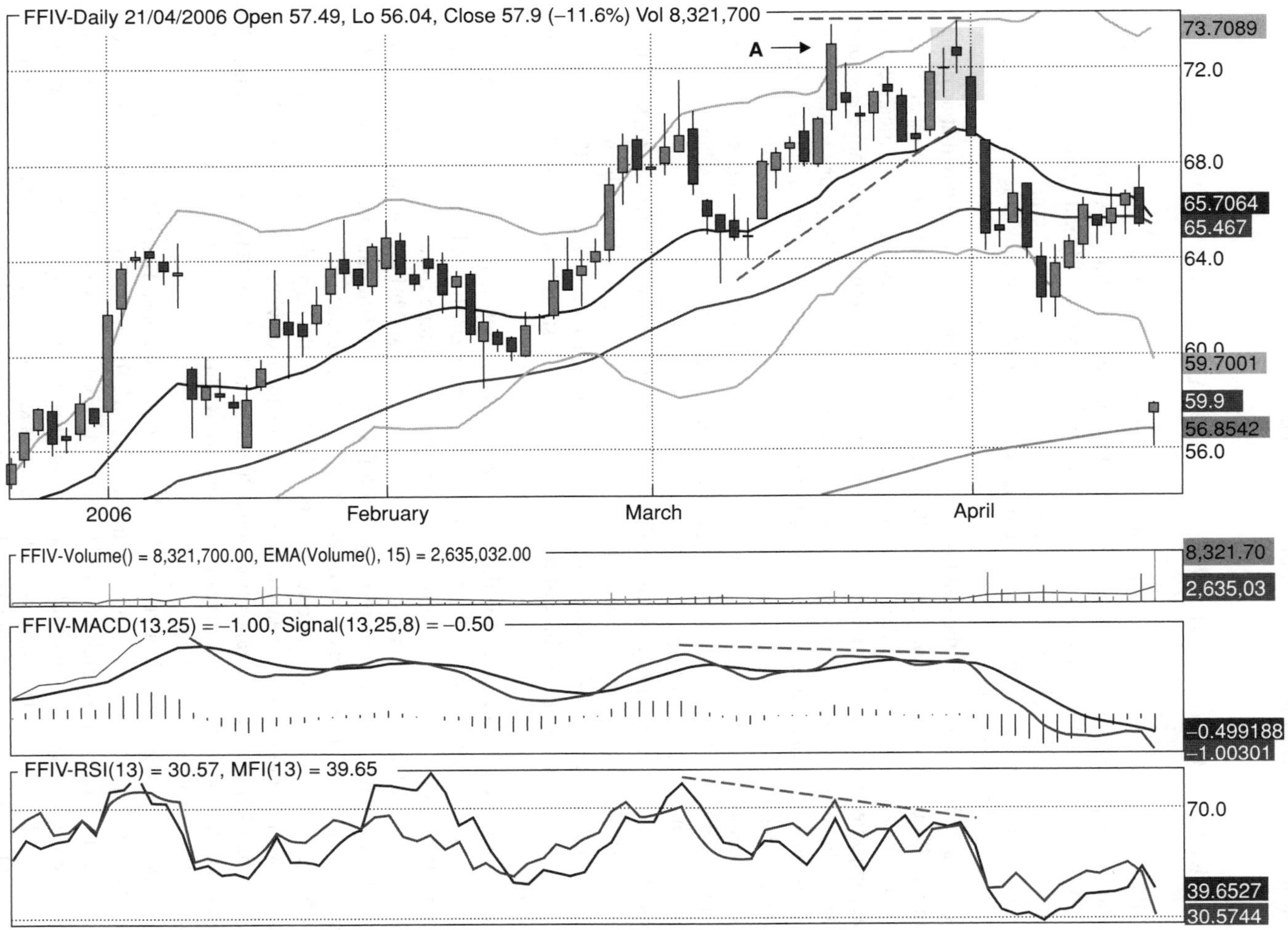

Figure 5.9 FFIV double top formation

on the second day shows clearly that the intraday high reaches up to the previous high from A but the close is below that of A. Meanwhile as the momentum and money flow indicators are showing there is a clear lack of commitment behind this retest.

A CASE STUDY OF RUPTURE DYNAMICS: DORAL FINANCIAL (DRL)

To illustrate the case that we have been making that many price charts reveal patterns that contain clear precursors to major collapses and that can best be thought of in terms of the metaphors of a rupture we shall explore as a case study the plight of Doral Financial (DRL) in the early part of 2006. Figure 5.10 offers several instances of the pre-crash dynamics that become significant and possibly predictive of the actual "crash" that took place in the stock's behavior in mid-April 2006.

The first point of interest is the candlestick marked A which is an inside day that arose on February 17th. In itself this is not a pattern that has huge predictive power but it does often act as a precursor to bigger moves that lie ahead. An inside day takes on added significance if it is accompanied by very light volume and is in the proximity of other narrow range sessions and/or light volume days which is the case here. In fact the inside day on February 17th follows on from three Doji-like candlesticks and was actually the fifth day in a row of below average volume (using a 15 day SMA).

The action on the following session which was February 21st (there was long weekend for the President's day holiday – and a case could be made that what may have happened on February 17th was a case of bad news having been buried just before a long weekend) was marked by a bearish trend day on twice the average daily volume. The stock closed in the bottom quartile of its daily range and also closed below the 20 day EMA. The next session on the 22nd was a reversal day where the stock moved back 3% following the fall of 3.5% on the 21st but was on about one third of the volume from the 21st. This was the first pre-quake rupture.

The stock became quiescent for the next three sessions but then the second pre-quake rupture occurred on the 28th of February which was again a bearish trend day with clear range expansion on twice the average daily volume. This sets the stage for a cascade decline (not on heavy volume) that takes place over the next six sessions and brings the stock down from the $11 area to the $10 area where there is the first pullback from the bearish retreat. The subsequent pattern fails to register as a bear flag formation because there is no clear flagpole preceding it – the time-to-wait logic suggests that the "top" of the flagpole (in this case inverted because we are talking about a bearish formation) should arise within four sessions. There is another mini sell-off at the juxtaposition of the 20 and 50 day EMAs (B) but this is then faded rapidly as the stock puts in a concerted recovery effort ("trap") to attempt to regain the $12 level which was where the pattern began.

The point C on the chart is a critical level for several reasons. There is a strong gap up open that takes place on March 30th (window dressing for the end of Q1 2006) with the stock touching an intraday high of $11.79 (the mid-February closing high was $11.89) but then retreating to register a red candlestick with the close occurring approximately at the 50% level of the day's range. The candlestick formation is known as a Hanging Man formation as it resembles a Hammer candle but is at the top or close to a previous top (especially more significant it arises in connection with a double top with the second top being slightly lower

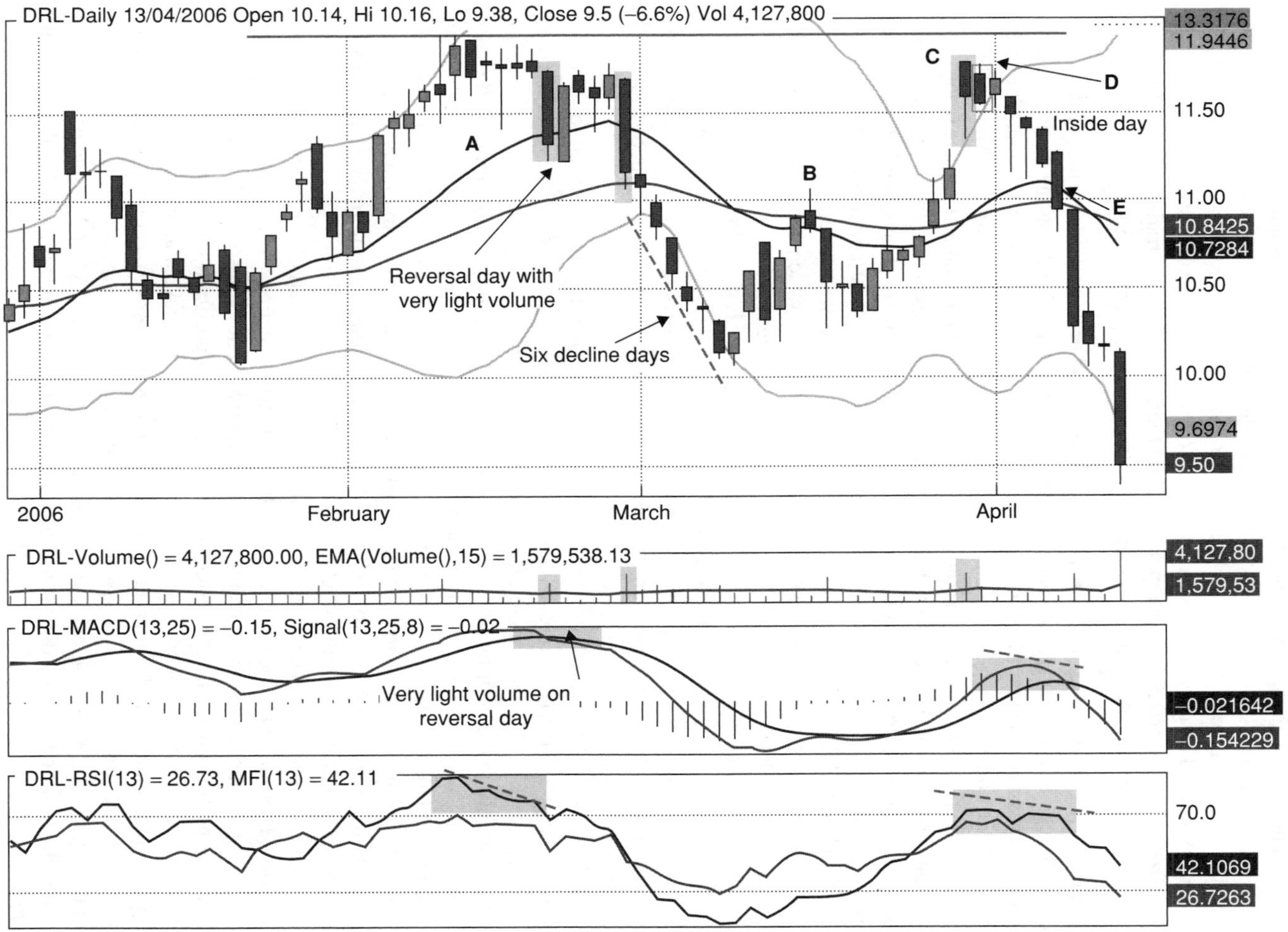

Figure 5.10 DRL failed flag formations

than the first – this is another divergence that increases the degree of dissonance in the pattern). One of the interpretations for the Hanging Man candlestick is as follows.

> Hanging Man candlesticks have the same appearance as a Hammer candle but what is required for this classification is that the pattern should occur at the top of a trading range or at chart locations that represent a significant high mark for the security. The long lower shadow or tail to this formation suggests, when it is associated with prices at upper extremes, that there will be many traders that could be left stranded should the price begin to falter in subsequent sessions.[10]

The following session was an inside day followed by another fairly critical clue to the puzzle which is the candlestick D which was an NR7[11] on extraordinarily light volume. In fact the volume for this session was just 615 000 compared to a moving average of 1.5 million. However, seen within the context of a possible pullback channel from the gap up move on March 30th it would be quite feasible to see this as conforming to the descending channel template in the context of building a bullish retracement. The next three sessions all exhibit below average volume which again could be construed as the unfolding of the retracement channel and could potentially be pointing towards a resumption of the impetus to regain upward momentum that was attempted on March 30th (although that was suspect for the reasons we have cited). The next day's candlestick is very crucial and is the one marked E on the chart, which occurred on April 7th.

On this day the candle shows that the base of the possible flagpole from the gap up on March 30th was violated and also the close was just below the 50 day EMA. This should have acted as confirmation that any attempt to interpret the previous six day pattern (i.e. extending back to March 30th) as a bullish descending channel formation was invalid. The failure on April 7th set up the next powerful downward moves that brought the stock down from $11 to $9.50 with the move on April 13th (just prior to the Easter break).

What lessons can be learned from this forensic analysis (anatomical dissection) of a crash, especially in relation to the rupture dynamics that we have advocated? We would maintain that the two rupture days that were mentioned should have alerted us to a possible crash scenario that could unfold in the coming sessions. But this raises the question of how long we have to wait for the potential entry signal. It is not possible to forecast this with any accuracy which is exactly analogous to the difficulty of forecasting major seismic events. The ruptures, like foreshocks, alert us to the possibility that a crash is possible and we can forensically examine the ensuing patterns with a view to finding further evidence that the ruptures were precursors to a more serious problem for the stock.

One of the key differences between earthquake dynamics and market dynamics is that in the latter case it is possible for the traders and participants whose actions "create" the daily prices in the financial markets to observe and influence the way that events unfold. The process is self-aware and reflexive. The interested parties range from portfolio managers holding long positions in their funds, traders who are long or short the stock, market makers who are trying to maintain an "orderly" market, algorithmic trading systems that are not "aware" of the dynamics but are programmed to respond to microstructural developments in the order book – all of these participants are following events with more or less "savvy" and trying to anticipate what the other participants are doing and what the likely direction is within their time frame of reference.

When did it become apparent to these participants that the final collapse of the stock which brought it down from $11 to $9.50 (at point E) on the chart was the path of least resistance? When did the normal fractious consensus shift to a coherent view that the stock should be sold?

In order to clarify the issue let us review Figure 5.11 which is a 60 minute intraday chart in the neighborhood of the point E that is found in Figure 5.10. Point B in Figure 5.11 represents the trading that occurred on April 7th.

However, we need to create the context for this critical day's action. The important precedent for the pattern originated at point A which commences with the long red candlestick that occurred at the open on April 4th and which coincided with a heavy volume thrust that brought the close right to the 50 period EMA. This also suggests that there is a growing conviction that the previous ruptures are pointing towards an eventual crisis for the stock. The pattern that then unfolds is a bearish descending wedge formation. From the larger-scale EOD charts this coincides with the pullback channel that we noted as having a possible claim to being a bullish flag in the making. A couple of other features are worth commenting on. First, there is clear evidence from the volume chart that the preponderance of volume is towards the downside. The second notable feature is the failure of the stock to close above its 20 and 50 period EMAs on the close on April 6th. The break below the 200 period EMA in the first hour of trading on the 7th also failed to bring any meaningful volume to rescue the violation of these critical levels and the stock closed the session below all three moving averages as well as below the base of the flagpole that we observed on the end of day chart (Figure 5.10).

The final resolution of this pattern can be seen in the eventual collapse which is shown in Figure 5.12. There is a waterfall pattern in which price keeps tumbling downwards with no attempt to arrest the decline. On the volume chart there are a succession of downthrusts on increasing volume which culminate in the heaviest volume of all which occurs on the close of April 13th when DRL closes at $9.50.

FLAGS AND HIKKAKE PATTERNS

Additional chart patterns associated with flag formations include pennants, diamonds, triangles and wedges and these have been widely discussed in the technical analysis literature. We have found some of these patterns to be useful and predictive but we would rather consider two less commonly discussed patterns that are often associated with pullbacks – the Hikkake pattern and the Gartley pattern.

The Hikkake pattern or template has been proposed by Dan Chesler in some online reference materials.[12] The defining characteristic of the pattern is that it follows an inside day, which, as we have seen before, is where all of the trading for a particular session falls within the range of the previous session. In other words the initial identification rule can be simply expressed as Current low > Previous low and Current high < Previous high. The inside day is the key marker for the bullish and bearish version of the Hikkake signal. Let us review the bearish version initially. Once an inside day has been identified the next screen is to look for a further bar which has a higher low and higher high than the inside day. At this point, after the two-session pattern, one can create a bearish entry rule which is that if price falls below the low on the inside day then one goes short with a stop above the high of the subsequent day to the inside day. Let us look at an example of when the Hikkake pattern has arisen in conjunction with a pattern which would have been classified as an emerging bear flag formation by our previously discussed pattern detection algorithms.

Figure 5.13 is a daily chart for Foundry Networks (FDRY) and the first inside day occurs on April 5th 2006 which we have noted on the chart. This was followed by a session that satisfied the conditions for a potential bearish setup and the entry target level for a short position would

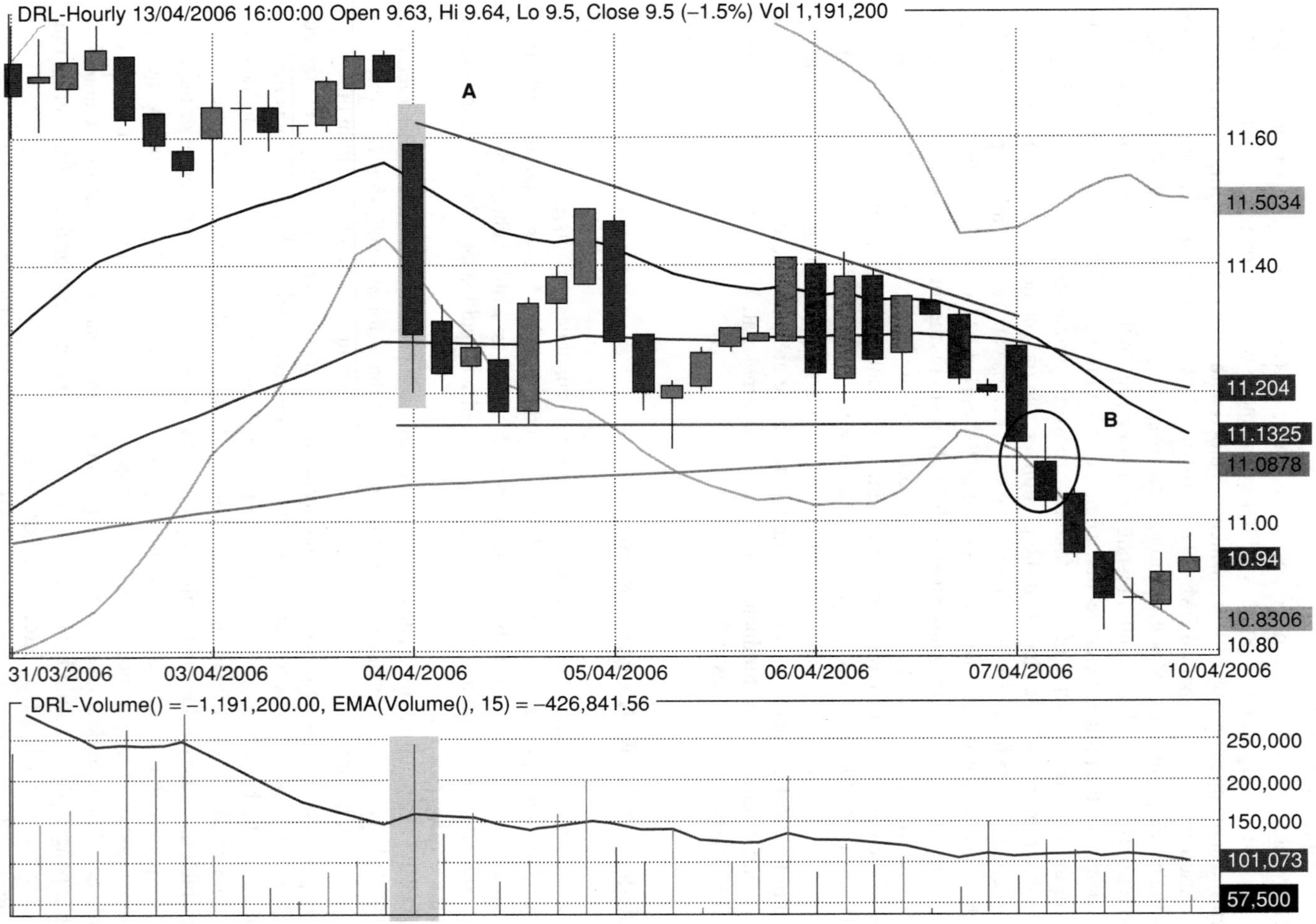

Figure 5.11 DRL 60 minute chart

Figure 5.12 DRL final collapse

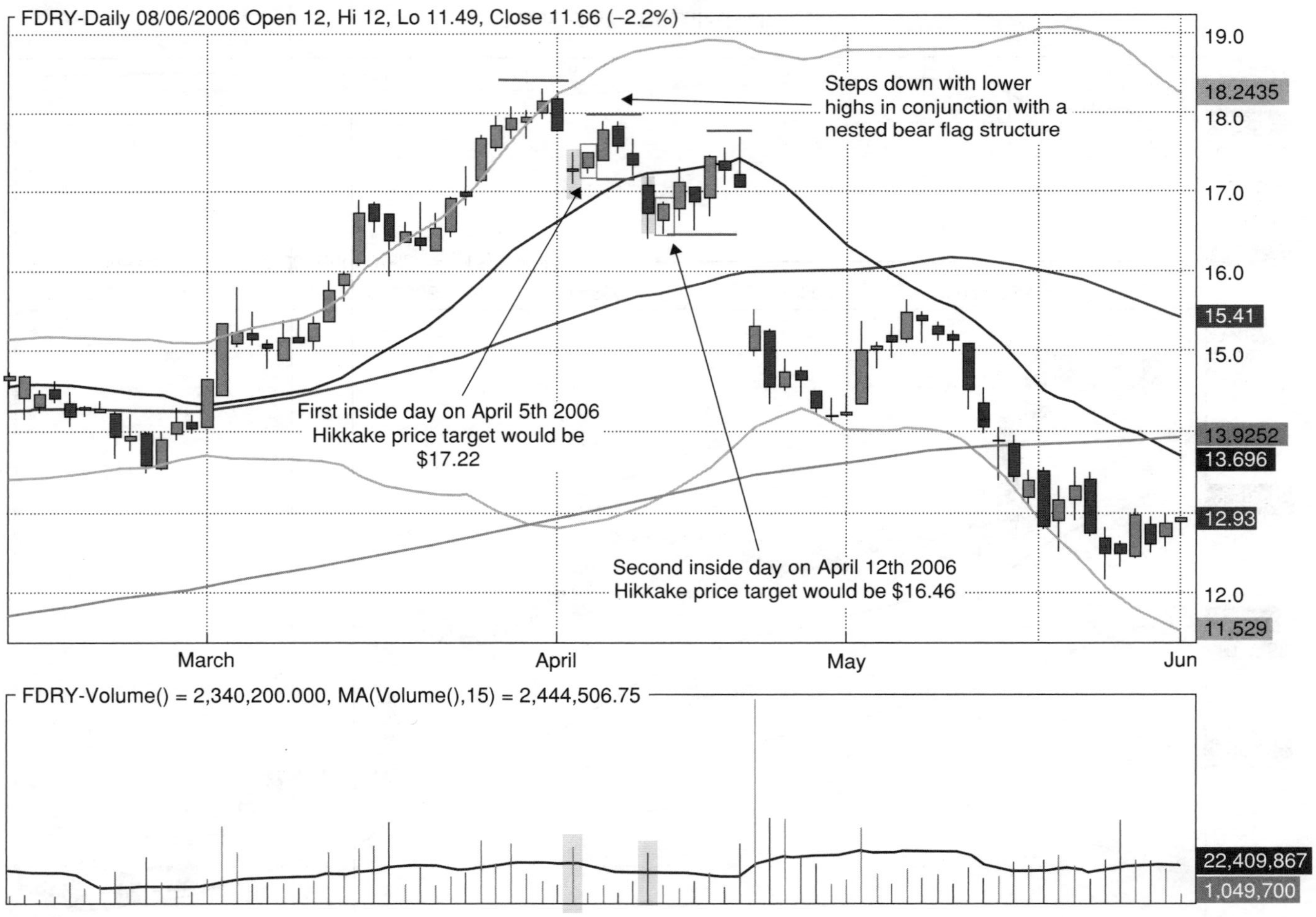

Figure 5.13 FDRY Hikkake patterns

have been set at the low on the inside day which was \$17.22. The low for the session of April 10th was \$17.20 which would have secured a fill and in the next session on April 11th a low of \$16.40 was realized which could have provided a 3% plus return from the entry point on the previous session's low. As can also be seen on the chart the Hikkake pattern is occurring within the context of an evolving bear flag formation. On the day preceding the inside day (April 4th) it can be seen that there had been a gap down on heavy volume and that would have alerted the screening algorithms to the potential of a bear flagpole forming.

After the initial profitable trade the situation becomes a little more complex as the day right after the first profitable session also qualifies as an inside day and is followed by another session which could lead to a further bearish entry signal. The second inside day has a low of \$16.46 which now becomes the entry stop if a reversal should occur in subsequent sessions. However, as can be seen from the chart this entry signal rule would not have proved to be of much value in the way that the price developed. The clue to why this second Hikkake signal was redundant can be seen in the way that, as is common in the evolution of the bear flag channel, the point of entry that one should be looking for is near the top of the channel and not near the "inverted top" of the flagpole. As is clear from the chart, by setting the sell entry at the second Hikkake point one would have missed the chance to get on board prior to the big gap down on April 21st and it is these kinds of powerful moves (notice the extremely heavy volume) that make the correct interpretation of a complex flag formation so rewarding. Also revealing in the Foundry chart are the two steps down from the recent high as each of the pullback channels "failed" just below the previously achieved high.

Another way of considering the value of a Hikkake signal when it occurs within an evolving flag formation is to think of the "time to wait" factor that was already discussed. The Hikkake signal tends to have a short time-span associated with it, whereas one of the key requirements of successfully trading flag formations is to be patient and set the entry level at a retracement point which is close to where the pattern would be declared invalid under the setup rules. As we have remarked before markets rarely behave predictably and it is not uncommon to find retracements that go right up to and sometimes slightly beyond where they should terminate if the classification rules for a particular pattern are to be strictly applied.

Pattern recognition using software algorithms require both precision and continuing refinement. From a computational point of view this involves an adaptable rule set or classification framework that screens and filters out the elements successively. In fact, it can best be implemented in software in the form a finite state machine that switches to different states with different logics based on the positive identification of specifically required attributes and if specified negative attributes are observed the finite state machine will branch to a different logic or rule execution procedure.

One of the techniques that is most constructive in refining the rules is to look at instances where there is an apparent flag but the pattern fails. Faced with this situation there are three possible paths one can take:

- Accept that the pattern has been correctly identified but also accept the failure as nothing more than the fact that no pattern is completely reliable.
- Recognize that the characteristics exhibited in a particular example of the supposed occurrence of the pattern lead to a misclassification and that the rules that allowed the pattern through the filtering process need to be adapted.
- Accept that a failed pattern is itself an important market signal which can be a useful addition to one's trading strategy.

Let us review these options in the light of the daily chart pattern in Figure 5.14 which is for Marvell Technology (MRVL) during late January/early February 2006.

We have highlighted the key candlestick for the issue of classification and it is the long tailed pattern that occurred on January 27th (A). There is clear range expansion and a dramatic volume increase with more than twice the average volume being registered on the day in question. The troublesome feature, however, is the long upper shadow or tail to the pattern. In fact the close was below the median value for the daily range revealing what could also be interpreted as a shooting star formation. Should this in itself invalidate the pattern? What would be our view if the gap between the close on the 27th and that session's high was partially filled in the next session? There are several qualifiers that could be introduced to the pattern classification logic. For the moment we shall suspend our doubts and consider that the pattern was correctly classified as a possible ingredient in the formation of the flagpole.

The next question arises in connection with the apparent breakout from the descending channel that took place on February 9th (B). This could have been the beginning of the expected move higher. But here we encounter an issue that separates our thinking on these patterns from the view of many others. We do not like the notion of a "beginning" in this context. If the bullish flag has one key ingredient it is that when the pattern is ready to break, when the trigger is pulled, the break is decisive and should produce a coherent move which will not enable latecomers to hitch a ride. Traders know that this is the resolution of the pattern and there is no mercy for doubters or no reason to leave anything on the table. The break should itself be a range expansion with strong volume and the close should be in the upper quartile of the daily range. This was clearly not the case with the candle at B. Interestingly there was almost a bearish Hikkake pattern observed in conjunction with the point B. The candle preceding the one we have discussed for the 9th was almost an inside day and if it had been then the break below the low for that day which is annotated on the chart would have provided the signal to get short on February 10th ahead of the more decisive move down on the 13th which clearly signals that the bull flag (if it had been one) had failed.

Looking at the pattern again we would suggest that the long upper tail to the flagpole candlestick should have raised a doubt about the validity of the pattern but not in itself overruled its classification. We would not have issued a signal to buy following the candle on the 8th (the one that we have commented was almost an inside day) as there was still some question about the channel duration. The "breakout" on the 9th would have made us very suspicious that this was a fake-out pattern (whether we would have been able to stretch the Hikkake rules a little is another question!) and the really important focus would have been on the intraday action on the 10th following the suspect breakout.

GARTLEY PATTERNS

The second kind of pattern that we want to focus on is a more specialized pattern that is not widely featured in the T.A. literature but which is worth reviewing because it can sometimes have bearing on the possible interpretations of where one is in relation to an evolving flag formation.

The pattern is named after H.M. Gartley who first published a discussion of the key elements of the pattern in a book entitled *Profits in the Stock Market*.[13] This book is not easy to find and there have been several followers of Gartley that have questioned the ways in which the

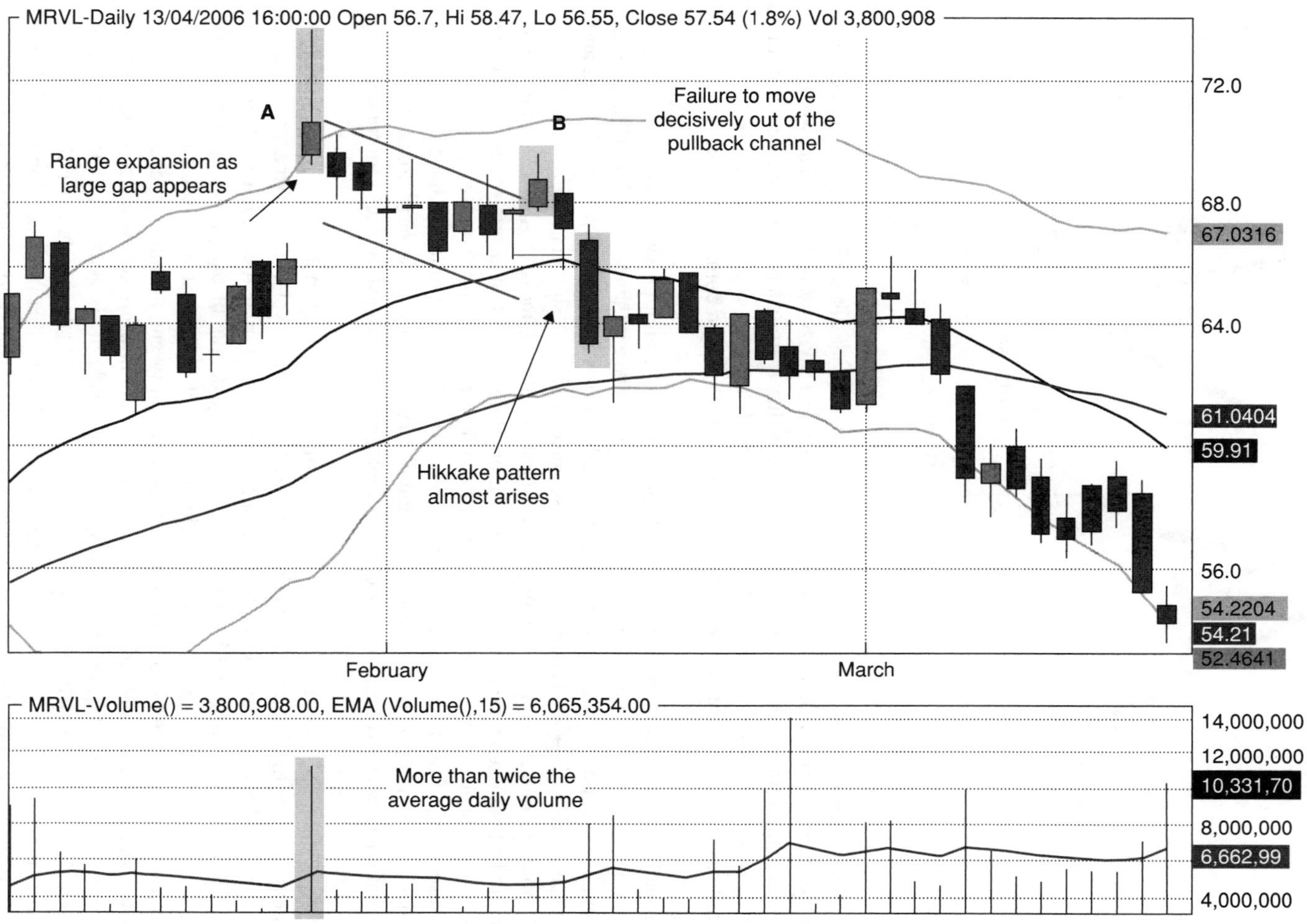

Figure 5.14 MRVL failed flag and Hikkake patterns

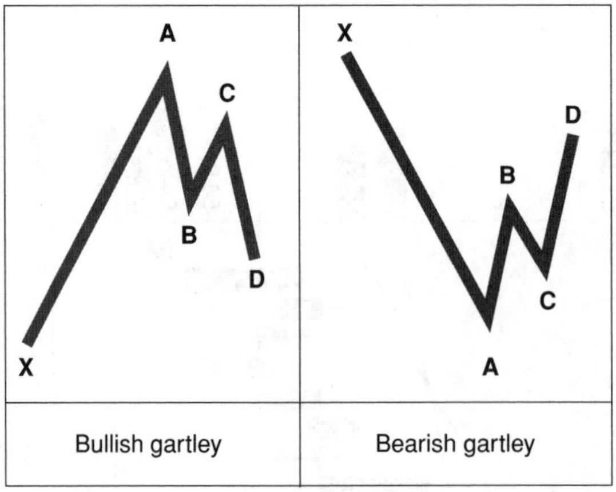

Figure 5.15 Basic Gartley patterns

original pattern has been "misinterpreted" in the subsequent discussions of it. To track the history of the development of this pattern and the subject revisions by "disciples" would take us beyond our current focus which is to explore whether there is any predictive power in the pattern, whether or not it is entirely in accordance with any one proponent of it.[14]

Reduced to its simplest components the basic Gartley pattern comes in two flavors as can be seen in Figure 5.15.

In each of the two cases, both bullish and bearish, there is an impulse wave which is reflected diagrammatically by the path from X to A. This impulse wave is then followed by a "pullback" or retracement move which consists of three smaller waves A → B followed by B → C and then followed by C → D. The original impulse wave of X → A should be the strongest move and should be greater than the eventual retracement or pullback move of A → D. At this point it might be legitimately asked why the pattern is anything more than an approximate template for most pullback patterns that follow on from an initial price impulse. As we have seen from our discussion of the basic flag formation there is already a valid template for considering a continuation of the original impulse after a temporary counterimpulse or pullback move. So why would we want to muddy the waters with another pattern that exhibits the same underlying structure?

This is where the pattern becomes more interesting and where even if Gartley himself did not address the issue his disciples have come forward with some novel use of Fibonacci numbers. Most traders have been introduced to the sequence named after the Italian mathematician who first discussed them and have read the obligatory couple of paragraphs discussing the proliferation of rabbits and the golden ratio so we will not repeat that exercise. The main reason why traders should be familiar with Fibonacci ratios and the number series is because many traders swear by their significance in understanding how markets work. Ralph N. Elliot was preoccupied with the key ratios 1.618, 0.618 and 0.382 in his work[14] and there are many other technicians that attach great importance to these ratios. At this juncture, we shall carefully avoid expressing any opinion about the validity of believing that price development follows a path that is "governed by" or "shaped by" some underlying mathematical law of growth, but we will return to this fascinating issue in another place.[15] What can be stated with great

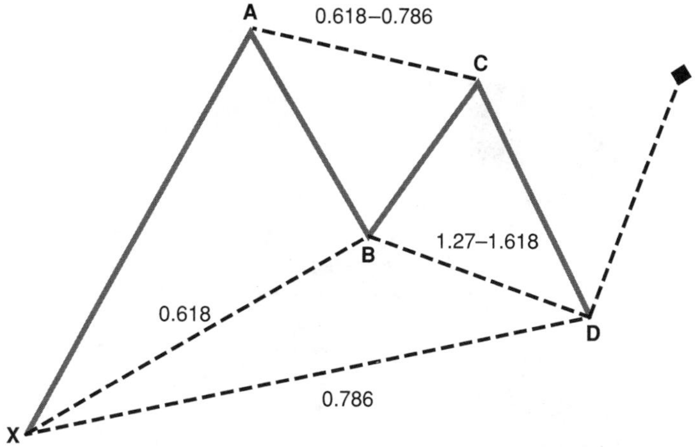

Figure 5.16 The Bullish Gartley pattern

confidence is that many traders both respect and disrespect these ratios and because of that it is always worth being aware of price levels that are based on a Fibonacci analysis of the key chart levels for an index, stock or commodity. One can be sure that the obvious price levels (e.g. a 38% or 62% retracement level from a widely acknowledged bullish impulse move) will become sensitive areas for traders as those who target them both out of conviction as to their validity, or out of a more predatory kind of opportunism, will be paying close attention as markets approach these key levels.

Figure 5.16 is a refinement of the stripped down Bullish Gartley pattern that was displayed in Figure 5.15. Some additional paths have been traced and some Fibonacci values have been applied to the pattern. It requires some careful explanation as the essence of the pattern's validity hinges on the achievement of targets that are bounded by key Fibonacci levels. The impulse move is represented in Figure 5.16 by the path XA. Price reverses at A, and applying Fibonacci ratios, the retracement AB should be 61.8% of the impulse wave (calculated as the price at A minus the price at X). This amount is shown on the dotted path between XB.

At B, the price reverses again. The retracement BC should be between 61.8% and 78.6% of the AB price range and is shown on the dotted path AC. At C, the price again reverses and, again using Fibonacci ratios, the retracement CD should be between 127% and 161.8% of the range BC and this is shown on the dotted path BD. Price D is the trigger to buy. The overall retracement XD is a crucial part of the pattern, and this should be thought of as the retracement of the range AD with respect to XA. XD should ideally be 78.6% of the range XA. One further ideal is for the length of CD to equal the length of AB.

The idealized template in Figure 5.16 shows that when all of the elements are in place for this fairly complex pattern the achievement of the target at point D should lead to a bullish breakout. The next chart (Figure 5.17) shows the template instantiated to a remarkable extent and also shows the predicted resumption of bullish activity following the extended and complex retracement or pullback that is traced out in the path from A to D. Figure 5.17 shows a daily chart of DIA, the exchange traded proxy instrument for the Dow Jones Industrials Average, from November 2003 to June 2004.

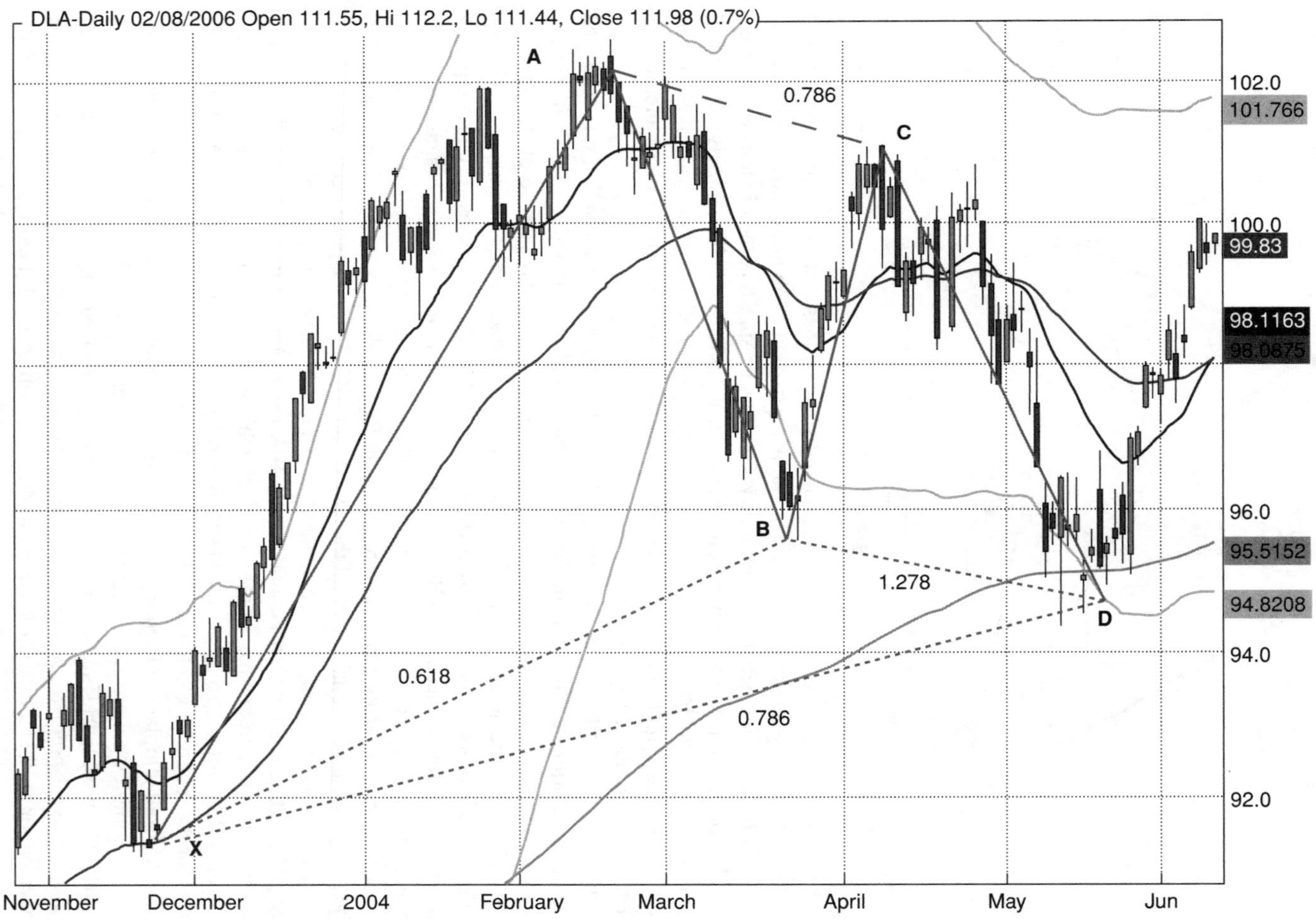

Figure 5.17 DIA Bullish Gartley example

The pattern in Figure 5.17 resembles the template diagram almost exactly and the relevant paths have been annotated on the chart. The impulse wave from X to A is the longest and most decisive pattern on the chart and the three wave retracement pattern from A to D brings the price down from A by 78% of the impulse wave. What is also very noteworthy about the chart is the length of time required to register the complete pattern. The path from X to D takes six months to complete and as promised the index takes off to the upside on achievement of the target at D in mid-May 2004. Also noteworthy is the fact that the length of path AB is very closely equal to the length of the path CD. Discovering such patterns is something of an intellectual delight and very often the trader that is patient enough to wait for the Gartley patterns to mature will be well rewarded.

A variation on the Gartley pattern has been developed by Larry Pesavento, and is outlined in his book *Fibonacci Ratios with Pattern Recognition*.[16] The pattern that we shall examine is called the Gartley Butterfly pattern and specifically we shall review the bullish version although very similar logic applies to the bearish version. The essential difference between the idealized pattern template that we looked at in Figure 5.16 and the modified pattern that is idealized in Figure 5.18 is the degree of retracement. In the original Gartley pattern the retracement or pullback would be targeting 78% of the original impulse wave – the move up from X to A. To this extent the pattern resembles one of the key detection rules for the flag formations which is that the pullback or corrective wave should not penetrate below the origin of the impulse wave (or in the case of the flag formation – the base of the flagpole). However, in the Butterfly variations on the basic pattern the retracement goes below the origin of the impulse wave in the case of the bullish pattern and above the origin of the impulse wave in the bearish version. Figure 5.18 shows that the retracement followed by A to D is actually either 127% of the original impulse wave or even 168% in limiting cases. The other Fibonacci values are shown on the dotted paths as before.

Figure 5.19 is a daily chart for Nordstrom (JWN) that depicts the Bullish Gartley Butterfly pattern again in almost text book fashion.[17]

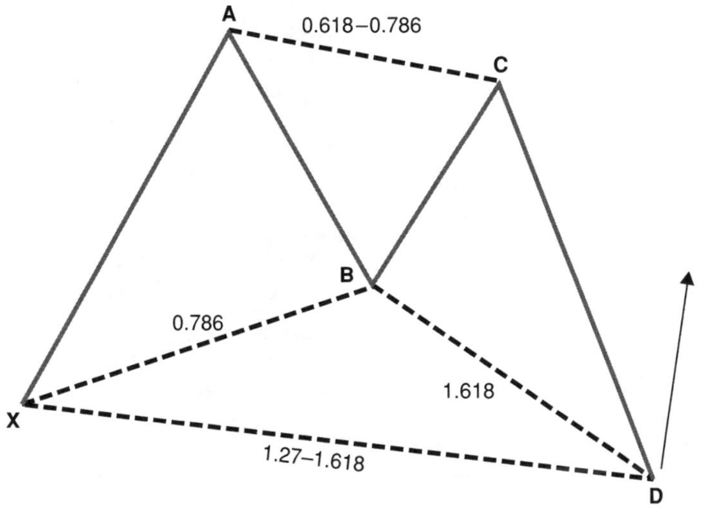

Figure 5.18 Bullish Gartley Butterfly pattern template

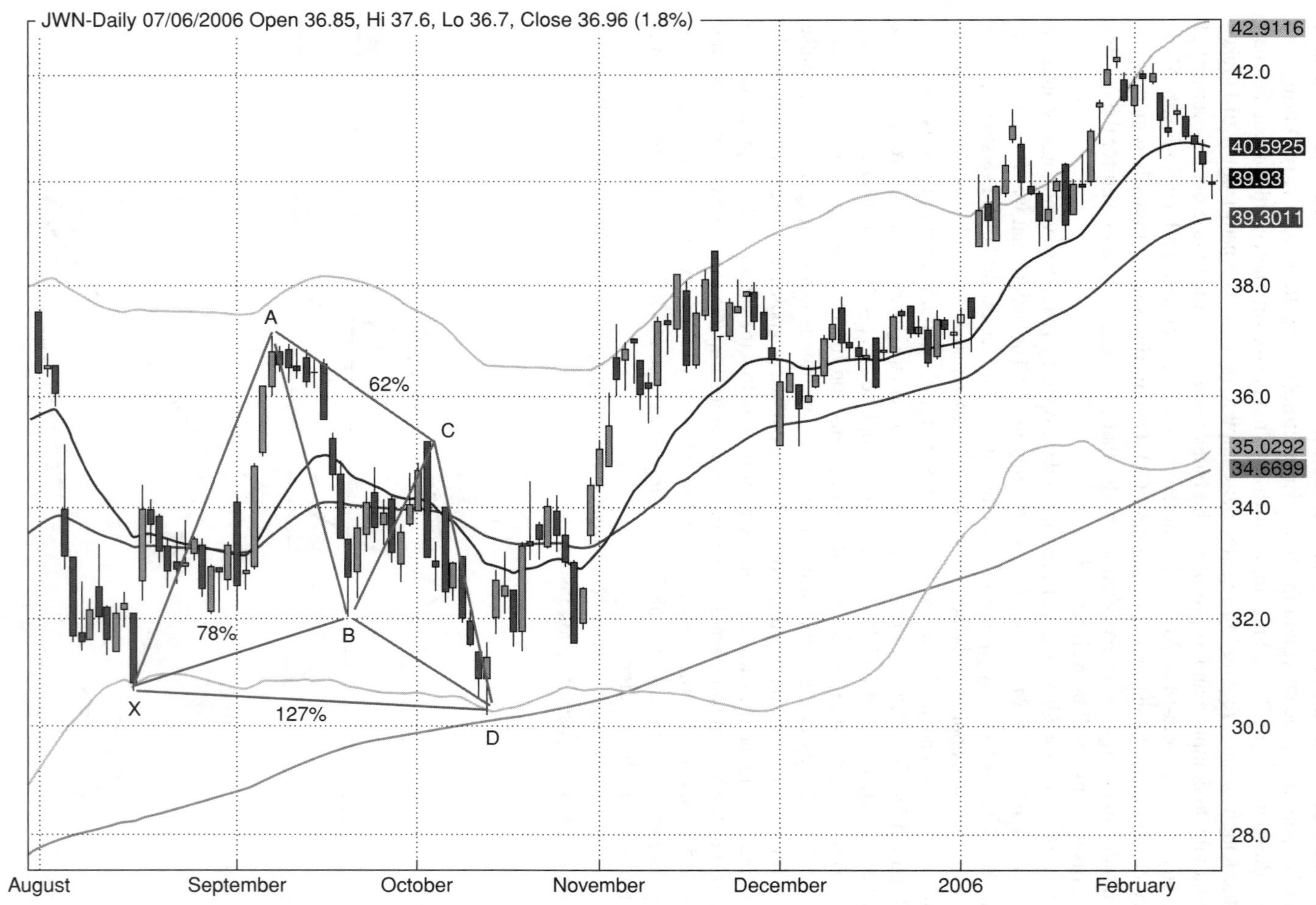

Figure 5.19 JWN Bullish Gartley pattern

The ratios match the template almost exactly, which is not always the case of course, and the October 2005 lows just above $30 mark a 127% retracement in A to D of the impulse move from X to A. The chart reveals clearly that the retracement target having been achieved at point D the trader who had recognized the unfolding pattern and taken a long position in October 2005 close to the $30 level would have been rewarded with a 40% ride by the end of January 2006.

6
Volatility

In this chapter we shall examine some riddles and puzzles that have to do with market volatility and the perception of it by the trading community and the popular imagination. There are many different opinions on what constitutes the best measurement of volatility ranging from the simplest, which is the variance in the log returns of an asset, or more commonly the standard deviation in the log returns, which is simply the square root of the variance, to more subtle measurements relating to the maximum drawdowns of an index or asset over a certain time period which we shall examine in connection with portfolio management issues.

We shall begin with implied volatility which has to be distinguished from the actual observed variance in the log returns that we just mentioned, and which is usually referred to as historical volatility. Implied volatility is the market's perception, at the time, of the likely variation in returns as expressed in the prices (which incorporate a variable premium value) that traders are willing to buy and sell options to counterparties. The broadest measure of the overall market's calculation of implied volatility is to be found in the Chicago Board Options Exchange's (CBOE) Volatility index which is often referred to simply as the VIX. It is fortunate that detailed daily records of the value of this index have been kept since 1990 so it is possible to take a good look, for a substantial period, at what has happened to the market's own perception of its likely volatility and risk.

Figure 6.1 shows the monthly values of the CBOE Volatility index for the period from 1990 until the middle of 2006. As can be seen immediately the VIX is itself highly volatile, showing that perceptions about the future course of volatility are subject to profound and dramatic changes depending on the prevailing market conditions, contemporaneous news events and "crises".

Several annotations have been made on the chart to provide the context and background for many of the spikes that took the VIX on some occasions above the 40% level and which coincided with such major events as the LTCM collapse in 1998 and the attack on the World Trade Center in September 2001. Many of the highest readings correspond with the more obvious crisis episodes but it is also worth reflecting that the very high values for the index that occur during the latter half of 2002 did not coincide with a specific critical event so much as the fact that the market was in a severe decline. In July and October 2002, the S&P 500 fell below 800 and on October 10th 2002 the index registered an intraday low of 768 which was a level it had not been at since 1997 and which was more or less a 50% retracement from the all time intraday high for the index of 1552 achieved on March 24th 2000. It is worth remembering that

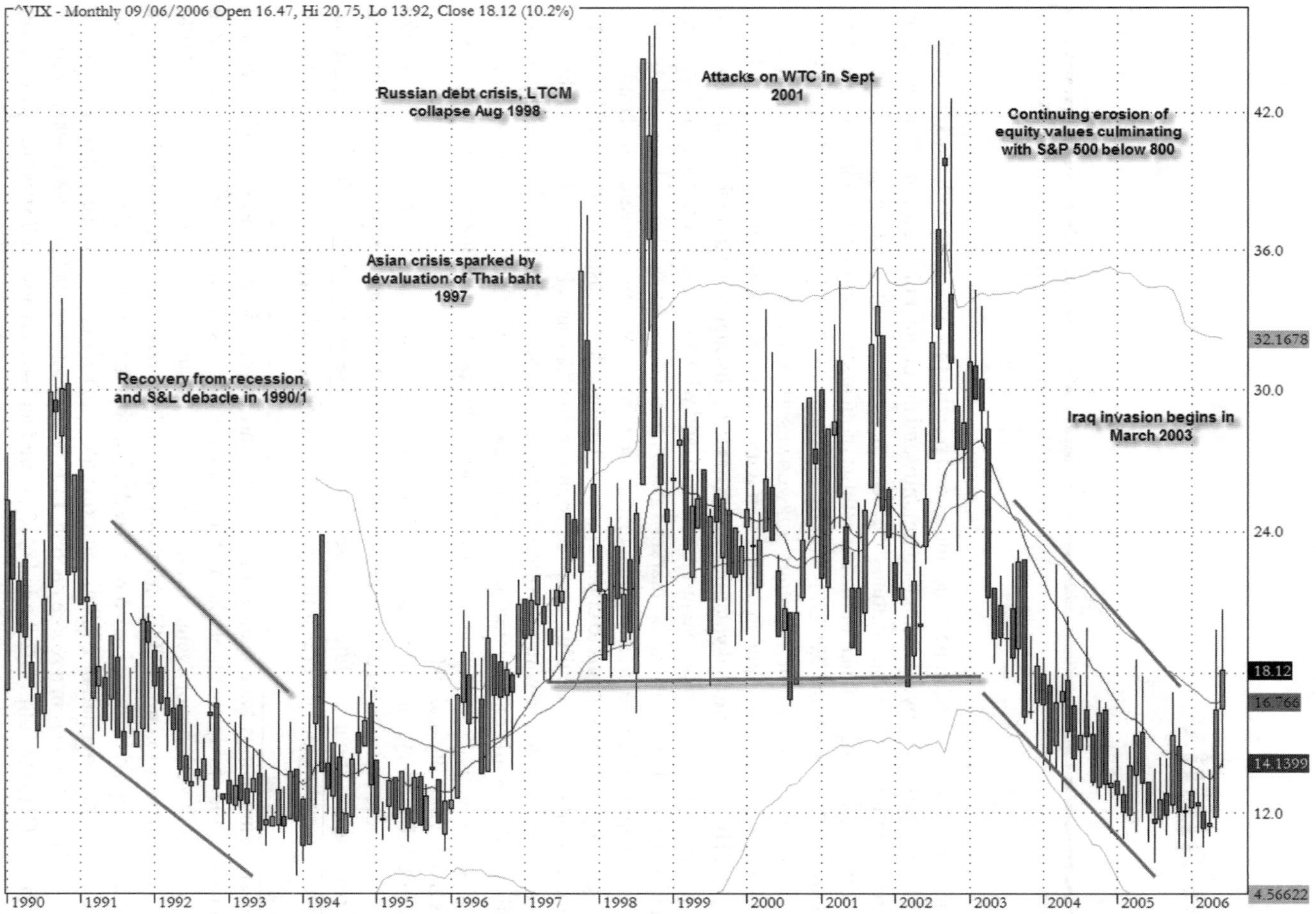

Figure 6.1 CBOE Volatility index monthly 1990–mid-2006

there is as much demand for option protection when markets are suffering sustained weakness as when there is an episodic crisis such as the Russian debt default or 9/11.

One further broad brush comment on the chart is the noticeable decline that shows on the index on both of the left-hand and right-hand sides of the chart. The period following the U.S. recession in 1990/1 until late 1995 (apart from a spike in the spring of 1994) as well as the period from the invasion of Iraq in 2003 (which almost coincides with the end of the S&P 500's deepest bear market lows) until the spring of 2006 show a persistent decline in the index. In both cases implied volatility as registered by the index based around 10%. This needs to be contrasted with the middle period on the chart, from 1997 to the end of 2002, which could be said to coincide with the build-up of the millennium technology bubble as well as its bursting. During this period the index rarely dropped below a value of 18 and more typically was around 24 which is twice the implied volatility for the typical readings observed throughout 2005 and even into 2006. As this book is being written the VIX is showing clear signs of moving upwards and away from the historically low readings that were achieved in the summer of 2005. As is often commented, the VIX chart has an inverse relationship to the chart of the underlying S&P 500 index but is perhaps even more revealing as it tends to highlight exactly those periods when the market's sense of risk is at extremes. It is for this reason that it is sometimes referred to as the "Fear Index", and conversely when readings have been consistently low it is claimed that the market is suffering from complacency. Many traders and market commentators pay very special attention to the VIX, and look for confirmations or divergences with the movements of the S&P 500 for clues as to how to "time the market". But increasingly, some commentators are beginning to question whether the index still has the predictive power that it once had.

We shall argue that because of the proliferation of long/short strategies there is reason to doubt whether the supposed gauge of investor fears still functions the way it is assumed to, but beforehand we need to look at historical or observed volatility. Historical volatility is not what is captured in the VIX as we have already noted, but rather it is a statistical property of the price development of a particular broad market index. We shall look at two separate broad indices for the U.S. equity markets, the Standard & Poor's 500 and the Russell 2000, and some interesting and perhaps surprising facts will be revealed from a comparison between them. In what follows we are discussing actual realized volatility and to begin we want to make some general remarks about the statistical nature of observed volatility.

VOLATILITY FOR THE S&P 500 SINCE 1985

We need to distinguish between the interday volatility for the S&P 500 index and the intraday volatility. Essentially the difference is as follows:

- Interday volatility requires us to subtract the log of today's price from the log of yesterday's price or, what amounts to the same thing we find the log of today's close/previous close.
- Intraday volatility involves subtracting the low price from the high price for each session to calculate the intraday range and then finding the log of today's intraday range/previous intraday range.

Let us begin with the interday volatility which is the more traditional technique for assessing volatility trends. If we examine the period from January 2nd 1985 until December 30th 2005

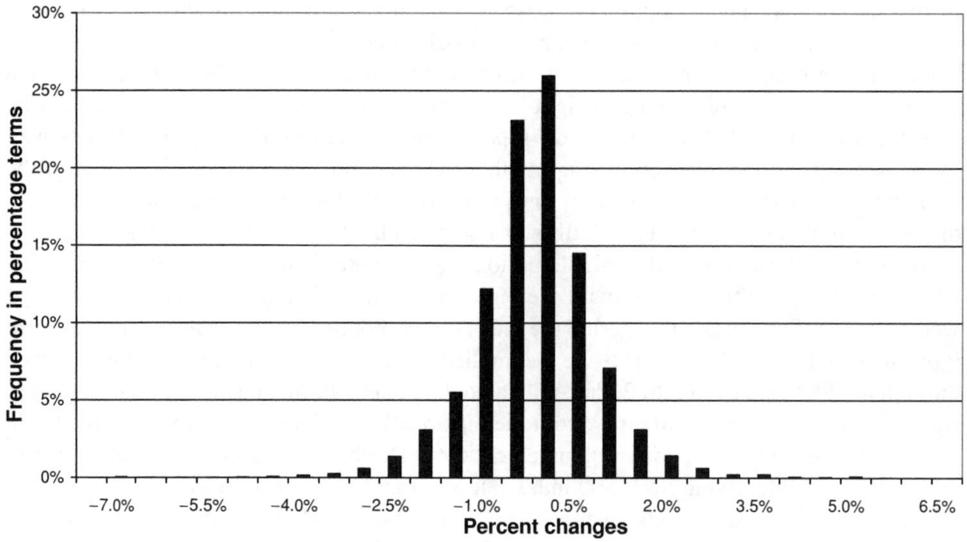

Figure 6.2 S&P 500 distribution of log changes

and then create a frequency histogram for the daily log changes we find that the changes are distributed as indicated in Figure 6.2

The first point to note about Figure 6.2, the diagram of the distribution, is that some of the more extreme movements have been excluded and the x-axis confines the range to the interval $\pm 7\%$ daily moves. There have been several daily changes that have fallen beyond this interval including most notably October 19th 1987 which registered a more than -20% change. It can also be clearly seen that the bulk of the distribution congregates around the unchanged level with a bias towards $+0.5\%$ moves. The distribution falls away quite noticeably as we move outwards toward the tails of the distribution but there is noticeable activity still within the tails (we shall examine this more in the context of the normalized distribution).

Figure 6.3 shows the above distribution transformed into the standard normal distribution which more clearly shows how the actual distribution differs from the theoretical values implicit in a normal distribution.

Again the diagram has been limited so that it shows only the interval ± 5 STDs from the mean value and it is worth contemplating that the z-value or standard normal variable value for October 19th 1987 was in fact more than -19 STDs which according to standard probability theory has a likelihood of occurring once in 1.22198E-83 times or one chance in several billion times the history of the Universe.[1]

In terms of how closely this distribution matches the characteristics of the theoretical normal distribution there are a few salient points which demonstrate that while the above chart reveals the archetypal bell curve the actual distribution of daily returns deviates significantly from the idealized normal distribution. First, with regard to the outlier events, it can be seen that these are much more likely than the normal probability distribution suggests. According to the theory only 0.3% of the events should lay beyond the ± 3 STD values from the mean. It can be seen from Table 6.1, which captures all of the index's extreme movements, that they arise with a frequency of 1.15%, almost four times more frequently than would be expected.

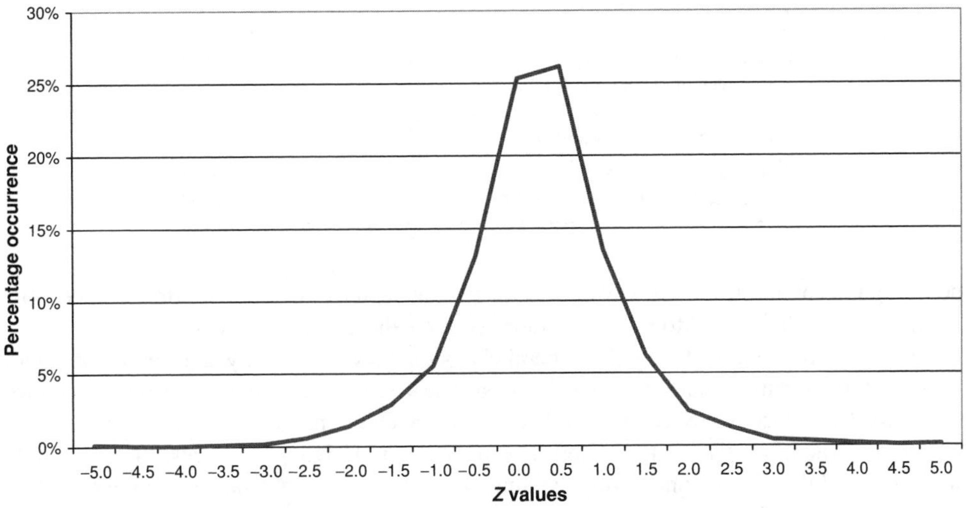

Figure 6.3 S&P 500 1985–2005 standardized normal distribution for daily log changes

Not only is there abnormality with respect to the tails of the distribution but there is also a marked difference with respect to the central tendency of the distribution. According to statistical theory 68% of the values should fall in the interval between plus one standard deviation and minus one standard deviation from the mean, whereas as can be seen from Table 6.2 there are almost 90% of the values that fit this criterion in the actual observed distribution. As a result of this discrepancy the observed distribution is sometimes referred to being leptokurtic.[2]

In general terms it can be seen that the broad equity market is, relatively speaking, less volatile on most occasions than is consistent with the data being normally distributed, but that the likelihood of extreme events is considerably higher than the normal distribution would suggest. This is not just an interesting statistical property of the S&P 500 but is echoed across the board for all financial time series. From a trading perspective there are important lessons to be drawn from this fact as it suggests that any input of historical price data into the various technical indicators and statistical tools commonly available to us is going to understate the possibility of "freak" or extreme events. Although markets are perhaps "tamer" than is often supposed, when they act erratically, and there are precious few leading indicators to alert us as to when this is likely to happen, they perform in a more extreme manner than probability theory founded on Gaussian assumptions would suggest. As will be seen in regard to money management this

Table 6.1 Left tail outliers

Left tail outliers (more than −3 STDs from mean)	27
Right tail outliers (more than +3 STDs from mean)	34
Total outliers	61
Percentage outliers	1.15%

Table 6.2 Central tendency

Left-hand central tendency (between mean and −1 STD)	2033
Right-hand central tendency (between mean and +1 STD)	2728
Central tendency values	4761
Central tendency as percentage	89.9%

poses significant hurdles in the way of quantifying the degree of risk of a portfolio, since most conventional tools will fail to reflect the more erratic behavior that can arise.

So far we have commented on the general characteristics of volatility distribution but there are three further matters that we want to focus on. The first is the tendency for extreme volatility events to cluster together. Second, we will examine the claim that there may be some periodic signature to the market's quieter episodes versus its more turbulent episodes. In other words we shall see if there is any underlying dynamic that explains the switches from periods of low volatility to high volatility, sometimes referred to as regime shifts.[3] Third, we want to examine the claim that the overall equity market has become less volatile in recent years (since 2003) and that this diminution of volatility represents a secular as opposed to a cyclical change in market conditions.

VOLATILITY CLUSTERING

Volatility clustering is one of the more widely acknowledged characteristics of financial time series data and its existence violates the notion that price development and the log changes from succeeding prices follow a random walk and are normally distributed. This subject will come to the forefront in subsequent discussions (in Chapter 9) and for present purposes it is sufficient to note that one of the underlying (Gaussian) assumptions about a normally distributed data series is that all of the data points are independent and identically distributed. This is the so-called i.i.d. assumption and it is best illustrated by examples from games of chance and rests on the notion that there is no "memory" in the sequence of independent events. The sequence of outcomes when we throw a fair die or spin a roulette wheel exhibits the quality of i.i.d. in the sense that no inferences can be drawn from any repetitive patterns. If the spins of a roulette wheel lead to five red outcomes in a row, the very next spin has an equal chance of being a red or black outcome. There is no dependency between each outcome, and the outcomes theoretically will follow a normal distribution. If they do not follow this distribution this should be seen as a purely contingent feature of the particular sequence and no predictive patterns can be inferred. We shall see that this is not true in the case of a sequence of financial returns. Volatile returns will cluster and when we find one exceptionally volatile trading session we are much more likely than suggested by chance to find others in close proximity. This has far reaching repercussions for the statistical analysis of financial data and once these have been acknowledged and understood there are potential payoffs for the active trader.

How can we illustrate volatility clustering? Figure 6.4 shows the daily log changes for the S&P 500 between January 2nd 1985 and July 31st 2006. However, only those returns that exceed on an absolute basis two standard deviations (i.e. ±2 STDs) are included in the chart. The vertical y-axis indicates the magnitude of the log changes in percentage terms. In Figure 6.4

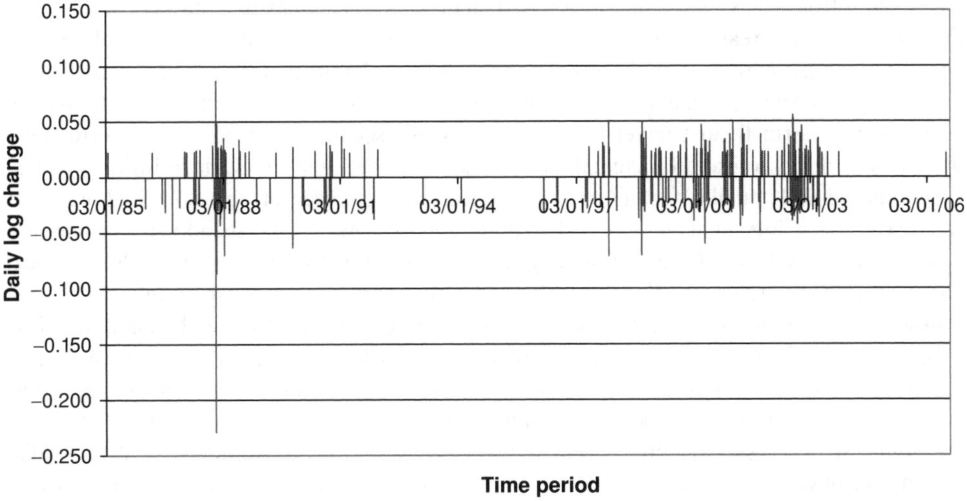

Figure 6.4 S&P 500 1985–mid-2006 daily log changes >2 STDs (absolute) using STD for whole period

the standard deviation value has been calculated from all of the returns for the whole 21 year period which is somewhat flawed since that statistic is only available at the end of the period and not contemporaneously; however, this issue will be addressed in the next chart.

By only plotting the more extreme periods we have highlighted the manner in which the broad market index has had extended, quiescent periods and then periods where the incidence of large fluctuations (on both sides of the y-axis) cluster. Some obvious periods that stand out on the chart are the 1987 market crash, the period in the late 1980s and early 1990s that coincided with the S&L problems, recessionary forces and the first Gulf War. There followed a period through the mid-1990s where there were few instances of abnormal fluctuations. There are periods in the late 1990s that correspond to the Asian market crisis in 1997, the Russian debt/LTCM crisis in 1998 and then a very large cluster in the early part of the new millennium that is related to 9/11 and more acutely to the mounting bear market throughout late 2002. This chart, because it focuses only on the extreme events, bears a striking resemblance to the spike events that we saw on the VIX chart.

As Figure 6.4 reveals, the most recent period since late 2003 has been a period of market quiescence and has many similarities to the volatility characteristics of the broad market in the mid-1990s period. During the period under review there were 5447 separate log change data points and 251 or 4.6% that exceeded the threshold of ±2 STDs. It is perhaps worth noting that the often cited confidence interval of 95% for measuring value at risk, for examples is based on the likelihood of an event happening 1 in 20 periods and we have seen that over the 21 year period under review the broad U.S. market has experienced an abnormal move almost 1 in 20 periods. That this frequency of 4.6% also concurs with the expectation from statistical theory that ±2 STD events should occur with 5% probability is discussed again below. But the distribution of these abnormal moves is itself far from random as assumed in a normal distribution. In other words there is a tendency for abnormal moves to cluster and not be distributed haphazardly across the time line.

Failure to properly acknowledge the clustering of volatility undermines much of the academic research that has been done in risk management and portfolio theory. Erroneous conclusions from applying assumptions based on i.i.d. have led many practitioners of orthodox theories of risk to greatly underestimate the financial risks associated with the likelihood of abnormally volatile trading conditions. The probability calculus that is used in statistics, or at least that part of statistics that most of us can understand, is based on assumptions that financial returns data is normally distributed but as we can clearly see this is not the case. Unfortunately there is a tendency to import financial data into spreadsheets, use all of the built-in statistical functions and pull out all kinds of bogus conclusions that are accurate to 15 decimal places. If we are rigorously logical in our approach to trading markets we should abandon the probability forecasting derived from Gaussian assumptions and admit that we have no reliable statistical basis for determining when volatility outliers will occur or how severe they might be.

Another source of confusion that arises in discussion about volatility is the claim that it is mean reverting. Periods of high volatility will eventually be succeeded by periods of normal volatility as extreme conditions will be superseded by reversion to more typical conditions. As with many discussions of mean reversion the weakness in this notion is that the key word *eventually* is hopelessly undefined. For the three year period from mid-2000 to mid-2003 waiting for observed volatility to revert to its long-term average would have required heroic patience. When we examined the VIX chart earlier in this chapter we saw that although the 2000–2003 period was particularly volatile it was a subset of a longer period dating back to 1997 that was characterized by much greater volatility than the other periods on the chart. There would seem to be two qualitatively different kinds of volatility epochs or regimes and the best description of prevailing market volatility conditions is best thought of as exhibiting one of these two possible states. A more accurate and useful way of thinking about the change from one volatility condition to the other is to think of this as like a phase transition, in the same way that ice becomes water or water becomes steam. Using this analogy or mental model one can dispense with the notion that the transition is from some average volatility state to some extreme volatility state which not only does not conform with the observed facts but which impoverishes our understanding of the nuances of volatility. We would even question whether the concept of an average or typical volatility level is even meaningful. It is one of those notions that seems innocuous enough at first glance but which clouds our thinking and obscures the real dynamics of the capital markets.

Following on from this revised understanding of the nature of underlying volatility conditions we can begin to make more sense of the fact if the market had a large move in one trading session it is *more not less* likely that it will have another large move in a forthcoming session. Until the market has moved from one phase or regime to another, we should be very hesitant about making any forecasts as to the intermediate term trend of volatility. Even then the variability in the actual data makes forecasting volatility as likely to be as accurate as trying to forecast major earthquakes or volcanic eruptions (indeed in the case of the latter it is probably simpler and likely to be more accurate).

Previously in Figure 6.4 we calculated the standard deviation value for the S&P 500 from all of the data available to us and commented at the time that this has the limitation that this data is only available at the end of the entire period. We want to correct that in the next diagram by being more adaptive and use a moving window calculation for the standard deviation value. In Figure 6.5 the same outlier volatility values (the ± 2 STD daily log changes) have been presented but this time based on a calculation of the standard deviation that looks back only at the preceding year of daily data. This approach allows us to monitor more sensitively the abruptness of large moves in the context of the market's typical and contemporaneously observed behavior prior to the occurrences.

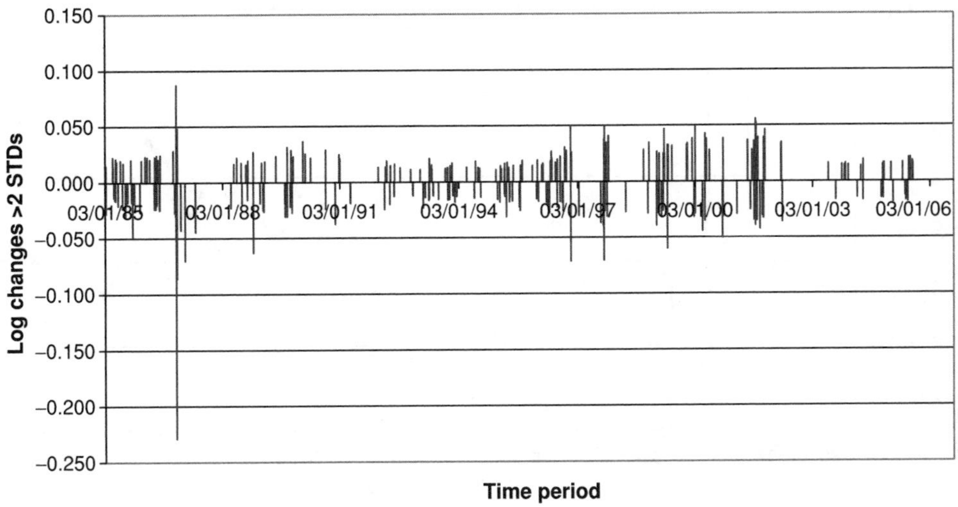

Figure 6.5 S&P 500 1985–mid-2006 log changes where greater than 2 absolute STDs using a one year trailing standard deviation

Using this different method of registering the extreme events we find that there is an increase in the number of occasions on which the plotted data points exceeded the ±2 STD threshold. The number of occurrences increases to 266 events for a reduced total set of log changes, the total tracked has fallen to 5197 (we could not begin counting until the first year had elapsed). The percentage has moved up slightly above 5% but as we noted already this is not the most salient feature of the statistical interpretation. There is still a very noticeable clustering but there has also been some thinning of the clusters, especially in the late 1990s to early 2000s period as some events slipped below the threshold because we were using an STD figure that was more closely tuned to recent market conditions. Interestingly we now see that there are some events showing in the 2003–2006 period, some of which were associated with the fall-out from convertible arbitrage accidents following the April/May 2005 GM downgrade (discussed in Chapter 10) and some having to do with the whipsaws in the 4th quarter of 2005 after the market corrected in September and then rallied strongly from mid-October to late November.

Figure 6.6 plots the standard deviation, on a trailing 52 week basis, of the daily returns for the S&P 500 index from January 1985 to the end of July 2006. The chart is very helpful in this context as it clearly illustrates the variability of the trailing standard deviation itself during the period. What is also revealed strikingly in Figure 6.6 is the manner in which the index's volatility in 2005 approached again the very low levels that were observed in 1995. Noticeably the volatility appears to be turning back up on the right-hand side of the chart as it fell short of attaining the same level of subdued volatility that occurred in the earlier period. However, it is the variability in the data series that is the primary focus for our present discussion. Yet again this is evidence that contravenes assumptions that stem from the view that price development follows a random walk and can best be analyzed using a traditional Gaussian inspired theory of finance. Stationarity (which will also be discussed in further detail in Chapter 9) is the assumption that a time series will show a persistent and (relatively) constant mean and variance. The instability of the variance for the S&P 500 time series is clear evidence that this series in nonstationary.

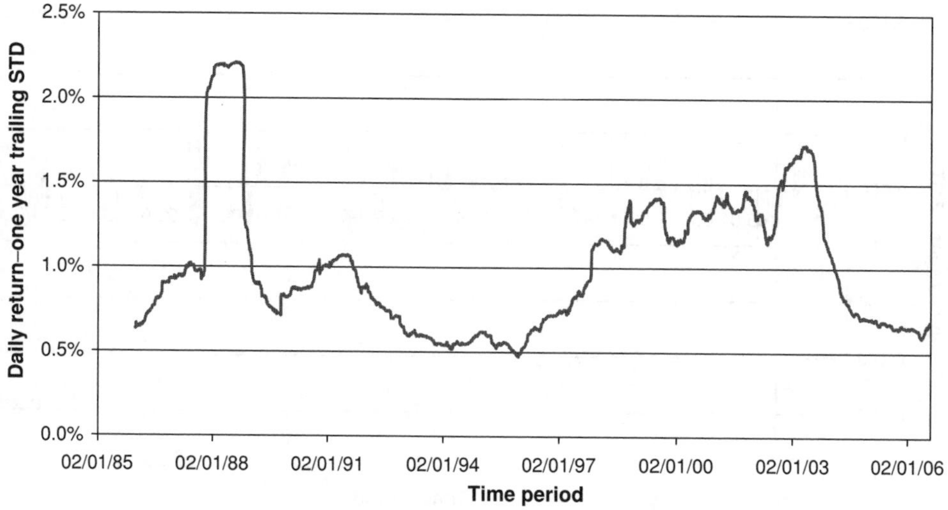

Figure 6.6 S&P 500 daily returns – one year trading STD – January 1985–July 2006

Figure 6.6 also reveals the highly unusual spike in the trailing STD that occurred in the 1987 period followed by another smaller rise in the 1991/1992 period which then led to a gradual decline through the mid-1990s until we see the build-up again into the turn of the millennium. The other most notable spike that is clearly evident on the right-hand side of the chart coincides with the late 2002/early 2003 bear market lows. During the latter half of 2002 there was a lot of institutional liquidation of portfolios as managers struggled with redemptions and asset/liability mismatching following the prolonged sell-off that began in 2000/2001 but which did not abate until after the Iraq invasion. The steady decline that can be observed following the invasion of Iraq in March 2003 brought the observed level of volatility back to the lowest levels observable on the chart that coincided with the 1993/1996 period.

Up to this point broad market volatility has been considered in the context of the S&P 500 but it will be instructive to extend the examination to consider volatility clustering in the Russell 2000 index which is probably the best gauge of the smaller capitalization stocks in the U.S. This index includes the kinds of companies and stocks that historically have tended to exhibit the most volatility and where there are more concerns about the liquidity of such issues. Large mutual funds place a premium on their ability to transact in liquid stocks, and some major asset managers are wary of taking large positions in stocks that have market capitalizations below certain minimum threshold levels.

Figure 6.7 takes a similar approach to the one that we initially used for the S&P 500. In this instance where we are focused on the small cap index we shall also confine ourselves to those daily log changes that exceed the ± 2 STD threshold where the standard deviation has been determined on a retrospective basis for the whole period. Statistics for the Russell 2000 began in September 1987 which somewhat fortuitously enables us to include the movements of the index during the October 1987 crash (although these would not be so useful to us for the trailing one year approach that we used). In accordance with what was observed for the S&P 500 there is clear evidence of clustering of the more volatile sessions, especially during the 2000–2003 period which coincides with the most persistently volatile period in the index's history. The mid-1990s again are characterized by relatively few extreme volatility events and

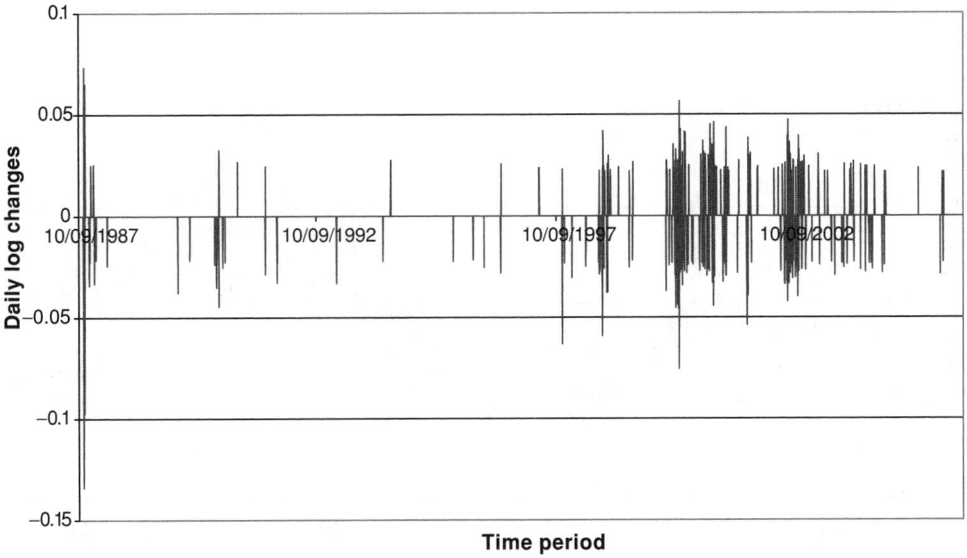

Figure 6.7 Daily log changes in price >2 STDs for Russell 2000 index

the incidence tapers off on the right-hand side of the chart from about mid-2003 onwards. There were 5.4% occasions on which the index produced an absolute movement of more than 2 STDs which again conforms to the notion that extreme events tend to occur about 1 in 20 trading sessions. But the same comment that we made before can be made again – the clustering of abnormally volatile sessions undermines the notion that price movements and returns in the index are independent and identically distributed.

Figure 6.8 offers a useful comparison of the relative volatility of the S&P 500 and the Russell 2000. In the case of the returns that are plotted in Figure 6.8 we have taken as the primary measure the standard deviation between the weekly returns on each index and then constructed a one year moving average from that. The year 1988 is omitted from this comparison because of the need to have one year of data to look back for the moving average calculation and as was noted records only exist for the Russell 2000 from late 1987 onwards.

Figure 6.8 shows the trailing one year standard deviation for the weekly returns on the two indices. Of particular interest on this chart are those periods when the standard deviation for the Russell 2000 jumps decisively above the line for the S&P 500. These periods of increased relative volatility for the Russell 2000 also tend to coincide with critical times for the overall market. The term critical is used to suggest that there is not necessarily a specific directional bias (although in many cases these periods are associated with a downward bias in prices) but also to cover other issues concerned with overall market liquidity and also periods when there are "flight to safety" concerns. Also apparent from the chart is how volatility for the S&P 500 has fallen back quite drastically from the higher volatility regime that was present in the early part of the new millennium and has since mid-2003 retreated to the levels of mid-1990s. The decline for the Russell 2000 during this same period has been more subdued. In order to understand further the interplay between these two indices a normalized graph has been presented in Figure 6.9 showing the relative performances of the two indices where the beginning of 1988 has been taken as the base period.

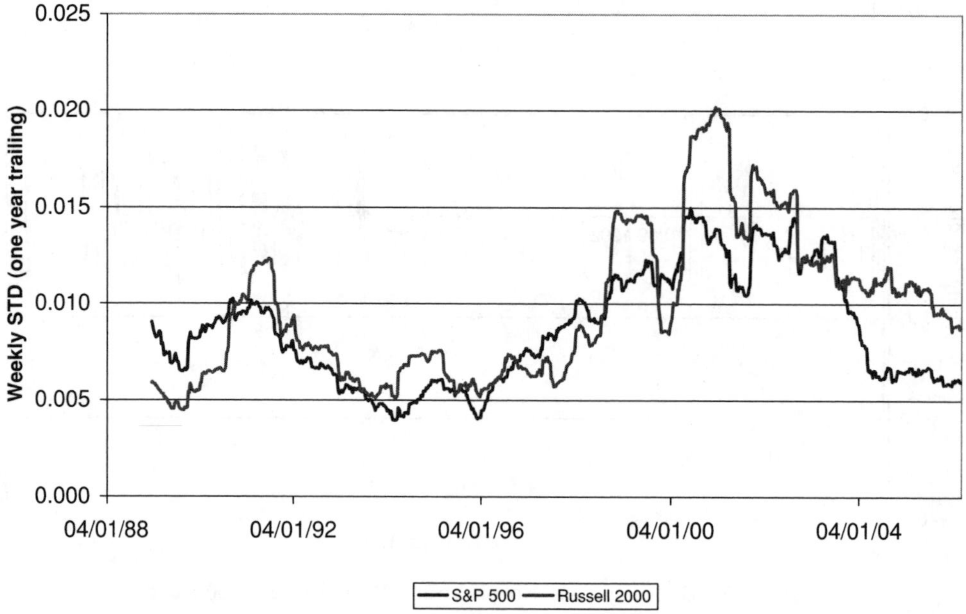

Figure 6.8 Comparison between the one year trailing standard deviations based on the weekly closes for the S&P 500 and Russell 2000 indices since 1988

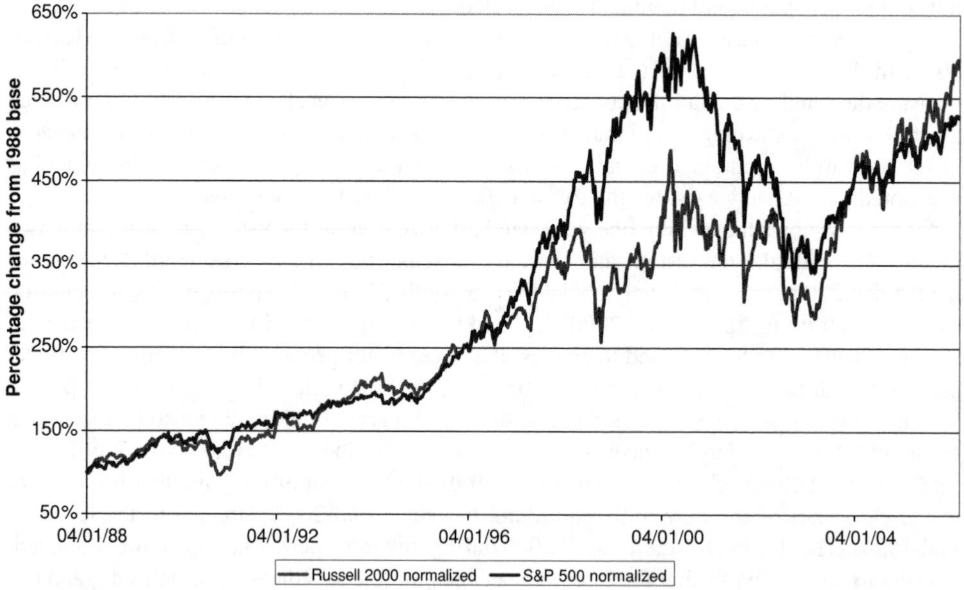

Figure 6.9 Normalized performance of the S&P 500 and Russell 2000 indices from 1988 to 2005

Several things emerge from Figure 6.9. First, there is the remarkably coincidental co-movement of the indices from the beginning of the period until 1998 when the S&P began to outperform the small cap index. Throughout the late 1990s until the apex of the two lines in late 2000 the larger cap stocks were clearly the best performing sector of the U.S. market. In price terms the S&P corrected more dramatically than the Russell 2000 despite the fact that the volatility chart shows that it was the smaller cap index which experienced the greater increase in volatility.

So here is perhaps one of the clues to the volatility enigma that we are trying to unravel. *There is a vital difference between the degree of fluctuations that prices undergo and the magnitude of the price movements.* It can be seen that price can decline more steadily and steeply as it did for the S&P 500 during the 2001–2003 period but the degree of the week to week fluctuations experienced by the smaller cap index indicate greater volatility. What is perhaps most remarkable about this chart is that since early 2004 there has been a clear outperformance in price terms by the smaller cap index which has been recording successive new all time highs since 2004 whereas the S&P 500 remains below the levels from late 2001. There is a paradoxical situation that most commentators of the market completely missed during the 2004–2005 period which is that the Russell 2000 displayed more volatility than it did during the 1990s but kept breaking out to new all time highs. During the same period the S&P 500 experienced a relatively quiet period with respect to its volatility but consistently lagged the smaller cap index in terms of price appreciation.

So far the two indices have been considered in isolation but the time has come to bring them together in a graphical procedure that will bring out the degree to which their price movements and returns are related. The technique we will be following employs a charting technique that is known as a scatter plot or diagram and the statistical procedure that allows us to quantify the degree of co-movement between the two series is known as linear regression.[4]

Figure 6.10 shows a scatter plot for all of the pairs of weekly log changes between the S&P 500 and the Russell 2000 during the entire period from 1987 to mid-2006. An intrinsic quality

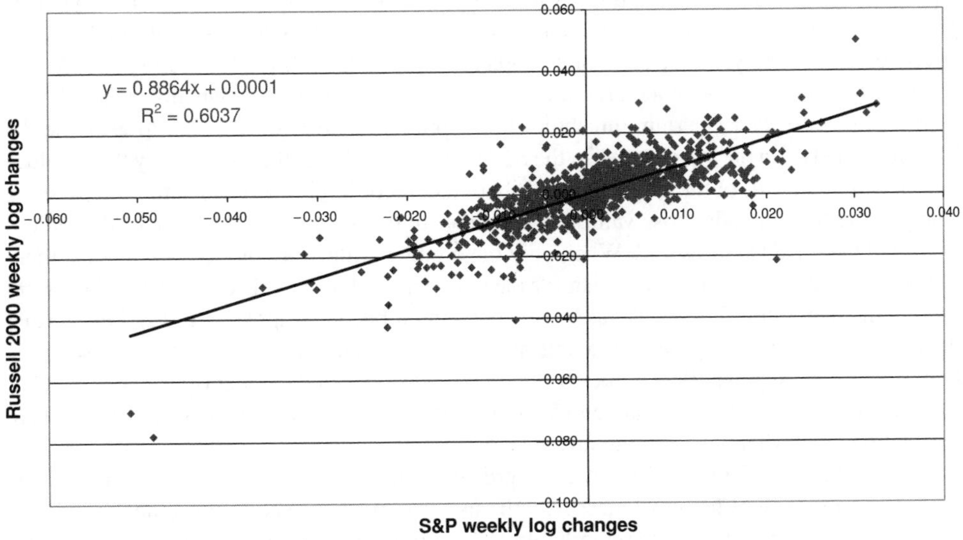

Figure 6.10 Scatter plot of weekly log changes in the S&P 500 and Russell 2000 indices

of this graphical technique is that the series of data points are not depicted historically. The pairs of points are obviously observations or samplings made of both series historically but when they are presented in the scatter plot fashion they lose their historical or time line dimension. Each point – each *XY* value – shows how each index performed, in terms of the log changes of successive periods, on a particular occasion but adjacent points on a scatter plot could be from very different moments in time and separated by long intervals. As is apparent from the diagram the vast majority of values are clustered around the intersection of the x- and y- axis in the middle of the scatter plot where both x and y are zero. The cloud of points that are centered on the origin reflect the fact most of the returns for both indices will be of small magnitude either side of the unchanged level and the denser cloud in the top right-hand quadrant reflects the fact that there are more changes that are slightly positive for both indices than any other possibility. The important value to interpret from this scatter plot is the degree of correlation between the movements of each index. Expressed slightly differently we are looking for a measure of the co-movement of the two indices. The measure that is most appropriate is the coefficient of determination or as it is usually expressed the R^2 value.[5] This value is the square of another widely used statistic which is the coefficient of correlation and it is squared because the correlation coefficient can take on values between -1 and 1.

Higher values of the R^2 value indicate that there is a relatively strong association between the two movements of each index. As the value of R^2 approaches its limit of one, a straight line drawn through all of the *XY* values in a scatter plot will closely capture the implicit trend of the entire *XY* series of points. If the line was to fit the data points perfectly we would have an R^2 value of 1 and if the value approaches zero it tells us that there is no implicit (linear) trend in the *XY* values and that the indices move in a completely indeterminate fashion with respect to each other. In fact, Figure 6.10 indicates an R^2 value of 0.6037 and this provides reasonably good support (about 60%) that movements of the independent index in the example (i.e. the S&P 500) can be used a basis for forecasting the associated movements in the other index (i.e. the Russell 2000).

Scatter plots are made up from a series of paired *XY* values as we have seen and they do not represent the association between the *X* and the *Y* values in a strictly historical fashion. This provides an excellent opportunity for being selective about the data that we want to subject to a linear regression analysis. We can, for example, focus only on outlier events and select for the determination of the slope of a regression or its R^2 value only those movements in the relevant security that exceeded a certain threshold. In the present context we decided to examine the association between the log changes in the S&P 500 and the Russell 2000 for only those values falling within the tails of the respective distributions. Accordingly we decided to screen the log changes and only include those values where either of the log changes for each of the indices exceeded the ± 2 STD threshold. When only these outlier values are plotted we find that there is a stronger degree of correlation than for the case where all of the observed pair values were used in the regression. The R^2 value rises to 0.77 and it becomes apparent in Figure 6.11 that the line of best fit through the data points appears to reconcile more closely with those in the bottom left-hand segment than it does for those paired values in the upper right-hand segment. Indeed if just the negative tails are considered we find the highest R^2 values, indicating more correlation, than when we examine just the positive tails.

The tendency for there to be a greater degree of co-movement in the negative tails reflects another vital feature of financial markets – the fact that in adverse conditions the correlations between assets tend to rise quite remarkably.[6] These much enhanced correlations and the general condition that there is a very noticeable asymmetry between the volatility and correlation characteristics of the positive and negative tails will move to center stage in Chapters 9 and 10.

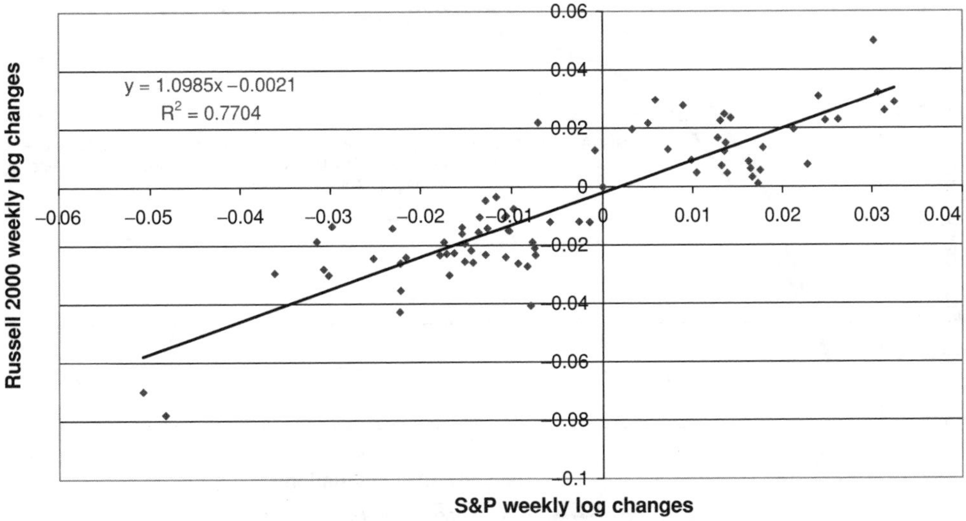

Figure 6.11 Scatter diagram for extreme weekly movements only in the S&P 500 and Russell indices since 1988

IS THE S&P 500 WITHIN A LOW VOLATILITY EPOCH?

In our earlier discussion of the nature of the volatility characteristics of the S&P 500 we proposed that the most useful way of thinking about underlying volatility of the markets is that there are (broadly) two kinds of epochs or regimes that best describe the prevailing conditions. There have been high volatility epochs such as that which covered the period from 1997 to the end of 2002 and there are low volatility regimes that, for example, best describe the kind of conditions found in the mid-1990s. As we have also observed the period from mid-2003 to early 2006 strongly resembles the low volatility regime of the mid-1990s.

What has also been commented upon by numerous market technicians is that the period following on from spring 2003 – coinciding closely with the resolution of the second Iraq war – has been uncharacteristically lacking in volatility. This is evident from the low readings of the CBOE Volatility index (^VIX) but also from observing the day to day (and intraday) fluctuations of the actual S&P 500 index.

To demonstrate the issue we have created cumulative frequency curves[7] showing the incidence of certain intraday fluctuation levels for two periods initially. The first period extends from January 1985 to March 31st 2003 and the second period extends from April 1st 2003 to the end of 2005. As can be seen from Figure 6.12, across the whole spectrum of intraday fluctuation levels, the post-April 2003 period has been consistently less volatile.

Further evidence for this conclusion is provided by examining the value for the frequency distribution at different quantiles as shown in Table 6.3.

Arguments have been proposed that this is not in itself remarkable since it followed on from a period from the beginning of 2000 until the time of the Iraq invasion when the markets had endured a prolonged period of turbulence associated with the collapse of the NASDAQ and the forced selling and partial capitulation by many institutional asset managers in late 2002 and early 2003. To highlight this possibility we have focused only on the 2000–2005 period

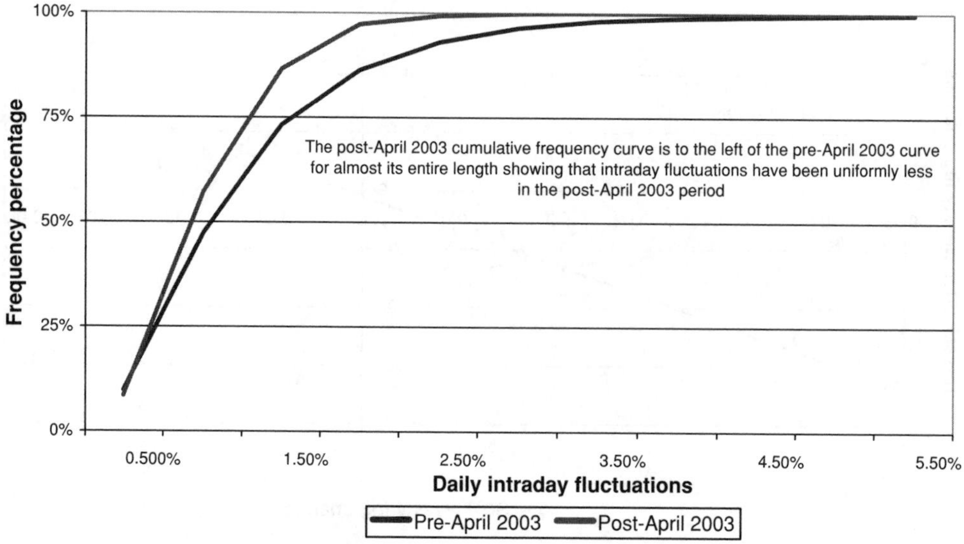

Figure 6.12 S&P 500 intraday volatility before and after April 2003 (cumulative frequency curve of intraday percentage fluctuations)

and divided the before and after periods as of the end of March 2003. Figure 6.13 shows how the frequency for the intraday fluctuations stacks up for the two time periods.

The longer solid columns on the left-hand side of Figure 6.13 show that the post-2003 period is more characteristically one of relatively low intraday volatility. In fact, it can be seen from the figure that the second column from the left contains almost 50% of all of the intraday fluctuations during the post-2003 period, and that this lies between 0.5% and 1%. Moving across the horizontal axis from left to right, it can be observed that the size of the patterned columns increases significantly in relation to the solid columns. For the pre-2003 period, 25% of the sessions show an intraday fluctuation between 2% and 2.5% whereas the corresponding value for the post-2003 period was just 10%. Also evident in Figure 6.13 is the fact that since April 2003 fluctuations of more than 3% have become almost nonexistent, whereas they clearly did arise in the pre-2003 period.

The drop in volatility in the post-April 2003 period can also be demonstrated most strikingly in Figure 6.14. The cumulative frequency curve for the post-April 2003 period lies substantially to the left of the 2000–2003 cumulative frequency curve. At the upper quartile value (i.e. the value where the cumulative frequency curve has subsumed 75% of the returns values) the difference is quite striking. For the 2000–2003 period the 75 percentile value for the

Table 6.3 S & P 500 volatility for upper quartile

Pre-2003	Upper quartile	1.55%
Post-2003	Upper quartile	1.33%
Pre-2003	Upper decile	2.22%
Post-2003	Upper decile	1.74%

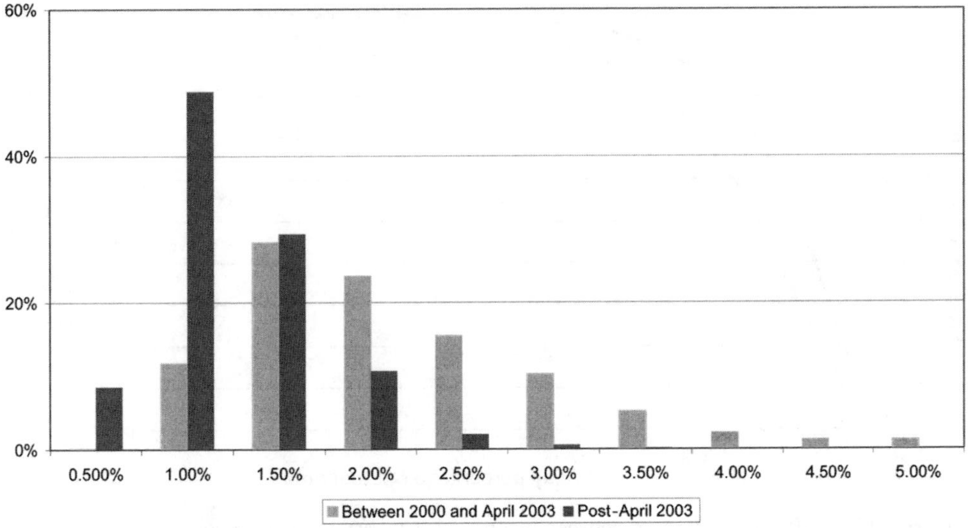

Figure 6.13 S&P 500 comparison of intraday fluctuations from January 2000 to March 2003 and April 2003 to end of 2005

distribution is 2.32% showing that 25% of the intraday fluctuations exceeded this amount whereas the upper quartile value for the post-April 2003 period the equivalent value is 1.24% indicating that only 25% of the intraday fluctuations in the later period exceeded this amount. This is quite a striking difference between the two periods and is well illustrated using the cumulative frequency curves or ogives.[8]

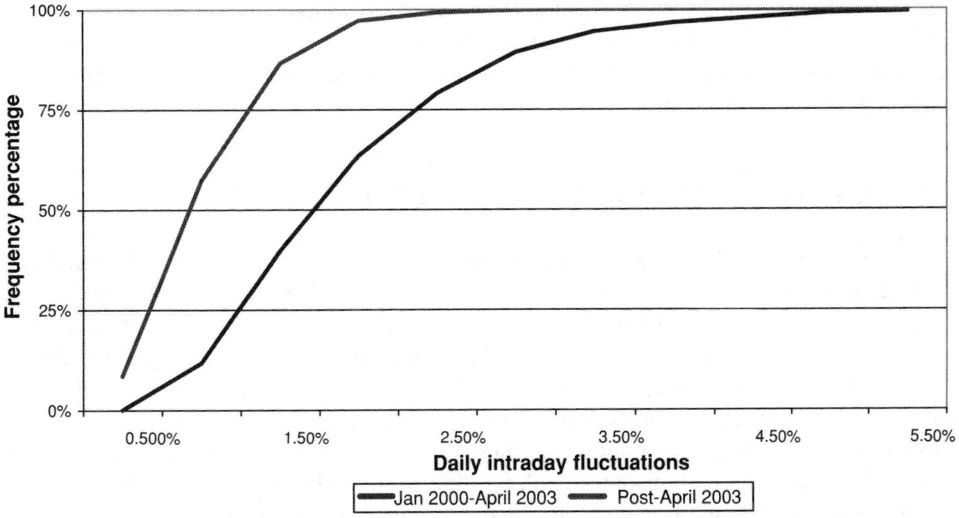

Figure 6.14 S&P 500 two period comparison of intraday volatility from January 2000 to April 2003 and April 2003 to December 2005 (cumulative frequency curve of intraday percentage fluctuations)

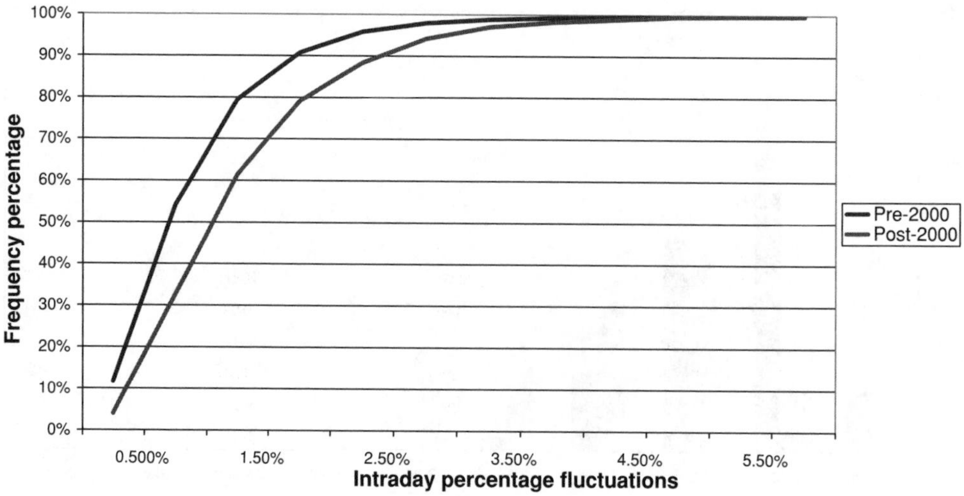

Figure 6.15 S&P 500 comparison between two periods contrasting intraday volatility from January 1985 to end of 1999 and January 2000 to end of 2005 (cumulative frequency curve of intraday fluctuations)

From analyzing the data with the benefit of the cumulative frequency graphs we believe that it can certainly be inferred that the first three years of the new millennium were a lot more volatile than the next three years. But how does the post-2000 period compare to the pre-2000 period? Taking the much longer period of January 1985–December 31st 1999 as our comparison benchmark we can now see that the post-2000 era has been uniformly more volatile than the earlier period across the whole spectrum of daily observed fluctuations.

Figure 6.15 again allows us to focus on the upper quartile value for each of the two periods as a useful benchmark for comparison purposes. In the pre-2000 period if we move up the vertical axis to the 75% level and then move across to the cumulative frequency curve for this period we can see by reading off the value vertically below on the *x*-axis that 25% of the intraday fluctuations were in excess of 1.38%. Performing the same operation for the post-2000 period this had jumped to almost 1.9%.

INCREASES IN RUSSELL 2000 INDEX VOLATILITY

It has already been noted that there are some distinctive properties for the Russell 2000 small cap index regarding its volatility signature and there is evidence that unlike for the S&P 500 index, the small cap index has become more volatile since the beginning of the new millennium than it was during the 1990s. Figure 6.16, applies the cumulative frequency charting techniques to illustrate this tendency towards greater volatility. Looking initially at the cumulative frequency line for the pre-2000 daily returns as we move across the horizontal axis we see that the line becomes steeper indicating that more and more of the daily returns have been subsumed by or included within the accumulating total. Starting from the left-hand side of the chart and moving across to the right (i.e. with progressively higher values on the horizontal axis), the fact that we reach all values on the pre-2000 line much sooner than we do for the post-2000 line shows that the post-2000 returns are uniformly more volatile.

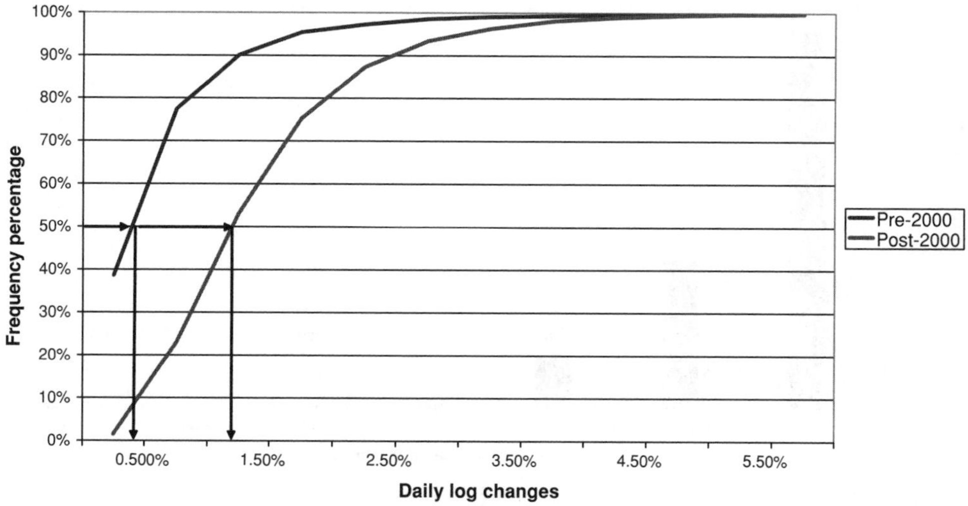

Figure 6.16 Russell 2000 contrast between volatility pre-2000 and post-2000 (cumulative frequency curve and daily log changes)

The median value for the pre-2000 period is 0.63% and the median value for the post-2000 period is more than twice as much at 1.4%. The upper quartile value (the 75%) value reveals a similar disparity with 75% of the daily volatility for the pre 2000 period falling below 1% whereas for the post-2000 period we need to move to 1.95% to cover 75% of the values.

If we were to focus on just the daily fluctuations that exceed 2% we can plot the percentages that these frequencies have with respect to the overall total counts for both the pre-and post-2000 periods. What should be immediately clear from Figure 6.17 is the limited amount of pre-2000 data that is actually displayed on the chart.

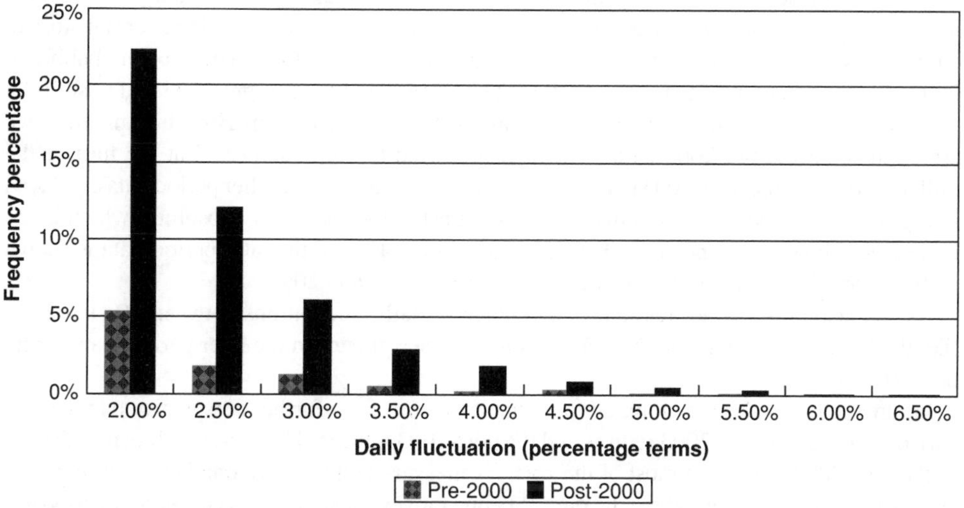

Figure 6.17 Russell 2000 comparison between large daily fluctuations pre-2000 and post-2000 (first value on left excludes changes below 2%)

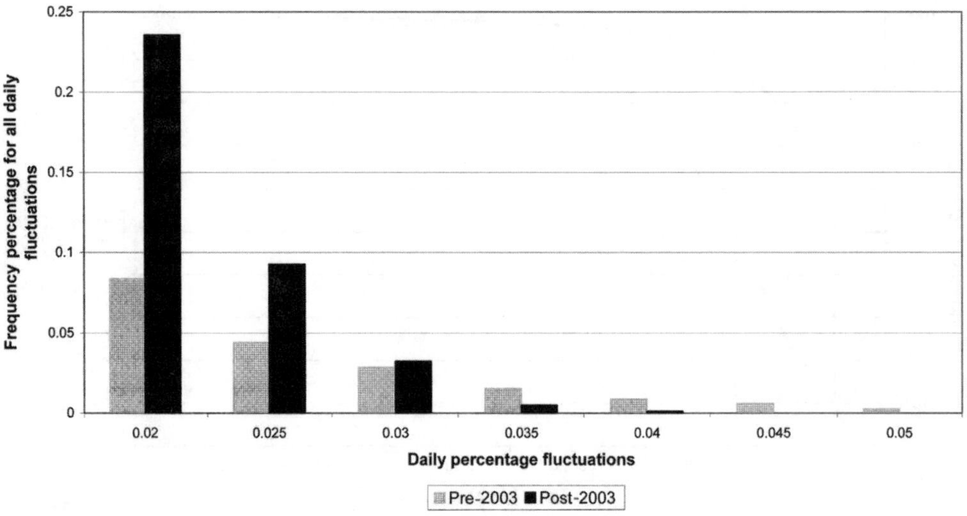

Figure 6.18 Russell 2000 comparison between large daily fluctuations pre-2003 and post-2003 (first value on left excludes changes below 2%)

Moving across the chart and observing the sizes of the patterned columns we can see that most of the returns data has been omitted from display because it falls below the threshold value of an absolute 2% fluctuation. This is confirmed by the fact that during the pre-2000 period only 10% of the daily fluctuations were in excess of 2% whereas in the post-2000 period this has risen to 47%. This is quite an extraordinary difference. Even if we take the columns at x-axis interval between 2% and 2.5% as the magnitude of the daily fluctuation we can see that for the pre-2000 data only 5% of the sessions fit within this interval whereas for the post-2000 data this is almost 25% of the sessions. So the story for the small caps is that they have become dramatically more volatile since 2000, but as we have observed from the long-term historical charts the smaller caps did get pretty badly roughed up during the bursting of the bubble in 2000–2002. So perhaps we need to confine the comparison between pre-2003 and post-2003.

Figure 6.18 follows the same procedure as for the previous comparison but this time we are contrasting the pre-2003 data (which includes the tumultuous period at the turn of the millennium) with the post-2003 period. As before there is a lot less earlier period data displayed in Figure 6.18 as the data also falls below the threshold value of 2% (absolute) which is the first value shown on the horizontal axis. In fact almost 40% of the later period data is shown on the chart whereas the figure for the later period is less than 20%.

As can also be seen the frequency percentage of daily fluctuations between 2% and 2.5% (i.e. the left most columns on the x-axis) is three times greater in the later period than during the earlier period.

Figure 6.19 provides the cumulative frequency curves for a further perspective on the comparison between the pre-2003 returns and the post-2003 returns. The pre-2003 line is to the left of the post-2003 line along most of the x values measured on the horizontal axis but there is a crossover at the 90% level where the pre-2003 line moves ahead. Because the earlier period has almost 10 times as many trading sessions it is to be expected that there will be more "outlier" events in the earlier period and this is what is observed. As of the time of writing, there have since 2003 been no six sigma events[9] (i.e. events that exceed minus three standard deviations

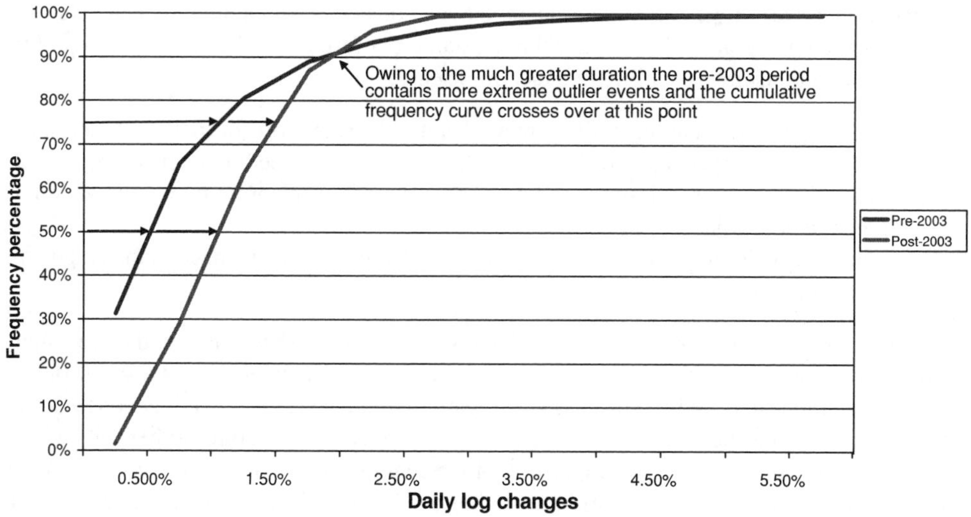

Figure 6.19 Russell 2000 contrast between volatility pre-2003 and post-2003 (cumulative frequency curve and daily log changes)

or plus three standard deviations) in the daily fluctuations of the Russell 2000 but for all daily fluctuations below 2.5% the post-2003 period is again showing relatively more volatility than for the pre-2003 period.

While the S&P 500 has been declining very significantly in volatility since 2003 the small capitalization stocks have been increasing in volatility. This is more remarkable in that during the three year subperiod of 2000–2002 the small cap index encountered its most turbulent period. One final statistic is worth pointing out – in the pre-2003 period the Russell 2000 experienced daily fluctuations greater than 2% on 19% of all of that period's trading days. In the post-2003 period the small cap has experienced daily fluctuations greater than 2% on 37% of all of that period's trading days. The story of the Russell 2000 index from the fall of Saddam Hussein until the summer of 2006 is that stellar returns and a succession of new all time highs for the index were accompanied by far greater intraday volatility.

HOW DOES ALGORITHMIC TRADING AFFECT VOLATILITY

We have discussed the growing adoption by institutional asset managers of algorithmic trading platforms. Order flow is increasingly being "sliced and diced" by different algorithms that focus on the distribution of transaction sizes that are sent to the electronic order books so as to mitigate the effects of large block trades. What are the consequences that these new platforms, which account for an ever increasing amount of trading volume, will have with respect to volatility? Do they increase or decrease the velocity of trading and if so does this make markets more or less liquid?

Advocates of algorithmic trading have claimed that one of the benefits of the execution technique that the approach uses is to provide additional depth to electronic order books. There will be more tiers at the micro-structural level to the organization of the limit orders and therefore it will be less likely to encounter pockets of illiquidity.

If we summarize our general findings about the relationship between liquidity and volatility as follows it could be argued that algorithmic trading platforms may be enhancing liquidity and therefore diminishing volatility in a localized sense:

- Volatility arises because, at different market horizons, in terms of trader's time frames of reference, supply at an available and executable price exceeds demand or vice versa.
- Volatility is greater or less depending on the "depth" of the order book relative to the size of a new order.
- The volatility of a security is a function of the depth of the order back in the neighborhood of interest.

What do we mean by the neighborhood of interest? This must surely relate to the prevailing view of "fair" or "best" price which is clearly very context dependent. If, as a result of the kinds of conditions that we have discussed in regard to trend days, the prevailing consensus is abruptly transformed and traders begin to reach more uniform views about another level which constitutes "fair" price (perhaps the retesting of a recent major low or the 200 day EMA) the depth that has been supplied by algorithmic trading platforms at the previous estimation of fair price will rapidly evaporate.

When market conditions change abruptly or it becomes obvious that traders want to move to another price neighborhood for conducting transactions, the tier of orders that may previously have been registering as limit orders or even market orders will rapidly disappear from the order books. Accordingly the focus for the algorithmic platforms will perhaps have a tendency to be hyperreactive to changes in the current "locale" for price execution and may exhibit a tendency to either freeze liquidity in certain locales or jump quite abruptly to new potential locales. In such circumstances the argument that is made for greater liquidity becomes suspect and there may even be a tendency for these new execution strategies to accentuate the coherent dynamics of trend days producing even more acceleration of the range expansion that traders are exploring.

BUY WRITE STRATEGIES AND VOLATILITY PREMIUMS

The period of quiescence that can be seen on the charts for both the S&P 500 and the CBOE Volatility index from the spring of 2003 more or less intact until the spring of 2006 has encouraged some commentators to believe that the market may have entered a new secular period of low volatility. Some of these same commentators and analysts will go on to claim that this more benign market environment (not all traders desire a more benign volatility environment, however) is a by-product of the financial engineering innovations that are taking place at a gathering pace in the capital markets. As just discussed, one of the alleged benefits of the burgeoning adoption of algorithmic trading platforms is that it contributes to greater market liquidity and therefore plays a part in reducing market volatility.

Claims are also made that the proliferation of long/short strategies and hedging techniques that are predicated on derivatives have the effect of dampening volatility and we are sympathetic to the first part of this claim. As we shall see towards the end of this chapter if a hedge fund manager is running a market neutral strategy or a net short fund in what sense can she be said to revealing fear when the market suffers an unexpected downturn? Perhaps the traditional notions that align the volatility index with fear and anxiety need to be recast in a market where many players are positioned to benefit from sell-offs and market crises.

There is a further factor that needs to be considered in the context of the market's reduced volatility which is the much greater supply of traders that are willing to sell or go short volatility. In other words there has been a substantial increase, in the wake of the major correction in the equity markets during the 2000–2002 period, of the number of institutional investors that are engaging in buy – write option strategies and even sellers of options based on more complex strategies known as dispersion trading. To set the background for this examination we would like to address again the remarkable decline in the implied volatility revealed by the CBOE Volatility index in the period following the beginning of the second Iraq war in March 2003 and extending into the early part of 2006.

Figure 6.20 shows the weekly values of the VIX since the end of 2002. The first thing to notice is the extraordinarily high levels of the VIX that are evident on the far left-hand side of the chart in the last quarter of 2002. As discussed earlier this coincides with the nadir of the S&P 500 in the post-millennium collapse (semantically it was not a "crash" as it extended over a two year period but it was far more severe than the 1987 episode that everyone thinks of in connection with a "crash"). To provide the necessary context a quick skim through the bubble years is in order.

Irrational exuberance saw the NASDAQ index move above 5000 in early 2000 and dot com companies with no revenues were routinely valued more highly than established businesses with sales and profits. The late 1990s were a fabulous time to have been a recent graduate of Stanford University's computer science department, a venture capitalist on the adjacent campuses to Stanford (and of course other universities) and a purveyor of software and hardware designed to prevent businesses grinding to a halt (and planes falling out of the sky) on January 1st 2000. But it had to end and it was not too early in the new millennium that it all began to unravel. The NASDAQ saw its largest one day plunge in March 2000. Y2K mania had come and gone, venture capitalists had realized most of their gains, the lock-ups on a number of late 1990's IPOs had run their course and there were far too many day traders who thought they had a hot hand by being on the long side of a raging bull market.

The bubble went into a protracted burst and in turn the fall-out was exacerbated by the events of 9/11, the investigations into illicit practices in the securities industry, the debacles involving Enron, Worldcom etc., lurid stories of double dealing and six thousand dollar shower curtains[10] and so much more left a major hangover for the world's financiers. The Federal Reserve had no option but to mount a major rescue operation with short-term interest rates to be set at historic lows of 1% (in effect a negative return on cash as inflation was higher than this). Another concern was the impending Iraq war in late 2002 as the political and diplomatic maneuvering unnerved the markets far more than the eventual hostilities. Major institutional investors, demonstrating their propensity for *occasional lapses* in market timing, were big sellers in late 2002 and early 2003 as the gloom mounted. On both sides of the Atlantic there were rumors of pension funds and insurance companies failing. This was time for some major asset reallocation. Major portfolio liquidations were taking place as custodians of pension fund assets sold out of the big tech stocks that they had seen crumble in the first two years of the millennium, some of them with 95% losses.

With hindsight, early 2003 was the very worst time to be liquidating stock portfolios and the very best time to be putting new money to work in stocks. But it would take another few thousand points on the Dow before many money managers were willing to believe it. In the meantime many portfolio managers faced with declining equity prices and historic low income from the Treasury market had dusted off an option writing strategy that had almost become obsolete during the raging bull market of the late 1990s.

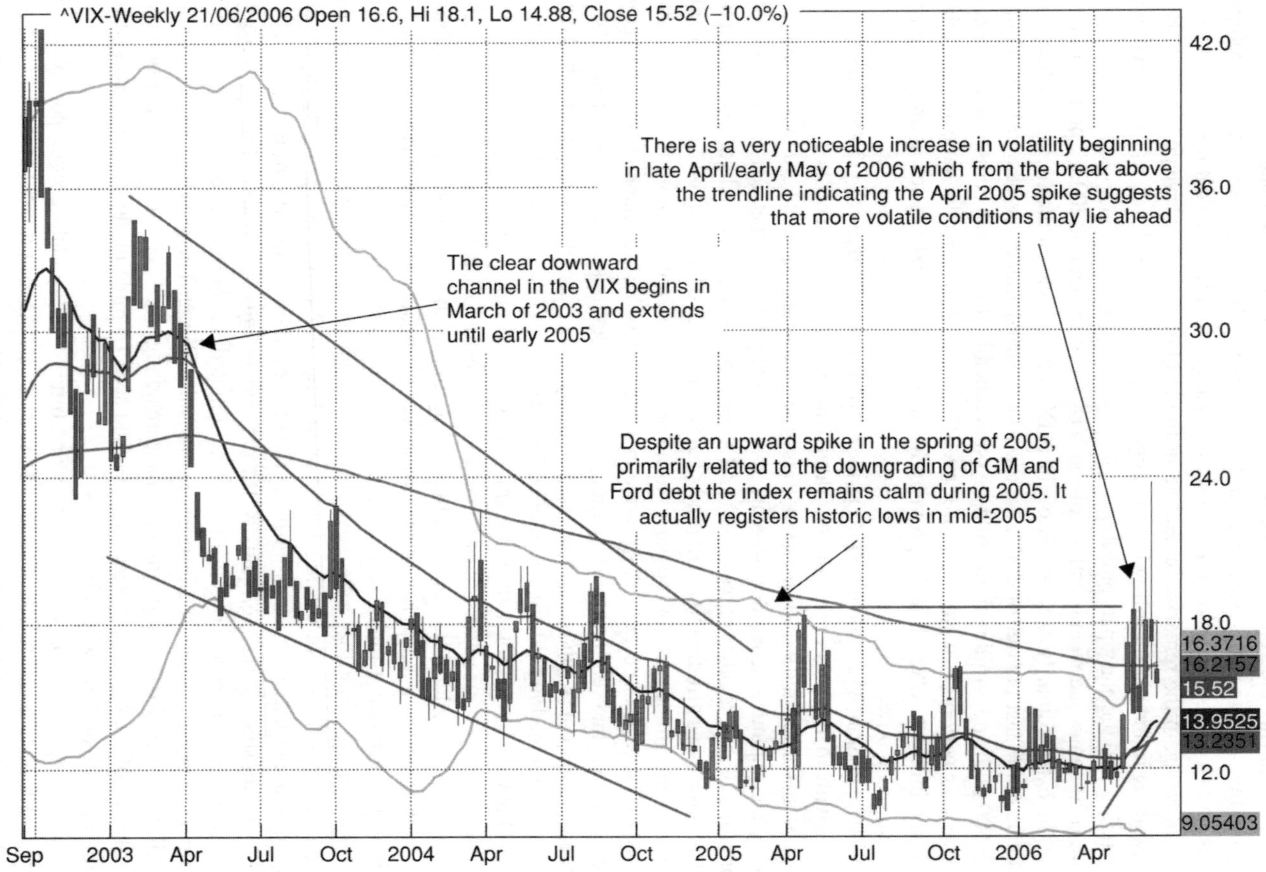
^VIX-Weekly 21/06/2006 Open 16.6, Hi 18.1, Lo 14.88, Close 15.52 (–10.0%)
There is a very noticeable increase in volatility beginning in late April/early May of 2006 which from the break above the trendline indicating the April 2005 spike suggests that more volatile conditions may lie ahead
The clear downward channel in the VIX begins in March of 2003 and extends until early 2005
Despite an upward spike in the spring of 2005, primarily related to the downgrading of GM and Ford debt the index remains calm during 2005. It actually registers historic lows in mid-2005
42.0
36.0
30.0
24.0
18.0
16.3716
16.2157
15.52
13.9525
13.2351
12.0
9.05403
Sep
2003
Apr
Jul
Oct
2004
Apr
Jul
Oct
2005
Apr
Jul
Oct
2006
Apr

Figure 6.20 VIX weekly since 2003

Let us examine this buy – write strategy. The central idea is to be long a portfolio, preferably one that matches closely to an index and then sell calls that are slightly out of the money on the index itself. The principal benefit of the strategy is that one is able to take in as income the premium on the calls and only if the market puts in a good performance would one have the stocks called away. In a downward or sideways market the strategy works well enough producing a more consistent return than just being long the stocks since there is also the premium income to supplement whatever dividend income there may be from the stocks. During a runaway bull market the strategy does not look so clever because the endless upward climb of the indices meant that the stocks would be called away and rather than enjoying upside capital appreciation surprises one would be looking at the relatively meager income from the call premiums.

Portfolio managers, including a number of the major investment banks, were taking the view from late 2002 onwards that there was a limited chance of major upside surprises, and increasingly they were keen to sell calls against their long holdings. As in any market where there is excessive supply the price, in this case the time premium that is a major component of the option price, will be under downward pressure. Major institutional investors such as pension funds and insurance companies had become big players in the options markets not as buyers but as writers. They were showing a much greater propensity to diversify their strategies as they could not rely solely on capital appreciation to realize positive returns.

On the other side of the equation, the scares that caused interest in puts to rise were not as frequent as the market pulled out of the doldrums in mid-2003. Moreover, because of the growing adoption of alternative asset management strategies exemplified by hedge funds there were enough players in the market with net short exposure or long/short stock and option strategies to ensure that there was a commensurate availability of puts at subdued premium prices.

So, to properly address the possibility that volatility is in secular decline we need to take account of the structural changes that have taken place in the markets during the period under review. We also need to consider that the recent renewed interest in buy – write strategies may be a passing phenomenon. As fixed income instruments yield more than inflation again there will be less reliance on generating income from the options market.

Furthermore the options market, which has always been a somewhat arcane and mathematically sophisticated market, has become even less frequented by retail investors in recent years compared to the 1990s. The volatility index (^VIX) measures the implied volatility in the S&P 500 index options; it reflects the amount of the extrinsic value (as opposed to the intrinsic value) that is being charged in the index options. While the sentiment will change in response to market scares, and premiums will ratchet up and down in sympathy with sell-offs and rallies, the underlying supply conditions had changed quite profoundly from the late 1990s when buy – write strategies were out of vogue and market makers in options had to encourage supply by pricing premiums more attractively. But these supply conditions are themselves a response to a certain kind of market environment and subject to change.

The financial engineering community have ushered in massive and wide ranging structural changes in the market's recent history but the claims that these innovations have produced more benign volatility conditions for financial markets is a claim too far.

PROBLEMS IN INTERPRETING THE VOLATILITY INDEX

As we have seen the CBOE Volatility index VIX measures market expectations of near-term volatility and this is directly reflected in the premiums that traders and investors are willing to pay. Since volatility often signifies financial turbulence, VIX is often referred to as the "investor fear gage". There is a clearly observed historical trend that during periods of financial stress, which are often accompanied by steep market declines, option prices – and therefore the VIX – tend to rise. From this one can begin to see that many traders and market analysts have formulated (at least subliminally) an expectation that there is a fairly simple (linear) relationship between fear and high VIX readings and complacency and low VIX readings. This "rule of thumb" is supported by macro behavior. When there are shocks or during periods of severe declines the long only fund manager will be keen to pay for protective put insurance and during periods of tranquillity when prices are essentially stable or moving upwards there will be far less willingness to pay for insurance and the VIX premium will fall. This is essentially the theoretical expectation that is well established within many sections of the financial and trading community and in terms of the overall validity of the hypothesis we would find it hard to disagree. But there are some nagging doubts about the validity of the theory in the context of the proliferation of long/short strategies.

How do you measure the fear levels of a hedge fund that specializes in net short strategies when prices are rising? Is there a separate index that captures the alternative asset management philosophy which shuns outright long exposure to markets? The traditional notion tends to simplistically assume that most market players are essentially long the market and their fear levels will rise during times of adversity. But as we have seen this rather simplistic view is not shared by several kinds of players. Those who see rising volatility as an opportunity to sell volatility (i.e. take short positions, especially on puts) will actually act as a counter to the notion that rising volatility will be a positive feedback process. Volatility dispersion strategists[11] and sellers of volatility will create a dampening effect on the premiums paid, especially in the aftermath of a temporary spike in volatility caused by a specific event such as 9/11. Even more significant is the fact that many fund managers are practicing market neutral strategies which means their exposure to adversity is less than for the long only managers (they may not have done their sums right and not be as neutral as they thought but overall they are, probably, more sheltered than a traditional pension fund or mutual fund). Second, there will be a large number of funds and traders that are net short the market and will be prospering from overall market declines and adversity. So, as we have suggested, these fund managers will not be fearful when prices are going down but will actually be more anxious when prices are going up. But their fear is not measured within the VIX calculation or if it is a factor it certainly will not obey the same functional relationship as that assumed by the traditional fear gage hypothesis.

From a larger perspective we think that it clearly can be useful to monitor the VIX charts for clues as to possible market turning points but we would suggest extreme caution in applying any micro analysis of its day to day movements. We want to illustrate the fallacy of overanalyzing the relationship between the S&P 500 index and the VIX from the work of a market commentator who was puzzled in the fall of 2005 by an episode where there was some unusual behavior in the VIX moving down quite decisively without there being an adequate "cause" from any obvious positive action in the S&P 500 index. The actual example comes from a regular commentator to the TradingMarkets.com website and we want to emphasize that our reasons for citing this example are purely to illustrate the kind of linkage that is often assumed between price action in the indices and specifically the S&P 500 and action in the VIX. There is no desire to discredit the author or the website (both of whom are worthy of the reader's attention) but simply to draw out erroneous logic in the reasoning within the article.

We shall quote from the article because we believe that the author is expressing quite lucidly the assumptions and mental "model" that are shared by many active traders and market commentators:

> I believe the market action on Friday was so unusual that it should be noted. The market had been oversold on a price basis and sentiment gauges like the VIX had been showing relatively extreme fear for several days, so a bounce was bound to occur. What was so unusual was the weakness of the bounce combined with the strong sell-off in the VIX.
>
> As a quick refresher, the VIX is a measure of the implied volatility of S&P options. A rising VIX is an indication of fear among options traders, while a falling VIX can be an indication of complacency. Much of the time a chart of the VIX will look like a mirror image of an S&P 500 chart. This is because fear levels tend to rise when the market sells off and lessen during an uptrend. Past studies have shown that when there are sharp spikes in the VIX, this often leads to a short-term rise in the market. The study I showed in last Wednesday's column used a 10-day moving average in looking at the relative level of the VIX. As we saw then, when the VIX gets substantially stretched above its 10-day moving average, there is a high likelihood of a bounce.
>
> Now back to Friday's unusual action. Here's what occurred. The market bounced, which was expected, but the bounce was weak. The S&P 500 didn't even gain 1%. Meanwhile, the VIX, which closed Thursday more than 12% above its 10-day moving average, dropped so sharply that it closed Friday below its 10-day moving average. In other words, it took just a very small move for people to lose their fear of the market.

As a market historian the author of the article then checked the following hypothesis against the historical data:

- The VIX closed yesterday at least 5% above its 10 day moving average.
- The VIX closed today below its moving average.
- The S&P 500 gained less than 1% today.

He found that these three conditions had occurred 38 times since the VIX was established. The results were as follows: 23 of those 38 times (61%) the market was trading lower two weeks later. He calculated the returns to the trader who went short as a result of the unusual coincidence of factors that he cited and claims that "Gross profits from shorting would have been more than twice the amount of the gross losses." He concludes his analysis with this conclusion: "These results helped to confirm my belief. The quick move south by the VIX helps put this bounce very much in doubt."

What makes the example so interesting is not that the author's forecast at the end of his commentary was wrong (it was) but his timing was also especially unfortunate. In mid-October 2005 the market was actually at an important inflection point and was about to begin a sizable rally. The S&P 500 experienced a major reversal formation on October 19th/20th where the index touched lows around 1170 and then forged ahead to achieve intraday highs just prior to Thanksgiving 2005 (less than six weeks later) almost 100 points higher.

What can be concluded from this detour other than that it is extremely ungracious to point out the erroneous conclusions of a fellow market commentator. What we suggest is that the traditional notion that there is a simple causal relationship between the zigs and zags of the VIX and the zigs and zags of the S&P 500 index are no longer valid. There are too many complex trading strategies and alternative agendas to the traditional notion of investors sitting with portfolios of only long positions. For this reason we suggest that one has to be increasingly skeptical of the premises that are presupposed by the VIX as fear gauge argument, and, at least in relation to short-term market movements, the VIX as fear gauge hypothesis has moved beyond its sell-by date.

7 The Morphology of Gaps

When you find one gap you are likely to find another soon afterwards.

Discontinuities in price behavior or "gaps" are one of the most intimidating characteristics of financial markets. Gaps or discontinuities arise because, and this is not properly acknowledged in academic texts on financial markets, price does not follow a trajectory in the same way that physical objects move continuously through spatial dimensions. We can plot the points that an apple falls from a tree in a three-dimensional Cartesian space with 3D coordinates showing at all times the position occupied by the apple at each fleeting interval during its fall. If the fall of an apple is recorded on film with the samplings of the spatial trajectory taking place at 24 frames per second we can replay the fall either forwards or backwards and reconstruct the continuous original motion or path of the fall.

Although price can be mapped into two- or even three-dimensional graphical surfaces to depict the movement of price "through" time, there will be discontinuities in the path of movement. Price does not literally move through time; rather it is sampled at different moments and we use the metaphor of a path to show its movement. To go back to the example of the film of the apple falling, the discontinuities in price would be analogous to examining the frames from one to the next and finding that the apple had disappeared. In other words discrete samplings of the "movement" of price will often contain no information as to the path followed. The problem has nothing to do with the granularity of the sampling technique but rather the fact that price does not have a physical existence within space and therefore does not have to obey the laws of physics. Leaving aside the issues of quantum particles, physical objects do not disappear from one spatial neighborhood at one instant only to reappear at the next instant in a completely different position, but prices often do. In other words "gaps" shatter the myth of price trajectories.

Let us now review some of the different notions about gaps to be found in the technical analysis literature. This is in no way intended to be a comprehensive summary but rather an overview that will allow us to dig out some less widely commented on features of price discontinuities. Several different kinds of gaps have been identified including breakaway gaps, common gaps and exhaustion gaps, but from a purely geometric perspective (i.e. how do they look on a chart) there are some basic common properties which are revealed by all gap events. Gaps occur when the lowest price traded is above the high of the previous day or, conversely,

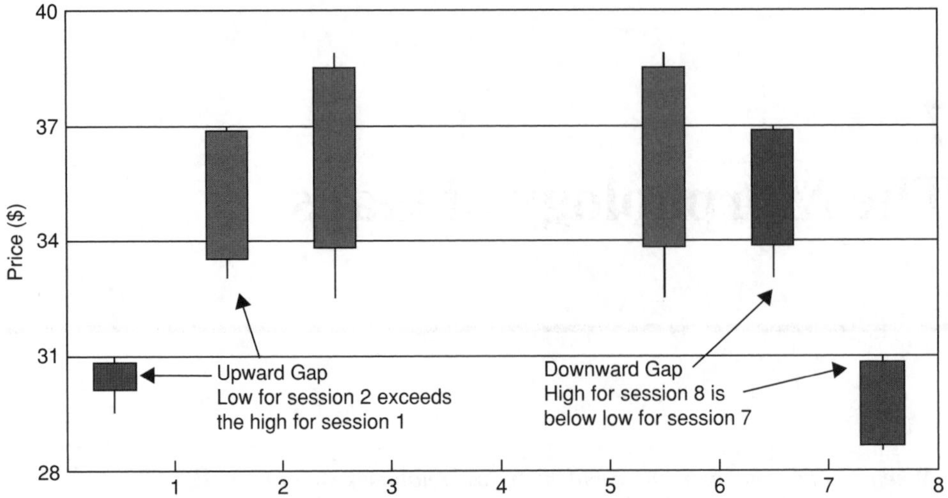

Figure 7.1 Simple illustration of price gaps

when the highest price traded is below the previous day's low. They can be simply illustrated as in Figure 7.1.

We want to take a slightly different approach and examine the phenomenon from the point of view of an *opening price break* which can be set to different thresholds and then we can classify the ensuing action as one that either leaves an actual price gap at the end of the day or one that does not. So in terms of the previous diagram not all of the gaps that we shall be considering will actually show the interval remaining unfilled at the end of the session. They will all begin with an interval but this could be filled in during the current session.

To clarify the distinction further the following definitions will be followed during the remainder of this chapter.

OPENING PRICE GAPS

A *bullish opening price gap* can be identified in connection with a threshold parameter. For example, at the 2% threshold, we can say that there is a bullish opening price gap when the opening price for the current session is at least 2% above the close for the previous session *and* the opening price is above the previous high.

A *bearish opening price gap* can be identified in connection with a threshold parameter. For example, at the 2% threshold, we can say that there is a bearish opening price gap when the opening price for the current session is at least 2% below the close for the previous session *and* the opening price is below the previous low.

OPENING PRICE BREAKS

A *bullish opening price break* can be identified in connection with a threshold parameter. For example, at the 2% threshold, we can say that there is a bullish opening price break when the opening price for the current session is at least 2% above the close for the previous session.

A *bearish opening price break* can be identified in connection with a threshold parameter. For example, at the 2% threshold, we can say that there is a bearish opening price break when the opening price for the current session is at least 2% below the close for the previous session.

In order to get a high level overview of the matter we shall initially compare two instruments, one focus will be on Qualcomm (QCOM) as it is fairly representative of a volatile NASDAQ 100 stock, and the other will be on SPY the SPDR trust proxy for the S&P 500. We have chosen a very similar period to review both stocks which covers the period of trading for QCOM which begins in 1993.

Between September 1993 and June 2006 QCOM has experienced an upward price gap on 3.6% of the total trading occasions and a downward price gap on 2.5% of the trading sessions. During exactly the same period SPY has seen upward gaps in 4.7% of the total sessions and downward gaps in 2.6% of the sessions. So there has been a price gap in 6.1% of the trading for QCOM and 7.3% of the trading for SPY. How can we make sense of that comparison? Does it suggest that the broad-based market index is somehow more erratic in its price behavior than a stock which has both a high beta and a high volatility rating?

We would suggest that it is precisely because the questions reflect the counterintuitive nature of the observed gaps that there is a lot more to gap analysis than might first seem apparent. The fact that a gap is left on the chart does not tell us much about the intraday activity of a stock which may, for example, have a tendency to frequently "break away" in price terms from the previous trading session, but which then subsequently fills in the break leaving a long range bar rather than the eye catching price "gap".

What explains this pseudo-dichotomy is that whereas the opening gap leads to the potential for an "unfilled" gap to exist on the chart there is a strong tendency for intraday volatility to push the boundary prices back within the range of the previous day's range. This is why it can be argued that stocks that show more intraday volatility, such as QCOM, are less likely to record frequent true gap events than those which may have a relatively high degree of inter day volatility but a lower degree of intraday volatility (such as SPY).

Let us now consider the following table which reveals the frequency of true gaps for a universe of 500 stocks which are among the most liquid stocks traded in the U.S. markets.[1] The observations cover true gaps and the magnitudes of the gaps have been shown in the table at two levels for both the upside gaps and the downside gaps. The table also reveals the frequencies expressed from the average values and median values taken from the 500 stocks. The average values will be more influenced by outliers and the median values could be claimed to be the most typical.

Overnight Gaps	>2%	>4%	<−2%	<−4%
AVG	3.6%	2%	2.9%	1.5%
Median	2.9%	0.9%	2.3%	0.8%

As is clear the incidence of large gaps at the $\pm$4% level is very low. Using the median value these events will occur in less than 1% of the trading. At the 2% level, for the typical stock in our universe of 500 (median value), the frequency of gaps of plus or minus is also relatively low with a combined frequency of just 5.2%. On the basis of this historical analysis covering more than 20 years of data for many securities the conclusion that can be reached is that true gap events are uncommon at the 2% level and become only a peripheral concern for trading purposes beyond that level. As will be seen there are far more occurrences to consider when we consider opening price breaks which have less exacting conditions.

OVERNIGHT PRICE BREAKS – A VERY SIMPLE MEASUREMENT OF RISK

In the scanning analysis that follows the criterion that we will use is to screen for opening price breaks only. This does not mean that price gaps will not be included as some of those sessions that begin with a price break will be followed by intraday trading activity which leaves a true price gap at the end of the session and some will not. Our reason for approaching the topic in this manner is because we feel that this most clearly reflects the interest of the trader. To be concrete, if one is holding a long position overnight and there is a *bearish opening price break* this poses immediate decisions for the trader which at the time they occur will not contain any information as to whether or not the session will register a true price gap. In fact depending on how one sets one's stops the *bearish opening price break* may already have triggered an exit.

The concept of overnight risk can be best illustrated by examining several stocks and comparing them with a benchmark performance for which we shall use SPY, the SPDR proxy for the S&P 500. We have used the proxy rather than the actual cash index as there are some data reporting issues regarding the cash index in which very frequently some data vendors will report the opening price for the cash index as the same as the previous close. Since it is important for our present purposes that we use a valid opening price that reflects any overnight developments we have decided to use the SPY data. The SPDR Trust is an exchange-traded fund that holds all of the S&P 500 index stocks and its performance matches the actual cash index very closely but as it is a separately traded security from time to time some interesting discrepancies may arise between it and the underlying S&P 500 index. SPY has been trading since September 29th, 1993 which allows us to have (in mid-2006) more than 3000 separate sessions for comparison purposes. In our comparisons we have, in most cases, used securities for comparison that have been trading at least as long as the SPY proxy.

In Table 7.1, the opening price break has been set to 1% so we are looking at those situations where QCOM or SPY has opened either 1% above its previous close or 1% below its previous close. We have calculated the number of occurrences both as a numerical count and also as a percentage of the total number of observations. There were 106 occasions (out of 3360) when the broad index, as represented by SPY, opened 1% higher than the previous close and 97 when it opened 1% lower than the previous close. Taken together these opening price breaks amount to only 6% of the total trading sessions whereas for Qualcomm (QCOM) the total for both kinds of opening breaks was 37.6%. Using a rather simple ratio it could be claimed that there is six times (approximately) more overnight risk associated with holding QCOM than

Table 7.1 Opening price breaks QCOM and SPY

Upward breaks			Downward breaks		
	SPY	QCOM		SPY	QCOM
Gap size	1.00%	1.00%	Gap size	−1.00%	−1.00%
Count	106	712	Count	97	551
Percent	3.1%	21.2%	Percent	2.9%	16.4%
Ratio	6.7		Ratio	5.7	

Table 7.2 Opening price breaks QCOM and SPY greater than 2%

Upward breaks			Downward breaks		
	SPY	QCOM		SPY	QCOM
Gap size	2.00%	2.00%	Gap size	−2.00%	−2.00%
Count	15	298	Count	19	226
Percent	0.4%	8.9%	Percent	0.6%	6.7%
Ratio	19.9		Ratio	11.9	

the broad market. If one is going to hold a position in QCOM overnight, more than one session in three, one would begin the session with a more than 1% jump from the close of the previous trading session. If one was holding the index proxy this kind of jump would take place in only one session in sixteen. Examining the differences between the upward and downward opening price breaks we can see that for both SPY and QCOM these are less frequent than the upward price breaks on the open. Also the ratio for downward breaks is slightly less between the two securities than for the upward price breaks.

Table 7.2 shows the situation when the opening break is expanded to 2% on either side of the previous close and the relative frequency of breaks has become dramatically different. Overall the broad market has experienced (absolute) opening breaks of 2% on only 34 occasions in the survey which covers almost 13 years. For QCOM this figure is 524 occasions, or 15.6% of the trading sessions, which represents an overall ratio with respect to the occurrences for SPY of more than 15:1. There are slightly more downward breaks for SPY and considerably fewer downward breaks for QCOM than upward breaks. The ratios for each show that the possibility of an upside break of more than 2% is almost 20 times more likely for QCOM than for the broad market index.

So that we can sample a few further securities with different characteristics Table 7.3 has the same framework as before and data extending back to 1993 for 3M company (MMM) which is a constituent of the Dow Jones Industrials and a far less volatile stock than QCOM. At the 1% level the percentage of occasions when MMM opens with a break either above that level or below it is slightly more than 10% of the time. There is remarkable symmetry between the upward and downward price breaks with both showing that the degree of overnight risk for MMM is 1.7 times larger than for the broad index alone.

At the 2% level for MMM the opening gaps conditions are met on only 1.9% of the trading sessions as revealed in Table 7.4 and the ratios with the broad market have not risen as dramatically as they did previously for QCOM. With less volatile securities the likelihood of price breaks of greater magnitudes than 1% diminishes rapidly whereas for many of the

Table 7.3 Opening price breaks SPY and MMM

Upward breaks			Downward breaks		
	SPY	MMM		SPY	MMM
Gap size	1.00%	1.00%	Gap size	−1.00%	−1.00%
Count	106	179	Count	97	166
Percent	3.1%	5.3%	Percent	2.9%	4.9%
Ratio	1.7		Ratio	1.7	

Table 7.4 Opening breaks (2%) MMM and SPY

Upward breaks			Downward breaks		
	SPY	MMM		SPY	MMM
Gap size	2.00%	2.00%	Gap size	−2.00%	−2.00%
Count	15	34	Count	19	30
Percent	0.4%	1.0%	Percent	0.6%	0.9%
Ratio	2.3		Ratio	1.6	

more volatile high growth and technology stocks it can be observed that even at the 3% level the number of occurrences can still be substantial. For example, in the case of QCOM when the opening price breaks are at 3% the number of occurrences at this level are almost 8% of the total trading sessions.

The final comparison in this section will be between two proxy securities as we shall continue with the SPY data and contrast this with QQQQ which is the exchange-traded proxy for the NASDAQ 100 stocks. QQQQ has only been trading since March 1999 so there will be fewer data points for the comparison; however, the percentage comparisons will still be meaningful.

When the opening break threshold is set at ±1% as indicated in Table 7.5 the data shows that on a percentage basis QQQQ experiences breaks of such magnitudes almost 24% of the time as compared to the 6% for SPY – providing an overall ratio of 4:1. There is a slight asymmetry between the upward breaks and downward breaks as QQQQ opens more than 1% upwards 12.8% of the time compared to downward breaks 11.1% of the time.

Table 7.6 illustrates the situation when the opening breaks have been increased to the 2% level. The ratios have expanded again more in line with the QCOM/SPY comparison. Opening breaks of more than 2% in absolute terms occur 6.9% of the time for QQQQ which is almost seven times more frequently than for SPY and this jumps to 8.7 times when only the opening gaps upwards are considered.

Returning to the larger-scale analysis of the 500 most liquid US stocks the table below shows the results of scanning for price breaks. As can be seen the frequency is considerably

Overnight price breaks	>2%	>4%	<−2%	<−4%
AVG	6.4%	1.9%	4.9%	1.5%
Median	4.4%	0.9%	3.7%	0.8%

Table 7.5 Opening breaks (1%) QQQQ and SPY

Upward breaks			Downward breaks		
	SPY	QQQQ		SPY	QQQQ
Gap size	1.00%	1.00%	Gap size	−1.00%	−1.00%
Count	106	234	Count	97	202
Percent	3.1%	12.8%	Percent	2.9%	11.1%
Ratio	4.1		Ratio	3.8	

Table 7.6 Opening price breaks (2%) QQQQ and SPY

Upward breaks			Downward breaks		
	SPY	QQQQ		SPY	QQQQ
Gap size	2.00%	2.00%	Gap size	−2.00%	−2.00%
Count	15	71	Count	19	54
Percent	0.4%	3.9%	Percent	0.6%	3.0%
Ratio	8.7		Ratio	5.2	

higher than the comparable table that was produced for true gaps. The median stock is likely to experience a ±2% gap on more than 8% of its trading days (the average performance suggests an even higher incidence). At the ±4% level the frequency of occurrence is still very low with less than 2% of the trading sessions resulting in such a price break. Interestingly the figures that are registered at the ±4% level are identical for opening breaks and opening gaps which intuitively is plausible since a large magnitude opening price break is almost certainly going to satisfy the opening gap criterion as well.

CO-OCCURRENCE OF GAPS

We now want to dig a little deeper and explore the question of gap co-occurrences. In the tables below we have calculated the number of times that an opening price break or an opening price gap (refer back to the beginning of the chapter for exact definitions) with specified magnitudes is associated with another similar directional gap of the same magnitude within a moving five day window. Table 7.7 illustrates the different scenarios with respect to QCOM and the time frames for the observations is the same as in the previous analysis in Table 7.1 (i.e. involves more than three thousand daily trading sessions).

To take as an example it can be seen that an opening price break of more than 2% will be followed by a similar event within five days more than half the time (51%) and an opening price break of more than 3% is followed by a similar event (i.e. another opening price break of more than 3%) more than one third of the time (34%). We now have some specific corroboration for the casual remark that when you see one gap you should expect another. If we now switch to downside opening price breaks there is still a tendency for one to follow another but that it is less probable than in the case of upside opening breaks. At the −3% level an opening price break will be accompanied by another of the same magnitude just less than one quarter of the time.

Table 7.7 QCOM price break and price gap co-occurrences (five day window)

QCOM	Upwards			Downwards		
Description	>1%	>2%	>3%	<−1%	<−2%	<−3%
Opening price break	70.0%	51.0%	34.0%	62.0%	41.0%	23.6%
Opening price gap	39.5%	28.4%	20.0%	29.0%	18.0%	12.5%

Table 7.8 QCOM price break and price gap co-occurrences (10 day window)

QCOM		Upwards			Downwards	
Description	>1%	>2%	>3%	<−1%	<−2%	<−3%
Opening price break	87.5%	71.2%	53.3%	83.9%	64.3%	48.3%
Opening price gap	63.3%	47.9%	33.7%	57.6%	45.3%	39.8%

Let us turn our attention next to the second row which examines opening price gaps. It will be recalled that an opening price gap has to satisfy the slightly more exacting criterion that not only is the price above the breakout threshold but, in the case of an upside price gap, the open must be above the previous day high and for a downside price gap the open must be below the previous low. The more exacting criterion for classification results in fewer opening gaps than opening breaks, and most interestingly even though the occurrence of an opening gap points to a more "abnormal" condition, as can be seen there is less follow-up across the spectrum for opening gaps.

So far we have examined the co-occurrence within a five day window but let us now extend that to a 10 day window to see how the percentages change. It should be emphasized with respect to Table 7.8 that there is a possibility that more than one follow-up event may have arisen within the 10 day window but according to the methodology used this would register as a single event.

There are several noteworthy features of Table 7.8. First, the likelihood of a follow-up has increased substantially across the spectrum for both scenarios – the opening price break and the opening price gap. Most notably the likelihood of a follow-up event in the case of the gaps is dramatically higher. This can be seen for example in relation to a downside opening gap of less than −2% which shows a follow-up 45% of the time within 10 days but only 18% likelihood within five days. Also the asymmetry between the upside and downside follow-ups for opening price breaks is much less noticeable when the time window is extended to 10 days.

In general the high percentages in Table 7.8 support the notion that price breaks and gaps have a tendency to cluster. While the likelihood of a follow-up diminishes in proportion to the magnitude of the break it is still very significant that for an upside break of ±3% there will be a similar follow-up event approximately 50% of the time. For price gaps this falls to the likelihood of a follow-up event occurring approximately one third of the time.

CONVERSE GAPS

As we have been keen to remind the reader gaps and price breaks have a tendency to cluster and the likelihood of follow-ups of similar events in the same direction has been demonstrated. But from a trading perspective a health warning has to be issued. Price breaks and gaps will often be accompanied by similar events but in a *converse direction* to the original impulse. This fits with the intuitions derived from the discussion of volatility, in which large-scale price fluctuations in alternate directions are to observed and to be expected during regimes of higher overall volatility. It should also serve to underline the fact that trading securities that are undergoing breakout patterns can often result in dangerous whipsaws.

Table 7.9 QCOM price break and price gap co-occurrences of contrary event (10 day window)

QCOM	Upwards			Downwards		
Description	>1%	>2%	>3%	<–1%	<–2%	<–3%
Opening price break	57.4%	30.9%	17.3%	67.9%	36.6%	17.5%
Opening price gap	21.9%	16.3%	10.5%	30.2%	11.4%	4.6%

Table 7.9 shows the results of a test for clustering of converse price breaks for QCOM. What has been tracked in this table is the observed frequency of an upward price break being followed by a downward price break (of similar but inverse magnitude) within a 10 session trading window or vice versa. To explain further it will be useful to take a particular instance as an example.

If we have observed a downside price break on the open of less than –2% this has been followed 37% of the time by an upside opening price break of more than +2%. If there has been an upside opening price break of 2% or more this has been followed within 10 days a converse break of the same magnitude in 31% of the cases. For the QCOM observations it can be seen that there was a greater likelihood that downside breaks would lead to converse events than the other way around. Also revealing is the fact that opening gaps in either direction are much less likely than opening breaks to lead to a converse event. In the case of a downside gap exceeding the 3% threshold this has only been followed by an upside gap in less than 5% of the observations.

Two other stocks have been included for comparative purposes in this regard. Table 7.10 shows the comparable percentages for Apple (AAPL) and Table 7.11 illustrates the same situation for Amazon (AMZN).

In general the table for AAPL shows less of a tendency than QCOM across the whole spectrum of cases for converse events to occur. In harmony with the QCOM table there is slightly more of a tendency for downward initial gaps and breaks to be followed by an upside event than the other way around. In examining breaks and gaps of more than 3% for AAPL it can be seen that in less than 10% of the cases will a contrary event be seen.

Table 17.11 illustrates the contrary events for AMZN and generally speaking there is a much higher propensity for opening price breaks to lead to a converse event. For example, an initial downside gap of greater than –2% lead to a converse break upwards in more than 50% of the cases. The behavior following opening gaps is also far more suggestive of a tendency towards producing converse reactions. A downside opening gap of more than –2% produced a converse response on 30% of the cases. Not shown in Table 17.13 are the actual numbers of such events. AMZN experienced an opening downwards gap of more than –2% on 132

Table 7.10 AAPL price break and price gap co-occurrences of contrary event (10 day window)

AAPL	Upwards			Downwards		
Description	>1%	>2%	>3%	<–1%	<–2%	<–3%
Opening price break	40.0%	17.1%	9.9%	49.7%	21.5%	6.7%
Opening price gap	20.3%	10.0%	3.0%	21.5%	9.6%	4.6%

Table 7.11 AMZN price break and price gap co-occurrences of contrary event (10 day window)

AMZN	Upwards			Downwards		
Description	>1%	>2%	>3%	<−1%	<−2%	<−3%
Opening price break	64.5%	37.5%	25.3%	68.3%	52.2%	31.6%
Opening price gap	26.3%	17.9%	14.3%	35.1%	30.3%	20.5%

occasions in the survey which was almost 6% of the total returns examined and on 40 of those occasions an upside opening gap of more than 2% was seen within 10 days.

So far we have relied on just three well-known NASDAQ stocks to provide some background to the discussion. However, we have analyzed a much larger universe of equities to fill out the survey. Using exactly the same approach that we took with QCOM, AAPL and AMZN we examined the opening gap events at the ±2% level for 500 of the most liquid stocks trading in the U.S. markets.[2] The next table shows the median values from all of the individual opening gaps that were found. As can be seen the incidence of gaps of the magnitude described are typically rare (the median values were selected to show the typical behavior) and interestingly for both of the upside and downside gaps the likelihood of converse events is 6%.

Median values	Upside gaps >2%	Downside gaps <−2%
Frequency of occurrence	2.9%	2.3%
Contrary event within 10 days	6.1%	6.2%

Needless to say there are some extreme individual instances that can be found among the stocks examined. For example, JDSU shows a much greater frequency of opening gaps and a very great propensity to produce a converse event after a downside opening gap.

JDSU	Upside gaps >2%	Downside gaps <−2%
Frequency of occurrence	9.3%	6.8%
Contrary event within 10 days	22.0%	34.9%

At the other end of the scale the proxy for the Dow Jones Industrials has produced opening gaps in either direction in only a handful of cases.

DIA	Upside gaps >2%	Downside gaps <−2%
Frequency of occurrence	0.3%	0.4%
Contrary event within 10 days	14.3%	0.0%

Among the stocks showing a tendency towards frequent reversal behavior our analysis yielded several that exhibit regular patterns to produce converse price breaks. One is Dynamic

Materials Corp which trades under the ticker BOOM and we have registered the observations below. There is a consistency between both the frequency of the signs of the gaps and the likelihood of a converse reaction. Traders looking for highly volatile stocks that produce whipsaw behavior will find similar patterns with the following stocks – FDRY, ERES, FRO, NTRI, TZOO and NOK.

BOOM	Upside gaps >2%	Downside gaps <−2%
Frequency of occurrence	13.1%	13.3%
Contrary event within 10 days	40.8%	40.1%

We think that it is fair to summarize these findings with the recommendation that traders would be well advised to screen for overnight price breaks and gaps as they are also a clustering phenomenon. The clustering of price breaks takes on an additional dimension which is that there is a considerable probability that price breaks in both directions will tend to co-occur in close proximity. This provides further warning that in attempting to extract trading rules from this kind of analysis one has to be wary that overnight range expansion may be a precursor to trending behavior and market turning points but it can also be associated with whipsaw activity.

OPENING PRICE BREAKS FOLLOWED BY PRICE REVERSALS

We want to consider now cases where the opening price break pattern has intraday reversal characteristics. We shall identify the upward and downward opening price gaps, but we shall then go on to examine what takes place with respect to the relative positions of the opening and closing price. If the opening price has broken upwards by (say) 2% but the stock then closes below the previous session's close (or vice versa) it could be said to have displayed reversal characteristics.

The following table focuses on opening price breaks set at the ±2% level and the procedure has been designed to track how the stock closes in relation to its opening price. In the case of the upside breaks we are monitoring the situation where the closing price will be below the opening price for the very session when an opening break of greater than 2% has been observed. The median values for the 500 most liquid U.S. stocks have been taken as representative of typical behavior.

Median values	Upside breaks >2%	Downside breaks <−2%
Frequency of occurrence	4.2%	3.5%
Reversal to close above/below open	52.6%	55.3%

The first thing to notice is that typically an opening price break in either direction is rare as it occurs less than 5% of the time for the typical stock. But what is perhaps surprising is the likelihood that the close will represent some kind of intraday reversal as the close is below the opening price after an upside break 53% of the time and the close is above the open following a downside break 55% of the time.

One of the more remarkable findings that emerged from running this scan was the following result for the proxy for the S&P 500, SPY. The frequency of opening price breaks is, not too surprisingly, very low but what is remarkable is that on the occasions when the index opened 2% below the previous close it went on to close above its opening price on 84% of the cases. The downside opening break occurred 19 times out of 3367 separate trading sessions that were monitored and on 16 occasions the price closed above the opening level for that session.

SPY	Upside breaks >2%	Downside breaks <−2%
Frequency of occurrence	0.4%	0.6%
Reversal to close above/below open	46.7%	84.2%

Several stocks produce opening price breaks with much greater frequency than SPY but also reveal a strong tendency towards reversing the day's gains on the close. Pan American Silver (PAAS) is one as the table below shows.

PAAS	Upside breaks >2%	Downside breaks <−2%
Frequency of occurrence	16.6%	10.5%
Reversal to close above/below open	67.8%	61.7%

QQQQ which is the exchange-traded proxy for the NASDAQ 100 index shows less reversal behavior than the median values that we witnessed above and the frequency of gaps in either direction totals almost 7% of the trading sessions.

QQQQ	Upside breaks >2%	Downside breaks <−2%
Frequency of occurrence	3.9%	2.9%
Reversal to close above/below open	42.3%	43.4%

We have spent some time reviewing the evidence of reversals that follow opening price breaks in order to assess the validity of the often repeated claim that "fading" an opening gap is likely to produce a favorable outcome. All of the evidence from our rather simple scans seems to support this in that for the typical stock the price reverses from the opening bias in more than 50% of the cases.

OPENING PRICE BREAKS FOLLOWED BY ADDITIONAL STRENGTH

We have also examined a different scenario to the price reversal or weak closes that we just considered. We scanned the same 500 stocks as before to ascertain the cases where there was an opening price break of ±2% and then we wanted to find whether there was continued strength (or weakness) following the opening price break. The test that was performed checked to see if an opening price break of 2% or more was accompanied by a further uplift from the open to the close of that session of more than 2%. The median value that was achieved from the sample of stocks examined shows that this occurred 23% of the time. The converse situation where the closing price continued downwards by a further 2% or more after a downside price break occurred 20% of the time for the median value. Interestingly there was very little to choose between the median values returned from the scan and the average values.

A rather simple strategy suggests itself that would need quite a lot more exploration before one would want to act on the results of the simple scanning that has been outlined. If price reversals (i.e. where the close is below the open or above the open depending on which direction the break occurs) following price breaks have more than a 50% likelihood but if continuations of another 2% occur about 20% of the time there could be merit in "fading" overnight price breaks with a stop that is 1% removed from the open price that would hopefully have been one's entry point. More aggressive traders might even wish to consider a stop and reverse strategy after price has moved more than 1% away from the open. But as suggested this should be researched further to examine the win/loss ratio from adopting such a strategy and consideration should be given to the characteristics of the stocks that behave most like the median stocks that have emerged from our survey as opposed to the stocks that are nearer to the extremes.

GAPS, BREAKS AND THE INVERSE SQUARE LAW

Power laws will be discussed in considerable detail in Chapter 9 and rather than stealing the thunder from that discussion we want to introduce the subject here by sketching out a simple model to explain the kind of behavior that we have observed in measuring gaps. The incidence of price breaks and gaps appears to follow an inverse square law.

For the purposes of this brief explanatory model assume that your voice has a certain intensity which can be calibrated in the units of some variable such as decibels. The decibels can be quantified as an x value for a person standing, for example, 10 meters away and this distance is now considered as the y value. The question arises – what would be the x value if you increased the y value so that you were now standing 20 meters away from the person? If the voice intensity/distance follows the inverse square power law (which it does) the answer is $\frac{1}{4}$ X. The sound intensity is one quarter of what it was when you were 10 meters away. The situation would be exactly the same if the original distance was increased to 15 meters and we then wanted to track the change in intensity at 30 meters. Again the result would be that the intensity at 30 meters is $\frac{1}{4}$ of what it was at 15 meters. The inverse square law applies regardless of the initial distance, it is said to be scale invariant or the rule applies across all scales. Thus *if you double the distance, the effect will be* $\frac{1}{4}$ *of the initial intensity.*

What do we find from examining the incidence of gaps and breaks in time series data? Remarkably there is a lot of evidence that when we double the magnitude of the gap we find that the frequency diminishes in accordance with the inverse square law. So to take a hypothetical example if we took a gap of magnitude +2% and found that there were 100 occasions (or let's say 10% of our observations) that matched this criterion then we would expect that if we increased the gap size to 4% (i.e. it was doubled from its previous value) the frequency would drop to 25 occasions (or 2.5% of our observations). This can be extended further so that if we double again to testing for gaps of magnitude +8% then we should expect a frequency of only 0.625%.

Table 7.12 KLAC incidence of gaps of different magnitudes

KLAC gaps	Small up gaps	Large up gaps	Small down gaps	Large down gaps
Gap size	1.50%	3.00%	−1.50%	−3.00%
Count	482	126	372	99
Percent	14.5%	3.8%	11.2%	3.0%
Ratio		26%		26%

Table 7.12 shows interesting findings that suggest that an inverse square law appears to arise in connection with the observation of opening gaps for KLAC. The period covered in the table includes more than 3000 daily observations. Table 7.12 shows two sizes for the gaps – small gaps of ±1.5% and the larger gaps of ±3%. The magnitude of the gaps has been doubled and we can then examine whether the relative frequencies will conform to the characteristic required for the aptness of the inverse square description.

In interpreting Table 7.12 we find that opening gaps of +1.5% for KLAC are quite common with 482 occurrences during the time frame from 1993 to May 2006 which represents a 14.5% of the total sessions. With respect to the larger gaps (+3%) there were 126 occurrences which equates to 3.8% of the total. Having doubled the magnitude of the upward gaps the frequency ratio is 0.26 (126/482) which is remarkably close to the expectation from the inverse square law of 0.25. There seems strong prima facie evidence that an inverse square law relationship may be at work here. If we switch to the occurrence of down gaps we find again that there is just as strong evidence of a power law relationship. There were 372 instances where the open was more than 1.5% below the previous close (this would be 11.2% of the time) and 99 instances where the open was more than 3% below the previous close (equivalent to 3% of the time). Again the ratio is 0.26 (i.e. 99/372).

In Table 7.13 for KLAC we have amplified the magnitudes of the gaps slightly and again we still find some evidence pointing to the inverse square law. As we move from 2% upward gaps to 4% upward gaps we have doubled the magnitude and we find that the frequency ratio is now is 0.19 (57/307) and for the downward gaps the ratio is 0.2 (i.e. 49/247). What we are witnessing is the fact that as the magnitude of the gaps increases the power law exponent begins to decay and this is another interesting phenomenon that we shall discuss in Chapter 9.

Lest it be thought that the results we have observed are peculiar to KLAC and untypical we have used the same procedures to examine QCOM data for approximately the same period that we looked at for KLAC with more than 3000 observations.

To quickly summarize the most pertinent features of Table 7.14 we can see that the frequency ratio as we double the gap size for the upward gaps is 78/293 which is equal to 0.26 and equivalently for the downward gaps the ratio is 65/226 or 0.28. In fact QCOM is even more

Table 7.13 KLAC incidence of gaps of different magnitudes

KLAC gaps	Small up gaps	Large up gaps	Small down gaps	Large down gaps
Gap size	2.00%	4.00%	−2.00%	−4.00%
Count	307	57	247	49
Percent	9.2%	1.7%	7.4%	1.5%
Ratio		19%		20%

Table 7.14

QCOM gaps	Small up gaps	Large up gaps	Small down gaps	Large down gaps
Gap size	2.00%	4.00%	−2.00%	−4.00%
Count	293	78	226	65
Percent	8.8%	2.3%	6.8%	2.0%
Ratio		26%		28%

supportive of the inverse square law for gaps of these magnitudes than we observed for KLAC. In terms of clustering the 2% gaps in either direction are followed four times out of five by another similar gap but this drops away, particularly for the downward gaps as the magnitude of the gap increases.

SURVEY OF GAPS FOR MOST LIQUID STOCKS

We have been sufficiently intrigued by our findings regarding the apparent power law relationship matching the magnitude of the gaps to their frequency that we decided to undertake a larger-scale examination of the phenomenon to satisfy ourselves that the data revealed by the two case studies that we have examined, KLAC and QCOM, was not untypical. We used the same universe of 500 stocks that was examined in our previous scans.[3]

The procedure is as follows. The gap sizes were set at ±2% for the smaller gaps and at ±4% for the larger gaps and the gaps were determined based on the opening price versus the previous closing price and may or may not have left true gaps as we have described that term. This is consistent with our previous methodology and also consistent with the point that it is the existence of an overnight price break that is of most concern to the typical trader.

Small breaks ±2% Large breaks ±4%	Ratio of small upside breaks to large	Ratio of small downside breaks to large
Median ratio	4.23	4.06
AVG ratio	5.07	4.83
between 3 and 5	42%	48%

The values contained in the table appear to support the notion that an inverse square law describes the relative frequency of the opening breaks of the two magnitudes. The median ratio for both upside and downside gaps is approximately four which translated into the principles that we noted regarding a power law suggests that as the magnitude doubles the frequency halves. Expressed inversely the ratio of large gaps to smaller gaps would be approximately 0.25. The average ratio is higher in both cases with an inverse value that would be closer to 0.2. But the average value is influenced by a lot of outliers where, for example, Budweiser has a value of 35:1 with respect to the downside gaps. This arises because it has only once experienced a downside gap of more than −4% and 35 times that it experienced the smaller downside gap. So the ratio of 35:1 would have been factored into the computation of the average. If we set the boundary thresholds at those stocks that showed a ratio of at least three and less than five we obtained the figures of 42% for the upside gaps and 48% for the downside gaps.

SUMMARY OF A POWER LAW RELATIONSHIP FOR OPENING BREAKS

Almost half of the stocks surveyed reveal similarities in their comparable frequencies with respect to small and large gaps. We find this result to be very supportive of the notion that an inverse square relationship or power law holds for the magnitude of the break and the relative frequency of the break. If we take the median values which are more representative than the average value we find that for both the upward and downward gaps the ratio between the smaller gaps and the larger gaps is very close to 4:1 or expressed inversely $\frac{1}{4}$ which as we have seen is exactly what the inverse square law would suggest.

We think that this is rather a striking conclusion and one that has not been widely acknowledged by either researchers within the financial community or active traders. The fact that typical and actively traded stocks should reveal the same kind of behavioral characteristics in regard to breaks and gaps suggests that there are similar dynamics at work within financial time series as other kinds of phenomena where power laws are evidenced.

8
Correlation and Convergence

We would like to begin this chapter with three separate questions:

- Does strong correlation provide the basis for successful long/short trades?
- Does convergence provide the basis for successful long/short trades?
- Does cointegration provide the basis for successful long/short trades?

In order to answer each of those questions it will be necessary to examine each of the three premises that are mentioned – correlation, convergence and cointegration. In much of the finance literature there is a lot of confusion between the first two concepts and for many traders and investors there is perhaps less familiarity with the third – cointegration. Before following each of these three paths we want to provide the reader with the flavor of the issues we shall be examining as we tackle one of the most important topics in the whole philosophy of market neutral investing.

One of the intellectual underpinnings of the boom in the hedge fund industry has been the growing acceptance of the notion that adding a short component to an investment strategy not only has protective benefits but also allows funds to exploit, relatively speaking, low risk market opportunities that arise from statistically aberrant price behavior. We have used the qualification "relatively speaking" to emphasize that these opportunities may under normal conditions be properly thought of as low risk but because of the tendencies for markets to frequently behave abnormally these opportunities may in fact be associated with much higher degrees of risk than is sometimes acknowledged. Dispersion and convergence are general headings for two of the most widely implemented trading strategies that are designed to exploit cases of statistically irregular market behavior. According to a recent survey of European hedge fund prospectuses perhaps as many as 50% have been drawn to the practice of statistical arbitrage and convergence trading.[1] These practices will feature prominently in the following discussion.

Jim Simons is one of the most successful hedge fund managers of the last 20 years, probably eclipsing the track record of better known luminaries such as George Soros and Paul Tudor Jones. He has managed to stay under most people's radar screens by remaining somewhat elusive as he rarely grants interviews. However, in one of his rare interviews he was questioned about the failure of Long Term Capital Management (LTCM) and made the following very pertinent remark:

> The trouble with convergence trading is that you don't have a time scale. You can say that *eventually* things will come together. Well when is eventually?[2]

This warning of the potential perils of convergence trading should always be present in the minds of asset managers and traders who subscribe to these strategies. The more recent popularity of the term convergence trading has overshadowed the more traditional nomenclature of "spread" trading. Spread trading has a long history in the commodities markets and numerous books have focused on trading opportunities provided by being, for example, both long and short different delivery months or different exchanges for certain agricultural commodities. As the term convergence trading is employed in today's markets the trading orientation is more or less reliant on some kind of statistical arbitrage opportunity. We will eventually clarify the nature of statistical arbitrage but in essence the problem with relying on previously observed evidence of convergence between two separate instruments is twofold. The first problem is the general problem that can be summed up in the simple disclaimer to be found on all risk disclosure statements – past performance is no guarantee of future results. The second problem is that implied by Jim Simon's remark which is that even if the convergence that is being traded is "sound" it may take longer to realize than anticipated (to put it kindly). This can be because of factors peculiar to the behavior of the converging instruments, or more ominously, and this was the case with the Long Term Capital Management (LTCM) mishap, when the overall market is in crisis and the "normal conditions" do not apply.

We are further reminded of a quotation that is often attributed to John Maynard Keynes which seems particularly relevant in the present context – "The market can stay irrational longer than you can stay solvent." Even if the attribution is apocryphal which some believe it to be,[3] there is a peculiar resonance that the sentiment expressed has with many contemporary market manias. In particular it captures the supreme irony of the Nobel Laureates and the high powered quants that ran the LTCM trading desks creating a monumental financial crisis in the summer of 1998 by practicing low risk "arbitrage" strategies. Arbitrage is supposed to be about risk free or at least low risk trading and investment; it is not supposed to bring the global financial system to the brink of collapse.

The final introductory point that needs to be made and should be familiar to anyone who has taken an elementary statistics course is the observation that correlation does not unearth causation it simply describes previously observed co-occurrences. Just like the items in a risk disclosure notice, this is one of those comments that tend to get overlooked. When reading many discussions that cite high degrees of correlation between different variables one often finds the implicit assumption that there is some dependency between the two variables. Dependence is more than we should infer from correlation if by dependency we assume that previously observed strongly associated co-movement will continue into the future. It is all too tempting to open Excel, input some variables, apply the statistical function which calculates the correlation coefficient and then make exaggerated claims for the significance of this single numerical value.

CORRELATION – IS IT THE BASIS FOR HEDGING?

Because of the "spread trading" tradition in the commodities and financial futures area, there has developed the notion that long/short trades are intimately connected with exploiting the supposed tendency of financial instruments that have previously exhibited correlation to revert to their normal behavior and converge. This last sentence contains a serious non-sequitur because correlation and convergence are two entirely separate issues. While it can be true that two time series that have historically shown a high degree of correlation may diverge temporarily and then reconverge this is just accidentally true. In other words this tells us nothing that is necessarily true about either the correlation potential or the convergence potential. It is possible to observe two time series that show perfect correlation and yet will always be diverging as we shall see.

We want to explore some peculiarities of correlation that will hopefully muddy the waters enough with this statistical concept that we will learn not to rely too heavily on the value of the measurement. The coefficient of correlation is a very useful technique for seeing how two variables are associated but it is not a good technique for attributing any causal dependency between the variables. Historically observed co-movement between two variables is often very useful information to have but going on to infer that the same degree of co-movement is likely in the future can be a recipe for major unpleasant surprises.

To begin we shall examine a trivial situation of where one variable is directly dependent on another, exhibiting perfect correlation. The equation $y = 2x + 10$ expresses a functional relationship between two variables x and y that will always be 100% deterministically associated. If we plot several of the x and y points that follow from the equation we will have created a straight line and if we find the coefficient of correlation between all of the points it will have a value of one showing perfect positive correlation. That may seem like a statement of the obvious, which it is, but it can also lead to some other less obvious situations where the association is deterministic but perhaps not what we were expecting.

Figure 8.1 shows two hypothetical stocks which have been purchased at period one and which have "traced out two separate price paths" and also been combined 50:50 in a mini-portfolio. The stocks perform remarkably differently as can be seen. The holdings of an equal amount of each stock start out in period one at \$1000 each but after 10 periods, the holding of stock X is worth more than \$1500 while the holding of stock Y has declined to close to \$500. The net result for the portfolio is that it has made a slight loss. But the curious feature of the

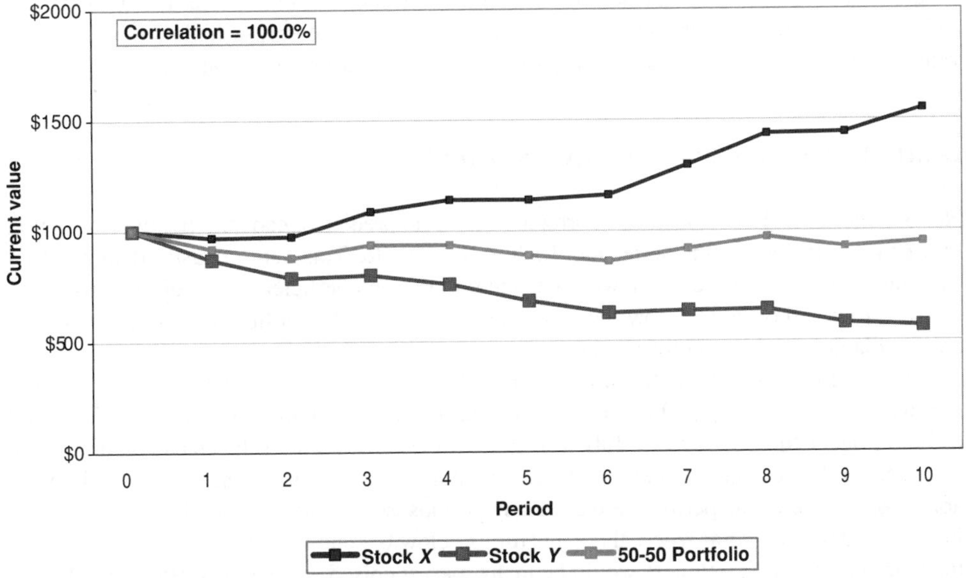

Figure 8.1 Anomaly of perfect correlation – two stocks are combined in a portfolio and have perfect correlation

chart is that there is 100% correlation between the co-movement of the two stocks. How can that be if one gains 50% and the other loses almost 50%? Very simply the returns path of stock Y has been "created" by using a simple linear equation expressing a functional relationship between X and Y. The returns path for stock X can be randomly generated but once the value for X is substituted into the $y = \text{slope} * x + \text{intercept}$ equation the path of Y is completely determined by the other variable x. This simple experiment is easy to reproduce in Excel[4] and one can play with different values of the slope and intercept of the linear equation to see how the "trajectories" diverge while still showing 100% correlation. It is worth commenting that if one sets a negative value for the slope then the coefficient of correlation becomes -1 indicating perfect negative correlation. Also revealing is playing with the intercept or alpha value as it is possible to have stock Y spectacularly outperform (or underperform) stock X by simply adjusting the intercept value in the linear equation. But even with spectacular discrepancies in the price paths the correlation remains at 100% (either positive or negative).

Correlation can be perfect even when the paths taken by the values under consideration are "perfectly diverging" as they are in the Figure 8.1. This is sometimes an unsettling and counterintuitive notion even for those who have taken their studies beyond elementary statistics. The conclusion is inescapable that what the correlation coefficient is measuring may have nothing to do with convergence. The association between two contingently related variables may show that they have a tendency to come together or even preserve their degree of separation but there is nothing intrinsically necessary about this. With this in mind we should be very careful how we use the terms and think about "convergence", "divergence" and "correlation". With real stock returns we must assume that there are no hidden deterministic equations that enable one master variable to drive the values of others. If there were we could discover not only 100% correlations as we have seen but also, because of the functional relationship there would be a genuine sense in which one variable displays a causal relationship over another. This of course, so far as we know, is not the case in the real world and what we are faced with in the actual analysis of two securities and their time series are varying degrees of co-movement and association. In summary, the correlation coefficient, no matter how high is the numerical value, does not reveal any predictive capability nor is it a harbinger of convergence.

CORRELATION CAN BE HIGHLY UNSTABLE

Not only does previously observed correlation have no predictive capacity but the correlation between two financial time series can be highly unstable. This can be easily demonstrated by running a moving time window across the correlation coefficient between two historical returns series and observing how the value varies over time. Very often the coefficient values are so volatile as to be effectively useless.

Figure 8.2 uses a 100 day window to track the correlation coefficient between the daily returns for the NASDAQ 100 index (^NDX) and the corresponding returns for the S&P 500 (^SPC) from October 1st 1985 to July 31st 2006. If the entire period is taken and all of the data is measured the correlation coefficient value is more than 0.9. However, observing the variability across the whole period there are many periods, some quite extended, where the value lies below 0.6 and several where the value drops below 0.4 and beyond. If one was to rely on the long-term value of 0.9 there would be many market episodes when this value would seem entirely inappropriate. Without the benefit of a historical overview if one was to measure the value at many times over the last 22 years from the trailing 100 day perspective one could be hopelessly inaccurate about extrapolating that value into a forecast value for the next 100 days.

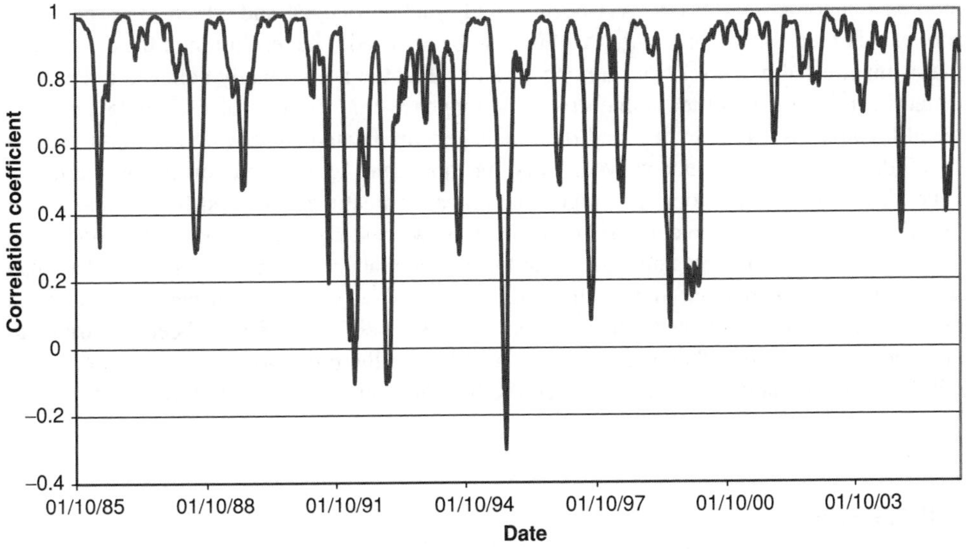

Figure 8.2 Moving correlation coefficient (100 day) between NASDAQ 100 returns and S&P 500 returns October 1st 1985–July 31st 2006

Under many "normal" trading conditions there will be value in tracking correlations between different assets. Observed correlations can often provide a helpful guideline as to the future paths of associated variables. Indeed much of modern portfolio theory is based on the assumption that these covariances and correlations are useful in enabling one to build diversified portfolio. But as we shall discuss later the Markowitz notion of diversification that was developed in the 1960s may be far less suited to a more globally interdependent financial system in which asset classes are more closely interwoven through complex trading strategies and derivatives than ever before. Our chief concern is that there is too high a reliance on the correlation coefficient value, an erroneous presumption as to its robustness and not enough attention paid to its inherent instability and volatility.

As an aside, the variability in correlation may be a more interesting feature of time series than the actual coefficient itself. Rather than looking for extremely positive or negative correlation and using that information as the basis for certain kinds of trading opportunities, evidence of sudden jumps or falls in correlation may have even more value to the trader. When correlations among assets all begin to rise noticeably this may be alerting us to a potentially critical market episode that lies ahead. Also quite valuable, and one that can be particularly useful in terms of identifying trading opportunities, is the discovery of unexpected correlations or sudden increases in the degree of correlation between two variables that have previously shown very poor correlation.

UNEXPECTED CORRELATIONS

While the focus in convergence trading may be to exploit wandering correlations there is real value in noting emerging and unexpected correlations. One of the obvious advantages of uncovering unexpected correlations is that one has an opportunity to exploit inefficiency in the market, something that has not yet been (widely) acknowledged and which often points to some kind of tension or conflict that will need to be resolved. The resolution of the dissonance that is manifested by correlations among variables that are not normally believed to be associated is one of the main ideas that drives the emphasis that we have placed on comparative quantiles analysis. Many traders and fund managers are fixated on looking for confirmations or validations of a particular view that one has about the future direction of the market in general, or a particular stock, and confirmations are sometimes supplied by the markets at exactly the times when the contrarian view is most warranted. One is more likely to have an edge in trading by noticing a divergence and acting on it ahead of the majority of traders than waiting for (say) a breakout to be confirmed. If the breakout is slightly suspect then there is a real possibility that it may better be described as a "fake-out", and if it has been confirmed to everybody's satisfaction then there remains no edge for the trader as the market participants will have already anticipated and realized the benefits simultaneously with the confirmation being provided.

ARBITRAGE

The methods used in statistical arbitrage techniques are some of the more arcane in modern finance. We want to look at least on the surface at some of the strategies and also some of the assumptions (to the extent that we understand them) that have developed in the contemporary trading community. There are many kinds of statistical arbitrage and some of the techniques do not really deserve the term arbitrage.

Arbitrage has been around as long as markets have. The very simple notion behind an arbitrage trade is that one performs a sequence of transactions in which one buys and sells a certain item for a profit without incurring any risk. How can this be possible? Well let us take a very simple example first that may be familiar to anyone who has shopped in a bazaar or souk. Let us suppose that you approach a merchant for a particular item and have agreed on the price for it but he does not have it in the color that you want. One of his stall attendants will enthusiastically offer to get it for you in no time at all. He will then disappear into the back streets and return with exactly the color you desired. He will have paid another merchant a specific amount x and you will be paying the merchant an amount y and $y > x$. This is a specific example where one has pre-sold something that one can buy at a lower price. The stall holder is in effect executing an arbitrage trade when he buys from another stall holder for a pre-sold item.

In arbitrage the important idea of simultaneity arises in the context of the purchase and sale. The risk exposure that could arise in connection with the twin activities has to do with the possibility that the prices expected for the purchase and sale could deviate over time or that the market for the sale side, that is the customer, could change his mind about the price or about the transaction altogether. One wants the certainty that the prices will be executable within a very short interval (or even pre-sold or pre-purchased at a specified price) before embarking on one of the legs of the arbitrage trade.

The more complex examples of an arbitrage trade have to do with the price of a cash instrument or the underlying and the price of a derivative such as a futures contract. The arbitrage possibilities can exist in multiple markets and even across markets. Because arbitrage is so readily available to large institutional traders that can execute with razor thin margins, the opportunities for observing mispricing opportunities in highly liquid markets have diminished dramatically. Some well-known examples of the more complex kinds of arbitrage involve the possible discrepancies that might temporarily arise between the trading in the S&P 500 futures pits in Chicago and the trading of the stocks that comprise the index in the actual cash market.

Another kind of arbitrage that is more complex, and that requires more sophisticated mathematics, involves an arbitrage between different U.S. Treasury bonds with slightly different maturities. This type of arbitrage has been practiced successfully by large investment banks for many years and is perhaps one of the "safest" forms of convergence trading. The traders at LTCM, most of whom had come from Salomon Brothers which had found considerable and sustained profitability from this kind of trading during the 1980s and 1990s, however, discovered just how unsafe this strategy could be in the wake of the Russian debt crisis of August 1998.

ON THE RUN ARBITRAGE

A classic example of an arbitrage trade that under most normal conditions should deliver profits with minimal risk is the phenomenon within the U.S. Treasury market involving the 30 year bond. The situation is described well by Roger Lowenstein in his very readable account of the collapse of Long Term Capital Management *When Genius Failed* (which also bears the subtitle *How one small bank created a trillion dollar hole*). As might be surmised the trade normally is an ultra-low risk arbitrage but in the summer of 1998 it spectacularly failed and helped contribute to the collapse of the hedge fund.

The essential characteristics of the trade involve a difference in the liquidity between the most recently issued 30 year bond which is given the term "on the run" and the next most recent which has perhaps already paid out on one of its coupons and instead of the 30 years to run it may only have another $29\frac{1}{2}$ years to run. It is called "off the run" and as it moves away from its issuance date it becomes a lot less liquid than the recently released bond. As Lowenstein remarks:

> A funny thing happens to thirty year Treasury bonds six months or so after they are issued: investors stuff them into safes and drawers for long term keeping. With fewer left in circulation, the bonds become harder to trade... Being less liquid, the off the run bond is considered less desirable. It begins to trade at a slight discount (that is, you can purchase it for a little less, or at what amounts to a slightly higher yield). As arbitrageurs would say, a spread opens.[5]

As Lowenstein also points out if the spread widens too far then it becomes illogical (he uses the word "silly"): "After all, the U.S. government is no less likely to pay off a bond that matures in $29\frac{1}{2}$ years than one that expires in thirty. But some institutions were so timid, so bureaucratic, that they refused to own anything but the most liquid paper."

There is a further issue here which deserves a brief mention which has to do with the delivery procedures for the CBOT Treasury Bond futures contracts which lay out a precise definition of the protocol to follow if one has to deliver actual bonds in fulfillment of a position in the futures market. A sophisticated technique has arisen as to calculating the so-called "cheapest to deliver" bonds and the traders at LTCM, many of whom had played this game for years, had devised arbitrage strategies to exploit the tiniest discrepancies in the pricing of these instruments. As Lowenstein remarks the margins that one is considering in this context are razor thin and effectively there are no real profit opportunities other than those available to institutional traders that are able to take on massive positions based on leverage and repo agreements with little or no financing costs. But if the yield difference between the "on the run" and "off the run" instruments opens up too far then there is an opportunity to exploit the spread by taking matched positions in which one sells the expensive bond and purchases an equal amount of the cheaper one. This is the basis of all convergence trades and LTCM used to boast that that was its forte. Lowenstein remarks:

> Long-Term dubbed its safest bets *convergence* trades [his italics], because the instruments matured at a specific date, meaning that convergence appeared to be a sure thing. Others were known as *relative value* trades in which convergence was expected but not guaranteed.[6]

As we now know, when the Russian debt crisis erupted in August 1998 there was a global evaporation of liquidity in which all assumptions about convergence were cast aside as investors and traders who were carrying massive positions in fixed income instruments from emerging markets panicked. Funds including LTCM that were used to hedging their exposure through the liquidity of the U.S. Treasury markets, both the cash and futures markets, found, when the default on Russian debt occurred, that the entire fixed income securities market had become erratic and illiquid. Unable to transact in a normal or typical fashion there was an avalanche of selling in a vast array of actual bonds, corporate, government and mortgage-backed as well as fixed income derivatives. The situation became one where you sold not what you wanted to, but what you could. And U.S. Treasuries were one market where too many traders were locked into positions of being long one bond that was deemed slightly less liquid than another and because of the liquidity meltdown there was no bid for the less liquid instrument. The circumstances were often more complex and had to do with knowledge by some of LTCM's competitors and even partners of the peculiar imbalances in their (i.e. LTCM's) positions and their vulnerability to sabotage by freezing certain transactions that would normally have posed no issues.

Lowenstein's book provides an excellent account of the numerous miscalculations that LTCM had made about the safety of their massive positions, their overconfidence in the notion that normal liquidity conditions will prevail even in critical market episodes, and the hazards of massive leverage. But perhaps most fundamentally the lesson to be learned is that even the safest of convergence trades can be perilous when the market is not trading "normally".

One of the main myths is that one can employ various arbitrage strategies that effectively remove risk or reduce it to a negligible amount. To highlight the fallacies that can lie buried in the assumptions behind certain supposedly market neutral strategies, we can consider a couple of often quoted examples of allegedly low risk investing. The first is a technique that has been widely followed in the hedge fund world and which goes under the heading of "convertible arbitrage". In a book entitled *Market Neutral Investing* by Joseph G. Nicholas[7] we find the following broad description:

> A convertible arbitrage trade is a relative value play on the relationship between a convertible security and the underlying stock. The strategy involves constructing long portfolios of convertible bonds and hedging these positions by selling short the underlying stock of each bond... *Usually* the price of the convertible bond declines less rapidly than the underlying stock in a falling equity market and mirrors the price of the stock more closely in a rising equity market. (p. 233)

The key word in the above brief description is the one italicized "*Usually*". We have no evidence to dispute the claim that these kinds of trades are much more likely to succeed than otherwise but when these trades go wrong they can sometimes go breathtakingly wrong. An example of how circumstances can go awry and disrupt the usual assumptions took place in May 2005 when Standard & Poor's downgraded $453 billion in outstanding debt of General Motors and Ford Motor Corporation to junk bond status and, in the same time frame, the maverick investor Kirk Kerkorian made a big purchase of GM's common stock. Arbitrageurs were caught out doubly since the bonds plunged and the stock surged. Several hedge funds suffered substantial losses including one or two that closed their doors.[8]

PAIRS TRADING

We have seen that convertible arbitrage can sometimes be far more risky than suggested from the assumptions underlying statistical arbitrage but let us know focus on another strategy which has received a lot of attention from traders – pairs trading. This is essentially a relative value arbitrage, although once again the term "arbitrage" seems to be used rather loosely. But also as noted before, we do not wish to be too skeptical as there are plausible assumptions behind the strategy and some traders have profited well from the practice.

Pairs trading can be or more or less complex. In its simplest form it will often consist of trading in two separate but related equities. There are more complex, and possibly "safer", versions of the trade that can involve exploiting discrepancies between stock market indices, including those that have overlapping memberships.[9] We shall consider the simplest form first, where the central idea is to find two stocks for companies that would be expected to show highly correlated returns that have wandered out of alignment with each other. In this circumstance one should buy the one that, on a relative valuation basis, appears to be the cheaper and to sell an equal dollar amount of the one that appears relatively expensive.

Often the screening process in looking for candidates not only scans for high correlation coefficients but sound "fundamental" reasons why there should be a correlated relationship. If there is, or there is supposed to be, a fundamental contributor to the high correlation then one can have greater confidence in betting on convergence when the historical association moves beyond the normally expected bounds. But sometimes the supposed fundamental "linkage" proves to be illusory, but that is to jump ahead. Advocates of a pairs trading strategy will tend to look for companies in the same sector and one of the obvious pairs is GM and Ford, two U.S. domiciled auto manufacturers whose fortunes are supposed to be "linked" because they both operate in the same business sector and would seem to be affected similarly by macro-economic factors. Sometimes the focus of the trade is expressed in the form that one is making a bet on mean reversion. To see just what this means and how the technique might be implemented we need to follow through with the GM/Ford example and see where the opportunity arises and how safe the trade actually is.

Figure 8.3 is a weekly chart showing the correlation between the return for General Motors and Ford for the period from January 1977 to June 2006. The particular period was chosen to coincide with the beginning of trading of Ford on the NSYE. We have plotted the coefficient of correlation between the two time series for the trailing 52 week period. There are some striking similarities in the unstable nature of the coefficient value to those that were seen between the NASDAQ 100 and the S&P 500 that was displayed in Figure 8.2. While the upper tendency of the line in Figure 8.3 shows that there are sometimes long periods where the value lies above 0.8 and even approaches 1.0, the line is also quite erratic. On three occasions the line actually drops below zero indicating negative correlation and there is an extended period from 1998 to 2002 where the correlation is noticeably weaker and more volatile. If we calculate the static correlation for the entire period, a total of 1535 weekly periods, the coefficient has a value of

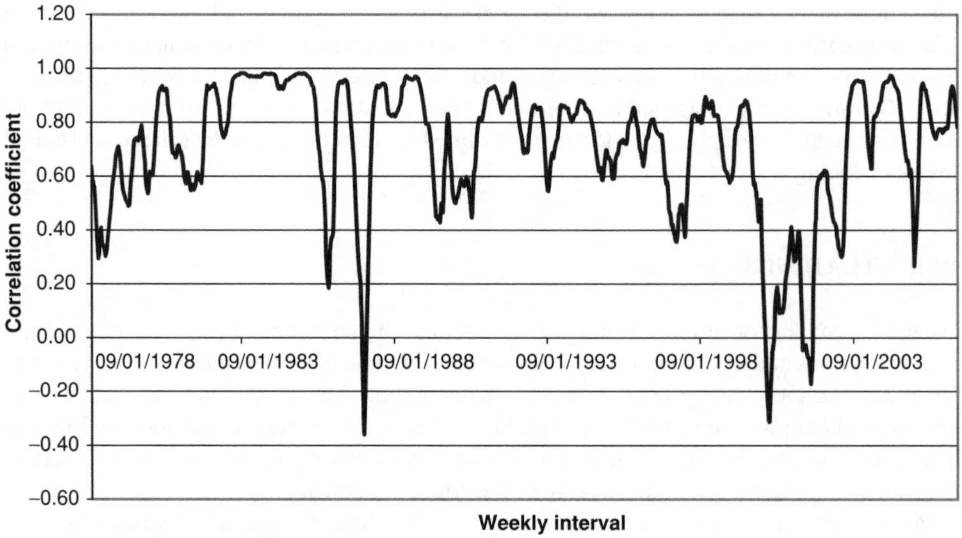

Figure 8.3 Correlation coefficient between GM and Ford – trailing 52 weeks

0.95 which clearly indicates very strong positive correlation. There is a plausible case that, over the long haul the co-movements have been so closely linked that *prima facie* there should be an opportunity to exploit the short-term deviations where the correlation drops below certain threshold amounts. We need to examine what short term means in this context and also what the thresholds for triggering a pairs trade might be.

Figure 8.4 shows the ratio of GM/Ford weekly prices during the period starting in January 2004 and extending to June 2006. The actual price ratio is shown along with the 50 week

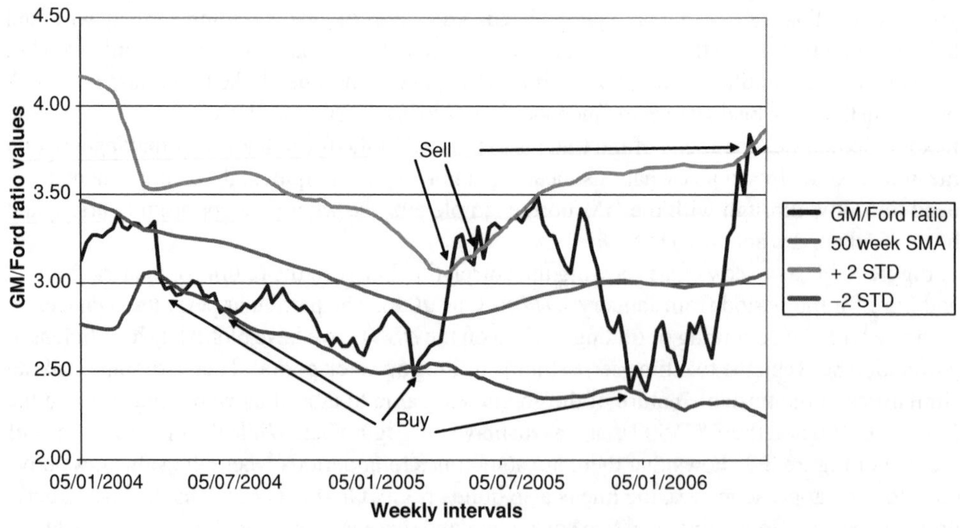

Figure 8.4 GM/Ford price ratio January 2004–June 2006

simple moving average (SMA) and the two volatility bands (Bollinger bands) which are set at ±2 STDs from the moving average. What we are exploring is the now familiar notion that when the ratio falls below the –2 STD band it suggests that the cheaper of the pair, in this case GM, should be purchased as a long holding and the more expensive of the pair, Ford, should be taken as a short position.

The obvious trigger points have been indicated in Figure 8.4 and it possible to devise more complex trading rules which would involve money management decisions about how to supplement an existing pairs position, if at all, when one already has been triggered within a certain time window. What can be seen is that the actual ratio line on the chart does move fairly sharply backwards and forwards through the channel or "envelope" that is bounded by the upper and lower volatility bands. To the extent that the ratio is largely confined within the bands it could be claimed that the relationship is showing a well-behaved convergence tendency which is to bounce off extreme values and then revert towards the mean. However, in examining the chart more closely it can be seen that the actual ratio line spends very little time in the vicinity of the mean and rather "whipsaws" back and forth from the lower volatility band up to the upper band and back again. The vertical axis on the chart represents the numerical value of the price ratio, in other words the value of dividing the weekly closing price of GM by that of Ford. As can be seen from the values on the *y*-axis there is some suggestion that the moving average runs approximately through a line that tracks the price ratio of 3, the lower band tracks approximately with 2.5 and the upper band with 3.5 but the lines are quite volatile which is to be expected given the volatility of the underlying price ratio itself.

Using a simplified version of the methodology one could propose a very simple pairs trading strategy which would be to open a long GM/short Ford position when the price ratio falls below 2.5 and exit or reverse the position when the price ratio rises above 3.5. For those who would prefer to pay closer attention to the actual trading conditions and prevailing volatility we have marked on the chart the places where one could instigate the trades. Other variations on this theme exist. One variation might be to enter a trade at the point where the pair have fallen below the −2 STD level and exit at the crossover point of the moving averages and then remain on the sidelines until the same situation unfolds again. Alternatively one could go short GM and buy Ford at the point where the pairs ratio goes above the +2 STD band and exit the position again where the ratio crosses the moving average of the ratio.

Let us examine what would have happened to a notional equal dollar amount committed to both stocks during the period shown in the chart in Figure 8.4. Our hypothetical portfolio contains $100 000, and even though one could use the proceeds of the short sale to finance the long position we shall simplify and set the dollar amounts committed to each "leg" of the spread to the $100K amounts. The trade is triggered on the week of April 19th, 2004 which is the point where the ratio first breaks below the lower boundary that is situated at twice the 50 week standard deviation subtracted from the 50 week moving average.[10] We have then traced the profit and loss account for this number of shares in each of the long and short positions for the ensuing period of almost one year. As can be clearly seen from Figure 8.5 the paired positions lose money immediately and continue to do so throughout the period. During the entire period the ratio essentially tracks the descending line that traces the declining lower volatility band for the GM/Ford ratio.

Around the turn of the year 2004/5 the losses have mounted to more than $13 000 and the trading rule for exiting the position has not once allowed one to abandon this deteriorating position. The GM/Ford ratio, in other words, has not in the entire period moved above the 50 week moving average which has been declining throughout. In early 2005 there is a

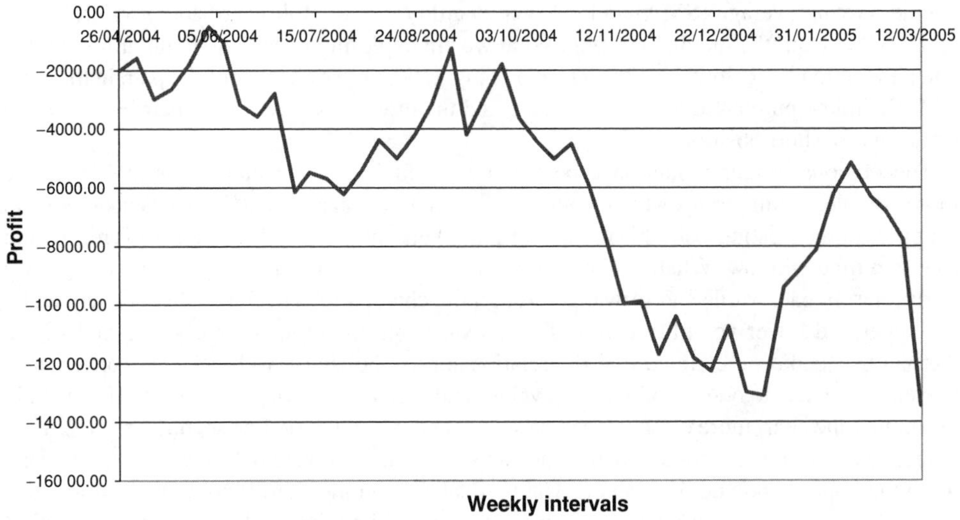

Figure 8.5 Profit from GM/Ford pairs trading 2004–2006

noticeable attempt at regaining the moving average level but this fades and reverses back to the −2 STD line and brings the losses from the hedge back down to the $13 000 level. The important question for the trader to address now is whether to abandon the trade or hang in there waiting (and hoping) for the mean reversion to eventually take place. Remember that this is an example of a low risk arbitrage trade in which the theory is that when the two correlated instruments diverge by more than what should be expected they will *eventually* revert to their historically confirmed ratio. How long does one wait for the eventual mean reversion? Is there any necessity that there will indeed be a mean reversion? These are difficult questions for pairs trading. But to be fair there are difficult questions that can be raised about any trading strategy and if one uses a robust money management technique one would have exited the pairs trade anyway as the losses exceeded one's comfort level.

We are not suggesting that pairs trading has no value among the numerous options available for long/short strategies but rather that pairs trading has no silver bullet that favors it among competing strategies. Even if mean reversion takes place, and historically in the case of GM and Ford and other classic pairs there is evidence that it does, there is no reliable guide as to how long one has to wait. More importantly there is no necessity or inevitability about the restoration of the historically observed mean ratio, which seems to be implied by the more enthusiastic advocates of statistical arbitrage. Just to fill out the rest of the trade history for the hypothetical portfolio we can see in Figure 8.6 that, shortly after the critical period that we previously observed where the account had suffered a $13 000 drawdown, the trade begins to recover and eventually delivers a profit, but the trade takes more than a year to do so. We are reminded of the quotation from Jim Simons regarding convergence trades – when is eventually?

From our examination of strategies based on statistical arbitrage we can find a variety of issues that suggest that traders should never rely imprudently on the "safety net" assumptions that are often implicitly made for them. Theoretically one can make the case that there is a spectrum of risk that is associated with each of the strategies that we have discussed, ranging from the long-term Treasury bond arbitrage which from a theoretical standpoint should be

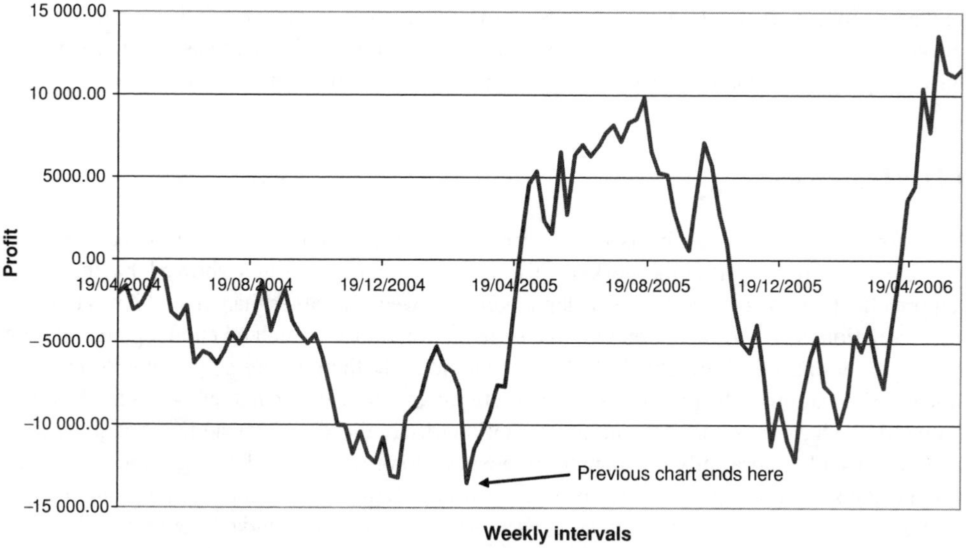

Figure 8.6 GM/Ford pairs trading P&L 2004–2006

the least risky to the more problematic relative value arbitrage assumed in pairs trading. But as our case studies have shown the strategies are far from riskless. In the case of LTCM's Treasury arbitrage that failed during August and September 1998 and contributed to the fund's prodigious collapse, the convergence between the "on the run" and "off the run" maturities did eventually come together again, as it surely should, when normal market conditions were restored. But there is an important difference between the two cases – the GM/Ford arbitrage and the "on the run/off the run" arbitrage which we need to explore more fully and that takes us beyond correlation into the statistical concept of cointegration.

Before introducing the concept of cointegration there is one further example of pairs trading that has some of the hallmarks that will enable us to differentiate between the kind of co-movements between price series that *necessarily* imply some dependency and those that do not. Royal Dutch and Shell are different trading entities of a hybrid conglomerate, the Royal Dutch/Shell Group. They conduct their own operations, have independently traded stocks and post different results but there is an interconnection or dependency between the financial status of each entity. A corporate charter stipulates that from the Group's overall operations, 60% of income received will ultimately belong to Royal Dutch and 40% to Shell. In these circumstances in tracking the correlation between the two time series there is more than a long standing historical co-movement phenomenon which makes the pair an attractive "spread trading" proposition. There is a fundamental reason why the two stocks should be "paired" as well. If the price ratio deviates too far from its historical average there is a fundamental organizational imperative that should prevent this deviation from wandering indefinitely further away from the mean. When two entities are connected in some fundamental or structural sense then it is legitimate to claim that there is a real dependency between their co-movements rather than just simply a historically observed association. Royal Dutch and Shell will not only exhibit a very high degree of positive correlation, their price series data are driven by or constrained by an underlying interdependence. A similar and more exacting interdependence is also be found in the co-movement of the Treasury bonds of different maturities and also in the co-movements of the S&P 500 futures contracts and the underlying cash index. In these cases the time series have a stronger link than correlation and they can be said to be cointegrated.

COINTEGRATION

The term cointegration and its associated methodology was introduced into the econometrician's tool box in 1987 after the work of Clive Granger and Robert Engle showed that there was a more effective way of ascertaining a dependency between variables than that which is implied by correlation only.[11] If there are two time series of log returns which taken independently are both nonstationary and effectively follow a random walk then it may be possible to create a linear combination of the two series which is stationary and which can then be said to be cointegrated. We have introduced the notion of stationarity in this definition and, although we will analyze this a lot more fully in Chapter 10, we need to provide a brief background to this important statistical concept and which is itself one of the major assumptions of Gaussian finance.

A stationary time series is one which has a constant mean and standard deviation. To revert to the notion of Brownian motion, the archetypal random walk, which Bachelier introduced into his theory of speculative markets, the log change data points from Brownian motion will fluctuate persistently but with a mean and standard deviation that settle down to a relatively constant value. One of the consequences of this is that if one was to partition a set of log changes that exhibit the same characteristics as Brownian motion into two separate subseries, and then calculate the mean and standard deviation for each series they should be approximately equal. Not only should they be equal but both should not significantly differ from the values calculated for the whole series itself.

It has already been demonstrated with Figure 8.3 that the 52 week trailing standard deviations for GM stock shows a high degree of variability and therefore the variation for the series cannot, in any meaningful sense, be considered to be a constant value. A chart showing the 52 week trailing calculation for the mean would show similar variability as well. It is also worth pointing out that the secular rise in equity prices is itself a factor that ensures that financial time series are not stationary. Most individual equities and the market indices have shown an underlying trend that is upwards which means that when we partition the price data for later periods and calculate the mean price it will be higher than for earlier periods. This is not a feature of a stationary time series such as Brownian motion or white noise, a theme that will be revisited in Chapter 10.

It has been argued, by Granger and others, that the fact that time series are nonstationary can give rise to many spurious kinds of correlation and in order to differentiate the spurious forms of correlation from the more meaningful forms a further statistical test was devised to determine whether there is a more "causal link" between the two time series. If we were to take the time series for (say) U.S. Treasury bonds of different maturities and were to combine them in a linear fashion to create a cointegrating vector we can then test to see whether this vector has a low order of integration. If it does, as would be the case for the Treasury bonds, the two original series can be said to be cointegrated.[12]

A rather simple example has been used to help in the visualization of the cointegration phenomenon and it recasts the analogy about the steps of someone who is drunk mapping the path of a random walk. The story requires the assumption that the random walker is somewhat intoxicated and has a tendency to wander aimlessly. However, in the modified version of the analogy that we are about to relate, the person is not drunk enough to be unable to act as a responsible dog owner. The inebriated dog owner leaves the pub or restaurant with her dog which is not initially on a leash. As she stumbles homewards, the dog will tend to wander off (as dogs do) and stray further away from the owner. Let us suppose that the journey homewards goes through a small park where owners are obliged to put their dogs on leashes. As she approaches the park the random walker calls out to her dog who eventually returns to her, whereupon she attaches her dog to the leash. The next segment of their paths, as they pass through the park, will proceed in a more coordinated fashion as the dog is confined to the leash. The point of the story is that the two paths of the owner and the dog are both random and can be said to be nonstationary but whereas they deviate and wander apart they will eventually come back together as the dog owner observes the park's by-laws. The combined paths will trace out a cointegrating vector and there is a causal dependency between the two separate itineraries.

One of the leading practitioners of applying cointegration techniques to financial modeling is Professor Carol Alexander who holds the chair of Risk Management at the University of Reading (ICMA center) in the UK. She has written several readable papers in leading journals on the subject as well as a fairly accessible book (to the nonspecialist that is) of econometric techniques that are useful in the analysis of financial time series:

> Cointegration measures long-run co-movements in prices, which may occur even through periods when static correlations appear low. Therefore, hedging methodologies based on cointegrated financial assets may be more effective in the long term... In summary, investment management strategies that are based only on volatility and correlation of returns cannot guarantee long-term performance. *There is no mechanism to ensure the reversion of the hedge to the underlying*, and nothing to prevent the tracking error from behaving in the unpredictable manner of a random walk. (My italics)[13]

This is a very clear statement, especially the italicized part, of the limitations of the correlation concept that we have been addressing in our discussion above. For those who are keen to understand the basis of hedging it is vital to clearly understand this distinction between correlation and the measurement of a more robust dependency, cointegration. Without some fundamental reason, such as that observed between Royal Dutch and Shell or between bonds of different maturities, then there is no mechanism or link between two time series to allow one to reach any firm conclusions about whether a hedge or arbitrage trade will eventually converge with the underlying instrument. If we use the notion of a tracking error to register the discrepancy between the hedge instrument and the underlying or the degree to which the pairs have strayed from their mean price ratio, then we can say that we have no assurances that the tracking error will diminish or grow larger. In other words, as the quotation above suggests, there is no compelling reason why the tracking error should not exhibit the unpredictable qualities of a random walk. This is most emphatically not assumed by the most enthusiastic advocates of statistical arbitrage techniques. To have any confidence that the tracking error will diminish and that the convergence or mean reversion assumptions are valid there needs to be a fundamental "link" between the hedge and the underlying. Exactly what is meant by the link is explained further by Alexander as she invokes the notion of "Granger causality":

> The mechanism which ties cointegrated series together is a "causality", not in the sense that if we make a structural change to one series the other will change too, but in the sense that turning points on one series precede turning points in the other. The strength and directions of this "Granger causality" can change over time, there can be bi-directional causality, or the direction of causality can change.[14]

So the link is something that "ties" a cointegrated series together (the aptness of the model of the intoxicated dog owner comes to mind) to produce a kind of causal relationship which is clearly much stronger than that which is implied in a correlation only relationship. We have seen that the only thing that can be inferred from a simple correlations analysis is an observed pattern of associations with no statistically valid basis for declaring causation or even underlying common dynamics. In the case of a relationship which has the property of cointegration there are underlying dynamics that will ensure that the paths of the related variables will preserve, over the longer term, a unified trend:

> Cointegrated asset prices have a common stochastic trend; they are "tied together" in the long run because spreads are mean reverting, even though they might drift apart in the short run.[15]

There are still some nagging questions about the exact nature of the linkage. In cases where there is a fundamental reason why two price paths should come together again after they may have deviated, such as the bonds of different maturity or even the prices of Royal Dutch and Shell, it is intuitively clear that there is a "mechanism to ensure" that the tracking error between the two price paths will have to converge at some point in the future. To this extent the prices are "tied together" and there should be a well-placed confidence in a trade that is made based on this cointegration. But if we do not know of the fundamental reasons that underlie the linkage it remains somewhat of a mystery as to what the factors are that enable cointegration "to augment the correlation analysis to include the dynamics and causal flows between returns". The problem is that we may only be able to extend the confidence that comes from a cointegration relationship to those cases where we know ahead of time that it exists and that returns and price paths are mean reverting. The following quote demonstrates the slightly circular notion that we can really only be sure that we have identified a stronger relationship than correlation if we assume what we were hoping to establish from our cointegration procedures, i.e. that the tracking error is mean reverting:

> It is not surprising that fixed-income markets are easily modelled with cointegration. Bond yields are random walks that are most probably cointegrated across different maturities within a given country. Wherever the 1 month yield is in 10 or 20 years time, the 3 month yield will be right along there with it, because the spread has finite variance. More generally, in a yield curve of n maturities, each of the $n-1$ independent spreads is a cointegrating vector, assuming it is mean reverting.[16]

Undoubtedly there is a class of assets where the co-movements of the returns are contained within relatively narrow parameters. This confinement is due to their need to revert towards historical norms because of the ultimately unifying nature of their fundamental dynamics or construction. But can we add to the known class of assets that are cointegrated solely on the results of a statistical test or do we need to know *a priori* about their shared fundamental dynamics?

For the uncontroversial members of the class of cointegrated assets (i.e. where we have an in principle understanding of the common dynamics), knowing that their returns have an underlying linkage it becomes possible to answer one of our opening questions in the affirmative. Cointegration clearly can provide, over the longer term (eventually?), a reliable basis for convergence trading and hedging. But under critical macro-circumstances, as the LTCM episode illustrates, in the short term the hedge basis can become unhinged. No convergence trade should ever be touted as a case of pure arbitrage and no trading methodology, no matter how sophisticated, should ever be promoted as "risk free".

TRACKING THE DOW

Now that we have covered the major caveats behind all convergence trading we can explore a strategy that carries minimal risk, is based on cointegration and has been well documented.

Carol Alexander and her colleague Anca Dimitriu present a convincing argument that there is an attractive trading opportunity to be found from exploiting the tracking relationship between the Dow Jones Industrial Average and a subset of stocks from that index. We shall examine this example in some detail as it has the right ingredients for a low risk and profitable long/short trading strategy.

What Alexander and Dimitriu have shown is that for a certain set of cointegrated instruments such as the time series for the DJIA index itself and the constituent securities, it is possible to financially engineer a smaller replica of the index that produces abnormal returns. The returns are abnormal in the sense that the replica outperforms the actual index. Although the authors do not explicitly make the point, it follows directly from their claims that if these abnormal returns are a persistent feature there exists an opportunity for a minimal risk trade based on a form of arbitrage. If one was to create the mini-index replica and use the periodic rebalancing techniques that they illustrate, and then take an equal dollar short position in the YM futures contract, then one would be able to generate a positive and virtually risk-free return.

The strategy involves the rebalancing of a tracking index which is created from a subset of the Dow's stocks.[17] The exact manner in which the subset is determined and the rebalancing logic are covered in some detail in the authors' articles. The key difference in the arbitrage is that we are not attempting to exploit pricing discrepancies between a cash index and a publicly traded standardized derivative that moves in tandem with it, rather we have to construct the derivative ourselves from a cointegration analysis and a periodic rebalancing of the subset of the DJIA constituents. The "edge" is provided by the fact that cointegration ensures that the replica constituents cannot, by virtue of their participation in the index, wander indefinitely far from the index itself. This provides the "safety net" that was lacking in the pairs trading situation that we examined and allows us to have confidence in the fact that the tracking index cannot follow a random walk with respect to the underlying index:

> In standard models, tracking errors may quite possibly be random walks, so the replicating basket can drift arbitrarily far from the benchmark unless it is frequently rebalanced. Portfolio replication strategies that can guarantee mean-reverting tracking errors must have cointegration as the basis, however obscured.[18]

Although the constituents cannot take truly independent paths with respect to the index and there is always the restraint that the replica will be periodically rebalanced, there is sufficient leeway for some items to exhibit untypical relative performance vis-à-vis the actual index. After a period of outperformance (or underperformance) the weighting of a particular index constituent will become nonaligned with its historical norm and during the periodic rebalancing exercise this "abnormal" weighting will be corrected. The interesting feature is that the replica index has, during the period reviewed by Alexander and Dimitriu, outperformed the actual index. During the bear market phase of late 2000 and 2001 the historically derived rebalancing techniques that are used to update the tracking index lead to the somewhat anomalous situation where the tracking index generates an excess return over the DJI index itself.

The exact rebalancing exercise goes into more details than we need to here but the technique hinges on the fact that there is obviously a cointegrating vector relationship between the replica and the index or as Alexander and Dimitriu put it "the price difference between the benchmark and the replica portfolio is, by construction, stationary", and furthermore when one performs the periodic rebalancing one can rely on the fact that "the stock weights, being based on a large amount of history, have an enhanced stability".

As we have already mentioned the reason for the abnormal returns or the replica's outperformance may have as much to do with the characteristics of overall market behavior as they do with the rebalancing exercise. Alexander and Dimitriu introduce the notion of "regime switches", which we will examine in some depth in Chapter 10, in order to explain the market dynamics that lead to the excess returns:

> The reason why the cointegration strategy has some periods when it significantly over-performs its benchmark but no periods when it significantly under-performs it, is the asymmetric behaviour of stock prices, the fact that prices tend to fall faster than they rise. The result is that the cointegration portfolio successfully exploits general stock market declines and recovery periods even though it is not specifically designed for this purpose.
>
> It can be interpreted as a relative pricing model with an implicit market timing element that pays off if the market switches from the regime with stable returns and low volatility to the high volatility regime when the benchmark returns are low.[19]

In their analysis they pay close attention to the underlying market conditions that accompany the back testing of the DJIA replica and they offer a good account of the time series modeling which allows different volatility and returns regimes to be identified. Based on econometric tests designed to identify structural breaks in time series data, the authors have identified a regime shift in the historical return of the DJIA that takes place in October 2000 (even precisely identified as October 16th 2000). At this point, the period of high returns that were consistent in the second half of the 1990s gives way to a period of much higher volatility and lower and negative returns. This is illustrated in Figure 8.7.

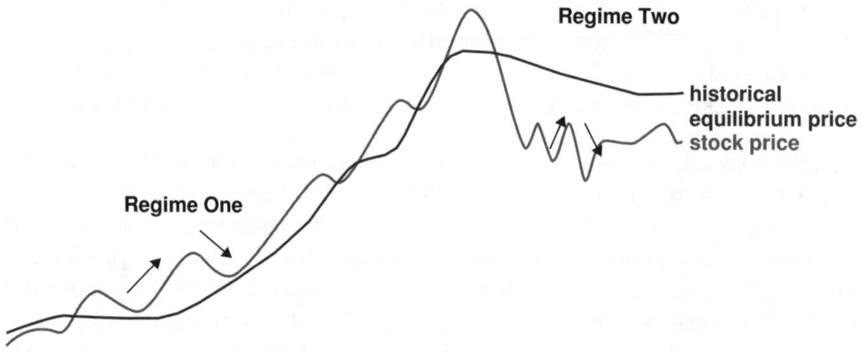

Figure 8.7 Market regimes. Reproduced by permission of Carole Alexander

To summarize how the replica can produce the excess returns it is simplest to consider the case of some of the high tech holdings in the DJIA replica. As the prices of the high tech stocks increased substantially in the late 1990s and because the rebalancing exercise looks at weightings from a longer cointegration perspective, the rebalancing will result in a relative underweighting of these components. As the markets entered regime two in October 2000 as the bubble burst the underweighting shielded the replica from the abnormal price declines as prices reverted to their more normal equilibrium levels as implied in the historical cointegration. Following the major correction, the stocks that had suffered the most would now have transitioned from being underweighted to being overweighted as the longer-term cointegration relationships begin to restore themselves, and as prices recover this overweighting will contribute further to excess returns:

> We have shown that, without any stock selection, solely through smart optimization that has an implicit element of market timing, the benchmark performance can be significantly enhanced in certain market circumstances.[20]

As a result of the smart optimization techniques and the observable characteristics of different market regimes it would seem that the authors have identified a special case where a meaningful positive return can be obtained from a long/short strategy involving a true arbitrage between an index and some of its components. So we have additional reasons, beyond the undoubted validity of the arbitrages involving fixed income instruments, to claim that we can provide a positive answer to our opening question concerning integration. We should, however, insert the proviso that mean reverting behavior is to be expected where asset returns are cointegrated but exactly when this will be achieved cannot be defined with any certainty. So it would be unwarranted to unduly rely on a definite timetable as to when the reversion will occur and this raises hazards that lie beyond what should be expected from a pure arbitrage trade.

But what about the other two questions that began this chapter. It can be said without qualification that correlation alone is not a basis for a riskless or low risk arbitrage trade or hedging strategy. This does not mean that there cannot be a successful track record generated by following a pairs trading strategy. What it does mean is that this kind of strategy is subject to much greater risk than is often implied by advocates of statistical arbitrage.

With regard to the question whether convergence can be the basis for a hedge strategy it is vital to clearly identify what kind of convergence is under consideration and also the time frame for the eventual convergence. Clearly the GM/Ford example suggests that the use of the term convergence in this context is misleading at best. The on the run/off the run strategy will lead to convergence eventually (almost certainly the U.S. Treasury is as unlikely to default on a bond with $29\frac{1}{2}$ years to run as one with 30 years to run) but as the events of August 1998 shockingly demonstrated "eventually" can seem like a very long time when one is in the midst of a global liquidity crisis.

MARKET TURNING POINTS AND COINTEGRATION

In the concluding section to this chapter we want to venture into slightly more controversial territory and discuss a conjectural view of why the view that there is mean reversion at work in the markets has persisted and why it may ultimately have much to recommend it.

Returning to the themes of Chapter 2 where trend days were examined there was an implicit realization that during the market's "quieter" and less coherent periods of trading prices will have a tendency to "wander away" from areas of chart support and resistance. Chart support and resistance levels take many forms, such as prior breakout levels, gaps or a previous historical or multi-period high or low. Astute traders are keenly aware of the major levels of support and resistance and from time to time they will want to test them but what is also apparent is that much of the time markets are not in the vicinity of these key levels. It might even be argued that there may be an aversion tendency at work so that traders can avoid having to confront too often critical decisions about what to do when a key support or resistance level is reached. If there is a specific reason or precipitating factor that arises to test a strategic price level for an index or security then the decision making can no longer be postponed, but for many market participants, especially short-term traders, there will be a relief that the market is not at a "defining moment". But how far can the markets wander away from the key support/resistance levels before other traders sense an opportunity to catch the unwary by surprise?

Looked at from this perspective markets can sometimes be construed as exemplifying the least edifying features of the predator/prey model of collective behavior. There are many traders that will find that this model is the most appropriate framework for making sense of the financial markets and we would be severely challenged to persuade them otherwise. Looked at from the more benign perspective that markets are a form of self-organizing intelligence, the occasional crashes or critical market episodes could be interpreted as a kind of self-regulating process that takes place periodically to eliminate excessive wanderings from historical norms. This same self-regulation could even be seen as the intervention of an "invisible hand" that seeks to restore more customary alignments between asset returns.

If we are right about this self-correcting process has to be clearly distinguished from the statistically rigorous concept of cointegration (in the precise sense that Clive Granger or Carol Alexander would approve of) but the results may take on some of the same characteristics. The correcting of excesses, the reversion to more established benchmark relationships that are often features of climactic trading periods, could be the result of a sudden admission to the excesses of what has been "allowed to happen" during the more unorganized and fractious market sessions. Constant disagreements over the suitability of short-term prices are a vital feature of markets. As we have previously commented it is fractiousness that enables the market to have the necessary liquidity to facilitate a high volume of transactions but as prices wander in some sense "incoherently" many kinds of dissonances and inconsistencies arise. Extreme trend days are the sudden realization by many traders that these dissonances are unsustainable and require resolution and this produces the kind of coherent price behavior that we have seen in trend days.

Perhaps it is also worth pointing out that some of the largest opportunities for trades based on statistical arbitrage arise in the aftermath of liquidity disasters. In other words when markets have wandered too far from historical equilibrium levels or from a loosely defined notion of cointegration (as opposed to the idea of there being some "fundamental" level based on earnings etc.) then the extremely coherent behavior that produces crashes and major corrections also offers great trading opportunities. After major disruptions traders will seek out areas of technical support as evidenced by both index and individual security price charts in an attempt to test the validity of recovery efforts.

We are all fascinated by blow-ups and crises but it is worth remembering that markets will, over extended periods, swing back and forth between different extremes or boundaries. They will reach too far in moments of overconfidence by building bubbles or taking on heroic levels of leverage to exploit convergence trades. But when they "correct" they will also overreact in purging excesses. Those who were able to sift through the debris of the LTCM accident were able to make enormous returns quickly as the "normal" relationships among securities that had underlying cointegration forces at work came to prevail again.

Even in the case of pairs trading which we have found wanting in many respects as the basis for an arbitrage-based long/short or spread strategy it has to be said that when markets are recovering from major corrective episodes there is more likely to be better opportunity to exploit large discrepancies. When major dissonance has been resolved and prices have overreacted towards extremes then traders will be looking to re-establish some previously observed relative value trades based on historical levels of price support and previously observed co-movements of securities. It is not that markets have any natural tendency towards equilibrium but rather that when things have come apart the best way to begin the reassembly process is to try to reassert previous prices and relative values that worked historically. Edward Thorp[21] makes the related point in relation to the aftermath of the 1987 market crash:

> [S]imulations showed that the crash and the few months thereafter were by far the best period ever for statistical arbitrage. It was so good that in future tests and simulations we had to delete this period as an unrealistically favorable outlier.

9
Random Walks and Power Laws

In Chapter 7 compelling evidence was provided for the existence of power law behavior in financial time series, at least with respect to the frequency of overnight price breaks and gaps. We discussed in general terms what the significance of this might be and touched on the nature of the power law relationship, specifically the inverse square law, which appears to describe the gaps phenomenon. We would now like to devote considerably more attention to the nature of power laws and look at some intriguing research that has been done by scientists, not specifically with finance or trading backgrounds, but which provides for a much richer understanding of market dynamics.

Clustering of volatility is one of the so-called stylized facts about market behavior that has been cited by critics of the orthodox view that price development is essentially a random process. Clustering suggests serial correlations or some kind of "memory" within the daily or finer grained observations and this runs counter to the i.i.d. assumption that was discussed previously.... Additional facts, such as the "fat tails" phenomenon whereby extreme behavior is far more likely than would be suggested if time series data is normally distributed, also present problems for those who advocate the random walk hypothesis (RWH). For present purposes we shall summarize in general terms why the clustering of volatility poses peculiar problems to one of the tenets of the RWH.

Research into volatility clustering supports the notion that markets seem to reveal two noticeably different kinds of phases or regimes – those periods that are relatively calm and those that are unusually turbulent. As we have seen from our own analysis and overview of the volatility of the S&P 500, the 1993–1996 period was on the whole a quiet period as was the more recent period from mid-2003 to the spring of 2006. At other times, there are periods when the markets exhibit greater volatility and clustering of the highly volatile sessions, for example much of the period from early 2000 to late 2002 falls into this category. Clustering can also be seen at finer granularities at the intraday level. Furthermore it can be empirically observed that within the more volatile clusters there are alternating periods of strong upward moves followed by downward moves. In fact this is the more probable scenario and the larger the magnitude of the volatility the more alternation from one period to the next is likely to be found. This leads to the suggestion that there is a correlation or "memory" inherent in the log returns for all financial time series and sometimes it is more apparent than others. Serial correlation does not fit well with the RWH as we shall soon discover.

We have also observed that on the trend days there is an unmistakable pattern or signature to the price behavior for such sessions. The closing price will tend to fall at one extreme or the other in terms of its intraday range after a sustained and coherent move within a single trading session. This phenomenon has been referred to as the Coherent Closing Bias. To state simply again the finding, we observed that when considering trading histories in bulk, the closing biases (i.e. the position of the closing price with respect to the intraday range) appear to follow a random distribution, being equally as likely to arise within each of the 10 deciles of intraday range. However, when we confine attention to only the coherent trend days there is nothing random about the distribution. Traders' opinions lose their normal fragmented quality and become much more consistent and closely aligned, liquidity dissipates and there is an internal coherence to the data which provides a clear challenge to the classical notions that time series data is independent and identically distributed and is effectively random. We have so far avoided discussing the random walk hypothesis because we feel that it has occupied too many opening chapters in the trading and finance literature and the reader has probably little appetite for a largely discredited notion anyway.

WHAT IS A RANDOM WALK?

The history of this notion goes back at least as far as Louis Bachelier, a French mathematician, who wrote his PhD dissertation on the nature of speculative markets at the turn of the 20th century. Largely unnoticed at the time, the underlying ideas of his thesis were that price movements within markets have similar characteristics to what is called Brownian motion and which, in effect, means that there is no pattern or signature to the development of price in a time series. It follows that if there are no underlying patterns or trends to price movements, then price development over time is a matter of "chance" rather than intention. But if this is the case there would seem to be no basis for prediction or anticipation of the way in which a market is going to behave in the future. Bachelier came to the conclusion that "The mathematical expectation of the speculator is zero."

If the speculator is unable to find any "edge" from studying the previous history of a time series then shouldn't we all abandon technical analysis? If price development is purely a chance process with no underlying intentionality, the analytical activities of the technician would be akin to those who look for patterns in the winning number sequences for lottery draws. This line of attack on technical analysis became one of the favorite hobby horses of sections of the academic community in finance and continues, in a less ebullient fashion, to this day. One of the best known statements of the "worthlessness" of T.A. or chartism is to be found in a classic paper by Eugene Fama:[1]

> Chartist theories implicitly assume that there is dependence in series of successive price changes. That is, the history of the series can be used to make meaningful predictions concerning the future. On the other hand, the theory of random walks says that successive price changes are independent, that is, the past cannot be used to predict the future. Thus the two theories are diametrically opposed, and if, as the empirical evidence seems to suggest, the random-walk theory is valid, then chartist theories are akin to astrology and of no real value to the investor... It is not enough for him (the chartist) to talk mystically about patterns that he sees in the data. He must show that he can consistently use these patterns to make meaningful predictions of future prices.

It is only fair to point out that Fama has modified his views since this early statement and may even have come under the influence of major critics of the random walk theory such as Benoit Mandelbrot. But there are still many in academic finance that would subscribe to the view that price development is essentially pattern-less and that to engage in techniques designed to unearth patterns is a form of self-delusion.

A classic popularization of the hostility to "technical patterns" and advocacy of the random walk hypothesis appears in the works of Burton G. Malkiel, specifically in his book *A Random Walk down Wall Street*, first published in 1975. The following is an excerpt in which he answers the question he has put – What is a random walk?:

> A random walk is one in which future steps or directions cannot be predicted on the basis of past actions. When the term is applied to the stock market, it means that short-run changes in stock prices cannot be predicted. Investment advisory services, earnings predictions, and complicated chart patterns are useless. On Wall Street, the term "random walk" is an obscenity... Taken to its logical extreme, it means that a blindfolded monkey throwing darts at a newspaper's financial pages could select a portfolio that would do just as well as one carefully selected by the experts.[2]

Often the random walk theory is illustrated by comparing the "path" followed by prices in a marketplace as similar to the path taken by a drunk who is trying to find his way home. The drunk staggers from one lamppost to the next in an entirely haphazard manner with no purpose or intentionality. This random stumbling motion is supposed to mirror the way in which the prices in a market develop over time. To be a little more specific, a random walk supposedly tracks the fact that on balance, the log changes in market prices tend to be purposeless and unpredictable. One moment they are moving this way, the next the other way, lurching back and forth in the manner of someone who is deeply intoxicated. One final point that is often made is that the best place to look for the drunk after several time intervals is close to where you found him the last time you looked. The suggestion here is that despite a lot of wandering back and forth prices have a tendency to change only slightly over the longer term.

Several consequences flow from this way of thinking about price development. Not only are the efforts of chartists and technical analysts likely to fail, according to the thesis, but also, and perhaps this was the secret agenda all along, the markets become much more susceptible to analysis using the statistical techniques founded on the theory of the normal distribution. The vast body of mainstream statistical concepts that ultimately hinge on Gaussian premises are now deemed the most suitable method for analyzing time series data. The fact that many kinds of assumptions about stationarity, serial independence and normally distributed data have proven to be erroneous when applied to actual time series has not deterred many practitioners and trading advisors in their enthusiasm for an uncritical application of statistical measurements to markets. The nonrigorous use of correlation and probability statements about the likelihood of extreme events are only two of the unfortunate consequences of this methodological bias.

What is also not widely commented on by those who have recognized the shortcomings of the random walk model for understanding price behavior is that there seem to be two other strands to the modeling exercise which affect our way of thinking about financial time series and which are also erroneous. The first is the view that price follows a walk or as it is often expressed a *trajectory*. The second and somewhat interconnected notion is that there are clearly discernible linear relationships between financial variables. We shall examine both of these metaphorical prejudices that accompany the random walk model.

THE PRICE AS A TRAJECTORY FALLACY

The metaphors that we use in describing concepts and ideas, especially as they become more remote from common experience, usually provide valuable "insight" into the strengths and limitations of these concepts and ideas. The first metaphors we encounter in the statement of the random walk hypothesis have to do with "paths" or "steps" in discussing the direction of prices. It may be claimed that the very usage of direction is metaphorical but we suggest that this is far less problematic than the terms path and steps. All of our concepts of direction are ultimately metaphorical involving references to a fundamental orientation framework. "In" and "out", "up" and "down", are terms we use and understand because we know how to position ourselves in relation to the world and others. But when we go on to talk about prices following a certain *path* we have moved into a more potentially troublesome use of spatial metaphors. We map price development over time in stock charts with graph coordinates and so on and it is tempting to think of these chart formations as depicting the trajectory of price.

This may be useful as a metaphor but that is all that it is. To go beyond this and apply some of the techniques from the physical sciences that pertain to bodies in motion and the trajectories that they follow is a fundamental misconception. Changes in market prices and a chronological record of their development over time is an ideational or virtual process, it is not a physical process. The laws of physics have been used with great effect to predict the development of a trajectory for a physical object (that's how NASA landed the lunar module) but *we cannot use the laws of physics to predict the development of price over time.* A simple demonstration of that is to be found in market gap events where a stock does not trade at all within the gap price interval. Physical objects necessarily move through all intervals (although quantum theories would dispute that and this is what gives rise to the phenomenon known as the *quantum jump*), prices, as ideational entities, do not have to.

THE LINEAR BIAS AND GRADUALISM

In organizing time series data for analysis and also for our common sense conceptual framework we inevitably use spatial metaphors. We organize events one after the other. We display time series on graphs with coordinates and we implicitly assume that there is a linear continuum of time along which price moves. All of these metaphors are required, how else would we be able to think about time series? But we need to be aware of how these metaphors subtly influence our understanding. Another implicit assumption that often follows in connection with the price as trajectory mental model is the notion that changes in a linear continuum are gradual and continuous. Disruptive changes and discontinuities are relegated to the margins whereas gradual incremental development is considered to be the norm.

We do not want to venture off too far into the history of ideas but there have been several advocates of gradualism; among the more prominent are two seminal writers and thinkers of the 19th century, Darwin and Lyell. The views of Charles Darwin are too widely known for there to be much discussion except to note the very general point that, in his view, the evolution of life forms took place gradually in conjunction with the logic of ecological adaptation. Less well known is the influence that the principal work of Charles Lyell, *The Principles of Geology*, had on his friend Charles Darwin.

Writing in the middle of the 19th century Lyell rebelled against the prevailing theories of geology of the time. At the time geology was largely nonscientific and to the extent that there were any firm views about the nature and history of the Earth and its geological formations, these were largely based on interpretations of the Bible and specifically the books of Genesis and Revelations. Lyell wished to exclude some of the apocalyptic thinking that had informed the thinking of early geologists and paleontologists and believed that the vast fossil record pointed towards a vast time scale for Earth's history. The study of geology, he maintained, should proceed on the assumption that the Earth formations that are evident need to be studied in the context of this vast time scale. Accompanying this perspective was the notion that all change takes place gradually and not dramatically. This is in very marked contrast to the views of catastrophists that place much greater emphasis on dramatic events and disruptive changes as accounting for many geological formations.[3]

Lyell's overall philosophical orientation came to be known as Uniformitarianism which is now a rather neglected premise in our common sense views of the world. Darwin is quoted saying, "The greatest merit of the *Principles* was that it altered the whole tone of one's mind, and therefore that, when seeing a thing never seen by Lyell, one yet saw it through his eyes." So if the "tone" of Darwin's mind was altered by Lyell's uniformitarianism it is hardly surprising that the meme of gradualism has pervaded much of subsequent thought about time series and change.[4] Linear thinking is also pervasive in the physical sciences but during the 20th century several intellectual breakthroughs so undermined the linear and gradualist bias that most scientists abandoned them altogether, at least when they were wearing their professional hats. Unfortunately some econometricians have been rather slow in catching on to the new thinking of complexity and nonlinear systems.

The Danish scientist Per Bak, who unfortunately passed away in his early fifties in 2002, was among the most influential advocates for a new way of thinking and a new methodology for the study of time series data within both the physical and financial world.[5] In both his academic writings and in a very readable book that was addressed to a mainstream audience, *How Nature Works*, Bak introduced some powerful new metaphors and models for thinking about the way that certain systems such as financial markets, which he characterizes as nonlinear, behave and evolve. As can be seen from the citations below Bak was not only a very accomplished physicist but also a student of intellectual history and in his work he often pointed to the origins of many implicit assumptions in our common sense notions about the world:

> However, the uniformitarian theory fails to realize that a simple extrapolation does not necessarily take us from the smallest to the largest scale. A physicist might represent Lyell's philosophy simply as a statement that we live in a linear world. The assumption that a large effect must come from a large impact also represents a linear way of thinking. However, we may be dealing with highly non-linear systems in which there is no simple way (or no way at all) to predict emergent behavior.[6]

The concept of emergence and emergent behavior is a very fruitful one and we shall return to it again but Bak's most important idea in this brief quotation is the notion that, and this is a corollary of the linear and gradualist view, a sudden large effect must require as an explanation the identification of a large cause. This tendency can be found in the literature on market crashes where many analysts are convinced that there needs to be some major precipitating event that precedes or causes a crash to occur. But as we shall see this may not be the case. Crashes emerge from the nonlinear dynamics of a complex system of interactions which is a pretty good description of what a market is. Before we can fully appreciate the benefits of Bak's insights we need to come to terms with two powerful ideas from his work (and the works of other scientists concerned with complexity) which are the idea of self-organized criticality and second the characteristics of power laws.

SELF-ORGANIZED CRITICALITY (SOC)

The following definition appears in the online encyclopedia Wikipedia and as a general introduction we are not tempted to try to improve on it:

> Self-organized criticality (SOC) is a term used in physics to describe (classes of) dynamical systems which have a critical point as an attractor. Their macroscopic behaviour thus displays the spatial and/or temporal scale-invariance characteristic of the critical point of a phase transition, but, unlike the latter, in SOC these features result without needing to tune control parameters to precise values.[7]

It would not be an exaggeration to suggest that SOC has become one of the most influential ideas to emerge over the last 20 years for scientists within many disciplines and especially those that take a multi-disciplinary approach to the study of complexity in its many forms.[8]

If the reader is still grappling with the abstractions in the definition above there is good news for Bak and his colleagues provided a compelling modeling tool that helps to explain SOC in a very accessible manner and in turn a way of visualizing the key elements of the SOC concept. Bak's example rests on thinking about a hypothetical sand pile; it is in fact a computer simulation of how a sand pile forms and the properties that it exhibits when it reaches a critical state. The computer simulation allows us to explore what happens within a sandbox when we add imaginary or simulated grains of sand to the box one at a time. Initially the grains are scattered across the box in no particular fashion until there are a sufficient number to begin to form a pile. As more grains are added the slope and contours emerge as it begins to take on more and more the appearance of a true sand pile. At a certain point the slope of the pile will have reached locally critical values such that adding more grains of sand will cause "avalanches" to occur. These avalanches can either be minor involving only the dislocation of a few grains of sand to massive in which the pile collapses causing almost a complete rearrangement of the grains that had previously been in the pile. The repeated avalanches eventually take up all of the available space in the sandbox, and as the "rain" of new sand grains into the box continues there will be constant overflows as the excess sand grains cannot be contained within the capacity of the container or sandbox. New imaginary sand grains continue to be added but there is equally an exodus of those grains which are overflowing from the box.

According to Bak and his collaborators, at this point the sandbox as a system could be said to have self-organized into a critical state. The nonlinear dynamics of the system have produced complex behavior in which the addition of a single grain may "cause" a major avalanche but as we have already intimated this is a misconception of the nature of nonlinear dynamics. The major avalanche emerges from the behavior of the entire system taken as a self-organized whole (we are tempted to use the metaphor of a network of sand grains here) and not from a single proximate cause. As Bak describes it:

> [M]icroscopic mechanisms working everywhere in a uniform way lead to intermittent, and sometimes catastrophic, behavior. In self-organized critical systems most of the changes often concentrate within the largest events, so self-organized criticality can actually be thought of as the theoretical underpinning for catastrophism, the opposite philosophy to gradualism.[9]

The phrase "most of the changes often concentrate within the largest events" captures one of the most powerful ideas that is relevant to the financial markets. As we have seen a major avalanche can wreak havoc on the previous arrangement of the sand grains and the impact on the system can thus be said to be concentrated in the largest events, yet they can be triggered, just as is the case for minor avalanches, by the simple addition of one more grain of sand. Could there be a resonance here with the remark that we have made noted previously that market crashes are simply corrections that don't stop in the same way that a major avalanche within the sand box could also be said to be a minor avalanche that didn't stop. The immediate or proximate cause of both the large and small avalanches is the same (i.e. the addition of one more grain of sand) but the scale and morphology of the events is radically different. Could there be parallels in the morphology of market crashes? This idea has motivated some fascinating, but mathematically challenging, work by another maverick "outsider" to the world of finance, Didier Sornette.[10] Sornette is Professor of Geophysics at the University of California, Los Angeles, and he has written and co-authored many research papers which attempt to unravel the underlying dynamics of market crashes. He published a book in 2005 called *Why Stock Markets Crash: Critical Events in Complex Financial Systems*, which is not for the faint hearted. In many respects there is a direct line of descent in this book from the ideas of Per Bak and the concepts of self-organized criticality and power laws feature heavily in Sornette's work. The tantalizing subtext of Sornette's research is that there may be underlying "signatures" to the more critical phases of price development in the capital markets that could provide an early warning system of potential crashes. Unfortunately Sornette has published several predictions about impending collapses that have been inaccurate. This only serves to underline the adage that market forecasters should never make predictions.

The second powerful idea that we need to examine inspired by the input from scientists of complexity such as Bak and Sornette is the notion that the distribution of the sizes of avalanches (i.e. the number of grains involved) follows a power law.

POWER LAWS

Roughly, an event is said to behave in accordance with a power law if the frequency of the event is inversely proportional to its magnitude. The dimension of the magnitude or scaling variable can be, as we have seen in the sand pile example, the size of the avalanches (i.e. the number of grains that are displaced), it could be the amount of energy released (or ground motion) in the case of an earthquake or in the case of the financial markets it could be the magnitude of price breaks associated with gaps and range expansion.

To illustrate the incidence of power laws in the financial market we can cite from a recent study that was published in an academic journal but which also managed to secure attention in some of the popular financial media.[11] After analyzing time series data from the financial markets, an interdisciplinary team, headed by Xavier Gabaix of the Department of Economics at the Massachusetts Institute of Technology and which included physicists from Boston University, reported their findings that large-scale events in the stock market adhere to distinct patterns which have all of the hallmarks of a power law relationship. Gabaix and his collaborators found that:

> the number of days when a particular stock price moves by 1 percent will be eight times the number of days when that stock moves by 2 percent, which will in turn be eight times the number of days when that stock moves by 4 percent, which will in turn be eight times the number of days that stock moves by 8 percent, and so on.

This relationship can be described as an inverse cubic law where the exponent of the power law is 3. This is a different exponent to the one previously discussed for the inverse square law (which is 2), so which of these two findings is more accurate? It may be that, as we shall see, they are both accurate within their terms of reference.

Gabaix and his team of physicists analyzed an enormous amount of high frequency financial data (i.e. tick by tick data for thousands of individual securities and indices), but it was confined to a five year period and it may be that their findings were somewhat untypical. We will eventually consider whether the inverse cubic law is a constant or universal relationship across the spectrum (there is reason to believe that it is not) of all price movements but let us finish off with the simple mathematics first. In the case of an inverse cubic relationship we can say that $y = ax^k$ or $y =$ some constant of proportionality (i.e. minus one) $* x$ raised to the power of 3 (the exponent). Power laws can be seen as a straight line on a log–log graph since, taking logs of both sides, the above equation is equal to

$$\log(y) = k \log(x) + \log(a)$$

which has the same form as the equation for a line $y = mx + c$. So for an inverse cubic law the simple line equation would be equal to $y = -3x + c$.

Graphically one can see how this appears on a log–log graph by plotting a series of paired data points that are in accordance with the equation for the power law. For Figure 9.1 the data points were functionally derived to illustrate the inverse cubic law in a mathematically ideal fashion. The points follow an exact straight line when mapped in a log–log fashion whereas in the world of real data we would expect to find a plot line which approximates a line with the exponent value that we have found to be in effect. The equation of the line drawn shows the slope value of -3 which is to be expected for the inverse cubic law.

Reverting back to the artificial avalanches in the sandbox, the distribution of the sizes of the avalanches can also be shown to follow a power law. Again this is best explained by looking at the data. Bak and his collaborators found, when their computers ran the sand pile simulations many thousands of times, that if one tracked the history of the avalanche sizes against their

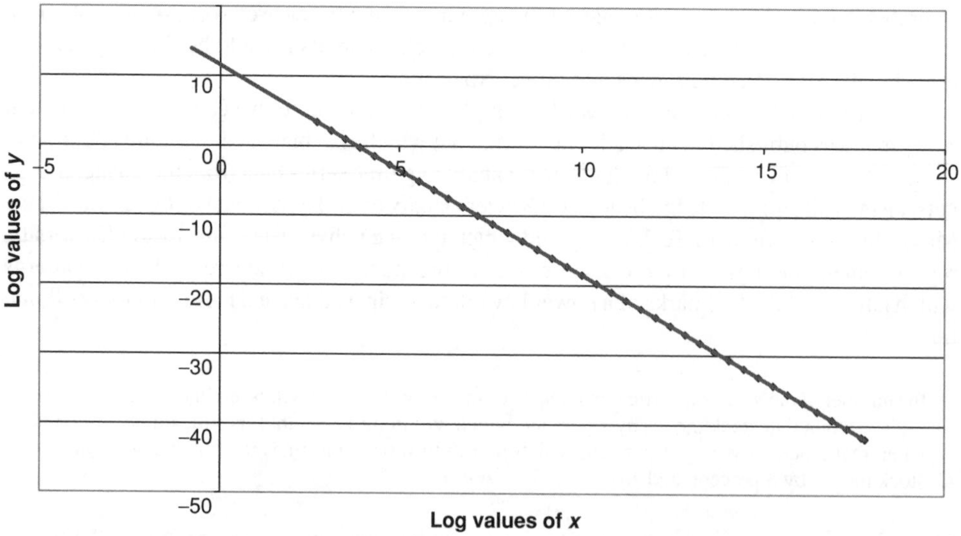

Figure 9.1 *XY* scatter graph illustrating the inverse cubic law – equation of the line is $y = -3x + 11.513$

frequency throughout the entire time line for each simulation, several interesting properties were observed. To summarize the results in a very general fashion what they found was that, on balance, for each simulation one would find that there was 1 avalanche which involved 1000 grains, 10 avalanches which involved 100 grains, 100 avalanches which involved 10 grains, and so on. The frequency of the avalanches was inversely proportional to the magnitude of the avalanche sizes. Based on their findings the exponent of the power law expressing the inverse proportionality was found to be close to 1.

This result received widespread interest from scientists engaged in the study of complex systems and especially from those involved in the earth sciences. The intuition seemed to suggest that there may be some underlying logic or principle of dynamics that could be explored and modeled through computer simulation that may eventually lead to a basis for making predictions for the evolution of complex nonlinear systems. Geoscientists have been challenged by the movements of tectonic plates which have not yielded too much of value as far as understanding when major seismic events are likely. Any modeling tool that might illuminate the mysterious and complex forces that lead to catastrophic earthquakes is worth serious attention and this has certainly been accorded to Bak's research. The next intellectual leap was to suppose that the logic of avalanches in controlled sand piles might also offer some clues as to the incidence of *price avalanches* in the financial markets. A perusal of the research papers at the website that is dedicated to the emerging world of econophysics (www.unifr.ch/econophysics) reveals that many research papers have been inspired by the works of Bak and Sornette among others.

SEISMICITY – A CASE STUDY OF POWER LAWS

Probably the most familiar example of the use of power laws is in relation to the frequency of earthquakes. Table 9.1 is compiled from statistics that are maintained by the U.S. Geological Survey and constantly updated. The table is based on actual observed data from 1900 for the more severe magnitudes and estimates for the minor ones. The U.S.G.S. estimates that several million earthquakes occur in the world each year. Many go undetected because they hit remote areas or have very small magnitudes. As can be seen from the table the magnitude of earthquakes can be stratified from great to very minor. It can also be clearly seen from the table that the frequency of an earthquake of a particular magnitude (measured on the Richter scale) is in a broad sense inversely proportional to its magnitude. Another simpler way of saying

Table 9.1 Frequency of earthquakes

Descriptor	Magnitude	Average annually
Great	8 and higher	1
Major	7–7.9	17
Strong	6–6.9	134
Moderate	5–5.9	1319
Light	4–4.9	13 000 (est.)
Minor	3–3.9	130 000 (est.)
Very minor	2–2.9	1 300 000 (est.)

Based on observations since 1900.

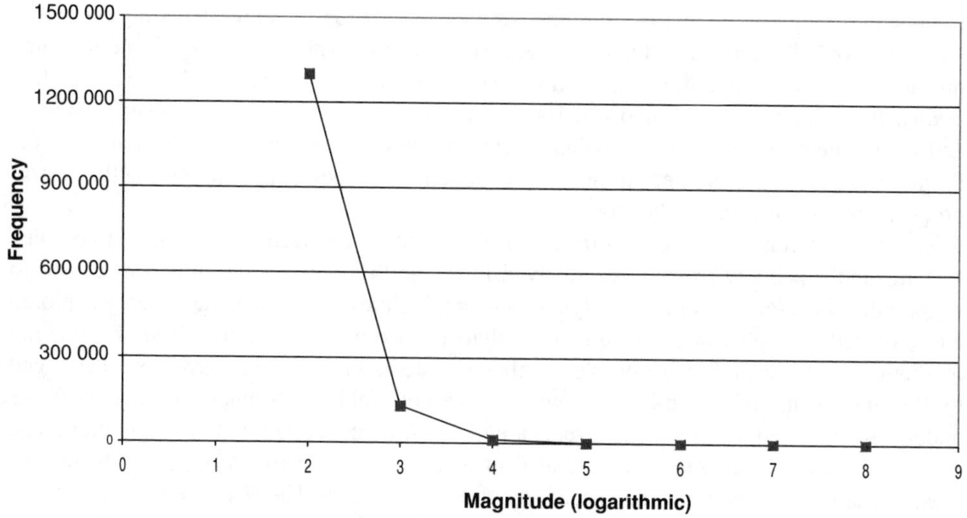

Figure 9.2 Frequency of earthquakes – http://neic.gov/neis/eqlists/eqstats.html

the same thing is that smaller earthquakes occur more frequently than larger earthquakes. But it is possible to be more precise about the nature of the inverse proportionality. There is a mathematical function which describes this relationship between the magnitude and the frequency. The equation has the form of a power law.

Figure 9.2 is based on the data from Table 9.1 and plots the actual frequency on the vertical y-axis while the magnitudes of the earthquakes are plotted on the x-axis. The magnitudes are expressed on the Richter scale which is a logarithmic scaling, as will be discussed further, whereas the frequency values in Figure 9.2 are natural numbers.

Something remarkable happens if we flip the y-axis of Figure 9.2 to a logarithmic scale. The result can be seen in Figure 9.3 and what has emerged in the log–log rendition of the variables (the Richter magnitudes were already in logarithmic form) is the unmistakable linear signature indicating a power law relationship between the frequency and magnitudes of earthquakes.

The magnitude or scaling factor of earthquakes was developed by the geologist Charles Richter. On the Richter scale, the magnitude of an earthquake is proportional to the log of the maximum amplitude of the Earth's motion. This can be illustrated by the following examples: If the Earth moves one millimeter in a magnitude 2 earthquake, it will move 10 millimeters in a magnitude 3 earthquake, 100 millimeters in a magnitude 4 earthquake, and 10 meters in a magnitude 6 earthquake. A magnitude 8 earthquake is by no means twice as powerful as a magnitude 4 earthquake as is sometimes mistakenly thought; in fact the ground is moving 10 000 times more in the magnitude 8 earthquake than in the magnitude 4 earthquake. Another slightly less awesome statistic is that a magnitude 7.2 earthquake produces 10 times more ground motion than a magnitude 6.2 earthquake, but it releases about 32 times more energy.

As promised it is possible to specify precisely the nature of the inverse proportionality between the frequency and magnitudes and this is implicitly revealed in the slope of the line of Figure 9.3. Simply stated, the Gutenberg Richter law expresses the nature of the power law relationship between frequency and magnitude and can be stated as follows: The number of

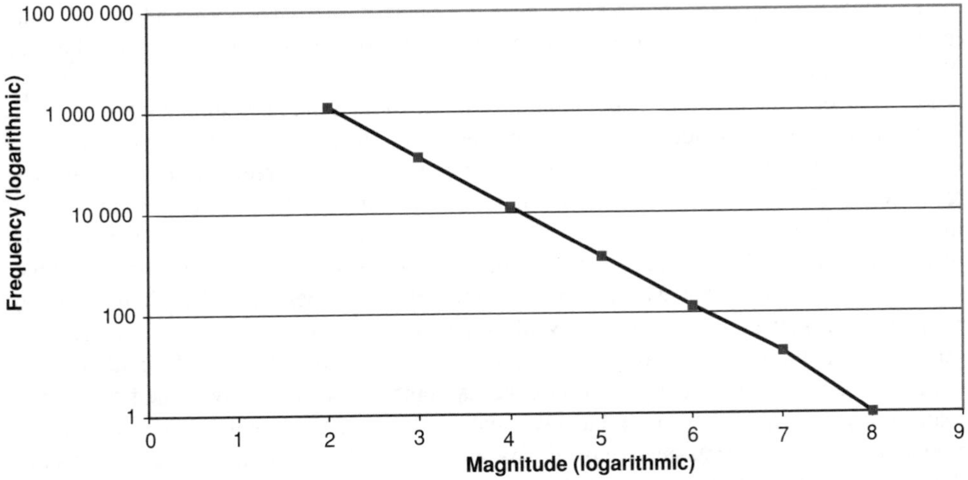

Figure 9.3 Log–log graph showing frequency and magnitudes of earthquakes compiled from data collected by the U.S. Geological Survey

earthquakes of magnitude M is proportional to 10^{-bM} where $b = 1$. It can also be noted that there is some evidence that the exponent in the power law relating the actual historical record of earthquake magnitudes and their frequency may not in fact follow a universal and constant exponent and may vary from one geographical location to another. Interestingly, as will be seen below, there appears to be some variability in the power law exponents that are observed in financial time series data and evidence that the background market conditions may affect the values of the exponent.

CAN POWER LAW RELATIONSHIPS YIELD PREDICTIONS?

This is an area of considerable controversy and in many ways is the key topic of the fascinating book by Didier Sornette that we referred to above. The subject matter of this fairly complex study (from a mathematical standpoint) would take us into territory that we do not need to venture but we can perhaps briefly summarize the controversy with the following very clear synopsis (hopefully) of the issue:

> A large number of papers have been written by physicists documenting an alleged signature of imminent financial crashes involving so-called log-periodic oscillations – oscillations which are periodic with respect to the logarithm of the time to the crash. In addition to the obvious practical implications of such a signature, log-periodicity has been taken as evidence that financial markets can be modeled as complex statistical mechanics systems. However, while many log-periodic precursors have been identified, the statistical significance of these precursors and their predictive power remain controversial.[12]

The reader may be happy to hear that we will not discuss the log-periodic oscillations any further but will take the rather simple minded approach which is to see whether there is any pattern to the actual frequency distribution of events that may follow a power law with respect to their relative frequencies. In other words, even if we have a pattern and formula for expressing relative frequencies does this enable us to say anything about the distribution in time of events of a certain magnitude?

Let us revert back to the safe and familiar example of the sand piles simulations to help us out with this rather abstract topic. An important finding that emerged from analyzing all of Bak's data was that there was no obvious common interval to the frequency of the avalanche sizes. Although there may have been 10 avalanches involving 100 grains within the duration of the simulation and these were 10 times more frequent than those involving 1000 grains, each of these avalanches did not occur at regular intervals of one tenth of the time line. There was just as much likelihood that events might cluster together and then wait a long interval before recurring as that the events would be evenly separated across the time line at roughly equal intervals. This finding is also very much in accordance with the classical observations from the earth sciences that there may be no frequency signature or cyclicality to the frequency of major seismic events. We know, relatively speaking, that major earthquakes will be a lot less frequent than minor events and we even have a constant of proportionality that can quantify that frequency ratio fairly precisely, but this does not mean that we have a way of anticipating when the major episodes will occur and no foundation for believing that they will be separated by common intervals.

Sometimes in the popular media in connection with articles about the likelihood of major earthquakes there is something like the following reasoning used to think about "the Big One". The logic (if it can be called that) goes as follows: Major earthquakes have affected the San Andreas fault approximately once in every 100 years and one has not been experienced since the 1906 San Francisco quake, therefore one is overdue. But this is based on an erroneous view of the Richter law and a confusion and misunderstanding of the nature of periodicity. It could be that another major quake will not happen for another 100 years and then there might be two that occur soon after each other. The average frequency figure would have been maintained but to the residents of San Francisco it makes a huge difference whether there is clustering or common intervals between the events.

A very similar kind of inappropriate use of reasoning is sometimes used in the attempt to forecast market crashes or bear markets. A very simple view might be that bear markets occur on average every seven years and since we are now eight years from the last (assuming that this statement happened to be a true statement at the time it was made), a new bear market is overdue. This conclusion is just as erroneous as the view that California is on the verge of a major seismic event (let us hope that it isn't). We are suspicious of any of these averaging principles to financial forecasting for several reasons. One of the most pertinent is that large fluctuations tend to cluster and are not evenly spread out around a mean. The clustering phenomenon is one that does not conflict with power laws, since the power law relationship does not and cannot make any predictions about when a certain sized event will occur only that it will have a frequency factor associated with its magnitude. Bak's work has produced an avalanche of research papers itself and, without going into the academic debates which it has provoked, there has emerged some evidence of clustering of the sizes of the avalanches and this has been related back to the fractal dimension of the sand piles but that is probably best left to the reader to pursue.

The notion that complex systems within the natural world, such as the movements of the Earth's tectonic plates, can be compared to a computer simulated sand pile may seem excessively simple. Likewise, on first reaction it may seem completely inappropriate to use the metaphor of an avalanche to model phenomena as complex as critical price changes in the financial markets. The essential link is that these phenomena both contain power law distributions, which is, in itself, a significant new insight into the nature of financial time series. The less than good news is that, as we have also seen, this link may not make us any the wiser as to when large-scale events will occur.

Perhaps the most important contribution that Bak has made to the understanding of finance is the recognition that nonlinear systems self-organize into critical states and that periodically they exhibit transitional shifts or discontinuities that are entirely explicable in terms of the system itself. There is no need to go outside the system to introduce exogenous events. This was the point that we made in relation to the gradualist bias in our common sense way of thinking about change and proportionality of cause and effect. It may be appropriate to explain a major phase shift within the financial markets in terms of a major event such as the attacks on the World Trade Center and the Pentagon in 2001, but perhaps in the case of other critical events, including the October 1987 crash, we should be examining the internal dynamics of the financial system and its susceptibility to major displacements and discontinuities.

In talking of discontinuities we are reminded of one of our starting out points for this chapter which was the price as trajectory fallacy. From the study of sand piles and avalanches we may now have the beginnings of a framework to explain why price development within a market exhibits discontinuities at all time scales. These can range from intraday gaps, overnight gaps through to market crashes or even major bullish gaps. The power law framework introduces the notion of scale invariance (see note 1, Chapter 7) and once again we could glibly remark that an overnight gap and a market crash may have more in common in terms of their underlying dynamics than would appear on the surface. But it is a definite *non sequitur* to suggest that, because we have observed power law relationships covering the magnitude of large price movements and their frequency we have secured a firmer basis for predictions.

We have learned a lot about the dynamics of avalanches from the sand pile simulations, Bak has discovered some compelling facts about their relative frequencies but it would be a step too far to claim that Bak has unearthed meaningful patterns as to the probability density function and actual distribution of any event of a specified magnitude. This is an important and critical distinction and one that is sometimes mistaken by those who should know better. For example, in the press release that was circulated to announce the findings of the academic research that was done by Gabaix and the Boston University physicists there is the following very misleading remark: "The stock market has its share of shakeups, but who would guess that large movements in this man-made system adhere to a similar pattern of predictability as earthquake magnitudes?"[13] As we have seen there is no pattern of predictability to earthquake magnitudes other than in the very narrow sense that we have seen. It goes without saying that there is likewise no known "pattern of predictability" in the financial markets.

POWER LAWS WITH DIFFERENT EXPONENTS

From our own analysis of historical data for security returns and the analysis of price breaks and gaps that we summarized in Chapter 7 we have found evidence which is in accordance with the view that there may effectively be different exponents applicable for the power laws that describe the fluctuations in markets. We found evidence with price breaks for individual security returns that at the intermediate level of fluctuations (i.e. gaps of magnitude ± 2 to $\pm 4\%$) the exponent of the power law is 2, in effect reflecting an inverse square law relationship. The exponent appears to move closer to 3 when larger fluctuations are considered (i.e. gaps of more

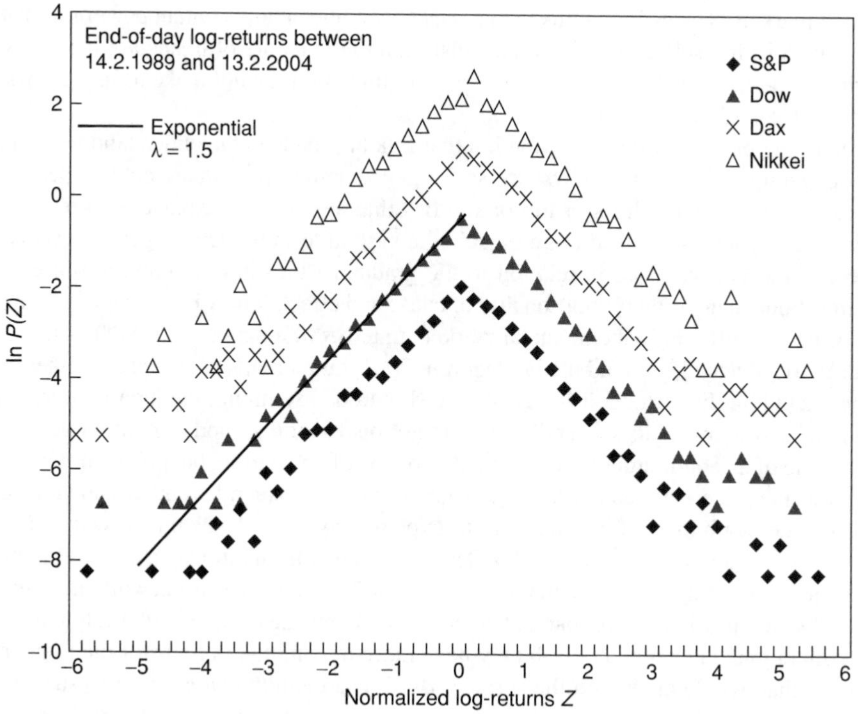

Figure 9.4 Returns of different world indices follow a power law. Reproduced by permission of P. Neu and R. Kühn

than ±5%) and this exponent value is also the one proposed in the study by Gabaix *et al.* that was cited previously.[14]

According to research conducted by Peter Neu and Reimer Kühn[15] we may be more accurate in seeing the exponent at the level of the major indices and in the case of intermediate sized fluctuations to have a value that more closely approximates to 1.5 rather than 2.

Figure 9.4 is quite revealing as it covers four major indices over a 15 year period and shows remarkable symmetry between the indices for three different economies. Both tails of the distribution have been shown and there is evidence that the power law exponent of 1.5 provides a "best fit" for the data.

Figure 9.5 is based on the end of day log returns, covering 15 years and more than 3500 data points in each case, for four major equity indices – the S&P 500, the Dow Jones Industrials, the German DAX index and the Japanese Nikkei 225 index. The horizontal axis of the scatter diagram shown in Figure 9.5 plots the normalized log returns for each index (i.e. where the returns have been adjusted to the standard normal variable or z-value for each index based upon the relevant mean and standard deviation for each index). The vertical axis is the standardized probability for each of the z-values expressed as a natural logarithm. In other words this is the same representational technique that was encountered previously when we examined the idealized graphical display of the inverse cubic relationship (see Figure 9.1).

Neu and Kühn have also suggested that a similar exponent can be found in the intermediate fluctuations that are found within time series of different granularity ranging from 1 minute

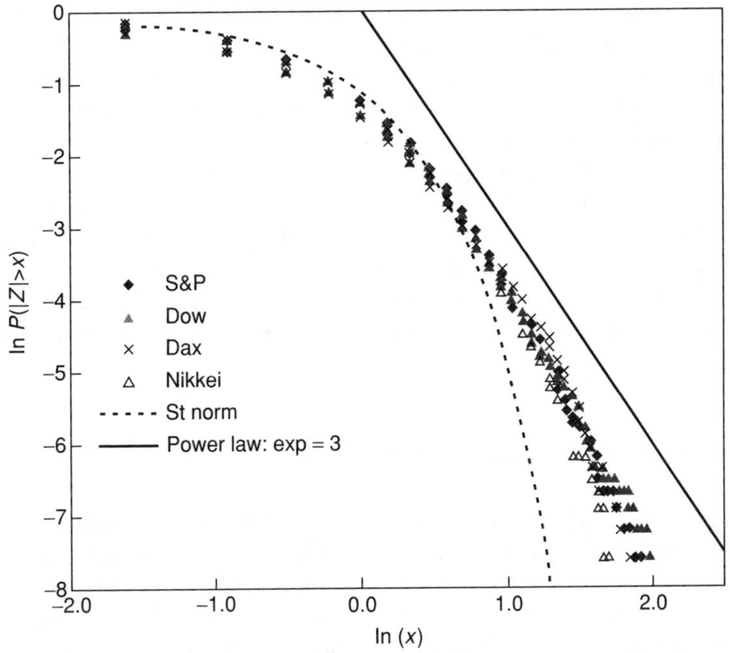

Figure 9.5 Large fluctuations follow a power law with exponent = 3

through larger granularities to 16 hour data. They claim that these findings are also consistent with Mandelbrot's view that the stable Levy distribution best describes the amplitudes of the fluctuations (Levy distributions will be discussed at the end of this chapter). Since there is a constant Levy scaling across all granularities they come to the conclusion that "the same market mechanisms are operating at all time levels".

Moving from intermediate sized fluctuations to larger-scale fluctuations, the suggestion is that the power law is best described and "fitted" with an exponent value of 3. The authors have not made a suggestion as to where the threshold lies that enables the fluctuations to be classified as large rather than intermediate. From our own research with several time series we have observed a phase transition that appears after the daily fluctuation exceeds ±4%. Below that threshold the exponent that best fits the relative frequencies appears to be 2 following the inverse square law and above the 4% threshold this moves to 3 following the inverse cubic law.

Just why this is found and what the phase shift may represent is not discussed by any of the authors who are focused on power laws in financial time series. From our own analysis we would suggest that the intermediate fluctuations with an exponent ≤ 2 mark the upper boundary to the extreme trend days that we analysed in Chapter 2. Trend days represent a range expansion and even though they can create significant price displacements and temporary loss of liquidity they are well behaved in the sense that liquidity is usually re-established at the end of a single trading session albeit at a price that may be far removed from the opening price. The price displacement can be quite sharp and abrupt but the dislocation does not get out of hand as the market stabilizes before the end of the current session. The suggestion is that the larger fluctuations (i.e. price breaks and gaps that are greater than 4 or 5%) may be more likely associated with large overnight gaps, responses to critical developments at the macro level and more serious liquidity concerns as assets become more highly correlated. In such cases the price dislocations and the loss of liquidity may not be contained so readily at the end of a particular session and may become a more persistent phenomenon. These larger fluctuations would then give rise to the higher exponent value for the power law relationship. All of this is highly conjectural and the reader may be asking just what do these power law exponents really indicate anyway? We cannot provide a convincing repudiation for those that find the notion of power laws to be mired in mystery and question its usefulness. However, we are of the view that there will be further intellectual breakthroughs that are motivated and inspired by econophysicists using similar modeling tools to those that have been pioneered by Per Bak. It would be as foolish to dismiss the value of this research in principle as to believe that it promises a financially engineered world in which crashes and market irrationality become obsolete.

THE MANDELBROT DISTRIBUTION MODEL

We have covered some fairly abstract notions in this chapter and ventured into territory that has not been addressed in most of the well-known technical analysis literature. Our main purpose in taking the reader on this journey was to expose some of the less widely known features of financial data and the treatment of these characteristics by researchers and scientists that are not yet in the mainstream of financial orthodoxy. Our secondary purpose has been to underline the inherent limitations of standard statistical techniques when applied to the peculiarities of asset returns. Let us summarize our findings in this chapter so far.

We have found the normal distribution to be severely lacking in its ability to capture the essential characteristics of time series. The random walk hypothesis which dismisses the idea that there can be useful patterns to assist the trader in anticipating price development clearly does not fit the fact that many traders have achieved great wealth from finding such patterns. The evidence of power laws is persuasive and yet it is somewhat frustrating as it held out the promise that it could be more useful than it appears to be. We should emphasize that our understanding of the true significance of power law relationships may take large steps forward as the state of knowledge on complex nonlinear systems continues to evolve. But we still do not have a robust, quantitatively grounded, account that allows us to describe the "shape" of the distribution of large-scale or critical events in a time series.

Let us conclude with one other suggestion that has been proposed for the manner in which time series data may be distributed and which would account for the tendency of such data to reveal "fat tails". Much of the influential work that has been done in this area is attributable to Benoit Mandelbrot who has been a student of the markets for much of his life and who is largely responsible, through his classical work *The Fractal Geometry of Nature*, for the position that fractals now occupy in the intellectual landscape. Mandelbrot has written numerous articles about the unsuitability of Gaussian assumptions to the understanding of financial markets. The most accessible treatment of his views on markets is to be found in a book that he co-authored with Richard Hudson entitled *The (Mis)behavior of Markets* which carries the subtitle *A Fractal View of Risk, Ruin and Reward*.[16] The book is a *tour de force* of all that Mandelbrot finds erroneous in the way that finance is still taught in universities and widely practiced in the investment community. Unfortunately the prescriptions for a new way of profiting from his insights are somewhat thin on the ground and his multi-fractal model of market behavior and application of techniques derived from studying the flooding of the river Nile[17] are probably not suitable for most traders. Nevertheless the contributions that Mandelbrot has made to the study of markets are enormous and his influence can be felt in the works of Per Bak and Didier Sornette who have already been acknowledged in our earlier discussion.

One of Mandelbrot's key insights, which is now widely accepted although when originally proposed it was quite revolutionary, is the observation that markets exhibit much more prominent "outliers" than should be expected from classical theory. It is in this sense that they can be said to misbehave. The fat tails phenomenon is the tendency of financial returns (i.e. the log changes in consecutive prices) to occur more frequently at extremes than would be expected if the returns were normally distributed. Events beyond three standard deviations either side of the mean (sometimes called the six sigma domain) should, according to the probability calculus which is based on the assumptions of a normal distribution, occur with a frequency of less than 0.3%. This is clearly contravened by examining the distribution of actual time series data. Mandelbrot's starting point and the motivating factor that has energized him to continue his criticism of academic orthodoxy in finance is the awkward conclusion that time series do not follow a normal distribution and yet we continue to apply statements about the probability of various occurrences including the likelihood of losses arising in a portfolio that are based on the assumption that there is a normal distribution. Apart from being logically indefensible the inconsistency of this position can also be hazardous to your wealth as he and others, including Nicholas Taleb, have pointed out.[18]

Why if there is such an obvious inconsistency has the assumption of a normal distribution been allowed to continue to circulate as a valid stance for the study of markets? The reason is pretty clear as one critic of Mandelbrot observed: "If we abandon the (normal distribution) assumption most statistical tools would be rendered 'obsolete' and past econometric work 'meaningless'."[19]

So is there another kind of distribution that could more accurately describe the nature of the distribution of large-scale events in time series and help us to predict when they might occur? There are actually two separate issues embedded in that question. We may have a better theoretical model for describing time series data and accounting for "fat tails" but we may not be able to make any better predictions from it than we can with using the obviously flawed assumptions of a normal distribution.

In describing Mandelbrot's view we need to bring together two separate models but one of which follows rather appropriately from our discussion of power laws. Mandelbrot describes in his book how he was very much influenced by the work of the Italian economist Vilfredo Pareto who developed a theory regarding income distribution that was one of the first models to reveal a power law relationship:

> Society was not a "social pyramid" with the proportion of the rich to poor sloping gently from one class to the next. Instead it was more of a social "arrow" – very fat at the bottom where the mass of men live, and very thin at the top where sit the wealthy elite . . . the data did not remotely fit a bell curve, as one would expect if data were distributed randomly.[20]

What in fact Pareto had shown, with the somewhat limited statistical data that he had access to, was the fact that the distribution of income followed a power law with an exponent of approximately 3/2. As Mandelbrot suggests "according to Pareto's formula . . . what percentage of Americans are earning more than ten times the minimum wage . . . the answer should be 3.2% (more) . . . what proportion are making more than $1.07 million and the answer is 1000 times more than make the minimum wage etc.". There is also the interesting remark that "according to Pareto's formula the conditional probability of making a billion dollars once you have made half a billion is the same as that of making a million once you have made half a million".

One important fact follows from the Pareto formula, which is true for all power law relationships, which is that the *distribution around the mean bears absolutely no resemblance to that of a normal distribution*. A rather provocative statement of the consequences of the Paretian view of income distribution is to be found in a research paper published by Sorin Solomon, a professor at the Hebrew University of Jerusalem:

> [T]he number of people $P(w)$ possessing the wealth w can be parametrized by a power law: $P(w) \sim w - 1 - \alpha \ldots$ where $\alpha = 1.4$ has been (shown to be fairly constant) throughout the last 100 years in most of the free economies. This wealth distribution is quite nontrivial in as far as it implies the existence of many individuals with wealth more than 3 orders of magnitude larger than the average. To compare, if such a distribution would hold for personal weight, height or life span it would imply the existence of individual humans 1 Km tall, weighting 70 tons and living 70 000 years.[21]

But knowing that a power law relationship exists in terms of relative frequencies does not really provide us with a means of predicting how the distribution will actually be shaped. We can draw a log–log graph showing the probability of someone being within certain income levels that are scaled logarithmically to the power of 3/2 but how will the actual distribution of income be structured, how will it look? Mandelbrot employs another mathematically based model, the Levy stable distribution, to assist with this question.

To contrast the differences between the Levy distribution and a Gaussian (normal) distribution it will be useful to return to the notion of a random walk. In a random walk where each step follows a Gaussian distribution the distance traveled from the origin of the walk can be expressed fairly simply by multiplying the number of steps by a step size that can be derived probabilistically from the average size of the steps and the standard deviation. Very roughly speaking the steps will be of differing sizes but the likelihood of a step that is three times the previous is about 0.3%. Graphically a random walk in two dimensions will tend to show a pattern that resembles Figure 9.6. Although, according to our model, the direction that the walker takes is random, the sizes of the steps are normally distributed with lot of small steps being the norm (i.e. 68% of the time) and large steps occurring infrequently. The path of the random walker and termination point would resemble the path taken in Figure 9.6. As we can see there are a lot of erratic changes in directions and despite many steps the walker has not covered a lot of territory.

With a random walk where the step sizes follow a Levy distribution the possibility exists of more extreme jumps for the step sizes. To explain this we need to consider the notion of a Levy flight which is the metaphor given to describe the fact that the step sizes can be of much greater magnitude and in fact have infinite variance.[22]

The behavior of a process governed by a Levy distribution is very different from that which follows a normal distribution as Figure 9.7 reveals. In a Levy flight, named after the French mathematician Paul Levy (1886–1971), a random walk would consist of a series of steps or flights whose lengths are cumulatively distributed according to a power law of the form: Power(step length) = Constant $*$ Length raised to the power law exponent.

To assist the reader who may find this all rather confusing there is a way of visualizing this behavior from the natural world. The wandering albatrosses live their lives by a Levy distribution. When looking for food, these seabirds fly for long distances, and then forage in a small area before flying off again. Unlike the foraging activities of many animals they do not only scurry around within a highly localized neighborhood but they from time to time displace

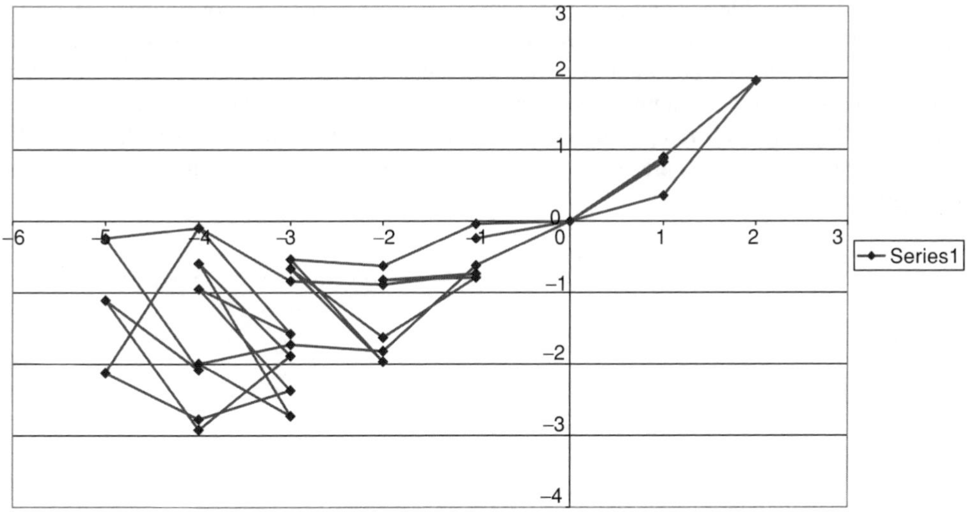

Figure 9.6 Simulation of a random walk

themselves a great distance to find new habitats and hunting ground.[23] The implication to this mental model is that markets also have this tendency from time to time. When a particular market locale or price neighborhood has been exhausted price will take a "flight" to some new locale where traders can continue to transact.

The probability function within the Levy distribution and which determines the likelihood of the large flights is determined by the tails of the distribution and therefore greater attention is paid to the extremes that are found in price behavior. While this approach may provide a more

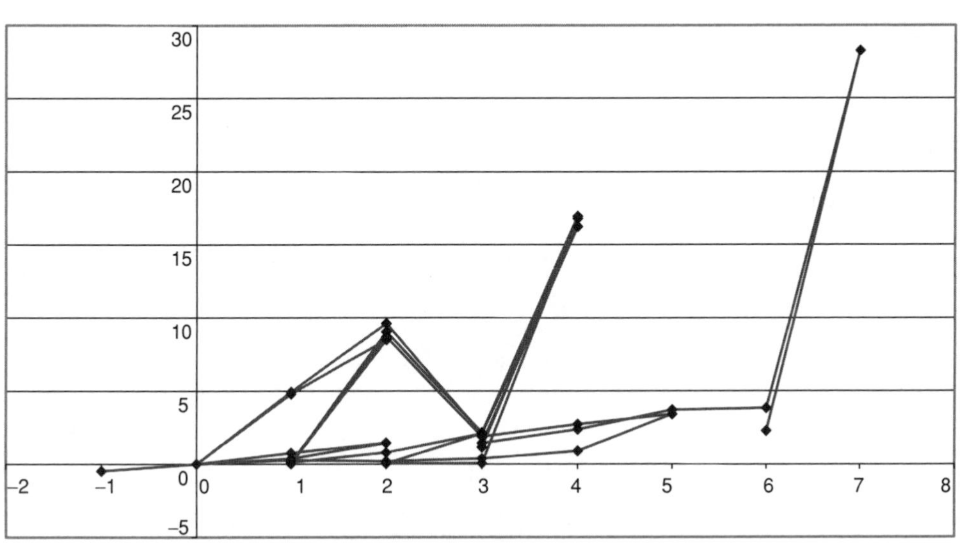

Figure 9.7 Simulation of a Levy flight

intellectually defensible account of the probability of large scale price movements it seems to be unable to yield any more satisfaction from its predictive qualities. We know that extreme movements will be more common than they are under a normal distribution but we may not have advanced our understanding much further as to when they are likely to occur. But there is one clear benefit to regarding time series distributions in this manner which is that it should influence our calculations of the probability of drawdown risks in portfolio management which we shall review in Chapter 11.

10
Regime Shifts and Stationarity

Trading activities are non-stationary: quiescent periods are followed by hectic periods resulting in the volatility bursts that are a striking characteristic of financial time series.

Stationarity is a property that may or may not be present in time series data. In its more general sense it provides an answer to the question of whether the time series preserves a constant mean and standard deviation over the entire series of data points and for any randomly chosen subset of data points. If the time series is stationary then it should reveal a constant mean and standard deviation. With regard specifically to financial time series, it becomes quickly clear that they do not preserve constancy of either value and therefore do not exhibit stationarity. Why should this characteristic be of interest to the trader and portfolio manager? This will be the focus of the discussion in this chapter and in particular we need to examine the consequences flowing from the fact that there is a serious question mark over attempts at applying probability assumptions from Gaussian statistics to the analysis of financial data.

An example of a time series that does have the property of stationarity is white noise which as can be seen from Figure 10.1 fluctuates in a random fashion but which manages to preserve a uniform mean and variance no matter which "section" of the image one takes. The sections are thus interchangeable, they have the same "fingerprint" or "signature" and this can be confirmed using certain statistical procedures. If we were to extract any section and compare its mean and variance to the whole series or any other section then a statistical t-test would indicate that, with a very high degree of probability, we could declare that the two sections came from the same population.

Stationarity is not a feature of data series or distributions that lack a temporal dimension as the following example will show. If we take a static data series based, for example, on some morphological characteristic of a population such as height, the order in which the individuals are sampled and stored in the statistician's database is unimportant. When we provide the summary statistics for the population, the mean and standard deviation will not be affected by the order of the sampling or storage protocol; the summary statistics express the characteristics independently of any ordering. The ranking of the individuals is not a concern until we begin to inquire about the median, lower quartile values and skewness, and even then when we apply

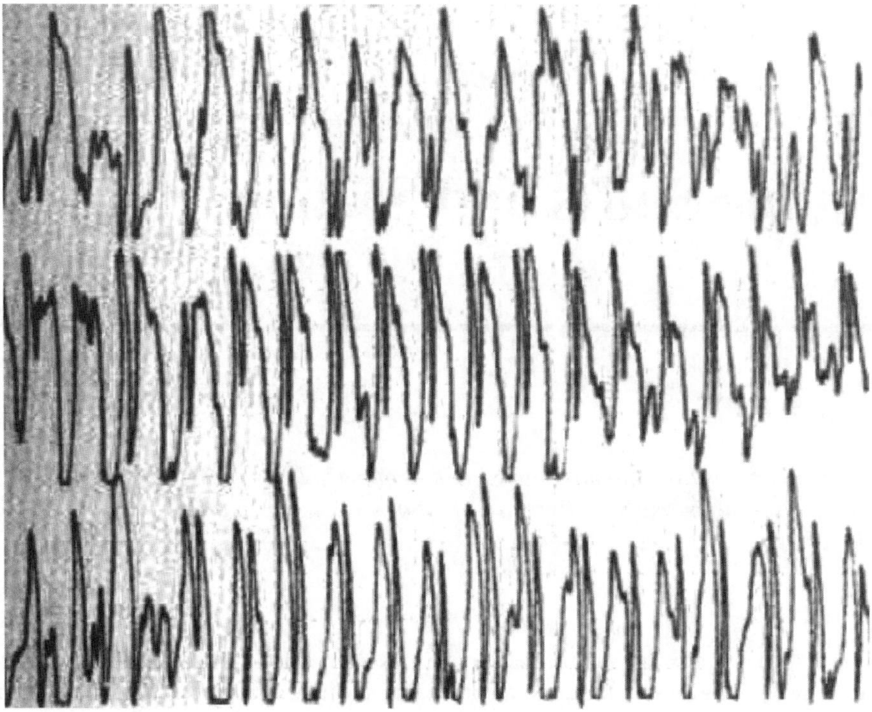

Figure 10.1 White noise

a ranking, we need not concern ourselves with the order in which the actual samples were collected. The order in which the data was gathered is a purely accidental feature of the series. For the case of time series data, the order in which the data is captured is critical, it is the defining characteristic of a time series and if we apply any intermediate sorting techniques to the data we then need to re-establish the original time-based sequence in order for the data to still be meaningful.

To illustrate the kind of testing for stationarity we shall use an analogy with a static data series of height measurements to expose, in its simplest form, the logic involved. Just for present purposes we should imagine that the order in which the series of individual heights were collected is important. Suppose that when the original sampling was being done heights were taken from people at a variety of venues – concerts, schoolyards, offices, basketball arenas etc. We know the population mean and standard deviation (for the entire data set) and we are going to select random clusters or consecutive sets of the originally collected sample data to compare its statistical characteristics against similar characteristics for the whole population. As we select the samples, say the first is for a concert venue, we will apply the t-test and almost certainly find that the probability that the two samples come from different populations is negligible and that we can therefore conclude that both samples are taken from the same population. But suppose that one of our samples, by chance, consisted only of basketball players gathered during a practice session. If we perform the t-test we would almost certainly find grounds for declaring that the sample differed enough from the statistical properties of the entire population that it would have to be declared as qualitatively different. The situation

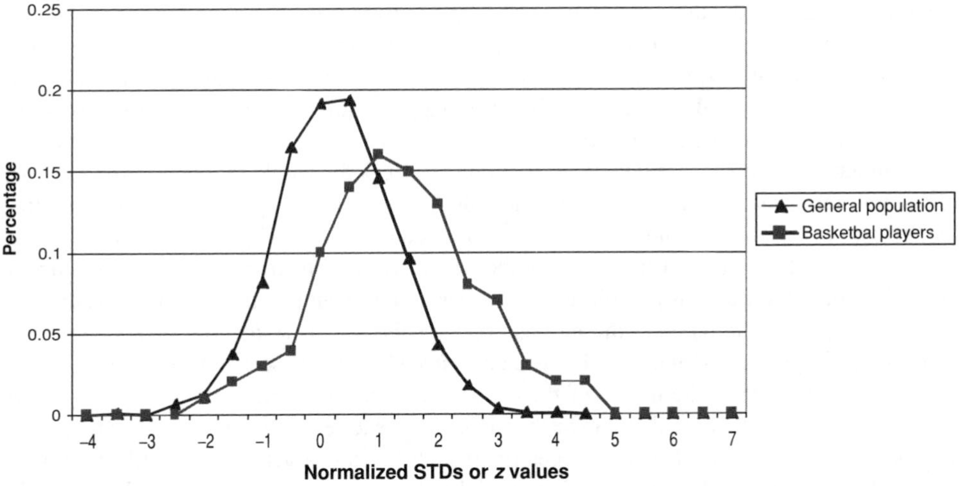

Figure 10.2 Statistical samples with different distributions – the general population and a group of basketball players

is exemplified by Figure 10.2. Without straining the analogy any further, the presence of the basketball players could be compared to a clustering of high volatility within an overall time series that shows, on the whole, tamer characteristics than for the volatile subset (of basketball players).

Where the original order of data capture is critical, which is always true for time series unlike a static series, if we were to select a consecutive set of 100 data points from a database of 20 years of daily market data and then test for the probability that these 100 dates have the same fundamental characteristics of the much larger dataset it is likely that we shall encounter the basketball players far more frequently. We can be almost certain that the original distribution will not show stationarity and that in fact there will be a clustering of "abnormal" occurrences. This also leads to the conclusion that the data is not independent and identically distributed in the same statistical sense as a sampling of the modulations within the white noise series.

REGIME SHIFTS

Financial time series not only exhibit stochastic volatility by which is meant that the standard deviations of the whole series (and therefore the samples as well) are themselves subject to an abnormal series of jumps and dispersion, but also there is clustering of high volatility periods. Accordingly there is a far greater than random chance that for any 100 period window of data there will be a collection or co-occurrence of deviant data points that do not fit well to the larger data set's characteristics. The problem is less acute than at others as time series do appear to exhibit quiet periods when the mean and standard deviation may, relatively speaking, be well behaved over extended periods. But the time series can then abruptly display a "wilder" side in which there is a sharp increase in the magnitude of the log changes and the standard deviation. It could be said, with the modifications to the simple Darwinian thesis in mind, that price development takes place for times in a gradual manner but this gradual quality is punctuated from time to time with bursts of volatility and "innovative" price behavior. However, and this is also true of the neo-Darwinian notion of punctuated equilibrium, it would be incorrect to describe these bursts in time series as revealing some oscillating forces at work. There do not appear to be underlying dynamics that give rise to any obvious signature or periodicity to the alternations. The stochastic volatility of financial time series certainly points to the fact their nonstationarity, which as previously observed undermines the whole rationale behind the use of the normal probability calculus in finance, but there does not appear to be an oscillating mechanism to account for this. Are there any procedures that could help us to analyze and anticipate when the financial time series are about to make the transition from quiescence to high volatility? In the terminology of climate scientists and econometricians are there techniques for detecting *regime shifts* or, as these transitions are also called, *structural breaks*?

There is a large body of work that has been produced by climate scientists who have focused on switches or shifts in the nature of the ecological time series data, often very long term, that they observe. One area that has been studied in great detail involves the oceanographic characteristics of the North Pacific Ocean and how these characteristics oscillate between different attractors. While much of this material is fascinating and covers such issues as the widely recognized "El Niño" climate effect which has been of value to traders in the Chicago agricultural pits, we do not want to go too far astray. We will illustrate one part of the findings for the marine ecology of the North Pacific which involves the number of salmon runs as well as the quality of the herring and pollock stock. As is now widely reported the marine environment is undergoing significant changes through the warming of the oceans and the melting of ice caps and these changes influence the activities of marine life. These changes can be plotted and analyzed statistically and, when the underlying characteristics of the time window "shift" from one period to the next, the underlying series is said to be going through a regime shift. This shift may be an oscillation with a periodicity signature (i.e. it is cyclical and "comes around" every so many years) or it may not have an obvious oscillation signature which is the case with some of the more recent observations and is becoming a matter of great concern for a much wider constituency than just climate scientists.

Figure 10.3[1] covers the 50 year period since 1955 and as can be seen with each of the three time series they alternate between different regimes or phases when the statistical properties of the data, as reflected in the amplitude, mean and fluctuations of the data points pass through a phase shift or qualitative change. Each of the three series depicted in Figure 10.2 has a resemblance in terms of their general contours to some of the volatility charts that we have reviewed. They may be more cyclical with more suggestion of underlying oscillations than we have observed for financial time series but it can said of both kinds of data that they lack stationarity and both kinds are subject to some form of stochastic volatility.

The important conceptual insight that climate scientists have recognized is that time series undergo structural breaks from one climate regime to another. These structural breaks are the equivalent in terms of the capital markets to the critical episodes that we have seen in such charts as the CBOE Volatility index or some of the case studies that have been examined. They are easy to observe in hindsight but the real challenge is to see if we can discover them when they are actually happening. Marine ecologists have proposed different algorithms that attempt to calculate in *real time* whether there is a transitional stage in progress but the exact details go beyond our remit.[2] Essentially the tests involve a continuing sampling of the environmental conditions and a statistical testing of the hypothesis that the present sample and the historical samples are qualitatively different in a manner that is unlikely to have arisen by chance. When a highly improbable transition is detected then the case can be made that the marine ecosystem

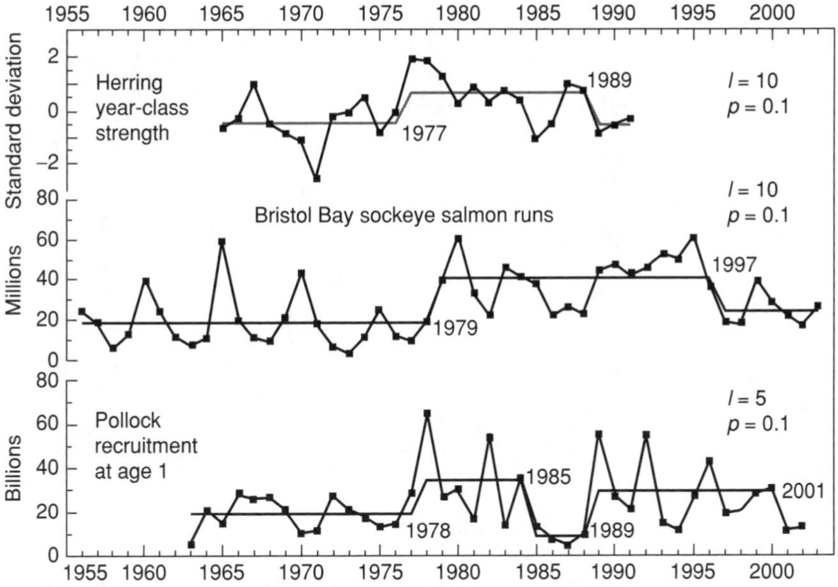

Figure 10.3 Regime shifts in herring year-class strength (top), sockeye salmon runs (middle) and pollock recruitment (bottom). Reproduced by permission of International Council for the Exploration of the Sea (ICES)

is transforming from one regime to another. But what do the fish stocks of the North Pacific have to do with trying to find an edge when trading the markets? As we shall see we will certainly have enhanced our understanding of market dynamics from applying the concept of a regime shift but will we have anything like a real time detection procedure for anticipating the market's major turning points? To answer this let us now turn our attention from marine ecology to the S&P 500 index.

EVIDENCE OF REGIME SHIFTS IN THE STOCK MARKET

From a high level perspective it should be apparent that the testing procedures that have been used by ecologists to detect regime shifts within ecosystems are generically suitable for the analysis of any temporal series. We can apply similar techniques to a uniquely segregated set of financial data, such as the daily log changes in the S&P 500 index over a 20 year period. For testing purposes we might extract, say, a 200 day sample from 1995 and compare it with a 200 day sample taken from 2002. Selecting these two periods would lead to the conclusion that the samples are from different populations, in the statistically significant manner required by a statistical *t*-test. However, since the two samples clearly came from the same original population of data points we should declare not so much that they came from a different population but rather that the original population lacks homogeneity with respect to its statistical characteristics. The disconnect in comparing the two sample periods is of such a degree that the underlying 20 year series should best be thought of as being partitionable into distinctive subperiods each with fundamentally different characteristics. These different partitions can be considered to be *regimes* and the identification of the demarcation zones becomes a matter of

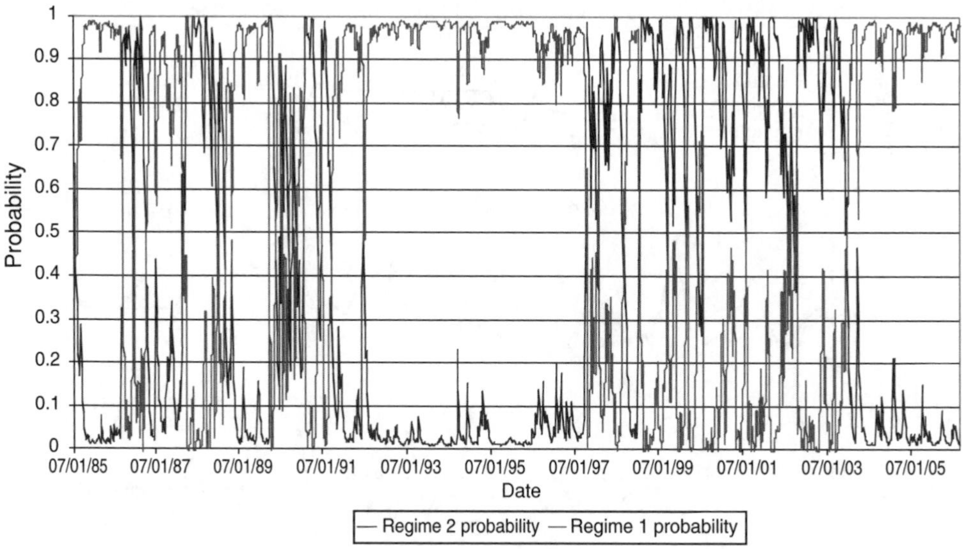

Figure 10.4 S&P 500 weekly log changes 1985–April 2006 – a regime switching model

testing for a so-called regime switch or structural break. More advanced procedures than the *t*-test have been proposed to conduct this test for regime switches in the world of finance. One of the pioneering works in this area was that proposed by Chow and other techniques have been based on use of the Wald statistic.[3]

Figure 10.4 tracks the weekly log changes for the S&P 500 from 1985 to mid-2006 and requires some interpretation. In the discussion of volatility clustering in Chapter 6 it was shown that we can identify periods of greater volatility by showing a histogram which is confined to log changes which cross above the ± 2 standard deviations threshold. We saw clear evidence of clustering and also demonstrated, by means of a moving window (of 52 weeks), that the trailing standard deviation and mean fluctuate erratically during certain periods and appear to "settle down" in others. Figure 10.4 provides us with a different methodology to examine the same phenomenon as well as a technique that allows us to determine which of two market regimes is prevailing at the time.

The vertical axis in the diagram measures a probability reading between zero and 100%. It plots the value that is returned by the Chow procedure that tests for the presence of structural breaks. The jumps from the bottom of the probability axis to the top reflect the transition from the applicability of two different scenarios or statistical models that provide different state descriptions for the prevailing market conditions. In some cases the switches are literally from top to bottom and at other times the jump may take the probability from say zero up to the 40% level at which point the probability may slip back to zero. In such circumstances the market conditions were displaying behavior that could have brought about a regime shift but this was short-lived and the market returned to the status quo with no switch between the two regimes or statistical models.

Additional modeling of the two regimes has yielded some notable differences in the vital statistical values for each regime. They differ most relevantly in their means and variances. The analysis has determined that regime 1 is characterized by relatively low volatility and relatively high mean returns, the standard deviation on an annualized basis is approximately 10% with an annualized mean return of 16%. This is in contrast to regime 2 which is characterized by relatively greater volatility and lower returns – the annualized standard deviation has risen to more than 20% and there is a small negative annual mean of approximately −1%. Some studies of the applicability of regime modeling to the broad market indices have proposed that there is a need to invoke more than two regimes. There are clearly intermediate values (and values beyond) that the mean and standard deviation could take on other than the characteristics of the two regimes so far identified. The problem with expanding the number of regimes is that the transitional paths become more complex which is why we prefer the simplicity that is provided by a two regime model. The real value in the regime modeling comes about from the definitive natures of the breaks rather than the certitude that the exact variance presumed by each of the regime models will fit the emerging market conditions.

We need to be careful when we say that the market switches regimes abruptly or that it passes from one regime to another as it could suggest that we are looking for some kind of "path" or "footprint" which shows the exact transition. This would be to extend the benefit of the helpful metaphors provided by the regime switching model too far and confuse our thinking about what the analysis provides. The regime switching model is a classification model which enables us to differentiate between two (or more) different qualities of market behavior. Each of the regimes can be described qualitatively (i.e. more volatile, lower mean returns etc.) and therefore we can make the classifications intuitively plausible. But the important point is that each regime has certain quantitative features such as a specific standard deviation and a specific mean that become in effect the regime's signature or template. The probability readings indicate whether, from a statistical significance perspective, regime 1 best describes the recent activity or regime 2. When the index "jumps" from one to the other all that we mean is that one of the two regimes' signatures more accurately fits the prevailing conditions or signature.

What can we say about how much time the S&P 500, during the more than 20 year period under review, spends in each of the regimes? If we set the threshold amount on the probability axis to 80%, for qualifying the market condition as being in either of the two regimes, then we find that the index spends approximately 53% within regime 1 (the quiet, moderate returns regime), 26% within regime 2 (the more volatile and negative returns regime) and the remainder of the time is in a transitional mode. So again we are able to become more quantitatively informed of our intuitions about the presence of volatility clustering. We can begin to attach a more viable probability to the likelihood of encountering turbulence over the long haul. However, the probability is a relative probability as to how much time will be spent in each regime, it does not permit any estimation as to the likelihood at any one time that the index is going to make a switch. Let us try to make the predicament clearer by taking a rather simple but familiar analogy from the world of aviation. Ultimately the analogy breaks down and for reasons that may suggest possible clues as to how the concept of regime switching and an early warning system might be harnessed in financial forecasting.

Let us suppose that the airline industry, having tracked the incidence of turbulence over the North Atlantic Ocean for many years, has established that there are two regimes in effect with regard to how much turbulence can be expected for the transatlantic traveler. The first regime is characterized by very occasional turbulence and an overall smooth flight, the second by much greater turbulence and a very bumpy ride. In terms of our illustration let us hope that regime 1 is far more common than regime 2 which seems to be the case, at least with respect to the current climatic conditions. Continuing with the analogy, for each flight we are going to compare the turbulence signature for that flight (i.e. how frequent are the "bumps") with the two regime templates to determine which of the two signatures best describes the current flight. But what if the current flight suddenly switches from one regime to the other? This is exactly analogous to the unwitting trader that sustains a large drawdown in the market when *current conditions* no longer apply. For the nervous flyer (such as the author) and typical trader it would be very useful information to know before a flight or trade whether it would be subject to "normal" or modest turbulence or likely to experience far more severe turbulence. It would not be of much comfort to the flyers if the captain was to announce to the passengers halfway through the ocean crossing that they had just entered a regime 2 turbulence pattern. So even a real time detection algorithm has limited benefit to anxious travelers. What would be far more useful would be a pre-flight detection system based on monitoring weather patterns and other background variables sufficiently closely that one can detect the kinds of signatures or patterns that precede aviation turbulence. In the case of aviation turbulence an early warning system seems very feasible and although it may not be 100% effective it would be possible to warn ahead of time of the most extreme forms of turbulence arising from major storms etc. But if we monitor the background variables in the capital markets sufficiently closely are we likely to be able to anticipate the more extreme episodes of market turbulence? Are there precursors to the large-scale critical events? According to one influential academic paper there are.

In a paper that first appeared in February 2006 entitled *Criticality and Phase Transition in Stock-Price Fluctuations*, the Japanese authors Kiyono, Struzik and Yamamoto claim to have discovered evidence that markets exhibit precursors and phase transition characteristics in the vicinity of critical behavior such as the stock market crash of 1987. They summarize their findings in the following extract from the abstract to their paper:

> The temporal dependence of fat tails in the PDF of a ten-minute log return shows a gradual, systematic increase in the probability of the appearance of large increments on approaching black Monday in October 1987, reminiscent of parameter tuning towards criticality.[4]

In the course of their article which has echoes of similar findings that have been documented by other researchers such as Didier Sornette they characterize the precursors and "markers" that preceded the crash as follows:

> (1) Strongly non-Gaussian behavior of the logarithmic returns of the U.S. S&P 500 index in the critical regime; (2) scale-invariant behavior (data collapse) of the PDF function in the critical regime ... From the observed non-Gaussian behavior of the index, we numerically estimate the unexpectedly high probability of a large price change in the critical regime. This probability estimate is of importance for risk analysis and a central issue for the understanding of the statistics of price changes.

The promise held out by this kind of research is that early detection of regime shifts may in principle be attainable in the same way that turbulent weather can be anticipated from studying meteorological conditions. But there is one big difference. When we are given early warning of major aviation turbulence we cannot alter the condition. The captain can take the plane to a higher altitude or steer a different course to avoid the worst of it but the turbulence will still be there. If traders were able to detect impending crashes and critical market episodes ahead of time they can do something about it – they can refrain from various strategies or remove themselves from the market. However, if the early warning system is accessible to all traders then it could be argued that if all traders are planning to avoid the condition it will not occur.

This raises some interesting questions about the nature of reflexivity in the way that markets behave and whether any early warning system would actually be accepted and followed by the majority of traders.

It is also relevant to distinguish between early warnings of increased volatility and an advance warning system for possible crashes. We doubt that the latter ultimately is a logically consistent concept whereas the former probably is. This leads to one further thought regarding greater understanding of regime switches. The classification of the different regimes does not in itself lead us to any simplistic notions of a bull market or bear market *per se* but rather can enable us to have a warning that the volatility backdrop to trading has changed and that strategies that worked effectively within one regime may no longer be profitable under the new regime or volatility scenario. In particular writers of options would be well advised to pay attention to the explanatory power of regime switching models.

OPTION WRITING DURING REGIME SWITCHES

The following brief excursion is designed to provide an illustration of the hazardous nature of regime switches to option writers who specialize in "selling or going short volatility". We want to emphasize that the model we are about to explain is highly simplified and rests, in its construction, on some of the very questionable assumptions taken from the normal probability calculus that we have been anxious to discredit in other contexts. Nevertheless we hope that the reader will bear with us as we believe that some interesting conclusions do actually surface from thinking through different aspects of the modeling exercise.

We will focus on the case of someone who sells out of the money puts and calls on the S&P 500 index because they wish to collect the premiums that are paid by the option buyers for the possible rewards that come from "unlikely" events happening. The classic example of a trader that likes to buy such options is Nicholas Taleb[5] while there are many other institutions who are willing to take the other side of the trade on the thesis that once in a while they will be required to make a big payout but this has to be offset by the knowledge that they are able to collect premiums consistently without payment as long as these "unlikely" events do not occur.

It is a strategy that rests upon the idea that although markets will behave erratically from time to time, when taking the long view, volatility will *eventually* (that is the key word) revert to more normal conditions. Given this "comfort" traders/option writers are willing to supply the market with protective or speculative puts and calls. If one does not have a counterbalancing position in the underlying security, in other words the position is "naked", there is an undefined risk to selling puts and/or calls, but it is similar to the actuarial risk that an insurance company makes when it writes life assurance policies. It knows that it will have to pay out on a certain portion of its portfolio but it also knows it will be collecting premiums constantly for that part of the portfolio where deaths are not incurred. The illustration that we will make suggests that an actuarial analysis of the risks incurred in option writing would be very well served by the regime switching model that we have reviewed. It might be tempting to build an elaborate framework based on the different volatility regimes for the S&P 500 factoring in the propensity to cluster for a while within one or other regime after they have switched back and forth. We said tempting but we will not be tempted into such an elaborate exercise because it would be a spurious undertaking anyway. We will simply illustrate how an index option writer can become exposed during a transition period by having written options within the assumptions of one regime only to find that the market is transitioning to the very different volatility conditions of the alternative regime.

To keep the example simple and relevant we shall confine our attention only to the different volatility conditions of the two regimes and, for our hypothetical situation, we shall use a historical mean for the S&P 500 of 13% per annum, and consider it to be independent of either of the regimes. The real purpose of the example is to illustrate the consequences of the doubling of volatility and accordingly the mean estimate will remain neutral within the scope of the analysis.

In the S&P 500 analysis above the annualized volatility for regime 1 was 10% and this jumps to 20% for regime 2. These annualized standard deviations can be converted to weekly figures by multiplying them by the square root of (7/365). Two other simplifying assumptions can also be introduced. If the weekly standard deviation of the returns is less than ±3 STDs from the mean the option writer pockets the premium income. The annual premium income represents a 25% return. If the weekly standard deviation of the returns exceeds an absolute 3 STDs from the mean the option writer has to make a payout which is equivalent to 25% of his income. Based on a normally distributed returns schedule (which we know to be erroneous) the chances of a payout are about 0.3% (i.e. 99.7% of the returns should fall within 3 STDs on either side of the mean). The index options writer who uses a weekly accounting framework would only make a payout approximately once in 300 weeks or about once in six years. From this we can infer that if the markets were well behaved, exhibited stationarity and followed a normal distribution (all of which are assumed in conventional options theory but which we have argued are erroneous) then the option writer should be able to make a consistent annual return of 25% for five years and then suffer one year in six with effectively zero income.

In relation to the regime identification issue the procedure we can adopt is as follows. We can set up two hypothetical weekly returns schedules for our index options writer with the characteristics of each of the regimes that we are interested in.

The following notation will be helpful:

- HIST_MEAN is the weekly return of the index based on long-term historical perspective – we have assumed 13% per annum.
- STD_R1 is the weekly standard deviation for regime 1.
- STD_R2 is the weekly standard deviation for regime 2.

Using the NORMINV function within Excel we can generate a random, normally distributed, sample of returns for both regimes for 312 periods to cover the six years that should produce at least one ±3 STD event. We can specify in the parameters to the function the following parameters which will allow us to simulate the volatility likely to be suffered during each regime. So we would have for the first regime =NORMINV(RAND(), HIST_MEAN,STD_R1) and for the second regime we would have =NORMINV(RAND(),HIST_MEAN, STD_R2).

We then calculate the standard normal variables or z values for each of the two sets of returns which is simply done by taking each return subtracting the HIST_MEAN and dividing the result by the STD_R1 or STD_R2 respectively. The z value tells us how many standard deviations we are away from the mean and if the absolute value of z exceeds three the option writer has to make a pay out.

Figure 10.5 is just one possible version of the scenario which can be generated repeatedly within an Excel workbook to create a Monte Carlo simulation of the scenario variables. As can be seen from the chart the line for regime 1 has no "cliffs", in other words the option writer does not have to make any payouts. This has arisen because the generated values from

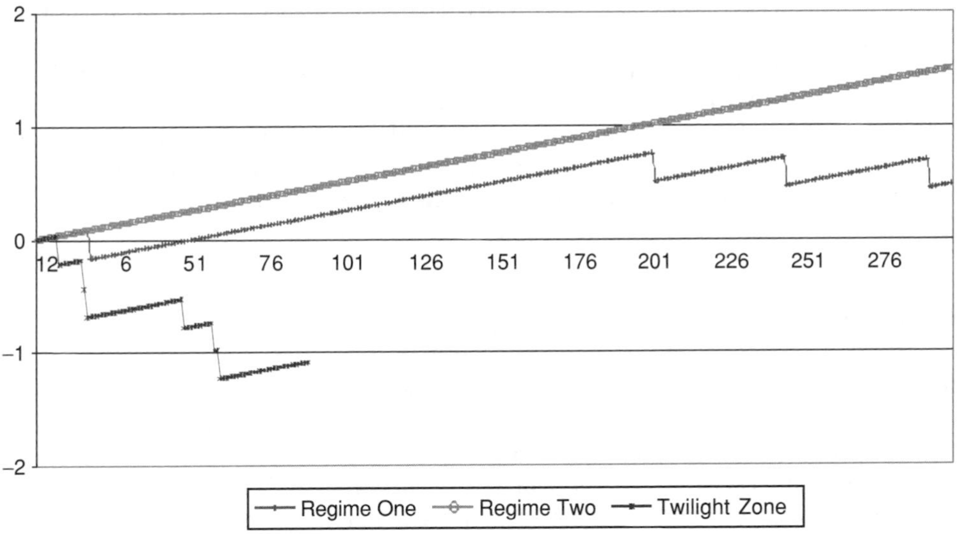

Figure 10.5 Equity curve for option writing strategies showing how regimes will critically affect the risk to the writer

the NORMINV function, which includes as one of its parameters the subsidiary RAND() function, has not produced a ±3 STD event. This is not exceptional as there is no necessity that it should produce an extreme event within six years but the balance of probability suggests that it will. When we examine the regime 2 line which would reflect trading with the volatility parameter of the second regime we can see that there are four "cliffs" reflecting the fact that four extreme events took place within the six year period under the more volatile regime. In this particular run of the simulation it can be seen that at the end of the six year period the option writer has still managed to achieve a 50% return despite the fact that the market environment is a lot less "friendly" to the option writing strategy.

The logic behind the third line requires a little more explanation. We have called this line the "twilight zone" and it is intended to show how the option writing strategy suffers from the transition from regime 1 (which we saw from our earlier discussion occurs more than 50% of the time) to regime 2 (which occurs slightly more than 25% of the time). During this period when the market is becoming a lot more volatile the strategy that has been based on the historical volatility observed during a regime 1 environment becomes hazardous. It may not yet be obvious to the index option writer that the market is in a transitional phase so the strategy of selecting which options to write (i.e. how far "out of the money" one should go and what volatility premium is "fair") will be mismatched with the emerging (yet still not properly visible) market volatility conditions. The twilight zone line is created from a series of returns that are the result of a random draw from either the regime 1 returns or the regime 2 returns. This is achieved by using a RAND() result to select from either of the two previously rendered returns from regime 1 or 2 depending on whether the result of the RAND() function is above or below 0.5. After the appropriate return has been selected we then use the following logic to determine its z value. The value is the (randomly drawn return – HIST_MEAN)/STD_R1. The reasoning behind this is that during the transition the option writer is still following the standard deviation of the regime which has been in effect and which is applicable for the majority of market circumstances.

As is obvious from the chart this twilight zone strategy fails abysmally as the market is alternating (randomly in the initial stages) between a low volatility regime and a regime which has double the volatility. The cliffs come very frequently and we have suspended the blue line after it becomes more than obvious that the market has completed a transition to a far more volatile state where the assumptions inherited from regime 1 are dangerous and need to be replaced by the much higher volatility presumptions of regime 2.

WHAT CAUSES MARKETS TO SWITCH REGIMES?

We shall see that this question is ultimately not properly formulated as it may inadvertently lead to the erroneous assumption that there are underlying objective market dynamics that generate price developments and that, by analyzing these dynamics, some logic or probability model will be discovered that will explain the "switching". This is a trap that is sometimes fallen into by econophysicists who employ agent-based modeling techniques:

> Regime switching allows the stock price process to switch between *K* regimes randomly; each regime is characterized by different model parameters, and the process describing which regime the price process is in at any time is assumed to be Markov (that is, the probability of changing regime depends only on the current regime, not on the history of the process).[6]

In the above quote the suggestion is that the process leading to a regime switch is "assumed to be Markov" which amounts to the same thing as saying that it is random and ultimately unexplainable. This is an unsatisfactory suggestion as it not only doesn't contribute to our further understanding of market behavior but saying that it is random also would seem not to be true. If we reformulate the original question and ask why do traders shift their trading strategies *en masse* in such a manner that the market as a whole undergoes a phase shift or regime switch then to answer that by saying that they do so in a Markov fashion goes against all of our assumptions about intentionality. It suggests that mass behavior as revealed in market movements may be as intentional as the way in which birds flock or fish all decide to switch direction at the same time. Swarming behavior is clearly a factor in market dynamics but we need to be a little more persistent in our search for the trigger that produces regime switches than simply assert that it is entirely contingent or accidental.

Once we have reformulated the question we can try again with the question which is why do traders abruptly change their strategies, or why does their behavior change in such a manner that price development becomes more erratic and volatile? This is not the same question as asking why they become "bullish" or "bearish" although similar issues may be involved. Regimes are characterized by the shift in the variance as well as the mean of market returns. The question is therefore not the same as the mystery of the "gestalt" switches that allow us to see a half full glass at one point and a second later a half empty glass. So can we answer the question in a more convincing manner than suggesting that it is merely a matter of chance? Are we back to the same point, but this time on a grander scale, that the advocates of random walk theory and Brownian motion start from? We believe that the answer is no and we suggest that we have offered at least a partial answer to this question in Chapter 2. There we discussed the results of a coherent view of price arising on trend days when the absence of the normal "fractious" market conditions leads to a temporary loss of liquidity and sharp price moves. This view of coherence vs fractiousness sits in sharp contrast to some of the commonsensical notions of the order and disorder in the financial markets. Markets move to extremes when they are most organized and when the participants are most aligned in their views. The sharing of a consensus view about the direction of price and the associated coherent market behavior, which causes liquidity to cease at one price and move to another (not always too readily), produces the most ordered behavior in price development. It may be painful if one is incorrectly positioned but to describe the behavior in terms of disorder and chaos is to reveal an emotional bias because long only portfolios will be suffering.

However, we still have not tackled the bigger question which is why do some market corrections stop with minor or moderate price displacements while others, less frequently, go on to produce crashes? Is it possible to provide a satisfactory account of the major shifts in sentiment that result in large-scale changes in behavior, the kind that are really expressed in the nomenclature of the regime switch model? Let us continue to explore some of the answers supplied by econophysicists and advocates of agent-based modeling techniques to this larger question. There are several different kinds of explanation that have been proposed for why traders switch their trading bias:

- They switch randomly or with a specified time-based probability (i.e. the Markov assumption that was seen in the previous quotation).
- They switch in the same manner that ants decide to forage another food source.[7]
- They switch based on herding (this is a different issue to foraging behavior and is sometimes expressed more fully in terms of swarming behavior).
- They switch when the markets reach a critical state (this is really the position taken by advocates of the view that markets self-organize into critical states).[8]

One of the leading exponents of applying computer simulations and what are generally referred to as agent-based modeling techniques to the study markets is Professor Doyne Farmer of the Santa Fe Institute in New Mexico, which is the home of the interdisciplinary approach to complexity theory and the study of complex adaptive systems.[9] Farmer also had a stint working for the Prediction Company as a co-founder, which was a company that was partly financed by UBS and whose mission was to apply sophisticated quantitative techniques designed to uncover exploitable patterns in financial time series.[10] Farmer eventually decided to return to academia after declaring that there were relatively few reliable setups and patterns that were revealed by the pattern detection algorithms developed by the Prediction Company and has done pioneering work in the area that is somewhat loosely called econophysics. In a paper entitled *Toward Agent-based Models for Investment,* first published in 2001,[11] Farmer outlines his agenda for the importation of software simulation techniques that had been used in numerous contexts at the Santa Fe Institute to the study of finance and investment. In the article we find a prospectus for the technique:

> An agent-based model involves a model for price formation and a model for agent behavior, including the models' information inputs and how the inputs behave, which could involve learning. From an investor's point of view, agent-based models represent a new direction that may or may not result in more practical investment models. From an academic's point of view, agent-based models are fascinating new tools that make it possible to investigate problems previously out of reach.[12]

Since this early work in the field Farmer has been joined by a growing number of practitioners that have made considerable progress in investigating the complex dynamics that emerge from relatively simple rules of engagement between traders within a simple market microstructure.

They have produced some important insights into the nature of the stylized facts (e.g. volatility clustering and the "fat tails" phenomenon) about markets that the more traditional/orthodox financial community had been unable to explain. In concluding his paper Farmer was perhaps a little too optimistic about the rate of progress but there seems to be no dissatisfaction with the methodology and the field is certainly a vital area of research:

> Agent-based modeling of markets is still in its infancy. I predict that as the models get better, they will begin to be useful for real problems... Within five years, people may be trading money with agent-based models.

With colleagues Paolo Patelli and Ilija Zovko, in a subsequent paper,[13] Farmer begins with the simplest model of all – their agents have bounded rationality approaching zero intelligence. These agents or virtual traders then place orders to buy and sell at random, subject only to the microstructural rules in a typical financial market. What emerges from these very simple interactions among the software-based traders is behavior that is quite complex and which takes on many of the characteristics of the stylized facts and the phase shifts that actual markets go through. This complex emergent behavior is reminiscent of other work that has been done at the Santa Fe Institute within artificial life (Chris Langton), cellular automata (Steven Wolfram), and complex metabolic systems (Stuart Kauffman). For the interested reader there is some fascinating and accessible material available that describes a lot of this work mentioned in the Bibliography.

Farmer's model assumed that the agents or traders effectively had zero intelligence and made their trading decisions in a random or Markov fashion which is a supposition we have previously resisted. Even though the model was able to generate complex behavior with these simplistic assumptions we sense that the real insights that agent modeling will yield require virtual traders with more sophisticated cognitive qualities than the primitive endowments assumed in Farmer's paper. More recent work has been based on providing the virtual traders with more sophisticated decision-making capabilities. A paper by Thomas Lux and Michele Marchesi[14] proposes that the software agents/traders can be divided into two broad categories – fundamentalists and chartists (noise traders). In essence Lux's work suggests that markets will produce abrupt switches when too many traders are following momentum strategies based on technical factors and that the "switch" will cause the restoration of "normal" conditions that are the outcome of strategies and valuations that are more in accordance with the software traders that are following fundamentalist strategies. Although the model is simple and begs questions about exactly what constitutes a fundamentalist strategy, the broad conclusions that are extracted from the way that the model functions have a certain intuitive plausibility. In broad terms the findings could provide an explanatory framework for such market episodes as the building of the internet/high tech bubble in the late 1990s and its subsequent bursting.

One further approach to the cognitive elements that are built into the software agents is worth attention as it rests on a large body of work that seeks to explain what is sometimes referred to as herding behavior. Herding is often also linked to contagion behavior that we shall examine in more detail in Chapter 14. The concept of financial contagion has its roots in the use of the terminology that explains the process by which diseases are propagated to form epidemics. The spread of viruses can be extraordinarily fast in a highly networked world and for instantaneous forms of communication such as those on which the capital markets are founded the contagion metaphor can be very apt to explain how crises can emerge and rapidly mesmerize the world's trading desks. Financial contagion models are usually based on the idea that traders occupy virtual "neighborhoods" and when enough of a trader's nearest neighbors are in the process of changing their views about the market or individual security there is a network feedback effect or "tipping point" reached in which the traders *en masse* suddenly form the same opinions. This is reminiscent of the discussion that we had in Chapter 2 of how coherent behavior emerges as market sentiment becomes highly aligned. Another metaphor or model that has been used to explain the way in which an effect spreads through a network topology is the percolation model. The seminal work in this regard is a book by Dietrich Stauffer[15] which provides an insight into percolation logic when considered in its most general form.

Stauffer demonstrates that for a pro forma network conceived as a two-dimensional grid or lattice the theoretical percolation value can be precisely determined. The best way to imagine this is to think of the lattice as analogous to a forest with each of the trees occupying sites on the lattice or grid. If all of the sites in the grid are occupied a fire which begins on the forest's boundaries will eventually consume all of the trees within the forest. But what is the threshold amount that will ensure that the fire will eventually spread from one boundary to the furthest boundary. It turns out that the threshold amount is approximately 59%. So if only 50% of the sites in the forest (or lattice) are populated with trees the fire will not spread from one side to the other but above 59% it will.

The exact value for the percolation threshold can be determined mathematically and can be tested and confirmed empirically using Monte Carlo simulation techniques in which the simulation runs thousands of fires with different site occupancies. We have mentioned Didier Sornette elsewhere[16] and he collaborated with Stauffer on a paper that pursues the agenda laid out by Doyne Farmer and which attempts to provide more robustness to the vague idea that herding takes place within financial markets:

> The simplest recipe to aggregate interacting or inter-influencing traders into groups is to assume that the connectivity between traders defining the groups can be seen as a pure geometrical percolation problem with fixed occupancy on a given network topology. Clusters are groups of neighboring occupied sites or investors. Then, random percolation clusters make a decision to buy or sell on the stock market, for all sites (corresponding to the individual investors and units of wealth) in that cluster together. Thus, the individual investors are thought to cluster together to form companies or groups of influence, which under the guidance of a single manager buy (probability a), sell (probability a), or refrain from trading (probability 1–2a) within one time interval.

Interested readers are again urged to follow through on some of this work in network topologies and percolation not because we have anything yet that approaches a tractable way of measuring the factors that produce contagion but because it is replete with novel insights into network dynamics. Sornette is preoccupied with the factors that lead to market crashes and following in a similar vein to the article that was cited earlier which has identified certain volatility signatures that preceded the 1987 stock market crash, he has produced his own evidence that financial markets may display mathematically detectable precursors to crashing behavior. As traders are forming extremely aligned views about the direction of price development there will be more or less subtle changes in the underlying market dynamics that may provide the clues as to impending critical episodes ahead. One of the reasons that we decided to focus on the nature of regimes and regime switching is that we believe that there is much promise in the mathematics of contagion and regime switching. Although these early efforts from econophysicists are still far from offering any real payoffs to traders we suggest that the astute trader will want to keep an eye on developments in this field as there is clearly a potential for developing profitable insights into what moves markets and how to identify turning points.

One of the real challenges for those looking for the underlying factors that produce critical market events and regime switches is to distinguish between the events that are precursors to "run of the mill" corrective behavior and those events which precede major crashes. As Sornette has pointed out a crash is a correction that didn't stop and this is both an arresting insight and at the same time a cause for some skepticism that the logic of crashes and corrections will be distinguishable. The types of minor crashes that the market as a whole experiences from time to time may be, after all, more than a lot of minor crashes in many individual stocks. If one starts with the assumption that a mini-crash is nothing more than a lot of stocks correcting severely at the same time this seems to employ a suspect kind of reasoning based on a linear combination of factors giving rise to a macro-event. But in fact the dynamics would seem to be the other way around – otherwise how can one explain the contagion aspects. There are important issues of additivity and emergence involved that may eventually be better understood by the efforts of those engaged in agent-based modeling. One of the benefits of these computer simulation techniques such as the creation of artificial sand piles and their avalanche dynamics is that they enable us to give a quantitative dimension to our modeling of emergence rather than using the qualitative language that was previously used in the "soft sciences". For example, as we briefly noted before terms like gestalt switching, although they have a lot of insightful characteristics, lack the kind of quantitative dimension that would make them effective in the modeling of time series data.

Another interesting conclusion that some agent-based modelers have considered is that the "interacting agents hypothesis", and the resulting complex behavior that is able to emulate some of the peculiar characteristics of actual markets, leads us to the prediction that eventually all informed market participants should become market timers. If the underlying market dynamics can be made more transparent and the inscrutable manner in which price develops can be demystified, the suggestion is that the astute trader will learn how to take her cues only from price development patterns in deciding how to trade. This reminds us of the dictum of Keynes that traders are engaged in making estimates of how average opinion has estimated what the average opinion of the market is.[17]

IS MARKET TIMING THE MOST LOGICAL TRADING STRATEGY?

Perhaps most traders and investors are market timers in disguise. Even though many claimed to be only influenced by the market's fundamentals (i.e. P/E ratios, interest rates etc.) it may be that beneath the surface most traders are watching other traders and this is the primary factor influencing their decisions about what and when to trade. This seems to be especially borne out by the way that the market bubble developed in the late 1990s. Contagion can work on the upside as well as the downside as the following shows.

Suppose that you are the manager of a traditional long only mutual fund (someone like the legendary Fidelity Magellan fund's Peter Lynch of the 1980s). You have a background in finance and have studied EMH, CAPM and have fairly orthodox views on the "fundamental value" of equities. You have familiarized yourself with stock market history and can recite all of the well-known benchmarks and ratios such as the prevailing and historical PE ratios, price to book, price to dividends etc. You are operating in an environment like the one that prevailed in the late 1990s. All of your models and instincts are pointing to the fact that the overall market is overvalued by a rather large degree. Dot com companies are trading at more than 600 times earnings (if they had any!) and popular analysts seem to be engaged in a scramble to publish even more ebullient outlooks than their competitors. Learned academics and financial commentators are writing widely quoted reports (especially in the popular business press such as *Forbes* and *Business Week*) that discuss the "New Economy" with new valuation techniques. There is a pervasive sense that stocks only suffer minor corrections which present a buying opportunity and that recessions have become obsolete owing to the power of financial engineering. Each day you see the prices of stocks like Amazon and Cisco advancing by 5% or more and you sense that there will be a meltdown ahead. But when is it going to happen? How much more froth can the market take? When are "investors" going to come to their senses and realize that the current valuations are unsustainable? When is the market going to revert to the mean?

Let us suppose that you become a cautious (prudent) manager and start to sell your more speculative holdings (not becoming a short seller because as the example sets out this is a traditional long only fund) and replace your holdings with more cash or defensive (low PE) holdings. Let us suppose that you are early in this decision. After all a "rational" investor (that believes in mean reversion) could have reached this decision at any time from about 1997 onwards (remember that Alan Greenspan made his "irrational exuberance" remarks in 1996). As a result of your caution your fund would have underperformed for at least three or four years. Managers are not paid to underperform. Fundholders would start to switch to better performing funds. Publications like Morningstar enable the retail investor to make cross-sectional evaluations of thousands of funds all of which can be measured with alpha, betas, R^2 etc. Once they see that a fund is underperforming they do not want to get left behind. Thousands of decisions will be made by individual investors to switch to a better performing fund and who would question their rationality?

It surely would have been rational for a retail fund investor to decide to switch his life savings from Fund X in 1998 that only delivered a 12% return to Fund Y that was heavily invested in tech and delivered a return of 35%? If he had been smart enough to sell in early 2000 he would have had two more additional years of superlative returns rather than sticking with the cautious fund manager.

The fund manager may also have time to pause as to whether his strategy of selling off his high tech exposure was such a good idea. With fund redemptions increasing and his bonuses diminishing he would be more rational to go with the flow and convince himself that because of his superior skills in reading the markets he will see when they are about to crumble and pull out his exposure at the right time. Such is the logic of market timing.

The scenario described is designed to show that it is not only hyperactive day traders and "crazy" chartists or technical analysts that engage in market timing, but even "long-term" fundamental investors that buy into mutual funds and the managers of such funds. The Keynesian dictum is remarkably prescient about the inevitability of market timing and reflects the fact that all market actors react more to market prices than fundamentals. We keep buying as long as prices are going up and some of us convince ourselves that we will be smart enough to know when the markets have stopped going up and will exit our positions.

But on the contrary in bubble market conditions we get used to buying the dips because prices always come back. Well in the late 1990s that was basically correct because they did come back.

In fact the simple rule of market timing could be simply stated – buy the dips. Prices always come back until they don't.

That sums up the ultimate irrationality of market timing. But is it better to be rational and to miss out completely on the kind of market conditions that prevailed in the late 1990s? In other words the rational investor will often perform poorly. Even worse the entirely rational investor will probably become insolvent. If one had taken the view in the dot com bubble years that the market was grossly overvalued, and with the benefit of hindsight that is the only conclusion that a "rational trader" could *now* reach, the best strategy would have been to be short those most overvalued sectors. It hardly needs to be pointed out how dangerous it would have been to have been short stocks like JDSU, EBAY, CSCO and others in the late 1990s.

So is the lesson from this that one should avoid the markets altogether or perhaps that one should avoid them only when they have exceeded certain thresholds of rational valuation? If one decides on the former course then the purchase of this book was probably not a good idea. One might also reach the same conclusion about the second choice since we are not aware of any widely accepted and definitive accounts of fair valuation.

BENEFITS OF THE REGIME SWITCHING MODEL

There is, in our opinion, one principal benefit of the regime switching model. It may have limited value as a forecasting tool, indeed it was not really designed for that purpose anyway, but it can be very useful in guiding the way that we approach portfolio management issues and calculations of possible drawdowns. For insurance companies and asset managers that need to make reliable forecasts about their long-term risk exposure it is much more realistic to contemplate their risk horizons on the basis of different market regimes rather than to employ risk metrics that have been erroneously founded on the simplistic assumptions of stationarity of the time series and the normal distribution. Correctly calibrating the extent of the holding period with historical regime modeling can provide a more realistic view of portfolio risk for the trader and fund manager. It is still subject to limitations regarding the inadmissibility of making distributional forecasts based on historical regime observations but it is far less error prone than forecasting with the assumptions of stationarity and the normal distribution.

The underlying structure of a financial time series is far from stationary and displays clusters of volatility and extreme price movement that are underreported by the simple Gaussian statistics that are often used in financial forecast. As we have discussed elsewhere the Value at Risk metric, which in its pure vanilla form rests upon taking a 95% quantile value from the normal distribution, is likely to seriously underestimate the likelihood of losses occurring in a portfolio. Over the short term and under normal conditions where there is a regime 1 type of environment it may be "safe" to plug in a specific mean and standard deviation to derive probability estimates for different scenarios but over longer time periods and especially if one is in a more volatile and critical regime 2 environment then using either nonregime specific summary statistics or statistics relating to a different regime than the one in focus is likely to seriously underestimate the magnitude of a loss.

We need to be careful that we don't overstate the benefits of our ability to classify markets into two different regimes. The fact that we can do after the fact has undoubted benefits but it is the transitional phase dynamics that are still largely a mystery, notwithstanding the recent work that we have considered. We have already noted that a crisis event could simply be a corrective event that does not stop but how do you recognize this quantitatively at the time? We may be in exactly the same situation as the passengers on the jet that encounter unexpected turbulence. From a trading perspective the previous discussion really brings into focus the notion that the structural breaks can best be seen as market turning points. To the extent that we can become more adept at identifying such turning points our trading performance will become ever more successful.

11
Money Management Techniques

I have learned many things from George Soros, but perhaps the most significant is that it's not whether you're right or wrong that's important, but how much money you make when you're right and how much you lose when you're wrong.

Stanley Druckenmiller, one time manager of Soros's Quantum Fund [1]

RISK

Risk arises from the uncertainty of outcomes. As traders each time we enter a trade the outcome is uncertain in the same way that any future event is. We are concerned that we might incur a trading loss if we have miscalculated the direction that the particular security we are trading will actually follow as opposed to the direction that we thought it would follow. At the macro-level we may be concerned about the risks of market crashes, terrorist incidents that cause markets to plunge and other critical events. All of this contributes to the potential for profit for the speculator and trader and the accompanying uneasiness that we all feel about the possibility of losses or adverse consequences from trading activities. This is our general notion of risk.

But financial theory tends to focus on a more restrictive and quantitative notion of risk which concerns the variability of returns in a market. The returns for a security or index are simply the changes from day to day and instead of examining actual price levels we examine the log changes for consecutive returns. This gives rises to a time series of what are called first order differences and it is this data series that can then be used to calculate the mean and variance of the series. All users of popular spreadsheets will know how easy it is to calculate these values. The variance is a measure of the dispersion of the data around the mean and is an indicator of the variability of the data. It provides a numerical answer to the question of how much variation there is in the daily log changes. It is more useful to discuss the variance initially since the term itself is more transparent as to its purpose. But in the analytical literature the statistical concept that is most often used is the standard deviation of the time series data which is nothing more than the square root of the variance. One of the reasons why the standard deviation is used more frequently is that it is required to normalize the dispersion of values and to compare the dispersion to a theoretically normal distribution.

In addition to the risks posed by the variability and unpredictability of price movements the trader has to contend with a variety of psychological factors that foster uneasiness. Fear and greed are very powerful emotions that can overrule reason and logic in the "mind" of the trader. No matter how cerebral one's approach to trading is, and no matter how much success one may have had with a particular style of trading or methodology, the possibility of becoming emotionally unsettled by a particular trading outcome is always present. Many traders, including this author, attempt to minimize the emotion in trading by following a systematic strategy which removes a lot of the anxieties that arise especially in having to act under duress. It is always much saner to have a plan that covers the important issues such as when to enter, when to exit with a profit and when to take a loss before placing a trade than "making it up as you go along". Some traders in fast moving markets, such as scalpers in the futures pits, trade on gut feeling and "feel the trade" but this is not a style that works well for many people.

There are some fascinating paradoxes and inconsistencies that have been observed in the literature of behavioral finance. These have to do with the asymmetric manner in which human beings approach the possibility (or probability) of incurring a possible loss versus the probability of a definite gain. In addition there are some very common expressions from the trading folklore that have become popular precisely because of the perverse way in which many people act when trading. How many times has one heard the expression "Cut losses and let profits run" and one of the reasons why it is repeated so frequently is because it goes against the way that most people instinctively behave and no matter how often it is repeated many people are unable to follow the prescription. We take profits too soon because we are fearful that they will evaporate and we sit with losses for too long because we are hopeful that our loss will eventually turn into profit and that the intuition that got us into the trade in the first place will turn out to have been valid. Taking losses quickly and unemotionally is one of the hardest lessons that any trader has to learn, as is setting one's expectations at the right level as to how often one is going to make a wrong call. Many people have great difficulty with owning up to mistakes, seeming to think that this is a sign of weakness, whereas for the trader it is a survival imperative.

Not only should we follow the simple rule that we get out of losing positions quickly, and without emotion, but we also need to pay close attention to the ratio of how much we make when we are right versus how much we lose when we are wrong. This goes back to the point of the quotation from Stanley Druckenmiller about the trading philosophy of George Soros, who, as almost everybody knows, has been a very successful hedge fund manager since the 1960s. Indeed it could be claimed that Soros's notoriety and the track record of his pioneering investment vehicle, the Quantum Fund, has been a large contributor to the fascination for hedge fund investing.

Keeping track of how much one is making on profitable trades versus how much capital is being lost requires scrupulous account management obviously, but, more importantly, it also requires a systematic framework for tracking one's trading performance. This chapter is designed to offer some guidelines as to how this framework can best be constructed.

THE WIN/LOSS MATRIX

Table 11.1 is one of the more important in this book in the sense that without a clear understanding of these key ratios there can be little benefit from any discussion about money management techniques. We will expand on this table to cover such issues as the Kelly ratio for position sizing, the reward/risk ratio and how to include "outlier" events in any

Table 11.1 Win/loss matrix

Win/loss ratio	Average gain	Average loss	Typical outcome
70%	$1500	$1000	$750
65%	$1500	$1000	$625
60%	$1500	$1000	$500
55%	$1500	$1000	$375
50%	$1500	$1000	$250
45%	$1500	$1000	$125
40%	$1500	$1000	$0

risk analysis. The table, which has deliberately been kept as simple as possible to introduce this section, could potentially be the summary of trading results for an active trader, but is best seen for current purposes, as a construct showing a series of hypothetical benchmarks and trading outcomes that will enable us to illustrate some vital features of managing risks.

Several levels of trade signal accuracy have been shown in the table. These levels of accuracy show the ratio of trades where the direction has been correctly anticipated and which delivered a profit versus those trades where a loss was sustained. This is called the win/loss ratio. It is important to note that any trade that ends in a profit (no matter what magnitude) counts as a winner and every trade that ends in a loss is called a loser. The actual profit on the winning trades will vary but on average it will equal the values shown in the second column of Table 11.1. Using exactly the same principle we have included a different amount for the average losing trade, which again becomes the typical losing amount. We shall consider dollar values and not gains/losses as percentage to keep it simple. We have then calculated the typical outcome – the formula is simple (Average gain ∗ Probability of winner) – (Average loss ∗ Probability of loser (i.e. 1 – probability of a winning trade).

All of this is highly simplified because we aren't talking about net outcomes – i.e. the gross outcomes minus transaction costs, slippage etc. We also aren't really addressing how the averages are derived and how the distribution is dispersed around the mean in statistical terms – we shall later.

In order to make sense of Table 11.1 we need to settle on a particular win/loss ratio and then determine what the typical outcome would be for that level of accuracy. If we are able to maintain an accuracy of 60% and our average gains and losses are as shown then the typical outcome shows $500. If we have a trading system that can generate many signals and the average gains and losses can be assumed to be constant as Table 11.1 (not realistic assumptions in the real world of course), we are well on our way to a trading fortune as from here on it becomes a matter of scaling the trading activity, maintaining the level of accuracy and using the correct money management techniques.

Even if the level of accuracy falls to 45% in Table 11.1 the typical outcome is still positive. We retain an edge because of the superior average gain in comparison to the average loss. At the 40% level of accuracy we have a zero expected outcome which is clearly not feasible as there will be transaction costs and slippage etc. in the real world that will ensure that we are keeping our broker happy but will sooner or later be out of business.

In the second model shown in Table 11.2 we shall assume that the average gain is exactly equal to the average loss. At the 60% accuracy level we are still meaningfully ahead with a $200 typical outcome. Observe that at the 50% accuracy we have a zero expectation for the

Table 11.2 Win/loss matrix – equal gains and losses

Win/loss ratio	Average gain	Average loss	Typical outcome
70%	$1000	$1000	$400
65%	$1000	$1000	$300
60%	$1000	$1000	$200
55%	$1000	$1000	$100
50%	$1000	$1000	$0
45%	$1000	$1000	–$100

typical outcome which is intuitively what we would expect. As we drop below the 50% level our typical outcome clearly turns negative.

In the third model as outlined in Table 11.3 we shall assume that we make less on our average winners than on our average losers. Again at the 60% level of accuracy we still have a positive typical outcome but below this we would be soon out of business.

At this stage the simple win/loss matrix has provided the beginnings of a framework for thinking about trading as a process over time and as a modeling tool that will allow as to anticipate certain key attributes of trading strategy and performance. The next modification that will be made to the win/loss matrix is to consider how a typical outcome level can be preserved throughout the table even as trading accuracy declines. The second column shown in Table 11.4 is a derived amount showing how steeply the average gain has to rise to compensate for a weaker win/loss ratio in order to preserve the typical outcome of $500.

There are two dimensions to the win/loss ratio. There is the most obvious ratio which is the one that expresses how often you win versus how often you lose and the assumption is that the higher this ratio is the better. While this may be true there is the further factor to consider which is how much is gained when you win versus how much is lost when you lose. This was exactly the point that Stanley Druckenmiller was making in the quotation that begins this chapter. If a trading system generates highly reliable signals that allow the trader to perform with a 60% accuracy level then almost certainly the system will turn out to be very profitable. If, however, the system only generates a 40% accuracy level but the typical gain is much higher (according to the table $2750 vs the $1500 gain that is assumed in Table 11.1) then the typical outcome figure can still be achieved. The relationship between the win ratio and the amount required to maintain a constant typical outcome is shown in Figure 11.1 and as can be seen as the win ratio diminishes the steepness of the slope on the left-hand side of the chart begins to rise rather sharply (at an exponential rate). At the 30% win/loss ratio one has to achieve

Table 11.3 Win loss matrix – losses exceeds gains

Win/loss ratio	Average gain	Average loss	Typical outcome
70%	$900	$1000	$330
65%	$900	$1000	$235
60%	$900	$1000	$140
55%	$900	$1000	$45
50%	$900	$1000	–$50
45%	$900	$1000	–$145

Table 11.4 Simple win/loss matrix preserving the typical outcome

Win/loss ratio	Average gain	Average loss	Typical outcome
60%	$1500	$1000	$500
50%	$2000	$1000	$500
40%	$2750	$1000	$500
30%	$4000	$1000	$500
20%	$6500	$1000	$500

167% more in terms of the typical gain than one is required to achieve at the 60% win/loss ratio.

The matrix shown in Table 11.4 and the graph in Figure 11.1 serve to illustrate a neglected subject in many discussions of trading strategy. The question can be simply put in terms of the slope in Figure 11.1 – should we be aiming to maximize the win ratio in our trading and be willing to accept lower average gains or would it be more desirable to seek out a lower win ratio but one that delivers much higher average gains? In a sense this question may seem not to be an either/or decision since there are different trading styles that may differ in how they achieve the desired goal but if the requisite outcomes can be achieved from either style does it really matter which is followed? We suggest that it does and that by not focusing on the fact that there are two dimensions (i.e. the win ratio and the typical gain) to be considered in evaluating a trading strategy there is a risk of uncritically acquiescing in substandard performance. The smarter trader is not only one that can take consistent profits from the market but one that knows how to seize the full opportunities that the chosen trading methodology is offering.

Many traders will target the highest achievable win ratio and, to their own detriment, be less focused on maximizing the actual typical gain from each of their profitable trades. This might be the result of having lower expectations in terms of setting profit targets. This is an insidious

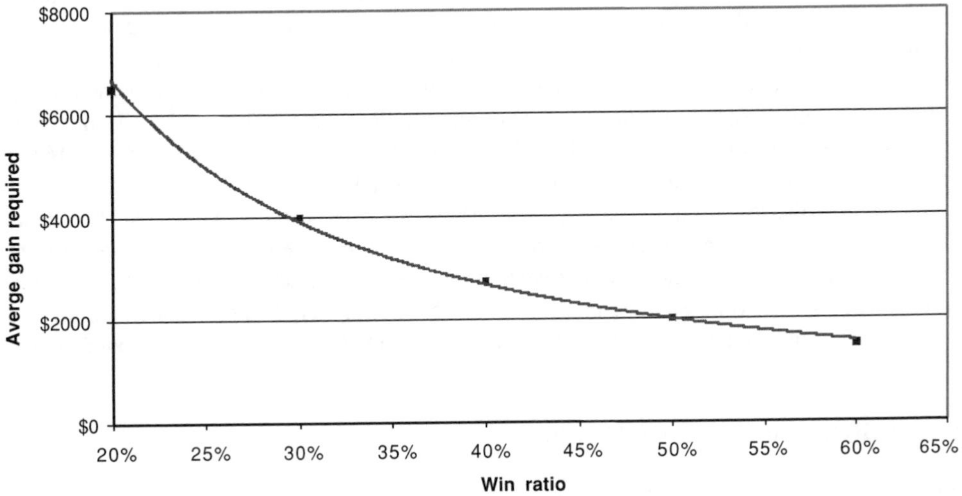

Figure 11.1 Win/loss ratio – amount required from average gain to maintain a constant outcome

version of one half of the maxim that was cited – that is not letting one's profits run. Scaling out of positions and setting the right profit targets are issues that will be considered later in this chapter but the general point is that if one is inordinately focused on the win ratio alone, then maximizing the full profit potential may become a secondary concern. The case could even be made that in seeking out the maximum win ratio there may be an unconscious motivation to take profits early to ensure that the win/loss statistics are as favorable as possible. Even more problematic is that the same driver may affect the selection criterion for which kinds of trades are most suitable for achieving the best win ratio.

Other traders may be far less driven by the win ratio *per se* and tend to look for trades that will win less frequently but when they do win the trades will produce larger typical gains. Paul Tudor Jones who we quoted earlier in the book is a trader that has no qualms about taking several small losses before he gets it right – "I may be stopped four or five times per trade until it really starts moving".[2] George Soros has also declared that he may shift his opinions about a particular trading position several times until he finds a powerful move that he can ride. This is again a difficult lesson for some traders to learn and many commentators write in a way that suggests that tapping into the same wellspring too frequently is a wasteful and inefficient trading style. But if one is close to a major market turning point and the exact timing is, as usual, hard to determine it is better to be wrong a few times but be persistent in chasing the turning point than to get discouraged after being stopped out a couple of times. If one is wrong four or five times at a turning point, as Paul Tudor Jones is willing to be, then one's win ratio can drop to 20/25% but if the final time you get it right, and the market produces an extreme trend day in the direction you anticipated, the gains can be sufficiently large that the inferiority of the win ratio fades into the background.

Being persistent at turning points can be very rewarding and suggests taking a relaxed view about win ratio deterioration; however, the critical question is how can one be sure that the market is at a turning point? This recalls the discussion from Chapter 6 regarding the possibility of identifying precursors to periods of increased volatility and transitions from one regime to another. The more reliably one can anticipate such turning points (and get the direction right!), the more appropriate will be the use of a trial and error approach to picking the right entry points. As was also revealed in the analysis of trend days it is vital to be patient when the market turns as it will almost certainly coincide with major range expansion days and the closing price will be near the limits of the intraday range in the direction of the breakout. In the absence of evidence that suggests that the market may be at a critical juncture and turning point there is good reason to reflect further on the implications of Figure 11.1. As the chart shows the steepness of the slope on the left suggests that one faces an increasingly difficult task to maintain the typical gain amount as the win ratio falls.

Returning to the definition of risk we have seen how the term is usually interpreted by analysts and academics – the standard deviation of returns – but there are some other approaches to thinking about risk which more closely match the concerns of the active trader. We shall briefly reconsider two factors that we have already discussed – overnight risk or gaps and losing streaks or clustering – and then we shall examine drawdowns, a pivotal metric in money management.

OVERNIGHT RISK AND OUTLIERS

The discussion of price breaks and gaps in Chapter 7 provided a rather simplistic but comparatively valid approach to the understanding of overnight risk. In examining opening price breaks and opening price gaps we were able to suggest a way, based on comparative historical data comparing a particular security to a benchmark such as the S&P 500, of quantifying or scaling in relative terms the degree of overnight risk. Opening gaps are relatively infrequent for the S&P 500 but for many individual stocks they are much more frequent and it is useful for traders, when combining portfolio positions and especially in setting stop loss levels, to be familiar with the extent to which individual securities reveal high levels of overnight risk on this comparative scale.

Outliers or extreme events such as "crashes" go far beyond the more "normal" phenomenon of a typical price gap which as was illustrated in Chapter 6 may occur more than 10% of the time for several large and liquid securities. It has been shown that outliers are far more common than would be expected by the normal distribution. The probability of encountering a human being that is three times as tall as the average human being is considered to be so remote that we would rule it out and even change our criteria for morphological classification if we ever encountered it. Yet the returns from financial markets do exhibit extreme outlier events. The infamous October 19th 1987 return was more than 20 standard deviations from the mean return and had a probability of occurring only once in several histories of the universe.

So how should the trader factor outliers into a risk analysis of the trading experience? This will bring us to one of the core ideas that are discussed in the concluding chapter of the book. At this stage we shall simply say that we need to always trade with a safety net and that this can only be properly ensured by always operating with a long/short strategy and applying systematic hedging techniques.

ADVERSE EVENTS COME IN CLUSTERS

Our previous analysis of volatility showed a very definite clustering characteristic for turbulent market conditions. Extreme price movements in either direction, including abrupt reversals, are a clearly visible feature of financial markets. In high level terms we can say that extreme returns tend to congregate, they do not arise by chance only to be followed by a return to normal. *Contrary to the fiction that time series returns have "no memory" and are serially independent, all trading experience shows that gaps tend to be followed frequently by further gaps and that volatility spikes are found in close proximity to each other.* Adverse returns and volatility spikes have an unfortunate habit of cropping up in clusters and any trading methodology that tries to accommodate the notion of extreme variability as a one-off or isolated phenomenon is in danger of seriously underestimating the damage that can be done to a portfolio during periods when the markets are exhibiting extreme behavior.

There is a simple technique for measuring the damage that can be done to a portfolio during its lifetime as a result of an extended period of adversity – "a losing streak" – and it involves measuring drawdowns and calculating maximum drawdown. Starting from the perspective of money management and portfolio construction, a primary motivation in risk management will be the avoidance of large drawdowns. In measuring standard deviations of log returns we only need to look at historical stock data but when we move to drawdowns we are focused on how *the actual sequence of returns* for the components of a portfolio will lead to more or less severe declines in account equity. There are several key issues that come into play here including the larger topic of how the combination of different positions will influence drawdowns which we shall come to, but let's begin with examining drawdown from the point of view of a very simple portfolio.

DRAWDOWNS

Very simply, a drawdown is the reduction in equity within a trading account following a losing trade. But this is not in itself very revealing since the trading account will consist of many trades, some profitable and some not and a constantly shifting equity curve. Accordingly a more useful notion of drawdown is that the measurement should be made from one peak in the equity to a trough in the equity curve over a specified period of time, which might be a month. Maintaining end of month balances in the amount of equity in a trading account enables one to calculate the monthly drawdown (if any) that has been experienced by the trader. This drawdown amount is often expressed in percentage terms. Collecting these monthly drawdown figures enables one to easily determine the maximum drawdown over a given period, perhaps one year. The maximum drawdown shows the greatest difference between neighboring peaks and troughs.

Table 11.5 shows a series of hypothetical returns for a portfolio over a two year period. The column headed "VAMI" reflects the returns expressed in terms of a Value Added Monthly

Table 11.5 Maximum drawdown

Holding periods	Return for period	VAMI	Account equity status	Drawdown
0	—	$1000	1	—
1	0.05	$1050	1.05	0.0%
2	0.08	$1134	1.13	0.0%
3	−0.11	$1009	1.01	−11.0%
4	0.2	$1211	1.21	0.0%
5	−0.24	$920	0.92	−24.0%
6	0.2	$1105	1.10	−8.8%
7	0.05	$1160	1.16	−4.2%
8	−0.14	$997	1.00	−17.6%
9	0.12	$1117	1.12	−7.8%
10	0.03	$1151	1.15	−5.0%
11	0.03	$1185	1.19	−2.1%
12	−0.12	$1043	1.04	−13.9%
13	−0.06	$980	0.98	−19.1%
14	0.02	$1000	1.00	−17.4%
15	0.1	$1100	1.10	−9.2%
16	0	$1100	1.10	−9.2%
17	−0.12	$968	0.97	−20.1%
18	−0.24	$736	0.74	−39.3%
19	0.1	$809	0.81	−33.2%
20	0.2	$971	0.97	−19.8%
21	0.02	$990	0.99	−18.2%
22	0.02	$1010	1.01	−16.6%
23	0.02	$1030	1.03	−14.9%
24	−0.03	$1000	1.00	−17.5%
Summary Statistics				
Maximum drawdown			−39.26%	
Minimum period return			−24.00%	
Maximum period return			20.00%	
Average period return			0.75%	
Standard deviation of returns			12.30%	

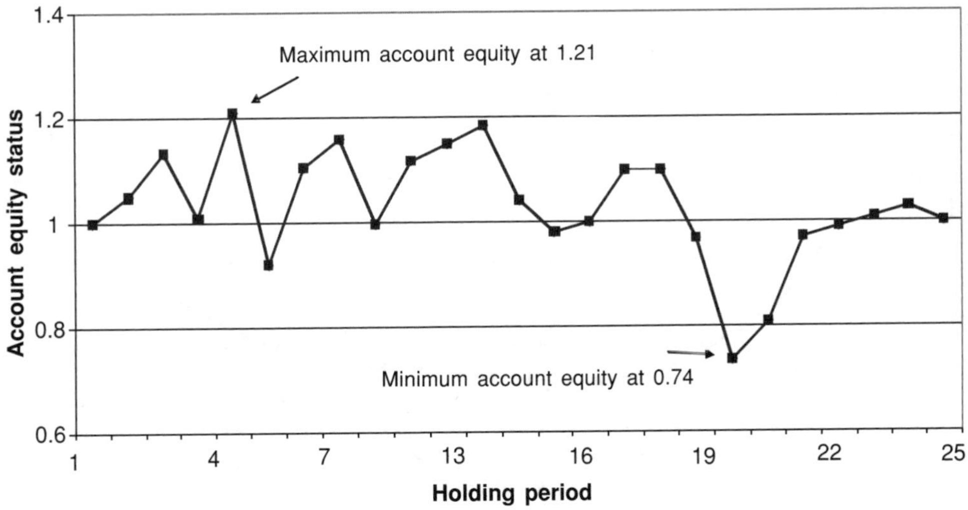

Figure 11.2 Account equity status – unsorted returns

Index where the starting amount for the notional account is a nominal \$1000. As can be seen from the column headed "Account equity status" in period 24 the portfolio equity has actually terminated at the same value that it began with. The series of values in this column can be plotted to show the progress of the account equity during the period under review and this has been shown separately in Figure 11.2. The position where the maximum account equity was achieved at 121% has been marked as well as the position when the account equity reached its minimum at 74%. The difference between these two points is referred to as the maximum drawdown of equity for the period and as can be seen in Table 11.5 this value is 39.3%. In reviewing the summary statistics underlying the trajectory of this equity curve it can be seen that the standard deviation of the returns is 12.3% with an average period return of 0.75%.

It is important to realize that the maximum drawdown value is completely independent of the mean and standard deviation values for the returns. This can be demonstrated by sorting the returns and then observing the changes to the drawdown columns and specifically the maximum drawdown amount. In Table 11.6 we show the summary statistics after the monthly returns have been sorted in an ascending fashion. In other words the poorest returns are confronted initially and then the returns get progressively better as time unfolds, and the following summary statistics can be extracted for the hypothetical portfolio.

Table 11.6 Summary statistics after returns – ascending sort

Maximum drawdown	68.9%
Minimum period return	–24.00%
Maximum period return	20.00%
Average period return	0.75%
Standard deviation of returns	12.30%

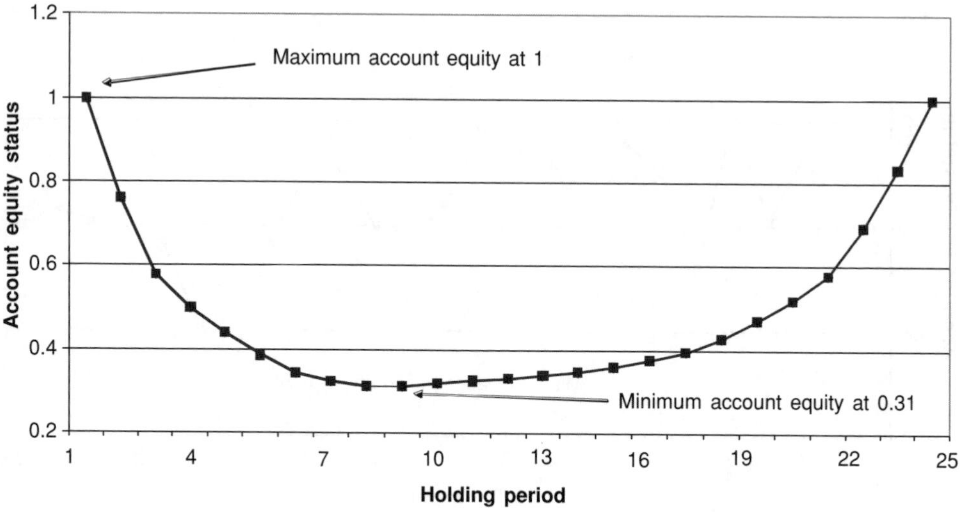

Figure 11.3 Account equity status – returns in ascending order

The statistics relating to the maximum and minimum returns as well as the mean and standard deviation have clearly not changed but the maximum drawdown has increased from 39% to 69%. In terms of the "ride" the portfolio equity curve is shown in Figure 11.3 and as can be seen the account nosedives for 10 periods and then recovers to the unchanged level at the end of the period.

If we now conduct a descending sort for the returns, ranking them from highest to lowest the situation looks dramatically different from the perspective of the equity curve as can be seen in Figure 11.4. It is worth recalling that in both cases we end up in the same place and

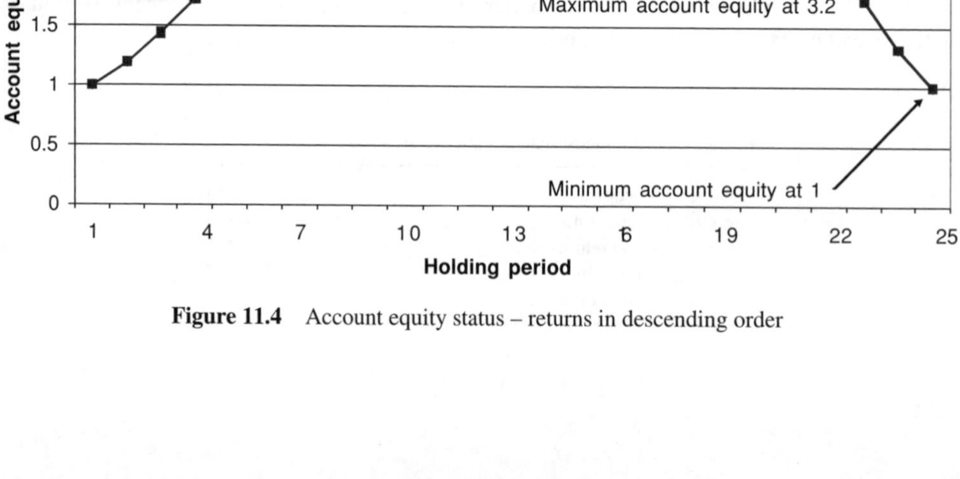

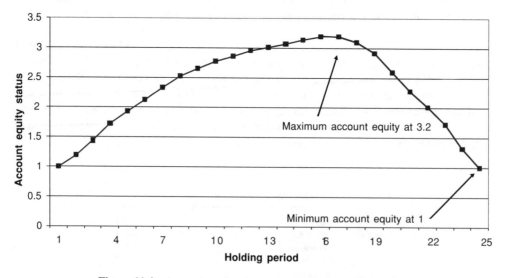

Figure 11.4 Account equity status – returns in descending order

the actual returns, and their accompanying statistical properties – their mean and standard deviations – remain unchanged. All that has changed is the sequence of the returns. The maximum drawdown figure remains as for the ascending sort that was tabulated in Table 11.3 at a rather breathtaking 69% and the equity curve rider has had to endure a very steep descent in the final eight months of the portfolio's lifetime.

What emerges from this comparison of hypothetical returns is that using the most commonly used measurement for the risk of a portfolio – the standard deviation of the returns – there is no way to distinguish between the three equity curves that have been depicted. In each case the standard deviation of the returns is 12.3% but the level of discomfort experienced by the trader has dramatically different profiles across the three different scenarios. This is why we propose that a much more meaningful measure of risk for a trader is the severity of drawdowns and that is highly influenced by the sequence of the returns. Using standard statistical techniques such as the standard deviation there is no way of separating the equity curve rides that have just been observed and there is a difference of 30% between the maximum drawdown from the returns when they are distributed in a purely contingent manner and when they are ranked from highest to lowest or vice versa.

Apart from this theoretical exercise which was intended to demonstrate the crucial role that returns sequencing has on trading risk, one of the other real benefits to traders of thinking about risk in terms of drawdowns is that this measure is more phenomenologically meaningful than a standard deviation calculation as it reflects the "pain" felt by the trader as he or she monitors portfolio performance at periodic intervals. Drawdowns are inevitable and managing the emotion associated with them is one of the keys to becoming a successful trader.

THE KELLY FORMULA

The Kelly Criterion was originally developed by AT&T Bell Laboratories physicist John Larry Kelly, based on the work of his colleague Claude Shannon, which applied to noise issues arising over long distance telephone lines. Kelly showed how Shannon's information theory could be applied to the problem of a gambler who has inside information about a horse race, trying to determine the optimum bet size. It is not important for us to delve too deeply into the historical development of the actual mechanics of the Kelly formula as this has been done very well in a highly readable book *Fortune's Formula* by William Poundstone.[3] Several interpreters of his work are well worth the attention of traders, including Edward Thorp[4] and William Ziemba[5] who is a finance professor at the University of British Columbia, and who has several fascinating papers showing the application of Kelly techniques not only to the stock market but also on the race track.

Before we cite the formula we need to think of the reasons why we should be concerned about it. Why should the calculation of gambling odds be relevant to the concerns of the typical trader? We are not surely suggesting that the trading activity is gambling after all. Well no, but they do share some common characteristics. Both activities have uncertain outcomes and both activities will occur within the context of a probability framework which will be more or less robust. We will not consider the formulation for the race track or the casino, but rather we shall follow on from win/loss matrix that we have previously examined. To frame the question in this context we now have the basis for the Kelly formula equation. What is the fraction of one's trading capital that should be allocated to a specific trading opportunity when the odds of success (the win/loss ratio) are available and we also have a knowledge of the average winning

Table 11.7 Win/loss matrix showing the Kelly formula values

Win/loss ratio	Average gain	Average loss	Typical outcome	Kelly formula
70%	$1500	$1000	$750	50.0%
65%	$1500	$1000	$625	41.7%
60%	$1500	$1000	$500	33.3%
55%	$1500	$1000	$375	25.0%
50%	$1500	$1000	$250	16.7%
45%	$1500	$1000	$125	8.3%
40%	$1500	$1000	$0	0.0%

amount (i.e. where our trades are profitable) and the average losing amount? To understand the solution that Kelly offers to this question the following notation will be useful:

- pW = the win ratio
- pL = the losing ratio or $(1 - pW)$
- aW = the amount of the average winner
- aL = the amount of the average loser (aW and aL can be expressed in either monetary terms or as percentages since it is the ratio between aW and aL that is required for the formula)
- fC = the fraction of capital to invest in the trade in question

The Kelly formula is: $fC = pW - pL/(aW/aL)$.

The best way to examine how this works out in practice is to re-examine the first section of the win/loss matrix that was introduced with Table 11.1 and substitute the appropriate values into the formula. As can be seen in Table 11.7 the most advantageous situation that we have shown is at the 70% level of winners to losers and it can be seen that the Kelly formula suggests that we should commit 50% of our trading capital to each trade if these circumstances apply. As we move down through the levels of accuracy, in other words the win/loss ratio is deteriorating while the ratio of average gain to average loss remains the same, we can see that the Kelly formula is showing that we should allocate progressively smaller amounts of our capital as the "edge" that we have declines.

Sometimes commentators fail to point out exactly what need the Kelly formula is really addressing. This can best be described by working through a specific example and showing what the formula is actually telling us. Let us take, purely for illustration purposes, the 55% win/loss ratio in Table 11.7 and the fact that the Kelly recommendation is that we commit 25% of our capital in these circumstances.

We can see that the typical outcome for trading at this level of accuracy (or with this win/loss ratio or odds) is $375 and we can interpret the Kelly formula as telling us in effect how many trades with this typical or "expected" outcome are required to realize the actual average gain of $1500, from which it should be obvious that the answer is 4. In order to be sure of achieving our aim we need to apportion our capital so that we can be sure of achieving the gain of $1500; in other words, we need to be able to allocate one quarter of our capital on each trade to achieve the goal.

Expressed differently and to extend the above formula, the expected gain (or typical outcome per trade) is $pW * aW - pL * aL$ and the number of trades required is simply $aW/(pW * aW - pL * aL)$. If we were to risk more than 25% of our current account equity, as we recycle our way through the iterations available to us within this odds and opportunity framework, then we would be in danger of missing our goal of achieving the average gain and would eventually go bust. If we were to commit less than 25% of our capital on an iterative basis then we would be "leaving profit on the table" as it were and failing to seize the full advantage from the risk/reward parameters.

But what happens if we encounter a losing streak? The good news is that if we follow the Kelly formula strictly we cannot go broke, because we only ever commit a fractional amount of our current capital to any trade. The bad news is that we may experience stomach churning drawdowns. The example that is often cited to illustrate this unfortunate consequence of the Kelly system is the massive drawdown sustained by Larry Williams as part of his effort in 1987 when he started with $10 000 and arrived at $1.1 million in a widely publicized real time trading championship, the Robbins World Cup Trading Championships. The gain that Williams achieved is clearly monumental but it did include a 67% drawdown at one stage during this effort which was broadly based on a Kelly approach to futures trading.

MANAGING DRAWDOWNS OR HOW SMOOTH IS THE RIDE?

It is often useful in reviewing a large area where so much has been written to look at some of the more provocative and extreme ideas that have been advanced as how to implement effective money management and to see how these will impact on the likelihood of experiencing drawdowns.

One of the most extreme discussions of money management is to be found in the work of Ralph Vince who wrote several books in the 1990s in which he advocated certain trading strategies based on his own idiosyncratic view of the mathematics of portfolio management. One of these books is titled *The Mathematics of Money Management*, which also carries the inappropriate subtitle *Risk Analysis Techniques for Traders*.[6] If there any followers of his strategies that are still solvent then they certainly would have some tales to tell as to the horrors of the risks of trading in the financial markets based on implementing his core ideas.

Vince creates the case for what is essentially an extreme version of a money management system which can be characterized as a fractional Kelly system. Vince is an advocate of committing a specified fraction of one's account equity on every trade which as a money management principle is fundamentally sound and a reasonable starting out point for the determination of position sizing. Unfortunately from following Vince's writings this is where reasonableness ends and recklessness begins. Vince proposes that the fraction of account equity to commit to each trade should be predicated on the most severe loss that the account may face, the so-called "Worst Case Scenario" (WCS). If we then scale this eventuality of achieving the worst case scenario in accordance with his optimization algorithm we shall arrive at the optimal fraction of equity to use in order to produce the highest geometric mean for a portfolio's growth. The difference between the final equity value in the account and the initial value expressed as a ratio is known as the Terminal Wealth Relative (TWR), which is analogous to the "Account equity status" column in Table 11.5. The number of trades that have been required to reach this final wealth value becomes the value of n that we use to calculate the geometric mean of the progression where the geometric mean = TWR^ $(1/n)$ in other words the nth root of the TWR.

There are two rather alarming consequences of this approach. The first, and this is more than a little bit reckless, is that one can never know ahead of time what the "worst case scenario" is going to be. However, this value is critically assumed at each stage in the progression. In other words, an uncertain and unknowable, in advance, maximum risk threshold is used to calculate the optimal *f* and thereby dictate how much of your capital to allocate to each trade. Since the worst case scenario is a moving value that can never be known with any certainty in advance there are no precautions as to how much risk exposure one is taking on. The trader who follows this money management strategy is in the peculiar position of not knowing ahead of time whether the optimal *f* value is in fact optimal for the very next trade because that trade could lead to a more severe "worst case scenario".

What Vince tells us is that

> It is important to note at this point that the drawdown you can expect with fixed fractional trading, as a percentage retracement of your account equity, historically would have been at least as much as *f* percent... This is so because if you are trading at the optimal *f*, as soon as your biggest loss *was* [my emphasis] hit, you would experience the drawdown equivalent to *f*.[7]

The convoluted nature of the last sentence in this quotation slightly obscures the fact that the *f* value or fraction of your capital to commit can never be set with any assurance as its value depends on the loss you might sustain in the next trade. This is like driving without a safety belt and only looking in the rear view mirror. Your worse case scenario, and the corresponding *f* value can only be specified with any precision after the losses which are in your future! An even more alarming proposition is that the optimal *f* method says nothing about drawdown. The results are the same no matter what the sequence of the trades. If the sorting of the two losses come one after the other then the worst drawdown is 76% but the TWR and optimal *f* are unchanged.

Vince fails to adequately address the issue of drawdowns and in the exposition of his methods he addresses their severity only obliquely:

> If you want to be in this (i.e. his scheme) and do it mathematically correct you better expect to be nailed for 30% to 95% equity retracements. *This takes enormous discipline, and very few people can emotionally handle this.*[8]

A little later he says, as if to reassure himself that this is all going to work out fine:

> So, like it or not, the question of what quantity to take on the next trade is inevitable for everyone. To simply select an arbitrary amount is *a costly mistake* [my emphasis]. Optimal *f* is factual, it is mathematically correct.

So we have to be heroically calm in the face of up to 95% equity retracements. But is this the worst that it can get? Well actually not quite. It is theoretically possible that it could be even more severe *but* we can take comfort that it cannot be 100% because the fractional equity reinvestment will never allow us to actually commit 100% of our capital. We can rest assured that we will always have a little bit of capital to try again! If you had seen your account equity go let us say from $1m to $50 000 and you were then expected to commit another $30 000 to your next trade, would you do it? Would you more likely be under severe medication? If you were managing a fund on behalf of your "stakeholders" do you expect that any of them would have the stomach for such drawdowns?

Theoretically one is protected (maybe) from insolvency by always recalculating your optimal *f* before each trade but in reality you will almost certainly lose your will to trade and perhaps even your will to live.

As the reader may have gathered we are not persuaded of any value to this optimal *f* technique but there are some other forms of portfolio and risk management strategy that do employ a fractional approach towards the sizing of positions and their combination within a portfolio, which are considerably more appealing and we shall soon consider them.

POSITION SIZING

One of the neglected areas in much of the literature designed to assist traders to gain an edge in the markets concerns one of the most fundamental decisions a trader has to make. The following questions are always at the back of the trader's mind and should be addressed by any good book about trading:

- How much of my capital should I risk on any individual trade?
- Is there a formula for determining position sizing?
- How can I combine positions in a portfolio so as to optimize my risk/reward ratio?

This last question appears to go a lot further than the first two questions and will lead us into a discussion of portfolio theory, diversification and different ways in which positions can be combined to manage risk. But it is intimately concerned with the two more fundamental questions. Indeed we would propose that the first two questions can only be properly addressed after there is some deeper understanding of the trader's overall exposure to risk from holding several positions in the market simultaneously. Some authors of trading books barely discuss the question of position sizing and others treat it as an afterthought. Simple rules of thumb for position sizing sometimes reflect the fact that the author feels obliged to deal with the issue but either has not thought through the larger contextual issues or thinks that his readers would prefer simpler answers. One of our main contentions is that it is only by having a framework or context for evaluating position risk that one can intelligently answer any of the three questions that were posed.

Before we outline the long/short framework that we believe all risk averse traders should follow we would like to discuss some of the answers that have been provided to the first two questions that we posed above. One such approach is known as the 2×2 rule, although there are many variations including the 3×3 rule. But essentially they have the same simple structure:

> Ensure your upside is twice (three times) your downside and never lose more than 2% (3%) of your trading capital on any single trade.

To take a simple example suppose you have \$100 000 trading capital and you think, based on favorable technical signals, that Apple Computers (AAPL) is poised to move up by 20% during the next month. If the stock is priced currently at \$50 your expectation is that the stock will be trading at \$60 within a month. You then have to contemplate the likelihood or expectation that the stock could lose 10% during the month and trade below \$45.

Assuming that you believe, on balance, that the reward/risk ratio of 2:1 fits your expectations modeling then you would proceed with the trade. But how large a long position would you take in Apple? The answer is provided by thinking of the downside and bringing in the second component to the simple rule which is that you should never risk more than 2% of your trading capital on a single trade. According to the assumptions that would amount to \$2000 and if you were to purchase more than 400 shares of Apple at \$50 and the loss was worse than your expectation you would be losing more than \$2000. So the position size is determined by the simple rule of not exceeding your maximum risk per trade (a moving total that can either adjust with your current trading capital or be set once and for all with your initial trading capital) and then factoring in your downside scenario based on the inverse ratio to your expected gain.

Table 11.8 Simple position sizing

Current portfolio equity	$100 000
Key ratio	2%
Current price for AAPL	$50
Predetermined profit target	$60
Predetermined stop-loss level	$45
Risk percent	10%
Reward percent	20%
Reward/risk ratio	2
Position size	400
Magnitude of the gain if all works according to plan	$4000
Magnitude of the loss if all works according to plan	−$2000

This can be expressed quite simply in the following formula:

$$\text{Position size} = \frac{\text{Portfolio equity} * \text{Maximum risk ratio}}{\text{Entry price for the stock} - \text{Predetermined stop-loss}}$$

The important idea with this approach is that your position size is determined not by how much you expect to make (or would like to make) on the trade but rather how much you are prepared to lose on the trade. The rule can obviously be used for instigating short positions and also there is no reason why the rule cannot have different parameters so that, for example, you may still be only willing to risk 2% of your capital on any trade but you will only act on trades where the reward/risk ratio is 3:1 or more. This simple rule has a lot to recommend it and if one was only to follow a simple model for determining position sizing, targeting profit levels and stop-loss levels this would be a good candidate. But as with all simple rules they do not stand up robustly in a complex marketplace and their limitations can be easily demonstrated.

The first and most obvious shortcoming is that there is no reliable technique for determining the likelihood of the expected outcomes, even determining a probability matrix from previous performance would be of little value or relevance. We may have a "hunch" that the reward/risk ratio implied in the expected outcomes for the Apple long position is valid but when all of pseudo probabilistic assumptions are stripped away we are left with little more than a positive "gut" feeling. But perhaps we should not be dismissive of "gut feelings" as many traders would claim that this is precisely the manner in which good trades are made. Our purpose is not to dismiss the validity of "gut feelings" or even to pretend that there are robust methods of determining the reward/risk ratio but rather to provide a safety net that will help to avoid large drawdowns.

The second major shortcoming of the 2×2 rule is that if offers the "false" hope that losses can somehow be contained from following this simple rule. It does not address the question of how accurate the trader is in making the decision to go long Apple and if the rule is followed for a series of trades it also does not take into account how many losing trades there will be to winning trades. This key ratio win/loss ratio will be addressed in the next section but it can be seen that if a trader's technical analysis skills are lacking then there could be a long series of 2% losses that would erode the trading capital and produce the kind of drawdown scenario that will often cause demotivation and defeat. But the situation is even worse than that because the trader is obviously exposed to more than "a series of 2% losses". Wouldn't it be very tidy if one could know exactly how much one would lose from every trade beforehand but in practice the frequency of overnight or even intraday gaps that see prices fall way below a stop-loss level (in the case of a long trade) suggests that the 2% loss may end up being a much larger loss in real time experience. If the trader thought that his risk on the Apple long position was limited to a \$5 loss as he cheerfully assumes that he would be cleanly stopped out of the position as it fell below \$45, from the trade as it fell below \$45 then a negative news story that caused a large overnight (or even intraday) drop from (say) \$46 to \$40 with no trading in between would trigger the stop-loss at (say) \$40 and the trader would end up losing \$10 or 20% on the trade.

The situation gets even worse if one had been combining positions in a trading account using the simple rule as the following drastic scenario illustrates. If the trader used the rule with (say) five long positions in his portfolio and had used the same logic as before then one could make a very simple and naïve assumption that the portfolio currently had a risk exposure of 10% of the account equity (i.e. 5 × 2%). Now let us suppose that the negative news scenario is not about any one or more of the holdings but a *critical macro event* that causes the whole market to gap down by 7%, how this would impact the trader's account. The (very) simple answer might be that the "mini-crash" would actually result in a 35% loss to the trading account (i.e. the five positions all falling by 7% each). But this assumes that all of the positions fall in exactly the same proportion as the overall market; for simplicity, let us assume that the crash had caused a 7% drop in the S&P 500. To imagine that each of the individual stocks that were being held exactly matched the market's downside risk would itself be illusory. The stocks have different beta values which indicate how much the individual stock is likely to fluctuate with respect to a benchmark index. If all of the stocks had a beta of exactly one then a case could be made that the overall 7% market drop would translate into the 35% loss that we previously calculated.

Unfortunately there is a further fundamental flaw with this logic which has been widely acknowledged in academic literature on "discontinuities", "crashes", or "correlated liquidity crises" to use some of the terminology that is used for the critical event scenario we have discussed. The problem is that when markets crash, the beta values and correlations among assets all tend to rise together. *The only thing that rises in troubled times are the correlations among financial assets.*[9]

So even if our trader had been taking some account of the degree of correlation between the five holdings and paid some regard to the beta values of the five stocks, when the market drops precipitously these previously observed beta values and correlations in a "tame" market go out of the window in a "wild" market. To take a rather simplistic view, let us suppose that during the pre-crash environment the five stocks did all have a beta of one and therefore moved exactly in line with the benchmark index, but when the market moves to wild extremes these beta values might all move up by 50% and in effect each stock would have a beta of 1.5. Now the trader could be looking at a loss of 35% * 1.5 or 52.5% as each of the stocks is losing half as much again as the benchmark index loss. To finish the point the trader thought that he was only exposed to a potential 10% loss of capital even if he turned out to be wrong about all five of his expectations of a positive outcome to the trades entered. But with an adverse market event that can arise with alarming alacrity the loss has turned into a loss of more than half of the trading capital and a psychologically devastating drawdown from which the trader may decide to abandon trading for a quieter pastime.

THE SIMPLEST LONG/SHORT FRAMEWORK

At this point we can introduce a simple but potentially powerful modification to the simple 2 × 2 rule. Let us now suppose that the trader has recovered from the previous shock and decided to continue trading but this time has realized that there are unacceptable dangers in

Table 11.9 Simple long short portfolio

Magnitude of crash −7%	Position size	Entry price	Initial position value	Tame beta	Wild beta	Price after	Position P/L
AAPL	400	$50	$20 000	1.5	2	$43.00	−$2800
INTC	−1000	$20	−$20 000	1.5	2	$17.20	$2800
Net balances			0				0

having a 100% long portfolio when there is the possibility, however low the probability, that a crash event can wipe out a substantial chunk of his trading capital in one fell swoop.

The trader has decided to combine long and short positions in the portfolio so that when the long positions are plunging along with the rest of the market the short positions in the portfolio are gaining in value as the price of the stocks shorted are also plunging. To keep things simple at this stage let us assume that we use exactly the same principle as before that all of the short positions are selected on the same reward/risk proposition and that the per trade capital risk is as before. As an example let us assume that the trader is bearish about Intel Corporation while remaining positive about Apple. The trader takes the view that Intel could fall by 20% in the coming month and is confident that the stock could not rise by more than 10%. If the stock is trading at $20 at the time, the same logic as before suggests that the trader will take up a short position of 1000 shares of INTC. If the stock should rise by more than 10% to trade at or above $22 the trader will be stopped out of the short trade with a loss of $2000 which is again equivalent to 2% of the account equity.

To keep life simple let us suppose that these are the only two holdings that the trader has – a long position of AAPL of 400 shares purchased at $50 and a 1000 share short position in INTC shorted at $20. The matrix outlined in Table 11.9 illustrates what would happen in the same crash scenario that we examined.

We have included a recognition that the beta value will escalate but we have assumed that for simplification both stocks have the same wild beta values. The magnitude of the crash has caused the price of both stocks to drop by 14% or twice the drop in the benchmark index but as can be seen the short position has gained as much as the long position has lost leaving the net balance on the P&L column at zero.

However, this matrix does not fully capture what would have happened to the positions as there were predetermined stop-loss levels established for both positions which would have been "hit" in the wake of the gap event or crash.

Table 11.10 shows that the trader would have exited both positions, the account would be flat and there would have been no loss incurred by the portfolio. This happy event has much to do with the simplifying assumptions and the fact that the stop-loss levels were both triggered

Table 11.10 Both positions have been exited

Magnitude of crash −7.00%	Position size	Entry price	Profit target price	Stop loss price	Initial position value	Tame beta	Wild beta	Price after crash	Exit price	Current position value	Position P/L
AAPL	400	$50	$60.0	$45.0	$20 000	1.5	2	$43.00	$43.00		−$2800
INTC	−1000	$20	$18.0	$22.0	−$20 000	1.5	2	$17.20	$17.20		$2800
Net balances					0					0	0

Table 11.11 One portfolio position remains after correction

Magnitude of crash −7.00%	Position size	Entry price	Profit target price	Stop loss price	Initial position value	Tame beta	Wild beta	Price after crash	Exit price	Current position value	Position P/L
AAPL	400	$50	$60.0	$45.0	$20 000	1.5	2	$43.00	$43.00		−$2800
INTC	−1000	$20	$18.0	$22.0	−$20 000	1	1.4	$18.04		−$18 040.00	$1960
Net balances					0					−18 040	−840

by the crash. But it is easy to construct a less happy scenario by simply changing a couple of values in the beta columns.

In the alternative scenario depicted in Table 11.11, the beta values were not identical to start with and the wild beta values did not track each other perfectly as before. In this new scenario the tame beta for INTC was 1 and it moves up to 1.4 during an extreme or critical market episode. As a consequence two things have happened that are less favorable to the trader. First, AAPL lost more than INTC gained on the short side, owing to the unmatched beta values, and second, the account is no longer flat but is showing a net short position in INTC as the stop has not triggered and therefore the position was not exited. The account has a current loss of $840 and if there is a relief rally the portfolio's net short exposure is going to produce further losses as the short position in INTC suffers. The trader has realized the loss of $2800 in AAPL but is still carrying an unbalanced short position in INTC.

The point of the previous examples is to show that portfolio construction logic and position management can never be reduced to simple rules of thumb. The task of managing a portfolio that wishes to preserve the correct balance of long and short positions requires more sophisticated logic which takes into account adjustable stop-loss levels and should also include a recognition of the conditional nature of beta values. These issues will be treated again in Chapter 13.

PORTFOLIOS AND DRAWDOWNS

We are going to review some more measures of portfolio performance in relation to drawdowns and the overall risk characteristics of a hypothetical portfolio. The exercise is primarily designed to consider the following ratios: the Sharpe ratio, the sterling ratio, the Sortino ratio and the Calmar ratio all of which have been used as benchmarks within the financial community and are especially used in the comparative analysis of portfolio performance. In particular many hedge fund managers pay particular attention to these ratios, especially the Sharpe ratio, as these are considered to be a principal element in the due diligence that a potential investor is likely to undertake before making a capital commitment.

We shall define each of the ratios in turn but to begin with we need to introduce some more fundamental terminology. We will introduce the following concepts – Terminal Wealth Relative (TWR), Value Added Monthly Index (VAMI), and Compound Annual Growth Rate (CAGR).

TERMINAL WEALTH RELATIVE (TWR)

Terminal Wealth Relative is simply defined as the return on an investment quantified as a multiple. A TWR of 1.55 means that one would have a final value to one's original investment of 155% which in effect means that one has made a profit of 55%. A TWR of 0.55 would suggest that one had lost 45% of one's original investment.

Table 11.12 CAGR explained

Year	VAMI	Annual return
0	1000	
1	1015	1.50%
2	1020	0.49%
3	1023	0.29%
4	1030	0.68%
5	1040	0.97%
Compound annual growth rate (CAGR)		0.79%

VALUE ADDED MONEY INDEX (VAMI)

This is also designed to express in simple notional terms how an investment grows on a monthly basis. It is expressed in the form of an index value which tracks how a hypothetical portfolio of $1000 will change from month to month. The calculation for the current month's VAMI is Previous VAMI × (1 + Current rate of return).

COMPOUND ANNUAL GROWTH RATE (CAGR)

The best way to understand this important concept is to use an example that can rely on the previously introduced notion of the VAMI. Let us suppose that we have the brief data in Table 11.12 showing the growth of VAMI over a five year period.

The VAMI at year zero is an index value of 1000 and it has grown to 1040 (i.e. a total 4% return). The annual returns are shown in the right-hand column but to calculate the CAGR we need to use the following formula CAGR $= (C_t/C_0)^{(1/t)} - 1$, where we can substitute VAMI for C and 5 the number of compounding periods for t.

We have periods of returns and we need to substitute into the following formula the VAMI at the end $(1040/100)^\wedge(1/5) - 1$. As can be seen this gives us the Compound Annual Growth Rate of slightly less that 0.8%. It should also be seen that if we start with the VAMI of 1000 and then multiply that by $(1 + \text{CAGR})^\wedge 5$ we will arrive at 1040.[10]

At this point we can consider several benchmarks or ratios that have been proposed in the finance literature to assess the risk/reward ratio characteristics of different portfolios. They differ slightly in their constructions but with the exception of one of those to be considered – the Calmar ratio – they are all insensitive to the sequencing of returns which our earlier discussion has shown to be a crucial shortcoming in the reliance on standard deviation alone as adequately portraying the risk profiles of a portfolio. We shall start with the most widely used ratio – the Sharpe ratio.

SHARPE RATIO

The simplest method to calculate the Sharpe ratio is to deduct the Risk-Free Rate of Return (RFR) from the CAGR and divide the result by the annualized standard deviation of the returns. So the formula is simply

$$[\text{CAGR} - \text{RFR}]/\text{Annualized standard deviation of returns}$$

There is a slightly different approach which is to deduct the average monthly return at the risk-free T bill rate from the average monthly return and divide the result by the monthly standard deviation of the returns. Once that figure is obtained the result is again multiplied by the square root of 12. The alternate formula is simply

$$\{[\text{Average monthly return} - \text{Average RFR}]/\text{STD of monthly returns}\} * 12\hat{}0.5$$

Now that we know how to calculate it we should briefly explore the significance of this value which was first proposed by the Nobel Laureate William F. Sharpe who is Emeritus Professor of Finance at Stanford University. The assumption behind the calculation and the reason why the standard deviation is used as the denominator to the equation is that since investors prefer a smooth ride to a bumpy one the higher the standard deviation the lower will be the Sharpe ratio. Accordingly high Sharpe ratios are to be preferred and positive values are obviously better than negative values reflecting the fact that returns are positive (obviously the denominator in the equation will always be a positive value).

As we have commented previously our intention is to use the various ratios and indicators, not necessarily in 100% compliance with how they may have been introduced into the financial literature, but in the manner that makes them most appropriate in today's market circumstances.

As an aside we should note that many analysts compute the Sharpe ratio using arithmetic returns. The main reason for this is because the basic theories of portfolio investment management such as mean-variance analysis and the Capital Asset Pricing Model (CAPM) are based on arithmetic means. However, the geometric mean is a more accurate measure of average performance for time series data as the following example shows. For example, if one has returns of +50% and −50% in two periods, then the arithmetic mean is zero which does not correctly reflect the fact that 100 became 150 and then 75. The geometric mean which is −13.7% is the correct measure to use. For investment returns in the 10–15% range, the arithmetic returns are about 2% above the geometric returns.[11]

There are a few other factors that need to be noted about the simple formula for the Sharpe ratio. Since the denominator of the formula is the standard deviation of the returns the ratio becomes numerically very unstable at extremes or in other words when the denominator is close to zero. The second and major problem is the one that we have witnessed previously with regard to the discussion of the different equity curves that arise from sorting the returns of a hypothetical portfolio so that they run in either ascending or descending fashion as opposed to their actual sequence in time. As the discussion above showed the equity curves are so dramatically different when ranked in an ascending or descending fashion and yet the means and standard deviations of the returns are the same. Therefore, depending on the exact time frame of reference, the Sharpe ratio would be the same in all three instances – the actual sequence, the ascending and the descending sequence. What this illustrates is that the Sharpe ratio is essentially insensitive to the clustering of returns. From our perspective this is a serious limitation of the value because not only would an investor be seriously perturbed by the extreme equity curves that we witnessed but would be concerned if there was a cluster of losing months in a returns schedule. Because of the calculation mode that underlies averages and standard deviations this clustering of losing months also he would no longer be apparent on a retrospective basis although *at the time* the volatility would have "felt" much worse than the Sharpe ratio suggests.

There is one further limitation of the procedure for calculating the Sharpe ratio which is that the simple standard deviation or variability of the returns includes not only the months when returns are negative but also those when returns are positive as well. The presence of a number of months with superior returns in an otherwise typically positive period of performance will increase the standard deviation but for reasons that hopefully the investor will not find unattractive. Risk is asymmetrical and we tend to equate negative or adverse returns as problematic, whereas the Sharpe ratio penalizes the fund manager who happens to show superior performance with higher variability caused by a higher frequency of big winners. This limitation was the inspiration for the next ratio we shall examine.

SORTINO RATIO

Named after its protagonist, this ratio is really no more than an adaptation of the Sharpe ratio to deal with the problem just observed that investors do not normally object to increased volatility when it leads to positive returns. The numerator of the Sortino ratio is the CAGR – the Risk-Free Rate (as before for the Sharpe ratio), but the denominator is based on a calculation of the standard deviations of only those returns that are below a minimum acceptable level. There is some disagreement on how that minimum threshold should be set so we prefer to simply calculate, for the denominator, the standard deviation of all the negative returns. The Sortino ratio, as it is heralded, no longer penalizes the superior fund managers for spectacular upside returns.

STERLING RATIO

As originally proposed the numerator of the equation for the Sterling Ratio is the CAGR for the past three years if available or pro-rated accordingly. The denominator for the formula is the average yearly maximum drawdown over the preceding three years less an arbitrary 10%; again it can be pro-rated accordingly if three years of returns are not available.

CALMAR RATIO

The Calmar Ratio is our preferred measurement of the risk/return relationship as it most matches the requirements of the active trader, and it is also becoming increasingly favored by some academics who are concerned with the limitations in the Sharpe ratio. Very simply it is the CAGR divided by the absolute value of the maximum drawdown for the period under consideration. The higher the ratio the better is considered to be the trade-off between risk and reward.

A brief discussion of the Calmar ratio will help in better understanding the interpretation.

	CAGR	Max drawdown (absolute value)	Calmar ratio	Expected maximum VAMI	Expected minimum VAMI
Fund A	25%	10%	2.5	1250	900
Fund B	40%	30%	1.33	1400	700

Although an investor in Fund B has a potential upside VAMI of 1400 this must be seen within the context that the drawdown figures show that Fund B also has the capacity to deliver a final or interim VAMI of 700 for any particular holding period. In terms of the reward/risk ratio this is less attractive than the expectations for an investor in Fund A which will not potentially deliver as big an upside as Fund B but which does not expose the investor to as much potential downside risk. Using the Calmar ratio an investment in Fund A is to be preferred.

We now have the tools we need to apply a risk analysis of the following hypothetical portfolio which is tabulated in Table 11.13. Let us review the summary of the performance in Table 11.13

Table 11.13 Hypothetical portfolio with risk/reward profile

Month	Monthly return	VAMI 1000	TWR 1	YTD P&L	Maximum drawdown
1	−1.7%	983.1	0.98	−1.7%	−1.7%
2	−2.7%	956.7	0.96	−4.3%	−4.3%
3	4.5%	999.2	1.00	−0.1%	−0.1%
4	9.4%	1092.8	1.09	9.3%	0.0%
5	−2.0%	1071.4	1.07	7.1%	−2.0%
6	−6.0%	1007.3	1.01	0.7%	−7.8%
7	8.7%	1095.2	1.10	9.5%	0.0%
8	7.1%	1173.2	1.17	17.3%	0.0%
9	5.4%	1236.0	1.24	23.6%	0.0%
10	4.3%	1289.3	1.29	28.9%	0.0%
11	19.5%	1540.6	1.54	54.1%	0.0%
12	3.8%	1598.6	1.60	59.9%	0.0%
13	0.2%	1602.6	1.60	60.3%	0.0%
14	−6.9%	1492.2	1.49	49.2%	−6.9%
15	−0.4%	1486.5	1.49	48.7%	−7.2%
16	−1.3%	1467.9	1.47	46.8%	−8.4%
17	−0.1%	1466.6	1.47	46.7%	−8.5%
18	−3.1%	1421.7	1.42	42.2%	−11.3%
19	5.4%	1498.2	1.50	49.8%	−6.5%
20	−13.5%	1295.3	1.30	29.5%	−19.2%
21	9.5%	1418.3	1.42	41.8%	−11.5%
22	15.8%	1642.2	1.64	64.2%	0.0%
23	2.7%	1686.0	1.69	68.6%	0.0%
24	0.4%	1692.2	1.69	69.2%	0.0%
Summary					
Maximum drawdown					−19.2%
Average annual maximum drawdown					−13.5%
Average monthly return					2.5%
Standard deviation of monthly returns					7.2%
Monthly annualized compound rate of return					2.2%
Compound annualized growth rate					30.1%
Annualized standard deviation of returns					25.0%
Standard deviation of negative monthly returns					3.2%
Annualized standard deviation of negative returns					11.0%
Assumed annual risk free rate of return					5.0%
Key risk ratios					
Sharpe ratio					1.00
Sterling ratio					1.28
Sortino ratio					2.27
Calmar ratio					1.57

Table 11.14 Summary of unsorted returns

Maximum drawdown	−19.2%
Average annual maximum drawdown	−13.5%
Average monthly return	2.5%
Standard deviation of monthly returns	7.2%
Monthly annualized compound rate of return	2.2%
Compound annualized growth rate	30.1%
Annualized standard deviation of returns	25.0%
Standard deviation of negative monthly returns	3.2%
Annualized standard deviation of negative returns	11.0%
Assumed annual risk free rate of return	5.0%
Key risk ratios	
Sharpe ratio	1.00
Sterling ratio	1.28
Sortino ratio	2.27
Calmar ratio	1.57

and look at each of the values in turn. There are 24 monthly returns and the closing VAMI of 1692 with a corresponding TWR of 1.69. The maximum drawdown over the 24 months – 19.2% – is simply the maximum value that appears in the running maximum drawdown column. The annual average maximum drawdown applies the maximum drawdown to each of the two years and then averages the two values. The average and standard deviations for the monthly returns are straightforward. The CAGR of slightly more than 30% is determined as we have seen in our previous discussion. The annualized standard deviation of the returns is calculated by multiplying the standard deviation for the monthly returns by the square root of 12.

In the summary section of the table we have calculated the standard deviation for the downside returns in order to determine the Sortino ratio. As previously noted, there are variations on this procedure where it has been suggested that only the negative deviations below some arbitrary threshold should be included in the computation but we have simply taken all of the negative returns and determined the standard deviation for them. This figure has also been annualized as before using the square root of 12. The final value that we have used is the Risk-Free Rate of Return which for a U.S. investor is the yield on three month Treasury bills and which for simplicity sake we have assumed to be equal to 5% per annum.

We are now in a position to calculate the risk ratios that we previously mentioned but we will first summarize them for the above portfolio. Table 11.14 repeats the summary statistics for the hypothetical portfolio and includes an expression of each of the key risk ratios we have examined. The table has been provided with the header "Unsorted returns" to emphasize that the sequencing of the returns is exactly as outlined in Table 11.13.

It may appear from a purely numerical perspective that there is not a lot of variation in the values for key risk ratios presented in Table 11.14 but each value should be interpreted within the proper framework. For example, it can be seen that the annualized standard deviation for all of the returns is 25% but for the negative returns only it is 11% and it is exactly for this reason that the Sortino ratio is considerably higher than the Sharpe ratio. The portfolio manager is only penalized from delivering adverse returns and therefore the denominator value to the risk/reward ratio is lower for the manager who is assessed with the Sortino ratio rather than the Sharpe ratio.

Table 11.15 Summary of ascending sort of portfolio returns

Maximum drawdown	−32.4%
Average annual maximum drawdown	−10.9%
Average monthly return	2.5%
Standard deviation of monthly returns	7.2%
Monthly annualized compound rate of return	2.2%
Compound annualized growth rate	30.1%
Annualized standard deviation of returns	25.0%
Standard deviation of negative monthly returns	3.2%
Annualized standard deviation of negative returns	11.0%
Assumed annual risk free rate of return	5.0%
Key risk ratios	
Sharpe ratio	1.00
Sterling ratio	1.44
Sortino ratio	2.27
Calmar ratio	0.93

HOW SENSITIVE ARE RISK RATIOS TO SEQUENCING OF RETURNS?

The final exercise in this chapter is one of the most revealing as it highlights the inherent limitations of many conventional risk measurements. What if we were to sort the returns that are outlined in Table 11.13? Would the four ratios that we have looked at adequately reflect the fact that the portfolio manager would have had very different experiences depending on the manner in which the sequence of returns is actually "lived"? In view of the tendency for returns to cluster, or for markets to exhibit "winning or losing streaks", we would hope and expect that our measures of risk/reward would be sensitive to this clustering phenomenon. We shall find out if this is the case by sorting the returns in both an ascending and descending fashion. In the real world this is highly implausible but as a theoretical exercise it will allow us to see what happens (if anything) to the ratios from which we can extrapolate how useful they would be in less dramatic resequencing scenarios.

Table 11.15 shows the summary statistics and key risk ratios after the returns have been ranked with an ascending sort. Most values in the summary statistics will not have changed and this is evident from comparing Table 11. 15 with Table 11.14. The two that have changed are the maximum drawdown which is more acute in the case of the sorted returns and accordingly the average annual maximum drawdown will also be different. But what is more revealing is to look at the values in the key risk ratios section of the two tables. Neither the Sharpe ratio nor the Sortino ratio has budged between the two different scenarios. This follows directly from the fact that the standard deviations and CAGR values remain unchanged between the two different scenarios. If we simply used the Sharpe and Sortino ratios we could not differentiate between the totally different equity curves that would be traced out under the different sequence of returns.

The sterling ratio has taken on different values for each of the different scenarios based entirely on the changes to the average annual maximum drawdown for each scenario. In fact under the ascending sort the average drawdown is slightly more benign and therefore the sterling ratio value has actually increased for this scenario. The only ratio that has shifted noticeably is the Calmar ratio which has moved down from 1.53 with the unsorted returns to a value of 0.93 for the returns subject to the ascending sort. The denominator for the Calmar

Table 11.16 Summary of descending sort of returns

Maximum drawdown	−32.4%
Average annual maximum drawdown	−16.2%
Average monthly return	2.5%
Standard deviation of monthly returns	7.2%
Monthly annualized compound rate of return	2.2%
Compound annualized growth rate	30.1%
Annualized standard deviation of returns	25.0%
Standard deviation of negative monthly returns	3.2%
Annualized standard deviation of negative returns	11.0%
Assumed annual risk free rate of return	5.0%
Key risk ratios	
Sharpe ratio	1.00
Sterling ratio	1.15
Sortino ratio	2.27
Calmar ratio	0.93

ratio is the maximum drawdown and this has jumped as a result of the sorting of returns and correspondingly the ratio has fallen. The Calmar ratio signals this additional risk whereas none of the other three ratios would bring it to our attention.

The final table to be considered is Table 11.16 which sorts the returns from Table 11.13 in a descending fashion so that the highest returns are encountered at the beginning of the lifetime of the portfolio and the returns get progressively more negative over the 24 months.

The only value to change among the summary statistics at the top of Table 11.16 is the average annual maximum drawdown which is worst under the descending sort than the ascending sort. Interestingly only one of the key ratios captures this change which is the sterling ratio as its denominator relies on average drawdown. So the sterling ratio is the only one of the key ratios to be sensitive to the sequencing of returns. The Calmar ratio is not influenced by the manner of the ranking of returns – either ascending or descending – because the maximum drawdown does not change under the two scenarios.

Well-respected risk ratios have performed unexpectedly under this exercise and hopefully the reader will now place a little less faith in the ability of the Sharpe ratio to adequately express the degree of discomfort that might actually be experienced from holding a portfolio in a market environment where clustering of abnormal returns is to be expected.

12
Portfolio Theory

Modern portfolio theory (MPT) originated with an article entitled "Portfolio Selection" by Harry Markowitz which appeared in 1952 in the *Journal of Finance*. The principles that were proposed in this highly influential paper now seem to be unremarkable, but at the time the emphasis on diversification and the mathematical model that enabled a portfolio manager to assemble positions that will provide the best level of expected return for a given risk tolerance, helped to usher in a period of great innovation in investment theory. The MPT foundations were a cornerstone of the work of William Sharpe which culminated in the Capital Asset Pricing Model (CAPM), and Markowitz, Sharpe and a further collaborator Merton Miller shared the Nobel Prize for Economics in 1980.[1]

Markowitz's seminal insight and contribution to asset allocation theory was his provision of a quantitative technique that encouraged the astute portfolio manager to focus on selecting portfolios based on their overall risk/reward characteristics rather than constructing portfolios from consideration of only their individual profit opportunities. In essence MPT stresses that a trader or investor should allocate assets based on the characteristics of a portfolio rather than the individual characteristics of the constituent securities considered separately. Prior to the MPT, the received wisdom on the manner to combine securities in a portfolio was to screen securities that offered the most attractive opportunities for gain with the least risk and then add these together in a portfolio. Bringing individual securities together in such a fashion would often lead to exposing the portfolio to too many securities from the same sector where the correlations between the returns among the securities selected would be imprudently high. In other words the portfolio would lack the benefits of diversification. Markowitz's major contribution was to articulate the logic of diversification and to focus attention on the manner in which the overall volatility of a portfolio (which is considered to be the suitable proxy for its degree of risk) is calculated from the covariance matrix of the returns of its constituents.

After Markowitz's paper the asset manager had a systematic procedure for evaluating different combinations of securities and selecting those combinations that provided the optimal reward for a given level of risk. The optimal allocations will be a trade-off between the risks a fund manager is willing to tolerate and the anticipated returns. The Markowitz procedure enables a fund manager to calculate the correlated portfolio volatility and the expected returns for numerous combination scenarios. From the logical space of possible portfolio combinations there are a series of combinations that will optimally balance the risk and reward. The optimal combinations that maximize the reward for the different possible levels of risk lie on what Markowitz termed the efficient frontier. The fund manager can settle on the level of risk

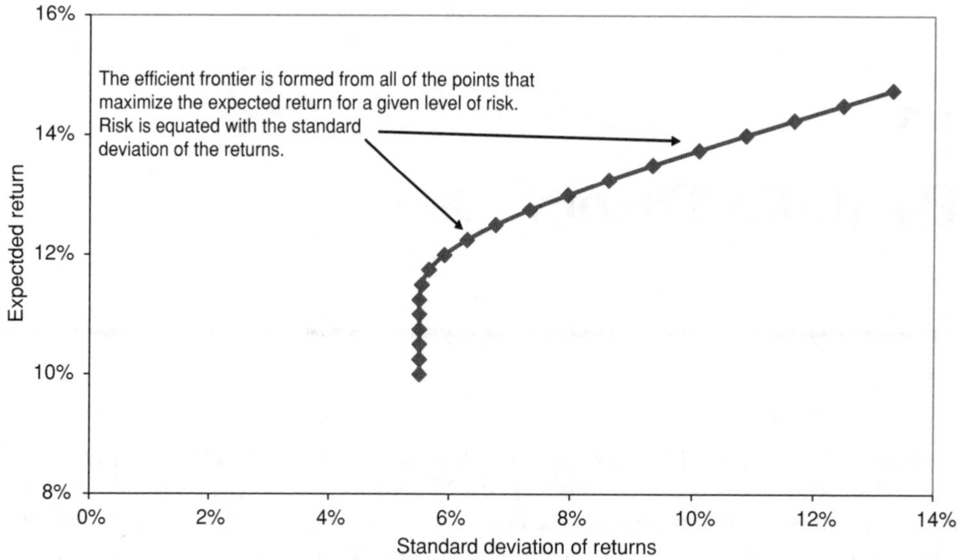

Figure 12.1 Portfolio theory – the efficient frontier

that is acceptable and then select the particular combination of securities that optimize the reward for this level of risk.

The efficient frontier can best be illustrated from the simple graphical presentation in Figure 12.1. The points on the frontier reflect the optimal allocations between the securities that match the two dimensions of the two axes of the chart. For example, at the level of risk equating to a 6% standard deviation in the portfolio returns the best reward is offered at just over 12% and the particular combination of positions that generated this point in the space of possibilities would be the optimal portfolio that satisfies the two constraints.

Points on the efficient frontier reflect those combinations of securities where no added diversification can lower the portfolio's risk for a given return expectation, or looked at from the other perspective no additional expected return can be gained without increasing the risk of the portfolio. From this we can define the Markowitz efficient frontier as "the set of all portfolios that will give you the highest expected return for each given level of risk".[2] Portfolios on the efficient frontier are optimal in both the sense that they offer maximal expected return for some given level of risk and minimal risk for some given level of expected return.

Typically, the portfolios that comprise the efficient frontier are the ones that reflect the most benign benefits of diversification. We will examine the methods that are required to compute the candidates for the efficient frontier in what follows but beforehand we want to introduce and explain an associated concept which has also become crucial in portfolio management–Value at Risk.

VALUE AT RISK

One of the extensions of the portfolio construction methodology inspired by the work of Markowitz is that it becomes relatively simple to extend the logic to calculate the likelihood of incurring a specified loss during a certain holding period with a given level of confidence.

Table 12.1 Two asset portfolio

	Asset A		Asset B
Expected monthly return	1.00%		1.50%
Relative allocation share	50%		50%
Standard deviation	5.00%		8.00%
Correlation coefficient		0.5	
Expected portfolio monthly return		1.25%	
t-statistic for confidence interval		1.645	
Portfolio variance		0.003225	
Portfolio standard deviation		0.057	
Monthly VaR		−8.1%	

All of the concerns that we have discussed previously about the suitability of using a normal Gaussian distribution and probability assumptions are once again brought into focus in the Value at Risk calculation. The VaR calculation does not answer the question: What is the largest amount that one can lose during a month? Rather it provides the answer to the following question: What is the amount that one would expect to lose (under normal distribution assumptions) with a probability of x% for a specified period?

Consider the problem of estimating how big a loss a portfolio could experience over the next month. Typically, the estimate of the maximum expected loss is defined for a given time horizon and a given confidence interval. Assuming for simplicity that the distribution of portfolio returns is normal, then a three standard deviation drop is possible, but not very likely. According to the probability density function it should arise only 0.3% of the time or once in approximately 300 months. Retreating to a more probable event, let us consider the type of loss that occurs once in 20 months. If you know the mean and standard deviation of the portfolio, and you specify the confidence interval as a 5% event (1 in 20 months) or a 1% event (1 in a 100 months) it is straightforward to calculate the Value at Risk.

Table 12.1 outlines the case of a simple portfolio which has two assets. The two assets could be two different stocks or one could be an asset class such as stocks and the other could be a different asset class such as bonds. Each of the assets has different historical returns and volatility characteristics (standard deviations). Based on the highly simplistic assumptions that we are using the expected return becomes (0.01 * 0.5) + (0.015 * 0.5) or 1.25%. Let us also assume that we have also observed that the linear correlation coefficient between the data for each of the assets is 0.5 for the lookback period that we have chosen (let us assume 20 periods). Because there are only two assets to consider the covariance matrix is trivially simple and the portfolio variance is easily calculated. The square root of the variance, the standard deviation, has been determined to be 0.057.

With the values for the expected return and portfolio volatility calculated it is possible to situate the first point on a graph that shows the derivation of the Value at Risk. Figure 12.2 provides a useful intuitive basis for the other steps involved in the procedure and requires further explanation. A confidence interval of 5% has been assumed in Figure 12.2 which means that 19 times out of 20 a loss of less than the VaR calculation would be the expected outcome but 1 in 20 times a loss of at least the VaR amount should be expected. The value used for the gradient of the linear equation that enables the y-intercept value to be precisely determined is dependent on the confidence interval and is derived from the t-statistic. The t-statistic represents the probability of an event's occurrence predicated on where the standardized value for the

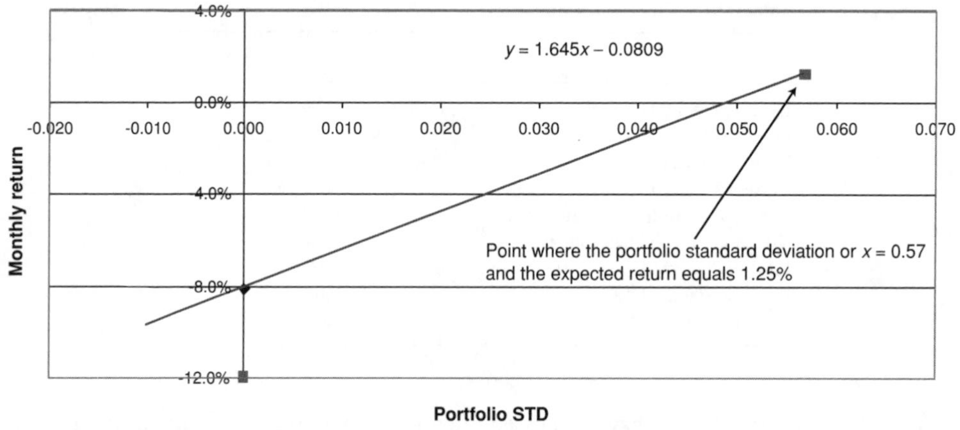

Figure 12.2 Value at Risk – simple two asset portfolio – 5% confidence

event falls within the normal distribution. If we are interested in a 95% confidence interval then we are concerned about the likelihood of an event which falls 1.645 standard deviations from the normalized mean. Thus 1.645 becomes the slope for the equation that we are interested in. As a result of substituting the values into the simple linear equation we can find that the VaR (i.e. the y-intercept value) is 8.1%.

How did we know to use the value of 1.645 for the slope of the line? This value is the inverse of the standard normal cumulative distribution for the assumed probability level of 0.95. This value can be found in various t-statistics tables or more usually through a simple computation in Excel. If one enters the function = NORMSINV(0.95) into a cell in Excel the value returned will be 1.645. Let us suppose that we are looking for a more extreme value which is the value associated with an event that might arise 1 in 100 months then we could determine the gradient value for the equation using the same procedure = NORMSINV(0.99) and we would use a value for the slope of 2.326.

Figure 12.3 illustrates the case of deriving the VaR for two different confidence intervals, the 95% level that was previously shown and the 99% level as well. The slope for the higher confidence interval is much steeper and as can be seen the value of the y-intercept value (i.e. the value of y where x is zero) falls slightly above the −12% level (i.e. 11.96%). All the previous qualifications apply again but from this chart, one can make the assumption that 99 times out of 100, a monthly loss of this magnitude will not be incurred but 1 time in 100 months a loss of almost 12% from this portfolio should be expected. To summarize the key features of the graphical representation of these two scenarios – the y-intercept value is the Value at Risk and the slope is the t-statistic for the given level of confidence.

The formula for the Value at Risk is simply:

$$\text{VaR} = \text{Expected return} - (\text{Portfolio volatility} \times t\text{-statistic for the confidence interval})$$

The expected return is customarily based on the historical mean returns for the individual securities with a weighting based on the relative allocations within the portfolio. At the moment we are only considering long positions and in Table 12.1 the expected return reflected positive

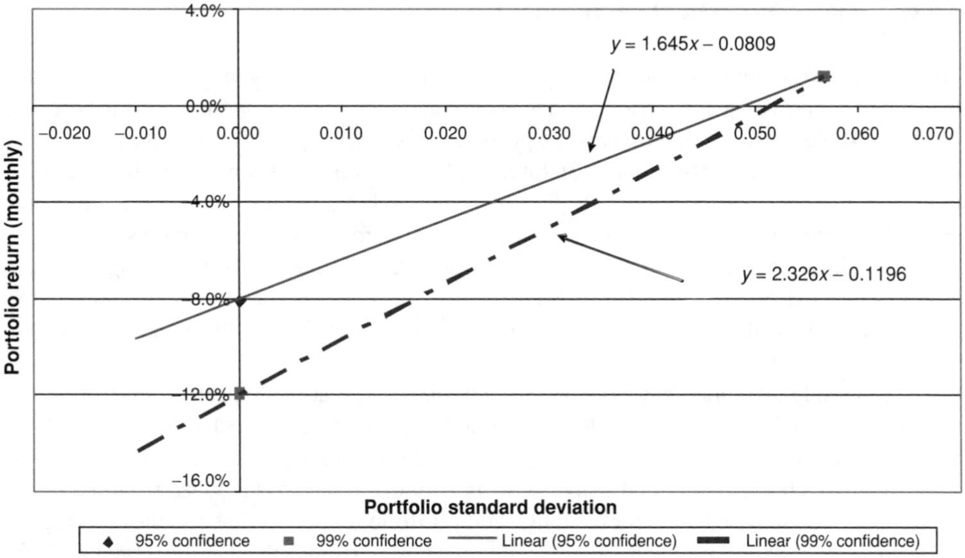

Figure 12.3 Value at Risk with different confidence intervals

returns for both of the securities and a portfolio return of 1.25%. The VaR will be higher if the positions are long and the mean returns for the individual securities and this can be simply illustrated in Table 12.2. The incremental increase in the VaR value for a two asset portfolio will be equal to the positive VaR and twice the negative monthly return, so in the case that we have considered the VaR deteriorates by a further 2.5% which is twice the portfolio return.

Table 12.2 Two asset portfolio – bull and bear markets

Bull market scenario	Asset A		Asset B	Bear market scenario	Asset A		Asset B
Expected monthly return	1.00%		1.50%	Expected monthly return	−1.00%		−1.50%
Relative allocation share	50%		50%	Relative allocation share	50%		50%
Standard deviation	5.00%		8.00%	Standard deviation	5.00%		8.00%
Correlation coefficient		0.5		Correlation coefficient		0.5	
Expected portfolio monthly return		1.25%		Expected portfolio monthly return		−1.25%	
t-Statistic for confidence interval		1.645		*t*-statistic for confidence interval		1.645	
Portfolio variance		0.003225		Portfolio variance		0.003225	
Portfolio standard deviation		0.057		Portfolio standard deviation		0.057	
Monthly VAR		−8.1%		Monthly VAR		−10.6%	

TWO ASSET LONG/SHORT PORTFOLIO

We now want to demonstrate the beneficial consequences of combining long and short positions in the very simple two asset portfolio as a way of reducing the risk as measured by the portfolio volatility. Table 12.3 contains two very simple portfolios – the long only version is a restatement of the scenario on the right-hand side of Table 12.2 which shows the consequences of negative returns to the two long positions. On the right-hand side of Figure 12.3 for the long/short portfolio, in order to keep the comparison as straightforward as possible, we have simply taken the two positions A and B and flipped the sign of the holdings for Asset B from being a positive 50% to a negative 50%. In all other respects the two scenarios are the same with a correlation coefficient of 0.5 and identical standard deviations for A and B in both the long only case and the long/short case.

The long only portfolio shows, as before in Table 12.2, that the expected return from the two assets is −1.25% whereas the long/short portfolio shows an expected return of 0.25%. This is entirely the result of Asset B being a short holding with equal absolute dollar value to Asset A. In this highly simplified scenario the portfolio variance has reduced from 0.0032 in the long only version to 0.0012 for the long/short portfolio. Figure 12.4 shows the comparison between the VaR values for the long only and long/short portfolios that are illustrated in Table 12.3 and the clear beneficial consequences for the VaR value that arises from the long/short portfolio. From the reduced volatility and the higher expected return the long/short scenario shows a VaR (in both cases at the 95% confidence interval) which is almost one half of the value for the long only portfolio. Interestingly if the actual returns and the expected returns coincide the long only portfolio not only is more risky from the VaR perspective but will also incur a loss whereas the long/only portfolio has less inherent risk and yields a small profit in the same circumstances.

So far in the illustrative scenarios the correlation coefficient between the two assets, A and B, has been maintained at 0.5 for no other reason than simplicity. It will now be instructive to follow the consequences of increasing this correlation value. Intuitively from the work of Harry Markowitz we should expect the increase in covariance or correlation between the two

Table 12.3 Long (left) and long/short (right) correlation coefficient 0.5

Bull market scenario	Asset A		Asset B	Bear market scenario	Asset A		Asset B
Expected monthly return	−1.00%		−1.50%	Expected monthly return	−1.00%		−1.50%
Relative allocation share	50%		50%	Relative allocation share	50%		−50%
Standard deviation	5.00%		8.00%	Standard deviation	5.00%		8.00%
Correlation coefficient		0.5		Correlation coefficient		0.5	
Expected portfolio monthly return		−1.25%		Expected portfolio monthly return		0.25%	
t-statistic for confidence interval		1.645		t-statistic for confidence interval		1.645	
Portfolio variance		0.003225		Portfolio variance		0.001225	
Portfolio standard deviation		0.057		Portfolio standard deviation		0.035	
Monthly VAR		−10.6%		Monthly VAR		−5.5%	

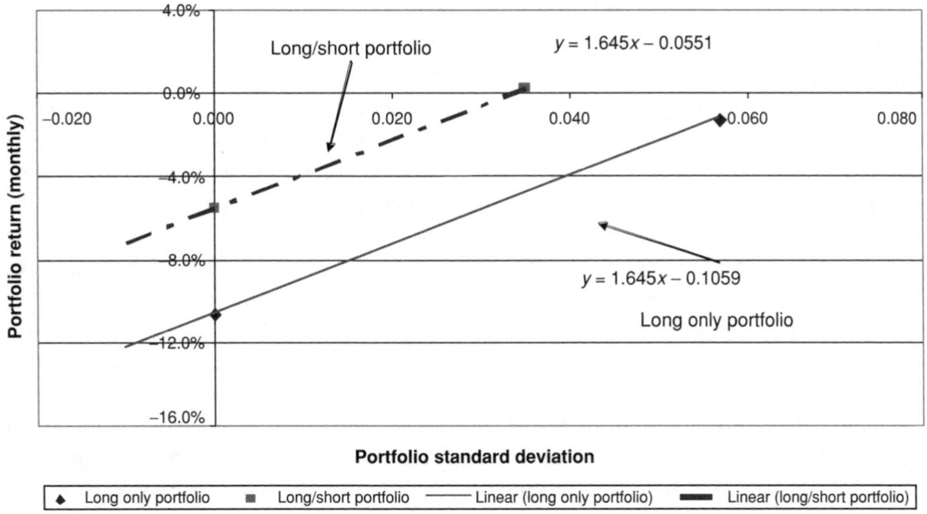

Figure 12.4 Long only and long/short two asset portfolios showing Value at Risk with different confidence intervals – correlation 0.5

assets to lead to less diversification, as the co-movements between A and B are more closely aligned, and higher risk as the degree of portfolio volatility will increase.

However, there are two very distinctive effects from increasing the correlation coefficient that can be highlighted in the contrast between the long only and the long/short portfolio. The first is to consider in Table 12.4 what happens to the long only portfolio where, as expected, the increase to 0.9 for the correlation coefficient leads to an increase in VaR from 10.6% to 11.7% (with all of the other factors remaining the same). Where both positions are long and the co-movements between them are more closely aligned the portfolio volatility will increase.

Table 12.4 Long only (left) and long/short (right) portfolios

Bull market scenario	Asset A		Asset B	Bear market scenario	Asset A		Asset B
Expected monthly return	−1.00%		−1.50%	Expected monthly return	−1.00%		−1.50%
Relative allocation share	50%		50%	Relative allocation share	50%		−50%
Standard deviation	5.00%		8.00%	Standard deviation	5.00%		8.00%
Correlation coefficient		0.9		Correlation coefficient		0.9	
Expected portfolio monthly return		−1.25%		Expected portfolio monthly return		0.25%	
t-statistic for confidence interval		1.645		t-statistic for confidence interval		1.645	
Portfolio variance		0.004025		Portfolio variance		0.000425	
Portfolio standard deviation		0.063		Portfolio standard deviation		0.021	
Monthly VAR		−11.7%		Monthly VAR		−3.1%	

This is the crucial lesson from the Markowitz framework as applied to the analysis of long only portfolios. In the early work in modern portfolio theory the refinements that were made to the quantification of the risk/reward analysis to determine optimal portfolio allocations were, in essence, predicated on long portfolios and deriving the best mix of positions from uncovering the greatest degree of diversification that could be achieved. This was driven by the goal of minimizing cross-position correlations. The radical breakthrough in applying the Markowitz techniques is to be found in its usefulness in constructing portfolios that have long and short positions.

Most strikingly the long/short portfolio on the right-hand side of Table 12.4 shows a VaR of only 3.1%. It can also be demonstrated easily that the higher the correlation coefficient between A and B the lower the portfolio volatility and VaR will be. The vital feature of the table is that by holding short positions in our simple portfolio the degree of diversification and the overall risk profile will actually be *reduced* from higher correlations between the assets. This highly simplified VaR analysis reveals the golden rule of risk management and one that we set out in this book to champion – the most effective way to shelter a portfolio from market risk is by combining long and short positions to achieve the optimal reward/risk ratio. We have further to go to describe how this optimization is achieved in practice but it should by now be clear in principle at least that assuming a long/short orientation goes much further than the diversification benefits that can ever be achieved with a long only portfolio strategy.

There is even more reason to celebrate the achievements of the long/short portfolio which is grounded in one of the frequently observed characteristics of contemporary markets. The phenomenon of increasing correlation among all financial assets in downside markets has been widely reported in the financial literature.[3] Studies have shown that across many asset classes the correlations that prevail under "normal" or typical conditions are replaced by much greater correlations when the overall market is suffering sustained or critical weakness. The following citation comes from a research paper by Andrew Ang and Joseph, both of Stanford University, entitled "Asymmetric correlations of equity portfolios":

> Correlations between U.S. stocks and the aggregate U.S. market are much greater for downside moves, especially for extreme downside moves, than for upside moves ... Conditional on the downside, correlations in the data differ from the conditional correlations implied by a normal distribution by 11.6%. We find that conditional asymmetric correlations are fundamentally different from other measures of asymmetries, such as skewness and co-skewness.[4]

The asymmetric nature of correlations is very bad news for portfolio managers that subscribe to a long only strategy. As we have discussed elsewhere there are serious methodological issues that make it difficult to determine a stable or fair-weather value for the cross-correlation between assets. The observed values for any pair of time series will show stochastic volatility in the correlation values across even short time-spans. So whatever value is selected to represent the historical correlation is going to be somewhat arbitrary and unsatisfactory. But, in fact, the situation is made even worse because, as Ang and Chen and others have documented, in times of market weakness (i.e. exactly the times when one requires the benefits that come from implementing smart diversification techniques) there will be a generalized tendency for all assets to correlate more strongly.

Let us pursue the notion of asymmetry a little further at this stage since it raises a couple of related issues that are relevant to the discussion ahead. We have noted that the covariance between two assets will tend to rise in downside markets and a related phenomenon is the fact that stocks will exhibit two kinds of beta. Downside beta will be higher than the beta values which apply in more typical market conditions. Beta values share the same limitations that correlation coefficients have – they are hard to measure with any reliability. Moreover the unstable nature of beta even under normal conditions gives way to severe modifications in the beta values when markets are falling. Some securities are more prone to experiencing abnormally high betas in troubled times and these are the very same constituents within a portfolio that can play havoc with the covariance matrix that has been generated from "normal" market observations. The disruptions to beta and the escalation in correlations in downside markets need to be accommodated in any robust portfolio construction methodology and this will be pursued further in the next chapter.

If a security strongly displays the kinds of asymmetry that has been noted, will not investors and traders tend to shun such assets in favor of "better behaved" securities? Ang and Chen have addressed this issue in a separate paper entitled "Downside risk":[5]

> If an asset tends to move downward in a declining market more than it moves upward in a rising market, it is an unattractive asset to hold because it tends to have very low payoffs precisely when the wealth of investors is low. Investors who are sensitive to downside losses, relative to upside gains, require a premium for holding assets that co-vary strongly with the market when the market declines. Hence, in an economy with agents placing greater emphasis on downside risk than upside gains, assets with high sensitivities to downside market movements have high average returns ... [they reflect] a premium for bearing downside risk.

The premium return that is offered as an inducement to holding securities that behave especially poorly in market downturns is yet another complication to the simple Markowitz framework that has been discussed so far. The situation is best considered in the light of the behavior of assets in a recovery phase following a severe correction or market downturn. The securities which have fallen the hardest will often rebound the most vigorously. So yet again the beta values and the covariances will display idiosyncrasies that are not easily captured in compiling an all-purpose covariance matrix. With all of these qualifications to fit specific circumstances it should be apparent that the application of the Markowitz methods is not a straightforward matter.

Returning to the scenario that is outlined in Table 12.4 we can also see on a scatter graph (Figure 12.5) how the long and long/short portfolios occupy very different positions in the risk/reward space. The negative conditions that are portrayed are relatively minor and yet the long only portfolio has a VaR of almost 12%. By contrast the VaR for the long/short portfolio is only 3.1%. Even more striking is what would be revealed if the magnitude of the returns for A and B were to be amplified. If A was to decline by 10% and B by 15% the long only portfolio would show a VaR of 22.9% whereas the long/short portfolio would show a VaR of just 0.9%. This can be attributed to the "safety net" that is provided by the short position in B for the second portfolio.[6]

We have illustrated the Value at Risk concept in a deliberately simplistic manner to bring out its essential features. As with many techniques it has been refined by portfolio managers and financial engineers to accommodate some of the special circumstances that have been discussed as well as many others. Just how useful is the VaR measurement? Before answering that we need to note that Value at Risk has become pervasive in the financial industry as a summary measure of risk. It melds well with the Markowitz framework and, to the extent that it provides a simple method of understanding the reward/risk dilemmas involved in trading and investment, it is worthy of serious study. In terms of limitations, it has many. Critically it depends on the key probability assumptions from the normal distribution. We need not reiterate

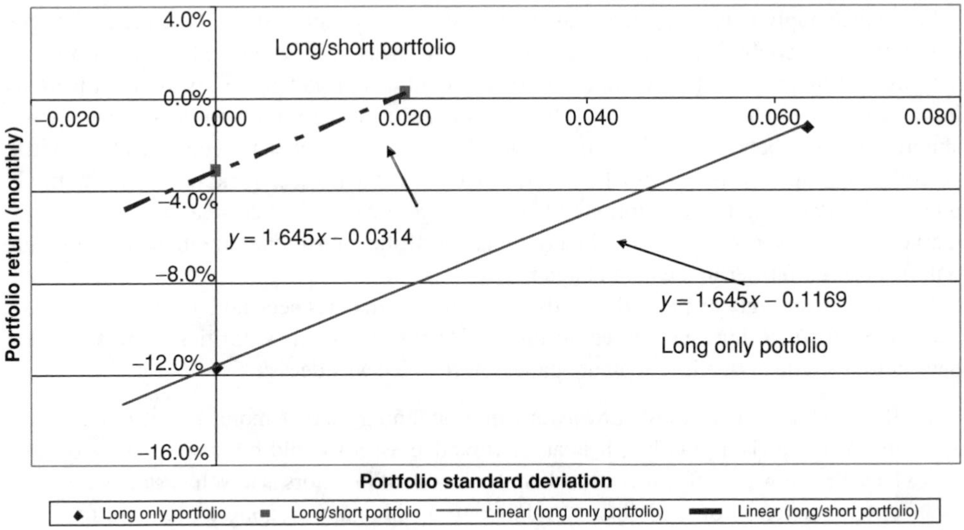

Figure 12.5 Long only and long/short two asset portfolios showing Value at Risk with different confidence intervals

general theoretical problems associated with this assumption and we have seen that there are idiosyncrasies that arise from the way that covariance works out in the real world. It is not ultimately a robust tool for risk management and needs to be supplemented by various other procedures that implement additional checks and safeguards.

OPTIMIZATION OF MORE COMPLEX PORTFOLIOS

Up to this point extremely simple portfolios have been considered and we want in this section to extend the framework somewhat to show what happens with slightly more complex situations involving more securities. However, many simplifying assumptions will be continued in what follows

Table 12.5 shows the case of a long only portfolio with four stocks A, B, C and D. The notional size of the portfolio is one million dollars and each stock is owned in equal proportions to the others. They were each purchased at \$50 and their recent trading history shows that each has a weekly standard deviation of 5% which will be the metric used for volatility. We have deliberately kept their mean return (based on recent history) at 0% so that we can simply focus on the VaR that arises from the portfolio volatility (recall that the VAR equals the mean return minus the portfolio volatility * the *t*-value which again is assumed to be 1.65 for a 95% confidence interval).

Some additional elements have been introduced into the table from the simpler versions that were previously reviewed. Although the weekly mean return has been set at zero for each of the four securities there is now an expected return row which comprises the forecast change for each during the time period in question. As can be seen two of the securities are expected to increase by 10% and two to decline by that amount. The net expected gain for all four of the securities which are long positions is also zero in this example (in further examples we shall

Table 12.5 Correlations matrix

	A	B	C	D
Number of shares	5000	5000	5000	5000
Price	\$50.00	\$50.00	\$50.00	\$50.00
Position value	\$250 000	\$250 000	\$250 000	\$250 000
Percentage of portfolio	25%	25%	25%	25%
Weekly volatility	5.00%	5.00%	5.00%	5.00%
Weekly mean return	0.00%	0.00%	0.00%	0.00%
Volatility component	\$12 500	\$12 500	\$12 500	\$12 500
Expected gain/loss percentage	10%	−10%	10%	−10%
Expected return	25 000	−25 000	25 000	−25 000

Correlations matrix

	A	B	C	D
A	1.0000	0.5000	0.5000	0.5000
B	0.5000	1.0000	0.5000	0.5000
C	0.5000	0.5000	1.0000	0.5000
D	0.5000	0.5000	0.5000	1.0000

Risk tolerance – t-statistic	1.65
Portfolio volatility	39 528
Portfolio mean	0
Net portfolio value	1 000 000
Absolute portfolio value	1 000 000
Portfolio Value at Risk for t-statistic	−65 222
Expected gain	0

explore how the expected gain becomes an important factor in optimizing the risk/reward ratio for the portfolio). The critical value that is determined in the table is the portfolio volatility which is calculated by performing matrix multiplication from the correlation values.[7] The VaR in this simple example, which has a zero mean return, is 1.65 times the portfolio volatility and is calculated at −6.5%.

Table 12.6 shows a very similar setup to the previous table but this time there are two stocks that are short – stocks B and D. The net portfolio value is zero as the two short positions are matched by the two long positions. The historical mean return remains at zero but in this new example the expected returns for each of the securities have been modified, A and C are both expected to gain 10% and B and D are expected to fall by 10%. The expected returns row provides an additional dimension to the analysis and allows for a simulation of the performance of the portfolio under specified conditions. As can be seen in Table 12.6 the portfolio now has an expected gain of 10% since the two short positions will now be profitable from their expected declines. By calculating the expected gain under different expected return assumptions it is possible to calculate the ratio of the expected gain to the VaR which is found to be 3.43. This ratio can be used to drive the optimization quest further as we shall see. It should be emphasized that the VaR calculation is based on the historical return rather than the expected returns. With the two short positions, the portfolio volatility has now reduced from \$39 528 in the case of the long only portfolio to \$17 678. This demonstrates once again the volatility dampening effect that arises from the combining of long and short positions. We have once again calculated the portfolio VaR at the 95% confidence level and found it this time to be \$29 168 which is less than half of the value that was seen in the long only portfolio.

Table 12.6 Long and short portfolio

	A	B	C	D
Number of shares	5000	−5000	5000	−5000
Price	$50.00	$50.00	$50.00	$50.00
Position value	$250 000	−$250 000	$250 000	−$250 000
Percentage of portfolio	25%	25%	25%	25%
Weekly volatility	5.00%	5.00%	5.00%	5.00%
Weekly mean return	0.00%	0.00%	0.00%	0.00%
Volatility component	$12 500	−$12 500	$12 500	−$12 500
Expected gain/loss percentage	10%	−10%	10%	−10%
Expected return	25 000	25 000	25 000	25 000
Correlations matrix				
	A	B	C	D
A	1.0000	0.5000	0.5000	0.5000
B	0.5000	1.0000	0.5000	0.5000
C	0.5000	0.5000	1.0000	0.5000
D	0.5000	0.5000	0.5000	1.0000
Risk tolerance – t-statistic	1.65			
Portfolio volatility	17 678	1.77%		
Portfolio mean	0			
Net portfolio value	0			
Absolute portfolio value	1 000 000			
Portfolio Value at Risk for t-statistic	−29 168	−2.92%		
Expected gain	100 000			
Ratio expected gain/Value at Risk	3.43			
Ratio expected gain/extreme event				
Portfolio beta	1.00			

The long/short (LS) portfolio has again convincingly outperformed the long only (LO) portfolio in this simulation. What is even more impressive, however, is the following diagram which illustrates what happens to the VaR values for both LO and LS when the values in the correlations matrix are uniformly changed. In Table 12.6 the correlation coefficient that was assumed was 0.5 but let us now use a spectrum of different coefficient values and plot the resulting VaR against the correlation coefficients. We cover the intervals from 0.1 to 0.9 correlation and then record the associated VaR value for each of these correlation levels for both the LO and LS portfolios.

Figure 12.6 shows the results of simulating each trial. On the horizontal axis are plotted the values of the coefficient of correlation that were assumed in the correlations matrix and on the vertical axis the VaR values that resulted from each of the specific coefficients. The situation could not be more positively biased toward the long/short portfolio as the increase on the correlation axis coincides with an improving VaR whereas for the long only portfolio the VaR gets progressively more negative as we move across the correlations axis. Figure 12.6 is the most revealing in this chapter as it shows very poignantly the benefits of using a long/short portfolio strategy. The LS portfolio is not only superior at the lowest levels of correlation, which is the circumstance that the Markowitz approach suggests is the most favorable for the highest risk/reward ratio, but even more striking is the fact that as the correlation among the assets rises – and hence the diversification for a long only portfolio diminishes and the risk/reward ratio deteriorates – the LS portfolio shows a progressively greater degree of outperformance

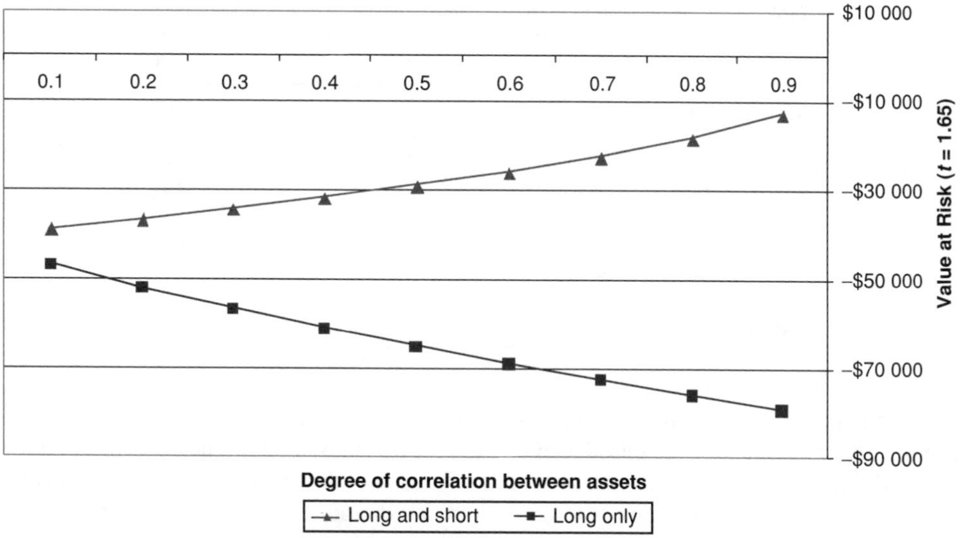

Figure 12.6 Asymmetry in Value at Risk between long only and long/short portfolios

over the LO portfolio. When we also recall that the correlations among assets will tend to increase during market downturns the LS portfolio provides exactly the right risk/reward characteristics.

RATIO OF EXPECTED GAIN TO VALUE AT RISK

The two elements that have been examined so far – the MPT methodology that originated with Markowitz and the Value at Risk metric – can be combined to provide one approach to optimizing portfolio returns. By following the fundamental lesson of this chapter that a long/short portfolio will offer far superior risk/reward characteristics to a long only portfolio and by simulating the risk/reward profiles as we have done, the next step is to settle on the best method to drive the optimization algorithm. We started off by considering the efficient frontier of portfolios each of which had a specific return and risk dimension. Following the precepts of the Markowitz method a decision needed to be made about which of the dimensions was the ultimate arbiter in selecting among the different portfolio combinations along the efficient frontier. But is there a procedure that can achieve an optimal allocation delivering the highest expected gain for the lowest level of risk? Can the optimization procedure be driven by maximizing a key ratio? The answer is yes and we propose that the ratio is expected return/Value at Risk.

When selecting among different securities for insertion into a portfolio the historical returns and volatility characteristics will be major contributory factors in the decision-making process and both of these are included in the Markowitz method but we are also basing a decision on the expected behavior of the assets in the future. If a security has reached the top of a trading range its historical return over several weeks may have been very positive but if it is now overdue for a correction the expected return or forecast values will be negative and a short position will be suitable. The model that is used to simulate the risk/reward profile needs to

Table 12.7 Performance characteristics for Goldman Sachs and Amazon.com

	GS	AMZN
Number of shares	−480	1120
Price	104.22	44.55
Position value	−50 026	49 896
Weekly volatility	2.37%	6.34%
Weekly mean return	−1.01%	2.75%
Volatility component	−1187	3164
Individual mean component	506	1370
Individual VaR	−2880	−4957
Expected dollar return	2501	2495

accommodate the expected future returns as well as the historical returns which is the reason that the expected returns were introduced into the previous discussion. The expected gain for the portfolio will result from the forecast returns for each of the securities in the portfolio and critically on whether the position is long or short and the position size. So the optimization issue restated becomes which of the many possible combinations of position sizes produces the optimal ratio between expected gain and the Value at Risk? We shall turn to position sizing and the related issue of hedge ratios in the next section.

POSITION SIZING AND HEDGE RATIOS

Hedge ratio calculation focuses on a number of parameters that measure different dimensions of the "risk profile" of the portfolio but, for the purposes of the discussion below, we shall simplify the examination of these parameters and examine the relatively well-accepted benchmark – Value at Risk. It should be emphasized, however, that relying on a one-dimensional approach such as this has severe limitations, and that we do not, in practice, attach great significance to this measure alone.

Let us suppose that the following two stocks have been alerted by our trade selection procedures – Goldman Sachs (GS) and Amazon.com (AMZN). Again, to simplify matters, we shall assume that each trade is accompanied by a forecast change of 5%, with GS expected to fall by that amount and thus a short sale recommendation while Amazon is expected to rise by 5% with a long recommendation.

Table 12.7 shows certain trading characteristics that are based on the most recent 25 day price activity of each stock. If the objective is to maximize the expected return the logic is very straightforward, we simply set the position sizes for each stock at the maximum permitted position size for an individual component (i.e. $50 000).

The correlations matrix for the portfolio is equally simple and shows that the two instruments are somewhat weakly correlated with a value of 0.324 which is unsurprising given that the companies operate in very different sectors of the economy.

	GS	AMZN
GS	1.0000	0.3240
AMZN	0.3240	1.0000

Table 12.8 Value at Risk for simple portfolio with GS and AMZN

Portfolio volatility	2997
Portfolio mean	1875
Portfolio VaR	−4119
Expected gain	4996
Ratio expected gain/VaR	1.21

Using matrix multiplication it is straightforward to derive the following overall measurements for the "portfolio" containing the two stocks and we can see from Table 12.8 that the VaR has been calculated at −\$4119 with the expected return more or less at the maximum of 5% (it is slightly less due to rounding off of share sizes). The simplest ratio of risk to reward shows that the expected gain is 1.21 times the VaR.

If the objective is now changed, so that we are aiming to maximize the ratio of expected gain/VaR, the composition of the portfolio changes quite significantly with respect to the position size for Amazon and this can be seen in Table 12.9 with the number of shares having been reduced to 330. The reduced position size reflects the fact that AMZN exhibits greater volatility and greater weekly mean return, both of which contribute to the individual VaR component for AMZN.

The expected gain for the portfolio has been reduced from \$4996 to \$3236 but there has been a proportionately larger decrease in the portfolio VaR from −\$4119 to −\$1590. The net result is that the reward/risk ratio, as measured by the expected gain/VaR, has risen from 1.21 to 2.04.

Portfolio volatility	1249
Portfolio mean	909
Portfolio VaR	−1590
Expected gain	3236
Ratio expected gain/VaR	2.04

To illustrate further the hedge procedures and introduce another measure of risk that will be accommodated within the reward/risk optimization routines, we shall examine a more complex portfolio that will contain six stocks that will be added contemporaneously. The six securities

Table 12.9 Maximizing the ratio of Expected Gain/VAR for the simple portfolio with GS and AMZN

	GS	AMZN
Number of shares	−480	330
Price	104.22	44.55
Position value	−50 026	14 702
Weekly volatility	2.37%	6.34%
Weekly mean return	−1.01%	2.75%
Volatility component	−1187	932
Individual mean component	506	404
Individual VaR	−2880	−1461
Expected dollar return	2501	735

Table 12.10 A more complex portfolio with six securities

	GS	AMZN	NEM	JBLU	PAAS	PG
GS (Goldman Sachs)	1.0000	0.3240	0.1357	0.0939	0.1383	0.3607
AMZN (Amazon)	0.3240	1.0000	0.1174	0.5825	0.2086	0.1983
NEM (Newmont Mining)	0.1357	0.1174	1.0000	0.1659	0.7988	0.2170
JBLU (Jet Blue Airways)	0.0939	0.5825	0.1659	1.0000	0.0537	0.4177
PAAS (Pan American Silver)	0.1383	0.2086	0.7988	0.0537	1.0000	0.0609
PG (Procter & Gamble)	0.3607	0.1983	0.2170	0.4177	0.0609	1.0000
BETA	0.829	1.748	1.140	1.521	1.301	0.701

and their matrix of correlation are listed in Table 12.10. Also included in the bottom row of the matrix are the beta coefficients of each security with respect to the broad market index – the S&P 500. The stocks that have been selected for the illustration are, with a couple of exceptions, quite weakly correlated which poses additional challenges for the hedging exercise. The two most strongly correlated stocks, NEM and PAAS, both mining stocks, have a strong degree of correlation at approximately 0.8. If one of these two is to be included as a long position and the other as a short position then the high degree of correlation makes this particular instance of long/short matching relatively benign.

Let us initially construct a portfolio where the objective is to maximize the expected return (again for simplicity, it is assumed that each position is forecasted to achieve a 5% profit). Table 12.11 shows the relative position sizing for the six securities and as can be seen there is an expected return for the portfolio of a little less than $15 000. In addition to the VaR calculations that we noted in the simple two-stock portfolio above, we will also consider a critical event scenario in which the broad market drops 10%. Derived from the beta values the critical event consequence for each stock can also be "anticipated" and the overall impact on the portfolio can be estimated. In the case of a 10% drop the effect on the portfolio would be a loss of −$9465. This calculation is based only on the beta value without regard to the other characteristics, such as individual mean values, that are used in the calculation of VaR.

Table 12.11 Position sizing for portfolio based upon maximizing the expected return

	GS	AMZN	NEM	JBLU	PAAS	PG
Number of shares	−480	1120	−1190	2350	3400	−895
Price	104.22	44.55	41.87	21.21	14.68	55.88
Position value	−50 026	49 896	−49 825	49 844	49 912	−50 013
Weekly volatility	2.37%	6.34%	3.15%	4.00%	4.57%	1.62%
Weekly mean return	−1.01%	2.75%	−1.31%	−2.80%	−1.58%	−0.21%
Volatility component	−1187	3164	−1570	1995	2282	−812
Individual mean component	506	1370	651	−1395	−791	104
Individual VaR	−2880	−4957	−3791	−5385	−5355	−1728
Expected dollar return	2501	2495	2491	2492	2496	2501
Price after critical event	95.58	36.76	37.10	17.98	12.77	51.96
Position value after critical event	−45 879	41 174	−44 147	42 263	43 419	−46 507
Beta	0.829	1.748	1.140	1.521	1.301	0.701
Profit/loss after critical event	4147	−8722	5678	−7581	−6493	3506

Table 12.12 Ratio of Expected Gain/VAR where position sizing is driven by goal of maximizing expected return

Critical event	−10%
Portfolio volatility	4710
Portfolio mean	444
Portfolio VaR	−8975
Expected gain	14976
Critical event P/L	−9465
Ratio expected gain/VaR	1.67
Ratio expected gain/critical event	−1.58

From Table 12.12 it can be seen that the critical event P/L of −$9465 is a slightly greater loss than the VaR value of −$8975. The ratio of expected gain/critical event is a signed value since the value would be quite different if the critical event was a positive scenario. The other ratio of expected gain/VaR is always expressed as a positive fraction since VaR will always be expressed as a negative magnitude.

The value of 1.67 for the expected gain/VaR is not unattractive but the critical event P/L suggests a level of risk that can be improved on through some loss of upside in the expected gain but for a more comfortable level of risk.

In order to improve the reward/risk ratio for the portfolio we need to perform an optimization procedure that will seek out a maximum value for the ratio between the gain that we expect to make from the six securities and the risk entailed from combining them as reflected in the VaR value. The optimization procedure can be undertaken with a software tool such as the Solver add-in for Excel and would need to be set up with the required constraints. However the task would be somewhat daunting for complex portfolios and there are more sophisticated tools using evolutionary computation techniques that are better suited to the task.[8] In essence the application of genetic or evolutionary algorithms to this optimization task involves the repeated testing of a large sample of randomly sized portfolios that obey constraints regarding the parameters for what would constitute an acceptable combination for the portfolio's composition. Each of the initial samples is evaluated to see how it has performed with respect to the key ratios and the superior performers are used to "seed" or act as templates for a successor generation of trial portfolios. Once again the superior performers are selected and allowed to pass through into the subsequent generation. The winners from each generation are allowed to cross-fertilize in a virtual process resembling genetic recombination. Eventually a stable winner will emerge in the sense that successive generations are unable to improve the key ratios. The process can thus be seen as a fitness contest which echoes the Darwinian process of natural selection.

After evolving many generations of portfolios and comparing the risk characteristics of each, the positions outlined in Table 12.13 demonstrate a more acceptable level of risk for the expected return. Not only has the critical event P/L actually turned positive but the ratio of expected gain/VaR as indicated in Table 12.14 has improved substantially to 3.12. It should be emphasized that the optimization algorithms do not disclose a "perfect" solution (indeed it is questionable what that actually means in this context) but will improve the ratios that are selected for optimization to a noticeable degree. It can be seen from Table 12.14 that the dollar value of the Expected Gain from the portfolio has declined to $8221 from the value of $14976

Table 12.13 Position sizing of portfolio when the goal is to maximize the ratio between the Expected Gain and the VAR

	GS	AMZN	NEM	JBLU	PAAS	PG
Number of shares	−330	270	−1100	510	1690	−650
Price	104.22	44.55	41.87	21.21	14.68	55.88
Position value	−34 393	12 029	−46 057	10 817	24 809	−36 322
Weekly volatility	2.37%	6.34%	3.15%	4.00%	4.57%	1.62%
Weekly mean return	−1.01%	2.75%	−1.31%	−2.80%	−1.58%	−0.21%
Volatility component	−816	763	−1451	433	1134	−590
Individual mean component	348	330	602	−303	−393	75
Individual VaR	−1980	−1195	−3504	−1169	−2662	−1255
Expected dollar return	1720	601	2303	541	1240	1816
Price after critical event	95.58	36.76	37.10	17.98	12.77	51.96
Position value after critical event	−31 542	99 26	−40 809	91 72	21 582	−33 776
Beta	0.829	1.748	1.140	1.521	1.301	0.701
Profit/loss after critical event	2851	−2103	5248	−1645	−3227	2546

that was observed in Table 12.12 but the VaR value has fallen more on a proportional basis and this has produced the much higher value of 3.12 for the ratio of the Expected Gain/VaR.

When employed on an iterative basis, the risk management routines that have been discussed will tend towards significant improvement of the reward/risk ratio for use of the trading capital. The accuracy of the trading signals is of course vital, but the management of the hedging activity and determination of hedge ratios are where a large part of the value is added by the risk/reward optimization algorithms.

Table 12.14 Key portfolio characteristics for the optimal portfolio based on maximizing the Expected Gain/Var ratio

Critical event	−10%
Portfolio volatility	1648
Portfolio mean	659
Portfolio VaR	−2637
Expected gain	8221
Critical event P/L	3670
Ratio expected gain/VaR	3.12
Ratio expected gain/critical event	2.24

13
Alpha

Alpha is usually defined as the degree to which a particular portfolio manager is able to outperform a benchmark index such as the S&P 500. Often for fund managers who are focused on particular equity strategies such as specialists in the small cap universe of stocks, the benchmark might be one of the many indices maintained by the Russell group,[1] most notably the benchmark that is often used is the Russell 2000. Alpha is eagerly sought after by hedge fund managers as it is typically the basis that is used for ranking asset management performance. Fairly obviously passive index tracking funds will not (if they are doing their job correctly) exhibit alpha with respect to their chosen benchmark.

We can also use the concept of alpha in regard to individual securities since in a comparable way to the manner in which a manager can outperform a benchmark index so we can observe the same kind of outperformance or underperformance in a security's returns relative to an index. Here we are not measuring managerial competence (or lack of it) but simply taking the returns of the stock versus the historical returns of an index and isolating the excess or deficit returns vis à vis the benchmark index.

Being able to quantify alpha is important if we want to separate the degree to which a particular asset is benefiting (or suffering) from the overall direction of the market and the degree to which it is displaying relative advantage or disadvantage to a benchmark or index. The saying that "all boats rise with the rising tide" is a useful analogy as it captures the notion that when the underlying dynamics of the market environment are rising then it should be expected that most market securities will enjoy similar buoyancy. The converse is equally true. When bearish conditions prevail in the overall market it is to be expected that most securities will be falling. If a security moves up and down completely in unison with the overall market it will have zero alpha, if it underperforms the overall market it can be said to have negative alpha and if it outperforms the overall market it has positive alpha.

In much the same way as the companion concept of beta which we shall examine later in this chapter, alpha is conveniently calculated as a by-product of the linear regression between the chosen asset that we are interested in and the benchmark that is appropriate. In the case of the U.S. equity markets the benchmark that is invariably chosen is the Standard & Poor's 500 index. The value of beta corresponds to the slope of the linear equation found from a least squares regression and the alpha value is what is often referred to as the intercept value or in other words the value of y where x is equal to zero. Once we have found the linear equation of best fit we know from determining the y-intercept whether the security either has a positive or negative alpha or possibly zero alpha.

Both the alpha and beta value of a security are found to be very unstable over long stretches in the returns history of a security and this poses pertinent questions as to how reliable either value can be in further statistical analysis or portfolio construction strategies. Nevertheless both values are widely used in modern finance and especially so within the hedge fund community and among practitioners of market neutral investing.

HANS – A CASE STUDY OF POSITIVE ALPHA

We shall illustrate how easy it is to calculate the alpha for a particular stock and we shall use as an example one of the best performing stocks since 2000 which is Hansen Natural Corporation (NASDAQ: HANS). The company had a market capitalization in August 2006 of approximately $2.5bn and the stock is a member of the S&P 600 small cap index.

Figure 13.1 reveals the spectacular performance of HANS from the beginning of 2000 until early 2006 and the extent to which it outperformed the S&P 500 during the period. Both price series have been normalized using a base of 100 in January 2000, and while the S&P 500 shows a value of 88 in August 2006 (indicating a 12% decline), the value for HANS indicates a stunning 5346 (and this was despite a 25% decline experienced in the first week of August 2006). The price at the end of the period was more than 50 times what it had been at the beginning of the period.

Another way of measuring the phenomenal growth that HANS has experienced is to use the technique that was illustrated in the last chapter to calculate the Compound Annual Growth Rate (CAGR) for a security.

Table 13.1 was constructed by calculating the VAMI values for each year end since 2000 and calculating the Compound Annual Growth Rate according to the formula that was provided on p.. A CAGR figure of 86% was determined for the returns as of the end of 2005, corresponding

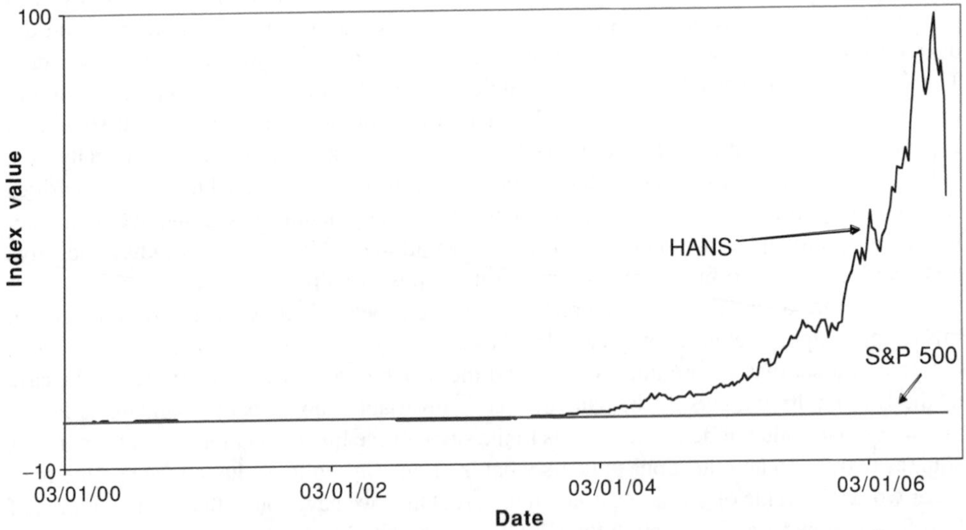

Figure 13.1 HANS and S&P 500 normalized price charts January 2000–August 2006

Table 13.1 HANS–CAGR

Year	VAMI	Annual return
0	1000	
1	981	−0.02
2	1038	0.06
3	1038	0.00
4	1942	0.87
5	8135	3.19
6	41 192	4.06
7	53 462	0.30
	6 yr CAGR	0.86
	7 yr CAGR	0.77

to year 6 in the table, and 77% if the August 2006 VAMI is considered to represent the seven year return.

Table 13.1 and Figure 13.1 have been computed using *simple returns* and it is worth a brief diversion to contrast simple returns with *log returns* which have been used most widely in this book so far. The simple return from one period to the next is calculated as (Current price – Previous price)/Previous price) whereas the log price is calculated as the natural logarithm of (Current Price/Previous price). Where the changes concerned are small there is not a significant difference between the two calculations, but when one is dealing with the dramatic changes that are shown in the price development of HANS there can be a very noticeable difference. For example, the simple return for the whole period is ($27.80 – $0.52)/$0.52 or 5346% whereas the log return is the natural logarithm of ($27.80/$0.52) which equates to slightly less than 4.

Having established the outstanding simple return that would have been enjoyed by someone who had purchased Hansen stock in 2000 and held it throughout the period we now need to switch to thinking about the weekly returns which is what the alpha value is measuring. In other words we are focusing on the changes from week to week in the price of HANS versus the comparable weekly changes in the S&P 500.

Figure 13.2 captures the accumulation values for the weekly changes of both the stock and the index and it is useful to examine again the difference between the accumulation of the simple weekly returns for HANS and the weekly log returns. As the changes in the S&P 500 were minor in comparison there would be little difference between the two calculation methods for the index and these are not shown in Figure 13.2. The dashed line in Figure 13.2 shows the cumulative simple returns and the solid upper line shows the cumulative log returns. Both are very impressive but again the simple returns line will result in an even better showing than the line based on log returns. From this it can be seen that a decision needs to be made in computing the alpha value as to which of the two returns – the simple or log series – should be used to derive the alpha value. As alpha is a comparative value the same series needs to be used for both HANS and the index. In the remainder of this chapter we shall focus on the log returns, but in the first instance to contrast the difference we will also show for HANS the alpha value that is derived from simple returns as well.

Figure 13.3 shows an *XY* scatter diagram of the weekly log returns for HANS plotted in conjunction with the weekly log returns of the S&P 500 index. The chart graphically illustrates the alpha value for the whole period. This value is returned as the *y*-intercept value and expresses

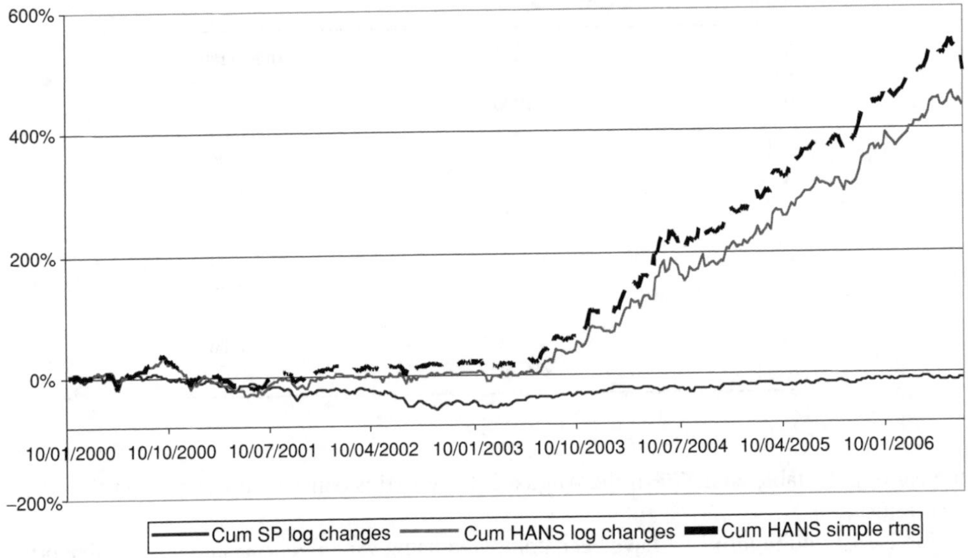

Figure 13.2 Cumulative weekly changes for S&P 500 and HANS January 2000–August 2006

the value for HANS' returns where the returns for the benchmark index are equal to zero. In other words we have neutralized the effects of the changes in the underlying benchmarks as far as the scatter range is concerned and extracted the excess return that is the result of the outperformance of the stock itself. What emerges from the scatter plot and a linear regression analysis is the equation for the line of best fit which includes the *y*-intercept value of 0.012.

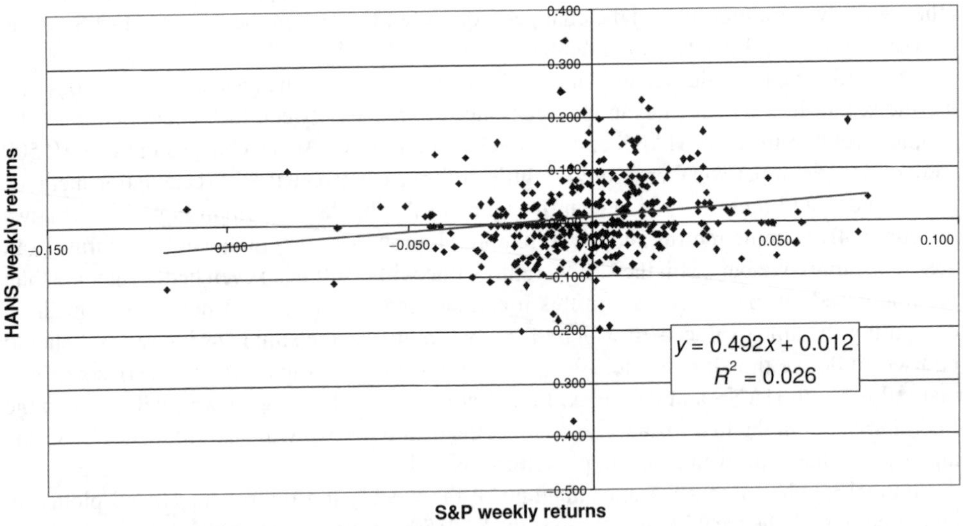

Figure 13.3 Scatter graph of weekly returns for S&P 500 and HANS January 2000–August 2006

What does this intercept value actually tell us? It tells us that during the entire period the stock, on a weekly basis, and on "average" has provided a 1.2% additional return higher than the index return. The "fit" between the returns is very poorly correlated as reflected in the extremely low value for the R^2 which also indicates that the co-movements between the two items are essentially independent of each other.[2] The value for the slope of the regression of 0.492 provides a further useful statistic for the stock which is known as the stock's beta and this value reflects the degree to which variability in the index is matched by variability in the stock itself, and will be discussed later in the chapter.

As we have discussed in previous contexts the associations and correlations between two financial variables are subject to considerable fluctuations and variability themselves. Figure 13.3 reflects the entire period under examination and a single value of alpha has been derived from the y-intercept value. This is a useful statistic if we want to get an overall feel for the degree to which the stock has outperformed the index, but we also need to examine the variability in the alpha values over time. We can use a moving window approach to the linear regression where we look back at the log change values of the stock and the index within a moving frame of the trailing 26 periods. This enables a calculation of the line of best fit for each of these moving windows as we move along the time axis and from the equations derived we can extract the alpha value (intercept) and the beta values (gradient).

Within Excel if we create columns with the weekly natural log changes for y the dependent variable HANS, and x for the benchmark index, we can then apply a moving window to the columns with the Excel function = INTERCEPT(y values, x values) where the cell references move down the columns with a 26 week lookback window. Figure 13.4 shows the results of this procedure.

As Figure 13.4 reveals there is considerable variability in the alpha values for HANS based on a trailing 26 week period calculation. During the early part of the period which covers the bear market period following the NASDAQ crash and the extended period of weakness until mid- 2003 period, there were periods of negative alpha (just reaching below −0.2% on

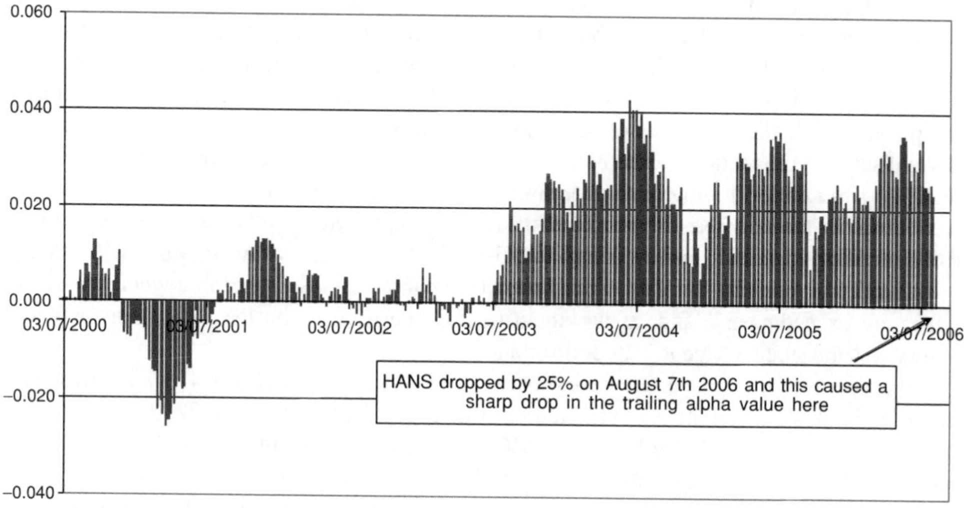

Figure 13.4 HANS alpha values for weekly returns as compared to the S&P 500 – trailing 26 week window

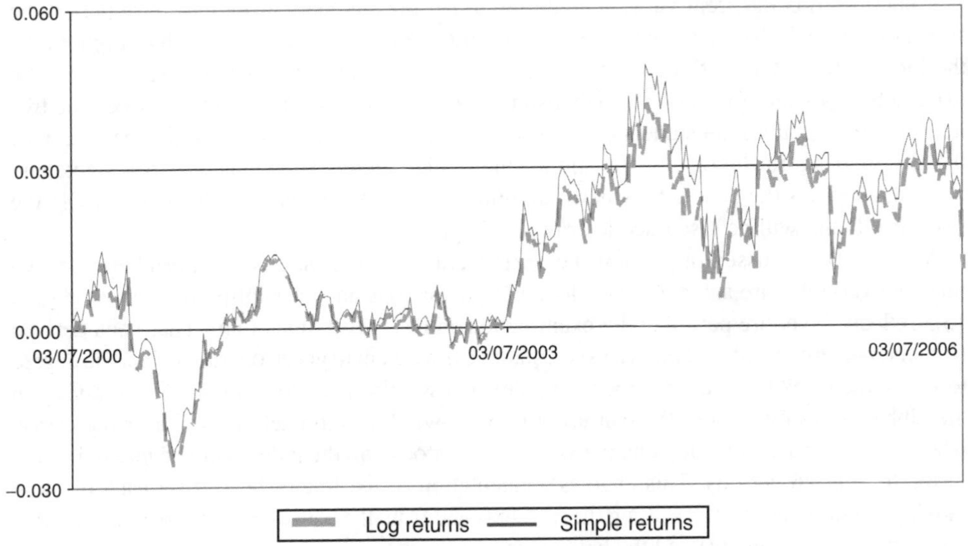

Figure 13.5 HANS January 2000–August 2006 – contrast between alpha constructed with simple returns and log returns

a weekly basis) or underperformance of the stock with respect to the index. Commencing in the latter part of 2003 the alpha has been consistently showing positive values at one point reaching as high as a 4% excess weekly return over the index and typically running in the vicinity of 2%. When this kind of excess return is achieved consistently on a weekly basis it is not hard to see how the stock has managed to realize such superlative returns.

On the extreme right-hand side of Figure 13.4 it can be seen that the alpha value suffers a rather steep drop and this is the result of a one day loss of 25% for HANS on August 7th 2006. This occurred literally as this book was being finalized and is perhaps a suitable warning that even stocks that have exhibited eye-popping returns over an extended period can produce very nasty surprises from time to time. It remains to be seen whether HANS can regain its composure or whether its period of outstanding outperformance may have come to an end.

We discussed the matter of computing alpha (which is a by-product of the linear regression analysis) from either the log returns or simple returns and Figure 13.5 shows the difference between using these different series for both HANS and the S&P 500 index. The dashed line shows the results of using the log returns and the solid line indicates how the value will usually be higher if we use the simple returns. The discrepancy is most noticeable when the alpha values are exceeding 3% and, as we noted before, the reliance on the log returns actually understates the stock's exceptional performance.

The excess return for the entire period between HANS and the index is 410% if calculated on the basis of the cumulative weekly log returns. Since the beginning of 2000 the S&P 500 index has shown a cumulative loss of 12.5% and HANS a cumulative gain of 397%. If one multiplies the "average" alpha for the period of 1.2% by the number of weeks for which we have observations we arrive at the figure of 406%. So over the six and one half year period there would have been a more than 1% relative advantage achieved by HANS over the S&P 500 every week! However, if one had purchased HANS during late 2000 period and held the stock during

2001 one would have underperformed the index. The underperformance was relatively mild during the early period covered in Figure 13.5, and the overperformance has been remarkable during the later period, but the fact remains that alpha is itself an unstable statistical measure which again poses important questions regarding the reliability of the statistic in stock selection and portfolio construction.

GRANULARITY OF THE ALPHA PERIOD

A question arises as to what is the most suitable time frame or granularity to time series data for determining the alpha values. Especially in the light of the variability of the data, if one is screening securities for their "edge" over the broad market, one wants to avoid fleeting episodes of outperformance but also not use such a coarse grained approach that one fails to spot a rising star until it has achieved most of its gains. We have used daily data and monthly data and each has its own merits and drawbacks. The daily data, as expected, shows greater variability – the standard deviation in the daily alpha readings can become very noisy but if one applies a filter to eliminate those cases where the values are too erratic, the discovery of emerging and consistent daily positive alpha can provide a leading indicator for stocks that may be entering phases where there is an emerging relative advantage. Monthly data has the disadvantage that one needs to be looking back at least three years to obtain a valid reading and this runs the risk that the factors that may have been in effect during the period when favorable values were recorded have ceased to be relevant.

The optimal situation seems to be a twin track approach. We suggest that one uses a 26 period window on weekly data to identify those stocks that have generated positive alpha values above a certain threshold. In addition, one should also be monitoring the variation in the weekly returns. A highly volatile reading for the previous 26 weeks would suggest that the relative outperformance may be too erratic. There is a presumption that a relative advantage which is well grounded should show a relatively stable weekly alpha. In fact it is preferable to find a stock that has a consistent positive alpha with low variability than one that may have a more highly volatile alpha.

As with all of the statistical values that one is tempted to use in assisting the search for superior returns there are different dimensions of variability that need to be factored into the methodology followed. A scanning technique which calculates the alpha reading on the periodic basis and reports on those that are showing consistency in positive alpha, or perhaps alerting about an emerging positive alpha scenario, then needs to be filtered further to assess the associated risk that will accompany selecting such stocks. For example, high alpha may be accompanied by high beta as well. If one is keen to avoid the possibility of having a portfolio that exhibits a far greater degree of volatility than the overall market then in general it is undesirable to include stocks that have relatively high beta values. What one is really looking for is relatively high alpha + relatively low beta. The following quote from Eric Sorensen, managing director and head of equity derivatives research at Salomon Brothers, captures the issue well:[3]

> "Alpha is supposed to be return to skill, not to asset class volatility. Often, the higher return from a manager isn't from insight, but from moving to higher beta areas." The manager of a corporate/government bond portfolio who outperforms his benchmark index by buying high-yield bonds isn't delivering alpha, he is taking more risk.

Let us examine how attractive HANS would have been from this perspective of offering high alpha, which it clearly did, and low overall volatility of returns. As we can see from the scatter diagram in Figure 13.3 and the linear equation, the beta value during the whole period has been modest at 0.49. However, this beta value does not reflect the volatility of the stock on a day to day basis but rather the degree to which the movements in the index and the stock are associated. To get a real handle on the volatility of HANS compared to the index we need to look at the standard deviations for the two. We find that the index has a standard deviation value of just 0.023 on a weekly basis whereas HANS has a corresponding value of 0.07. The achievement of high alpha for HANS would have come at the expense of considerably more volatility but, as we shall examine later in the chapter, the low beta characteristics for HANS help to make it an attractive candidate for including in a portfolio where achieving beta neutrality is the desired goal.

NEGATIVE ALPHA AND HIGHER BETA RISK

Let us now move our attention to a much less attractive stock from both of the points of view that we have just been examining. One of the stocks that not only shows poor alpha values but has a high beta is Amazon (NASDAQ: AMZN). Figure 13.6 covers the period from January 2000 to August 2006 and we have calculated the regression coefficients for the entire period showing that for the overall period the alpha is negative at −0.002 and the beta value is 1.64. The relatively high beta value shows that AMZN will tend to rise or sink about 65% more than the overall market. Also relevant are the standard deviation figures which were 0.023 for the index (this is the same value that was observed in connection with HANS as the periods covered are identical) and 0.1 which is the value for AMZN indicating that AMZN is four times more volatile than the index and even more volatile than HANS. The fact that the alpha

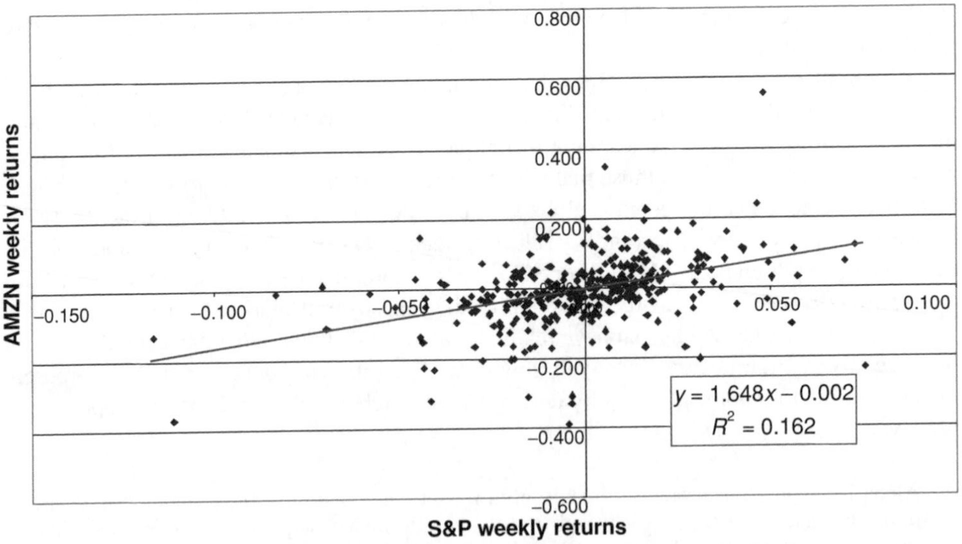

Figure 13.6 Scatter graph of weekly returns for S&P 500 and AMZN January 2000–August 2006

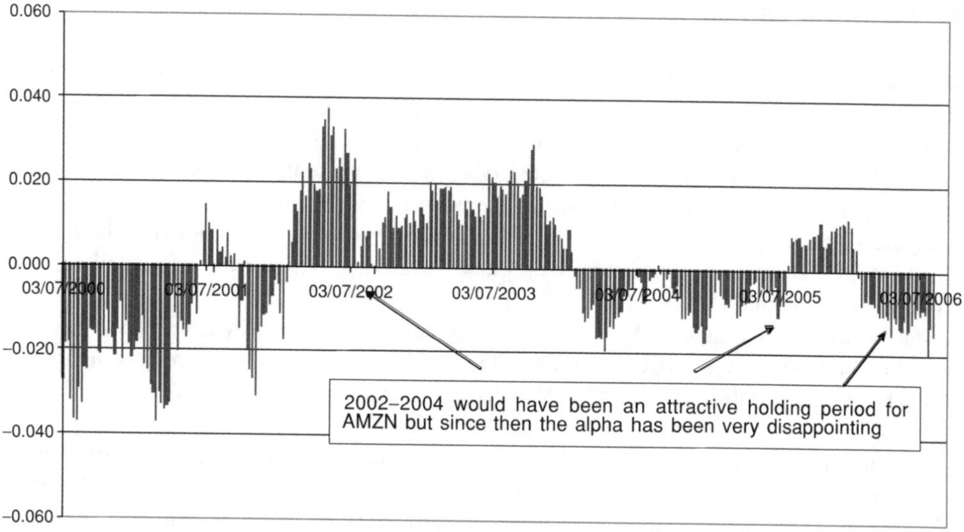

Figure 13.7 AMZN alpha values for weekly returns as compared to the S&P 500 – trailing 26 week window

value is only modestly negative at −0.002 should not obscure the fact that measured over a six year period even a slightly negative amount can lead to considerable underperformance. In fact during the period when the S&P 500 has shown a −12.5% return, when measured using the cumulative weekly log returns, Amazon has delivered a remarkably negative return of −98% (using the same cumulative weekly log returns) which gives a net underperformance by the stock of −86%.

The alpha value revealed in the equation shown in Figure 13.6 obviously smoothes out a lot of episodic variability in the short-term alpha values. If we now use the same technique of calculating the trailing 26 week period in a moving window frame approach, we can plot the variability of the alpha readings over time, as before. From Figure 13.7 we can see that there is far greater variability in the observed alpha over time than we saw on the equivalent chart for Hansen (Figure 13.4).

Amazon has enjoyed some extended periods when it has been in favor especially during the middle period that is shown in Figure 13.7 covering 2002–2004 but has seen this relative advantage disappear to be followed by lengthy periods when negative alpha prevails. Since the beginning of 2004 the stock has underperformed the benchmark for most of the period with a brief respite in the second half of 2005.

It would be hard to attach the same confidence in the reliability of the observation of periods of positive alpha for Amazon as can be granted for HANS. This can be seen in the tendency of AMZN to flip back and forth more abruptly across the zero line and this also has to be considered in the context of the greater volatility (standard deviations) of AMZN as compared to HANS, and most strikingly the much higher beta values of AMZN. From the point of view of holding AMZN rather than HANS in a long-term portfolio, which clearly needs to be distinguished from a short-term trading perspective where AMZN can often be an attractive stock to trade, there would be a clear win for HANS as it offers higher and more consistent alpha with lower volatility and exceptionally low beta values.

THE VARIABILITY OF ALPHA

A further dimension to the alpha picture needs to be considered which has to do with the variability of the alpha values themselves. The most appropriate technique to assess this dimension will be to use the trailing standard deviation to measure this. The reader may be forgiven for finding this somewhat obscure as we are beginning to enter the realms of statistical abstraction but hopefully the simple chart will illustrate the point that we are making.

Figure 13.8 shows the standard deviation for a moving window (20 periods) to the trailing alpha values that were calculated for HANS and AMZN and which were already pictorially represented in Figures 13.4 and 13.7.

The dashed line in Figure 13.8 tracks the standard deviation of the AMZN alpha values and the solid line tracks the standard deviation of the HANS alpha values. Our previous intuitions about the greater variability of the AMZN alpha values are confirmed from this chart although in the latter period this is far less evident than for the earlier period.

One further stock that we shall consider has an interesting alpha profile because of its relative consistency, at least since the end of the 2000–2002 bear market. Figure 13.9 is for Haliburton (NYSE: HAL) and shows the trailing 26 week alpha values. During the challenging conditions of the 2000–2002 period, the first two years shown on the chart, HAL basically shows alpha in negative territory and severely so in late 2001 and early 2002. During difficult times for the overall market HAL was performing even more poorly than a broad market index. However, since mid-2002 the situation has become much more favorable and there have only been very occasional brief episodes of negative alpha in the weekly returns.

The alpha values since mid-2002 are not as impressive as the excess returns that we observed in the Hansen chart but they have been remarkably stable with little variation from the median alpha during the period of approximately 0.5% on a weekly basis. This is the kind of pattern

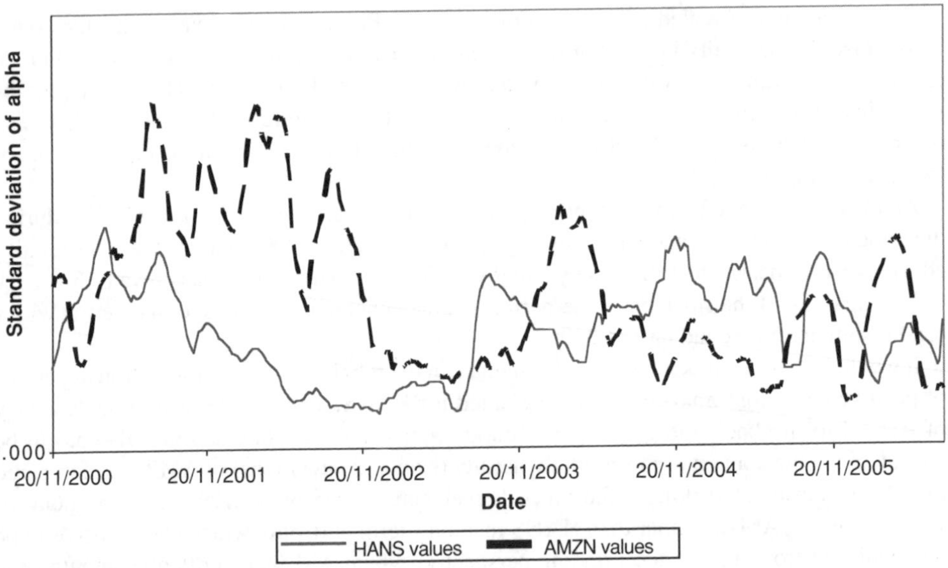

Figure 13.8 HANS and AMZN standard deviation of the alpha values – 26 weeks – January 200–August 2006

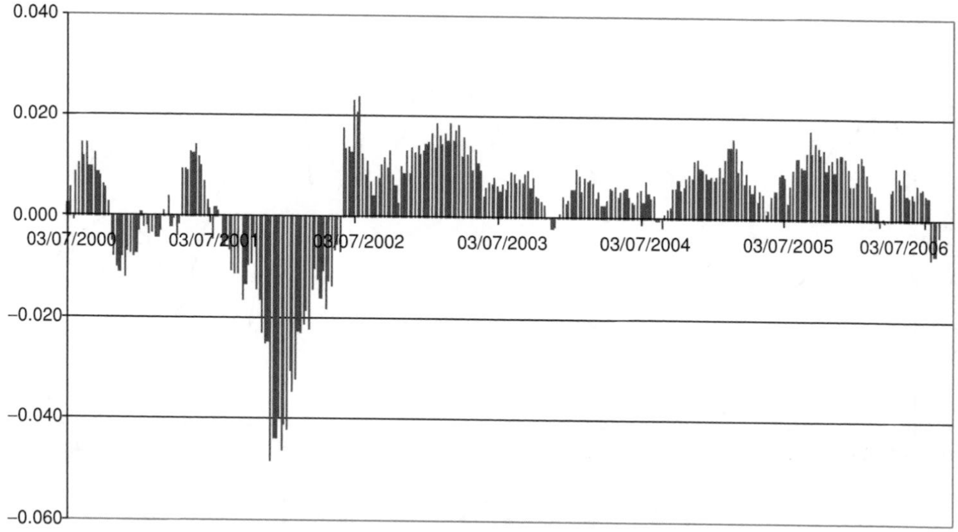

Figure 13.9 HAL alpha values for weekly returns as compared to the S&P 500 – trailing 26 week window

that is indicative of steady accumulation by institutional investors and points to a sustaining relative advantage for the stock which has enabled it to outperform the index by 75% during this period. To illustrate the relative calmness of the alpha values for Haliburton we shall show the standard deviations of the alpha values for HANS and HAL that have arisen since the broad market recovery in 2003.

Figure 13.10 illustrates very well how stable the alpha values have been for Haliburton since the middle of 2003. The comparison with HANS which as we know performed very well during the period shown in Figure 13.10 exhibits much more variability in the alpha, so if the requirement for a stable alpha is sought after in portfolio construction Haliburton would be a more attractive proposition than Hansen. Interestingly both stocks exhibit very similar week to week volatility but Haliburton shows a beta value of exactly one showing that its movements track the S&P 500 almost perfectly.

DOUBLE ALPHA

One of the much heralded promises of a long/short trading or investment strategy is that it may be possible to achieve a double alpha performance. By selecting both long and short positions, which are expected to deliver absolute returns and because of the protection from overall market risk that is provided by being "hedged", the long/short trader and fund manager may be able to have two bites of the cherry. A long only trader or fund manager who is either restricted from, or refrains from, selling short only has the opportunity to generate alpha by buying or not buying stocks. However, a trader who can also sell stocks short has the possibility of generating alpha from the short sales as well. There has been a certain amount of controversy among financial analysts about how significant this double alpha advantage, which is claimed by many hedge funds, actually is.

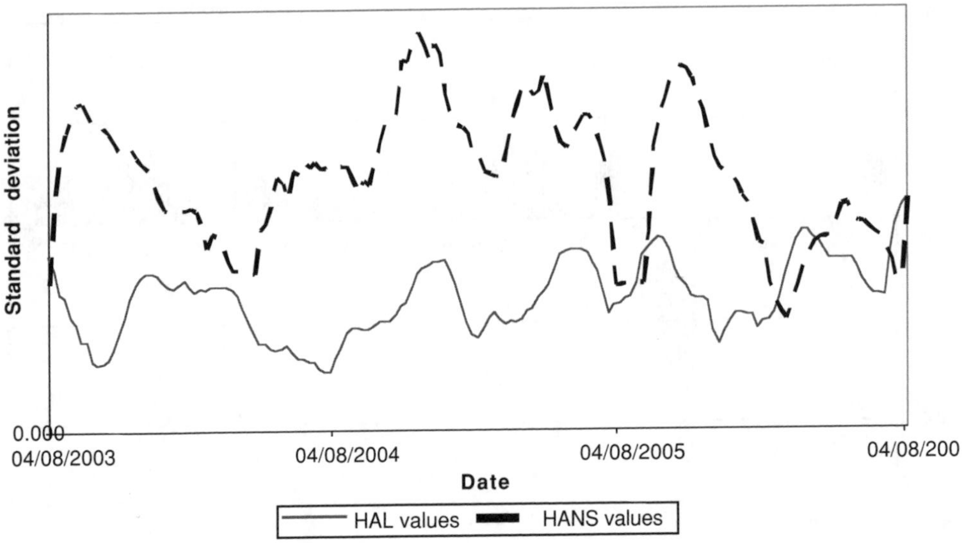

Figure 13.10 HANS and HAL standard deviation of the alpha values – 26 weeks – January 200–August 2006

One of the arguments used is that long/short strategies do not really differ from long only strategies because the long only trader or fund manager has the opportunity to underweight certain securities which it is then claimed is equivalent to effectively having a short position in the underweighted security. But this argument seems to be completely misconceived and to ignore the real benefits from having outright short positions. We agree completely with the following statement and especially the last sentence:

> Some market observers argue that this "double alpha" argument is faulty because an active long-only manager can over- and underweight securities, which means he is short relative to benchmark when underweight. We do not share this view because we believe there is a difference between selling short and being underweight against a benchmark. Long/short strategies can capture more alpha per unit of risk. If a stock has a weight of 0.02% in the benchmark index, the possible opportunity to underweight is limited to 0.02% of the portfolio. We would even go as far as portraying short selling as a risk management discipline of its own.[4]

The double alpha claim has to be considered separately from the risk management claim and we would maintain that both are crucial. The positive "safety net" features that are provided by a long/short methodology will have to be implemented with very different protection techniques by the long only trader or fund manager. Hedging strategies for a long only manager will involve the purchase of puts or the selling of futures contracts in the underlying index whereas for the long/short trader there is intrinsic protection supplied by the presence of positions on both sides of the market.

We do want to consider whether the achievement of a double alpha return is inconsistent with the achievement of a market neutral hedge strategy. We are actually considering whether the following proposition is true or not: "constraining long/short portfolios to have zero net holdings or zero betas is generally suboptimal". In other words the allegation is that the possibility of achieving superior alpha characteristics may suffer if the portfolio construction imperative is to achieve a zero beta portfolio (see the discussion below). Some purveyors of market neutral strategies emphasize that the financial engineering that underlies their security selection is designed to achieve the supposed optimal state where beta values of the long and short holdings are effectively counterbalanced to achieve a zero beta status for the portfolio as a whole. We have already voiced our general uneasiness with the notion that betas can be reliably estimated for a portfolio, and especially in times of market stress the beta values and also the covariance matrix values for a portfolio of stocks can shift quite dramatically. We are equally uneasy with the view that one needs to separate, from a portfolio management perspective, the long holdings and the short holding into two separate notional portfolios each with their own covariance matrices and portfolio betas. Advocates of such a viewpoint then also suggest that if the correlation between the long alpha and the short alpha characteristics approaches one then the long/short portfolio does not substantially improve on the long only portfolio. We cannot find much merit in this claim since it seems to have the same problems – that beta values are notoriously unstable and that it is difficult to make any robust claims about alpha correlations.

In general we would want to distinguish between two broadly different kinds of philosophy for long/short investing:

- Portfolios are constructed by looking for attractive opportunities that arise for specific securities on both sides of the market. These specific circumstances may have to do with identifying candidates for selection which it is believed are going to deliver alpha in their own right. In other words each selection is considered to have stand-alone on its own merits. Let us suppose that we have a short selection that is based on a well-defined bear flag formation – all we have to consider is whether, taken on its own merits, that trade is going to lead to a positive return. We are not considering whether the security is necessarily going to underperform the index as a successful short or even underperform in comparison with another security that has been selected via a zero beta selection technique. Once all of the potential long and short candidates have been identified then the portfolio construction logic takes over and brings the positions together to achieve the appropriate hedge ratios which are guided by estimates regarding the overall variance and beta of the portfolio.
- The alternative approach is to start from the portfolio construction angle first and allow this to become the primary selection mechanism in deciding on the merits of the individual components of the portfolio. The emphasis has shifted so that the competing candidates for individual positions are screened less for whether they have compelling individual supporting circumstances and more for how well they can be integrated into a market neutral portfolio.

The two approaches differ in the emphasis that they place on the different selection criteria. We contend that the double alpha scenario is more likely to arise in the case of the first approach than in the second. If we set out to engineer a market neutral portfolio there is a risk that we will achieve a portfolio that performs in line with the overall market.

The primary motivation for combining long and short positions should be the attractiveness of the specific opportunities and the inherent risk management characteristics that such a combination provides. We can apply beta and correlations analysis to the selection candidates to refine the eventual hedge ratios within the portfolio but this is a different motivation than setting out to achieve a market neutral portfolio.

BETA

Beta can be thought of as a measure of the co-movement between a security and an underlying index such as the S&P 500. This important statistical value is used extensively in portfolio management as we shall see, and it is important to be clear what it does not measure. It is not equivalent to the volatility of a security but rather provides an answer to the question – if the overall market moves up (or down) by (say) 3% what movement should one expect to see in the security in question? It is based on historical observations showing the manner in which log changes in the index have been associated with log changes in the security. We thus create a series of paired data points showing the log change in the index and the security and can then use an *XY* scatter plot to show how the pairs are associated. We can then use the least squares regression method to calculate the slope of the linear equation of best fit. Expressed simply we take the slope value returned from a linear regression of the changes of the security with respect to changes in the index. The slope value derived is equivalent to the beta of the security.

Figure 13.11 shows a scatter plot of the associated daily log changes between SPY and GE since March 1999. There are almost 2000 data pairs to consider and as the chart illustrates the line of best fit has an R^2 value of 0.44 which suggests that we need to be somewhat cautious in making claims about the strength of the linear relationship. Nonetheless, this is the statistical procedure that is widely used in the financial community for calculating the beta values for securities. As can be seen from the equation of the line, the slope value is 1.09 which is equivalent to the security's beta. Essentially what has been revealed is that GE is very closely aligned in terms of its overall co-movement with the underlying index.

This result is unsurprising in many respects as GE is one of the "bell-weather" stocks for the U.S. (and world) economy and its fortunes and price patterns tend to be in broad sympathy with the broad market. One could even make the case that GE is one of the most representative components of the S&P 500 and it is somewhat reassuring to see that the beta value shows this. Also clear from Figure 13.11 is the fact that the great majority of data pairs are in the center

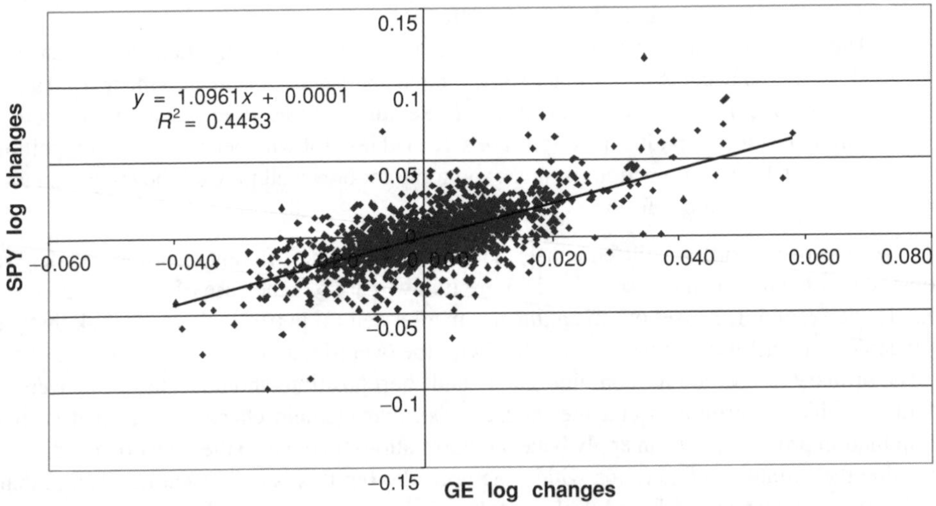

Figure 13.11 SPY and GE scatter plot of log changes March 1999–June 2006

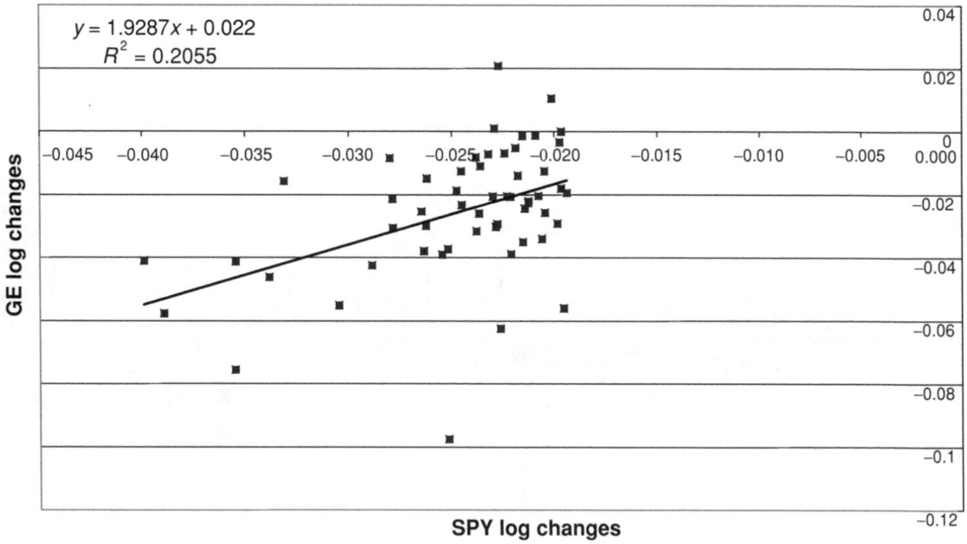

Figure 13.12 SPY and GE scatter plot showing negative outliers

of the graph around the origin. In most trading sessions the index and GE will show minor values in their log changes and these will tend to cluster around the unchanged value. More importantly we can see several "outlier" events where the log changes for either the stock or the index take on more extreme values and it is these more extreme values that we want to explore.

Extreme values or "outliers" will be registered in a quantile approach to the log change series for both GE and SPY and we can therefore segregate just those values in the upper and lower quantile that we are interested in. Let us focus on the negative outlier values. Shown in Figure 13.12 are the 50 largest negative log changes in the S&P 500 (corresponding to the 97 percentile) and the associated values for GE. One of the fortunate properties of an *XY* scatter plot is that the original sequence of the occurrences is unimportant; all that is required is that the coincidental pairing of the values is preserved. Accordingly one can calculate the beta value for the cases where the index is suffering its worst declines. As can be seen from the linear equation the beta value has almost doubled from 1 to close to 2. Again the R^2 value is not sufficient to give us great confidence in the result but in conducting beta tests there is a tendency for these R^2 values to be generally low.

What can we conclude from Figure 13.12? The result suggests that when the index is seeing its most severe declines (the worst 3% of its sessions) then the GE is likely to move twice as far in relation to the index as it does under more typical conditions. Interestingly the results are asymmetrical because if we plot the pairings based on the worst sessions for GE the slope of the regression line falls to 0.2 with virtually a zero R^2. When we reverse the scenario and examine the 50 best performances for SPY during the period the beta value is 1.25 and the R^2 is very similar to that found for the negative sessions.

The benefit of this approach is that we can give a quantitative perspective on the notion that has been much discussed by portfolio managers and academics which is the tendency of markets to exhibit very different behavior during critical phases from those that accompany

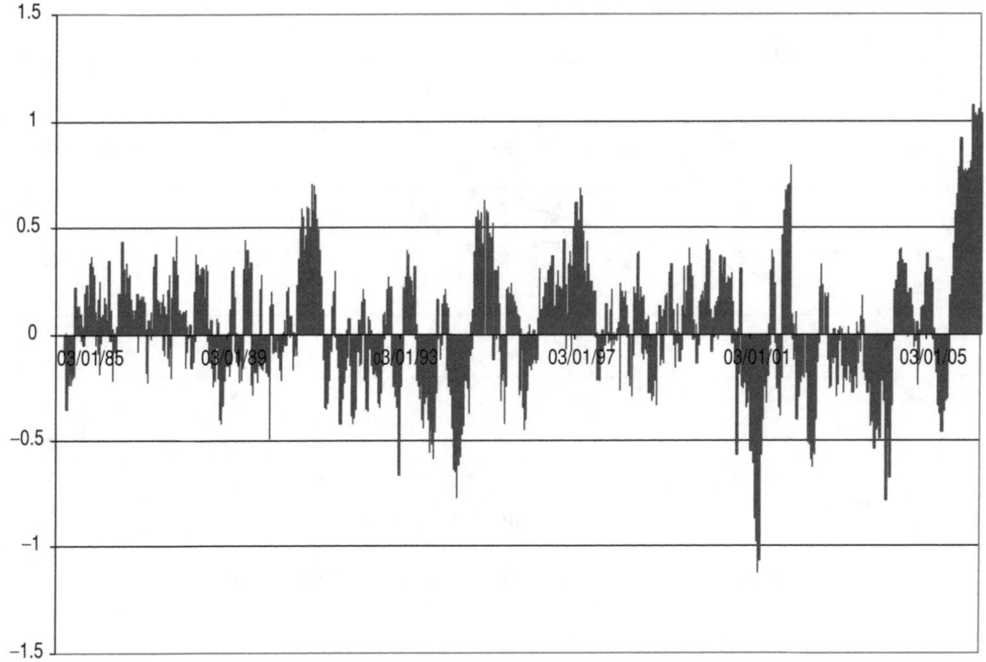

Figure 13.13 GE trailing 50 day beta values

more typical sessions. In particular there is considerable value in identifying a beta value which is more characteristically found when the markets are passing through critical downside periods as the beta can be more applicable in developing portfolios that are more immune to overall market risk.

Alas, the theoretical underpinnings that are often assumed in portfolio construction logic are on shaky ground when it comes to quantifying beta with any precision. Just as we observed in our discussion of alpha the actual observed measurements of beta taken periodically show a great variability. Figure 13.13 registers the beta readings taken using a trailing 50 day window on the data over more than 20 years.

In Figure 13.13 the beta value has been all over the map with large fluctuations and discontinuities occurring frequently. At times the stock has shown negative beta with values sometimes as high as −1 and at other times it has been +1 with many periods during which it appears to fluctuate wildly. Interestingly the period on the extreme right-hand side of the chart which corresponds to late 2004–2006 is showing the most stability in the value as the beta value has remained in the vicinity of one for some time.

Beta values can also be usefully determined between different equity indices and we shall briefly consider the relationship between the Russell 2000 index and the S&P 500 index.

In Chapter 6 we contrasted the two indices with respect to volatility and reached some surprising conclusions. If we create an *XY* scatter plot for the daily log changes of both of the indices from mid-2000 to mid-2006 we can also perform a linear regression as we have done in Figure 13.14. Three salient features should be mentioned in connection with this plot. First, the R^2 value is far greater for the regression than any of the values that have been observed

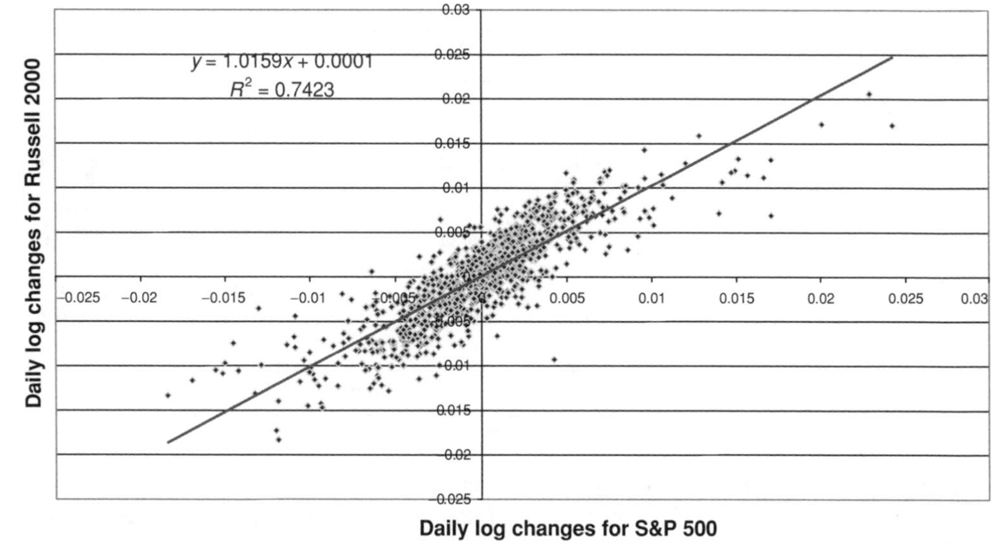

Figure 13.14 Linear regression of Russell 2000 daily log changes versus S&P 500 mid-2002–March 31st 2006

in the case of an individual security and the S&P 500. Even in the case of General Electric, which is a very representative stock of the broad market, the R^2 value that was observed in Figure 13.12 was less than 0.5. The value that we see in Figure 13.14 of almost 0.75 shows the tendency for indices to show greater association in their co-movements even if they are comprised of very different stocks as are the Russell 2000 and S&P 500. Visual inspection of the line that runs through the cloud of data points reveals that there is a much better fit than for most of the other diagrams in this chapter.

The second noticeable feature of the equation expressed in Figure 13.14 is the y-intercept value showing a marginally positive value. As our previous discussion of alpha would suggest this is evidence that the small cap index was consistently outperforming the S&P 500 index during the period. And remembering that daily log changes have been plotted, even a marginal positive value can accumulate sizable gains. The third interesting feature of the linear regression is that the slope of the line is almost one which suggests that the two indices track each very closely in terms of their co-movements.

BETA NEUTRALITY

Our exploration of immunizing a portfolio from market risk will begin with a simple model portfolio that has been constructed with very controlled conditions to enable us to see in a series of steps the consequences of aiming for beta neutrality. The first model is expressed in Table 13.2 and shows a long only portfolio.

Let us walk through the assumptions that are contained in the model portfolio outlined in Table 13.2. The portfolio holds four stocks A, B, C and D and all are held as long positions. Each of the four holdings has equal weighting contributing to a net balance of holdings of \$1 million. For the initial version of the model all of the stocks have beta values of one,

Table 13.2 Model portfolio long only

Model portfolio	A	B	C	D
Number of shares	5000	6250	3125	2500
Price	$50.00	$40.00	$80.00	$100.00
Position value	$250 000	$250 000	$250 000	$250 000
Percentage of portfolio	25%	25%	25%	25%
Price after extreme event	45.00	36.00	72.00	90.00
Position value after critical event	225 000	225 000	225 000	225 000
Beta	1.000	1.000	1.000	1.000
Beta * weighting	0.250	0.250	0.250	0.250
Profit/loss after critical event	−25 000	−25 000	−25 000	−25 000
Market driver	0.9000		Critical event P/L	−100 000
Extreme event	−10%		Portfolio beta	1.00

meaning that their movements are entirely in harmony with the overall market. The portfolio beta is calculated as the combined sum of the products of each of the individual beta values multiplied by their respective weightings in the portfolio. In the limiting case that begins our analysis it can be seen that the portfolio beta is unsurprisingly equal to one.

We have included an item called market driver which is like a master volume switch for the model portfolio. We can turn it up or down to indicate whether an extreme event is affecting the overall market. In Table 13.2 it can be seen that the market driver is set at 0.9 which means that the market is down by 10%, and since each of the stocks has a beta of one their prices will also reflect this and in the row entitled "Price after extreme event" it will be seen that each of the stocks has been marked down by 10% as well. It can also be seen that what we have called the "Critical event P/L" is showing a loss of $100 000 which is equal to 10% of the total portfolio value. None of this may seem too surprising to the reader but the purpose of the model will become clearer as we move forward. At this stage we want to illustrate the degree to which a portfolio beta, derived from the constituent's betas and the weightings, leads to an anticipated gain or loss depending on the condition of the overall market.

Table 13.3 shows what happens if we switch two of the positions B and D to being short positions with equal absolute dollar values to the other two positions A and C.

Table 13.3 Model portfolio – long and short

Model portfolio	A	B	C	D
Number of shares	5000	−6250	3125	−2500
Price	$50.00	$40.00	$80.00	$100.00
Position value	$250 000	−$250 000	$250 000	−$250 000
Percentage of portfolio	25%	−25%	25%	−25%
Price after extreme event	45.00	36.00	72.00	90.00
Position value after critical event	225 000	−225 000	225 000	−225 000
Beta	1.000	1.000	1.000	1.000
Beta * weighting	0.250	−0.250	0.250	−0.250
Profit/loss after critical event	−25 000	25 000	−25 000	25 000
Market driver	0.9000		Critical event P/L	0
Extreme event	−10%		Portfolio beta	0.00

Table 13.4 Model portfolio showing increased portfolio beta

Model portfolio	A	B	C	D
Number of shares	5000	−6250	3125	−2500
Price	$50.00	$40.00	$80.00	$100.00
Position value	$250 000	−$250 000	$250 000	−$250 000
Percentage of portfolio	25%	−25%	25%	−25%
Price after extreme event	42.00	36.80	62.40	85.00
Position value after critical event	210 000	−230 000	195 000	−212 500
Beta	1.600	0.800	2.200	1.500
Beta * weighting	0.400	−0.200	0.550	−0.375
Profit/loss after critical event	−40 000	20 000	−55 000	37 500
Market driver	0.9000	Critical event P/L		−37 500
Extreme event	−10%	Portfolio beta		0.38

Two key values have changed in Table 13.3. First the portfolio beta has become zero as two of the portfolio weightings have become negative amounts and the critical event P/L is also now zero. The portfolio has become immunized to market risk, at least to the extent that the beta values accurately capture the manner in which each of the stocks will behave in a 10% correction.

Figure 13.4 shows the same model portfolio as before except in this version the beta values have been changed (arbitrarily). In the case of holding B the beta value has fallen below one and for each of the other three holdings the beta value has been increased.

Changing the beta values without making an adjustment to the portfolio weighting values results in the portfolio losing its zero beta status and this has moved from zero to 0.375. It can also be seen that the critical event P/L is now showing a loss of $37 500, which of course is to be expected from multiplying the beta value by the total portfolio value.

The issue that we now have to confront is how to restore the portfolio's immunity from market risk, in other words how to adjust the position sizes or weightings within the portfolio so that an overall zero value can be regained for the portfolio. One procedure that can be adopted with an optimization within constraints problem such as this is to use Solver, the built-in tool that is part of the Microsoft Excel package. For the interested reader the procedure is discussed further in footnote.[5]

The results of rebalancing the respective sizes of the positions in order to achieve a zero portfolio beta can be seen in Table 13.5.

Short positions have been retained in B and D and it can be seen that the short positions are relatively larger than the long positions. This can be explained from reviewing the beta values of A and C which are both larger than the beta values for B and D. The two long positions will sustain relatively more damage in an overall market decline because of their higher beta values and therefore the two short positions need to have a higher weighting in the portfolio to compensate for this.

Our brief excursion into portfolio beta is simply the tip of a rather large iceberg. In our previous discussion of portfolio construction we focused largely upon the logic derived from the Markowitz model of diversification. We pointed to the inherent limitations of the covariance approach because of the unstable nature of the cross -correlations between securities. An alternative, or sometimes complementary, strategy that can be integrated into more sophisticated

Table 13.5 Model portfolio – restoring a zero value for the portfolio beta

Model portfolio	A	B	C	D
Number of shares	2664	−7680	2946	−3239
Price	$50.00	$40.00	$80.00	$100.00
Position value	$133 185	−$307 216	$235 696	−$323 903
Percentage of portfolio	13%	−31%	24%	−32%
Price after extreme event	42.00	36.80	62.40	85.00
Position value after critical event	111 875	−282 638	183 843	−275 318
Beta	1.600	0.800	2.200	1.500
Beta * weighting	0.213	−0.246	0.519	−0.486
Profit/loss after critical event	−21 310	24 577	−51 853	48 586
Market driver	0.9000	Critical event P/L		0
Extreme event	−10%	Portfolio beta		0.00

portfolio construction methodologies is to perform optimizations of different holding scenarios with different position sizes and hedge ratios that are designed to yield the required reward/risk ratios within a complex matrix of constraints. One of those constraints could involve an attempt to approach a zero value for the overall portfolio beta and this objective needs to be achieved within a framework of other competing constraints. Needless to say a proper discussion of these kinds of optimization routines could take us on a fascinating detour exploring areas of computational finance from which we shall have to resist.[6]

14
Markets as Networks

In this concluding chapter we shall weave several of our previously discussed threads together and present the reader with an overview of a conceptual model of financial markets based on the dynamics and logical structure of networks. While this may seem like an abstract and theoretical exercise we believe that many of the trading opportunities that we have identified are provided with stronger foundations as a result of this model. We emphasize that this is just a first step in what may become a larger undertaking.

In several sections of the book and specifically in Chapter 9 we have spent considerable time in articulating the aptness of the power law relationships that have been revealed within the fluctuations of financial time series. We have suggested that there are surprising and counter-intuitive consequences that are captured by the power law description. Rather than seeing the price behavior of markets as random and disorganized we have seen that, at the macro level, there is an *underlying scaling and ordering* of price development. Although there are good reasons to be cautious about how likely it is that we can harness the power law relationship to provide precise predictions there is the tantalizing possibility that there may eventually be a way of accessing and gaining explanatory insights into the deep structure and dynamics of price development.

We have suggested in our discussion of the "logic" of trend days and critical contagion episodes in markets that they are, contrary to the popular view, displaying more organized and more coherent behavior during such large movements. They are not behaving chaotically or randomly (not that those two descriptions are the same). Rather it is the day to day minor fluctuations of the financial markets that are the manifestation of the least organized, and to that extent, the most random behavior. So the question arises as to whether we can gain greater understanding of the emergence of the more coherent and orderly episodes of market behavior by combining insights provided, on the one hand, by the invariant scaling feature of power law relationships and, on the other hand, some explanatory tools that have been used to analyze how complex behavior emerges from the dynamics of interacting agents within a network.

Power laws have been shown to be revealing features of many other domains in the physical and social sciences. Some of the more illuminating instances are the Paretian insights into the distribution of wealth and income that we reviewed in chapter 9, the evidence of power laws in avalanche sizes in Per Bak's simulated sand piles, the frequency of earthquakes, the occurrence of English words in a typical text, and even the sizes of cities around the world.

All of these examples provide compelling evidence that there may be a hidden order in the growth and underlying dynamics of complex behavior.[1]

Financial markets are in our opinion best considered as complex, nonlinear networks of interacting agents. More specifically modern financial markets are examples of a reflexive and self- conscious virtual network which has many similarities with the World Wide Web. The internet has been recognized as a great facilitator of commerce and some of the more profitable uses of internet technology have been the development of electronic marketplaces ranging from consumer applications such as the online auctioneer eBay through to intra-business facilitators such as supply chain management.

The interacting agents within financial markets considered as virtual networks are the innumerable screen based traders, scattered all over the world, that hardly ever meet and yet who enter into vast numbers of transactions each trading day. What emerges from all of this day to day interaction and the resulting transactions is *a meaningful price narrative.* It is the development of price over time and all of the accompanying technical characteristics of the market that constitute the story line. This is why technical analysis is so vital to understanding what the markets are telling us.

The *physical network of financial markets*, the work stations, the mainframes, relays and other IT infrastructure that interconnects all of the market's participants is the medium in which trades are executed. However it is at the virtual level that markets reveal their real purpose and intentions. *A financial market is a virtual community that carries on an endless dialogue about pricing.* The history of the community's conflicting and changing views of price development is the narrative and thread that holds the community together. Moreover the story line is being constantly adapted by the changing circumstances as traders react to events that may sometimes be external to the market but often to events that are internal to the market. As we have suggested the single most important factor that will influence the *future development* of price is the way that price is *presently evolving*. For most trading sessions price will be evolving in a relatively haphazard fashion as there is no consensus amongst traders on near term direction. From time to time however, the next direction of price suddenly becomes very clear to many market participants as the market's internal behavior changes. For example volume and range might be expanding or important chart levels are being violated, and there is an immediate and coherent alignment of views on where the market wants to go next. It turns out, as we hope to show soon, that on many of these occasions when the market produces the most decisive and interesting behavior, this can largely be explained by the internal dynamics and logic of the market considered purely in its guise as a network.

Just to summarize our view so far, *a market is a virtual community in which price behavior becomes aware of itself.* Prices, volume and all of the other behavioral features that are tracked by traders, market technicians and software algorithms are the "mental landscape" in which the market operates and understands itself. Markets do not meaningfully exist on Wall Street or in the City of London. Those are just hubs where traders and investors congregate to watch screens and have a drink at the end of the trading day. The watching of screens can occur in any place from Greenwich, Connecticut, to a remote island serviced by a satellite feed service. In this sense markets do not exist anywhere but everywhere. They have a similar existence to the World Wide Web. It is entirely unimportant and incidental where an internet server or router is located when conducting business online. Millions of pairs of eyes (and computer workstations) scattered geographically are constantly monitoring the development of price and, by their reactions to what they see, influencing the subsequent price development. Seeing markets like this provides the reflexivity dimension that is, unfortunately, absent in much of the work of econophysics which seems to attach an objective existence to the dynamical processes that create pricing. In our opinion there is no data generating process which can then be compared and analysed in accordance with statistical physics, rather the pricing process is an emergent property of network dynamics involving human beings interacting with each other to create an organized narrative about price. Like the individual human mind that needs some temporal organization to function properly, the collective mind of the markets is supplying a narrative to, and temporal organization of, a vast amount of separate, yet related, agendas and intentions.

One of the more interesting statements concerning the idea of markets as networks comes from an unlikely source. John Allen Paulos is a mathematician who has written several books designed to make his subject more accessible to a wide audience. A recent book of his, *A Mathematician Plays the Market,*[2] describes his exploits in the stock market throughout the bubble years. He has clearly taken to heart some of the lessons from that era and the losses that he sustained "playing" the market. The following quote from the book contains several attractive ideas that are echoes of many issues that we have tried to cover in this book:

> What is the relevance of power laws, networks to extreme price movements? Investors, companies, mutual funds, brokerages, analysts and media outlets are connected via a large vaguely defined network whose nodes exert influence on the nodes to which they are connected. This network is likely to be more tightly connected and to contain more very popular (and hence very influential) nodes than people realize. Most of the time this makes no difference and price movements, resulting from the sum of a myriad of investors' independent zigs and zags, are best characterized by the normal distribution.

The key insight that is lurking in this citation is the contrast between the myriad of "independent zigs and zags" that are characteristic of most trading sessions and the more coherent structure of extreme price movements. Paulos does not actually use the term "coherent" as we have done throughout this book but his context makes clear that it is the alignment of opinions and sentiment that is the source of the market's more critical behavior:

> But when the volume of trades is very high, the trades are strongly influenced by relatively few popular nodes – mutual funds, for example, or analysis of media outlets – becoming aligned in their sentiments and this alignment can create extreme price movements . . . That there exist a few very popular very connected nodes is a consequence of the fact that a power law and not the normal distribution governs their frequency. A contagious alignment of this handful of very popular, very connected, very influential nodes will occur more frequently than people expect, as will therefore, extreme price movements.

In this quotation Paulos is drawing a parallel between the power laws that can be used to explain the popularity of nodes on the World Wide Web, and the frequency of links to them versus other less popular sites, and the relative frequencies of large-scale events that we have spent much time examining. While the parallel is appealing it does not quite have the explanatory power that we would like. As the quote from Paulos says "when the volume of trades is very high, the nodes become aligned and the market becomes one sided", but there is something missing from the explanation and it is this which would frustrate our attempts to use a clear understanding of network dynamics as a possible anticipatory mechanism for anticipating extreme price movements.

But we believe that with further elaboration of the idea we can get about as close as we can to a satisfying account. The challenge is to make the context between the activities of network dynamics and the action of markets as robust as possible. We believe that is the mediation process that was discussed in detail in Chapter 2 in connection with the nature of liquidity at turning points that can give us the additional dimension to an explanation involving network dynamics. The first evidence of coherent price moves is likely to emerge in the order flows that are witnessed by the major players in today's markets – the proprietary trading desks of the major investment banks, the activities of very large hedge funds and to some extent the behavior of the large mutual funds. To this extent the visibility of other players and especially those at key nodes or hubs on the network will feed quickly into price dislocations and changes in order flow, as well as increasing volumes associated with larger price changes.

Volume pick-up in itself is not the cue but rather the effect of some more underlying reason as to why the markets begin to exhibit powerful and coherent alignments. When these alignments cross a certain critical threshold there can be sudden and abrupt changes to the liquidity conditions. The order flow transforms from one in which there is a tiering and hierarchical structure to one in which there is uniform opinion about the near-term direction of price across all time frames and an absence of bids except at the price that reflects the new consensus of where the market wants to go. It becomes circular and self-fulfilling.

Markets expect the necessary amount of liquidity to transact, to engage in cross-asset hedging etc. and at the first sniff of a dissipation in liquidity, based on the emerging coherence of opinions, there is an abrupt rethinking of strategies and trading assumptions that prevail under more typical conditions. This is the catalyst that provides the more rapid percolation of opinions and sentiments and causes alignments to arise where normally there would be a more adversarial tone to the market's price discovery process. The abrupt change in sentiment has some similarities with a phase shift in a physical system, but owing to the reflexive nature of the market as network the process is more like a transformation in the self-consciousness of the market. For traders and market participants there is a sudden and sometimes shocking realization that one is no longer observing an objective system on the screen that is exhibiting unusual behavior but that one is deeply implicated and accountable in the way that the price discovery proceeds. As we have said before nothing influences the price development process more than price development.

NETWORK DYNAMICS AND FINANCIAL CONTAGION

Let us pursue further the role that power law distribution characteristics, which are evident in network topologies such as the World Wide Web, may have on the emergence of coherence and alignment in market sentiment. There are undoubtedly important trading hubs that are visible on the network and considered more influential than others. Among the more obvious would be large asset management funds and the trading desks of major banks.

When there is, under more typical market conditions, continuing disagreement about market direction the opportunistic strategies that normally prevail in a noncritical market session do not draw undue attention to these major hubs. Indeed with various strategies such as algorithmic trading, statistical arbitrage, long/short and market neutral strategies the emphasis will be on providing the markets with two sided activity to encourage and promote liquidity and thereby facilitate transactions. The ongoing rotation or movement of funds from one asset class to another class generates transaction fees. Many players in the market derive their incomes from the decision of asset managers to keep moving money. This also explains the nature of sector rotation strategies that are instigated by large institutions and aided and abetted by brokers trading for their own account. The velocity of trading flows is enhanced by the creation of opportunities for constantly monitoring the markets for reallocation opportunities. All of this is consistent with the fractious markets hypothesis that we have outlined.

At times, however, there are very large players in the markets that have specific reasons to transgress the normal *modus operandi* because of shifts in liquidity conditions or because of miscalculations about major arbitrage strategies. Such was the case with the Long Term Capital Management (LTCM) debacle and other emerging markets crises. It is often the exposure to the less developed and less liquid capital markets that can occasion market crises. Concerns that the velocity of trading may be about to slow down with a tendency towards a dissipation of liquidity on the margins may trigger the first signs of a crisis.

Let us make a case study of a liquidity scare that produced some dramatic price movements in the equity and commodity markets in the early part of May 2006. Are there some footprints and leading indicators that could have tipped us off to the sharp falls that were experienced in several markets globally within a short period? Figure 14.1 reveals the scope of the downdraft in the most widely followed U.S. index, the S&P 500. At the beginning of May the index made a break to new multi-year highs as it managed to break above a price congestion zone that had been in force for several weeks. Coincidentally the Dow Jones Industrials in the same time frame was rapidly approaching the previous all time high that it had previously recorded on January 14th 2000 of 11 722 and was less than 1% from this milestone event. After registering the breakup to 1325 the S&P 500 recorded three tiny candlestick sessions that we have highlighted on the chart (Figure 14.1) which were for the trading sessions of May 8th, 9th and 10th. Within the next six sessions the market dropped almost 5% and there were three extreme trend days marked by the long red candlesticks on May 11th, 12th and then followed by the largest drop on May 17th which saw the index move down by 1.7% which has been a rare occurrence since the market's recovery in 2003.

What is most revealing is the performance of the broker/dealer sector in the period immediately prior to the S&P sell-off. As Figure 14.2 shows a spike up to new highs for this sector index had occurred in the two weeks prior to the May sell-off for the broader market indices.

As also highlighted in Figure 14.2 on May 1st the ^XBD sustained its second strong downward thrust which brought it below the 50 day EMA for the first time in several months. There was an attempt to recover from this but as can also be seen on the chart this effort lacked conviction and the selling resumed coincidentally with the weakness in the broader market as we saw previously in the S&P 500. While we are not prepared to attribute any form of direct causal relationship between the earlier sell-off and top formation for the ^XBD sector it does seem to us that there is scope for suggesting that some factors may have become evident to certain sections of the marketplace that were not going to properly manifest themselves to the broader market for another two weeks. What may have caused the broker dealers to show weakness? Perhaps it became evident to the major financial players that there were some signs in the global financial system that portended a correlated liquidity crisis ahead.

Is there perhaps further evidence that could be adduced to support the notion that circumstances were about to change. Well, perhaps the chart of the Nikkei 225 (Figure 14.3) during April could provide some clues as to the possibility that global liquidity was undergoing a critical transformation. The Japanese market had been in a strong bullish move for most of 2005 and as can be seen from the chart the index broke above previous resistance at 16 800 in late March. But during the month of April the index is beginning to show signs of an intermediate topping-out process which predates the emergence of the topping process on the ^XBD chart we reviewed. As the markets entered the month of May the Nikkei is looking decidedly vulnerable with three lower highs in short order and some recovery failure patterns.

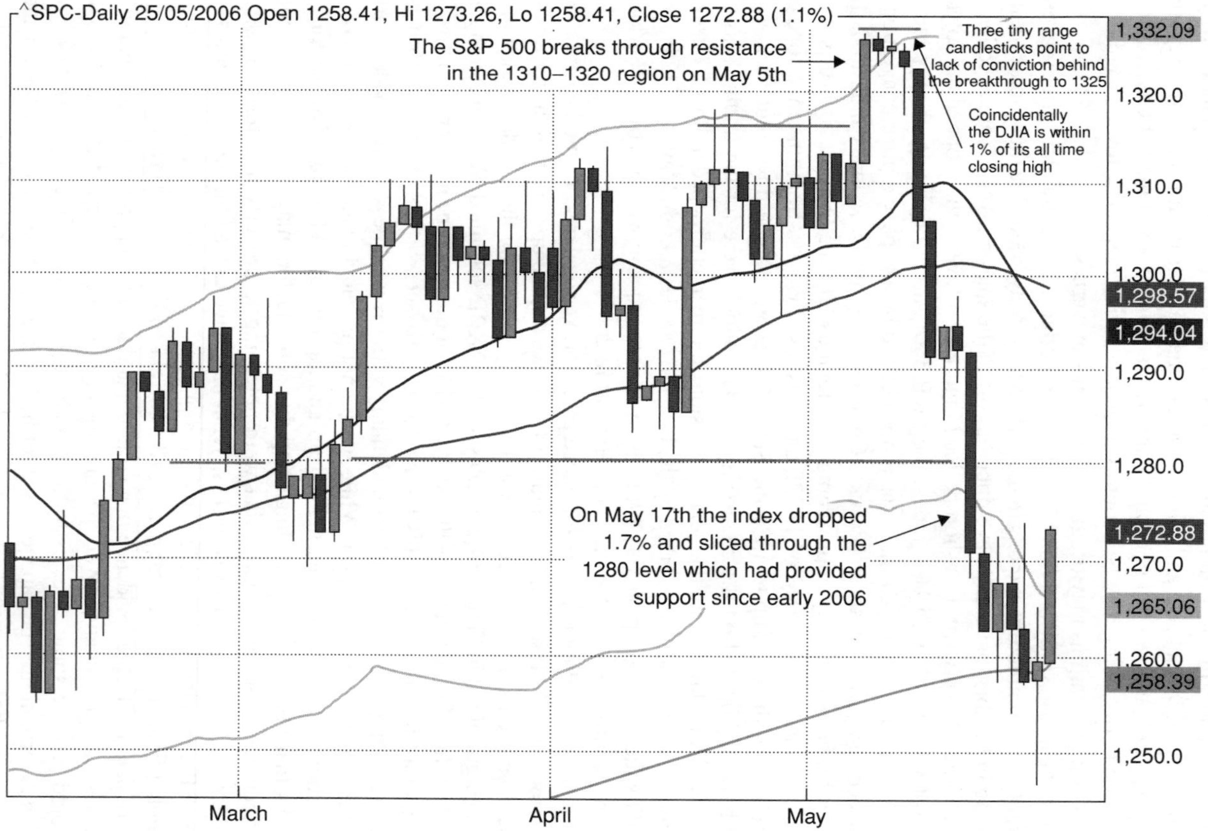
^SPC-Daily 25/05/2006 Open 1258.41, Hi 1273.26, Lo 1258.41, Close 1272.88 (1.1%)
The S&P 500 breaks through resistance in the 1310–1320 region on May 5th
Three tiny range candlesticks point to lack of conviction behind the breakthrough to 1325
Coincidentally the DJIA is within 1% of its all time closing high
On May 17th the index dropped 1.7% and sliced through the 1280 level which had provided support since early 2006
1,332.09
1,320.0
1,310.0
1,300.0
1,298.57
1,294.04
1,290.0
1,280.0
1,272.88
1,270.0
1,265.06
1,260.0
1,258.39
1,250.0
March
April
May

Figure 14.1 S&P 500 during spring/early summer of 2006

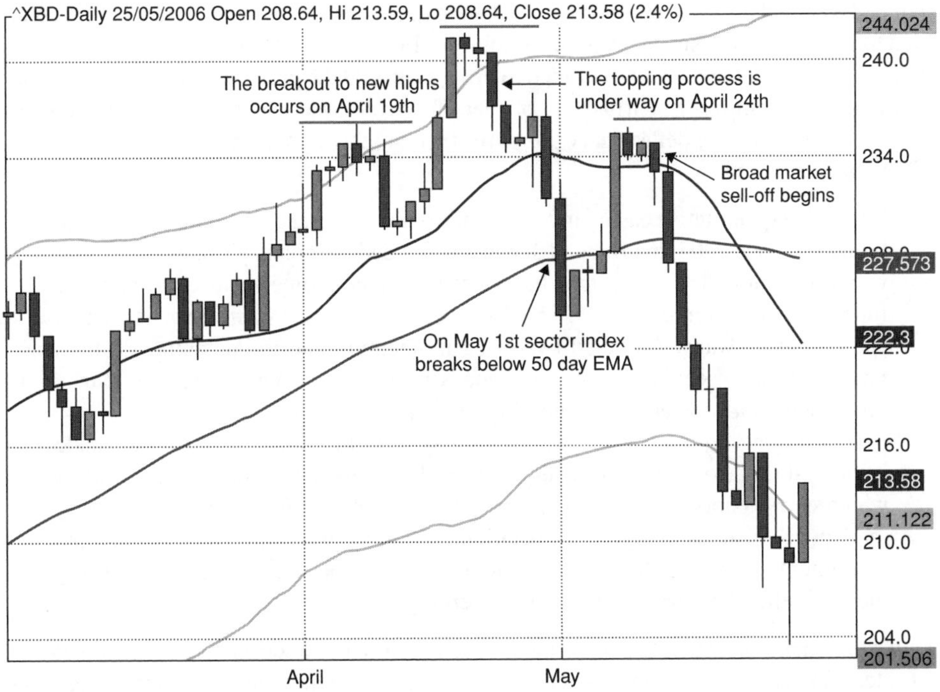

Figure 14.2 Broker dealer sector April/May 2006

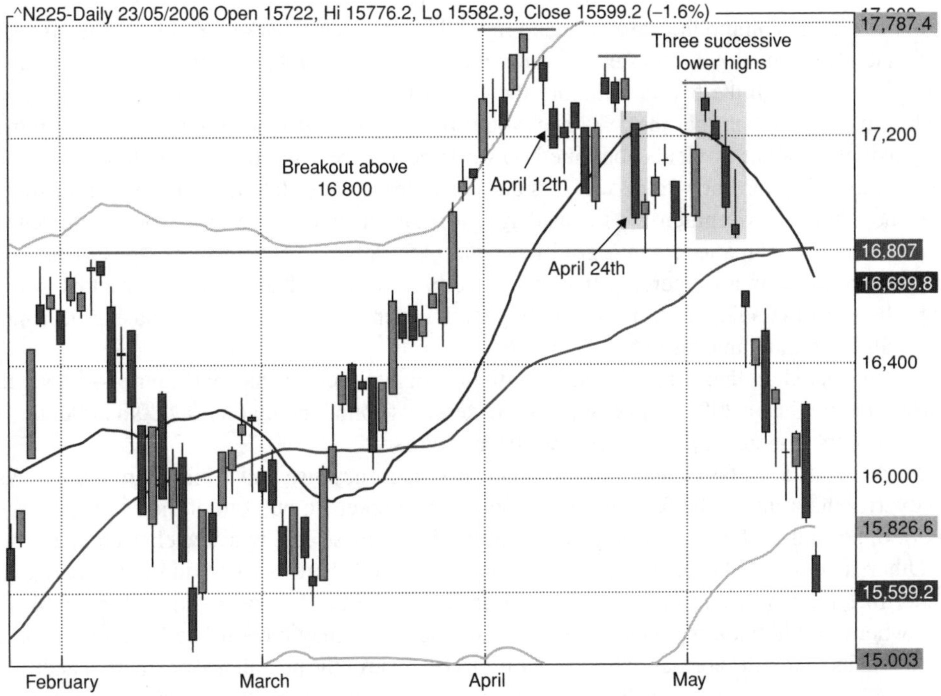

Figure 14.3 Nikkei 225 in early 2006

What had changed during the month of April were decisions by the central banks in Japan and China to introduce more stringent credit conditions. In the case of the Bank of Japan there were announcements that the bank had decided to bring to an end the prolonged period of extremely easy monetary conditions which had been in place for several years so that the nation's economy could avoid the systemic deflationary pressures that had threatened an outright recession.

One observer noted:

> The end of quantitative easing in Japan is the most important factor draining global liquidity. Since 2003, the Bank of Japan has flooded the country's banking system with excess liquidity. Rather than being used to finance domestic investment, these funds have been lent by Japanese banks to foreign investors in the form of interest and currency swaps. Attracted by strong momentum and the potential for high returns, these exceedingly cheap yen loans have been primarily used to finance investment in a wide array of emerging market assets.
>
> By draining liquidity from the banking system, the Bank of Japan has made it increasingly expensive for investors to roll over their yen loans, almost all of which carry tenors of one year or less. This, combined with sinking emerging market asset values and yen appreciation, will force more investors to liquidate investments overlying ultra-cheap yen loans. Liquidation means selling, and selling means further downward pressure on emerging market assets.[3]

Against this backdrop of constraints being imposed on the carry trade and increasing discomfort for traders that had made substantial bets in the industrial commodities sector including metals such as copper, zinc and even the so-called precious metals there were the beginnings of major asset reallocation decisions being made by large institutional investors including global hedge funds. Evidence of the beginnings of some shifts away from certain "hot" sectors was already being felt in the commodities markets and in the U.S. Treasury market. Yields on the 10 year note had also been moving up steadily throughout the month of April 2006 (Figure 14.4) and had passed through the 5% level before the end of the month. There had been an unspoken "whisper" assumption that the 5% level would provide a relief plateau but it was becoming increasingly evident as yields continued onwards beyond 5% that this assumption was open to question. The yen carry trade was less attractive, there were statements purported to show that the Chinese government was considering a small diversification in its foreign currency reserves to shift some assets into gold from the U.S. dollar and there were signs of unease in the debt markets for emerging markets. Whether this crisis had been supported by some ingredients from trading desks implementing tactics such as "financial contagion engineering" we shall leave as a mute point.

One further chart that we shall cite is for the Bombay Stock Exchange (Figure 14.5) which suffered more than a 20% decline in just eight sessions commencing on May 20th 2006 in the context of the contagion phenomenon we have discussed.

Markets fall a lot faster and more dramatically than they rise and while there are always recoveries that remove the fear and panic that cause markets to pull out of their tail spins the profit opportunities for those well positioned to ride out these selling avalanches are massive.

Other than all of the other factors that we have cited there is one additional chart that underlines the severity of the "crisis" and it is for the CBOE Volatility index (Figure 14.6). Elsewhere in this book we have discussed how the ^VIX may have limited usefulness as a technical indicator in "normal" market conditions because of the prevalence of "market neutral" and long/short strategies as well as innovative volatility dispersion strategies. But when fear

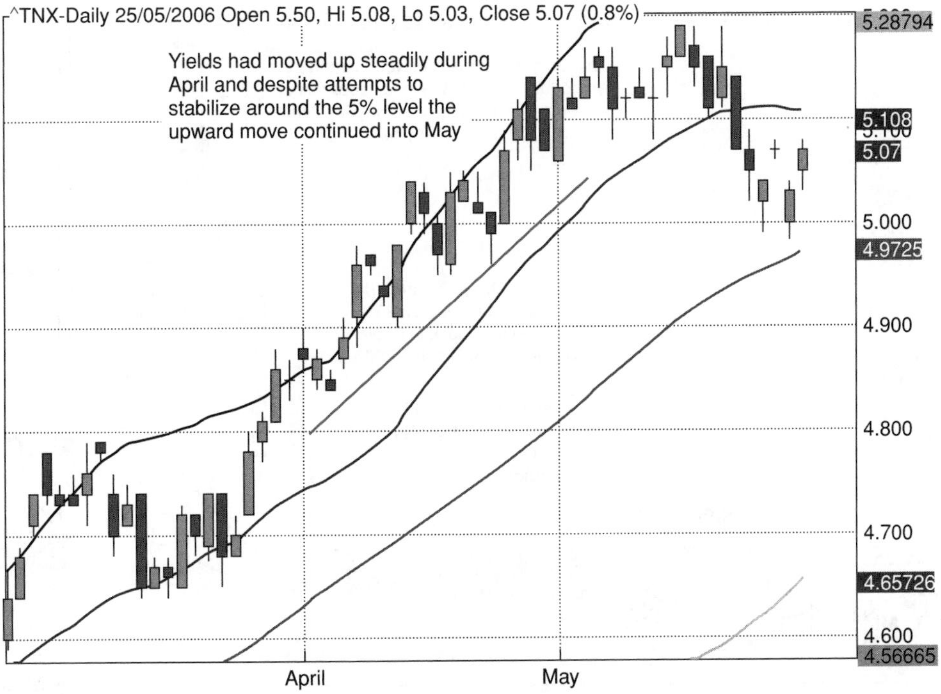

^TNX-Daily 25/05/2006 Open 5.50, Hi 5.08, Lo 5.03, Close 5.07 (0.8%)
Yields had moved up steadily during April and despite attempts to stabilize around the 5% level the upward move continued into May
5.28794
5.108
5.07
5.000
4.9725
4.900
4.800
4.700
4.65726
4.600
4.56665
April
May

Figure 14.4 Yields on the 10 year Treasury notes

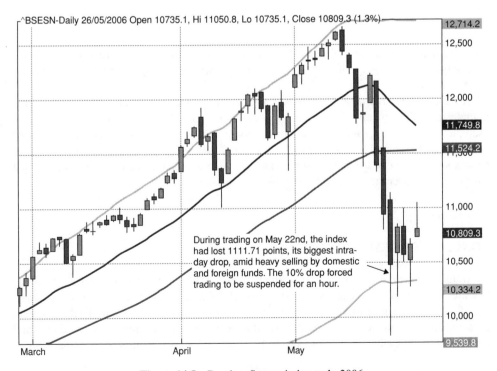

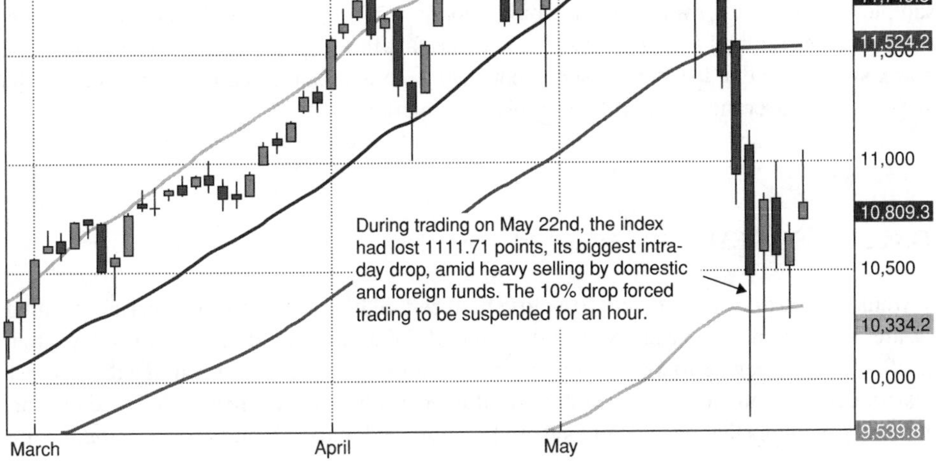

^BSESN-Daily 26/05/2006 Open 10735.1, Hi 11050.8, Lo 10735.1, Close 10809.3 (1.3%)
12,714.2
12,500
12,000
11,749.8
11,524.2
11,000
10,809.3
10,500
10,334.2
10,000
9,539.8
During trading on May 22nd, the index had lost 1111.71 points, its biggest intra-day drop, amid heavy selling by domestic and foreign funds. The 10% drop forced trading to be suspended for an hour.
March
April
May

Figure 14.5 Bombay Sensex index early 2006

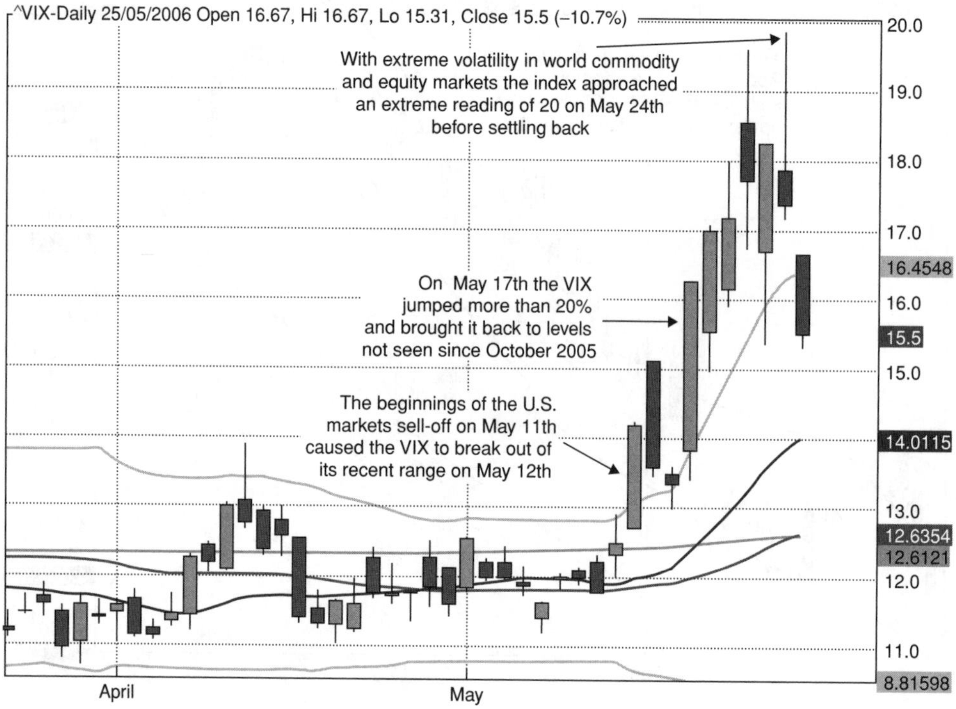

Figure 14.6 The CBOE Volatility index in April/May 2006

grips the markets and the markets move into *critical modes* there is a rush by traditional long only asset managers to implement protective put strategies which send implied volatility dramatically higher.

We have presented evidence that we believe may have some explanatory force in attempting to understand the dynamics behind the May 2006 correlated liquidity crisis. We see it as an example of a contagion event and we would rather examine it in that light than try to pretend that it was the result of a single cause such as the fact that Ben Bernanke made an informal remark suggesting that the FOMC statements had been misinterpreted by the markets or that one particular government report had spooked the markets.

CONCLUDING REMARKS

We would like to draw this chapter to a close with certain high level observations and opinions that are the outcome of our analysis and survey of the underlying dynamics of today's markets. Some have been deliberately framed somewhat provocatively to encourage the reader to possibly disagree, and as we have proposed, it is precisely the existence of disagreement and conflicting opinions that enables markets to function, and makes them such a fascinating area of collective human behavior:

- Markets have no fair or fundamental value.
- Mean reverting behavior may have some empirical basis and perhaps in the long run it will arise – but how long is the long run? How long will prices remain irrational?
- Collectively investors will exhibit swarming (or more crudely herding) behavior and when taken to extremes this will cause markets to enter supercritical states in which they produce bubbles and crashes.
- There may be precursors, during these critical states, which could provide warnings of abrupt discontinuities ahead. But to the extent that these precursors are robust and can be well identified and measured they may have a tendency to cancel their own efficacy.
- When markets are not at supercritical states and the normal fractiousness applies then there is normal market liquidity and tradable opportunities for those operating in all time frames.
- When behavior becomes too coherent, normal volatility will begin to be superseded by more coherent directional spikes (usually downwards) in which there is a significant jump in the degree of correlation among assets that under normal conditions have shown less correlation.
- In extremely critical stages the market will reverse its normal practice of exhibiting greater beta among illiquid stocks (those that trade less frequently) and in fact the beta can reverse as the largest and most liquid stocks will be those that are used to raise cash to meet margin calls and customer redemptions.
- When things get really critical for the stability of the financial system major financial players such as investment banks are incentivized by the U.S. Federal Reserve (by implementing negative real short-term interest rates if necessary) to carry inventories of unwanted assets.
- Hedge funds that want to hold illiquid assets benefit from the fact that they can use mark to model techniques rather than mark to market.
- Correlation and convergence strategies such as those practiced by LTCM and other convertible arbitrage funds in April/May 2005 in conjunction with GM and Ford are based on dubious foundations about the nature of convergence or the omnipresence of market liquidity. But for some opportunistic hedge fund managers that can have several good years before their strategies blow up this is not necessarily a great concern.
- The standard procedure that is practiced for calculating the Value at Risk proposition is seriously flawed and the Gaussian assumptions that underlie most of statistics do not accurately reflect what happens in the real world of finance.
- One has to be careful of not falling into the trap of thinking that just because something is easy to calculate with Excel and because it is a number that can be fed into another series of numbers or algorithms that it provides one with a robust safety net.
- Especially avoid strategies that are based on mean reversion, historical correlation estimates, and all-weather beta estimations.
- Be eclectic and use whatever tools and techniques have produced results. Too many traders carry prejudices or biases for or against certain kinds of techniques that are based more on ideological conviction than efficacy. There is nothing incongruous, in our opinion, between finding value in Japanese candlestick techniques as well as insights from cutting edge econophysics.[4]

For the typical trader and investor, and perhaps even the typical institutional players as well, there is only one broad trading philosophy that will allow one to survive in modern financial markets which is to engage in a form of long/short positioning that allows one to prosper from finding positive alpha opportunities but shelters one from what we like to call "correlated liquidity crises":

- Select trades for a long/short portfolio primarily on whether they can be justified on a stand-alone basis.
- Actively seek out the most attractive opportunities on both sides of the market without having to take a firm view about the underlying direction of the market.
- When combining positions within a portfolio the conventional tactics that are useful such as historically observed correlations and betas can be used as a guide to calculating the applicable position sizes and hedge ratios, but they should not be followed to a spurious level of accuracy. There is no point in calculating the Value at Risk to five decimal places or pretending that one has an accurate measurement of a stock's correlation with the market, or even its standard deviation since these are highly unstable and volatile measurements that cannot be determined with a high degree of accuracy.
- Maintain, at all times, a collection of positions within the market that will alleviate the fear/anxiety element that causes one to tamper with positions prematurely. Knowing that one is not subjected to catastrophic drawdowns and that there are built-in shock absorbers allows one to be stoical about sudden moves.
- Apply profit target and stop-loss targets judiciously so that in volatile conditions the balance between long and short positions is maintained even if the market whipsaws quickly. This should also guide the manner in which positions are exited with profits. There needs to be an overall portfolio exit logic which ensures that positions are retired in a coordinated fashion so that the remaining positions are not overly skewed in either direction.

Notes

CHAPTER 1

1. A very good example of the kind of mathematician/physicist who has found great success on Wall Street is Emanuel Derman who has a PhD in theoretical physics from Columbia University. At one point Derman worked at AT&T Bell Laboratories but he was eventually recruited as a quant at Goldman Sachs where he became a managing director. He has written a very readable account of his journey to Wall Street entitled *My Life as a Quant: Reflections on Physics and Finance*, John Wiley & Sons, 2004.
2. This is cited in *Hedge Funds Losses, Credit Derivatives and Dr. Li's Copula*, by Kevin Dowd, PhD. Available online at http://www.fenews.com/fen46/one_time_articles/copula/copula.html
3. Taken from an article entitled "Managing Risk in Real-time Markets" by Adam Sussman, TABB Group publication, February 2005. Also available online at http://www.sybase.com/content/1034521/Real-TimeRisk-Tabb_WP.pdf
4. Cited in an article entitled "Cracking the Street's New Math – algorithmic trades are sweeping the stock market. But how secure are they?" by Mara Der Hovanesian, April 18th 2005. Available online at http://www.businessweek.com/magazine/content/05_16/b3929113_mz020.htm
5. Quoted in "The New Sell-side Trader", by Ivy Schmerken, *Wall Street & Technology*, July 1st 2005. Also available at http://www.wallstreetandtech.com/showArticle.jhtml?articleID=164903111
6. Quoted in "Cracking the Street's New Math" – see note 4.
7. Quoted in "Managing Risk in Real-time Markets" – see note 3.
8. Reports featured in the London *Daily Telegraph* from June 9th 2006. Available online at http://www.telegraph.co.uk/money/main.jhtml?xml=/money/2006/06/09/cncine09.xml
9. This idea arises in the work of Didier Sornette discussed elsewhere in the book. Some of his many insights into the financial markets are to be found in *Why Stock Markets Crash: Critical Events in Complex Financial Systems*, Princeton: Princeton University Press, 2003.

CHAPTER 2

1. The following entry for Paul Tudor Jones can be found in the Forbes 400 list for 2005:

   #133 Paul Tudor Jones II

   Net Worth: **$2.0 billion ↑**
   Source: Finance, hedge funds
   Self made

Age: **51**
Marital Status: **Married, 4 children**
Hometown: **Greenwich, CT**
Education: **University of Virginia**

Traded cotton after studying economics at U. of Virginia. Started Tudor Investment 1985. Early success predicting 1987 market crash; turned prescient short positions into 201% gain. Never a down year; worst performance in 2000, when offshore Tudor BVI Global Portfolio fund delivered 11.6%. Said to charge 23% of profits and 4% of assets. Now focusing on Asia: last year created Australian affiliate, opened Singapore trading office. Avid pheasant hunter, bass fisherman, owns property around the world, including getaways in Florida Keys and Zimbabwe. Founder New York City's Robin Hood Foundation.

See http://www.forbes.com/lists/2005/54/L6IH.html

2. Jack D. Schwager, *Market Wizards: Interviews with Top Traders, New York Institute of Finance*, Simon & Schuster, 1989, p. 135.
3. Larry Williams and Toby Crabel are both featured later in this chapter. Linda Bradford Raschke has been a successful trader and is co-author of *Street Smarts: High Probability Short-Term Trading Strategies*, M. Gordon Publishing, 1995, with Laurence Connors.
4. Linda Bradford Raschke, "Capturing Trend Days", LBRGroup.com. See http://www.traderslog.com/capturing-trend-days.htm
5. William H. Janeway, "Risk *versus* Uncertainty: Frank Knight's 'Brute' Facts of Economic Life". See http://privatizationofrisk.ssrc.org/Janeway/pf/#9#9
6. Overnight gaps as well as opening price breaks are discussed in much detail in Chapter 7.
7. J.M. Keynes, *The General Theory of Employment, Interest and Money*, Macmillan, 1973, p. 156.
8. See the Bibliography for Dietrich Stauffer (1992).
9. Larry Williams, *The Definitive Guide to Futures Trading*, Windsor Books, 1988.
10. Toby Crabel, *Day Trading With Short Term Price Patterns and Opening Range Breakout*, Traders Press, 1990.
11. The following is taken from Alan Farley's excellent website HardRightEdge.com and explains Crabel's NR7 formation.

    Short-term traders should closely examine small price bar formations. Narrow and wide range bars signal measurable change within the crowd and impending price movement. One classic pattern is NR7, the narrowest range bar of the last 7. These predict breakouts that can be safely traded in the direction of the first impulse.

    Movement out of a NR7 tends to continue in the direction the NR7 bar is first violated. This tendency allows for a tight stop just beyond the range extreme opposite to the position taken.

    See http://www.hardrightedge.com/tour/spring.htm
12. Alan Farley, *The Master Swing Trader. Tools and Techniques to Profit from Outstanding Short-term Trading Opportunities*, McGraw-Hill, 2000.
13. Cited in *The Master Swing Trader*, p. 283 – see note 12.

CHAPTER 3

1. The example has been deliberately chosen with an odd number in the data set as the median value is then derived from the item that has as many predecessors as successors. If there is an even number of numbers in the data set, then the median is calculated from the average value of the *two* numbers in the middle. This is the method that is used by Microsoft Excel.
2. Suppose we want to find the 25th percentile value for a set of eight numbers. We will need to use interpolation since 25 is not a multiple of $1/(n-1)$, where n is the number of values in the set. Here is the procedure that would be followed by the Excel function =PERCENTILE(array, 0.25) to calculate the value for the small array of ranked numbers in the table below.

1	12
2	15
3	16
4	19
5	21
6	23
7	45
8	56

The first step is to compute the rank (R) of the 25th percentile. This is done using the following formula: $R = P/100 \times (N - 1)$ where P is the required percentile (25) and N is the size of the array (i.e. 8 in the present case). Therefore, $R = 25/100 \times (8 - 1) = 7/4 = 1.75$.

If R were an integer, the Pth percentile would be the number with rank R.

When R is not an integer, as is the case here the Pth percentile is determined by interpolation as follows:

- Define I_R as the integer portion of R (the number to the left of the decimal point). For this example, $I_R = 1$.
- Define F_R as the fractional portion of R. For this example, $F_R = 0.75$.
- Find the values in the table with Rank I_R and with Rank $I_R + 1$. In this case, we take the values with Rank 1 and Rank 2. The scores are 12 and 15.
- Multiply the difference between these two values by F_R and add the result to the value of Rank 1. For this array, this is $(0.75)(15 - 12) + 12 = 15.75$.

Accordingly the 25th percentile is 15.75.

3. Linear regression is a statistical technique that when applied to time series data allows one to determine how strongly associated the co-movements of two separate variables are. As with so many statistical techniques it can be traced back to the German mathematician Carl Friedrich Gauss (1777–1855), who developed the simple method of *least squares* which seeks to mimimize the squared differences between the associated data points of two variables, one of which is considered to be the independent variable and the other the dependent variable. The line which moves through the data points with the smallest sum of squared differences between itself and the data is called the line of best fit. The coefficients of the line are equal to the slope and the intercept. It can be used to measure the alpha and beta values when a security is compared to a benchmark index. For more information on the technique there is a full explanation at http://en.wikipedia.org/wiki/Linear_regression

CHAPTER 4

1. See, for example, *Granville's New Strategy of Daily Stock Market Timing for Maximum Profit*, 1976. Granville was hired by E.F. Hutton in October 1957 to write their daily stock market letter. He quit Hutton in August 1963 to start the Granville Market Letter which is still published.

   During his heyday he made a series of notorious market calls some of which were accurate but many of which were not. Perhaps the most serious error was made in 1982 when Granville's charts told him that the stock market was going to crash. He advised his newsletter subscribers and the world at large through media coverage that not only should they sell all of their stocks, but they should go *short*. He made the call as the Dow hit 800, but within a year it had risen to more than 1200. This was the beginning of the longest bull market in history.
2. The construction of the On Balance Volume index is covered at the following http://support.microsoft.com/default.aspx?scid=kb;en-us;222503

   The On Balance Volume Index is based on the average trade volumes, average trade volumes for days when the stock price increased, and final stock prices for the last four weeks compared to the same information for the previous four weeks. The On Balance

Volume Index for a stock increases as the prices and trade volumes for the stock increase. This can be an indication of significant buying activity.

The On Balance Volume Index is based on this formula:
300 × (S1 × P1 × V1)/(S0 × P0 × V0)
These values are defined in the following table:

Value	Definition
S1	The average daily volume of shares traded in the last 4 weeks.
S0	The average daily volume of shares traded in the previous 4 weeks.
P1	The stock price at the end of the last 4 weeks.
P0	The stock price at the end of the previous 4 weeks.
V1	The average daily shares traded in the last 4 weeks on days when the stock price increased.
V0	The average daily shares traded in the previous 4 weeks on days when the stock price increased.

Note The most significant increases in this index occur when stock price and trading volume both significantly increase.

3. The concept of falsifiability is rooted in the work of Karl Popper a strong advocate of the empiricist or scientific method of testing the validity of any hypothesis. He discusses the notion that various theories proposed by philosophers and social theorists fail the test of being open to being shown to be false. If a theory cannot be subjected to such a test it should be dismissed as a dogmatic or ideological assertion rather than a scientific statement. His works include the *Poverty of Historicism* and *The Open Society and Its Enemies – Plato, Hegel and Marx*. One of the better known followers of Popper's philosophy is the eminent investor George Soros.
4. Norman Fosback, *Stock Market Logic*. The book has been through several editions and was originally published by The Institute for Econometric Research in 1976 but is now out of print. We should point out that we are not so concerned with following all aspects of the techniques laid out by Fosback but rather want to capture the core ideas and insights that accompany the procedure.
5. The Smart Money Index is a composite sentiment indicator that is based on intra-day price patterns in the Dow Jones Industrial Average. This index was described by Lynn Elgert in the February 22nd 1988 issue of *Barron's*. According to the Hertler Market Signal website, which has a proprietary interest in the index, the indicator is credited with correctly signaling in advance the 1982 stock market bottom and the 1987 market top.
6. Hertler Market Signal, Inc. tracks this indicator for investors. See http://www.hertlermarketsignal.com
7. The author has made no investigation into the authenticity of any of the claims that are made on behalf of the Smart Money Index.
8. J. Welles Wilder discusses true range in his very influential "New Concepts in Technical Trading Systems", *Trend Research*, June 1978. J. Welles Wilder is credited with the introduction of many technical indicators that are widely followed today and implemented in most software packages for charting the markets. Some of the most useful are the Relative Strength Index (RSI), the Average Directional Index (ADX) and Parabolic SAR. The following website provides good introductions to most technical indicators including the ones just mentioned http://www.investopedia.com/

CHAPTER 5

1. Moving Average Convergence/Divergence (MACD) was developed by Gerald Appel and is one of the most reliable technical indicators available. MACD uses moving averages to derive a momentum oscillator that subtracts the longer moving average from the shorter moving average. The resulting plot forms a line that oscillates above and below zero, without any upper or lower limits.

   The most popular formula of the MACD is the difference between a 26 day and a 12 day exponential moving average. Appel and others have experimented with different time periods to come up with an indicator that is more flexible and to analyze securities with different volatility characteristics and market conditions. Using shorter moving averages will produce a quicker, more responsive indicator, while using longer moving averages will produce a slower indicator, less prone to whipsaws. In the canonical version of the formula that make up MACD, the 12 day EMA is called the fast period and the 26 day EMA is called the slow period. The daily closes are used in the exponential moving average calculation. Traditionally, a 9 day EMA of the MACD value itself is plotted alongside to act as a signal line. A bullish crossover occurs when MACD moves above the signal line and a bearish crossover occurs when MACD moves below the signal line. The histogram represents the difference between MACD and its signal line. The histogram is positive when MACD is above the signal line and negative when MACD is below the signal line.

If MACD is positive and rising, then the gap between the 12 day EMA and the 26 day EMA is widening. This indicates that the rate of change of the faster moving average is higher than the rate of change of the slower moving average. Positive momentum is increasing and this would be considered bullish. If MACD is negative and declining further, then the negative gap between the faster moving average and the slower moving average is expanding. Downward momentum is accelerating and this would be considered bearish.

The definition can be found in a glossary of trading terminology that is found on the author's website at http://www.tradewithform.com/Notices/PatternsGlossary.html

2. S.A. Nelson, *The ABC of Stock Speculation*, Fraser Publishing Company, 1903.
3. The following brief biography is found on Richard Russell's own website:

> Richard Russell began publishing Dow Theory Letters in 1958. Dow Theory Letters is the oldest service continuously written by one person in the business.
>
> Russell gained wide recognition via a series of over 30 Dow Theory and technical articles that he wrote for Barron's during the late-'50s through the '90s. Through Barron's and via word of mouth, he gained a wide following. Russell was the first (in 1960) to recommend gold stocks. He called the top of the 1949-'66 bull market. And almost to the day he called the bottom of the great 1972-'74 bear market, and the beginning of the great bull market which started in December 1974.

Available online at http://ww2.dowtheoryletters.com/DTLOL.nsf/htmlmedia/body_about.html

4. John Murphy, *Technical Analysis of the Futures Markets*, New York Institute of Finance, 1986.
5. *Technical Analysis of the Futures Markets*, see note 4.
6. The question was put to Mark Hulbert who answered it in the following citation:

> Why pay attention to what Russell says, given that he has been wrong on more than one occasion in recent years? A number of you e-mailed me this question after previous columns in which I quoted him. In fact, one of you suggested helpfully that Russell must be paying me under the table to quote him.
>
> The answer, of course, is that I quote Russell because he has a good track record. In fact, when ranked on the basis of the performance of just their stock market timing recommendations, Russell is in second place among all the newsletters the Hulbert Financial Digest has tracked since 1980.

See http://www.marketwatch.com/News/Story/Story.aspx?guid=%7B4C83BBC8-9259-422C-8FC9-583A18C049D9%7D&print=1&siteid=mktw

7. Alan Farley, *The Master Swing Trader. Tools and Techniques to Profit from Outstanding Short-term Trading Opportunities*, McGraw-Hill, 2000, p. 183.
8. See note 7.
9. Didier Sornette is Professor of Geophysics in the Department of Earth and Space Sciences at the University of California, Los Angeles

> In addition to the articles listed in the bibliography he has published *Why Stock Markets Crash: Critical Events in Complex Financial Systems*, Princeton: Princeton University Press, 2003.

His views and predictions regarding the financial markets can be found at http://www.ess.ucla.edu/faculty/sornette/

10. The definition can be found in a glossary of trading terminology that is found on the author's website at http://www.tradewithform.com/Notices/PatternsGlossary.html
11. NR7 refers to the narrowest range in seven sessions which is a concept developed by Toby Crabel and which Farley has covered in his own work.
12. Dan Chesler's work, including his discussion of Hikkake patterns, can be found at http://www.chartricks.com
13. H.M. Gartley, *Profits in the Stock Market*, Lambert-Gann Publishing, 1935.
14. For further information on the "controversy" surrounding the Gartley pattern, see http://www.harmonictrader.com/gcontroversy.htm
15. Ralph N. Elliot's work has been edited and covered for many years by Robert Prechter, see, for example, *The Elliott Wave Principle*, New Classics Library, 1978.
16. The Gartley Butterfly patterns are an extension to the basic Gartley patterns and were introduced in Larry Pesavento's, *Fibonacci Ratios with Pattern Recognition*, Traders Press, Inc., 1997.
17. The author thanks Alan Farley for allowing him to use this example which was featured in one of Farley's columns.

CHAPTER 6

1. Mark Rubinstein, "Comments on the 1987 Stock Market Crash: Eleven Years Later, Monday, October 19, 1998", published in *Risks in Accumulation Products*, Society of Actuaries, 2000.
2. The online encyclopedia Wikipedia defines leptokurtic as follows:

   > A distribution with positive kurtosis is called **leptokurtic**. In terms of shape, a leptokurtic distribution has a more acute "peak" around the mean (that is, a higher probability than a normally distributed variable of values near the mean) and "fat tails" (that is, a higher probability than a normally distributed variable of extreme values).

3. Econometricians have developed techniques that permit the classification of broad market conditions according to the statistical characteristics including volatility. The techniques of classification and further consequences of regime switches are covered in detail in Chapter 10.
4. Refer to note 3.
5. The coefficient of determination is a statistical value that features prominently in linear regression analysis and is usually denoted by the symbol R^2. The value is calculated simply from the square of the correlation coefficient. The latter value can take on positive and negative values so a correlation coefficient of –1 which represents perfect negative correlation will have an R^2 of $+1$ as will the correlation coefficient value of $+1$.
6. Andrew Ang and Joseph Chen make the following point in their paper *Asymmetric Correlations of Equity Portfolios*:

   > Correlations conditional on "downside" movements, which occur when both a U.S. equity portfolio and the U.S. market fall, are, on average, 11.6% higher than correlations implied by a normal distribution.

   Journal of Financial Economics, 2002.
7. A cumulative frequency curve is used to show graphically the total number of time or frequency of occurrence for values that result from a simple frequency table. The advantage of the curve is that is allows easy identification of key quantiles such as the median and interquartile range.
8. The term "ogive" is sometimes used as an alternative name for a cumulative frequency curve.
9. Six sigma event refers to the fact that sigma is the designated symbol within statistics for the standard deviation. If one takes the interval ± 3 STDs – hence six sigmas – this should contain more than 99% of all expected outcomes.

10. The extraordinarily expensive shower curtains are mentioned in "The Rise and Fall of Dennis Kozlowski. How did he become so unhinged by greed?" A revealing look at the man behind the Tyco scandal (Business Week Online, December 23rd 2002).

    > With every passing month, Tyco International Ltd.'s (**TYC**) Leo Dennis Kozlowski looms larger as a rogue CEO for the ages. His $6,000 shower curtain and vodka-spewing, full-size ice replica of Michelangelo's David will not be soon forgotten. At the office, too, Kozlowski's excess was legendary.

    Available online at http://www.businessweek.com/magazine/content/02_51/b3813001.htm
11. Volatility dispersion trading is a hedge strategy designed to take advantage of relative value differences in implied volatilities between an index and a basket of component stocks. This strategy typically involves short option positions on an index, against which long option positions are taken on a set of components of the index.
12. Rob Hanna, "We're in a pattern not seen since 1992 and 1987", from the website TradingMarkets.com, October 17th 2005.

CHAPTER 7

1. The sample size was 500 and the selection criteria were those U.S. stocks which have market capitalizations of at least $500 million and/or trading volumes of at least 500 000 shares per day. The time series data was then scanned for at least 3000 periods of daily data if available, or as many as possible if the stock has not traded that long.
2. See note 1.
3. See note 1.

CHAPTER 8

1. The following is taken from a survey by Eurexchange.

    > Industry estimates suggest that approximately 50 percent of all funds are long/short, 35 percent convertible bond and event driven arbitrage, ten percent macro and the remainder made up of primarily fixed income arbitrage with newer fund styles such as volatility arbitrage coming to the forefront.

    Available online at http://www.eurexchange.com/download/brochures/Xpand51_Hedge_Fonds_E.pdf
2. Quote is found in "The Secret World of Jim Simons by Hal Lux", *Institutional Investor Magazine*, November 1st 2000. Available online at http://www.charttricks.com/Resources/Articles/jim_simons.pdf
3. In an article by John Quiggin found on his website the following suggests that perhaps Keynes never made the remark that is often attributed to him.

    > I haven't been able to find an actual citation, and the informal use of "you" leads me to suspect that these are not Keynes' actual words.

    See http://www.johnquiggin.com/archives/000957.html
4. Two columns of hypothetical values can be entered into an Excel spreadsheet. In column A one can use a random series of values generated by the function RAND(). In cell B1 one can enter the formula =(slope constant * a1) + intercept value. Copy this down the remainder of column B. The two sets of values can then be plotted using a line graph and most surprisingly by using the function

=CORREL(column A values, column B values) the result returned should be +1 or −1 depending on the constants that were entered.

5. Cited in Roger Lowenstein, *When Genius Failed: The Rise and Fall of Long-term Capital Management*, Random House, 2000, p. 43.
6. Cited in *When Genius Failed*, p. 52 – see note 5.
7. A fairly high level overview of market neutral and long/short strategies is to be found in Joseph Nicholas' *Market Neutral Investing: Long/Short Hedge Fund Strategies*, Bloomberg Professional Library, 2000.
8. The following was reported in Randall Dodd, *Rumors and News: Credit Derivatives Trigger Near System Meltdown*, Director Financial Policy Forum, August 5th 2005.

> Rumors started circulating two months ago concerning the possible failure of several large hedge funds and massive losses by at least one major global bank. The source of the troubles was a free-fall in prices in the credit derivatives market that was triggered by the downgrading of GM and Ford. The financial system ended up dodging a systemic meltdown, but without proper coverage and analysis of the events there will be no lessons for policy makers to learn.
>
> During these May events, there were only rumors because this "near-systemic meltdown" – in the words of a senior representative of the securities industry – occurred in OTC derivatives markets where there are no reporting requirements and hence no real transparency.
>
> Instead of news and facts, it was rumors that circulated. First the rumors were of one hedge fund failing, and then another. As the New York Times (May 12, 2005) put it, "One firm that was the subject of rumors was Highbridge Capital Management." Highbridge, which manages a reported $7 billion in hedge fund investments, had to send out a reassuring letter to investors denying the rumors. GLG Partners – a London hedge fund owned by Lehman Brothers known to have suffered enormous losses – was also the subject of such rumors. More alarming were rumors that Deutsche Bank had lost $500 million on its own account from trading in credit derivatives and that it faced further losses through a default from its prime broker relationship with an unnamed hedge fund – its stock slid 3% as a result.

Available online at http://www.financialpolicy.org/fpfspb26.htm

9. Some indices contain obvious overlaps such as the Dow Jones Industrials and the S&P 500 but others contain no overlaps, for example the Russell 2000 is selected from a completely different universe than the S&P 500. It is also interesting that there are some omissions from the S&P 500 that are included in the Russell 1000. The Russell organization points this out as follows.

> Many think the S&P represents the 500 largest companies in America. Not so. It's a selection from the market, chosen by a closed-door committee.

A list of 110 of the largest 500 companies in the U.S. that are not included in the S&P 500 can be found at:
http://www.russell.com/us/indexes/us/followtheleader.asp

10. The positions as of this date show that one would go long 2245 shares of General Motors at a weekly closing price of $44.56 and take a short position of 6845 shares in Ford which had a corresponding weekly close as of this date of $14.61.
11. R.F. Engle and C.W.J. Granger, "Co-integration and Error Correction: Representation, Estimation and Testing", *Econometrica* 552: 251–276, 1987.
12. The "on the run" and "off the run" bond arbitrage is an obvious example of cointegrated assets. The tracking error between different maturities should not follow a random walk and this should be true across the whole Treasury yield spectrum.
13. C. Alexander, "Optimal Hedging using Cointegration", *Philosophical Transactions of the Royal Society, London, Series A* 357: 2039–2058.
14. Quoted in "Optimal Hedging using Cointegration" – see note 13.
15. C. Alexander, I. Giblin and W. Weddington, "Cointegration and Asset Allocation: A New Active Hedge Fund Strategy", *Research in International Business and Finance* 16: 65–90, 2002.

16. Quoted in "Optimal Hedging using Cointegration" – see note 13.
17. C. Alexander and A. Dimitriu, "Indexing, Cointegration and Equity Market Regimes", *International Journal of Finance and Economics* 10: 213–231, 2005.
18. Quoted in "Optimal Hedging using Cointegration" – see note 13.
19. Quoted in "Indexing, Cointegration and Equity Market Regimes" – see note 17.
20. Quoted in "Indexing, Cointegration and Equity Market Regimes" – see note 17.
21. Ed Thorp, "A Perspective on Quantitative Finance: Models for Beating the Market", *Quantitative Finance Review*, 2003.

CHAPTER 9

1. Eugene F. Fama, "Random Walks in Stock Market Prices", *Financial Analysts Journal*, September/October 1965 (reprinted January–February 1995).
2. Burton G. Malkiel, *A Random Walk Down Wall Street*, W.W. Norton and Company, 2003, p. 24.
3. The proposal that a giant asteroid impact in the Yucatan peninsula was responsible for the extinction of the dinosaurs, and Wegener's theories regarding continental drift and tectonic plates, were initially shunned as they conflicted with the broad prejudice of gradual uniformitarianism.
4. The idea of meme as a cultural counterpart to DNA has been popularized by Richard Dawkins. See, for example, *The Selfish Gene*, Oxford University Press, 1976:

   > ... there is something, some essence of Darwinism, which is present in the head of every individual who understands the theory. If this were not so, then almost any statement about two people agreeing with each other would be meaningless. An 'idea-meme' might be defined as an entity that is capable of being transmitted from one brain to another. The meme of Darwin's theory is therefore that essential basis of the idea which is held in common by all brains that understand the theory. The *differences* in the ways that people represent the theory are then, by definition, not part of the meme. If Darwin's theory can be subdivided into components, such that some people believe component *A* but not component *B*, while others believe *B* but not *A*, then *A* and *B* should be regarded as separate memes. If almost everybody who believes in *A* also believes in *B* – if the memes are closely 'linked' to use the genetic term – then it is convenient to lump them together as one meme.

5. The following comes from an obituary notice for Per Bak in PhysicsWeb.

   > Per Bak, a theoretical physicist who helped to develop the concept of "self-organized criticality", has died at the age of 54. Self-organized criticality, which was first used to study the behaviour of sand piles, can also predict phenomena as diverse as earthquakes, forest fires and stock-market prices. Bak developed the concept in 1987 with Chao Tang and Kurt Wiesenfeld while working at the Brookhaven National Laboratory in the US.
   >
   > Bak, who was based at Imperial College London since 2000, wrote the ambitiously titled *How Nature Works* in 1996. He also wrote "Why Nature is complex" with his second wife Maya Paczuski in the December 1993 issue of Physics World. Bak died on 16 October in Copenhagen.

   See http://physicsweb.org/articles/news/6/10/18/1
6. Per Bak, *How Nature Works: The Science of Self-organized Criticality*, Copernicus Press, 1996, p. 131.
7. See the article on self-organized criticality at http://en.wikipedia.org/wiki/Self-organized_criticality
8. A good general treatment of SOC, complexity theory and associated ideas is to be found in Stuart Kauffman's *At Home in the Universe: The Search for the Laws of Self-Organization and Complexity*, Oxford University Press, 1996.
9. Quoted in *How Nature Works*, p. 131 – see note 6.
10. See Sornette's mathematically demanding work *Why Stock Markets Crash: Critical Events in Complex Financial Systems*, Princeton University Press 2002. Also several of his articles are mentioned in the Bibliography.

11. Xavier Gabaix, Parameswaran Gopikrishnan, Vasiliki Plerou and H. Eugene Stanley, "A Theory of Power Law Distributions in Financial Market Fluctuations", *Nature* 423: 267–270, 2003. See http://econ-www.mit.edu/faculty/download_pdf.php?id=529. A press release was put out by Boston University to publicize the research and this can be found at http://www.bu.edu/phpbin/news/releases/display.php?id=526
12. Quoted from George Chang, "A Bayesian Analysis of Log-periodic Precursors to Financial Crashes", 2005.
    Available online at http://www.nd.edu/~meg/MEG2004/Chang-George.pdf. Also available from http://www.gloriamundi.org/picsresources/gcjf.pdf
13. This is quoted directly from a press release put out by Boston University to publicize the research mentioned in note 11 and this can be found at http://www.bu.edu/phpbin/news/releases/display.php?id=526
14. Quoted in "A Theory of Power Law Distributions in Financial Market Fluctuations" – see note 11.
15. P. Neu and R. Kühn, "Statistical Mechanics of Financial Time Series and Applications in Risk Management", Presentation at the Math Finance Workshop Hochschule für Bankwirtschaft, Frankfurt, April 2004. See http://workshop.mathfinance.de/2004/papers/neu/slides.pdf
16. One of the most readable works by Mandelbrot is *The (Mis)behavior of Markets* which carries the subtitle *A Fractal View of Risk, Ruin and Reward*. It was co-authored with Richard Hudson. Basic Books, 2004.
17. Mandelbrot cites the work of J. Hurst, a British hydrologist who studied flooding patterns in the Nile and produced a technique called rescaled range analysis which has been used by some market analysts to determine whether financial time series data shows persistence – see Peters (1994) and (1996) in the Bibliography.
18. See Nicholas Taleb, *Fooled by Randomness: The Hidden Role of Chance in Life and in the Markets*, Random House, 2005.
19. Taken from P.H. Cootner, *The Random Character of Stock Market Prices*, MIT Press, 1964.
20. Quoted in *The (Mis)behavior of Markets*, p. 153 – see note 16.
21. The example comes from the following paper – "Stochastic Lotka-Volterra Systems of Competing Auto-catalytic Agents Lead Generically to Truncated Pareto Power Wealth Distribution, Truncated Levy Distribution of Market Returns, Clustered Volatility, Booms and Crashes" by Sorin Solomon of the Racah Institute of Physics, Hebrew University of Jerusalem and can be found in *Decision Technologies for Computational Finance*, edited by A.-P. Refenes, A.N. Burgess and J.E. Moody, Kluwer Academic Publishers, 1998. Available online at http://xxx.lanl.gov/abs/cond-mat/9803367
22. Levy flights are discussed further in an accessible manner at the Wikipedia website:

    > A Lévy flight is a type of random walk in which the increments are distributed according to a "heavy tail" distribution. A heavy tail distribution is a probability distribution which falls to zero as $1/|x|^{\alpha+1}$ where $0 < \alpha < 2$ and therefore has an infinite variance.

    See http://en.wikipedia.org/wiki/L%C3%A9vy_flight
23. See Ivars Peterson's article "Trails of the Wandering Albatross – Patterns of Flight Resemble Levy Flights", *Science News*, August 17th 1996. Available online at http://www.findarticles.com/p/articles/mi_m1200/is_n7_v150/ai_18621169

CHAPTER 10

1. S.N. Rodionov and J.E. Overland, "Application of a Sequential Regime Shift Detection Method to the Bering Sea Ecosystem", *Journal of Marine Sciences* 62: 328–332, 2005.
2. S.N. Rodionov, "A Sequential Algorithm for Testing Climate Regime Shifts", *Geophysical Research Letters* 31: L09204, doi:10.1029/2004. Available online at http://www.beringclimate.noaa.gov/regimes/Regime_shift_algorithm.pdf
3. G.C. Chow, "Tests of Equality Between Sets of Coefficients in Two Linear Regressions", *Econometrica*, 1960.
4. K. Kiyono, Z. Struzik and Y. Yamamoto, "Criticality and Phase Transition in Stock-Price Fluctuations", *Physical Review Letters* PRL 96, 068701, February 17th 2006.

5. See Nicholas Taleb, *Fooled by Randomness: The Hidden Role of Chance in Life and in the Markets*, Random House, 2005.
6. Mary Hardy, "A Regime-switching Model of Long-term Stock Returns", *North American Actuarial Journal*, April 2001.
7. See, for example, the discussion of ant foraging behavior by Paul Ormerod in *Butterfly Economics: A New General Theory of Social and Economic Behavior*, Basic Books, 2001.
8. This is really the suggestion in "Criticality and Phase Transition in Stock-Price Fluctuations" – see note 4.
9. The Santa Fe institute in New Mexico is renowned for its interdisciplinary approach to the study of many kinds of complex systems. Pioneering work in artificial life, genetic algorithms, cellular automata and finance and artificial markets has been conducted by the many scientific luminaries that have been associated with the Institute over the last 20 years. They have included Per Bak, Chris Langton, Stuart Kauffman, J. Doyne Farmer, W. Brian Arthur, John Holland, Murray Gell-Mann and Duncan Watts.
10. There is a readable account of the Prediction Company's work to be found in Thomas A. Bass, *The Predictors*, Henry Holt, 1999.
11. See the seminal article by J. Doyne Farmer, "Toward Agent-based Models for Investment", 2001. Available online at http://www.santafe.edu/~jdf/papers/aimr.pdf
12. Cited in "Toward Agent-based Models for Investment" – see note 11.
13. J.D Farmer, P. Patelli and I. Zovko, "Predictive Power of Zero Intelligence in Financial Markets", 2003.
    Available online at http://xxx.lanl.gov/abs/cond-mat/0309233
14. Thomas Lux and M. Marchesi, "Volatility Clustering in Financial Markets: A Micro Simulation of Interacting Agents", *International Journal of Theoretical and Applied Finance* 3: 675–702, 2000.
15. D. Stauffer, D and A. Aharony, *Introduction to Percolation Theory*, Taylor & Francis, 1992.
16. D. Stauffer and D. Sornette, "Self-organized Percolation Model for Stock Market Fluctuations", *Physica A* 271: 499–506, 1999.
17. The following is the classic quotation from J.M. Keynes' *The General Theory of Employment Interest and Money*, 1936.

    > It is not a case of choosing those [faces] which, to the best of one's judgment, are really the prettiest, nor even those which average opinion genuinely thinks the prettiest. We have reached the third degree where we devote our intelligences to anticipating what average opinion expects the average opinion to be. And there are some, I believe, who practise the fourth, fifth and higher degrees.

CHAPTER 11

1. Stanley Druckenmiller was hired by George Soros to manage his funds when Soros decided to focus his energies on philanthropy. Eventually Druckenmiller moved on to set up his own asset management company called the Duquesne Fund. The quotation is found in an interview with Jack Schwager in his book, *The New Market Wizards: Conversations with America's Top Traders*, Harper Business, 1992, p. 207.
2. This quotation is attributed to Paul Tudor Jones in the following article by Dmitry Tolstonogov, "Money Management: The Foundations of Money Management". The present author cannot vouch for its authentic attribution, however. Available online at http://www.tsresearch.com/public/money_management/money_management1/
3. An excellent book by William Poundstone, deals with the Kelly formula and many more fascinating ideas relating to systems designed to find an edge in trading and gaming. William Poundstone, *Fortune's Formula: The Untold Story of the Scientific Betting System that Beat the Casinos and Wall Street*, Hill and Wang, 2005.
4. Ed Thorp, "A Perspective on Quantitative Finance: Models for Beating the Market", *Quantitative Finance Review*, 2003.

5. Dr William T. Ziemba is the Alumni Professor of Financial Modeling and Stochastic Optimization, Emeritus in the Sauder School of Business, University of British Columbia, where he taught from 1968 to 2004. He now teaches as a visiting professor. A good source for his publications is found at http://www.interchange.ubc.ca/ziemba/
6. The source of much of the discussion in this section is from the following work by Ralph Vince, *The Mathematics of Money Management*, John Wiley & Sons, 1992.
7. Cited in *The Mathematics of Money Management*, p. 38 – see note 6.
8. Cited in *The Mathematics of Money Management*, p. 39 – see note 6.
9. The quotation comes from the website of one of the pioneers in alternative asset management, the J.W. Henry Company, which is one of the largest managed futures advisors in the world. See http://www.jwh.com/templ006.cfm?id=006AB&left=1&tid=006AB
10. For users of Excel there is a technique for calculating the CAGR by using the geometric mean function. If the returns are in cells C3:C7 of a spreadsheet we can calculate the CAGR by using the following formula {=GEOMEAN(1+C3:C7)-1}. The external brace brackets are required and this can be achieved with the following Excel array function procedure:
    Type: =GEOMEAN(1+C3:C7)-1 in a cell but don't press the Enter key right away.
    Hold down the Ctrl and Shift keys and then hit the Enter key. The formula will change to {=GEOMEAN(1+C3:C7)-1}.
11. The following is an explanation of the value of using the geometric mean as a way of expressing returns and is found in" William T. Ziemba, "The Symmetric Downside-Risk Sharpe Ratio and the Evaluation of Great Investors and Speculators", *Journal of Portfolio Management*, Fall 2005.

> Typically the Sharpe ratio is computed using arithmetic returns. This is because the basic static theories of portfolio investment management such as mean-variance analysis and the capital asset pricing model are based on arithmetic means. These are static one period theories. However, for asset returns over time, the geometric mean is a more accurate measure of average performance since the arithmetic mean is biased upwards. The geometric mean helps mitigate the autocorrelated and time varying mean and other statistical properties of returns that are not iid. For example, if one has returns of +50% and –50% in two periods, then the arithmetic mean is zero which does not correctly reflect the fact that 100 became 150 and then 75. The geometric mean, which is –13.7%, is the correct measure to use. For investment returns in the 10–15% range, the arithmetic returns are about 2% above the geometric returns. But for higher returns this approximation is not accurate. Hence, geometric means as well as more typical arithmetic means are used in this paper. Lo (2002) points out that care must be used in Sharpe ratio estimations when the investment returns are not iid, which they are for the investors discussed here. For dependent but stationary returns he derives a correction of the Sharpe ratios that deflates artificially high values back to correct values using an estimation of the correlation of serial returns. The Sharpe ratios are usually lower when geometric means are used rather than arithmetic means with the difference between these two measures a function of return volatility.

CHAPTER 12

1. See Markowitz's paper "Portfolio Selection", *Journal of Finance* 7(1), 1952.
2. Taken from a good introduction to Markowitz's work at Wikipedia. See http://en.wikipedia.org/wiki/Harry_Markowitz
3. A. Ang and J. Chen, "Asymmetric Correlations of Equity Portfolios", *Journal of Financial Economics* 63: 443–494, 2002.
4. Cited in "Asymmetric Correlations of Equity Portfolios" – see note 3.
5. A. Ang, J. Chen and Y. Xing, "Downside Risk", *Review of Financial Studies*, 2005.

6. The following table illustrates the safety net provided.

Long only two asset portfolio			Long/short two asset portfolio		
Bear market scenario	Asset A	Asset B	Bear market scenario	Asset A	Asset B
Expected monthly return	–10.00%	–15.00%	Expected monthly return	–10.00%	–15.00%
Relative allocation share	50%	50%	Relative allocation share	50%	–50%
Standard deviation	5.00%	8.00%	Standard deviation	5.00%	8.00%
Correlation coefficient	0.9		Correlation coefficient	0.9	
Expected portfolio monthly return	–12.50%		Expected portfolio monthly return	2.50%	
t-statistic for confidence interval	1.645		*t*-statistic for confidence interval	1.645	
Portfolio variance	0.004025		Portfolio variance	0.000425	
Portfolio standard deviation	0.063		Portfolio standard deviation	0.021	
Monthly VAR	–22.9%		Monthly VAR	–0.9%	

7. Matrix multiplication can be achieved within Excel by using the function =MMULT (etc.). It is an array function and requires special handling as described in note 10 of Chapter 11.
8. The impetus behind evolutionary computation techniques came from the work of John Holland who pioneered the use of genetic algorithms in solving a certain class of problems that are not capable of being solved using algorithms that explore the space of possible permutations of the constraining variables. One of the most accessible of his works is "Emergence" (1998), Addison Wesley. See also below for note 6 of chapter 13 for a further reference to evolutionary algorithms.

CHAPTER 13

1. See http://www.russell.com for an explanation of the many indices that the Russell Company has created and manages. There are some interesting differences between the largest stocks that are included in the Russell 1000 index and the S&P 500 and sometimes the 100 or so stocks that are not common to both indices display *interesting* trading characteristics. See also note 9 in Chapter 8.
2. The R^2 value is one of the more important corollary statistics arising from a linear regression and indicates the strength of the observed correlation between two variables. It equates to the squared value of the correlation coefficient and can sometimes be thought of as expressing in percentage terms the confidence of any expectation of future association from a previously observed correlation. For example, an R^2 value of 0.75 is sometimes treated as providing a 75% confidence of the expected co-movement between two variables.
3. The quotation appears in an article by Miriam Bensman entitled "Moving Alpha" which appeared at DerivativesStrategy.com. Available online at http://www.derivativesstrategy.com/magazine/archive/1995-1996/0796fea2.asp?print
4. Quoted in Alexander M. Ineichen, "CFA Market-neutral versus Long/Short Equity". Available online at http://www.blumontcapital.com/downloads/articles/wp_whoslong_0701.pdf
5. Users of Excel should make sure that the Solver tool has been added to their installation as it is a very useful tool for producing many optimization solutions that are often required in finance. Set up a table with the various weightings of the securities as the array of variables that will be changed by the Solver tool. Another row of the table should include the individual beta values of the relevant securities in the portfolio. A key cell will be the cell which calculates the portfolio beta and this cell should include the following function =SUMPRODUCT(cells with weightings, cells with individual

betas). The result returned in this cell will be the portfolio beta value. In the Solver dialog box this cell address should be set as the Target Cell and one can specify that it should match the level of zero. When Solver runs it will experiment with different portfolio weightings in an attempt to satisfy any other constraints that have been incorporated in the spreadsheet and to achieve the desired goal which is a portfolio with a beta value equal to zero. Solver will not always find a solution and sometimes it will provide one solution out of several that may be applicable as well. A useful Excel file and guide for traders wanting to experiment with Solver in portfolio construction is found online at http://www.solver.com/solutions/Investment%20Examples.xls

6. A helpful way of visualizing the evolutionary algorithm process is to imagine a virtual trading environment populated by a number of virtual traders. The traders operate with rules that are encoded at the programmatic level so that a series of rule following dispositions are expressed in machine instructions that resemble the DNA code. During program execution, each trader is exposed to the time series data on a sequential basis. If the trader detects an observation pattern that corresponds to its rule description then it executes a trade (either long or short depending on further rule parameters) and stores the trade in its portfolio. The portfolio management techniques including hedge ratios, stop-loss and take profit logic are also encoded in further strings of DNA.

   At the end of a single iteration of the program, which may have exposed all of the traders to (say) 200 periods of data, the relative performance of the traders can be evaluated by examining each trader's portfolio for such characteristics as profit ratios, Sharpe ratios, maximum drawdown etc.

   The traders that exhibit superior performance with respect to the evaluation criteria are then given prominence in the reproductive cycle that produces the next generation of traders for the next iteration of the program. The new generation of traders will incorporate the recombined DNA of the previous generation, with a bias toward the superior performance of their parents but also with the introduction of novelty from "random" crossover of the parent's genomes. This new generation is then exposed to the same time series data and their trading performance is assessed at the end of the iteration.

   After running the program through many generations (typically 50 or so) it is possible to identify those traders that have encoded the best pattern detection rules that enable them to excel at trading.

   The DNA of the most successful traders represents the sets of rule descriptions that capture those market behavior patterns that will yield the greatest profitability.

CHAPTER 14

1. A fascinating book covering power laws and how they reveal themselves in many unexpected places in both the physical world and the world of culture is by Manfred Schroeder, *Fractals, Chaos and Power Laws*, Freeman, 1991.
2. John Allen Paulos, *A Mathematician Plays the Market*, Penguin Books, 2004.
3. Quoted from Jephraim P. Gundzik, President of Condor Advisers, Inc. Condor Advisers provides investment risk analysis to individuals and institutions globally. Available online at http://www.atimes.com/atimes/Global_Economy/HE27Dj01.html
4. An indication of how misguided some people's prejudices are in this regard is found in the following review that was posted at the amazon.com website for another author's book.

   > I didn't read the book, but took a look at the table of contents. I don't think that any decent Quant Finance writer would include a chapter on Japanese candlesticks in his book, so I don't recommend buying it. If that chapter was included just to show what NOT to do, please correct me.

   Available online at http://www.amazon.com/gp/product/0471584282. Needless to say the current author does not expect the writer of the review to purchase this book either!

Bibliography

Alexander, C. (1999), "Optimal Hedging using Cointegration", *Philosophical Transactions of the Royal Society, London, Series A* 357: 2039–2058.

Alexander, C. (2001). *Market Models – A Guide to Financial Data Analysis.* Chichester: John Wiley & Sons.

Alexander, C. and A. Dimitriu (2005). "Indexing and Statistical Arbitrage: Tracking Error or Cointegration?", *Journal of Portfolio Management* 31(2): 50–63.

Alexander, C. and A. Dimitriu (2005). "Indexing, Cointegration and Equity Market Regimes", *International Journal of Finance and Economics* 10: 213–231.

Alexander, C., I. Giblin and W. Weddington (2002). "Cointegration and Asset Allocation: A New Active Hedge Fund Strategy", *Research in International Business and Finance* 16: 65–90.

Anderson, P.W., K.J. Arrow and D. Pines, eds (1988). *The Economy as an Evolving Complex System.* Redwood City, CA: Addison-Wesley.

Ang, A. and G. Bekaert (2000). "International Asset Allocation with Time-varying Correlations", *Review of Financial Studies* 15: 1137–1187.

Ang, A. and G. Bekaert (2002). "Regime Switches in Interest Rates", *Journal of Business and Economic Statistics* 20: 163–182.

Ang, A. and J. Chen (2002). "Asymmetric Correlations of Equity Portfolios", *Journal of Financial Economics* 63: 443–494.

Ang, A., J. Chen and Y. Xing (2002). "Downside Correlation and Expected Stock Returns", working paper, Columbia Business School.

Arthur, W.B., S.N. Durlauf and D.A. Lane, eds (1997). *The Economy as an Evolving Complex System II.* Redwood City, CA: Addison-Wesley.

Axelrod, R. and M. Cohen (2000). *Harnessing Complexity*. Free Press.

Bachelier, L. (1900) "Théorie de la Spéculation", *Annales Scientifique de l'École Normale Supérieure* III-17: 21–86 (English translation in Cootner, P.H., ed. (1964). *The Random Character of Stock Market Prices*. Cambridge, MA: MIT Press, 17–78).

Bak, P. (1996). *How Nature Works: The Science of Self-Organized Criticality.* New York: Copernicus Press for Springer-Verlag.

Bak, P. and K. Chen (1991). "Self-organized Criticality", *Scientific American* January, 46–53.

Bak, P. and C. Tang (1989). "Earthquakes as a Self-organized Critical Phenomenon", *Journal of Geophysical Research* 94: 15 635–15 637.

Bak, P., C. Tang and K. Wiesenfeld (1987). "Self-organized Criticality: An Explanation of the 1/f Noise", *Phys. Rev. Lett.* 59: 381–384.

Bak, P., K. Chen, J. Scheinkman and M. Woodford (1993). "Aggregate Fluctuations from Independent Sectoral Shocks: Self-organized Criticality in a Model of Production and Inventory Dynamics", *Ricerche Economiche* 47: 3–30.

Barabasi, A-L. and R. Albert (1999). "Emergence of Scaling in Random Networks", *Science* 286: 509–512.

Black, F. and M. Scholes (1973). "The Pricing of Options and Corporate Liabilities", *Journal of Political Economy* 81: 637–654.

Brock, W.A. and S.N. Durlauf (2001). "Discrete Choice with Social Interactions", *Review of Economic Studies* 68: 235–260.

Bouchard, J., M. Mezard and M. Potters (2002). "Statistical Properties of Stock Order Books: Empirical Results and Models", *Quantitative Finance* 2(4).

Burton, G.M. (2003). *A Random Walk Down Wall Street.* Completely revised and updated Eighth Edition. W.W. Norton and Company.

Crabel, T. (1990). *Day Trading With Short Term Price Patterns and Opening Range Breakout.* Traders Press (out of print).

Darvas, N. (1986). *How I Made $2,000,000 in the Stock Market.* Reissue Edition. Carol Publishing Corporation.

Derman, E. (2004). *My Life as a Quant, Reflections on Physics and Finance.* New York: John Wiley & Sons.

Farley, A. (2000). *The Master Swing Trader.* McGraw Hill.

Dunbar, N. (2000). *Inventing Money.* Chichester: John Wiley & Sons.

Embrechts, P., A.J. McNeil and D. Straumann (1999). "Correlation: Pitfalls and Alternatives", *Risk* 69–71.

Embrechts, P., A.J. McNeil and D. Straumann (2001). "Correlation and Dependency in Risk Management: Properties and Pitfalls", in Dempster M., ed., *Value at Risk and Beyond.* Cambridge University Press.

Engle, R.F. and C.W.J. Granger (1987). "Co-integration and Error Correction: Representation, Estimation and Testing", *Econometrica* 55, 251–276, 987–1008.

Engle , R.F. and C.W.J. Granger, eds (1991). *Long-run Economic Relationships: Readings in Cointegration.* Oxford: Oxford University Press.

Farmer, J.D. (2001). "Toward Agent-based Models for Investment", reproduced and republished from *Benchmarks and Attribution Analysis* with permission from the Association for Investment Management and Research. The article is available at http://www.santafe.edu/~jdf/papers/aimr.pdf

Farmer, J.D. and A.W. Lo (1999). "Frontiers of Finance: Evolution and Efficient Markets", *Proceedings of the National Academy of Science USA* 96: 1991–1992.

Farmer, D. and F. Lillo (2004). "On the Origin of Power-law Tails in Price Fluctuations," *Quantitative Finance* IV C7–11.

Farmer, J.D. and S. Joshi (2002). "The Price Dynamics of Common Trading Strategies", *Journal of Economic Behavior and Organization* 49: 149–171.

Gabaix, X. (1999). "Zipf's Law for Cities: An Explanation", *Quarterly Journal of Economics* 114: 739–767.

Gartley, H.M. (1935). *Profits in the Stock Market.* Lambert-Gann Publishing.

Gleick, J. (1987). *Chaos: Making a New Science.* New York and London: Penguin Books.

Gopakrishnan, P., V. Plerou, L.A.N. Amaral, M. Meyer and H.E. Stanley (1999). "Scaling of the Distributions of Fluctuations of Financial Market Indices", *Physical Review E* 60: 5305–5316.

Gopikrishnan, P., V. Plerou, Y. Liu, L.A.N. Amaral, X. Gabaix and H.E. Stanley (2000). "Scaling and Correlation in Financial Time Series", *Physica A* 287: 362–373.

Granville, J.E. (1976). *Granville's New Strategy of Daily Stock Market Timing for Maximum Profit.* (Hardcover), Simon & Schuster.

Hamilton, J.D. (1989). "A New Approach to the Economic Analysis of Nonstationary Time Series and the Business Cycle", *Econometrica* 57: 357–384.

Hamilton, J.D. (1994). *Time Series Analysis.* Princeton: Princeton University Press.

Holland, J. (1995). *Hidden Order.* Reading, MA: Addison-Wesley, pp. 1–40 on elements of a complex adaptive system.

Holland, J. (1998). Emergence: From Chaos to Order, Addison Wesley.

Hull, J. (1993). *Options, Futures and Other Derivative Securities.* Second Edition. Englewood Cliffs: Prentice Hall International Editions.

Johnson, S. (2001). *Emergence: The Connected Lives of Ants, Brains, Cities and Software.* Scribner.

Jorion, P. (1996). "Risk2: Measuring the Risk in Value at Risk", *Financial Analysts Journal* November/December: 47–56.

Kahneman, D. and A. Tversky, eds (2000). *Choices, Values and Frames*. Cambridge: Cambridge University Press.

Kelly, J.L. Jr. (1956). "A New Interpretation of Information Rate", *Bell Systems Technical Journal* 35: 917–926.

Kelly, K. (1994) *Out of Control: The New Biology of Machines, Social Systems, and the Economic World*. Reading, MA: Addison-Wesley, pp. 22–25 and 468–472.

Keynes, J.M. (1973). *The General Theory of Employment, Interest and Money*. London: Macmillan.

Kirman, A. (1993). "Ants, Rationality, and Recruitment", *Quarterly Journal of Economics* 108: 137–156.

Kiyono, K., Z. Struzik and Y. Yamamoto (2006). "Criticality and Phase Transition in Stock–Price Fluctuations", *Physical Review Letters* PRL 96, 068701, 17 February 2006.

Kodres, L. and M.G. Pritsker (1999). "A Rational Expectations Model of Financial Contagion", mimeo, Federal Reserve Board, May.

Kritzman, M. and D. Rich (2002). "The Mismeasurement of Risk", *Financial Analysts Journal* May/June: 91–99.

Leland, H. (1999). "Beyond Mean Variance: Performance Measurement in a Non-symmetrical World", *Financial Analysts Journal* January/February: 27–35.

Lévy, P. (1925). *Calcul des Probabilités*. Paris: Gauthier-Villars.

Levy, M. and S. Solomon (1997). "New Evidence for the Power-law Distribution of Wealth", *Physica A* 242: 90–94.

Lhabitant, F. (2002). *Hedge Funds: Myths and Limits*. Chichester: John Wiley & Sons.

Lo, A. (1991). "Long-term Memory in Stock Market Prices", *Econometrica* 59: 1279–1313.

Lo, A. (2002). "The Statistics of the Sharpe Ratio", *Financial Analysts Journal* July/August: 36–52.

Lo, A.W. and C. MacKinlay (1998). "Stock Prices Do Not Follow Random Walks: Evidence from a Simple Specification Test", *Review of Financial Studies* 1: 41–66.

Loretan, M. and W.B. English (2000). "Evaluating 'Correlation Breakdowns' during Periods of Market Volatility", *BIS Conference Papers, Vol 8*, Bank for International Settlements, March.

Longstaff, F.A. (2004). "Financial Claustrophobia: Asset Pricing in Illiquid Markets", NBER Working Paper Series 10411.

Lowenstein, R. (2000). *When Genius Failed: The Rise and Fall of Long-term Capital Management*. New York: Random House.

Lux, H. (2002). "Risk Gets Riskier", *Institutional Investor* October: 28–36.

Lux, T. (1998). "The Socio-economic Dynamics of Speculative Markets: Interacting Agents, Chaos, and the Fat Tail of Return Distributions", *Journal of Economic Behavior and Organization* 33: 143–165.

Lux, T. and M. Marchesi (1999). "Scaling and Criticality in a Stochastic Multi-agent Model of a Financial Market", *Nature* 397: 498–500.

Lux, T. and M. Marchesi (2000). "Volatility Clustering in Financial Markets: A Micro Simulation of Interacting Agents", *International Journal of Theoretical and Applied Finance* 3: 675–702.

MacLean, L.C. and W.T. Ziemba (1999). "Growth versus Security Tradeoffs in Dynamic Investment Analysis", in Wets, R.J-B. and Ziemba, W.T., eds, *Stochastic Programming: State of the Art 1998*. Amsterdam: Balzer Science Publishers, pp. 193–226.

Mandelbrot, B.B. (1963). "The Variation of Certain Speculative Prices", *Journal of Business* 36: 394–419.

Mandelbrot, B.B. (1983). *The Fractal Geometry of Nature*. San Francisco: W.H. Freeman.

Mandelbrot, B.B. (1997). *Fractals and Scaling in Finance*. New York: Springer-Verlag.

Mandelbrot, B. and R. Hudson (2004). *The (Mis)behavior of Markets: A Fractal View of Risk, Ruin and Reward*. Basic Books.

Mantegna, R.N. (1991). "Lévy Walks and Enhanced Diffusion in Milan Stock Exchange", *Physica A* 179: 232–242.

Mantegna, R.N. and H.E. Stanley (2000). *An Introduction to Econophysics: Correlations and Complexity in Finance*. Cambridge, UK: Cambridge University Press.

Markowitz, H.M. (1959). *Portfolio Selection: Efficient Diversification of Investments*. New Haven, CT: Yale University Press.

Merton, R.C. and P.A. Samuelson (1974). "Fallacy of the Log-normal Approximation to Optimal Portfolio Decision-making over Many Periods", *Journal of Financial Economics* 95: 67–94.

Michaud, R.O. (2003). "A Practical Framework for Portfolio Choice", *Journal of Investment Management* 1(2): 1–16.
Neftci, S. (1996). *Mathematics of Financial Derivatives*. San Diego: Academic Press.
Neu, P. and R. Kühn (2004). "Statistical Mechanics of Financial Time Series and Applications in Risk Management", presentation at the Math Finance Workshop Hochschule für Bankwirtschaft, Frankfurt, April 2004.
Nicholas, J.G. (2000). *Market Neutral Investing*. Bloomberg Professional Library.
Nison, S. (2001). *Japanese Candlestick Charting*. Second Edition, Prentice Hall Press.
O'Hara, M. (1995). *Market Microstructure Theory*. Oxford: Blackwell.
Paulos, J.A. (2003). A Mathematician Plays the Market, Penguin Books.
Peters, E.E. (1994). *Fractal Market Analysis: Applying Chaos Theory to Investment Economics*. New York: John Wiley & Sons.
Peters, E.E. (1996). *Chaos and Order in the Capital Markets*. New York: John Wiley & Sons.
Poundstone, W. (2005). *Fortune's Formula, The Untold Story of the Scientific Betting System that Beat the Casinos and Wall Street*. New York: Hill and Wang.
Rodionov, S.N. and J.E. Overland (2005). Application of a Sequential Regime Shift Detection Method to the Bering Sea Ecosystem", *Journal of Marketing Science* 62: 328–332.
Rosser Jr., J.B. (2000). *From Catastrophe to Chaos: A General Theory of Economic Discontinuities*. Boston: Kluwer.
Scheinkman, J.A. and B. LeBaron (1989). "Nonlinear Dynamics and Stock Returns", *The Journal of Business* 62(3): 311–337.
Schwager, J.D. (1989). *Market Wizards: Interviews with Top Traders*. New York Institute of Finance (Simon & Schuster).
Schwager, J.D. (1992). *The New Market Wizards: Conversations with America's Top Traders*. Harper Business.
Sharpe, W. (1964). "Capital Assets Prices: A Theory of Market Equilibrium under Conditions of Risk", *Journal of Finance* 19: 425–442.
Sharpe, W.F. (1994). "The Sharpe Ratio", *Journal of Portfolio Management* 21(1): 49–58.
Shiller, R.J. (2000). *Irrational Exuberance*. Princeton: Princeton University Press.
Sornette, D. (2000). "The Nasdaq Crash of April 2000: Yet Another Example of Log-periodicity in a Speculative Bubble Ending in a Crash", *European Physical Journal B* 17: 319–328.
Sornette, D. (2002). "Endogenous versus Exogenous Crashes in Financial Markets", eprint arXiv:cond-mat/0210509.
Sornette, D. (2003). *Why Stock Markets Crash: Critical Events in Complex Financial Systems*. Princeton: Princeton University Press.
Sornette, D. (2005). "Endogenous versus Exogenous Origins of Crises", in Monograph on Extreme Events, V. Jentsch ed., Springer.
Sornette, D. and A. Johansen (2001). "Significance of Log-periodic Precursors to Financial Crashes", *Quantitative Finance* 1: 452–471.
Sornette, D. and D. Zajdenweber (1999). "Economic Returns of Research: The Pareto Law and its Implications", *European Physical Journal B* 8: 653–664.
Sortino, F.A. and L.N. Price (1994). "Performance Measurement in a Downside Risk Framework", *Journal of Investing* (Fall).
Sortino, F.A. and R. van der Meer (1991). "Downside Risk", *Journal of Portfolio Management* (Summer).
Spurgin, R.B. (2000). "How to Game your Sharpe Ratio", *Journal of Alternative Investments* 4(3): 38–46.
Stauffer, D. and A. Aharony (1992). *Introduction to Percolation Theory*. Taylor & Francis.
Stauffer, D. and D. Sornette (1999). "Self-organized Percolation Model for Stock Market Fluctuations" *Physica A* 271: 499–506.
Taleb, N. (2005). *Fooled by Randomness: The Hidden Role of Chance in Life and in the Markets*. Random House.
Thorp, E. (2003). "A Perspective on Quantitative Finance: Models for Beating the Market", *Quantitative Finance Review*.
Vince, R. (1990). *Portfolio Management Formulas: Mathematical Trading Methods for the Futures, Options, and Stock Markets*. New York: John Wiley & Sons.
Vince, R. (1992). The Mathematics of Money Management: Risk Analysis Techniques for Traders. New York: John Wiley & Sons.

Waldrop, M.M. (1993). *Complexity: The Emerging Science at the Edge of Order and Chaos*. Touchstone Books.
Watts, D.J. (2003). *Six Degrees: The Science of a Connected Age*. W.W. Norton & Company.
Williams, L. (1988). *The Definitive Guide to Futures Trading*. Windsor Books.
Wilmott, P. (1998). *Derivatives*. Chichester: John Wiley & Sons.
Wolfram, S. (2002). *A New Kind of Science*. Campaign, IL: Wolfram Media.

Index

Indexed compiled by Terry Halliday